Praise for

The Historical Jesus

Class 3   xvii — xxxiv,   90 - 124
3 - 30,
427 - 466.

The Historical Jesus

A Comprehensive Guide

Gerd Theissen and Annette Merz

Fortress Press

Minneapolis

THE HISTORICAL JESUS
A Comprehensive Guide

Translated by John Bowden from the German
Der historische Jesus: Ein Lehrbuch,
copyright © 1996 Vandenhoeck & Ruprecht,
Göttingen. English translation copyright © 1998
John Bowden. Bibliographies for this edition have
been revised and updated by Robert Morgan.

Cover design by Cheryl Watson, Graphiculture.

ISBN 0–8006–3123–4 (hardcover);
0–8006–3122–6 (paperback)

Manufactured in Great Britain   1–3123 (hc); 3122 (pb)

02   01   00   99   98   1   2   3   4   5   6   7   8   9   10

For Christoph Burchard
on his sixty-fifth birthday

Foreword

In the previous generation study of the historical Jesus was often combined with the message that it was not theologically important to engage in a detailed critical examination of his person. The Christ who was proclaimed was the decisive figure, and the only important thing was to be sure that he was not in opposition to what we know of the historical Jesus – which was very little. This message was very influential. Many people today are at a loss if they become engaged in an argument and have to explain what we know of the historical Jesus, what we can only conjecture, and what we cannot know. This gap in the knowledge market is filled by books which claim to expose the true Jesus behind the false guise in which the church has presented him, and by edifying works which create a new Jesus from the religious longings and ethical values of our time. Both sides underestimate the patient work of scholarship. Yet there is no alternative to this work in a post-Enlightenment society and an open church which wants to give an account of its own foundations.

This comprehensive guide sets out to present the way in which scholars study Jesus – not only the results they arrive at but also the process by which they acquire their knowledge. It is written in the conviction that two centuries of historical-critical study of Jesus along with an enormous increase over this period in the sources relating to Jesus and the world in which he lived have provided important insights. However, much that is involved in the process of scholarly work requires patience from readers who are primarily interested in immediately illuminating results.

Scholars do not say, 'That's what it was', but, 'It could have been like that on the basis of the sources.' So we discuss all the relevant sources – not just the canonical Gospels but the apocryphal Gospels; not just the Christian texts which mention Jesus but also the non-Christian ones. Elsewhere, too, we always give the textual basis for conclusions and hypotheses.

Scholars never say, 'That's it', but only, 'It looks like this at the present stage of research' – which means 'at the present stage of our knowledge and error'. So on each important theme we have provided a brief survey of research. The classic positions, which keep recurring in varied forms, are reported briefly. That should also help readers to locate, evaluate and relativize the decisions which are put forward in this book.

Scholars do not say, 'That is our result', but 'That is our result on the basis of particular methods.' For them the way by which they have reached their goal is as important as the goal itself – often even more important. For the way can be right, even if the goal proves to be an intermediate stage which has to be left behind again. So in this book there are frequent methodological and hermeneutical reflections. That is appropriate, given the scepticism about whether we can know anything at all about the historical Jesus. A whole section (§4) is devoted to this question.

Finally, scholars know that their results are more transitory than the problems to which they attempt to give answers. That is also the case with research into Jesus. Despite the enormous wealth of opinions and positions, some basic problems keep recurring. They form constants. So our account is orientated on problems. However, simply for the sake of comprehensibility and clarity we say each time where the solutions could lie – in the present state of our knowledge and ignorance.

Because scholars cannot simply 'narrate' reality, but reflect on sources, the state of research, methods and problems, theirs is a complicated business. We see this as a challenge to those who teach. Our book sets out to communicate the different degrees of our knowledge of problems as clearly as possible and also to convey something of the enjoyment scholars have in seeking truth and correcting their mistakes. We have also kept in mind as potential readers interested lay people who want to get information about Jesus. So a translation has been provided for all Greek and Hebrew quotations and words. We have also tried hard not to succumb to the academic tendency to confuse profundity with a lack of clarity. Consequently this book is governed above all by educational concerns. It has developed out of intensive courses on the New Testament given by Gerd Theissen as a teacher and taken a long time ago by Annette Merz as a student. We have deliberately written a comprehensive guide suitable for study either in small groups or by individuals.

Each section begins with a short introduction and preparatory tasks which often serve to introduce important texts. Here texts outside the Old and New Testaments are usually quoted in full. These texts should be noted even by readers who have no time to engage in the tasks which are suggested, because they are important for the basic problems. On the other hand, the suggestions for further reading which are occasionally given here are not necessary for an understanding of the section in question. However, anyone who wants to make a detailed study of a topic, perhaps for examination purposes, should note them.

The main part of each section contains a survey of texts and problems relating to the topic in question, set out as clearly as possible. Tables, comparisons and sketches are meant to illustrate important problems. Divisions into headings and sub-headings – with the key words emphasized – should help readers to remember complicated issues.

At the end of each main part there is a summary, which has no artificial division into headings and sub-headings. This is meant to indicate how the results of scholarship can be translated into language which can speak to schools, churches and society generally. Suggestions for hermeneutical reflection follow. On the one hand they are meant to make the presentation of topics easier, since historical investigation is not directly concerned with the question of how we can deal with its results today. On the other hand, they form part of our teaching method: knowledge becomes living knowledge only if we grapple with it personally and communicate it through our thought and experience.

At the end of each section there are tasks which are meant to check how much has been learned. Each task also raises new problems, especially where it is necessary to transfer what has been explained to a new and unknown area. These additional tasks are also part of the treatment of the topic. Solutions to all the tasks are given at the end of the book.

Our aim in shaping each of the sections was to make each topic self-contained. So anyone who wants to study, for example, Jesus' last supper will find a self-contained account of the problems without having to read the whole book. This means that it is possible to skip sections in reading the book. Anyone who thinks that any study of the historical Jesus must begin with the Easter faith can even begin there.

Even a comprehensive guide which seeks to communicate research into Jesus, and not the pet ideas of the two authors, is stamped by a particular picture of Jesus. This is a contextual picture of Jesus. Jesus is understood in the context of Judaism and the local, social and political history of his time. There are 'pre-understandings' and 'interests' behind this book, too. Thus we are convinced that through the historical Jesus one can find an approach to Judaism which is a sympathetic one, that grappling with his message sharpens the social conscience and that encounter with him changes the question one asks about God.

The book is a joint work. Both authors are responsible for all the sections in their final form, but we have shared the work between us. The greater part of chapters 1, 4–5 and 7–16 come from Gerd Theissen. Annette Merz has written chapters 2, 3–6. She has also devised the tasks and the solutions given to them on pp. 573–612, along with individual sections in the other chapters.[1] The manu-

---

[1]These relate to the following sections: 1: 1.1.1–2 (part of the history of research); 7: 1.1–3 (Nazareth); 3.5 (the religious character of Galilee); 8: 4.1.1–3 (John the Baptist: sources, teaching and understanding of himself); 7.1–2 (Jesus and the women); 9: 5.1 (Jesus' preaching of judgment); 10: 4.2 (Jesus as magician?); 11: 1.4–6 (part of the history of research); 3.6 (Matt. 20.1–12 in the framework of the rabbinic parables of reward); 12: 2.1–2 (Jesus as teacher); 5.1–6 (the commandment to love); 15: 2.5.2 (the first appearance of Jesus); 3 (Hermeneutics). In all, Annette Merz wrote around one-third of the book.

script was finished in September 1995. Literature which appeared after that date could not be taken into consideration. However, more recent works have been added in the bibliographies as adapted for English-speaking readers. This work has been done by Robert Morgan of the University of Oxford.

We have tried out parts of the book on others. For suggestions and for reading parts or all of the book we are grateful to Petra von Gemünden (Geneva), Michaela Höckel (Göttingen) and Christa Theissen (Heidelberg). Dörte Bester (Heidelberg) has studied large parts of the book thoroughly and has suggested a wealth of improvements from a student's perspective which we have gratefully adopted. We are also grateful to Matthias Walter and Heike Göbel for reading the proofs and Dörte Bester for helping with the index. Our publisher, Dr Arndt Ruprecht, has supported and encouraged the book from the beginning to which there was a long prelude, ultimately going back to work on the supplementary volume to Rudolf Bultmann's *History of the Synoptic Tradition*. We are grateful to him for this.

We have dedicated the book to Christoph Burchard on his sixty-fifth birthday, as a thank-you to a colleague and teacher whom all of us treasure and many of us love.

Heidelberg, January 1996   Gerd Theissen
                                                         Annette Merz

Contents

Frequently Quoted Literature

Sources and collections of sources

Where not otherwise indicated, the translations are quoted from the following editions of texts, collections of sources and translations (short title in brackets). Where earlier translations are quoted, the orthography has sometimes been modernized.

(a) Collections of sources

Barrett, C.K. (ed,), *The New Testament Background*, London ²1988 (Barrett)

(Strack, H. and) Billerbeck, P., *Kommentar zum Neuen Testament aus Talmud und Midrasch* (4 vols), Munich 1922–28 (Bill.)

Charles, R.H., *The Apocrypha and Pseudepigrapha of the New Testament* (2 vols), Oxford 1913 (Charles)

Charlesworth, J.H. (ed.), *Old Testament Pseudepigrapha* (2 vols), New York and London 1, 1983; 2, 1985 (Charlesworth)

Lohse, E., *Die Texte aus Qumran* (2 vols, Hebrew and German), Darmstadt 1971

Schneemelcher, W., and Wilson, R.McL., *New Testament Apocrypha, 1. Gospels; 2, Acts, Apocalypses, etc.*, Philadelphia and Cambridge ¹1963, ¹1965; Louisville and Cambridge ²1991, ²1993 (*NTApoc*)

Sparks, H.F.D. (ed.), *The Apocryphal Old Testament*, Oxford 1984 (Sparks)

Stern, M., *Greek and Latin Authors on Jews and Judaism* (3 vols), Jerusalem 1974–1984 *(GLAJJ* + no. of the source cited)

Vermes, Geza, *The Complete Dead Sea Scrolls in English*, London 1997 (Vermes)

(b) Individual sources

The Apostolic Fathers, ed. Kirsopp Lake, Loeb Classical Library (2 vols), London and Cambridge, Mass. 1912 and 1913

The Babylonian Talmud, Soncino edition, general editor I. Epstein (35 vols), London 1933–52, reprinted in 18 vols, London 1961

Dio Chrysostom, Loeb Classical Library (5 vols), London and Cambridge, Mass. 1932–51

The Ethiopic Book of Enoch: A New Edition in the Light of the Aramaic Dead Sea Fragments, ed. Michael Knibb, Oxford 1979; Charles II, 163–281; Charlesworth 1, 5–90; Sparks, 169–319

Epictetus, *Epicteti Dissertationes*, ed. H. Schenkl, Bibliotheca Teubneriana, Tübingen 1894

Eusebius of Caesarea, *Church History*, Greek: E. Schwarz (ed.), Leipzig 1914, reprinted 1955; H.J. Lawlor and J.E.L. Oulton (eds.) (2 vols.), London 1927; G.A. Williamson (ed.), Harmondsworth 1987

IV Ezra, Charles II, 542–624

Josephus, Flavius, *Life, Against Apion* (1926); *The Jewish War* (2 vols, 1927–8); *Jewish Antiquities* (5 vols, 1930–43), Loeb Classical Library, London and Cambridge, Mass.

Jubilees, Charles II, 1–82; Charlesworth 2, 35–142; Sparks, 1–139

I Maccabees, Charles I, 59–124

The Mishnah (ed. H.Danby), Oxford 1933

Philo, *Works* (10 vols), Loeb Classical Library, London and Cambridge, Mass. 1929–43

Philonis Alexandrini opera quae supersunt, ed. L. Cohn, editio minor, I–VI, Berlin 1888–1915

The Works of Philo, ed. C.D. Yonge, Peabody, Mass. 1993

Philostratus, *The Life of Apollonius von Tyana* (2 vols), Loeb Classical Library, London and Cambridge, Mass. 1912

Plutarch, *Lives* (11 vols), Loeb Classical Library, London and Cambridge, Mass. 1914–26

The Psalms of Solomon, Charles II, 625–52; Charlesworth 2, 630–707; Sparks, 649–82

Seneca, *De Clementia, De Beneficiis*, ed. R.C. Herzog 1876

Suetonius, *The Twelve Caesars*, trans. R. Graves, Harmondsworth 1957

Tacitus, *The Annals of Imperial Rome*, ed. M. Grant, Harmondsworth 1956

Testamenta XII Patriarcharum, ed. M. de Jonge, Leiden 1964

Testaments of the Twelve Patriarchs, Charles II, 282–367; Charlesworth 1,775–828; Sparks, 505–600

(c) Modern works

Throughout the book, titles listed below are quoted with a short title and asterisk.

Bornkamm, G., *Jesus of Nazareth*, London and New York 1960 (*Jesus**)
Bultmann, R., *The History of the Synoptic Tradition*, Oxford ²1968 (*HST**)
id., *Jesus and the Word* (1926), London and New York 1934, reissued London 1958 (*Jesus**)

id., *Theology of the New Testament* (2 vols), New York and London 1953, 1955 (*Theology**)

id., 'The Primitive Christian Kerygma and the Historical Jesus', in *The Historical Jesus and the Kerygmatic Christ*, ed. C.E. Braaten and R.A. Harrisville, Nashville 1964 ('Kerygma'*)

Burchard, C., 'Jesus of Nazareth', in: J. Becker (ed.) , *Christian Beginnings*, Louisville 1993 ('Jesus'*)

Crossan, J.D., *The Historical Jesus. The Life of a Mediterranean Jewish Peasant*, San Francisco and Edinburgh 1991 (*Jesus**)

Dibelius, M., *From Tradition to Gospel*, London 1934, reissued Cambridge 1971 (*Tradition**)

Evans, C.A., *Noncanonical Writings and New Testament Interpretation*, Peabody, Mass. 1992 (*Noncanonical Writings**)

id., *Jesus and his Contemporaries* (AGJU 25), Leiden, New York and Cologne 1995 (*Jesus**)

Flusser, D., *Jesus*, Hamburg 1968 (*Jesus**)

Hengel, M., *The Zealots. Investigations into the Jewish Freedom Movements in the Time from Herod I to 70 CE*, Edinburgh 1988 (*Zealots**)

Käsemann, E., 'The Problem of the Historical Jesus' (1953), in *Essays on New Testament Themes*, London 1964, 15–47 ('Problem'*)

Kümmel, W.G. *The New Testament. The History of the Investigation of its Problems*, Nashville 1972 (*NT**)

Meier, J.P., *A Marginal Jew. Rethinking the Historical Jesus*, Vol.1: *The Roots of the Problem and the Person*, New York 1991; Vol.2: *Mentor, Message, and Miracles*, New York 1994 (*Marginal Jew 1/2**)

Sanders, E.P., *Jesus and Judaism*, London and Philadelphia 1985-1991 (*Jesus**)

Schmidt, K.L., *Der Rahmen der Geschichte Jesu*, Berlin 1919 (*Rahmen**)

Schürer, E., *Die Geschichte des jüdischen Volkes im Zeitalter Jesu Christi*, I–III, Leipzig 1901–1909 (*Geschichte* I–III*, [4]1901, etc.)

Schürer, E., *The History of the Jewish People in the Age of Jesus Christ* (175 BC–AD 135), *A New English Version Revised and Edited by G. Vermes & F. Millar*, Vol.1, Edinburgh 1973; Vol.2, 1979; Vol.3.1, 1986; Vol.3.2, 1987 (Schürer, *History* 1*; 2*, etc.)

Schweitzer, A., *Geschichte der Leben-Jesu-Forschung*, Tübingen1984 (*Geschichte**) – *The Quest of the Historical Jesus*, London [3]1950, reissued 1981 (partial translation of *Geschichte** = *Quest**)

Stegemann, H., *Die Essener, Qumran, Johannes der Täufer und Jesus. Ein Sachbuch*, Freiburg, Basel and Vienna 1993 (*Essener**)

Studying the Historical Jesus. Evaluations of the State of Current Research, ed. B. Chilton and C.A. Evans, Leiden, New York and Cologne 1994 (*Studying**)

Theissen, G., *The Miracle Stories of the Early Christian Tradition*, Edinburgh 1982 and Philadelphia 1983 (*Miracle Stories**)

id., *The First Followers of Jesus*, London 1978 (US title, *The Sociology of the Earliest Jesus Movement*) (*First Followers**)

id, *Social Reality and the Early Christians*, Minneapolis 1992 and Edinburgh 1993
(*Social Reality**); this includes
'The Wandering Radicals', 33–59 ('Wandering Radicals'*)
'Jesus' Temple Prophecy', 94–114 ('Temple Prophecy'*)
id., 'Jesusbewegung als charismatische Weltrevolution', *NTS* 35, 1989, 243–360
('Jesusbewegung*')
id., *The Gospels in Context*, Edinburgh and Minneapolis 1992 *(Gospels*)*
id., 'Theologie und Exegese in den neutestamentlichen Arbeiten von Günther Born-
kamm', *EvTh 51*, 1991, 308–32 ('Theologie*')
id., 'Gruppenmessianismus. Überlegungen zum Ursprung der Kirche im Jüngerkreis
Jesu', *JBTh* 7, 1992, 101–123 ('Gruppenmessianismus*')
Vermes, G., *Jesus the Jew*, London and New York 1973 (*Jesus**)
Vielhauer, P., *Geschichte der urchristlichen Literatur*, Berlin and New York 1975
(*Geschichte**)

(d) Other references to select bibliographies and methods of quotation

At the beginning of each chapter and sometimes at the beginning of individual
sections there are also blocks of bibliography with select titles on particular
topics. Reference is made to these within the chapter by a short title. Comprehen-
siveness has not been sought. These bibliographical surveys do not contain titles
and literature published before c.1930 which are mainly about another topic.
Complete references to such works are given in the notes.

Abbreviations

ABD	*Anchor Bible Dictionary*
AGJU	Arbeiten zur Geschichte des antiken Judentums und der Urchristentums
ANRW	*Aufstieg und Niedergang der römischen Welt*, ed. H. Temporini and W. Haase, Berlin and New York
ASNU	Acta seminarii neotestamentici Upsaliensis
AThD	Acta Theologica Danica
ATLA	American Theological Library Association
BAR	*Biblical Archaeological Review*
BBB	Bonner Biblische Beiträge
BEvTh	Beiträge zur Evangelischen Theologie
BETL	Bibliotheca Ephemeridum Theologicarum Lovaniensium
Bib	*Biblica*
BibInt	*Biblical Interpretation*
BSt	Biblische Studien
BThSt	Biblisch-Theologische Studien
BWANT	Beiträge zur Wissenschaft vom Alten und Neuen Testament
BZAW	Beihefte zur Zeitschrift für die alttestamentliche Wissenschaft
BZNW	Beihefte zur Zeitschrift für die neutestamentliche Wissenschaft
CBQ	*Catholic Biblical Quarterly*
CIL	Corpus Inscriptionum Latinarum
CNT	*Coniectanea neotestamentica*
CThM	Calwer theologische Monographien
EdF	Erträge der Forschung
EK	Evangelische Kommentare
EKK	Evangelisch-katholischer Kommentar zum Neuen Testament
EtB	*Études bibliques*
EThL	*Ephemerides Theologicae Lovanienses*
EvTh	*Evangelische Theologie*
ExpT	*Expository Times*

FRLANT   Forschungen zur Religion und Literatur des Alten und Neuen Testament
FS   Festschrift

GTA   Göttinger Theologische Arbeiten

HDR   Harvard Dissertations in Religion
HTR   *Harvard Theological Review*
HThK   Herders theologischer Kommentar zum Neuen Testament
HThSt   Hamburger Theologische Studien
HTS   Harvard Theological Studies
HUT   Hermeneutische Untersuchungen zur Theologie

ICC   International Critical Commentary
IEJ   *Israel Exploration Journal*
IMWKT   *Internationale Monatsschrift für Wissenschaft, Kunst und Technik*

JBL   *Journal of Biblical Literature*
JBTh   *Journal of Biblical Theology*
JFSR   *Journal of Feminist Studies in Religion*
JJS   *Journal of Jewish Studies*
JSJ   *Journal for the Study of Judaism in the Persian, Hellenistic and Early
          Roman Period*
JSNT   *Journal for the Study of the New Testament*
JSNT SS   Journal for the Study of the New Testament Supplement Series
JTS   *Journal of Theological Studies*

KT   Kleine Texte

LCL   Loeb Classical Library
LD   Lectio Divina
LThK   *Lexikon für Theologie und Kirche*
LXX   Septuagint

MT   Massoretic Text
MusHelv *Museum Helveticum*

NEAEHL *New Encyclopaedia of Archaeological Excavations in the Holy Land*
NF   Neue Folge
NS   New Series
NT   *Novum Testamentum*
NTA   *Neutestamentliche Abhandlungen*
NTA NF *Neutestamentliche Abhandlungen Neue Folge*

NTG	*Novum Testamentum Graecum*
NTOA	Novum Testamentum et Orbis Antiquus
NTS	*New Testament Studies*
NZSTh	*Neue Zeitschrift für Systematische Theologie*
OBO	Orbis biblicus et orientalis
ÖTK	Ökumenischer Taschenbuchkommentar
Ph.S	*Philologus.* Supplementary volume
PJ	*Palästinajahrbuch des deutschen evangelischen Instituts*
QD	Quaestiones Disputatae
RAC	*Reallexikon für Antike und Christentum*
SBB	Stuttgarter Biblische Beiträge
SBS	Stuttgarter Bibelstudien
SBT	Studies in Biblical Theology
SC	Sources chrétiennes
SJ	Studia Judaica
SJT	*Scottish Journal of Theology*
SNTS MS	Society for New Testament Studies Monograph Series
SNTU	Studien zum Neuen Testament und seiner Umwelt
SPAW.PH	Sitzungsberichte der preussichen Akademie der Wissenschaften – Philosophisch-historische Klasse
StANT	Studien zum Alten und Neuen Testament
StNT	Studien zum Neuen Testament
StUNT	Studien zur Umwelt des Neuen Testaments
TANZ	Texte und Arbeiten zur neutestamentlichen Zeitalter
ThBl	*Theologische Blätter*
TEH	Theologische Existenz heute
ThL	Theologische Lehrbücher
ThR	*Theologische Rundschau*
TRE	*Theologische Realenzyklopädie*
TU	Texte und Untersuchungen
UTB	Uni-Taschenbücher
VigChr	*Vigiliae christianae*
WdF	Wege der Forschung

WMANT	Wissenschaftliche Monographien zum Alten und Neuen Testament
WuD	Wort und Dienst
WUNT	Wissenschaftliche Untersuchungen zum Umwelt des Neuen Testaments
ZDMG	Zeitschrift der deutschen morgenländischen Gesellschaft
ZKG	Zeitschrift für Kirchengeschichte
ZNW	Zeitschrift für die neutestamentliche Wissenschaft
ZSRG	Zeitschrift der Savigny-Stiftung für Rechtsgeschichte
ZSTh	Zeitschrift für systematische Theologie
ZThK	Zeitschrift für Theologie und Kirche

The Quest of the Historical Jesus

M.J. Borg, *Jesus in Contemporary Scholarship*, Valley Forge 1994; H. Braun, 'The Meaning of New Testament Christology' (1959), in *Journal for Theology and Church* 5, 1968, 89–127; J.D. Crossan, *The Cross that Spoke: The Origins of the Passion Narrative*, San Francisco 1988; id., *Jesus**; G. Ebeling, 'Jesus and Faith', in id., *Word and Faith*, Philadelphia and London 1963, 201–46; E. Fuchs, 'The Quest of the Historical Jesus', in *Studies of the Historical Jesus*, London 1964, 11–31; D. Georgi, 'Leben-Jesu-Theologie/ Leben-Jesu-Forschung', *TRE* 20, 1990, 566–75; E. Käsemann, 'Problem'*; id., 'Blind Alleys in the "Jesus of History" Controversy', *New Testament Questions of Today*, Philadelphia and London 1969, 11–31; id., *Jesus Means Freedom*, London and Philadelphia 1969; W.G. Kümmel, *Vierzig Jahre Jesusforschung (1950/1990)*, BBB 91, Weinheim 1994 (with bibliography); S. Neill and T. Wright, *The Interpretation of the New Testament 1861–1986*, Oxford 1988; S.J. Patterson, *The Gospel of Thomas and Jesus*, Sonoma, CA 1993; E.P Sanders, *Jesus**; K.L. Schmidt, *Rahmen**; A. Schweitzer, *Quest**; G. Theissen, 'Theologie'*; W. Wrede, *The Messianic Secret in the Gospels* (1901), Cambridge 1971.

Introduction

The quest of the historical Jesus has a dynamic all of its own. A whole culture has grown up to direct all its thoughts to a single figure, and in this figure to worship the incarnate God, to fear the eschatological judge, and to love the redeemer. What intellectual independence it shows to make this figure the object of historical criticism! First came the *criticism of the sources*. The question here was whether everything in the Gospel accounts was historical or authentic. It was not just a matter of whether a few 'satanic verses' had found their way into the sources, but whether in a great many verses Jesus has been surrounded with an unhistorical aura of myth and poetry. To source criticism was added *historical relativism*. Even if we had a historically reliable picture of Jesus, the problem would remain that this figure was deeply embedded in history and was less singular and absolute than people believed. In addition, finally, there was the awareness of *hermeneutical otherness*: even if we had historically reliable reports and in them encountered an irreplaceable person – this Jesus, who was as close to many people in childhood as a good friend, removed himself into his past world in which demons were driven out and there were strange anxieties about the end of the world.

Despite such distancing by source criticism, historical relativism and hermeneutical otherness, our culture still clings to this figure. Even where he is no longer regarded as 'Lord', people seek in the rabbi from Nazareth the great brother as an ally. Where people press for a socialist form of society, Jesus becomes the forerunner of socialism, since he criticized the rich and rejected mammon. For those who promote joy in life Jesus becomes the Galilean artist who had the art of living, taunted by narrow-minded contemporaries as a 'glutton and winebibber, a friend of publicans and sinners'. Where an existential decision is urgently called for, Jesus becomes the preacher of a call to decision who summons individuals from their forgetfulness of life. Where people advocate a humanism which emancipates itself from supervision by the church, Jesus becomes the one who challenges religious institutions. Was it not his claim to be *the* human being, the 'Son of Man'?

The quest of the historical Jesus and of portraits of Jesus is a history of constantly new approaches to Jesus and distancings from him. In what follows, only the most important phases of scholarly concern with Jesus will be sketched out – with fundamental and methodological insights which are still influential today. Precisely for that reason it should be emphasized that the history of pictures of Jesus is richer than the history of scholarly pictures of Jesus.

Suggested reading

Schweitzer, *Quest* *, 396–401, and Bultmann, *Jesus**.

1. Five phases of the quest of the historical Jesus

1.1 First phase: the critical impulse towards the question of the historical Jesus: H.S. Reimarus and D.F. Strauss

1.1.1 Hermann Samuel Reimarus (1694–1768)

H.S. Reimarus, a professor of oriental languages in Hamburg, was during his lifetime a literary champion of the religion of reason proposed by English deism. However, he made the historical-critical foundation of his ideas in his 'Apologia or Defence of the Rational Worshippers of God' available only to close friends. After his death, G.E. Lessing published seven fragments from this work (1774–1778) without indicating the identity of the author.[1] Reimarus marks the

---

[1]Especially the sixth and seventh fragments in *Reimarus: Fragments*, ed. C.H. Talbert, Philadelphia 1971 ('On the Resurrection Narratives'; 'On the Intentions of Jesus and His Disciples') are important for the question of the historical Jesus.

beginning of preoccupation with the life of Jesus from a purely historical perspective with Reimarus.

1. The methodological starting point is above all pioneering: Reimarus distinguishes the preaching of Jesus from the apostles' faith in Christ: 'I find great cause to separate completely what the apostles say in their own writings from that which Jesus himself actually said and taught.'[2]

2. The historical insight that the preaching of Jesus can be understood only from the context of the Jewish religion of his time corresponds to this starting point. Reimarus sees the centre of Jesus' preaching in the preaching of the imminence of the kingdom of heaven and the call to repentance which follows from that. This is to be understood 'in accordance with the Jewish way of speaking'. Jesus promises a worldly kingdom, 'the kingdom of Christ or Messiah, for which the Jews had for long waited and hoped'.[3] Jesus is a Jewish prophetic and apocalyptic figure, while Christianity, which detached itself from Judaism, was a new creation of the apostles.

3. Reimarus explains the discrepancy between the political and messianic message of Jesus and the apostles' proclamation of a Christ who brings redemption from suffering, who rises and comes again, by an objective theory of deception. The disciples of Jesus had stolen the body (cf. Matt. 28.11–15), so that they did not have to feel that they had failed, as Jesus had done, and after fifty days (when the body could no longer be identified) they had proclaimed his resurrection and imminent return.

Whereas the methodological separation between the historical Jesus and the apostles' belief in Christ is still normative today, and Jesus is once again being put in his Jewish context, the explanation of belief in Christ in terms of 'deception' was corrected at a very early stage by a second great critic, D.F. Strauss.

1.1.2 *David Friedrich Strauss (1808–1874)*

The philosopher and theologian D.F. Strauss, a pupil of F.C. Baur and F.W. Hegel, published his sensational *Life of Jesus*[4] in 1835/36. It provoked a flood of attempts at refutation and earned its author lifelong social ostracism; however, scholarship can never go back behind its basic thesis of the mythical transformation of the Jesus tradition.

1. Strauss' main achievement is to have applied to the Gospels the concept of myth which was already current in the Old Testament scholarship of his time. He demonstrates the mythical approach to the Jesus tradition as a synthesis (in the

---

[2]'On the Intentions of Jesus and His Disciples', §3, p.64.
[3]Ibid., §4, p.66.
[4]D.F. Strauss, *The Life of Jesus Critically Examined* (1835/36), ed. P.C. Hodgson, Philadelphia 1972 and London 1973.

Hegelian sense) of the inadequate interpretations of supranaturalism on the one hand and rationalism on the other.

> The main interest of the rationalistic accounts of the life of Jesus lies in their 'rational' explanation of the miracles of Jesus and the miraculous features in the Gospels. H.E.G. Paulus (1789–1851) might be mentioned here as an example.[5] More or less perceptive reflections are meant to make the miracles comprehensible to the 'enlightened' consciousness (resurrection as a pseudo-death, walking on the lake as a vision of the disciples); the account of the evangelists is excused as a concession to the 'Jewish desire for miracles'. Strauss enjoyed refuting this kind of interpretation of miracles far more than arguing with traditionally naive (super-naturalist) credulity. In every section of his life of Jesus he first plays the two trends off against each other, points out their deficiencies and then shows that the mythical approach solves all the problems.

Strauss sees myth, 'the saga which is poetic without a purpose', at work wherever the laws of nature are contravened in the Gospel accounts, the traditions contradict each other, or motives widespread in the history of religion, and especially in the Old Testament, are transferred to Jesus.[6] In contrast to Reimarus, he no longer explains the unhistorical by deliberate deception but by an unconscious process of mythical imagination.

2. For Strauss, a declared Hegelian, the inner nucleus of Christian faith is not touched by the mythical approach. For in the historical individual Jesus is realized the idea of God-humanity, the highest of all ideas. Myth is the legitimate 'history-like' garb of this universal human idea.[7]

3. Strauss was also the first to recognize that the Gospel of John is composed on theological premises and is historically less trustworthy than the Synoptics. F.C. Baur helped this thesis to make a breakthrough. The weakness of Strauss's criticism lay in the literary relationship between the Synoptic Gospels for which he argued: he put forward the view that Matthew and Luke are the earliest Gospels, and that Mark is an excerpt from both of them (the so-called Griesbach hypothesis). Therefore by clarifying the relationship between the sources through the two-source theory, liberal theology could hope to cope with the 'shock' caused by Strauss.

---

[5]H.E.G. Paulus, *Das Leben Jesu als Grundlage einer reinen Geschichte des Urchristentums*, Heidelberg 1828.

[6]Certainly Strauss does not dispute that the narratives also contain historical reminiscences, but he is not interested in these; he is solely concerned to demonstrate the omnipresence of myth.

[7]It would take us too far to outline Strauss's speculative christology. Reference need only be made to his conclusion, which was highly offensive to his orthodox contemporaries, that an idea is not realized in one example, and therefore that the classical attributes of Christ (the union of divine and human nature, etc.) are to be attributed to humankind as a whole.

1.2   Second phase: the optimism of the liberal quest of the historical Jesus

In Germany, the period of the Wilhelmine empire was the hey-day of theological liberalism and the classical 'quest of the historical Jesus'. Scholars hoped that by reconstructing the authoritative person of Jesus and his history through historical criticism they could renew Christian faith and thus leave the church's dogma of Christ behind. Heinrich Julius Holtzmann (1832–1910) can be regarded as a prime representative.

1. The methodological basis of the liberal study of Jesus is the literary-critical exploration of the earliest sources about Jesus: F.C. Baur demonstrated the priority of the Synoptic Gospels over the Gospel of John, and H.J.Holtzmann helped the two-source theory developed by Gottlob Wilke and Christian Hermann Weisse to achieve lasting success.[8] Mark, a source which hitherto had been overshadowed, and Q, a source first reconstructed by scholars, were now regarded as the earliest, largely reliable sources for the historical Jesus. An emancipation from the traditional church picture of Jesus seemed possible on his basis.

2. Holtzmann took over from the Gospel of Mark the outline of the life of Jesus, reading out of it a biographical development with a turning point in Mark 8; Jesus' messianic consciousness had formed in Galilee, and in Caesarea Philippi he showed himself to the disciples as Messiah. The authentic sayings of Jesus reconstructed from the Logia source were inserted into the biographical framework derived from Mark.

3. The liberal 'lives of Jesus' are the result of a combination of the aprioristic notion of a development of the personality of Jesus reflected in the sources with an acute literary-critical analysis. They believe that they can rediscover the ideal personality of their author in the sources about Jesus.

1.3   Third phase: the collapse of the quest of the historical Jesus

In the final phase of theological liberalism around the turn of the century, three scholarly insights led to the collapse of the quest of the historical Jesus.

1. A. Schweitzer's book *The Quest of the Historical Jesus* showed that the images in the lives of Jesus were projections.[9] Schweitzer demonstrated that each

---

[8]H.J. Holtzmann's work *Die synoptischen Evangelien. Ihr Ursprung und geschichtliche Character,* Leipzig 1863, won the day. The two-source theory is briefly described on p. 25 below.

[9]The first German edition appeared in 1906 under the title *Von Reimarus zu Wrede. Eine Geschichte der Leben-Jesu-Forschung,* and this was translated into English as *The Quest of the Historical Jesus,* London 1910. The title of the considerably enlarged second edition of 1913 was *Geschichte der Leben-Jesu-Forschung;* unfortunately the additions made in this edition have never appeared in English. Schweitzer added a new preface to the fifth edition of 1951, which appeared in the English edition of 1953.

of the liberal pictures of Jesus displayed the personality structure which, in the eyes of its author, was the ethical ideal most worth striving for.

2. W. Wrede in 1901 demonstrated the tendentious character of the earliest extant sources for the life of Jesus. He argued that the Gospel of Mark is an expression of community dogma. The post-Easter faith in the messiahship of Jesus is here projected on to the intrinsically unmessianic life of Jesus. Wrede claimed that the unhistorical 'messianic secret theory' shaped the whole of the Gospel of Mark.[10] This destroyed the confidence that it was possible to distinguish between the history of Jesus and the image of Christ after Easter by recourse to two ancient sources.

3. The fragmentary character of the Gospels was demonstrated by K.L. Schmidt. He showed that the Jesus tradition consists of 'small units' and that the chronological and geographical 'framework of the story of Jesus', to quote the title of his book, was created secondarily by the evangelist Mark. This destroyed the possibility of reading a development in the personality of Jesus from the sequence of pericopes. Moreover form criticism recognized that even the 'small units' have been primarily shaped by community needs and only secondarily by historical reminiscence – the kerygmatic character of the Jesus tradition governs even the smallest pericope (Dibelius, *Tradition**; Bultmann, *HST**).

The scepticism provoked by these insights was partly absorbed and partly intensified programmatically by theological motives, as for example in the work of R. Bultmann (1884–1976), the most significant exegete of dialectical theology, which had its heyday in the period between 1919 and 1968.

1. Dialectical theology opposes God and the world so radically that they touch only at one point – as a tangent touches a circle: in the 'that' of Jesus' coming and the 'that' of his departure, in the cross and resurrection. It was not what Jesus had said and done which was thought to be decisive but what God had said and done in the cross and resurrection. The message of this action of God, the New Testament 'kerygma', is not the historical Jesus but the 'kerygmatic Christ'.

2. According to the view of existentialist philosophy, human beings first achieve their 'authenticity' in decision, which cannot be guaranteed by objectifiable arguments (like historical knowledge). For a Christian existentialism, this decision is the answer to God's call in the kerygma of the cross and resurrection of Jesus, which men and women give by an existential dying and living with Christ.

3. The two most prominent sketches of New Testament theology show little interest in the historical Jesus. In II Cor.5.16 Paul denies that it is of theological significance to have known Jesus after the flesh.[11] In the Gospel of John the

---

[10]Wrede, *Messianic Secret*.
[11]II Cor. 5.16 is probably to be understood to be about not 'Christ after the flesh' but about 'knowing after the flesh'.

revealer reveals only *that* he is the revealer. Both develop the kerygma, i.e. a post-Easter faith which in the light of cross and resurrection has 'recast' the pre-Easter memory. If D.F. Strauss saw the truth of the Christ myth in the 'idea', Bultmann sees in the 'kerygma' a 'call of God' coming from outside.

4. Research into the history of religions made it clear that theologically Jesus belongs to Judaism[12] and that Christianity begins only with Easter. From this Bultmann drew the conclusion that the teaching of Jesus is of no significance for a Christian theology.[13] However, he did concede that post-Easter christology is 'implicitly' presented in Jesus' pre-Easter call to decision. That was the starting point for his pupils to put the question of the historical Jesus afresh.

1.4 Fourth phase: the 'new quest' of the historical Jesus

Whereas the (old) liberal quest of the historical Jesus played him off against the proclamation of the church, 'the new quest',[14] which developed in the circle of Bultmann pupils, began from the kerygmatic Christ and asked whether his exaltation, grounded in the cross and resurrection, has any 'support' in the proclamation of Jesus before Easter.[15]

1. The christological kerygma commits itself to the 'quest of the historical Jesus', as (in a stand against enthusiasm[16]) it refers to an earthly figure and speaks of it as an earthly figure in the Gospels. The identity of the earthly Jesus and the exalted Christ is presupposed in all the earliest Christian writings.

2. The methodological basis of the 'quest of the historical Jesus' is the confidence that a critically ensured minimum of 'authentic' Jesus tradition can be found, if everything is excluded that can be derived from both Judaism and earliest Christianity. Methodologically the place of the literary-critical reconstruction of the earliest sources in the 'old' quest of liberal theology is replaced by a comparison which makes use of the history of religions and the history of tradition: the 'criterion of difference'.

---

[12]Cf. Wellhausen's dictum, which has become famous: 'Jesus was not a Christian but a Jew', *Einleitung in die ersten drei Evangelien*, Berlin ²1911, 102.

[13]As is well known, Bultmann's *Theology** begins with the statement: 'The message of Jesus is a presupposition for the theology of the New Testament rather than a part of that theology itself' (3).

[14]The 'new' quest was sparked off by E.Käsemann's lecture 'The Problem of the Historical Jesus', given in Marburg in 1953.

[15]The expression 'return to the historical Jesus', which has become a technical term, is characteristic of this line of questions.

[16]The thesis that anti-enthusiastic/anti-docetic motives played a role in the writing of the Gospels has been put forward especially by Käsemann (e.g. 'Problem'*, 30–4).

3. The quest for pre-Easter support for the kerygma of Christ is independent of whether Jesus used christological titles (like Son of Man, Messiah, Son of God). Rather, this claim is implicit in his conduct and his proclamation:

- as a call to decision by Jesus in the face of the presence of God in the beginning of the rule of God (Bultmann);[17]
- as Jesus' criticism of the Law, which puts in question the foundations of all ancient religion, a 'call of freedom' (Käsemann);[18]
- as the immediacy of Jesus by which he is distinguished from the apocalyptic and casuistry of his environment (Bornkamm);[19]
- as the claim of the love of God for sinners, both in Jesus' conduct and in his proclamation (Fuchs);[20]
- as the paradoxical unity of radicalized Torah and radical grace, in which God's will occurs and takes place in Jesus (H. Braun);[21]
- as 'Jesus' faith', which makes it possible for him to participate in God's omnipotence: 'all is possible to the one who believes' (Ebeling).[22]

4. The theological intention to discover the germ of the kerygma of Christ already in the preaching of Jesus, combined with the criterion of difference, necessarily led to seeing Jesus in contrast to Judaism.[23]

Excursus: Jewish research into Jesus

P. Winter, *On the Trial of Jesus*, Berlin 1961; D. Catchpole, *The Trial of Jesus*, Leiden 1971.

Whereas Christian theology devalued the quest of the historical Jesus by turning away from theological liberalism, the beginning of scholarly Jewish research into

---

[17]However, Bultmann himself, in contrast to his pupils, did not attach any essential significance to the fact 'that Jesus' appearance and his preaching imply a christology in so far as he called for a decision over against his person as the bearer of the word of God'. For this claim to authority remains a historical phenomenon, and no decision can be made about its appropriateness. The unity in content of the proclamation of Jesus and the kerygma of Christ discloses itself only to existentialist interpretation: both force a decision and make a new existence possible. However, after Easter the kerygma has taken the place of the proclamation of the historical Jesus – to refer back to him is essentially superfluous. Cf. Bultmann's critical discussion with his pupils in 'Kerygma'* (the quotation above comes from p.28).
[18]Käsemann, *Jesus Means Freedom*.
[19]Bornkamm, *Jesus**, passim.
[20]Fuchs, 'The Quest of the Historical Jesus'.
[21]Braun, 'The Meaning of New Testament Christology'.
[22]Ebeling, 'Jesus and Faith'.
[23]Theissen, 'Theologie'*, esp. 319–25.

Jesus which began at the same time continued the liberal tradition. In so doing, it emphasized aspects to which insufficient justice was done in Christian research, namely the Jewish character of the life and teaching of Jesus – a process which is part of 'bringing Jesus home to Judaism'. Because the conflict with the Jewish Law was no longer located at the centre of Jesus' life, other possibilities of interpreting Jesus' violent death historically were considered. Was he perhaps a political rebel against the Romans? The three classical accounts of Jesus in Jewish research from the beginning of this century represent Jesus as a ethicist, prophet and rebel.

1. Jesus as *ethicist*. J. Klausner, *Jesus of Nazareth* (Hebrew 1907, English 1925), saw Jesus as the representative of an impressive Jewish ethic. He could call him an extreme nationalist (413) – but with a 'new concept of God' (379), which detached God from his bond to people and history.

2. Jesus as *prophet*. C.G. Montefiore (*The Synoptic Gospels*, 2 vols, London 1909, [2]1927 and many other publications) is probably the most significant of these first Jewish scholars concerned with Jesus: for him Jesus continues the series of the great prophets, but in a different historical situation. The old prophets did not yet have to grapple with the Law as a finished, completed entity. They uttered polemic against the sacrificial cult. But in the time of Jesus this was limited to the Jerusalem temple, whereas other rites – sabbath, food regulations, purity regulations – were externalized. Therefore Jesus attacked these rites.

3. Jesus as *rebel*. the thesis at the beginning of research into Jesus that Jesus had wanted to found a worldly kingdom (cf. above pp 2f. on Reimarus) was revived by R. Eisler (ΙΗΣΟΥΣ ΒΑΣΙΛΕΥΣ ΟΥ ΒΑΣΙΛΕΥΣΑΣ, 2 vols, Heidelberg 1927/30);[24] in the first half of his life Jesus had presented a non-violent teaching, but then seized and occupied the temple violently and finally came to grief in conflict with the Romans.

Jewish research into Jesus has also kept away from the specifically theological questions of the 'new quest' of the historical Jesus. Thus two more recent representatives became forerunners and representatives of the 'third quest' (see 1.5 below): D. Flusser (*Jesus*, 1969) represented Jesus as a Jew who was faithful to the Law. His preaching was governed not by criticism of the Law but by the commandment to love, the overcoming of the notion of retribution and the expectation of the kingdom of God – all Jewish traditions. G. Vermes (*Jesus the Jew**, 1973) put Jesus in a charismatic milieu in Galilee: we also find miracles and wisdom sayings combined in Hanina ben Dosa in Galilee at that time. He gives the christological titles an interpretation which fits into the framework of Judaism: Son of man simply means 'a man' – a thesis which had already been put forward by Wellhausen – or is a periphrasis for 'I'.

---

[24]The translation of the title of the book is: 'Jesus a King who did not become King'.

1.5 Fifth phase: the 'third quest' of the historical Jesus

With the fading out of the Bultmann school, the one-sidednesses of the 'new quest' of the historical Jesus became increasingly clear. It was primarily governed by a theological interest in finding a basis for Christian identity by marking it off from Judaism and in safeguarding this identity by marking it off from the earliest Christian heresies (like Gnosticism and enthusiasm). The 'new quest' therefore preferred 'orthodox' sources. In the 'third quest',[25] which first emerged predominantly in the English-speaking world, a sociological interest replaced the theological interest, and the concern to find Jesus a place in Judaism replaced the demarcation of Jesus from Judaism; an openness to non-canonical (sometimes 'heretical') sources also replaced the preference for canonical sources.

1. *The interest in social history*. Tensions characteristic of the Jewish society of the first century CE are reflected in the appearance and fate of Jesus. Comparable 'millenarian' renewal movements[26] in other cultures are always shaped by a dominant prophetic figure. We can also draw conclusions from them for primitive Christianity: there is a social continuity between the pre-Easter circle around Jesus and Christianity after Easter.[27] The earliest Christian itinerant charismatics continued the preaching and life-style of Jesus.[28]

2. *The place of Jesus in Judaism*: Jesus is the founder of a 'renewal movement within Judaism', whose intensification of Torah and eschatology corresponds to 'radical theocratic' movements which took another form.[29] In terms of content the preaching of Jesus is 'restoration eschatology'. It aims at restoring the Jewish people.[30] There is also greater theological continuity between Jesus and the

---

[25]The term 'third quest' was coined by S. Neill and T. Wright, *Interpretation*, 379ff.

[26]'Millenarian' comes from 'millennium' (= 1000) and originally refers to the thousand-year kingdom of Rev.20. Movements which expect a fundamental change of things are called millenarian (or chiliastic).

[27]H. Schürmann, 'Die vorösterliche Anfänge der Logientradition', in H. Ristow and K. Matthiae (ed.), *Der historische Jesus und der kerygmatischer Christus*, Berlin 1960, 342–73; id., *Jesus. Gestalt und Geheimnis*, Paderborn 1994, 85–104, was the first to recognize this social continutiy between Jesus and primitive Christianity, even before the beginning of the 'third quest'.

[28]Theissen, 'Wandering Radicals'*; id., *First Followers**.

[29]Theissen, *First Followers**.

[30]Sanders, *Jesus**.

kerygmatic Christ, since the status of Jesus after Easter was articulated with the help of the Jewish-biblical pattern of interpretation.[31]

3. *The attention to non-canonical sources.* The Logia source reconstructed from the canonical sources is taking on increasing significance, as is the Gospel of Thomas, discovered around 1945, in so far as it is thought to be independent of the Synoptic Gospels.[32] There is a consensus that the multiplicity of pictures of Jesus must be explained independently of the limits of the canon (H. Koester, J.M. Robinson).[33] However, there is a dispute over whether non-canonical sources are to be preferred to canonical sources, as they are by J.D. Crossan. He does not count any of the canonical Gospels as primary sources, preferring to them the earliest stratum of the Gospel of Thomas, the Egerton Gospel, the Gospel of the Hebrews, the Logia source and a 'Cross Gospel' reconstructed from the Gospel of Peter.[34]

Meantime the Jesus research within the 'third quest' has split into different trends (cf. M.J. Borg, *Jesus*). The most important differentiation is that on the one hand there is a return to a 'non-eschatological picture of Jesus' in which Jesus becomes the advocate of a paradoxical existential wisdom influenced by Cynicism – a 'Jewish Cynic' who, shaped by Hellenistic influences, moves to the periphery of Judaism (B.L. Mack; J.D. Crossan). On the other hand, as in previous research, Jesus is interpreted in the framework of his eschatology and placed at the centre of Judaism, for the restoration of which he hoped (E.P. Sanders). The interpretation of Jesus presented here belongs with the second tendency. The 'non-eschatological Jesus' seems to have more Californian than Galilean local colouring.

However, it is true of all the currents within the 'third quest' that research into Jesus dissociates itself clearly from the 'criterion of difference' as a methodological foundation of research and tends towards a historical criterion of plausibility: what is plausible in the Jewish context and makes the rise of Christianity understandable may be historical (see 4 below).

---

[31]P. Stuhlmacher, 'Jesus als Versöhner. Überlegungen zum Problem der Darstellung Jesu im Rahmen einer biblischer Theologie des Neuen Testaments', in id., *Versöhnung, Gesetz und Gerechtigkeit. Aufsätze zur biblischen Theologie*, Göttingen 1981, 9–26, is representative of this.

[32]Patterson, *Gospel*.

[33]See §2.1.3, pp. 23f. below.

[34]Crossan, *Jesus**; id., *Cross*.

2. Summary and survey: the quest of the historical Jesus

	Critical stimuli to research into Jesus	The liberal quest of the historical Jesus	Collapse of the quest of the historical Jesus	The 'new quest' of the historical Jesus	The 'third quest' of the historical Jesus
Important representatives	Reimarus; Lessing; Herder; Strauss	Holtzmann; Hase; Beyschlag	Schweitzer; Bultmann; Dibelius; Schmidt; Wrede	Käsemann; Bornkamm; Fuchs; Ebeling; Braun	Sanders; Vermes; Theissen, Burchard; Crossan
Main statements	H.S. Reimarus: • Distinction between the historical Jesus and the church's Christ • Objective theory of deception explains the discrepancy • Jesus interpreted in a Jewish context D.F. Strauss: • Myth theory: the Jesus tradition (especially John) is heavily overlaid with myth	• Historical-critical reconstruction of the life of Jesus on the basis of the earliest sources: – The Gospel of Mark as the framework (biographical development: turning point Mark 8) – Teaching of Jesus reconstructed on the basis of Q is inserted	• The character of the portraits of the life of Jesus as projections (A. Schweitzer) • The fragmentary character of the Jesus tradition; small units, framework secondary • Kerygmatic character of the Jesus tradition	• Believed identity of the earthly Jesus with the exalted Christ necessitates the quest of the historical Jesus • The basis of the kerygma of Christ is found in Jesus' claim to authority ('implicit christology') • Consequence: Jesus is perceived in contrast to Judaism	• Jesus in the Jewish context perceived as the founder of a 'renewal movement within Judaism' (Sanders) • Continuity between Jesus and Christ: – theological: application of Jewish-biblical pattern of interpretation, – sociological: itinerant charismatics continue Jesus' lifestyle
Method/ criterion	• Reimarus: purely historical question • Strauss: mythical approach (form criticism)	Literary criticism (two-source theory)	• Form criticism • Redaction criticism • History of religions	• Criterion of difference (removing Jesus from Judaism and earliest Christianity)	• Criterion of historical plausibility (with respect to the Jewish context and the influence of Jesus on Christianity)
Theological and philosophical context	• The Enlightenment calls for the application of historical critical methods to biblical texts • Hegel's philosophy influences Strauss	• A motif of liberal theology critical of the church: to liberate faith from dogma and renew it in the light of history	• Dialectical theology (the 'that' is enough) • Existentialism (against reassurance through historical facts) • The history-of religions-school (locates Jesus in Judaism)	• Later representatives of dialectical theology are concerned to bridge the gulf between revelation and history	• Christian–Jewish dialogue – Jews discover Jesus as part of their history – Christians make sure of their Jewish roots

3. Hermeneutical reflections

The multiplicity of pictures of Jesus is reason to suspect that they are in reality self-portraits of their authors. That they are certainly more than this can be shown by the following experiment. Take all the biographical accounts in world history and make them anonymous by deleting proper names (of persons, places and institutions). Even so, all the books about Jesus would clearly stand out. For they had to use the same sources, indicate the same constellation of persons, and quote the same core sayings of Jesus. The key phrases 'twelve disciples', the admonition 'love your enemies' and mention of the crucifixion would be enough for a clear identification.

Nevertheless, there is a wide range. For all the accounts of Jesus contain a constructive element which goes beyond the data contained in the sources. Historical imagination with its hypotheses creates an 'aura of fictionality' around the figure of Jesus, just like the religious imagination of earlier Christianity. For in both cases a creative power of imagination is at work, sparked off by the same historical figure. In both cases it seems incomplete: religious symbols, images and myths can continually be reinterpreted, historical hypotheses constantly corrected. Here neither the religious nor the historical reconstruction of the history of Jesus proceeds arbitrarily, but on the basis of axiomatic convictions. The religious imagination of primitive Christianity is guided by the firm belief that through Jesus it is possible to make contact with God, the ultimate reality. The historical imagination is governed by the basic convictions of the historical consciousness: all sources come from fallible human beings and must therefore be subjected to historical criticism. Furthermore, they must all be interpreted in the light of a historical relativism which knows that everything is correlated with everything else; everything has analogies. Finally, the maxim is true that historical distance prohibits an anachronistic interpretation of the sources within the framework of present-day values and convictions. Scholarly accounts of Jesus governed by such ideas are constructs of historical imagination: relatively free of arbitrariness, capable of being corrected by sources and portraits the presuppositions of which can be seen. If the religious imagination is concerned with access to God, the historical imagination is concerned with access to a past reality. Therefore historical sources are the decisive criterion for its work. Everything must be measured by these sources, and every thought subjected to them. Therefore any scholarly description of Jesus must begin by presenting the sources on the historical Jesus.

4. Tasks

4.1 Five phases of the quest of the historical Jesus

Here are five texts each of which belongs to one of the five phases of the quest of the historical Jesus. Assign the texts to their period and give reasons for this by briefly noting the most important identifying features. Make a guess at who the author could be.

Text 1:

> 'All exegesis is agreed that the authenticity of the first, second and fourth antitheses in the Sermon on the Mount cannot be doubted . . . The determining factor, however, is that the words ἐγὼ δὲ λέγω [= but I say] embody a claim to an authority which rivals and challenges that of Moses . . . To this there are no Jewish parallels, nor indeed can there be. For the Jew who does what is done here has cut himself off from the community of Judaism – or else he brings the Messianic Torah and is therefore the Messiah . . . The unheard-of implication of the saying testifies to its genuineness . . . [Jesus] was a Jew and made the assumption of Jewish piety, but at the same time he shatters this framework with his claim.'

Text 2:

> 'We must take into account the overwhelming impression which was made upon those around him by the personal character and discourse of Jesus, as long as he was living amongst them, which did not permit them deliberately to scrutinize and compare him with their previous standard. The belief in him as the Messiah extended to wider circles only by slow degrees; and even during his lifetime the people may have reported many wonderful stories of him . . . After his death, however, the belief in his resurrection, however that belief may have arisen, afforded more than sufficient proof of his messiahship; so that all the other miracles in his history need not be considered as the foundation of the faith in this, but it may rather be adduced as the consequences of it . . . It is to be considered that in ancient times, and especially amongst the Hebrews, and yet more when this people was stirred up by religious excitement, the line of distinction between history and fiction, prose and poetry, was not drawn so clearly as with us . . . The only question that can arise here is whether to such fictions . . . we can give the name of myths. If we regard only their own intrinsic nature, the name is not appropriate; but it is so when these fictions, having met with faith, come to be received amongst the legends of a people or religious party, for this is always a proof that they were the fruit, not of any individual conception, but of an accordance with the sentiments of a multitude.'

Text 3:

> 'I do indeed think that we can now know almost nothing concerning the life and personality of Jesus, since the early Christian sources show no interest in either, are moreover fragmentary and often legendary; and other sources about Jesus do not exist. Except for the purely critical research, what has been written in the last hundred and fifty years on the life of Jesus, his personality and the development of his inner life, is fantastic and romantic . . . I have in this book not dealt with the question at all – not so much because nothing can be said about it with certainty as because I consider it of secondary importance.'

Text 4:

> 'Whatever else Jesus was, he was a Jew from Galilee, and the Jesus movement was, at least in its beginnings, Galilean Jewish or, at any rate, Palestinian Jewish . . . Hence, one has access to Jesus in two ways: first, by the the history of primitive Christianity, insofar as it can be understood as the history of Jesus' influence; and second, the history of Palestine, insofar as it was the place of Jesus' ministry . . . The points of access complement each other and sometimes overlap. Both Jesus and the beginnings of early Christianity are part of the history of Judaism in Palestine.'

Text 5:

> 'Finally, attention must also be drawn to the way in which both sources [Mark and Q] deal with the material in so completely a homogeneous way that they offer further attempts to define the moral character of Jesus. In both, a harmonious picture of his mind is developed, the basic feature of which is the force of his consciousness of God which was always and everywhere present: a development in his life which progressed in many directions, the driving principle of which forms the religious and moral factor.'

Part One: The Sources and their Evaluation

2

Christian Sources about Jesus

R. Cameron (ed.), *The Other Gospels. Non-Canonical Gospel Texts*, Philadelphia 1982 (bibliography); id. (ed.), *The Apocryphal Jesus and Christian Origins*, Semeia 49, 1990; J.H. Charlesworth, 'Research on the New Testament Apocrypha and Pseudepigrapha', *ANRW* II 25.5,1988, 3920–68 (bibliography); id., *The New Testament Apocrypha and Pseudepigrapha: A Guide to Publications, with Excursus on Apocalypses*, ATLA Bibliography Series, no.17, Metuchen, NJ and London 1987; id. and C.A. Evans, 'Jesus in the Agrapha and Apocryphal Gospels', in *Studying**, 479–533; J.D. Crossan, *Four Other Gospels. Shadows on the Contours of Canon*, Minneapolis 1985; J.K. Elliott, *The Apocryphal Jesus*, Oxford 1996; C.A. Evans, *Noncanonical Writings**; S. Gero, 'Apocryphal Gospels: A Survey of Textual and Literary Problems', *ANRW* II 25.5, 1988, 3969–96; J. Jeremias, *Unknown Sayings of Jesus*, London 1957; C.W. Hedrick (ed.), *The Historical Jesus and the Rejected Gospels*, Semeia 44, 1988; H. Koester, 'Apocryphal and Canonical Gospels', *HTR* 73, 1980, 105–30; id., *Ancient Christian Gospels. Their History and Development*, Philadelphia and London 1990; id. and J.M. Robinson, *Trajectories through Early Christianity*, Philadelphia 1971; J.P. Meier, *Marginal Jew* 1*, 41–55, 112–166; U. Schnelle, *The History and Theology of the New Testament Writings,* Minneapolis and London 1998; B.H. Streeter, *The Four Gospels. A Study of Origins*, London 1924, ⁵1936; D. Wenham (ed.), *The Jesus Tradition Outside the Gospels*, Gospel Perspectives 5, Sheffield 1985; R. McL. Wilson, 'Apokryphen II', *TRE* 3, 1978, 316–62.

Introduction

In assessing the sources for the historical Jesus we need to note two characteristics: their historical proximity to the historical Jesus and their independence.

The closer a source brings us to the historical Jesus, the more important it is. Therefore it is important to determine the age of the sources. But age is not identical with historical proximity. The letters of Paul are older than the Synoptic Gospels, yet the latter are historically closer to the historical Jesus. This is first of all because they contain many individual traditions which are older than the letters of Paul, but above all because they are free of the Pauline 'tendency' to see Jesus as a pre-existent, mythical being. The tradition of the early church attempted to guarantee the historical proximity of the Gospels to Jesus by attributing their authorship to apostles: accordingly the Gospels of Matthew and

John were said to come from apostles of Jesus (i.e. eyewitnesses), Mark and Luke from disciples of the apostles (i.e. people who had access to eyewitness traditions). At present there is a tendency in part to rehabilitate this early church tradition and to attribute Mark to John Mark, Luke to Luke the companion of Paul, John to a disciple of Jesus and presbyter, John. But we can also attempt to determine how near to or far from Jesus a source is independently of that.

Here the second characteristic, the independence of the sources from one another, plays an important role. For we can never test our sources by direct comparison with historical reality; this always has to be done by comparison with other sources. When the agreement between the sources is all too great, we assume that they are dependent on one another. When the sources contradict each other all too sharply, we have to conjecture that one (or more) distorts reality heavily and is valueless. The position over sources is good where inconsistencies between the sources guarantee their independence but they can nevertheless be interpreted coherently as evidence of one and the same historical reality.

In writings which incorporate traditions, the independence of several sources from one another can extend to these traditions – regardless of whether the author who collected them perhaps knew the other Gospels. It is decisive that he follows a tradition autonomous from the other Gospels. Here it makes no difference whether we have canonical or non-canonical sources. Initially all the sources have the same potential for a historical approach, but that need not mean that the same historical value can be attributed to them after a historical examination. As this equal status for the canonical and the non-canonical Jesus tradition is by no means undisputed, this survey of the sources begins with a sketch of tendencies and phases in scholarly evaluation of the so-called apocryphal tradition.

Task

From the Table of Contents in Schneemelcher and Wilson, *New Testament Apocrypha*, Vol.1 (see opening general bibliography), discover the range of the extra-canonical Gospel literature. Read some of the source texts, e.g. the Gospel of Thomas, the papyrus fragments of unknown Gospels (POx 840; Papyrus Egerton), the fragment of the Gospel of Peter, the Apocryphon of James, the fragments of the Jewish Christian Gospels and the fragment of the secret Gospel of Mark.

1. The significance of extra-canonical Christian literature for the study of Jesus: tendencies and phases of research

First of all we need to explain some terminology. Traditionally, several groups of writings are distinguished among the extra-canonical sources, but the names given to them are now increasingly been recognized as being problematical:

New Testament apocrypha: all the early Christian writings which were not accepted into the canon, do not belong to the Apostolic Fathers, yet relate to the New Testament in either content or genre. However, an assumed relationship to the New Testament does not fit most of these writings. 'Apocryphal' (from ἀπόκρυφος = hidden) is used neutrally ('not part of the canon'), pejoratively ('heretical', 'forged', thus the church fathers), or esoterically ('secret' – as some Gnostic writings term themselves).

Apostolic Fathers: this term denotes a group of early Christian writings defined in the seventeenth century and extended several times since then; it was assumed that they were written in the apostolic age or (as this applies to none of the writings) were composed by early guarantors of apostolic doctrine. The main criterion is the assumed 'orthodoxy' and reliability of these writings as opposed to the apocrypha. They include I Clement, the letters of Ignatius and Polycarp, the Didache, the Letter of Barnabas, II Clement, the Letter to Diognetus and the Shepherd of Hermas.

Agrapha (or in the singular *agraphon*, from ἄγραφος = unwritten): sayings of Jesus not contained in the canonical Gospels. These are sayings of Jesus handed down by word of mouth in the church fathers or in apocrypha, the Apostolic Fathers or in the New Testament outside the Gospels. Sometimes 'agraphon' is also used as a positive counterpart to 'apocryphon' (an authentic saying of Jesus).

The historical-critical study of Jesus so far has almost exclusively used the canonical Gospels as sources, as the survey of the history of the quest of the historical Jesus (§ 1) showed. Scholars were convinced that the earliest and best Christian sources have been preserved in the canon. The apocryphal Gospels were regarded as chronologically late and inferior in content: at best fantastic and at worst heretical. This conviction has begun to waver in recent decades, among other things because over the course of the last century several early Christian writings and fragments have been discovered and edited; their composition dates to considerably before the consolidation of the New Testament canon and could in part have taken place parallel to the canonical texts.

Thus the Didache was discovered in 1873 and published in 1883; the Gospel of Peter was discovered in 1886/7 and published in 1892; after 1897 the important papyrus discoveries from Oxyrhynchus came to light; Egerton Papyrus 2 was published in 1935; the Nag Hammadi writings (including the Gospel of Thomas) were discovered around 1945 and edited in the following decades; the fragment of the Secret Gospel of Mark was discovered in 1958 and published in 1973.

The external attestation of canonical and extra-canonical literature about Jesus is almost equal for the first two centuries, in respect both of mentions and quotations in the early church fathers and of the manuscript evidence.

However, up to the end of the second century only two papyri each were known of the Gospel of John (P^{52}, P^{66}) and the Gospel of Matthew (P^{64}, P^{67}) on the one hand and the unknown Egerton Gospel, the Gospel of Peter (POx 2949, 4009) and the Gospel of Thomas (POx 1) on the other. From the third century we have several papyri of all the canonical Gospels and fragments of the Gospel of Thomas (POx 654, 655), the Protevangelium of James (Bodmer Papyrus V), the Gospel of Mary (POx 3525) and an unknown Gospel (Rainer Papyrus/Fayyum Fragment).The church fathers cite a good dozen further Gospels alongside the canonical Gospels.[1]

Nevertheless, there is still a vigorous debate about the value of extra-canonical literature for the study of the history of early Christianity and the story of Jesus. Scholars adopt one of three rival positions. The first states that non-canonical writings could not make any relevant contribution to the study of Christian beginnings; the second concedes that they can supplement the canonical writings; the third holds that canonical and extra-canonical Christian writings are to be used as sources which in principle are of equal value.

1.1 'Apocryphal' writings yield nothing for research into the life of Jesus

Occasionally it is denied that the early Christian writings outside the canon have any value for the reconstruction of the beginnings. As more recent examples, we might mention the monographs written by J.D. Crossan and R. Schnackenburg,[2] which appeared in 1991 and 1993 respectively. They base their restriction to the canonical Gospels on three 'classic' arguments:

- The *argument from age*: it is presupposed that the extra-canonical Gospels were composed considerably later than the canonical Gospels. It is not thought that there are any early traditions in them which can be identified. Conversely, Schnackenburg puts the canon of the four Gospels as early as the beginning of the second century.
- The argument of *greater historical reliability*. Although it is granted that the Synoptic Gospels were shaped by community needs, they are accorded relative historical credibility. By contrast, the apocryphal Gospels are said to be 'overlaid with legend and in part fantastic stories'.[3]

---

[1]Cf. Koester, 'Apocryphal and Canonical Gospels', especially 108–11.

[2]Crossan, *Jesus* *; R. Schnackenburg, *Jesus in the Gospels*, Louisville 1995, 323. But there are also other voices in the framework of Catholic exegesis like that of A.Läpple, *Ausserbiblische Jesusgeschichten, Ein Plädoyer für die Apokryphen*, who proposes the collective term 'Fifth Gospel' for all the extra-biblical Gospels 'which are already known today or are expanded in the future by the discovery of new manuscripts' (40). He expressly points out the value of the Gospel of Thomas for research into 'the time before the Gospels' (46).

[3]Schnackenburg, *Jesus*, 323.

- The argument of the *apostolic tradition* (the argument of orthodoxy): only the canonical Gospels 'guarantee the apostolic tradition';[4] by contrast the apocryphal Gospels are due to later 'excrescences and false developments' of the early tradition 'which stemmed partly from fantasy and partly from heresy'.[5]

This argument arouses the suspicion of being a confession of the priority of the canon and the picture of history handed down by the church which has only a thin cloak of scholarship. We might compare with the above arguments the formulation of Athanasius in the thirty-ninth Easter festal letter of 367. After enumerating the canonical books he says: 'These are the springs of salvation . . . In them alone is the doctrine of piety proclaimed. Let no one add anything to them . . .' There follows a warning against the apocrypha: they are 'a fabrication of the heretics, who write them down when it pleases them and generously assign to them an early date of composition, in order that they may be able to draw upon them as supposedly ancient writings and have in them occasion to deceive the guileless.'[6]

Important historical and methodological objections can be made to all three arguments:

- To the *argument from age*: certainly it is extremely difficult to date the relevant texts, as the following remarks will continually show. But in the present state of scholarship we must think it probable that traditions from the first century can be detected in some extra-canonical sources.
- To *historical reliability*: we must be careful to use our criteria in both directions. The Synoptic Gospels, too, contain 'legends' and 'fantastic narratives'. Distinctions should always be made only on the basis of individual texts – independently of whether they belong in the canon.
- To *orthodoxy*: the idea that the originally pure apostolic teaching was *later* distorted by heresies is a dogmatic construct. 'Orthodoxy and heresy' developed chronologically in parallel, and each borrowed from the other. The groups which were later excluded as heretical also (at least in part) refer to the earliest Christian traditions and developed these in accordance with their needs – here in principle they were no different from the 'orthodox' communities .

1.2 Research into the agrapha: the search for unknown sayings of Jesus to expand the Synoptic picture of Jesus

Most frequently extra-Christian sources are used selectively to support results which have been gained from the New Testament texts. In the study of the

---

[4]Ibid.
[5]J. Gnilka, *Jesus von Nazareth*, HThK Suppl. III, Freiburg, Basel and Vienna 1990, 25.
[6]Quoted from *NT Apoc* I, 1963, 60; 1991, 50.

teaching of Jesus this basic attitude has had its scholarly heyday in research into the so-called agrapha. The most important stages of this research are as follows:

- The first collection on a scholarly basis of all the extra-biblical sayings of Jesus then known[7] was made in 1889 by Alfred Resch under the title *Agrapha, Ausserkanonische Evangelienfragmente.*[8]
- Since 1897 the study of the agrapha has been enlivened by striking papyrus discoveries, which have brought to light hitherto unknown sayings and stories of Jesus, fragments of lost Gospels. In 1897 B.P. Grenfell and A.S. Hunt published Oxyrhynchus Papyrus 1 (POx 1);[9] shortly after this followed POx 654 and 655. These fragments contain several logia introduced by 'Jesus said', some of which have New Testament parallels and some of which were completely new. In 1905 the same scholars found POx 840, a Gospel fragment which relates a hitherto unknown dispute.[10] In 1935 a further fragment of an unknown Gospel was published, so-called Egerton Papyrus 2.[11]
- J. Jeremias summed up the numerous contributions to the debate on the agrapha which appeared over the following decades in his book *Unknown Sayings of Jesus*, which appeared in German in 1948. It aroused wide interest. He discussed 21 agrapha, 10 of them 'authentic' logia which probably come from Jesus. The principle of selection according to which he separates possibly authentic material from certainly inauthentic material is explicitly derived from the canonical writings: 'We shall discuss those agrapha which in content, form and tradition history can be set alongside the sayings of Jesus in the Synoptic Gospels.'[12]
- With the publication of the manuscripts found in Nag Hammadi around 1945, especially the Gospel of Thomas, many new agrapha have become known. Oxyrhynchus Papyri 1, 654, 655 with their sayings about Jesus proved to be Greek fragments of the extensive Gospel of Thomas which now exists in Coptic. Synoptic discourse traditions now existed in large numbers in a further

---

[7]A critical examination of these sayings with a view to determining their possible authenticity was made by the American J.H. Ropes in a work which appeared in 1896: *Die Sprüche Jesu, die in den kanonische Evangelien nicht überliefert sind. Eine kritische Bearbeitung des von D.Alfred Resch gesammelten Materials.*

[8]The second, thoroughly revised edition (Leipzig 1906, reprinted Darmstadt 1967) bears the slightly different title *Agrapha. Aussercanonische Schriftfragmente.*

[9]The very title of their book aroused widespread expectations: Λόγια Ἰησοῦ: *Sayings of Our Lord from an Early Greek Papyrus.*

[10]B.P. Grenfell and A.S. Hunt, *Fragment of an Uncanonical Gospel from Oxyrhynchus,* Oxford 1908.

[11]H.I. Bell and T.C. Skeat, *Fragments of an Unknown Gospel,* London 1935.

[12]Jeremias, *Unknown Sayings,* 33.

version, which sometimes gave the impression of being archaic, and sometimes seemed clearly to have been revised by the Gnostics. Study of the Gospel of Thomas began to shake the hitherto almost uncontested priority of the canonical writings for the reconstruction of beginnings – the possibility of an independent extra-canonical strand of tradition came into view.

1.3 Canonical and extra-canonical sources are in principle of equal value in the study of Jesus

The insight into the need to go beyond the limits of the canon in New Testament exegesis is relatively recent. It is grounded in the recognition that as far as the time of their composition is concerned, neither in content nor in form are the canonical writings in principle to be set apart from extra-canonical early Christian writings. Historical, form-critical and genre-critical works have prepared the way for this awareness.

- *Historically*, it has been recognized that the Christianity of the church, to which we owe the selection and establishment of the canon, is the result of a lengthy process within which other traditions, with writings which similarly went back to the beginnings, were excluded. The reconstruction of the history of early Christianity put forward by Walter Bauer in his 1934 book *Orthodoxy and Heresy in Earliest Christianity*, which stood the picture of history handed down by the church on its head, was pioneering here. According to Bauer, in some areas like Egypt and East Syria (Edessa), forms of Christianity later regarded as heterodox chronologically preceded the 'orthodox' communities. 'Catholic' and 'heretical' views existed side by side for decades in the same communities in Asia Minor and Macedonia, before orthodoxy established itself under Roman influence in the second century.
- In *form criticism*, the effect of the free Jesus tradition was discovered. Classical form criticism had initially worked out the importance of oral tradition for the prehistory of the writing of the Gospels. In his investigation on 'Synoptic Tradition in the Apostolic Fathers', which appeared in 1957, H. Koester demonstrated that oral or written free Jesus tradition, independent of the Gospels which existed in written form, was still used in liturgy, catechesis and church order in the first half of the second century.
- In terms of *genre*, the canonical Gospels and the sources underlying them are not to be understood in isolation from the extra-canonical Gospel literature. In his article 'LOGOI SOPHON. On the Genre of the Sayings Source Q', J.M. Robinson traced the development of the genre of the 'sayings collection' in earliest Christianity through canonical and extra-canonical sources. Its beginning lies in the early collections of the sayings of Jesus, which have their roots in

the Jewish wisdom tradition and can still be detected indirectly: as well as the known sayings source Q used by Matthew and Luke there are also collections of wisdom sayings, e.g. behind Mark 4 and I Clement 13.2. An advanced stage of the history of this tradition is to be found in the Gospel of Thomas: the claim of the wisdom teacher has been reshaped by that of the revealer of esoteric Gnostic knowledge – a development suggested by the genre which is already making its way in Q. Other genres have developed in both the canonical and the extra-canonical Gospels: dialogues (John, Egerton Gospel and Gnostic dialogue Gospels), infancy narratives (Matt. 1–2/Luke 1–2 and infancy Gospels), passion narratives (canonical Gospels and the Gospel of Peter).

In the framework of the new premises which have just been described, especially in the English-speaking world over the past decade scholars have begun intensive research into the early extra-canonical sources. Their age and place in the history of tradition is often defined radically differently from before. There has been some hesitation over accepting the results of this research in Germany, partly because there are justified reservations about all too early datings. In 1990 H. Koester produced the outline of a history of the development of the Gospel literature which gave a balanced assessment of these individual studies, entitled *Ancient Christian Gospels. Their History and Development*. Here for the first time canonical and extra-canonical Gospels and their sources are treated on an equal footing. Regardless of his judgments on individual questions, this is a methodological milestone which scholars must never go back from.

So far only the beginnings of the results of this new assessment of the sources have proved fruitful for the study of Jesus; here we can still expect developments in the future.[13]

From the wealth of early Christian canonical and extra-canonical sources, in the following sections we shall be discussing only those which could *possibly* be relevant for the reconstruction of the teaching and life of Jesus. As a rule these are texts which were composed in the first or second centuries or contain traditions which go back to this time.

2. The Synoptic sources

The Synoptic sources comprise the first three Gospels with their underlying sources. They are called 'Synoptic' because they sketch out a picture of Jesus

---

[13]Crossan, *Jesus**, is a major example of the use of extra-Christian sources in reconstructing the life and teaching of Jesus. However, Crossan's extremely early dating of extra-canonical sources has not gained acceptance.

which is clearly different from that of John and in part are dependent on one another in literary terms. Matthew and Luke had the Gospel of Mark (or a slightly revised Deutero-Mark) as a source, and in addition both use the Logia source (Q), which can be reconstructed from them. The two-source theory which is presupposed here means that for the study of Jesus we have two ancient sources (Mark and Q) which are independent of each other, and in addition large complexes of Matthaean and Lukan special material, each of which represents an independent tradition (oral or written?).

It is important for the study of Jesus that the content of these four independent sources (or complexes of tradition) are related: here we encounter the same forms and genres, themes and motives. All the sources agree in presenting Jesus as an eschatological preacher who in word and deed, in parables and miracles, proclaims and represents the breaking in of God's kingly rule as a turning towards the poor and sinners. Because of the great antiquity and the breadth of the dispersion of the Synoptic traditions, which also appear outside the sphere of Synoptic tradition in the narrower sense (e.g. in the Gospel of John, the Gospel of Thomas and in the earliest Christian epistolary literature), there is a broad scholarly consensus that we can best find access to the historical Jesus through the Synoptic tradition.

2.1 The Gospel of Mark

P.J. Achtemeier, 'Toward the Isolation of Pre-Markan Miracle Catenae', *JBL* 89, 1970, 265–91; id., 'Origin and Function of Pre-Markan Miracle Catenae', *JBL* 91, 1972, 198–221; M. Hengel, *Studies in the Gospel of Mark*, London and Philadelphia 1985; M.D. Hooker, *The Gospel according to St Mark*, London 1991; H.C. Kee, *Community of the New Age*, Philadelphia and London 1977; R.H. Lightfoot, *History and Interpretation in the Gospels*, London 1935; G. Strecker (ed.), *Minor Agreements*, Göttingen 1993; P. Stuhlmacher (ed.), *The Gospel and the Gospels*, Grand Rapids 1991, 209–51; W.R. Telford (ed.), *The Interpretation of Mark*, Edinburgh 1995.

1. *The text.* The Gospel of Mark is the earliest extant Gospel, and is the basis of Matthew and Luke. However, there are indications that the version which became canonical and is first attested by manuscripts from the third century is not the only form of the text that was in circulation:

- The *instability of the text*: Mark 6.45–8.26 is absent from Luke; as this section in particular contains doublets, it was perhaps not an original ingredient of the Gospel. As early as the second century the abrupt ending in Mark 16.8 (the women do not hand on the message of the resurrection) led to the composition of a secondary conclusion to Mark. The Secret Gospel of Mark was probably a longer version of Mark, but one which offered early material from the tradition (see below, 4.2).
- Some of the *minor agreements* between Matthew and Luke against Mark in texts which they have taken over from Mark could indicate a common original which diverged from the canonical Gospel of Mark.
- Markan special material, i.e. Markan texts which Matthew and Luke give no recognizable reason for not offering (e.g. Mark 2.27; 4.26–29; 9.48; 12.32–34; 15.44ff.), was perhaps not in their original.

So there were presumably several editions of the Gospel of Mark.[14] However, Matthew and Luke demonstrably had the greater part of the text before them.

2. *Place and time of composition.* According to the earliest church tradition the Gospel of Mark was written down in Rome, on the basis of oral teaching from Peter, by his interpreter John Mark (cf. I Peter 5.13: Mark and Peter in Rome).[15] Above all the heterogeneous source material which the evangelist has worked over tells against this account, which for example M. Hengel thinks to be essentially credible.[16] In the Gospel of Mark we find Palestinian Jesus traditions with rich local colouring alongside pre-Pauline Hellenistic traditions (e.g. eucharistic words, catalogue of vices in Mark 7.21f., the term εὐαγγέλιον [gospel]). This combination is most likely in the cities of Syria, which adjoins Palestine, for example in Antioch, where the authority of John Mark was originally based. This could explain the attribution to him.[17] Mark was composed around 70,[18] as the Jewish–Roman War (66–74 CE) is clearly reflected in the Gospel, for example in sections which relate to the time of the author and his first readers. There is a dispute as to whether the destruction of the temple announced in Mark 13.2 has already taken place,[19] or is still expected.[20]

---

[14]There are numerous explanations for the situation sketched out here, but basically it can be attributed to two models (presupposing that the two-source theory is valid in principle): to Proto-Mark or Ur-Mark theories, according to which *earlier* forms of the canonical Mark were used by Matthew and Luke, or to Deutero-Mark theories, according to which Matthew and Luke used *revised* versions of the Mark which later became canonical.

[15]Note by Papias in Eusebius *HE* 3, 39, 15, 16; Irenaeus, *Haer.* 3.1.1; Clement of Alexandria in Eusebius 2.15.1f.

[16]M. Hengel, in Stuhlmacher (ed.), *Gospels**, 229–43.

[17]For the locating of Mark in Syria cf. Theissen, *Gospels**, 236–49.

[18]Extremely early datings are not considered here.

[19]Thus e.g. Theissen, *Gospels**, 258–71.

[20]Thus for example Hengel, *Studies in the Gospel of Mark*, 14ff.

3. *Underlying sources*: the author of Mark is a collector, in so far as he demonstrably takes up written and oral material from the tradition which varies in both form and theology. This includes:

- a consecutive *passion narrative* which probably already existed in written form (its precise extent is disputed);
- oral or written (collections of) *miracle stories;*[21]
- apocalyptic traditions, especially the '*Synoptic apocalypse*', Mark 13, which had probably already been fixed in writing;[22]
- *disputations and didactic sayings* for which sometimes a written basis is conjectured;[23] in addition a further tradition of sayings, e.g. the probably already traditional collection of parables and metaphors in Mark 4. Some Markan logia are parallel traditions to Q.[24]

4. *Theological shaping*: the author of Mark is a theologian who shapes his material, bringing together traditional material under overarching christological ideas and creating something new: a Gospel which could be described as a passion narrative with an extended biographical introduction. In it Jesus is surrounded by a mystery which is successively disclosed

5. Mark as a *source for the study of Jesus*. The chronological and geographical outline of Mark is secondary to the individual traditions; its form is determined by the author's theological premises and therefore historically worthless (the same goes for Luke, Mark and John). However, some of the material from the tradition presented in Mark goes back a very long way and represents an important source for the reconstruction of the teaching and the life of Jesus.

2.2 The Logia source

D. Catchpole, *The Quest for Q*, Edinburgh 1993; R.A. Edwards, *A Theology of Q*, Philadelphia 1976; J.S. Kloppenborg, 'Tradition and Redaction in the Synoptic Sayings Source', *CBQ* 46, 1984, 34–62; id.,*The Formation of Q. Trajectories in Ancient Wisdom Collections*, Philadelphia 1987; id. (ed.), *The Shape of Q*, Minneapolis 1994; id., *Conflict and Intention*, Valley Forge 1995; D. Lührmann, *Die Redaktion der Logienquelle*, WMANT 33, Neukirchen-Vluyn 1969; B. Mack, *The Lost Gospel*, Shaftesbury 1993; A. Polag, *Fragmenta Q*, Neukirchen-Vluyn 1979, ²1982; V. Taylor, 'The Order of Q', *JTS* 4, 1953, 27–31 (*New Testament Essays*, London 1970, 90–4); C.M. Tuckett, *Q and the History of Early Christianity*, Edinburgh and Peabody, Mass. 1995.

---

[21]Achtemeier, 'Isolation'; 'Origin', assumes written collections of miracles in Mark 4–6; 6–8.

[22]Cf. E. Brandenburger, *Mk 13, 21–73 und die Apokalyptik*, FRLANT 134, Göttingen 1984; Theissen, *Gospels**, 125–65.

[23]H.-W. Kuhn, *Ältere Sammlungen im Markusevangelium*, StUNT 8, Göttingen 1971.

[24]Cf. R. Laufen, *Die Doppelüberlieferungen der Logienquelle und des Markusevangeliums*, BBB 54, Königstein/Bonn 1980.

1. *The text*. The so-called Logia source Q (short for German *Quelle*, source) is an entity that has been inferred. In addition to their Markan material Matthew and Luke have many texts in common, predominantly sayings material, which they have demonstrably included independently of each other. In all probability the source came to them in Greek and in writing.[25] Only the material attested by both Matthew and Luke in common can be assigned with some certainty to Q; here Luke has presumably kept the original sequence more than Matthew.[26] It is conceivable that some of the remaining special material in Matthew and Luke comes from the Logia source, but that cannot be proved.[27]

2. *Traditions incorporated, genre and Sitz im Leben*. Q contains almost only sayings of Jesus, e.g. wisdom sayings, prophetic and apocalyptic sayings, sayings about the Law, community rules and parables. Some of them certainly go back to Aramaic logia and thus to the beginnings of the tradition. There is no passion narrative or other narrative traditions; the only exceptions are the pericopes about the temptation of Jesus (Matt. 4.1–11/Luke 4.1–13) and the centurion of Capernaum (Matt. 8.5–13/Luke 7.1–10), but in them the emphasis lies on the sayings. Form-critically the Logia source is to be described as a collection of sayings in which the teaching of Jesus has been preserved. The sayings were probably collected and disseminated by the earliest Christian itinerant charismatics, who continued the lifestyle and preaching of Jesus. The central concern of the preaching is to call people to discipleship of Jesus in the face of the kingdom of God which is breaking in. As Son of God, Jesus is the teacher of God with full power and is expected as eschatological judge in the form of the Son of Man who will come again. His death is interpreted as a prophetic fate: he is one of the many messengers of wisdom who have been rejected (Luke 13.34f.; 11.49ff.)

3. *Time and place of origin*. Q has recognizably grown out of smaller collections. However, any reconstruction of the stages of growth and the redactions and tradents which belong to them must remain hypothetical.[28] Reliable statements can at best be made about the final redaction, by concentrating on the composition as a whole and the selection and linking of the different

---

[25]Kloppenborg, *Formation*. An oral source was proposed by J. Jeremias, 'Zur Hypothese einer schriftlichen Logienquelle Q', *ZNW* 29, 1980, 147–9.

[26]Taylor, 'Order'.

[27]It is frequently assumed that Matthew and Luke had different recensions of Q – however, this hypothesis leads into a methodologically uncontrolled field.

[28]On the basis of traditio-historical criteria, S. Schulz, *Q – Die Spruchquelle der Evangelisten*, Zurich 1972, wants to distinguish earlier Palestinian traditions from traditions shaped by Hellenism. Kloppenborg, *Formation*, 317–28, offers an analysis of three stages: he argues that as a originally pure wisdom book Q secondarily included prophetic-apocalypic sayings and began the transformation to a biographical genre by the integration of the narrative tradition.

themes. Thus Q certainly came into being before the Jewish War and the destruction of the temple, as the coming of the Son of Man is expected at a time of profound peace, and the threat is uttered that God will leave the temple. The temptation story has clear allusions to the surmounting of the Caligula crisis (39/40 CE). The image of the Pharisees as persecutors of Christians is to be located historically in the 40s and early 50s; the same goes for the preaching and mission orientated on Israel which is presupposed in Q. Q was probably composed in Palestine.[29]

4. *The Logia source and the historical Jesus.* Q is certainly the most important source for reconstructing the teaching of Jesus. However, here too the authentic traditions of Jesus occur in, with and under the sayings of generations after him. Therefore very different pictures of Jesus can also be reconstructed from the Q tradition. For example, B.L. Mack sketches his picture of Jesus as a Galilean Cynic on the basis of the seven thematic groups of logia which he assigns to the earliest stratum of Q.[30] By contrast, if the apocalyptic sayings are thought to come from Jesus, a quite different picture arises.

2.3 The Gospel of Matthew

D.L. Balch (ed.), *Social History of the Matthean Community*, Minneapolis 1991; H.D. Betz, *Essays on the Sermon on the Mount*, Philadelphia 1971, 37–50; G. Bornkamm, G. Barth and H.J. Held, *Tradition and Interpretation in Matthew*, London and Philadelphia 1963; W.D. Davies, *The Setting of the Sermon on the Mount*, Cambridge 1966; G.D. Kilpatrick, *The Origins of the Gospel According to St. Matthew*, Oxford 1946, [2]1950; U. Luz, *Matthew in History*, Minneapolis 1994; id., *The Theology of the Gospel of Matthew*, Cambridge 1995; J.A. Overman, *Matthew's Gospel and Formative Judaism*, Minneapolis 1990; A. Sand, *Das Matthäus-Evangelium*, EdF 275, Darmstadt 1991; E. Schweizer, *Matthäus und seine Gemeinde*, SBS 71, Stuttgart 1974; D. Senior, *What Are They Saying About Matthew?*, New York and Ramsey, NJ 1983; G. Stanton, 'The Origin and Purpose of Matthew's Gospel: Matthean Scholarship from 1945 to 1980', *ANRW* II 25.3, 1984, 1889–951; id., *A Gospel for a New People. Studies in Matthew*, Edinburgh 1992; id. (ed.), *The Interpretation of Matthew*, Edinburgh 1995; K. Stendahl, *The School of St Matthew and its Use of the Old Testament*, Uppsala 1954; G. Strecker, *Der Weg der Gerechtigkeit. Untersuchungen zur Theologie des Matthaus*, FRLANT 82, Göttingen 1962, [3]1971; W. Trilling, *Das wahre Israel. Studien zur Theologie des Matthäus-Evangeliums*, StANT 10, Munich 1964.

1. *The text.* The Gospel of Matthew is admirably attested by early papyri (from c.200) and quotations in the church fathers (from the middle of the second

---

[29]Cf. Theissen, *Gospels**, 203–34.
[30]Mack, *The Lost Gospel*, San Francisco 1993.

century). There is no question of the integrity of the text, which is composed in Greek, despite the view put forward since Papias and Irenaeus (in Eusebius, *HE* 3, 39, 16; 5, 8, 2) that Matthew originally wrote in Aramaic (or Hebrew).

2. *Sources and structure.* The Gospel of Matthew is based on Mark, the Logia source and special material of various kinds,[31] the value of which as sources has to be checked by examining individual texts: as well as sayings traditions (only eight parables) there is legendary material (like the prehistory in Matt. 1–2 or 14.28–31; 17.24–27; 27.3–10, 19, 24f.) and pericopes which have largely been shaped by the redactor (e.g. Matt. 28.16–20). In his outline Matthew predominantly follows Mark, but has done some regrouping from thematic perspectives within Mark 1–13 (e.g. the summary of Jesus' actions in Matt. 8–9). Matthew has worked in five great speeches at appropriate places or at places indicated by Mark, which use material from all three groups of sources: the Sermon on the Mount (5–7),[32] the mission discourse (9.35–10.42), the parable discourse (13), the community discourse (18) and the eschatological discourse (23–25).[33]

3. *Time and place of origin.* Matthew presupposes the destruction of the temple (Matt. 22.7); the *terminus ante quem* is given by Ignatius of Antioch (c.110–117), who in Smyrn. 1.1 quotes a redactional phrase from Matt. 3.15. The Didache (c.100?) also seems to refer to Matthew under the designation 'the Gospel' (15.3 etc.).[34] It is most probable that the Gospel was composed in the 80s, or the 90s at the latest. It suggests an eastern or north-eastern local perspective on Palestine: Matt. 19.1 puts Judaea '*beyond* the Jordan'; in Matt. 4.24 the author introduces the statement, contrary to Mark, that Jesus' call reverberated 'throughout Syria'. Matthew may have been composed somewhere within the Syrian interior, perhaps in the region of Damascus or the Decapolis.[35]

4. *Sitz im Leben.* The clear combination of Jewish–Christian and Gentile–Christian traditions in Matthew on the one hand and the intensive polemic of the Matthaean Jesus against the Jewish authorities on the other reflect the author's current relationship to Judaism. However, it is disputed whether Matthew reflects a conflict within Judaism, in other words whether the Matthaean community is still living within the synagogue community,[36] or whether this is a conflict after the

---

[31]Streeter, *Four Gospels*, 223–70, postulates a special written source (= M) for Matthew, but the heterogeneity of the material concerned tells against this.

[32]According to Betz, *Essays*, the composition of the Sermon on the Mount does not go back to Matthaean redaction. Rather, this is a Jewish–Christian epitome of the teaching of Jesus from the 50s, which Matthew took over almost unchanged.

[33]Each of these speeches ends with a concluding formula: 'And it happened after Jesus had finished (Matt. 26.1) all these words . . .' (7.28; 11.1; 13.53; 19.1; 26.1).

[34]K. Wengst (ed.), *Schriften des Urchristentums: Didache usw.*, Darmstadt 1994, 24–30.

[35]Cf. Theissen, *Gospels**, 249–52.

[36]Thus e.g. Kilpatrick, *Origins*; Bornkamm, 'End-Expectation and Church' (1956!), in id. et al., *Tradition and Interpretation*, 15–51; R. Hummel, Die *Auseinandersetzung zwischen Kirche und Judentum im Matthäusevangelium*, BETh 33, Munich ²1966; Davies, *Setting*.

separation,[37] concerned with the legitimacy of the basic decisions taken, i.e. the significance, role and interpretation of the Torah, belief in the Messiah, etc. The latter is more probable.

5. *The Matthaean picture of Jesus and the historical Jesus.* Matthew emphasizes the dignity of Jesus more strongly than Mark. Matthew interprets Jesus' life as a fulfilment of the Law and the Prophets (Matt. 5.17): the reflective quotations[38] demonstrate individual features of Jesus' life and conduct as the fulfilment of prophetic promises. Jesus fulfils the Torah through his conduct (cf. 3.15; 12.1–14), and above all his teaching is regarded as fulfilment, i.e. as the authentic exegesis of the Torah. Jesus is therefore depicted above all as the teacher who unfolds the will of God in some lesser discourses and especially in the five great discourses. The Risen Christ himself makes it clear in the important conclusion to the Gospel that the commandments of Jesus brought together in the Gospel of Matthew are to be taught through the world by the missionaries and observed in the life of the community (28.20; cf. 7.21, 24–27). Matthew has interpreted the sayings of Jesus contained in these discourses for his own time by bringing them together in a new context and working over them redactionally, while at the same time preserving them.

2.4 The Gospel of Luke

F. Bovon, *Luke the Theologian: Thirty-Three Years of Research (1950–1983)*, Princeton 1987; H.J. Cadbury, *The Making of Luke-Acts*, London 1927; H. Conzelmann, *The Theology of St Luke*, London and New York 1960; id., 'Luke's Place in the Development of Early Christianity' (1966), in L.E. Keck and J.L. Martyn, *Studies in Luke-Acts*, Nashville and London 1966, 298–316; M. Hengel, 'Luke the Historian and the Geography of Palestine in the Acts of the Apostles', in *Between Jesus and Paul*, London and Philadelphia 1983, 97–127; R.J. Karries, *What Are They Saying About Luke and Acts?*, New York, Ramsey and Toronto 1979; R. Maddox, *The Purpose of Luke-Acts*, Edinburgh 1982; W. Radl, *Das Lukas-Evangelium*, EdF 261, Darmstadt 1988; M. Rese, 'Das Lukas-Evangelium. Ein Forschungsbericht', *ANRW* II 25.3, 1984, 2258–328; V. Taylor, *Behind the Third Gospel*, Oxford 1926; C.M. Tuckett, *Luke*, Sheffield 1996; P. Vielhauer, 'On the "Paulinism" of Acts', in Keck and Martyn, *Studies in Luke-Acts*, 33–50.

1. *Text, sources and structure.* As far as we can tell from the history of the text, the Gospel of Luke, conceived as the first of the two parts of the Lukan history (Luke-Acts), has always been handed down separately from Acts. As sources Luke uses not only Mark and Q but also extensive special material, which makes up almost half the Gospel. In outline it follows Mark with few changes and two

---

[37]Thus Bornkamm, 'Authority to Bind and Loose' (1970!), in Stanton, *Interpretation*; Schweizer, *Matthäus*; Stanton, *Gospel*.

[38]Matt. 1.22f.; 2.5f., 15, 17f., 23; 4.14–16; 8.17; 12.17–21; 13.35; 21.4f.; 27.9f.

significant omissions (Mark 6.17–29; 6.45–8.26: great omission/lesser omission). The prehistories and Easter stories frame the Markan material, which is interrupted by two insertions composed of material from Q and special material: Luke 6.20–8.3; 9.51–18.14. However, the Lukan compilation of the extensive travel account (9.51–19.27) is clearly based on the travel chapter Mark 10; the relevant Markan material appears from Luke 18.15 on.[39]

2. *Author.* According to church tradition, Luke the physician and travelling companion of Paul, mentioned in Philemon 24; Col. 4.14; II Tim. 4.11, is said to have composed the Gospel and Acts (Irenaeus, *Haer.* 3.1.1). Contrary to this view, which is occasionally still put forward today, a critical consensus emphasizes the countless contradictions between the account in Acts and the authentic Pauline letters.[40] For example, in the Acts account of the life of Paul the second trip to Jerusalem before the Apostolic Council in 11.30; 12.25 contradicts what Paul himself says in Gal. 1.17–2.1. Luke denies Paul the title apostle, which was central to his own self-understanding. Genuinely Pauline theology appears only sparsely. The unknown author of Luke-Acts was certainly not a companion of Paul.

3. *Time and place of origin.* The Gospel of Luke was composed between 70 CE – the destruction of the temple (Luke 21.20–24; 19.43f.) and the Gospel of Mark are presupposed – and 140/150 CE, when it can certainly be demonstrated in Marcion and Justin; because of the independence from Matthew, more in the first half of this period. Luke will have been composed in a large city west of Palestine. The author knows the cities of the Mediterranean well, and his horizon embraces the whole inhabited world (already Luke 2.1; 3.1). For him the sea (θάλασσα) is the Mediterranean (Acts 10.6 etc.); Mark's 'Sea of Galilee', Lake Gennesaret, is described more appropriately as λίμνη (lake). Luke 12.55 indicates a perspective on Palestine from the west. The fact that the south wind is mentioned as the bringer of heat there corresponds to the wind conditions in the western Mediterranean. By contrast, in Palestine the east wind was regarded as the bringer of burning heat.[41]

4. *Luke and the historical Jesus.* Luke designates Jesus the saviour anointed with the Spirit of God, who accepts the weak and outcast in the name of God and proclaims salvation to them. This is indicated by the Nazareth pericope which is put at the beginning of Jesus' activity (Luke 4.16–30) with the programmatic

---

[39]The Proto-Luke theory put forward by Streeter, *Four Gospels*, and Taylor, *Third Gospel*, offers an alternative interpretation of the source question. It argues that Luke first composed a complete Gospel (without Luke 1–2) from Q and Luke[S] and later expanded this with Markan material. The fact that a separate passion tradition underlying Luke cannot be demonstrated and that the Lukan travel account is based on Mark 10 tells against this.

[40]Hengel, 'Historian'; C.-J. Thornton, *Der Zeuge der Zeugen*, WUNT 56, Tübingen 1991.

[41]Theissen, *Gospels**, 252–8.

quotations from scripture, Isa 61.1f.; 58.6. This picture of Jesus is drawn with Markan traditions (e.g. Luke 4.38f.; 5.27–32; 8.40–56), but above all large parts of the Lukan material are shaped by a concern for the poor (14.12–14; 16.19–31), the tax collectors (18.9–14; 19.1–10) and sinners (5.1–11; 7.36–50; 15.11–32; 23.39–43), women (7.11–17; 8.2f.; 7.36–50; 10.38–42; 13.10–17; 23.27–31) and Samaritans (9.52–56; 10.29–37; 17.11–19). While Luke has certainly deliberately chosen his tradition and also revised it to suit himself, in so doing he also brings out a picture of Jesus which already underlay these traditions.

3. Sources close to Gnosticism

In addition to the Synoptic sources, a series of major sources have come down to us which either stand close to Gnostic faith or are Gnostic through and through. Within the canon, mention must be made here of the Gospel of John, which in its structure corresponds most closely to the Synoptic Gospels: narratives about Jesus and discourses by him lead to the passion. Outside the canon, mention should be made of a Gnostic counterpart to the Logia source which was discovered in 1945, the Gospel of Thomas. A third genre is represented by a specifically Gnostic form of Gospel: the dialogue of the Risen Christ with his disciples.[42] Common to these sources is the fact that Jesus is seen as the revealer of a transcendent message which calls for special understanding. This understanding ('Gnosticism') is the decisive act of redemption. However, in contrast to the four Synoptic sources, these sources which are close to Gnosticism present no coherent picture of Jesus.

> This can be illustrated by an example: the Logia source contains clear references to Jesus doing miracles (and narrates two miracles, Luke 7.11ff.; 11.19f. Q). Thus the Gospel of Mark, which is so rich in miracles, and the Logia source provide a coherent picture despite the difference in genre and the different status given to miracles. The Gospel of Thomas does not contain any reference to the miracles of John at all. The Gospel of John, which is rich in miracles, when taken with the Gospel of Thomas does not produce a coherent picture (although they are both close to Gnosticism).

3.1 The Gospel of John

> J. Ashton, *Understanding the Fourth Gospel*, Oxford 1992; id., *Studying John*, Oxford 1994; J. Becker, *Das Evangelium nach Johannes*, ÖTK 4/1 and 2, Gütersloh and Würzburg

---

[42]The *Epistula Apostolorum* is a catholic reaction to the Gnostic revelation dialogues; it takes the form of a secret letter from the risen Christ, allegedly to the eleven disciples, with anti-docetic and anti-Gnostic tendencies. The work, which was composed around 150, contains traditions drawn from the canonical Gospels along with theological discussions (cf. *NT Apoc* I, 1963, 189–277; 1991, 249–84).

1979/1981, ²1984/85; R.E. Brown, *The Community of the Beloved Disciple*, London 1979; R. Bultmann, *The Gospel of John*, Oxford 1971; C.H. Dodd, *The Interpretation of the Fourth Gospel*, Cambridge 1953; id., *Historical Tradition in the Fourth Gospel*, Cambridge 1963; R. Fortna, *The Fourth Gospel and its Predecessors*, Edinburgh 1988; M. Hengel, *The Johannine Question*, London and Philadelphia 1989; R. Kysar, 'The Fourth Gospel: A Report on Recent Research', *ANRW* II 25.2, 1985, 2389–480; D. Rensberger, *Overcoming the World*, London 1988 (US title, *Johannine Faith and Liberating Community*, Philadelphia 1988); E. Ruckstuhl, *Die literarische Einheit des Johannesevangeliums*, Fribourg CH and Göttingen ²1987; id. and P. Dschulnigg, *Stilkritik und Verfasserfrage im Johannesevangelium*, Fribourg CH and Göttingen 1991; W. Schmithals, *Johannesevangelium und Johannesbriefe*, BZNW 64, Berlin and New York 1992; R. Schnackenburg, *The Gospel According to St John* (3 vols.), New York and Tunbridge Wells 1968, 1980, 1982; E. Schweizer, *Ego Eimi. Die religionsgeschichtliche Herkunft und theologische Bedeutung der johanneischen Bildreden, zugleich ein Beitrag zur Quellenfrage des vierten Evangeliums* FRLANT 56, Göttingen 1939, ²1965; H. Thyen, 'Johannesevangelium', *TRE* 17, 1987, 200–25; K. Wengst, *Bedrängte Gemeinde und verherrlichter Christus*, BThSt 5, Neukirchen-Vluyn 1981.

1. *The text and its integrity.* The Gospel of John is very well attested by several early papyri from the first half of the second century on (P⁵²). Apart from the pericope 7.53–8.11, which is clearly secondary, according to the manuscript evidence the text has never circulated other than in its present form. Stylistic investigations demonstrate the coherence of the work.[43] Over against this observations have been made which show that the text has grown, and not all the tensions which result from the history of its origin have been removed:

- The double conclusion to the book is unmistakable. John 20.30f. once concluded the Gospel. Chapter 21 is a supplement at the end of which a group of editors mentions as the author of John 1–20 the Beloved Disciple, whose unexpected death immediately beforehand (21.20–23) is specifically discussed. In 21.25 there follows a second conclusion to the book by an individual redactor which is based on 20.30. It seems natural to infer further insertions by the same redactional hand in the text of the Gospel, but there is no consensus about their number and extent.
- Chapter 15–17 interrupt the thread of the action which runs from 14.31 to 18.1 and scenically are left hanging. These are passages which were either put in the wrong place or inserted later, and could no longer be satisfactorily integrated into the narrative.
- There are obvious geographical and chronological inconsistencies in chs. 4–7: the sabbath healing in Jerusalem at the time of the Passover reported in John 5 is followed in 6.1 by the nonsensical remark that after that Jesus went to the other side of the Sea of Galilee. In John 7 Jesus is back in Jerusalem again for the Feast of

[43]Ruckstuhl, *Einheit*; id. and Dschulnigg, *Stilkritik*; Schweizer, *Ego Eimi*, 82–112.

Tabernacles. 7.15–24, however, clearly refer to the healing at the time of Passover reported in John 5. The order 4; 6; 5; 7.15–24; 7.1–14, 25ff. resolves these contradictions and many scholars therefore regard it as original. In some other passages, too, there is a suspicion that parts of the text are in the wrong order.

2. *Sources and traditions used.* Although the author gives the activity of Jesus a different structure from the Synoptics (prologue as an introduction, several journeys to Jerusalem, chronology of the festivals) and is concerned to shape larger narrative complexes, in taking over the Gospel form he is presumably indicating a knowledge of at least one Synoptic Gospel. Despite the marked differences in theological shaping it is also clear that John presupposes sources with a Synoptic stamp both in the narrative tradition and in the sayings tradition. But he seems to refer back to them independently of the Synoptics.[44]

Here is an example. The Johannine version of the 'centurion of Capernaum' (John 4.46–54) can hardly be understood as a direct revision of the corresponding miracle story in Q (Matt. 8.5–13; Luke 7.1–10), because the part which goes beyond Q (John 4.52f.) expresses that naive view of miracle which the redactional passage John 4.48 criticizes.

Larger complexes of written sources which have been used can be inferred to be:

- A passion and Easter tradition independent of the Synoptics (and close to the Lukan passion).
- Possibly a collection of miracle stories which have been massively heightened by comparison with the Synoptics, the so-called Semeia source. This probably contained all seven of the miracles narrated in John 1–11 and further narrative material. The original enumeration of the signs (σημεῖα) can still be recognized in 2.11 and 4.54 (and contradicts 2.23; 4.45!); the conclusion of the source is probably in John 20.30f., as the term σημεῖα which recurs here can hardly relate to the whole of the Gospel with its discourses and the passion narrative.[45]
- The question of the prior stages of the great discourses and dialogues in John has not been clarified.

3. *Author, time and place of origin.* The editors of the Gospel refer in 21.24 to the Beloved Disciple as the author of the Gospel and the guarantor of its truth and seem to be interested in his literary anonymity. Early church tradition saw John,

---

[44]There is some dispute about this. In numerous articles in *Evangelica* I–II e.g. F. Neirynck seeks to demonstrate that John knows all three Synoptics.

[45]Cf. the excursus on the Semeia source in Becker, ÖTK 4/1, 112–20; also D. Nicol, *The Semeia in the Fourth Gospel*, Leiden 1972.

son of Zebedee, as the author (Irenaeus, *Haer.* 3, 1, 1; Eusebius, *HE* 5, 8, 4). On a critical inspection we can hardly infer more from John 21.20–25 and other passages about the Beloved Disciple than that the Christian group from which the Gospel of John arose derived its tradition from a disciple of Jesus who was not all that well known; he had long survived Peter but had died before the parousia of the Lord.[46] The time of origin is to be put around the turn of the century: P[52] rules out extreme late datings.[47] We have no certain information about the place of origin. The earliest attestation and reception points to Egypt, but an early and successful reception of John has also been demonstrated by Hengel in Western Asia Minor, where the tradition of the Gospel is located (Ephesus). Finally, the close relationship to the Baptist movement, the proximity to the Odes of Solomon, Ignatius of Antioch and the Mandaean writings, and the abrupt opposition to 'the Jews' in a prehistory of the community in the synagogue suggest Syria as a place of origin.[48]

4. *The Johannine picture of Jesus and the historical Jesus.* The Gospel of John clearly presents the Jesus of the Gospels who is most stylized on the basis of theological premises. Jesus speaks and acts as the revealer who is aware of his pre-existence (John 8.58), but – as the author is aware – he can be recognized as the revealer only after Easter and through the influence of the Spirit; then he can be remembered anew (cf. 2.22; 7.39; 12.16; 13.7). Nevertheless, the Gospel of John, which is independent of the Synoptics, is not worthless. At some usually quite unemphatic places it hands down data which diverge from the Synoptics, and can go back to old traditions.

- According to 1.35ff. the first disciples were former disciples of John the Baptist.
- Peter, Andrew and Philip came from Bethsaida (1.44).
- The political expectations aroused by Jesus and the political motives which led to his execution are stated more clearly in John than in the Synoptic Gospels (cf. John 6.15; 11.47–53; 19.12).
- Instead of a Jewish trial of Jesus, John 18.19ff. reports a hearing of the Sanhedrin which preceded the accusation before Pilate.

---

[46]Hengel, *Johannine Question*, sees the elder (ὁ πρεσβύτερος) who composed II and III John as the author of the Gospel.

[47]F.C. Baur (*Über die Komposition und den Charakter des johanneischen Evangeliums*, 1844; *Kritische Untersuchungen über die kanonischen Evangelien . . .*, 1847) argued that it was composed only late in the second century; recently W. Schmithals, *Johannesevangelium*, has put the final redaction after 140.

[48]Wengst, *Bedrängte Gemeinde*, dates the Gospel of John around 90 and puts it in Gaulanitis (Transjordan), which was part of the territory of Agrippa II, because here 'the Jews' also functioned as magistrates until 93, as is sometimes presupposed at the level of the text of John (John 1.19; 5.15; 9.22; 18.12). Only here was an exclusion from the synagogue with fatal consequences conceivable (John 9.22f.; 12.42f.; 16.1–3).

• According to Johannine chronology, Jesus died before the Passover (18.28; 19.31), which many scholars think more probable than an execution on the festival itself (§6.4.1; §13.3.2).

3.2 The Gospel of Thomas[49]

J.B. Bauer, 'Echte Jesusworte?', in W.C. van Unnik, *Evangelien aus dem Nilsand*, Frankfurt 1960, 108–50; R.E. Brown, 'The Gospel of Thomas and St. John's Gospel', *NTS* 9, 1962/63, 155–77; J.D. Crossan, *Four Other Gospels*, Winston 1985; S.L. Davies, *The Gospel of Thomas and Christian Wisdom*, New York 1983; F.T. Fallon and R. Cameron, 'The Gospel of Thomas: A Forschungsbericht and Analysis', *ANRW* II 25. 6, 1988, 4195–251; M. Fieger, *Das Thomasevangelium. Einleitung, Kommentar und Systematik*, NTA 22, Münster 1991; R.M. Grant and D.N. Freedman, *The Secret Sayings of Jesus*, Garden City and London 1960; C.-H. Hunzinger, 'Unbekannte Gleichnisse Jesus aus dem Thomasevangelium', in W. Eltester (ed.), *Judentum, Urchristentum, Kirche (FS J. Jeremias)*, BZNW 26, Berlin 1960, 209–20; A.E.J. Klijn, 'Christianity in Edessa and the Gospel of Thomas', *NT* 14, 1972, 70–7; H. Koester, *Ancient Christian Gospels*, Philadelphia and London 1990, 75–128; H. Montefiore, 'A Comparison of the Parables of the Gospel according to Thomas and of the Synoptic Gospels', in H.E.W. Turner and H. Montefiore, *Thomas and the Evangelists*, SBT 35, London 1962, 40–78; S.J. Patterson, *The Gospel of Thomas and Jesus*, Sonoma, CA 1993; W. Schrage, *Das Verhältnis des Thomas-Evangeliums zur synoptischen Tradition und zu den koptischen Evangelienübersetzungen*, BZNW 29, Berlin 1964; R. McL. Wilson, *Studies in the Gospel of Thomas*, London 1960.

1. *The text.* Hippolytus (died 235) and Origen mention that heterodox groups use a 'Gospel of Thomas'.[50] This Gospel was rediscovered in 1945 among the writings in the library found at Nag Hammadi. The second codex contains a Coptic collection of sayings (NHC II/2) which begins with the words 'These are the secret sayings which the living Jesus spoke and which Didymos Judas Thomas wrote down', and the subscription runs 'The Gospel of Thomas'. Three papyri found in Oxyrhynchus around the turn of the century (POx 1, 654, 655) could be identified on this basis as Greek fragments of the Gospel of Thomas, but divergences in the wording and the sequence of the logia show that these cannot be the originals from which the Coptic text was directly translated.

2. *Content and structure.* The Gospel of Thomas contains 114 logia[51] of Jesus,

---

[49]Introduction and English translation by H.C. Puech and R.McL. Wilson, *NTApoc* I, 1963, 278ff.; 1991, by B. Blatz, 110–33; J.M. Robinson, *Nag Hammadi Library*, 124–36. Fallon and Cameron, *Gospel,* give a good more recent survey of research and literature on the Gospel of Thomas.

[50]Hippolytus, *Ref.* 5, 7, 20f.; Origen, *in Luc. hom.* 1.

[51]This (intrinsically random) modern division into 114 logia has become established; no sentence units are marked in the text.

but no narrative material and no reference within the sayings tradition to Jesus' actions (miracles!). Genres include wisdom sayings, parables, sayings about the Law, brief dialogues and prophetic sayings. A good half of the logia have parallels in the canonical Gospels. Strikingly, christological titles, references to Jesus' death and resurrection and apocalyptic sayings are almost completely absent. The logia are evidently arranged mostly by word association.[52] Doublets can be recognized, as the collection was successively enlarged.[53]

3. *Age and place of origin*. The Oxyrhynchus papyri guarantee that c.140 CE is the latest possible date of composition. The final redaction will have taken place after the destruction of the temple in 70 CE (logion 71),[54] though whether this was in the first century is disputed. There is relative agreement that the Gospel of Thomas was probably composed in Syria; this is indicated above all in the name of the fictitious author: Judas Didymus Thomas appears only in writings of East Syrian origin.[55]

4. *Age and independence of the traditions of the Gospel of Thomas*. The Gospel of Thomas is the extra-canonical Gospel which most probably has preserved traditions which are autonomous (independent of the canonical Gospels) and old. But there is no scholarly consensus about this. Supporters of independence[56] cite as an argument above all the genre, the sequence of the logia and traditio-historical observations about individual sayings:

• As a collection of sayings the Gospel of Thomas embodies one of the earliest genres of framework in which the Jesus material was handed down. Other early collections of sayings (Q; the collection of logia behind Mark 4) have been inserted into the canonical Gospels and swallowed up in them. No collections of sayings have come down to us from a later period.[57] The

---

[52]Patterson, *Gospel*, 100–2 offers a list of 'potential catchwords'. These are not always directly recognizable, as sometimes they become invisible in the course of the translation from Greek to Coptic.

[53]E.g. Gospel of Thomas 5/6; 21/103 (thief); 22/106; 41/70; 51/113; 56/80; 81/110; 87/112.

[54]The early dating to 60–70 CE put forward e.g. by Davies, *Gospel*, emphasizes too one-sidedly the features of old tradition which are indisputably present in the text.

[55]This, too, is not undisputed: B. Ehlers (Aland), 'Kann das Thomasevangelium aus Edessa stammen?', *NT* 12, 1970, 284–317, argues against composition in Edessa (Klijn, 'Christianity', attempts to refute her arguments); Davies, *Gospel*, 18–21, suggests that the Thomas tradition widely attested (later!) in East Syria could have begun with the *popularity* (and not necessarily the origin) of the Gospel of Thomas in Syria.

[56]The independence of the Gospel of Thomas is argued for by e.g. Blatz, in *NTApoc* I, 1991, 110–14; Vielhauer, *Geschichte**, 618–35; Koester and Robinson, *Trajectories*, esp. 71ff., 130ff., 166ff.; Koester, *Ancient Christian Gospels*, 75–128; Patterson, *Gospel*, 7–110; Davies, *Gospel*; Crossan, *Four Other Gospels*, 13–62.

[57]The Gnostic revelation dialogues are probably a further development of the genre of sayings collections, cf. H. Köster, 'Dialog und Spruchüberlieferung in den gnostischen Texten von Nag Hammadi', *EvTh* 39, 1979, 532–56, esp.544–56.

beginnings of the Gospel of Thomas therefore certainly lie in the first century: Koester conjectures that the collection of sayings which finally became the Gospel of Thomas is the eastern counterpart of the western Logia source Q.

- The order of the logia in the Gospel of Thomas is completely independent of the Synoptic Gospels; this is a strong indication that the logia which they have in common have not been taken over from the Synoptic Gospels.
- Often the Gospel of Thomas offers logia in a form which in terms of the history of the tradition is earlier than the Synoptics. Here are two examples:

– Logion 31 and POx 1 offer the following two-membered saying of the Lord: 'No prophet is accepted in his own village; no physician heals those who know him' (οὐκ ἔστιν δεκτὸς προφήτης ἐν τῇ πατρίδι αὐτοῦ, οὐδὲ ἰατρὸς ποιεῖ θεραπείας εἰς τοὺς γινώσκοντας αὐτόν). Form criticism shows that this logion is more original than the apophthegmatic garb which Mark 6.1–6 gives to the first half in the framework of Jesus' visit to Nazareth; it cannot in any way be a secondary derivation from Mark 6.1–6 par.[58]

– In Logion 65 the parable of the wicked husbandmen (Mark 12.1–12 par.) runs: 'He said, "There was a good man who owned a vineyard. He leased it to tenant farmers so that they might work it and he might collect the produce from them. He sent his servant so that the tenants might give him the produce of the vineyard. They seized his servant and beat him, all but killing him. The servant went back and told his master. The master said, 'Perhaps he did not recognize them.' He sent another servant. The tenants beat this one as well. Then the owner sent his son and said, 'Perhaps they will show respect to my son.' Because the tenants knew that it was he who was the heir to the vineyard, they seized him and killed him. Let him who has ears hear."' This version proves to be more original by comparison with the Synoptics,[59] as it is free of allusions to the Old Testament (Isa. 5.1f.) and of improbable and allegorical features.[60]

---

[58]This was demonstrated by E. Wendling, *Die Entstehung des Marcus-Evangeliums*, Tübingen 1908, 53–65 and Bultmann, *HST**, 31f., by means of POx 1, even before the discovery of the Coptic Gospel of Thomas. By contrast, Schrage, *Verhältnis*, 76f., thinks, hardly convincingly, that the redactor of the Gospel of Thomas detched the saying from its narrative context and (again) made it a floating logion.

[59]Even before the discovery of the Gospel of Thomas, Jeremias had demonstrated that the allegorization of the parable, beginning before Mark and increasing in the Synoptics, is a sign of its secondary interpretation in terms of salvation history and christology (*Parables of Jesus*, ¹1954, 55ff.). The discovery of the Gospel of Thomas confirmed this interpretation (cf. the revised version, 66–89, and Patterson, *Gospel*, 48–51). A. Lindemann, 'Zur Gleichnisinterpretation im Thomas-Evangelium', *ZNW* 71, 1980, differs; he wants to explain Gospel of Thomas 65 as a de-allegorized form of the Synoptic original used for the Gnostic interpretation.

[60]Individual agreements between Thomas and Luke against Mark cannot be traced back to literary dependence, but represent a variant of tradition (oral?) common to Luke and Thomas (against Schrage, *Verhältnis*, 137–45).

By contrast, those who argue for the dependence of the Gospel of Thomas on the Synoptists[61] attempt to demonstrate that the form of the Logia in the Gospel of Thomas can be derived from a Gnostic revision (handed down in written or oral form) of Synoptic discourse traditions.

5. *Theological shaping.* Central theological motives of the final redaction of the Gospel of Thomas can be recognized in the selection and redactional treatment of the logia:

- Jesus as revealer: Jesus the living one is the bringer of salvation simply through his (several) words of revelation:[62] 'Anyone who finds the interpretation of these words will not taste death' (logion 1). Identity between the revealer and the one who is enlightened by him is the goal (108).
- Dualistic anthropology: the world and with it the human body are devalued and become a synonym for death. The Father's kingdom of light, knowledge and eternal life are to be attained only by radical 'fasting from the world' (27): 'Whoever finds himself is superior to the world' (111).[63]
- Present eschatology: the kingdom (the kingdom of the Father, of Heaven) is an entity which is beyond time, the origin and goal of human beings who have come to know themselves. For self-knowledge is the knowledge of the real divine self and its place in the sphere of the divine light. Therefore the kingdom of heaven is both within human beings and outside them, and equally present at all times (cf. 3, 49, 50, 113).[64]
- Discipleship is achieved as turning away from the world (i.e. from dependence on possessions, family, sexuality, religious practices like fasting, circumcision, alms). The disciples are the individuals (*monachoi*), the elect of the living Father, who are reached by the call of Jesus. A Christian community hardly comes into view here.

The Gospel of Thomas reflects a Gnosticism in the state of growth, without a developed cosmology, doctrine of aeons, etc., which can be explained as a further

---

[61]In the German-speaking world mention should be made above all of E. Haenchen, *Die Botschaft des Thomas-Evangeliums*, Berlin 1961, and Schrage, *Verhältnis*; for the parables Lindemann, 'Gleichnisinterpretation' (n.58 above). Cf. also Grant and Freedman, *Secret Sayings*. Fieger, *Thomasevangelium*, offers a new commentary on this basis.

[62]Here we are not to think of sayings of the Risen Christ as in the dialogues of the Risen Christ with his disciples; rather, the words of the historical Jesus are understood as revelations of the one who is alive for ever.

[63]E. Haenchen, 'Die Anthropologie des Thomas-Evangeliums', in H.D. Betz and L. Schott-roff (ed.), *Neues Testament und christliche Existenz (FS H. Braun)*, Tübingen 1973, 207–27.

[64]Haenchen, *Botschaft* (n.61 above).

development of a gnosticizing tendency which is inherent in the wisdom tradition.[65]

6. *The Gospel of Thomas and the historical Jesus.* If we presuppose that the Gospel of Thomas includes an independent strand of tradition containing sayings from primitive Christianity which goes back to an early period, its great historical importance is evident, especially because of the breadth of the content of the tradition. As in the case of the Synoptic Gospels, the prehistory of the sayings material can be traced through tradition, form- and redaction-critical investigations. Since the discovery of the Gospel of Thomas, two different interests have governed the discussion:

- Various investigations[66] seek to extract authentic sayings of Jesus from the logia (especially the parables) of the Gospel of Thomas. They are interested in the further developments of the tradition only in so far as these have to be recognized in order to be excluded. Here there is always a danger, quite apart from the inherent problems of the attempt to establish *ipsissima verba* of Jesus by exegesis, of remaining dependent on a (prior) judgment of what Jesus could have said which is derived from the Synoptics.[67]
- By contrast, works more strongly orientated on form criticism emphasize that the development in the Gospel of Thomas of the sayings tradition which begins from Jesus, quite independently from the Synoptics, has to be compared with the Synoptic development as a whole. By surveying the common material and its different developments, new insights can be gained into the process of the formation of the tradition which can also illuminate its beginning, the preaching of Jesus.[68]

Two results relevant to the study of the historical Jesus might be mentioned: the Gospel of Thomas has a high christology – but almost without christological titles. By contrast with other Gnostic writings the title Messiah is absent. The term 'Son of Man' occurs only once, in the general sense of 'human being' (86). Does not this state of affairs tell against the claim to christological titles by Jesus? Furthermore (according to S.J. Patterson), the Gospel of Thomas suggests an original itinerant charismatic movement if we do not understand the instructions contained in it in a 'spiritualized way': it confirms the hypothesis that from the beginning sayings of Jesus were handed down above all by itinerant charismatics (a form of radical social Christianity).

---

[65]Cf. above all the contributions by Robinson and Koester mentioned above.
[66]Bauer, *'Echte Jesusworte?'*; Hunzinger, 'Unbekannte Gleichnisse'.
[67]Cf. Patterson, *Gospel*, 220–5.
[68]Ibid., 225–41 (further bibliography).

3.3 Gnostic dialogue Gospels

R. Cameron, *Sayings Traditions in the Apocryphon of James,* HTS 34, Philadelphia 1984; B. Dehandschutter, 'L'Epistula Jacobi apocrypha de Nag Hammadi (CG 1, 2) comme apocryphe néotestamentaire', *ANRW* II 25.6, 1988, 4529–50; S. Emmel, H. Koester and E. Pagels, *Nag Hammadi Codex III,5: The Dialogue of the Savior (NHS XXVI),* Leiden 1984; C.W. Hedrick, 'Kingdom Sayings and Parables of Jesus in the Apocryphon of James: Tradition and Redaction', *NTS* 29, 1983, 1–24; H. Köster, 'Dialog und Spruchüberlieferung in den gnostischen Texten von Nag Hammadi', *EvTh* 39, 1979, 532–56; D.R. MacDonald, *There Is No Male and Female. The Fate of a Dominical Saying in Paul and Gnosticism,* HDR 20, Philadelphia 1987; C.M. Tuckett, *Nag Hammadi and the Gospel Tradition,* Edinburgh 1986, esp. 87–97, 128–35; F.E. Williams, 'The Apocryphon of James', introduction and English translation in J.M. Robinson (ed.), *The Nag Hammadi Library,* Leiden 1988, 29–37.

We seem to have a further development of the early Christian sayings collections in the so-called 'Dialogue Gospels' (to use Koester's term) which interpret and shape earlier sayings material.[69] These include:[70]

1. The *Letter of James* (*Epistula Jacobi,* also Apocryphon of James, NHC 1/2)[71] from the early second century is a secret teaching in dialogue form handed down in the framework of a letter which James and Peter are said to have received 550 days after Jesus' resurrection. In addition to logia clearly interpreted in Gnostic terms, the Letter of James contains sayings which emphasize the suffering of Jesus and the following of him by the disciples in suffering. Moreover a number of parables are mentioned and quoted, including three otherwise unknown kingdom of God parables of a Synoptic type. One example is: 'The kingdom of heaven is like an ear of grain after it had sprouted in a field. And when it had ripened, it scattered its fruit and again filled the field with ears for another year.'[72] The sayings traditions which have been worked over are close in part to Q, Mark and the Gospel of Thomas and in part to the Johannine dialogues, but seem to be independent of them.[73]

2. The *Dialogue of the Redeemer* (NHC III,5)[74] is a revelation dialogue of the Saviour with his disciples, men and women, which was composed in the second

---

[69]Koester, *Early Christian Gospels,* 173–200; id., 'Dialog'.

[70]Some Gnostic writings which bear the title 'Gospel' (e.g. Gospel of Philip, Gospel of Truth) are theological treatises which contain no information about sayings or actions of Jesus.

[71]Introduction and translation by F.E. Williams in J.M. Robinson (ed.), *The Nag Hammadi Library,* 29–37.

[72]NHC I, 12, 22–27, ibid., 35.

[73]Thus Cameron, 'Sayings Traditions'; Hedrick, 'Kingdom Sayings', Koester, *Ancient Christian Gospels,* 187–200.

[74]Introduction by H. Koester and E.H. Pagels and translation by S. Emmel and J.M. Robinson in Robinson, *Nag Hammadi Library,* 244–55.

century, into which a number of sources have been incorporated. E. Pagels and H. Koester reconstruct among other things a dialogue source which could go back to a sayings collection close to the Gospel of Thomas.[75]

3. To judge from the few extant fragments, the *Gospel of the Egyptians* similarly seems to have been one of the gnosticizing dialogue Gospels.[76] Jesus teaches his conversation partner Salome an Encratistic soteriology (based on sexual asceticism): only if women cease to give birth and male and female again become one does death no longer have power and is knowledge possible.[77] This Gospel of the Egyptians was presumably written in the first half of the second century in Encratistic circles in Egypt. Clement of Alexandria (c.200) quotes it often and interprets the logia ethically by allegorizing them – evidently he could not just reject the Gospel.[78]

4. Gospel fragments with Synoptic and Johannine elements

Independently of the Synoptic Gospels and those near to Gnosticism which have been mentioned so far, mere fragments of other Gospels have come down to us which are hard to assess because of their fragmentary character. Despite the scanty textual basis, however, four of these fragments indicate that Johannine and Synoptic elements are combined in them. That need not necessarily be an indication that they are contemporaneously dependent on the Synoptics and John. In the Synoptic sayings source we find as a kind of erratic foundling a saying with a Johannine stamp: 'All things have been delivered to me by my Father; and no one knows who the Son is except the Father, or who the Father is except the Son and any one to whom the Son chooses to reveal him' (Luke 10.22 Q). Here Q documents a stage at which the Synoptic and Johannine tradition are not yet (wholly) separate. In principle this could also be the case with the following Gospel fragments – but with clearly different degrees of probability. The most probable is Egerton Papyrus 2. However, the combination of Johannine and

---

[75]Emmel, Koester and Pagels, Nag Hammadi Codex III 5.2ff.; Koester, *Ancient Christian Gospels*, 173–87; against, Tuckett, 'Nag Hammadi', 128–35. Koester regards some sections of the dialogue as prior forms of the related but even more complex Johannine discourses.

[76]There is an introduction and translation of the certain (and some uncertain) fragments in Schneemelcher, *NTApoc* 1, 1963, 166–78 (with bibliography); 1991, 209–15; cf. Vielhauer, *Geschichte**, 662–5. The Gospel of the Egyptians (εὐαγγέλιον καθ᾽ Αἰγυπτίους) quoted in Clement has nothing to do with the Sethian-Gnostic tractate of the same name found at Nag Hammadi (NHC III/2: IV, 2).

[77]There are parallels to the logia of the Gospel of the Egyptians in II Clem. 12.2; Thomas 22, 37 (+ POx 655).

[78]A generation later, Origen could call the Gospel of the Egyptians a Gospel rejected by the church (*Homily on Luke 1*).

Synoptic elements can also be interpreted as an expression of a late stage.

4.1 Egerton Papyrus 2 (Egerton Gospel)

J.B. Daniels, *The Egerton Gospel: Its Place in Early Christianity*, Claremont, CA dissertation 1989; C.H. Dodd, *A New Gospel*, Manchester 1936; D. Lohrmann, 'Das neue Fragment des P Egerton 2 (PKöln 255)', in F. Van Segbroeck et al. (ed.), *The Four Gospels 1992 (FS F. Neirynck)*, Vol. Ill, BETL 100, Louvain 1992, 2239–55; G. Mayeda, *Das Leben-Jesu-Fragment Papyrus Egerton 2 und seine Stellung in der urchristlichen Literaturgeschichte*, Bern 1946; F. Neirynck, 'Papyrus Egerton 2 and the Healing of the Leper', *EThL* 61, 1985, 153–60 (= *Evangelica* II, 773–784).

1. *The text.* So-called Papyrus Egerton 2 consists of two and a half sometimes heavily damaged leaves from a codex of unknown origin which was first published in 1935.[79] Palaeographers disagree over the dating of the papyrus: the date of 150 CE put forward earlier is now increasingly questioned in favour of a date around 200. If we draw conclusions for the original work from the four pericopes contained in the Egerton Papyrus, which are only loosely connected, then this was a Gospel composed of different pieces of tradition that ended with a passion narrative.

2. *Content.* The first fragment is a dispute between Jesus and experts on the Law and leaders of the people about a transgression of the Law by Jesus. It has a marked Johannine stamp and ends with an unsuccessful attempt to stone Jesus. Then follow two narratives with close Synoptic parallels, the healing of a leper and the question of tax. Finally Egerton 2 offers a miracle of Jesus at the Jordan which is not otherwise attested ('apocryphal'). However, the text is so damaged that it is impossible to reconstruct it with any certainty.

3. The *relationship between the fragment and the canonical Gospels* and the age of the traditions worked over in the Egerton fragment are disputed. On the one hand the pericopes which stand close to the Synoptics are steeped in Johannine phrases, and on the other the presence of Synoptic linguistic elements also in the dispute, which is markedly reminiscent of the Gospel of John, are characteristic. Three possible explanations are discussed:

* *Dependence on all the canonical Gospels* (Jeremias et al.):[80] the author quotes all four Gospels from memory, as associations of words have demonstrably

---

[79]Introduction, bibliography and translation in *NTApoc* I, 1963, 94–7; 1991, 96–9.

[80]Jeremias in *NTApoc* I, 1963, 94–7; 1991, 96–9. The same assessment can be found in Vielhauer, *Geschichte**, 636–9. F. Neirynck, 'Papyrus Egerton 2', attempts to demonstrate that the fragment about the healing of the leper is post-Synoptic and especially dependent on Luke.

governed the combination of materials. There are also influences from the oral development of the tradition.

- *Independence from the canonical Gospels* (G. Mayeda, H. Koester et al.): Mayeda[81] regards a great many oral and written traditions about the life of Jesus as sources and tends to see the whole of the Egerton papyrus as being late in the history of the tradition. Koester[82] thinks that an early stage of the tradition can be recognized here in which 'Synoptic' and 'Johannine' traditions have not yet developed away from each other.[83]
- C.H. Dodd (*New Gospel*) infers *literary dependence on the Gospel of John* from the observation that the closest agreements in PEg 2 are with John. By contrast the pericopes close to the Synoptics come from independent oral tradition.

4. *Age and place of origin.* Since the time of the composition of the papyrus cannot be defined more closely and the relationship to the canonical Gospels cannot be said to have been clarified, the time of origin must be left open. The text was not written in Palestine, since it is certainly not familiar with circumstances there. The mention of 'kings' (in the plural) points to the East.[84]

4.2 The Secret Gospel of Mark

R.E. Brown, 'The Relation of "the Secret Gospel of Mark" to the Fourth Gospel', *CBQ* 36, 1974, 466–85; H. Koester, 'History and Development of Mark's Gospel (From Mark to Secret Mark and "Canonical" Mark)', in B. Corley (ed.), *Colloquy on New Testament Studies*, Macon, GA 1983, 35–57; S. Levin, 'The Early History of Christianity, in Light of the "Secret Gospel" of Mark', *ANRW* II 25.6, 1988, 4270–92; H. Merkel, 'Auf den Spuren des Urmarkus? Ein neuer Fund und seine Beurteilung', *ZThK* 71, 1974, 123–44; M. Smith, *Clement of Alexandria and a Secret Gospel of Mark*, Cambridge, Mass. 1973; id., *The Secret Gospel: The Discovery and Interpretation of the Secret Gospel According to Mark*, New York, etc. 1973; id., 'Merkel on the Longer Text of Mark', *ZThK* 72, 1975, 133–50.

1. *The text.* In 1958 Morton Smith found a fragmentary copy of a hitherto

---

[81]Mayeda, *Leben-Jesu-Fragment.*

[82]Koester, *Ancient Christian Gospels*, 205–16; id., 'Apocryphal and Canonical Gospels', 119–23.

[83]Crossan, *Four Other Gospels*, 65–87, attempts to show that the version of the tax question in PEg 2 represents an earlier stage than Mark 12.13–17.

[84]The leper's remark that he had been infected by travelling and eating with lepers in an inn betrays ignorance of conditions in Palestine. The tax question is not focussed on the alternative 'God or Caesar', which is decisive in Judaea, but is a quite general question as to whether taxes may be paid to 'the kings'.

unknown letter from Clement of Alexandria to a certain Theodorus in the Greek Orthodox monastery of Mar Saba near Jerusalem.[85] In this letter (which on the basis of investigations of style can probably be regarded as authentic), Clement is answering enquiries about a 'secret' Gospel of Mark which is used in liturgies in Alexandria.[86] Clement confirms its existence, saying that it is a second more spiritual version of Mark's Gospel composed by the evangelist himself to encourage knowledge (γνῶσις) among more advanced Christians. However, he disputes that there are certain passages in it to which the Carpocratians, a Gnostic–Christian group, had appealed against Theodore.

2. *Content and structure*. In the extant fragment Clement quotes only one complete passage from the Gospel, the story of the resurrection of a youth from a tomb in Bethany (following Mark 10.34). The context and content of this pericope correspond to the resurrection of Lazarus according to John 11, but the linguistic form is Markan. The narrative ends: 'and in the evening the young man came to him, clothed only with a shirt on his bare body (cf. Mark 14.51). And he remained with him all night; for Jesus taught him the mystery of the kingdom of God (cf. Mark 4.11) . . .' The Carpocratian version of the pericope to be inferred from Clement's letter presumably offered an expansion at this point which referred to a baptismal ceremony[87] performed in the nude. A further insertion following Mark 10.46a ran: 'And the sister of the young man whom Jesus loved and his mother and Salome were there, and Jesus did not receive them.' Here too the Carpocratian version offered more text, but Clement does not say what.

3. Thus (presupposing the authenticity of the letter of Clement) it can be presumed that a 'secret' longer Gospel of Mark was being used by the Carpocratians in Alexandria (c.125–170). It is not completely certain whether Clement really knew two different versions of Mark, as he claims. F.F. Bruce conjectures that Clement knew only the Carpocratian version, but declared this to be a

---

[85]Morton Smith has told the story of its discovery and offered an interpretation of the letter in both a scholarly monograph and in a work addressed to a wider readership: *Clement of Alexandria and a Secret Gospel of Mark* (1973); *The Secret Gospel* (1973). There is a survey of all the relevant problems and the state of discussion in Levin, 'Early History'.

[86]Photographs, Greek transcription and English translation in M. Smith, *Clement of Alexandria*, 446–53. In *NT Apoc* 1, 1991, 106–9, Merkel gives only fragments of the Secret Gospel (and not the whole letter).

[87]Smith, *Clement of Alexandria*, 195–278, drew far-reaching conclusions from the words γυμνὸς γυμνῷ (a naked man with a naked man) cited by Clement as a Carpocratian expansion; he thinks they relate to a magical baptismal practice of Jesus as a mystical union of the baptizer and the one being baptized (possibly with homosexual connotations) for initiation into the mysteries of the kingdom of God, which puts an end to the law. Thus Jesus becomes the author of primitive Christian and later Gnostic libertinism. However, Smith is quite alone in this view; it must already be regarded as debatable whether the Carpocratians really practised the libertinist customs attributed to them, so we can hardly see this as a credible statement about the life of Jesus. For Smith's magic thesis see pp. 289 and 305f. below.

heretical falsification of a genuinely Alexandrian 'secret' Mark written for Gnostics who were faithful to the church (*Jesus and Christian Origins Outside the New Testament*, London 1984).

4. The relationship between this Gospel of Mark and the canonical Gospel of Mark is difficult to define because of the scanty textual basis. The picture is governed by two opposed judgments:

- Morton Smith, who discovered the Secret Gospel, regarded it as an early expansion of the Gospel of Mark on the basis of material from the Markan tradition in which Jesus was still clearly recognizable as a magician.[88] Leaving aside this problematical thesis, Koester and Crossan have presented studies according to which the Secret Gospel is a preliminary stage of the canonical Gospel of Mark.[89] Common to these positions is that they regard the pericope of the raising of the young man as an early variant, independent of John 11, which had its home in the Markan stream of tradition.
- By contrast, the majority of exegetes regard the Secret Gospel as a Gnostic revision of the canonical Mark composed in the second century. This is supported by an emphasis on its 'secret' character and its use in Carpocratian circles, which evidently employed it to legitimate particular liturgical customs. Merkel explains the linguistic form of the pericope as a retelling of John 11 which borrows language from all four Gospels.[90]

5. Even if the pericope of the raising of the young man represents a variant tradition independent of John 11, one cannot infer hitherto unknown knowledge about Jesus from the Secret Gospel.

4.3 The Gospel of Peter

N. Brox, '"Doketismus" – eine Problemanzeige', *ZKG* 95, 1984, 301–14; R.E. Brown, 'The Gospel of Peter and Canonical Gospel Priority', *NTS* 33, 1987, 321–3; J.D. Crossan, *Four Other Gospels*, Winston 1985, 91–121; id., *The Cross that Spoke: The Origins of the Passion Narrative*, San Francisco 1988; J. Denker, *Die theologiegeschichtliche Stellung des Petrusevangeliums. Ein Beitrag zur Frühgeschichte des Doketismus*, Bern and Frankfurt 1975; M. Dibelius, 'Die alttestamentlichen Motive in der Leidensgeschichte des Petrus- und

---

[88]See n.87.

[89]Koester, 'History and Development of Mark's Gospel'; id., *Ancient Christian Gospels*, 293–303; Crossan, *Four Other Gospels*, 91–121; against Neirynck, *Evangelica* II, 59–73; *Evangelica* I, 215–38.

[90]Merkel, 'Spuren', 130–40; but see the excellent reply by M. Smith, 'Merkel'; also R.E. Brown, 'Relation', and F. Neirynck, *Evangelica: Gospel Studies* (2 vols), BETL 60, 99, Leuven 1982, 1991: I, 215–28; II, 715–72.

des Johannes-Evangeliums', in *FS von Baudissin*, BZAW 33, 1918, 125ff. (= *Gesammelte Aufsätze* 1, 1953, 221–47); A. Fuchs, *Das Petrusevangelium. Mit 2 Beiträgen von F. Weissengruber und unter Mitarbeit von Chr. Eckmair*, SNTU B 12, Linz 1978; J.B. Green, 'The Gospel of Peter: Source for a Pre-Canonical Passion Narrative?', *ZNW* 78, 1987, 293–301; A. von Harnack, *Bruchstücke des Evangeliums und der Apokalypse des Petrus*. TU IX 2, Leipzig ²1893; B.A. Johnson, *The Empty Tomb Tradition in the Gospel of Peter*, Diss. Harvard University 1966; A. Kirk, 'Examining Priorities: Another Look at the Gospel of Peter's Relationship to the New Testament Gospels', *NTS* 40, 1994, 572–95; H. Koester, *Ancient Christian Gospels*, Philadelphia and London 1990, 293–303; D. Lührmann, 'POx 2949: EvPt 3–5 in einer Handschrift des 2./3. Jahrhunderts', *ZNW* 72, 1981, 217–26; id., 'POx 4009: Ein neues Fragment des Petrusevangeliums?', *NT* 35, 1993, 390–410; M.G. Mara, *Evangile de Pierre. Introduction, texte critique, traduction, commentaire et index*, SC 201, Paris 1973; J.W. McCant, 'The Gospel of Peter: Docetism Reconsidered', *NTS* 30, 1984, 258–73; P. Pilhofer, 'Justin und das Petrusevangelium', *ZNW* 81, 1990, 60–78; L. Vaganay, *L'Evangile de Pierre*, EtB, Paris 1930; T. Zahn, *Das Evangelium des Petrus*, 1893.

1. *The fragment of the Gospel of Peter.* Towards the end of the nineteenth century the Gospel of Peter[91] was known only by name on the basis of statements in the church fathers, particularly from a letter of Bishop Serapion of Antioch (in Eusebius, *HE* 6, 12, 2–6). On a visit he had allowed the community of Rhossos to use the Gospel of Peter, but revoked this permission by letter because he had been informed that some passages had given rise to docetic (mis)interpretations.[92] A largish fragment of a Gospel, the first-person narrator of which is Peter, was discovered in 1886/87 in the tomb of a Christian monk in Akhmim in Upper Egypt and published in 1892. It is almost beyond dispute that the manuscript, dating from the eighth or ninth century, presents the text of the Gospel of Peter which was disseminated in Syria around 200 CE, especially as two papyrus fragments from Oxyrhynchus (POx 2949) attest the dissemination of the text in Egypt in the second and third centuries.[93] In 1993 D. Lührmann was able to identify a further fragment of the Gospel, dating from the second century (POx 4009).

2. *Content.* The Akhmim fragment contains a report of the passion of Jesus beginning with Pilate washing his hands, the burial and the guard on the tomb, Jesus' resurrection before witnesses, the discovery of the empty tomb by the women, the return of the disciples to Galilee and the introduction to an appear-

---

[91]Maurer in *NTApoc* 1, 1963, 179–87, with introduction, translation and bibliography (1991, 1, 216–27, M.L. Schneemelcher); the Greek text is in E.Klostermann, *Apocrypha* I, Kleine Texte 3, Bonn ²1908; cf. also Vielhauer, *Geschichte**, 641–8; J.K. Elliott, *The Apocryphal New Testament*, Oxford 1993, 150–8.

[92]There is much discussion as to whether the Gospel of Peter really had docetic tendencies or was only interpreted in a docetic way, and what kind of docetism the intended recipients held; cf. Denker, *Stellung*; McCant, 'Gospel of Peter'; Brox, 'Doketismus'.

[93]Lührmann, 'POx 2949'.

ance of Jesus to Peter, Andrew and Levi by Lake Gennesaret. P O x 4009 presents a dialogue between the first-person narrator, Peter, and Jesus, which is akin to Matt. 10.16 and II Clem.5.2–4.

3. *Age and place of origin.* The *terminus a quo* for the composition of the Gospel of Peter is 70 CE, as the destruction of Jerusalem is presupposed (7.25); the *terminus ad quem* can hardly be put later than 190 CE (the letter of Serapion).[94] It was most probably composed in the first half of the second century CE; various indications point to Syria as a possible place of composition.

4. *Age and independence of the traditions in the Gospel.* The relationship of the traditions worked over in the Gospel of Peter to the canonical Gospels has been disputed, since in 1893 Adolf von Harnack considered the Gospel of Peter to be largely independent.[95] That is above all because early and late elements of tradition are demonstrably combined in the Gospel.

- Early tradition is represented by the references to the Old Testament in the passion narrative.[96] The event is narrated with words from the Old Testament without direct reference to a fulfilment of scripture. Here the Gospel keeps to Old Testament models more frequently and more directly than the Synoptic Gospels do. For example, 5.16 reports that on the cross Jesus was given 'gall with vinegar' (Ps. 69.22) to drink (Matt. 27.34,48 presents two different acts).
- Late elements of tradition, in addition to numerous individual features in the narrative, are the fictitious author (Peter as narrator), the exoneration of Pilate from responsibility for the crucifixion of Jesus (Herod and the Jews are responsible), and finally the fantastic depiction of the resurrection of Jesus from the tomb before many witnesses. Here a cross speaks, the preaching in Hades is mentioned, the figures of Jesus and two angels tower above the heavens, etc. However, today it is sometimes questioned whether the presence of a resurrection account at this point is intrinsically a secondary feature (as Vielhauer thinks; see below on Koester).

This evidence allows various interpretations of the history of the origin of the Gospel of Peter. Two rival models are worth sketching out briefly.

- According to H.Koester,[97] the features shared by the Gospel of Peter and the

---

[94]Cf. Denker, *Stellung*, 9–30. Pilhofer, 'Justin', lists some arguments for supposing that Justin knew the Gospel, which would put the date of origin at 130 CE at the latest. However, we cannot be completely certain here.

[95]von Harnack, *Bruchstücke* (however, Harnack thinks it probable that the Gospel of Peter knew Mark).

[96]Dibelius, 'Motive'; Denker, *Stellung*, 58–77.

[97]Koester, *Ancient Christian Gospels*, 216–40; id., 'Apocryphal and Canonical Gospels', esp. 126ff.

canonical Gospels rest on common old traditions, each of which was developed differently. Certainly the Gospel of Peter has undergone a relatively late redactional revision which accounts for the late features in the tradition, but according to Koester the basic stratum of the tradition is independent of the canonical Gospels and in the passion narrative often represents the earlier form. The basic core of the Easter epiphany story in the Gospel of Peter is similarly early and was eliminated by Mark for theological reasons.[98]

• With M. Dibelius,[99] many exegetes regarded it as proven that the Gospel of Peter presupposes all four canonical Gospels, reproduces their material from memory and has combined it with oral material, especially Old Testament exegetical traditions.

5. *Information about Jesus*. The historical value of the Gospel of Peter is slight, even if we assume that it is based on a version of the passion and resurrection tradition independent of the canonical Gospels. A crass ignorance of events in Palestine at the time of Jesus, Jewish feasts and customs, and the Law which applied at the time is combined with a massive anti-Jewish polemic in the interest of which the text has been heavily revised.

4.4 The so-called Oxyrhynchus Papyrus 840

J. Jeremias, 'Der Zusammenstoss Jesu mit dem pharisäischen Oberpriester auf dem Tempelplatz', *CNT* 11,1947 (*In honorem A. Fridrichsen*), 97–108; J. Jeremias and K.F.W. Schmidt, 'Ein bisher unbekanntes Evangelienfragment', *ThBl* 15, 1936, 34–45.

1. *The text*. POx 840, found in Oxyrhynchus in 1905, is a parchment leaf (thus not a 'papyrus') measuring only 8.8 by 7.4cm, and inscribed in tiny writing. It comes from a little codex made around 400 CE, which was presumably worn round the neck as an amulet and contained an unknown Gospel of a Synoptic type, to judge from the fragment.[100]

---

[98]Crossan, *Four Other Gospels*, 125–81; id., *Cross*, even attempted to show that the passion and resurrection narrative underlying the Gospel of Peter (the 'Cross Gospel') was used by the canonical Gospels. However, this demonstration can hardly be regarded as successful, cf. Brown, 'Gospel'.

[99]Dibelius, 'Motive'; thus also Vielhauer, *Geschichte**; the two French commentaries on the Gospel of Peter by M.G. Mara, *Evangile*, and L. Vaganay, *L'Évangile*; and also Kirk, 'Priorities'. Schneemelcher, *NTApoc* 1, 1991, 180; 1993, 218, leaves the decision open.

[100]Introduction and translation by Jeremias in *NTApoc* 1, 1963, 92–4; 1991, 94–6; cf. Vielhauer, *Geschichte**, 639–41; Jeremias, *Unknown Sayings*, 15f., 50ff. For the Gospels as amulets cf. John Chrysostom, *Homilia de statuis* XIX 4: 'Women and little children are in the habit of wearing Gospel books around their necks in place of a large amulet' (quoted from Jeremias, *Unknown Sayings*, 18).

2. *Content.* In 45 lines the leaf contains parts of two loosely connected pericopes located in Jerusalem; these are the conclusion of a discourse of Jesus to his disciples in which he warns them against committing injustice, and a dispute with a senior Pharisaic priest in the area of the temple which is subject to laws of cleanness. In analogy to Mark 7 and Matt. 23, this is a confrontation between different notions of cleanness. The priest accuses Jesus and his disciples of making the temple place unclean, because they have not performed the prescribed cultic purifications. In reply to Jesus' question whether he himself is then clean, the priest enumerates the washings and the rituals that he has performed. Thereupon Jesus utters a woe on him and all those who are blind, because he does not see that external cleanness can go with wickedness of all kinds (cf. Matt. 23.27f.; Mark 7.15ff.). In a heavily damaged conclusion Jesus seems to have spoken of baptism with living water (cf. John 4.10ff.; 7.37) as a purification from sins.

3. *Age and significance.* In form and content POx 840 represents a variant to corresponding Synoptic texts; it shows familiarity with the ritual of the Jerusalem temple,[101] and therefore could well come from the first century. But it should be noted that there is only a tiny fragment of this unknown Gospel and no well-founded statements can be made about its age, content and tendency.

Further papyrus fragments will not be discussed. Because in most cases the text is in a fragmentary state, no certain reading can be made. However, reference should be made to one agraphon which some scholars think valuable: the heavily damaged POx 1224 contains the following saying of Jesus: '(Whoever) is far (today), will be (near to you) tomorrow.'

5. Jewish Christian Gospels

G. Howard, 'The Gospel of the Ebionites', *ANRW* II 25.5, 1988, 4034–53; A.F. Klijn, 'Das Hebräer- und das Nazoräerevangelium', *ANRW* II 25.5, 1988, 3997–4033.

Alongside the Synoptic Gospels and those close to Gnosticism, the Jewish Christian Gospels represent a group held together by a comparable religious milieu. The few extant fragments do not allow us to recognize a clear common picture of Jesus in them. However, the ethical accent is unmistakable. The Gospel of the Nazarenes reinforces social aspects over and above the Synoptic tradition; the Gospel of the Ebionites shows interest in vegetarianism, which is connected with a repudiation of animal sacrifices as a criticism of the cult; and the Gospel of

---

[101] Jeremias, 'Zusammenstoss', has pointed this out.

the Hebrews combines gnosticizing motives with a high esteem for brotherly love: 'And never be joyful except when you look on your brother with love' (frag. 5).

The problems in investigating the Jewish Christian Gospels are particularly complex since the writings of Jewish Christian groups have largely been lost. Only fragments of these Gospels have been preserved as quotations in the church fathers. But the fathers are sometimes inaccurate in indicating their sources, sometimes contradictory, and sometimes obviously give false attributions to quotations out of ignorance. Therefore there is little agreement among scholars about the number of Jewish Gospels (estimates range from one to three) or about the attribution of individual fragments. The following survey is based on the solution proposed by Vielhauer and Strecker, according to which we are to suppose that there are three Jewish Gospels, since this solution seems to command most consensus at present.[102]

1. The *Gospel of the Nazarenes*[103] was closely akin to Matthew, but composed in Aramaic or Syriac. Since the Middle Ages it has been named after the group which handed it down, the so-called Nazarenes or Nazoreans, Jewish Christians from Beroea (Aleppo) in Coele Syria.[104] The church fathers did not regard it as heretical and it is to be dated in the early second century, as Hegesippus (c.180) already knew it. 36 fragments have survived, which often represent divergent readings of the text of Matthew. Novellistic elaborations and legendary expansions are characteristic of the shaping of the narrative materials (the garments of the Magi are described precisely; the man with a withered hand is a builder and asks for healing so that he can continue to pursue his trade); the form of the logia also points to a later stage of the tradition.[105] The Gospel of the Nazarenes in no way presents the Hebrew Ur-Matthew, as some church fathers think; we should follow Vielhauer in describing it as a 'targum-like rendering of the canonical Matthew'.[106]

2. The *Gospel of the Ebionites*[107] is attested by Irenaeus (c.180); seven fragments have been preserved in the *Panarion* of Epiphanius of Salamis (ch. 30).

---

[102]Vielhauer, *NTApoc* 1, 1963, 107–65; 1991, Vielhauer and Strecker, 134–78; Vielhauer, *Geschichte**, 648–55.

[103]Introduction and translation of the fragment in *NTApoc* 1, 1963, 139–53; 1991, 154–65.

[104]In modern works it is sometimes called Gospel of the Nazarenes. In the church fathers we have as titles 'the Syrian Gospel' (according to Hegesippus, quoted in *HE* 4, 22, 8), 'the Gospel which is disseminated among the Jews in Hebrew' (Eusebius, *Theoph.* 4.12). Mediaeval manuscripts speak of 'the Jewish [Gospel][τὸ Ἰουδαϊκόν]'. Jerome identifies the Gospel of the Nazarenes wrongly with the Gospel of the Hebrews.

[105]This is occasionally disputed; thus Jeremias, *Unknown Sayings*, 84, argues for the originality of frag.25a over against the parallel Matt.18.21f.

[106]Vielhauer, *Geschichte**, 652.

[107]Introduction and translation of the fragment by Vielhauer and Strecker, *NTApoc* 1, 1963, 153–8; 1991, 166–71.

This is a Gospel, composed in Greek, of the Jewish–Christian group of Ebionites who probably lived in Transjordan and adjoining territories. It, too, seems to be a revision of Matthew, but it also takes into account Lukan and Markan material and makes theologically substantial deletions and alterations which allow us to infer the theology of the group:

- *Rejection of the virgin birth*: the infancy narrative is deleted; the Gospel of the Ebionites begins with the appearance of John the Baptist and the baptism of Jesus, by which he became son of God (frag. 3).[108]
- *Vegetarianism*: the Ebionites consistently refrained from eating meat and also attributed the same attitude to the leading figures of the Gospel. Instead of eating wild honey and locusts (ἀκρίς, Matt. 3.4), John the Baptist eats only honey, 'the taste of which was that of manna, as a cake (ἐγκρίς) dipped in oil' (frag. 2).[109] To their question where they are to prepare the Passover lamb the disciples receive the dismissive answer: 'Do I desire with desire at this Passover to eat flesh with you?' (frag.7).
- *Hostility to the temple cult*: the Gospel of the Ebionites says about the goal of Jesus' mission: 'I am come to do away with sacrifices, and if you do not cease from sacrificing, the wrath of God will not cease from you' (frag.6).

3. The *Gospel of the Hebrews*[110] (probably also the first half of the second century) seems to be a Jewish Christian Gospel with a mythical-Gnostic bent which deviates more widely from the canonical Gospels. By way of qualification it should be pointed out that the attribution of the fragments is particularly difficult and controversial; only seven fragments remain of a work which was almost as long as Matthew, to form the basis of any judgment. As the Gospel of the Hebrews is known mainly from quotations in Clement of Alexandria and Origen, it will have been used among the Jewish Christians of Egypt; its proximity to Gnosticism would be compatible with an origin in this region.

- The *Jewish–Christian origin* of the Gospel is attested by its title ('the Gospel according to the Hebrews'), which identifies the circle of its users. 'Hebrews' can also denote Greek-speaking Diaspora Jews. The appearance reported in frag. 7 of the Risen Christ to James, who is thought to have taken part in the Last Supper and thus to be a disciple of the earthly Jesus, is a personal legend

---

[108]It is disputed whether the entry of the Spirit into Jesus at the baptism described in Fragment 3 allows us to infer a (gnosticizing) christology which diverges from the Synoptics.

[109]The alteration of ἀκρίς into ἐγκρίς visibly rests on a Greek text; the idea comes from Ex. 16.31; Num. 11.8 (LXX).

[110]Introduction and translation of the fragment by Vielhauer and Strecker, *NTApoc* i, 1963, 158–65; 1991, 172–8.

about the brother of the Lord spun out of I Cor.15.7; James became one of the most important guarantors of Jewish–Christian theology. Finally, the notion of the Holy Spirit as a female figure is to be understood against a Semitic linguistic background (cf. frag.3, where the saviour says: 'Even so did my mother, the Holy Spirit, take me by one of my hairs and carry me away on to the great mountain Tabor').

- The *proximity to Gnosticism* is shown in a catena about the stages of the revelation of salvation: 'He that seeks will not rest until he finds; and he that has found shall marvel; and he that has marvelled shall reign; and he that has reigned shall rest' (Frag.4b; similarly POx 654/Thomas 2). The baptism of Jesus is described as a descending of the 'whole fount of the Holy Spirit' on Jesus in which the Spirit (!) speaks to the pre-existent firstborn Son and attains eschatological rest through union with him (frag.2). The first fragment, which reproduces cosmic speculations about the birth of Jesus, also presupposes the pre-existence of Jesus.

6. Further sources: floating traditions about Jesus

D.C. Allison, Jr, 'The Pauline Epistles and the Synoptic Gospels: The Pattern of the Parallels', NTS 28, 1982, 1–32; E. Best, 'I Peter and the Gospel Tradition', NTS 16, 1969/70, 95–113; D.B. Deppe, *The Sayings of Jesus in the Epistle of James,* diss. Amsterdam 1989; P.J. Hartin, *James and the Q Sayings of Jesus,* JSNT SS 47, Sheffield 1991; H. Köster, *Synoptische Überlieferung bei den Apostolischen Vätern,* TU 65, Berlin 1957.

6.1 Sayings of Jesus in the New Testament outside the Gospels

1. In Paul's farewell speech before the elders of Miletus, which has been shaped by the author of Acts, Paul uses a saying of the Lord to justify his practice of working to support himself: '. . .remembering the word of the Lord Jesus, who himself said, "It is better to give than to receive"' (Acts 20.35; cf. Did.1.5).

2. Paul himself only rarely makes *explicit* reference to sayings of Jesus,[111] thus in I Cor.7.10 to the prohibition against divorce (cf. Mark 10.11f. par.) and in I Cor.9.14 to a mission rule (cf. Matt. 10.10 par.). In I Cor. 11.24f. he quotes the eucharistic words (Mark 14.22–24 par.). It is disputed whether Rom. 14.14 is to be taken as a quotation (cf. Mark 7.15 par.). Finally, I Thess. 4.15–17 is clearly introduced as a saying of the Lord, but the wording also allows the interpretation

---

[111]Allison, 'Pauline Epistles', and Koester, *Ancient Christian Gospels,* 52ff., give a survey.

that Paul is handing on a word of the Exalted Christ given to him in a revelation.[112]

3. Outside the Gospels, *anonymous traditions* are occasionally taken up in the New Testament writings which otherwise have been handed down as sayings in the mouth of Jesus. There can be no methodologically guaranteed way of discovering whether they were known to their several authors as sayings of the Lord.

- In the Letter of James[113] and I Peter[114] numerous parenetical traditions can be indicated which belong to the preaching of Jesus in the Sermon on the Mount or the Sermon on the Plain.
- In I Cor. 1–4 numerous possible *allusions* can be found *to wisdom logia* of Jesus which have parallels in Q, Mark and the Gospel of Thomas.[115] For example, in I Cor 2.9 Paul gives an alleged quotation from scripture, the origin of which cannot be clarified. Gospel of Thomas 17 hands down a very similar revelation saying of Jesus:

I Cor.2.9 ' . . .as it is written, "What no eye has seen, nor ear heard, nor the heart of man conceived, what God has prepared for those who love him"' (cf. Matt. 13.16/Luke 10.23f.).	Gospel of Thomas 17: 'I shall give you what no eye has seen and what no ear has heard and what no hand has touched and what has never occurred to the human mind.'

The attempt to infer an early collection of secret wisdom revelation sayings of Jesus on this basis must be regarded as hypothetical, as a secondary transfer of traditions to Jesus is equally conceivable.

6.2 Later additions to New Testament manuscripts

Some passages from the floating Jesus tradition have been added to the Gospels in the course of the manuscript tradition. Some of them have found their way into present-day editions of the Bible.

---

[112]Jeremias, *Unknown Sayings*, 64–7, interprets I Thess. 4.16f. as an authentic apocalyptic logion of Jesus, only slightly modified in the tradition and by Paul; by contrast, Hofius, 'Unbekannte Jesusworte', 357–60, argues that this is presumably a revelation saying given to Paul.

[113]Deppe, *Sayings*; Hartin, *James*; and Koester, *Ancient Christian Gospels*, 71–5.

[114]Best, 'I Peter'; and Koester, *Ancient Christian Gospels*, 64–6.

[115]Cf. Koester, *Ancient Christian Gospels*, 55–62.

- The pericope about the woman taken in adultery (today John 7.53–8.11) does not appear in the best manuscripts, and in the rest appears in different places (after John 7.52; 7.36; 21.24 and Luke 21.38).
- In Codex D (fifth century) after the logion on the Sabbath in Luke 6.5 the following apopthegm has been inserted: 'Man, if you know what you are doing you are blessed. But if you do not know, you are cursed and a transgressor of the Law.'[116]
- Luke 23. 34a ('Father, forgive them; for they know not what they do') is possibly an earlier expansion, since important textual witnesses do not have the logion.[117]
- Some textual witnesses add after Luke 9.55a: 'And he said: "You do not know what manner of spirit you are of; for the Son of Man came not to destroy men's lives but to save them." '
- The conclusion of Mark with its summary of Easter appearances, mission charge and ascension (Mark 16.9–20), is similarly a secondary addition. Within this passage a revelation saying of the risen Christ, the so-called Freer Logion, appears after 16.14 in the Codex Freerianus.[118]

6.3 Papias and the Apostolic Fathers

In the first half of the second century there were already some writings about the life and teaching of Jesus; however we cannot talk of a pre-eminence of the Gospels which later became canonical. Numerous Gospels later excluded as 'apocryphal' and further traditions about Jesus were received and handed on in the communities in oral and written form. They are recorded in a group of writings of this period for which the collective term 'Apostolic Fathers' has become established.

1. Papias, who was Bishop of Hierapolis in Asia Minor at the beginning of the second century, set himself the aim of bringing together the oral traditions of Jesus, whatever 'derives from a living and abiding voice' (παρὰ ζώσης φωνῆς καὶ μενούσης), by interrogating people who would still have known the disciples of Jesus. He presented the results of his investigations in five books of 'Exegesis of Sayings of the Lord' (Λογίων κυριακῶν ἐξηγήσεως συγ-γράμματα πέντε), but these are lost apart from some quotations above all in Irenaeus and Eusebius, which do not arouse a great deal of trust.

---

[116]Quoted from Jeremias, *Unknown Sayings of Jesus*, 49.

[117]Jeremias, *Unknown Sayings of Jesus*, 26f., argues for an expansion; by contrast O. Hofius, 'Unbekannte Jesusworte', in P. Stuhlmacher (ed.), *Das Evangelium und die Evangelien*, WUNT 28, Tübingen 1983, 360f., argues that the verse is an original part of the text.

[118]Introduction and translation by Jeremias in *NTApoc* I, 1963, 188ff.; 1991, 248f.

2. In I Clement 13.2 a catechetical collection of the teaching of Jesus has been handed down in seven logia which seem very close to the Sermon on the Mount/Sermon on the Plain, but cannot be directly dependent on Matthew, Luke or Q. Presumably they go back to an original which these had:

'. . . especially remembering the words of the Lord Jesus which he spoke when he was teaching gentleness and longsuffering. For he spoke thus: "Be merciful, that you may obtain mercy. Forgive, that you may be forgiven. As you do, so shall it be done to you. As you give, so shall it be given to you. As you judge, so shall you be judged. As you are kind, so shall kindness be shown you. With what measure you mete, it shall be measured to you"' (I Clem. 13.1b, 2).[119]

3. The letters of Ignatius are also still in the middle of a living process of shaping and handing down material from the 'Synoptic' tradition alongside the Synoptics. In Smyrn. 3.2, Ignatius reports the encounter of the Risen Christ with his disciples in a form which is close to Luke 24.36–43, but probably independent of it:[120]

'And when he came to those with Peter he said to them: "Take, handle me and see that I am not a phantom without a body." And they immediately touched him and believed, being mingled both with his flesh and spirit . . . And after his resurrection he ate and drank with them as a being of flesh, although he was united in spirit to the Father.'

4. In II Clement there are (mixed) quotations from Matthew and Luke (or a logia collection dependent on them) alongside sayings of Jesus from floating tradition, presumably from a lost Gospel. These include, for example, the following logion:

II Clem. 4.5: 'For this reason, if you do these things, the Lord said, "If you are gathered together with me in my bosom and do not my commandments, I will cast you out, and will say to you, 'Depart from me, I know not whence you are, you workers of iniquity'"' (cf. II Clem. 5.2ff.; 8.5; 12.2).

5. Occasionally community rules, sayings about the Law and liturgical sayings occur in the Apostolic Fathers for which the authority of Jesus is not claimed, although they are cited by the Synoptics as sayings of Jesus. Here sometimes it seems likely that these became sayings of Jesus only in a secondary development.

Mention should be made of the twofold commandment to love (cf. Barn. 19.2, 5 with Mark 12.30ff.), the Golden Rule (cf. Did. 1.2b and Acts 15.20, 29D with

---

[119]Quoted from Kirsopp Lake, *The Apostolic Fathers*, I, LCL, London 1914, 31. For further Jesus traditions in I Clement independent of the Synoptics see Koester, *Ancient Christian Gospels*, 66–71.
[120]Köster, *Synoptische Überlieferung*.

Matt. 7.12/Luke 6.31 and I Clem. 13.2), the tradition of the power of prayer (cf.
Ignatius, Eph. 5.2/Hermas VI, 3, 6b with Matt. 18.19f. and Mark 11.22–24 par.),
the sin against the Holy Spirit (cf. Did. 11.7 with Mark 3.28f.) and the trinitarian
baptismal formula (cf. Did. 7.1 with Matt. 28.19).[121]

6.4 Other 'agrapha' and narratives about Jesus

There are 'dispersed sayings of the Lord' and narrative traditions of Jesus with
increasingly legendary forms in the church fathers, in early Christian liturgies and
church orders, in pseudepigraphical stories and letters of apostles and numerous
other writings. With very few exceptions they are of no use as sources for the
earliest forms of the Jesus tradition. Three examples of agrapha the content of
which O.Hofius does not regard as suspicious and which cannot be derived from
the history of the tradition might be mentioned in conclusion:

'As you are found, so will you be led away [viz., to judgment]' (*Syr. Liber Graduum*,
Serm III 3; XV 4).

'Ask for the great and God will add to you the little' (Clement of Alexandria, *Strom.*
I, 24, 158)

'Be bold moneychangers' (*Ps. Clem. Hom.* II, 51, 1; II, 50, 2; XVIII, 20, 4).

---

[121]Cf. ibid., 261ff.

7. Summary Survey

	Place	Time	Dependence	Picture of Jesus
Synoptic sources				
Logia source (Q)	Palestine	after 50 before 70	Q and Mark = old dependent sources	Jesus as eschatological preacher of the kingdom of God
Gospel of Mark	Syria/Rome	around 70		
Gospel of Matthew	Syria	75–100	Matt[s] and Luke[s] = independent complexes of tradition	
Gospel of Luke	Aegean/ Rome	75–100		
Gospels close to Gnosticism				
Gospel of John	Syria/ Ephesus?	75–100	Independent traditions	Jesus as mediator of an esoteric revelation
Gospel of Thomas	East Syria	75–140		
Jewish–Christian Gospels				
Gospel of the Nazarenes	Syria	2nd century	Use of Synoptic Gospels	(Picture of Jesus with ethical accents)
Gospel of the Ebionites	Southern Syria	2nd century		
Gospel of the Hebrews	Egypt	2nd century	Synoptic and Gnostic traditions	
Gospel fragments with Synoptic and Johannine elements				
Pap. Egerton 2	?	1st/2nd century	Combination of Synoptic and Johannine traditions (Egerton 2?) or after the separation of the spheres of tradition	(No uniform picture of Jesus)
Gospel of Peter	Syria	2nd century		
Secret Gospel of Mark	Egypt	1st/2nd century		
P Ox 840	?	1st/2nd century	Independent tradition	

8. Summary and hermeneutical reflections

In many respects a survey of the Christian sources about Jesus has a sobering effect. First of all it shows that even in the earliest sources at our disposal we do not encounter the historical Jesus, but pictures of Jesus, memories which have been shaped by theological and social interests and convictions and the history of the groups which handed them down. Moreover the earliest more extensive sources available to us were written down only in the second Christian generation. Despite isolated assertions to the contrary, none of the non-canonical sources is older than the Gospel of Mark either. Certainly many of the writings from primitive Christianity go back to traditions, sometimes written, which preceded them, but the originals have been lost (presumably without recall). We can partially reconstruct their form by careful analysis (see above 2.2 on Q and § 4 on methodological procedures), but the results remain hypothetical, and the exact wording of the earliest sources about Jesus is unknown.

What is perhaps most irritating is the knowledge that, as the large number of Gospels preserved in fragments indicates, we know only a small section of the range of traditions about Jesus which existed e.g. in the year 150 CE – and this is probably not a 'representative cross-section'. For the selection that we have today owes itself only to a slight degree to 'blind chance'; it has been governed considerably more strongly by church-political processes like the canonization of the Synoptic Gospels and John and the deliberate elimination of 'apocryphal' Gospels. For example, the picture of Jesus current in strict Jewish–Christian trends has been largely lost. Only in a very few fortunate instances have the Jesus traditions of Christian groups which were regarded as heretical by the church circles that gained the upper hand been preserved in such completeness that they can be of significant use in the historical reconstruction of the life and preaching of Jesus (above all the Gospel of Thomas). However, even that does not happen often. This is either because of an objection in principle to 'heterodox sources' which is historically highly questionable and all the more trust in the reliability of the church's process of selection and tradition, or because of a more unconscious continuation in the mainstream of a long exegetical tradition which, once F.C. Baur recognized that the Gospel of John was historically unreliable, from then on almost exclusively relied on the Synoptics. Thus the protest against the 'tyranny of the Synoptic Jesus'[122] which has been made by scholars who argue that more note should be taken of the extra-canonical sources is supported by a correct analysis and a justified concern. However, the solution cannot be an unthinking farewell to the Synoptic Jesus and a new 'tyranny of the apocryphal Jesus', especially as

---

[122]C.W. Hedrick, 'The Tyranny of the Synoptic Jesus', introduction to id. (ed.), *The Historical Jesus and the Rejected Gospels*, Semeia 44, 1988, 1–8.

Synoptic traditions occur in many extra-canonical Jesus traditions. 'The' Synoptic tradition already combines a broad spectrum of the most different forms and contents; otherwise it could hardly have become so influential in the church. But there were rival pictures of Jesus, for example in the Gnostic sphere and in circles close to Gnosticism, which are similarly based on the revision of old traditions about Jesus. These must be evaluated more consistently than before. That leads to new insights into the process by which the traditions about Jesus were handed down, insights which could possibly lead to a re- evaluation of Synoptic traditions. However, on individual and indeed even on central points there is an even greater variability in the pictures of Jesus, for example over the question whether Jesus shared apocalyptic ideas (Synoptics) or not (Thomas). In such cases reflections on the time, the locality and the religious background often make the Synoptic sources seem historically more reliable. In a historical approach to Jesus they remain the decisive sources simply because of the wealth of their material. That makes it all the more important to be aware of their selective character and to use other sources as possible correctives.

9. Tasks

9.1 Extra-canonical sources and the study of Jesus

Use the following quotations to remind yourself of possible attitudes about the value of extra-canonical sources for the study of Jesus (make a guess at who the author could be). Each of the three positions is worth criticizing. Formulate obvious objections of a historical or methodological kind.

Write out your own views on the question what significance extra-canonical sources have in the study of Jesus.

Text 1:

> The author sums up how he arrives at 'authentic' sayings of Jesus: 'By a process of elimination we are left with twenty-one sayings whose attestation and subject matter do not give rise to objections of weight, which are perfectly compatible with the genuine teaching of our Lord, and which have as high a claim to authenticity as the sayings recorded in our four Gospels.'
>
> The conclusion he comes to is: 'The extra-canonical literature, taken as a whole, manifests a surprising poverty. The bulk of it is legendary, and bears the clear mark of forgery. Only here and there, amid a mass of worthless rubbish, do we come upon a priceless jewel. The range of material which is of any use to the historian is remarkably small.'

The author arrives at the overall verdict that 'the real value of the tradition outside the Gospels is that it throws into sharp relief the unique value of the canonical Gospels themselves. If we would learn about the life and message of Jesus, we shall find what we want only in the four canonical Gospels. The lost dominical sayings may supplement our knowledge here and there in important and valuable ways, but they cannot do more than that.'

Text 2:

'We can begin from the assumption that the decisive aspects of the activity and words of Jesus, those which are to be noted for our faith, have been preserved in the Gospels.

The fact that we find some tradition, though not much, outside the Gospels, suggests that some Jesus material has been lost. Scholars speak of agrapha, unwritten traditions . . . [Acts 20.35 follows as an example]. Small groups of sayings of the Lord can be found in the Apostolic Fathers which seem not to have been quoted from a Gospel, but to have still been in circulation as independent small traditions. But here there were later excrescences and false developments which arose partly from narrative fantasy and partly from heresy, and led to the composition of the apocryphal Gospels. The Gnostic Gospel of Thomas, which was discovered in Upper Egypt in 1947, is a particularly evocative example of this.

Text 3:

'It seems quite unlikely that any of the apocryphal texts was written during the apostolic period, but some of these writings may have been composed as early as the end of the first century and a very large number are products of the second centry. The New Testament apocrypha are therefore sources for the history of early Christianity which are just as important as the New Testament writings. They contain many traditions which can be traced back to the time of the origins of Christianity. They provide us with a spectrum that is much more colourful than that of the canonical writings and permit insights into the manifold diversity of early Christian piety and theology, in short, a perspective which the the polemical orientation of the New Testament often obstructs or seeks to limit.'

3

The Non-Christian Sources about Jesus

F.F. Bruce, *Jesus and Christian Origins outside the New Testament*, London 1984; C.A. Evans, *Noncanonical Writings**; R. Eisler, ΙΗΣΟΥΣ ΒΑΣΙΛΕΥΣ ΟΥ ΒΑΣΙΛΕΥΣΑΣ (2 vols), Heidelberg 1929/30; J. Klausner, *Jesus of Nazareth*, London 1925; J.P. Meier, *Marginal Jew* 1*, 56–111.

Introduction

The non-Christian testimonies to Jesus are open to the twofold danger of being either overestimated or underestimated. They are overestimated if one hopes through them to find a 'neutral' approach to the historical Jesus which is free from a Christian 'overlay'. Tacitus does not give an account which goes back to the Acts of Pilate, nor Josephus an account which goes back to the protocol of the Sanhedrin. The extra-Christian sources are probably a reaction to Christian statements. But one should not put their value as sources too low either. First, they go back to Christian statements which are probably independent of our Gospels. They are independent testimony. Secondly, they document the ambivalent attitude of both Jewish and pagan contemporaries: from both spheres we have positions which are sometimes benevolent (Josephus [?], Mara bar Sarapion) and sometimes dismissive (rabbinic sources; Roman authors). Thirdly, they show that contemporaries in the first and second century saw no reason to doubt Jesus' existence.[1]

Suggested reading and task

Read F.F. Bruce, *Jesus and Christian Origins*, 19–65. Bruce discusses the essential sources and quotes them in translation.

In looking at the sources, note everything that makes it possible to give them a historical context and to judge what is said in them. Questions to ask are:

- When was this source composed? Is it authentic or could it be a forgery?

---

[1]The Greek and Latin quotations in this chapter are based on J.B. Aufhauser, *Antike Jesus-Zeugnisse*, Kleine Texte 126, Bonn [2]1925.

- What do we know about the author (What religious or philosophical view did he hold? In what function was he dealing with Christ/the Christians, etc.)?

- What references are given by the literary context and why does it mention Jesus?

- Where does the information come from (Is it dependent on Christian statements? Does it go back to earlier sources, etc.)?

- What is actually said about Jesus and how does it relate to Christian accounts of him?

1. Josephus on 'Jesus who is called the Christ'

E. Bammel, 'A New Variant Form of the Testimonium Flavianum', *Judaica*, WUNT 37, Tübingen 1986, 190–3; id., 'Zum Testimonium Flavianum', in ibid., 177–89; Z. Baras, 'Testimonium Flavianum: The State of Recent Scholarship', in M. Avi-Yonah and Z. Baras, *Society and Religion in the Second Temple Period*, The World History of the Jewish People VIII, Jerusalem 1977, 303–13, 378–85; S.G.F. Brandon, *Jesus and the Zealots*, Manchester 1967, 59–368; L.H. Feldman, *Josephus and Modern Scholarship 1937–1980,* Berlin and New York 1984 (esp. 679–703); L.H. Feldman and G. Hata (eds.), *Josephus, Judaism and Christianity*, Detroit 1987; D. Flusser, *Die letzten Tage Jesu in Jerusalem*, Stuttgart 1982, 155–63; C.Martin, 'Le "Testimonium Flavianum". Vers une solution définitive?', *Revue belge de philologie et d'histoire* 20, 1941, 409–65; S. Mason, *Josephus and the New Testament*, Peabody, Mass. 1992; J.R. Meier, *Marginal Jew* 1*, 56–88; A. Schalit (ed.), *Zur Josephusforschung*, WdF 84, Darmstadt 1973, 27–69; S. Pines, *An Arabic Version of the Testimonium Flavianum and its Implications,* Jerusalem 1971; G. Vermes, 'The Jesus Notice of Josephus Re-Examined', *JJS* 38, 1987, 1–10; P. Winter, 'Josephus on Jesus and James', in E. Schürer, *History* 1*, 428–41.

The Jewish historian Josephus (37/38 CE – after 100), son of a priest and Pharisee from a well-to-do family, was first of all a commander in Galilee during the Jewish War and then became a Roman prisoner of war. He prophesied that Vespasian would become emperor and when this actually happened, Vespasian freed him. From then on Josephus lived in Rome under the protection of the Flavians and there composed his historical and apologetic writings. Amazingly Josephus does not speak of Jesus in his *Jewish War*, but he does mention him twice in the *Jewish Antiquities* (*Antt.* 18,63f.; 20,200). Only the second of these passages comes from him with any certainty; the first, the so-called 'Testimonium Flavianum', is under suspicion of containing Christian interpolations or at least of having been worked over by Christians.

1.1 The mention of Jesus as brother of James (*Antt.* 20,200)

In *Antt.* 20, 200, Josephus mentions the condemnation and stoning of James and others for transgressing the Law (ὡς παρανομησάντων) after a session of the

Sanhedrin under the high priest Ananus in 62. Josephus introduces James as 'the brother of Jesus who is called Christ' (τὸν ἀδελφὸν Ἰησοῦ τοῦ λεγομένου Χριστοῦ), and thus identifies him by his brother who is either better known or has already been mentioned.[2]

1. The *authenticity* of the text may be taken as certain; it is improbable that it is a Christian interpolation.[3]

- The text is closely connected to its context, though the designation 'brother of Jesus, the so-called Christ' could be secondary.
- However, this note shows no interest in Jesus himself, but mentions him only to identify his brother, a procedure which we often find in Josephus.
- The formulation ὁ λεγόμενος χριστός (who is called Christ) implies neither assent nor doubt (cf. Matt. 1.16). The surname 'Christ' merely appears to distinguish Jesus from the countless people of the same name[4] (cf. in the New Testament Col.4.11: Ἰησοῦς ὁ λεγόμενος Ἰοῦστος = Jesus with the surname Justus).

2. The talk of Jesus who is called Christ reflects Jewish rather than Christian terminology, since in Christianity χριστός soon became a proper name (and appears in Roman sources as such).

3. The tendency of the report on James is neutral to friendly: Josephus indicates that the condemnation was not legal, was disapproved of by those faithful to the Law (i.e. probably the Pharisees) and finally led to the deposition of Ananus.

1.2 The 'Testimonium Flavianum' (*Antt.* 18, 63f.).

The text of the disputed testimony of Josephus to Jesus Christ which is given by all manuscripts of Josephus with no deviations worth mentioning runs:

Γίνεται δὲ κατὰ τοῦτον τὸν χρόνον Ἰησοῦς σοφὸς ἀνήρ, εἴγε ἄνδρα αὐτὸν λέγειν χρή· ἦν γὰρ παραδόξων ἔργων ποιητής, διδάσκαλος ἀνθρώπων τῶν ἡδονῇ τἀληθῆ δεχομένων, καὶ πολλοὺς μὲν Ἰουδαίους, πολλοὺς δὲ καὶ τοῦ Ἑλληνικοῦ	Around this time there lived Jesus, a wise man, if indeed one ought to call him a man. For he was one who did surprising deeds, and a teacher of such people as accept the truth gladly. He won over many Jews and many of the Greeks. He was the Messiah.

---

[2]The text is quoted complete on p.470 below.

[3]The authenticity is assumed by the majority of scholars; Schürer, *Geschichte* I*, 1901, 581, is an exception.

[4]Josephus mentions around thirteen people called Jesus, cf. Winter, 'Josephus', 431 n.5; also Schürer, *History* I*, 581.

ἐπηγάγετο· ὁ χριστὸς οὗτος ἦν· καὶ αὐτὸν ἐνδείξει τῶν πρώτων ἀνδρῶν παρ'ἡμῖν σταυρῷ ἐπιτετιμηκότος Πιλάτου οὐκ ἐπαύσαντο οἱ τὸ πρῶτον ἀγαπήσαντες. ἐφάνη γὰρ αὐτοῖς τρίτην ἔχων ἡμέραν πάλιν ζῶν τῶν θείων προφητῶν ταῦτά τε καὶ ἄλλα μυρία περὶ αὐτοῦ θαυμάσια εἰρηκότων. εἰς ἔτι τε νῦν τῶν Χριστιανῶν ἀπὸ τοῦδε ὠνομασμένον οὐκ ἐπέλιπε τὸ φῦλον.

When Pilate, upon hearing him accused by men of the highest standing among us, had condemned him to be crucified, those who in the first place came to love him did not give up their affection for him, for on the third day he appeared to them restored to life. The prophets of God had prophesied this and countless other marvellous things about him. And the tribe of the Christians, so called after him, have still to this day not died out.

Since the sixteenth century the Testimonium Flavianum has been the subject of vigorous argument. First of all we must discuss whether the section is to be regarded as authentic testimony of Josephus or as a Christian interpolation. In the twentieth century the debate increasingly shifted to the question whether the Testimonium Flavianum is based on an earlier report by Josephus, which has been worked over by Christians, and whether one still can reconstruct the wording or tendency of this original report. The three possible hypotheses (authenticity, interpolation, revision) will be discussed below.

1.2.1 The hypothesis of authenticity

The hypothesis of unqualified authenticity is rarely put forward now.[5] But such significant historians as von Ranke and Harnack regarded the Testimonium as essentially authentic.[6] They excluded only the following parenthesis as a probable insertion: 'on the third day he appeared to them restored to life. The prophets of God had prophesied this and countless other marvellous things about him.' In fact, there are some quite illuminating arguments – at first sight, at least – for the substantial authenticity of the Testimonium:

　　1. *The wider and narrower context*: the passage about James in *Antt.* 20, 200 presupposes an earlier mention of Jesus. *Antt.* 18, 55–89 deals with Pilate's time in office: this was the place to mention Jesus.

　　2. *The testimony of the church fathers*: the attestation of the Testimonium goes back to Eusebius (260–339).[7] There are no earlier manuscripts or certain quotations.

---

　　[5]These are named by Meier, *Marginal Jew*, 1*, 73f.
　　[6]L. von Ranke, *Weltgeschichte* III, 2, Leipzig 1883, 40f.; A. von Harnack, 'Der jüdische Geschichtsschreiber Josephus und Jesus Christus', *IMWKT* 7, 1913, 1037–68.
　　[7]Eusebius, *HE* 1,1, 7–8; *DemEv* 3, 5, 105–6; *Theoph.* 5, 44 and numerous examples in other church fathers after Eusebius; cf. H. Schreckenberg, *Die Flavius-Josephus-Tradition in Antike und Mittelalter*, Leiden 1972.

3. *Content and language*: numerous formulations suggest Josephus more than a Christian author.

- The designation of Jesus as σοφὸς ἀνήρ (wise man) is not common in Christianity, but corresponds to Josephus' terminology. The same goes for the description of Jesus' miracles as παράδοξα ἔργα (surprising deeds).[8]
- The formulation ἡδονῇ τἀληθῆ δέχεσθαι (accept the truth gladly) would be unusual for a Christian as ἡδονή (pleasure) almost always has negative connotations. ἡδονῇ δέχεσθαι (accept gladly) is a favourite phrase of Josephus's; perhaps here it is meant ironically.
- That Jesus attracted Jews and Gentiles accords with Christian sources, but can easily be explained on the assumption that Joseph had in mind the Roman Christianity of his time, which also had pagan members.
- The execution of Jesus by Pilate on the denunciation of the Jewish authorities shows acquaintance with legal conditions in Judaea and contradicts the tendency of the Christian reports of the trial of Jesus, which incriminate the Jews but play down Pilate's responsibility.
- The designation of Christians as φῦλον (tribe) perhaps has derogatory connotations and betrays a Jewish rather than a Christian perspective.

However, it should be noted that the arguments are not clear: agreements with the language and ideas of the Jew Josephus could also be a sign that the forger was imitating his author (interpolation theory). It would also be conceivable that a reviser kept as much as possible of Josephus' own diction (revision hypothesis).

1.2.2 *The interpolation hypothesis*

As early as the sixteenth century, Reformed and Lutheran philologists recognized that the Testimonium contains so many clear confessions of Christian beliefs that it could not come from a Jew: '*Si enim Josephus ita sensisset . . . Josephus fuisset Christianus,*' thought Lukas Osiander.[9] Now as Josephus indubitably remained a Jew all his life, it seemed obvious that a Christian copyist must have forged and interpolated the section.[10] Good arguments can also be adduced for this thesis:

1. The *context*. E. Norden has demonstrated by a detailed analysis of the

---

[8]Cf. G. Vermes, 'Jesus Notice', though he regards only these formulations, and not the whole of the Testimonium Flavianum, as authentic.

[9]'Had Josephus been so inclined . . . Josephus would have been Christian', quoted from Eisler, ΙΗΣΟΥΣ, I,19.

[10]Thus e.g. H. Conzelmann, *Jesus*, Philadelphia 1972, 14; E. Norden, 'Josephus und Tacitus über Jesus Christus und eine messianische Prophetie' (1913), in A. Schalit (ed)., *Zur Josephusforschung*, WdF 84, Darmstadt 1973, 27–69.

context that the Testimonium is an isolated block which disrupts a carefully structured whole. In accord with a favourite pattern of composition in annals, Josephus depicts Pilate's time in office as a series of revolts; key compositional words which appear at the beginning and end of each of the sub-sections are θόρυβος (revolt) or the relevant verb θορυβεῖν and στάσις with the same meaning. Only in the section on Jesus are this topic and the corresponding key words missing.

2. The *testimony of the church fathers*. None of the Apologists of the second and third centuries quotes the Testimonium, though they use Josephus as a source of information about the exegesis of the Old Testament. Origen (c.185–254) states a century before Eusebius that Josephus did not believe that Jesus was the Christ (ἀπιστῶν τῷ Ἰησοῦ ὡς χριστῷ, *Contra Celsum* 1, 47).[11] So he certainly did not find the sentence 'this was the Christ'. Further conclusions are difficult. Did Origen have another more critical text instead of the present Testimonium, or was *Antt.* 20, 200 enough for his conclusion? At any rate one may suspect that the general acceptance of the Testimonium is to be attributed to knowledge of the works of Eusebius and not the integrity of the text.

3. *Content and language*. At least three statements are so clearly Christian that they cannot be attributed to a Jewish author:

- The doubting question whether Jesus may be named a man at all (εἴγε ἄνδρα αὐτὸν λέγειν χρή) is only understandable as a dogmatic correction which did not see the divinity of Jesus guaranteed by the formulation.[12]
- ὁ χριστὸς οὗτος ἦν (this man was the Christ) cannot be other than a definite confession of Jesus as the Christ (cf. Luke 23.35; John 7.26; Acts 9.22).
- 'For on the third day he appeared to them restored to life. The prophets of God had prophesied this and countless other marvellous things about him.' Here too a Christian is speaking.

1.2.3 *The revision hypothesis*

Neither the arguments for the substantial authenticity of the text nor those for an interpolation are convincing. The former are not sufficient explanation of the

---

[11]Cf. also *Commentary on Matthew* 10.17: Ἰησοῦν . . . οὐ καταδεξάμενος εἶναι χριστόν (he [Josephus] does not recognize that Jesus is the Christ); quoted from Winter, 'Josephus', 432 n.8.

[12]By contrast, von Harnack, 'Geschichtsschreiber' (n.6), 1053, thinks that this is just a widespread theme of the θεῖος ἀνήρ (divine man) which has been transferred to Jesus. As an analogy one could cite *Ap* 1, 232, 236. Here Josephus reports about an Egyptian whom he calls a wise man entrusted with soothsaying (σοφὸς καὶ μαντικὸς ἀνήρ) and reports that he had the reputation of a man related to the deity because of his wisdom and prophetic gifts (θείας δὲ δοκοῦντι μετεσχηκέναι φύσεως κατά τε σοφίαν καὶ πρόγνωσιν τῶν ἐσομένων). However, unlike the Testimonium Flavianum, the formulation leaves it open whether the author shares this belief.

Christian features; the latter do not do justice to the fact that there are clear echoes of Josephus' terminology. Therefore various revision theories have been proposed, some on the basis of newly discovered sources. The simplest theory reckons with very few Christian insertions into the otherwise intact text of Josephus. Thus J.P. Meier regards only the three clearly Christian statements mentioned above as additions. If we remove them we get the following text.[13]

Γίνεται δὲ κατὰ τοῦτον τὸν χρόνον Ἰησοῦς σοφὸς ἀνήρ· ἦν γὰρ παραδόξων ἔργων ποιητής, διδάσκαλος ἀνθρώπων τῶν ἡδονῇ τἀληθῆ δεχομένων, καὶ πολλοὺς μὲν Ἰουδαίους, πολλοὺς δὲ καὶ τοῦ Ἑλληνικοῦ ἐπηγάγετο· καὶ αὐτὸν ἐνδείξει τῶν πρώτων ἀνδρῶν παρ' ἡμῖν σταυρῷ ἐπιτετιμηκότος Πιλάτου οὐκ ἐπαύσαντο οἱ τὸ πρῶτον ἀγαπήσαντες· εἰς ἔτι τε νῦν τῶν Χριστιανῶν ἀπὸ τοῦδε ὠνομασμένον οὐκ ἐπέλιπε τὸ φῦλον.

At this time there appeared Jesus, a wise man. For he was a doer of startling deeds, a teacher of people who receive the truth with pleasure. And he gained a following both among many Jews and among many of Greek origin. And when Pilate, because of an accusation made by the leading men among us, condemned him to the cross, those who had loved him previously did not cease to do so. And up until this very day the tribe of Christians (named after him) has not died out.

Its simplicity supports this solution. But questions remain open.

- According to this reconstruction Josephus would not have said that Jesus was worshipped as Christ. But this is required both by *Antt.* 20, 200 (see above) and the last sentence about the Christians named after Jesus.
- The remaining text contains a number of vague terms which can be interpreted either positively or negatively. According to Meier, Josephus' intention was to compose an ambiguous text. However, this ambiguity could also be the result of a complicated history of the origin of the text.

Among the numerous reconstructions which reckon with further Christian insertions in the text, two basic types can be recognized. These display major parallels in method and results. According to one, Josephus judged Jesus neutrally or slightly positively; according to the other in a hostile way.

1.2.3.1 Reconstruction of an original form of the Josephus text hostile to Jesus

Numerous scholars conjecture as the original content of *Antt.* 18, 63f. a report on the attempted revolt by the political religious (mis)leader Jesus, which the Jewish

---

[13]Translation, Meier, *Marginal Jew* 1*, 61.

authorities nipped in the bud by handing over the troublemaker (Eisler, Beinert, Brandon).[14]

1. Crucial to this basic assumption is the context, which presents Pilate's time in office as a sequence of suppressed revolts (see p. 68 above). In this sense insertions of the following kind are suggested at the beginning and towards the end:

- 'Now around this time a certain Jesus appeared as leader of a new revolt' (= Γίνεται δὲ κατὰ τοῦτον τὸν χρόνον ἑτέρας στάσεως ἀρχηγὸς Ἰησοῦς τις).[15]
- The note that 'they had loved him previously' and thus 'did not cease to do so' (οὐκ ἐπαύσαντο οἱ τὸ πρῶτον ἀγαπήσαντες) becomes 'the adventurers who had followed him from the beginning did not cease to stir up tumults' (οὐκ ἐπαύσαντο θορυβεῖν οἱ τὸ πρῶτον ἀκολουθήσαντες λῃσταί).[16]

2. The method of reconstruction depends on the prior decision that the basis is a report with negative colouring. It is assumed that the Christian reviser primarily replaced hostile expressions with positive or neutral ones:

- Thus the designation of Jesus as σοφὸς ἀνήρ (wise man) goes back to an original σοφιστὴς καὶ γόης ἀνήρ (e.g. eloquent troublemaker and magician).[17]
- Instead of πολλούς ... ἐπηγάγετο (he gained a following of many) the text would have had πολλούς ... ἀπηγάγετο (he led many astray).[18]
- According to Josephus Jesus would not have taught his followers the truth (τἀληθῆ) but 'unusual things' (ἀήθη).[19]

3. The model according to which Josephus is said to have portrayed Jesus is that of the leaders of the resistance movement, who are portrayed as robbers, magicians and those who lead the people astray.

- The repertoire of terms applied to such political or religious leaders is: σοφιστής (someone learned in scripture who leads the people astray);[20]

---

[14]Eisler, ΙΗΣΟΥΣ; W. Bienert, *Der älteste nichtchristliche Jesusbericht. Josephus über Jesus. Unter besonderer Berücksichtigung des altrussischen 'Josephus'*, Halle 1936; *Brandon*, Jesus, 359–68. With reservations, Bammel, 'Testimonium', is also be included in this group, but he is more methodologically aware than Eisler and Bienert.

[15]Bienert, *Jesusbericht*, 252f.   [16]Ibid.; similarly Eisler, ΙΗΣΟΥΣ I, 87f.:

[17]Eisler, ΙΗΣΟΥΣ I, 51–4.   [18]Ibid., I, 39, 87f.; Bammel, 'Testimonium', 11f.

[19]Eisler, ΙΗΣΟΥΣ I, 63f.

[20]E.g. Judas of Galilee and his son Menahem (*BJ* 2, 118, 433); Judas and Matthias are also called *sophistai* (*BJ* 1, 648).

(ἄνθρωπος) γόης (deceptive miracle worker);[21] γόητες καὶ λῃστρικοί (miracle workers and robbers).[22] Common to all of them is that they rally the masses of the people behind them (according to Josephus, they 'deceive' and 'lead astray'), thus drawing the suspicion of the Romans upon them and provoking military intervention.

- ἡδονῇ δέχεσθαι occurs twice in such a context: both the speech of Judas of Galilee and the lying story of the false Alexander (a putative son of Herod) are 'received with pleasure' by those who are deceived (*Antt.* 18, 6; 17, 328f.)
- According to the model of the report of an Egyptian prophet who planned revolt against the Romans from the Mount of Olives (*BJ* 2, 261–3 [quoted below p. 89]; *Antt.* 20, 167–72), Bienert reconstructs the following Josephus text: 'And this so-called Christ led many Jews and Greeks to the Mount which is called the Mount of Olives, from where he intended to invade Jerusalem by force.'[23]

5. The text as an expression of the relationship between Judaism and earliest Christianity. The hostile attitude of Josephus is put in parallel to that of the Talmudic sources. Moreover apologetic motives are attributed to Jesus which led him to compose a text hostile to the Christians: he wanted to indicate to the Romans that the Jews had done their bit in fighting the Christian sect.[24]

1.2.3.2 The reconstruction of a neutral original form of the 'Testimonium Flavianum'

Recently there have been an increasing number of attempts to reconstruct an

---

[21]E.g. the false prophet from Egypt who led those whom he had deceived to the Mount of Olives, from there to engage in a revolt against the Romans (*BJ* 2, 261–3; *Antt.* 20, 167–72) or Theudas (*Antt.* 20, 97f.), a miracle worker (γόης τις ἀνήρ) who called himself a prophet (προφήτης γὰρ ἔλεγεν εἶναι).

[22]*BJ* 2, 264; cf. *Antt.* 20, 160.

[23]Bienert, *Jesusbericht*, 252f. Bienert attempts to support his reconstruction by incorporating the Old Russian translation of the Jewish War, the so-called Slavonic Josephus (11th/12th century); this contains a number of legendary interpolations, but its last revision is Christian. The beginning of one of them, the so-called Testamentum Slavianum (quoted below, pp. 87f.), clearly echoes the Testimonium Flavianum, so Bienert (similarly Eisler) conjectures that here the remnants of the original version have been preserved under a great many secondary insertions, e.g. also a reference to a planned rebellion by Jesus from the Mount of Olives. However, it is far more probable that this very late text is in turn based on a secondary combination of the Mount of Olives episode in Josephus and the notes in the Gospels about Jesus' time on the Mount of Olives, and already presupposes the Christian Testimonium Flavianum. Cf. Bruce, *Outside the Gospels*, 42–53, and J. Maier, *Jesus von Nazareth in der talmudischen Überlieferung*, EdF 82, Darmstadt ²1992, 46f.

[24]Brandon, *Jesus*, 364. Bammel, 'Testimonium', goes even further and accuses Josephus 'of having perpetrated the earliest literary denunciation of the Christians', with the aim of enabling and persuading the Roman authorities to separate out the dangerous tribe of Christians (21f., 18).

original text of Josephus which is neutral or even decidedly positive towards Jesus (thus already J. Klausner, in more recent times P. Winter, G. Vermes).[25]

1. This assumption too finds support in the context, since the section *Antt.* 18.65 which follows the Testimonium begins with the words: 'At the same time another misfortune stirred up the Jews' (καὶ ὑπὸ τοὺς αὐτοὺς χρόνους ἕτερόν τι δεινὸν ἐθορύβει τοὺς Ἰουδαίους). So it looks as if Josephus regarded the execution of Jesus as a δεινόν, a disturbing incident.[26]

2. The method used in reconstructing the original text is to exclude and reshape clearly Christian statements, weighing up the content and considering text-critical questions.

- Thus it is assumed that the reviser found 'around this time lived Jesus, a wise man', and corrected this description which, though respectful, he nevertheless found inadequate, by adding, 'if indeed it be lawful to call him a man'.
- The statement 'this was the Christ' is either deleted completely as a Christian interpolation or turned into a neutral statement, e.g. 'he came to be called Christ' (by analogy with *Antt.* 20, 200).[27]
- The same goes for the statements about the resurrection and the testimony of the prophets: they must either be deleted or so transformed that they can be imaginable in the mouth of Josephus, for example by being introduced as sayings of the disciples: φάσκοντες ὅτι κτλ ('they said that . . .').[28]

3. The text which can be produced in this way corresponds strikingly to an Arabic version of the Testimonium which Agapius the bishop of Hierapolis (tenth century) quotes in his Christian universal history. This text was first introduced into the discussion of the Testimonium in 1971 by S.Pines (*Arabic Version*). It runs:

> 'Josephus . . . says that at that time there was a wise man who was called Jesus, who led a good life and was known to be virtuous (or learned) and had many people of the Jews and other peoples as disciples. Pilate had condemned him to crucifixion and death, but those who had become his disciples did not give up his discipleship (or teaching) and related that he appeared to them three days after the crucifixion

---

[25]Klausner, *Jesus of Nazareth*; Winter, 'Josephus'; Vermes, 'Jesus Notice'.

[26]E.g. Winter, 'Josephus', 440f., puts forward this obvious solution. Bammel, 'Testimonium', 18, advances the opposite view; he thinks that for Judaism δεινόν is 'virtually the lack of punishment for the separable φῦλον'.

[27]Traces of this formulation have been preserved in the textual tradition of the Testimonium Flavianum, e.g. in Jerome, who writes *credebatur esse Christus*, and in Michael the Syrian (twelfth century); he was held to be/perhaps he was the Messiah. Quoted from Pines, *Arabic Version*, 40, 26f., 29 and n.109.

[28]Thus Bammel, 'Testimonium', 20.

and was alive, and therefore perhaps was the Messiah in connection with whom the prophets said marvellous things.'

- This text lacks all the elements which are suspect of being Christian interpolations: the humanity of Jesus is not put in question; his messiahship is only considered a possibility by the disciples; and the resurrection and testimony of the prophets are only reported indirectly via the testimony of the disciples.
- Strikingly there is also no reference to a denunciation of Jesus to Pilate by the Jewish authorities – could this report also derive from a Christian insertion?[29]
- The last statement of the Greek Testimonium Flavianum is not quoted, probably because in the context Agapius is quoting only sources about Jesus' life and death, and so the statement about the Christians would be superfluous.

Since unfortunately it is impossible to discover where Agapius got his source from, we cannot make any certain judgment on the authenticity of the text. It either came into being in the controversy with Islam, in which case its basis was the Testimonium in the form known to us today (Bammel).[30] Or Agapius's version is a version of the original text with slight Christian revisions, and thus a prior or parallel form of the Testimonium. Or is Agapius offering Josephus' original text about Jesus with a pinch of salt?

4. The model on which Josephus could have painted a positive picture of Jesus is John the Baptist (*Antt.* 18, 116–19, quoted below pp. 187f.).[31]

- John is depicted as a noble man (ἀγαθὸς ἀνήρ), who won over the crowds by his teaching. This is matched by the description of Jesus as a wise man (σοφὸς ἀνήρ) and teacher (διδάσκαλος) of many Jews and Gentiles.
- According to Josephus, John fell victim to a judicial murder by Herod. The reason given for the execution of John the Baptist is Herod's fear that he could lead the people to revolt – John is executed on mere suspicion (ὑποψίᾳ). Since it is relatively improbable that Josephus had no reason at all for mentioning Jesus' crucifixion, we can assume that a similar note about a feared revolt by Jesus or his followers was part of the original text.[32]
- It would be understandable for Christian copyists to suppress this section, since they must have been concerned to eliminate any suspicion of Christian disloyalty towards the Roman state.

---

[29]This is conjectured by Flusser, *Letzte Tage in Jerusalem*, 155–63.

[30]Cf. Bammel, 'Variant Form', 190–3. So far Bammel has not produced conclusive evidence for this theory, which goes beyond individual observations, cf. the critical remarks in Baras, 'Testimonium', 303–13, 378–85, esp. 305.

[31]Thus already Klausner, *Jesus of Nazareth*, 71. The testimony about the unjust execution of James (*Antt.* 20, 200), which is by no means hostile, should also be recalled.

[32]Flusser, *Letze Tage*, 155–63, with reference to John 11.47–53.

5. The text as an expression of the relationship between Judaism and primitive Christianity. According to Vermes, the description of Jesus as a 'wise man' and as 'one who did startling (miraculous) deeds' (παραδόξων ἔργων ποιητής) reflects the picture of Jesus which was going the rounds in Palestine as a popular tradition. The Pharisee Josephus[33] took it over still without an evaluation, whereas the rabbis later interpreted the same tradition as testimony about a magician and deceiver.[34]

Conclusion: the second version of the revision hypothesis is the most probable. Josephus reported on Jesus in as neutral and objective a way as he did on John the Baptist or James the brother of the Lord. His picture recalls that of Jesus in the Lukan writings. In both places Jesus is called 'man' (ἀνήρ). In both places there is a report on him in summary form and a distinction is made between his Jewish accusers and Pilate's responsibility. However, the idea that Jesus had pagan followers cannot be derived from Luke-Acts. Perhaps Josephus had contact in Rome with a Christianity of a Lukan stamp. But his roots in Palestine make it seem possible that he also used reports and popular traditions current in Jerusalem.

2. The rabbinic sources: Jesus as one who leads the people astray (bSanh 43a)

G. Dalman, *Jesus Christ in the Talmud, Midrash, Zohar and the Liturgy of the Synagogue* (1893), New York 1973; J. Maier, *Jüdische Auseinandersetzung mit dem Christentum in der Antike*, EdF 177, Darmstadt 1982; C. Thoma, 'Die Christen in rabbinischer Optik: Heiden, Häretiker oder Fromme?', in H. Frohnhofen (ed.), *Christlicher Antijudaismus und jüdischer Antipaganismus. Ihre Motive und Hintergründe in den ersten drei Jahrhunderten*, HThSt 3, Hamburg 1990, 23–49.

Whereas Josephus hands on a popular and sympathetic picture of Jesus, among the rabbis we have a picture of Jesus which attests to his rejection. However, assessments of the value of the (rare) rabbinic reports about Jesus as sources vary widely. Thus after a thorough investigation Maier comes to the conclusion: 'Analysis of the context, and study of the tradition, the material, the motifs and the form suggest that there is not a single rabbinic "Jesus passage" from Tannaitic times (up to c.220 CE).'[35] Rather, he claims, the name of Jesus was first inserted into the existing contexts in the process of the formation of the Talmud, which

---

[33] Jewish–Christian and Pharisaic groups maintained friendly relations for even longer, cf. Winter, 'Josephus', 441.

[34] Vermes, 'Jesus' Notice', esp. 9f.

[35] Maier, *Jesus* (n.23), 268; cf. also id., *Auseinandersetzung*.

extended over centuries, as a reaction to Christian provocations. Thus the passages have no independent historical value. In contrast to this, other authors, e.g. Klausner,[36] believe that they can discover at least some old and historically reliable traditions in the Talmud.

As representative of many possible texts, we shall quote only one important text on the execution of Jesus and his five disciples, which perhaps comes from the Tannaitic period (bSanh 43a):[37]

> On the sabbath of the Passover festival Jesus (Yeshu) the Nazarene was hanged. For forty days before execution took place, a herald went forth and cried: 'Here is Jesus the Nazarene, who is going forth to be stoned because he has practised sorcery and enticed Israel to apostasy. Anyone who can say anything in his favour, let him come forth and plead on his behalf.' But since nothing was brought forth in his favour, he was hanged on the eve of the Passover. . . .
>
> Our rabbis taught: Yeshu had five disciples: Matthai, Nakai, Nezer, Buni and Toda. When Matthai was brought [before the court], he said to them [the judges]: Shall Matthai be executed? Is it not written: [*matthai*] When shall I come and appear before God!? [Ps. 42.3]. Thereupon they retorted, Yes, Matthai shall be executed, since it is written: When [*matthai*], when will he be killed and his name perish? [Ps. 41.6] (similar word-plays follow for the other four 'disciples' of Jesus).

If we begin by assuming – though this is not beyond dispute – that this text comes from the early second century and always referred to Jesus,[38] the following statements are of historical interest:

1. The eve of the Passover is given as the *time of the execution of Jesus*; this contradicts the Synoptic chronology but corresponds to the information given in the Gospel of John.

2. Since this is an explanation of a rabbinic legal procedure, *the accusers and those who carry out the verdict* are of course exclusively Jewish authorities, and that is certainly historically inaccurate.

- Accordingly, Jesus is *stoned* and after that the body is *hung up*. The 'hanging on the eve of the Passover' is strongly emphasized over against stoning, perhaps to assimilate the report to the known fact that Jesus was crucified (by the Romans).
- It is also emphasized that, unusually, a crier sought witnesses for the defence forty days before the execution. Here we can perhaps see an apologetic answer to the Christian charge that Jesus had been tried over-hastily.

---

[36]Klausner, *Jesus of Nazareth*, 18–46.   [37]Quoted from Dalman, *Jesus Christ*, 85.
[38]Maier, *Jesus* (n.23), 219–37, comes to the conclusion that the name Jesus was inserted only secondarily into the account of the execution of some magician and deviant teacher who by chance had been killed on the eve of the Passover. If we follow this view, of course no historical conclusions are possible.

3. *Two reasons for the verdict* are given:

- Jesus practised sorcery – a charge that was circulating at a very early stage since it already appears in the Beelzebul pericope (Mark 3.22f.). It was natural to interpret Jesus' miracles as diabolical sorcery and magic, if God was not seen to be at work in him. However, it is very improbable that this accusation is connected with the execution of Jesus.
- Jesus is said to have led Israel astray and made it apostate – this accusation in no way reproduces the attitude of Jesus' accusers. Here, rather, a later historical situation is projected back into the life of Jesus. Only in retrospect, after the Christians had detached themselves as a religious group from Judaism and given up observing the Law (especially circumcision, the celebration of the sabbath and food regulations) and come to worship Jesus Christ as Kyrios and God, could Jews present Jesus as someone who led Israel astray to idolatry.

4. The mention of only five disciples of Jesus (instead of the twelve who might be expected), whose names may with much imagination remotely recall the names of disciples in the Christian tradition,[39] hardly derives from historical knowledge. Rather, here a list of names seems to have been applied secondarily to disciples of Jesus.[40]

3. Mara bar Sarapion: a Syrian Stoic on the 'wise king of the Jews'

A. Baumstark, *Geschichte der syrischen Literatur*, Bonn 1922; F. Schulthess, 'Der Brief des Mara bar Sarapion. Ein Beitrag zur Geschichte der syrischen Literatur', *ZDMG* 51, 1897, 365–91.

Just as presumably a benevolent report about Jesus has been preserved for us by the Jewish historian Josephus, so too we have one in the pagan philosopher Mara bar Sarapion. Here both in the Jewish and the pagan sphere probably earlier statements about Jesus have been given a positive colouring; only later do we have the negative counterparts. Remarkably, what is probably the earliest pagan testimony to Jesus is little known. It appears in a private letter by the Syrian Stoic Mara bar Sarapion, who came from Samosata, which he wrote to his son Sarapion from a Roman prison (in an unknown place). The letter contains numerous admonitions and warnings which Mara inculcates into his son in view of his own possible condemnation. Above all he commends wisdom to him as the

---

[39]Matthai has been interpreted as Matthew, Nakai as Nicodemus or Nicanor, Toda as Thaddaeus; Nezer and Buni are interpreted in a wide variety of ways.

[40]Thus Maier, *Jesus* (n.23), 234.

only possession and thing of substance in life which is worth striving for. The wise, too, may be persecuted in a world full of violence and calumny, but wisdom itself is eternal. To illustrate this notion he cites a series of paradigms in which not only Socrates and the sculptor (!) Pythagoras[41] but also Jesus appears, though Jesus' name is not mentioned:

> What good did it do the Athenians to kill Socrates, for which deed they were punished with famine and pestilence? What did it avail the Samians to burn Pythagoras, since their country was entirely buried under sand in one moment? Or what did it avail the Jews to kill their wise king, since their kingdom was taken away from them from that time on?
>
> God justly avenged these three wise men. The Athenians died of famine, the Samians were flooded by the sea, the Jews were slaughtered and driven from their kingdom, everywhere living in the dispersion.
>
> Socrates is not dead, thanks to Plato; nor Pythagoras, because of Hera's statue. Nor is the wise king, because of the new law which he has given.[42]

1. The *dating* of the letter is disputed.[43] Probably it was composed soon after 73 CE.[44]

- In the letter the father reminds his son of the flight to Seleucia of citizens of the city of Samosata, which was hostile to Rome.[45] This event seems to be identical with the deposition and expulsion of King Antiochus IV of Commagene (whose capital was Samosata) by the Romans in 73, reported by Josephus, *BJ* 7, 219–43.
- The 'punishment' of the Jews by loss of their self-administration, killing and dispersion 'from that time on', mentioned in the above text, must refer to the Roman–Jewish war of 66–74 CE. But in that case we must assume that the author does not yet know of the renewed clashes in Palestine which broke out in 132 CE.[46]

---

[41]The information about Pythagoras, the Samians and the Athenians is historically extremely inaccurate. Perhaps Mara thinks that the philosopher and the sculptor Pythagoras are one and the same person.

[42]Schulthess, 'Mara bar Sarapion', 371f. Cf. W. Cureton, *Spicilegium Syriacum*, London 1855, 43–8.

[43]Baumstarck, *Geschichte*, does not give a date, since the chronological indications do not seem sufficiently clear to him.

[44]Thus e.g. J. Blinzler, *The Trial of Jesus*, 35f., and E. Barnikol, *Das Leben Jesu der Heilsgeschichte*, Halle 1958, 251.

[45]Schulthess, 'Mara bar Sarapion', 368f., lines 478–74.

[46]There is just one difficulty here: the Jews were forbidden to enter Jerusalem only after the Bar Kochba War (c.132–135). However, the Jewish War (66–70) was already associated with so many deportations that one could have the impression that the Jews had been driven out of their kingdom.

2. The *author* is a Syrian Stoic; he is certainly not a Jew nor a Christian (for example, he speaks quite openly of 'our gods'). However, he is open towards Christianity.

3. The statements about Jesus are partly dependent on Christian sources:

- That the Jews are made exclusively responsible for the execution of Jesus corresponds to New Testament statements like I Thess. 2.15; Acts 4.10 etc.[47]
- It is similarly a widespread Christian interpretation to understand the Jewish defeat by the Romans as punishment for the crucifixion of Jesus (cf. Matt. 22.7; 27.25).
- The fact that Mara calls Jesus the 'wise king' of the Jews similarly derives from Christian sources. The title king plays an important role in the birth tradition (Matt. 2.1ff.: the wise men seek the new-born king of the Jews) and in the passion tradition (especially in the entry into Jerusalem, the mocking scene, the hearing before Pilate [John] and the *titulus* on the cross).

4. However, on some points Mara shows a clear external perspective in his assessment of Jesus and Christianity:

- In Mara's series of paradigms Jesus appears as one of three wise men, an exalted man among others.
- Mara either knows nothing of the resurrection of Jesus or he tacitly reinterprets it in keeping with his world-view. He had described this view earlier in his letter as: 'the life of human beings, my son, goes from the world; their praise and gifts abide in eternity.'[48] That is true of Socrates in the same way as it is of Jesus.
- For Mara, Jesus is significant above all as a new lawgiver; he lives on in his laws. Mara apparently sees the Christians as those who walk according to the laws of their 'wise king'. This well explains the positive attitude of the Stoic towards them.

If we ask where the Syrian Stoic Mara bar Sarapion got his information about Jesus from, we are directed towards earliest Syrian Christianity. At around the same time as the letter of Sarapion, the Gospel of Matthew, with a similar picture of Jesus, was composed there. In Matthew, too, the catastrophe of Judaism in 70 CE is punishment for the execution of Jesus. There too Jesus is the 'wise king of the Jews', who in the antitheses gives 'new laws'. Thus in the letter of Sarapion we probably do not have testimony about Jesus independent of Synoptic Christian-

---

[47]However, it is also conceivable that Mara knew of the role of the Romans in the crucifixion of Jesus, but kept quiet about it because of his own precarious situation.

[48]Schulthess, 'Mara bar Sarapion', 370, lines 106f.

ity, but evidence that the 'king of the Jews' depicted by Matthew also attracted pagan sages, as is depicted in legendary form in Matt.2.1ff.

4. Roman writers and statesmen on 'Christus', the founder of the Christian sect

R. Freudenberger, *Das Verhalten der römischen Behörden gegen die Christen im 2. Jahrhundert dargestellt am Brief des Plinius an Trajan und den Reskripten Trajans und Hadrian*, Munich 1967; id., 'Christenverfolgungen', *TRE* 8, 1981, 23–9 (Roman empire); H. Fuchs, 'Tacitus über die Christen', *VigChr* 4, 1950, 65–93; id., 'Nochmals: "Tacitus über die Christen"', *MusHelv* 20, 1963, 221–28 ; R. Hanslik, 'Der Erzählungskomplex vom Brand Roms und der Christenverfolgung bei Tacitus', *Wiener Studien* 76, 1963, 92–108; R. Klein (ed.), *Das frühe Christentum im römischen Staat*, WdF 267, Darmstadt 1971; A.N. Sherwin-White, *The Letters of Pliny. A Historical and Social Commentary*, Oxford 1966; J. Speigl, *Der römische Staat und die Christen. Staat und Kirche von Domitian bis Commodus*, Amsterdam 1970; M. Whittaker, *Jews and Christians: Graeco–Roman Views*, Cambridge Commentaries on Writings of the Jewish and Christian World 200 B.C. to A.D. 200, 6, Cambridge 1984; R.L. Wilken, *The Christians as the Romans Saw Them*, New Haven 1984; A.Wlosok, *Rom und die Christen. Zur Auseinandersetzung zwischen Christentum und römischem Staat*, Stuttgart 1970.

Three brief mentions of 'Christus' have been preserved for us in the works of Roman authors from the period between 110 and 120 CE. Pliny the Younger, Tacitus and Suetonius report on 'Christus' (or 'Chrestus') more in passing; they do not seem to be aware that they are taking a messianic title as his proper name ('Jesus' does not occur). There is always a connection with a public intervention against the Christians, so we are reading the sources against the grain if we look for information about Jesus in them. The three Romans, who are close to one another, all come from state circles, had all held government office and in addition had literary ambitions. Whereas the Stoic philosopher Mara bar Sarapion sitting in prison feels links with Jesus, their unanimous view of Christianity is that it is an abhorrent superstition and therefore a danger to the state. Despite what they have in common, their short statements about 'Christus' clearly differ from one another.

4.1 Pliny the Younger (61–c.120)

1. *Person.* C. Plinius Caecilius Secundus was a member of the Roman nobility (senator); he was an advocate and held various state offices. His literary fame rests on the letters he wrote, a ten-volume collection of which has survived.[49]

---

[49]There is a detailed commentary on the letters of Pliny in A.N.Sherwin-White, *Letters*; for the letter about the Christians and Trajan's rescript see 691–712, 772–87.

2. The *occasion* for his concern with 'Christus': around 111 CE Pliny was sent by the emperor Trajan (98–117) as an imperial legate with the powers of a governor to the province of Bithynia and Pontus. One type of case on which he had to pass judgment in one of the larger cities of Pontus was the denunciation of Christians.

3. *Literary context.* Pliny carried on an extended official correspondence with Trajan (*Letters,* Book X). When the denunciations of Christians increased, he also turned to the emperor over this question *(Ep.* X, 96): 'In investigations of Christians I have never taken part; hence I do not know what is the crime usually punished or investigated, or what allowances are made.'[50]

4. *Statements about 'Christus':* the information Pliny gives about the Christians and the way he deals with them cannot be discussed in detail here.[51] Pliny speaks of 'Christus' only twice in a cultic context.

- Anyone who was falsely accused of being a Christian could refute this charge by paying homage to the statues of the gods and the image of the emperor, sacrificing incense and wine to them and blaspheming 'Christus' (*Christo male dicere*), since it was well known that true Christians could not be compelled to do these things.
- Some of those denounced to Pliny asserted that they had not been Christians for long time, and demonstrated this by sacrifices and blasphemy. They told Pliny of the harmlessness of their former faith.

. . . quod essent soliti stato die ante lucem convenire carmenque Christo quasi deo dicere secum invicem seque sacramento non in scelus aliquod stringere, sed ne furta, ne latrocina, ne adulteria committerent, ne fidem fallerent, ne dspoeistum adpellati abnegarent.	. . . that it was their habit on a fixed day to assembly before daylight and recite by turns a form of words to Christ as a god; and that they bound themselves with an oath, not for any crime, but not to commit theft or robbery or adultery, nor to break their word, and not to deny a deposit when demanded.

5. Pliny's information is clearly based on different sources:

- Widespread rumours about Christians: Pliny at first assumed that crimes were necessarily associated with the name Christian *(flagitia cohaerentia*

---

[50]Translation of Pliny letter in J. Stevenson, *A New Eusebius,* second edition revised W.H.C. Frend, London 1987, 18.

[51]Cf. the survey in Wlosok, *Rom,* 27–39, and the comprehensive investigation by Freudenberger, *Verhalten.*

nomini) and investigated above all anything that could point to a group of political conspirators. These conjectures proved untenable, as Pliny explicitly states.[52]

- Official knowledge of the identification and punishment of Christians.[53] Although Pliny had no personal experience of trials of Christians, he carried out proceedings (with death sentences) before Trajan's answer arrived. He took the confession of being a Christian (*confessio nominis*) as sufficient identification and condemnation of Christians. However, anyone who performed the sacrifice and blasphemed Christus was acquitted. Here Pliny could refer to a fact generally known to the authorities that Christians – 'as they say' (*dicuntur*) – can never be compelled to do this.

- Statements by (former) Christians: Pliny interrogated defendants who claimed no longer to be Christians about their former faith. However, he did not believe their descriptions and in addition interrogated two women slaves, deacons of a community (*ministrae*), under torture. In his view, their statements, too, did not contain anything more than 'perverse and extravagant superstition' (*superstitio prava, immodica*), the content of which he did not think worth reporting.

6. There is not much direct knowledge of Christus in Pliny: he regards Christus as a cultic deity of the Christians, a kind of anti-god to the Roman state gods. He seems to know that the one worshipped in the cult was a man; this is indicated by the formulation '*carmen . . . quasi deo dicere . . .*', which suggests that Pliny sees Christ only as a quasi-god, precisely because he was a man.

4.2 Tacitus (55/56–c.120)

1. *Person*: P. Cornelius Tacitus, a member of the senatorial aristocracy, held the usual offices (e.g. in 112/113 he was Proconsul of Asia) and has become famous above all for his two great historical works critical of the Principate, the *Histories* (c.105–110) and the *Annals* (c.116/117).

2. The *occasion* for Tacitus to speak of the Christians is the burning of Rome in 64 CE (*Ann.* 15.38–44), for which Nero made the Christians responsible to divert suspicion from himself.[54]

3. The *context*: In his biography of Nero (*Ann.* 13–16), Tacitus makes a sharp contrast between the first five peaceful years of Nero's rule (the so-called quinquennium 54–58 CE, *Ann.* 13) and the reign of terror which followed (*Ann.* 14–16); the description of the cruel execution of the Christians in *Ann.* 15.44.2–5

---

[52]Cf. Wlosok, *Rom*, 28, 32f.

[53]There is much dispute over the legal basis of the trials of Christians, cf. Freudenberger, 'Christenverfolgungen', esp. 23–6.

[54]Cf. Fuchs, 'Tacitus', 65–93, and id., 'Nochmals: Tacitus'; Wlosok, *Rom*, 7–26.

is an illustration of this.[55] Tacitus' assessment of the event is ambivalent. He shares the abhorrence of the Christians but regards them as guilty not of the arson but of 'hatred against the human race' (*odium humani generis*, *Ann.* 15.44.4). He condemns Nero's motives: 'Hence, even for criminals who deserved extreme and exemplary punishment, there arose a feeling of compassion; for it was not, as it seemed, for the public good, but to glut one man's cruelty, that they were being destroyed' (*Ann.*15.44.5).[56]

4. *Statements about Christus.* Tacitus reports briefly and precisely what he knows about the founder (*auctor*) of the superstition in order to illuminate the origin of the *Christiani/Chrestiani*[57] who are allegedly hated among the people for their vices (*Ann.*15.44.3):

Auctor nominis eius Christus Tiberio imperitante per procuratorem Pontium Pilatum supplicio adfectus erat; repressaque in praesens exitiabilis superstitio rursum erumpebat, non modo per Iudaeam, originem eius mali, sed per urbem etiam, quo cuncta undique atrocia aut pudenda confluunt celebranturque.

Christus, from whom the name had its origin, suffered the extreme penalty during the reign of Tiberius at the hands of one of our procurators, Pontius Pilate, and a most mischievous superstition, thus checked for the moment, again broke out not only in Judaea, the first source of the evil, but even in Rome, where all things hideous and hateful from every part of the world find their centre and become popular.

5. There is no agreement over Tacitus' *source(s)*; there are several rival considerations:

- It is to be assumed that Tacitus was confronted with the question of the Christians during his governorship in Asia Minor (in parallel to his friend Pliny) and informed himself through hearings and investigations. Thus he could have arrived at the conviction quoted above that 'Christians were guilty' and 'deserved the most extreme punishment' in the public interest.

---

[55]Suetonius (*Nero* 16, 2) also mentions the persecution of Christians under Nero, but does not connect it with the burning of Rome: 'Punishment was inflicted on the Christians, a class of men given to a new and wicked superstition' (*Afflicti suppliciis Christiani, genus hominum superstitionis novae ac maleficae*), quoted from Stevenson, *A New Eusebius* (n.50), 3. Suetonius introduces this measure by Nero in the section in which he enumerates Nero's praiseworthy actions, not in the later part about his crimes.

[56]Translation in Barrett, 16.

[57]The reading *Christianos* is not certain, as it has been corrected into *Chrestianos* in the earliest and most reliable manuscript. *Chrestiani* is the vulgar form of the name for Christians ('the useful'), probably derived from the most widespread Greek slave's name, 'Chrestos' ('the useful one'), which is attested often: Tertullian, *Nat.* I, 3, 9; *Apol.* 3.5; Lactantius, *DivInst* IV, 7, 4f.; Justin, *Apology* I, 4, 5 etc.; cf. Fuchs, 'Tacitus', 563–9.

- In the *Annals* Tacitus draws on earlier historical works which have been lost. For example, for the burning of Rome he could have used the account by Pliny the Elder, but this cannot be proved. Harnack's assumption that Tacitus drew his knowledge of Jesus from Josephus' *Antiquities* is relatively improbable.[58]
- Scholars have also thought in terms of an official source (senate acts, etc.), which Tacitus could have seen in a Roman archive. This is particularly suggested by the note of the temporary suppression of the superstition, which indicates an official perspective and in no way is based on Christian statements. However, in that case one would not expect a mistake of the kind which occurs in lines which sound so precise: Pilate was prefect, not procurator, of Judaea.[59]

6. Result: Tacitus offers widespread prejudices about the Christians together with a few, albeit quite precise, pieces of information about Christus and the Christian movement, the origin of which remains unclear. He knows:

- 'Christus' is a Jew executed as a criminal under Pontius Pilate.
- 'Christus' is the author of a new religious movement which comes from Judaea; its adherents are called 'Christians' after him and were already known and widespread in Rome at the time of Nero.

4.3 Suetonius (70–c.130)

1. *Person.* C. Suetonius Tranquillus was a member of the equites, and worked as a lawyer until his patron Pliny the Younger smoothed his way to higher administrative office under Trajan and Hadrian. After that Suetonius had access to all the archives and thus obtained the information he needed for the composition of his biographies of the emperors (*De vita Caesarum*). These *Vitae,* which have been preserved almost complete, describe the lives of all twelve emperors from Caesar to Domitian in an entertaining way, in eight volumes. They were presumably written between 117 and 122.

2. The *occasion* for mentioning Christus is an expulsion of the Jews from Rome under Claudius (41–54); this is also mentioned in Acts 18.2 as the reason why Aquila and Priscilla had to move from Rome to Corinth: 'Claudius had commanded all the Jews to leave Rome (διὰ τὸ διατετάχεναι Κλαύδιον χωρίζεσθαι

---

[58]A von Harnack, 'Geschichtsschreiber' (n.6), 1058ff.: Josephus reports, just like Tacitus, that the Christians name themselves after Christ, Christ was executed under Pontius Pilate, but the Christian movement nevertheless did not cease. However, the differences between Tacitus and Josephus are important: Josephus does not report a temporary suppression of the movement. Christus appears in Josephus as a messianic title of a man whose civic name ('Jesus') is given; by contrast Tacitus regards the surname 'Christus' as Jesus' own name.

[59]This has been proved beyond any doubt by the Pilate inscription discovered in Caesarea in 1961; cf. Barrett, 155.

πάντας τοὺς ᾽Ιουδαίους ἀπὸ τῆς ῾Ρώμης).' This so-called edict of Claudius is probably to be dated to the year 49 CE.[60]

3. The *context*: Like all the Lives, the *Vita Claudii* is divided into a chronological part, which describes the career of the emperor, and an account of his activities, which is arranged by subject-matter. In *Claudius* 25, Suetonius enumerates the attitude of the emperor towards various foreign peoples and in so doing also comes to speak of the Jews.[61]

4. The statement about Christus, who will be meant by 'Chrestus',[62] runs as follows (*Claud.* 25.4):

Judaeos impulsore Chresto assidue tumultuantes Roma expulit.	He drove from Rome the Jews who, stirred up by Chrestus, continually caused unrest.[63]

5. Suetonius's source is unknown, but is certainly not Christian. Either the report is based on a vague rumour, or Suetonius has seen and misunderstood an official report.

6. Suetonius has no historically accurate knowledge of Christus, since he apparently assumes that 'Chrestus', the instigator of the unrest, was in Rome at the time of Claudius. But in fact there may have been disturbances among the Jews of Rome because of Christian mission preaching about the Messiah (= Christus), whereupon Claudius had the spokesmen banished.

Appendix: Thallus

F. Jacoby, *Die Fragmente der griechischen Historiker* II B, Berlin 1929.

A Roman or Samaritan historian named Thallus probably mentioned the crucifixion of Jesus as early as the first century CE.[64]

1. The *author*. All we know of Thallus is that he composed a three-volume history of the world after 52 CE, which has almost completely been lost. Possibly this Thallus is identical with the [Θ]αλλος Σαμαρεύς, a rich freeman of Tiberius, who is mentioned by Josephus (*Antt.* 18,167).[65]

---

[60]P. Lampe, *Die stadtrömische Christen in den ersten beiden Jahrhunderte*, WUNT, 2 Reihe 18, Tübingen ²1989, discusses the problems connected with the edict of Claudius.

[61]Cf. Barrett, no.9, p.14, where the wider context is given.

[62]'*Chrestiani*' was a popular designation for Christians (see above n.57); a shift from the unknown '*Christus*' to the familiar name '*Chrestus*' is easily imaginable.

[63]Translation based on Lampe, *Stadtrömische Christen* (n.60), 6f.; as an attribute to *Judaeos, impulsore . . . tumultuantes* limits the circle of Jews expelled: only the troublemakers were exiled (Acts 18.2 speaks of 'all Jews').

[64]Cf. Schürer, *History* II*, ii, 241.

[65]The traditional text ἄλλος Σαμαρεύς does not make sense; Θάλλος is an illuminating conjecture, supported by inscriptions which often mention the name Thallus among those in the service of Claudius.

2. *Context and occasion for mentioning Jesus.* The chronographer Julius Africanus (c.170–240) hands down Thallus' interpretation of the darkness which covered Judaea and the whole world at the crucifixion of Jesus:

τοῦτο τὸ σκότος ἔκλειψιν τοῦ ἡλίου Θάλλος ἀποκαλεῖ ἐν τρίτῃ τῶν Ἱστοριῶν· ὡς ἐμοὶ δοκεῖ, ἀλόγως.[66]	In the third book of the histories Thallus calls this darkness an eclipse. This seems to me to be irrational.

3. *Authenticity.* It cannot be proved beyond all doubt that Thallus mentioned the crucifixion of Jesus. However, the context in Julius Africanus suggests that contrary to the Christian assertion of a supernatural darkness at the crucifixion of Jesus, Thallus had advanced a 'rational' counter-proof by referring to an explicable and datable[67] natural event. Julius Africanus for his part 'proves' the miracle by recalling that Jesus was crucified at the Passover, i.e. at the spring full moon – and there cannot be an eclipse at the full moon.

4. *Source and historical value* of the note: Thallus is referring to an oral or written Christian tradition about the passion. In the second half of the first century a non-Christian historian felt challenged to refute 'false' historical information in it.

[handwritten: Too much.]

5. Summary

The value of these independent extra-Christian reports on Jesus is twofold. First we must note that both opponents and neutral or sympathetic observers of Christianity presuppose the historicity of Jesus and do not indicate a shadow of doubt about it. Furthermore the non-Christian notices allow us to check individual dates and facts in the primitive Christian tradition about Jesus. Thus Josephus confirms that Jesus had a brother named James. Josephus, Tacitus and Mara (and the rabbinic sources) report that Jesus' death was violent; here the Roman makes Pilate alone responsibile, Mara (and the rabbinic sources) the Jews alone, and Josephus presumably the Romans in co-operation with the Jewish authorities. Josephus and the rabbis report Jesus' miracles, the former in a neutral way, the latter under the charge of sorcery. Josephus, who calls Jesus a 'wise man' and 'teacher', and Mara, who mentions the 'new laws' of the 'wise king', know that Jesus worked as a teacher. As titles attributed to Jesus we have 'Christ/

---

[66]Quoted from Jacoby, *Fragmente* II B, 1157.
[67]According to Phlegon of Tralles (early second century), who derived his knowledge from Thallus, this eclipse of the sun took place in the 202nd Olympiad, which astronomers calculate to be 24 November of the year 29 CE (= fifteenth year of Tiberius).

Messiah' in Josephus – the Roman historians already use Christus as a proper name – and 'wise king' in Mara.

This picture which, given the nature of the interests of the non-Christian authors, can only be a rough one, is quite compatible with that in the Christian sources. Only the Christian traditions contain details about the life and teaching of Jesus. But can we filter out historically reliable statements from the tradition overlaid by belief in Christ? The next section is devoted to this question.

6. Tasks

6.1 Josephus' testimony about Jesus according to the Religious Dialogue at the Sasanid Court

> E. Bratke, *Das sogenannte Religionsgespräch am Hof der Sasaniden*, TU NF IV, 3, Leipzig 1899; id., 'Ein Zeugnis des Josephus über Christus I–II', *ThL* 15, 1894, 183–8, 193–7.

A version of the Testimonium Flavianum not discussed so far is a report from the fifth or sixth century about a(n alleged) disputation between Greeks, Jews and Christians at the Persian court, the so-called 'Religious Dialogue at the Sasanid Court'.[68] In this dialogue the Christians present to the Jewish participants testimony to Jesus' messiahship (mostly from the New Testament). The following testimony of Josephus forms the climax:

Ἰώσιππος ὁ συγγραφεὺς ὑμῶν, ὅς εἴρηκε περὶ Χριστοῦ ἀνδρὸς δικαίου καὶ ἀγαθοῦ, ἐκ θείας χάριτος ἀναδειχθέντος σημείοις καὶ τέρασιν, εὐεργετοῦντος πολλούς.	Josephus your historian, who has spoken of Christ as a just and good man, who by divine grace was made known by signs and wonders and did much good.[69]

1. Compare this text with the Testimonium Flavianum and the Agapius version (language, content and tendency).

2. Are there arguments to support the theory that this is the original testimony of Josephus? What tells against this? Sum up what conceivable relationships there can be between this text and the other versions (Testimonium Flavianum, Agapius) and the presumed original of Josephus. A hint: compare also Luke 23.47; Acts 2.22; 10.38.

---

[68]Edited with commentary by E. Bratke, *Religionsgespräch*, 1899.

[69]Translation based on ibid., 224. Bratke's translation of ἐκ θείας χάριτος ἀναδειχθέντος σημείοις καὶ τέρασιν as 'by divine grace through signs and miracles shown [to be the Messiah]' is too strongly a Christian interpretation of the words and has therefore been changed to match Bratke's original view, cf. id., 'Zeugnis', 183–8, 193–7.

6.2 The Old Slavonic Version of the Jewish War as a source for the teaching and death of Jesus and the original form of the Testimonium Flavianum[70]

A. Berendts, 'Die Zeugnisse vom Christentum im slavischen "De bello Judaico" des Josephus', in TU 29, 4, Leipzig 1906, 1–79; A. Berendts and K. Crass, *Flavius Josephus vom Jüdischen Kriege nach der slavischen Übersetzung deutsch herausgegeben und mit dem griechischen Text verglichen*, Dorpat 1924–1927; E. Bickermann, 'Sur la version vieux de Flavius-Josèphe', in *Mélanges Franz Cumont*, 1936, 53–84 (= AGJU IX/3, 172–95); Bienert, *Jesusbericht* (see above); R.Eisler, ΙΗΣΟΥΣ (see above); M. Goguel, *Jesus*, London 1933, 82–91; M. Hengel, *Zealots**, 16–18.

A variant of Josephus' testimony about Jesus which has at times been vigorously discussed appears in the Slavonic translation of the Jewish War which was probably made in the eleventh century CE; this contains some passages which go beyond the Greek text. Two texts which relate to Jesus (though his name is not mentioned) and his followers are quoted below.

Between *BJ* 2, 174 and 175, i.e. in two incidents from Pilate's period in office which are closely connected in the Greek text (namely the unsuccessful attempt to put standards with images of the emperor in Jerusalem and the building of an aqueduct with money from the temple treasury which was carried out forcibly), there is the so-called Testimonium Slavianum:

> At that time there appeared a man, if indeed it is fitting to call him a man. His nature (φύσις) and his form (εἶδος) were those of a man, yet his appearance was more than that of men. But his works were divine, and he worked miracles wonderful and mighty. Again if I look at his nature common with that of men (κοινὴ φύσις), I will not call him an angel. And whatsoever he did, he did it by some invisible power through word and command. Some said of him that our first lawgiver had risen from the dead and performed many healings and arts; others thought that he was sent from God. Howbeit in many things he disobeyed the law and kept not the Sabbath according to the custom of our fathers. Yet, on the other hand, he did nothing shameful, nor did he do anything with aid of hands, but by word alone did he provide everything.
>
> And many of the multitude followed after him and hearkened to his teaching; and many souls were in commotion, thinking that thereby the Jewish tribes might free themselves from Roman hands. Now it was his custom in general to sojourn before the city upon the Mount of Olives; there also he bestowed his healings upon the people. And there were gathered unto him servants, and a multitude of the people. When they saw his power, that whatever he would he wrought by a word, they urged him to enter the city, slay the Roman army and Pilate, and reign over them

---

[70]This task is more suitable for advanced students: it presupposes knowledge of the questions discussed in § 14 (evaluation of the sources for the trial of Jesus).

(καὶ βασιλεύειν αὐτούς). But he heeded it not.[71] And when afterwards news of it was brought to the Jewish leaders, they assembled together with the high priest and said: 'We are weak, and unable to oppose the Romans, as if the bow were bent; we will go and tell Pilate what we have heard, and we shall be clear of trouble, lest he hear it from others, and we are robbed of our substance and ourselves slaughtered and our children scattered.' And they went and told Pilate. And he sent and slew many of the people, and had that wonder-worker brought up. And after inquiring of him, he learnt that he was a benefactor, not a malefactor, and not seditious, nor yet desirous of kingship. And he let him go, for he had healed his dying wife. And he went to his wonted place and did his wonted works. And when more people again assembled round him, and he was glorified for his work before all, those who were learned in the law were smitten with envy, and gave thirty talents to Pilate that he might put him to death. And he took the money and gave them his counsel that they should fulfil their wish. And they took him and crucified him contrary to the law of their fathers.[72]

On the occasion of the death of Agrippa I (44 C E) and the assumption of office by both Cuspius Fadus and Tiberius Julius Alexander (a misunderstanding which rules out Josephus as author), there follows an insertion about the followers of the miracle worker (which replaces *BJ* 2, 221f.):

And when at the time of those two [governors] many had proved to be servants of the aforementioned miracle-worker, and when they spoke to the people of their teacher that he was alive, though he had died, and that he would free them from their servitude, many of the people listened to the aforenamed and accepted their commandments; not because of their fame, since they were from the humble folk: indeed some were even shoemakers, others sandal-makers, and yet others manual workers. And what marvellous signs they performed: in truth, what they wanted! But when those noble landowners saw the people being led astray, they took counsel with the scribes to seize them and kill them, so that the small matter should not be small, if it ended in great things.[73] And they were ashamed and were terrified of the signs, saying: such miracles do not take place in a straight way. If they do not come from God's counsel, they will soon be convicted. And they gave them authority to act as they would. And after being molested by them they let them go, some to the emperor, others to Antioch, and yet others to distant lands, to test the matter.[74]

---

[71]Thus the most probable text. The variant reading 'he does not despise us' is surely corrupt.

[72]Translation based on Bienert, *Jesusbericht* (n.14), diagram between 128 and 129; the Greek equivalents of some words relevant to dogma have been introduced back into the Old Russian text from his retrotranslation into Greek.

[73]Text possibly corrupt. Berents, 'Zeugnisse', 61, thinks that the meaning is 'that the little is not to be thought of as little because it can perfect itself in the great'.

[74]Quoted from Berendts, 'Zeugnisse', 1of.

The view originally put forward (by Berendts, 'Zeugnisse', 38ff.), that these could be authentic texts coming from Josephus, is untenable. The text must at least have been worked over by Christians, if it does not come completely from a Christian pen.

1. Justify this by (a) mentioning statements which Josephus, as a Jew and critical contemporary, could not possibly have made and which (b) indicate a clearly Christian interest.

2. Large parts of the text can be read as a 'montage' of New Testament and extra-canonical[75] motifs and linguistic forms:
   (a) Indicate the most important passages and contexts from the New Testament which provide key words (an exercise in Bible study).
   (b) Where is it possible to demonstrate the heightening of tendencies which already govern the NT sources?

3. Finally, there are close points of contact with other Josephus texts. Compare the Testimonium Slavianum with the Testimonium Flavianum from *Antt.* 18.63f. (see above, 65f.) and *BJ* 2, 261–3:

> A greater blow than this was inflicted on the Jews by the Egyptian false prophet. Arriving in the country this man, a fraud who posed as a seer, collected about 30,000 dupes, led them round from the desert to the Mount of Olives, and from there was ready to force an entry into Jerusalem, overwhelm the Roman garrison, and seize supreme power with his fellow-raiders as bodyguard. But Felix anticipated his attempt by meeting him with the Roman heavy infantry, the whole population rallying to the defence, so that when the clash occured, the Egyptians fled with a handful of men and most of his followers were killed or captured; the rest of the mob scattered and stole away to their respective homes.

4. What theory of the origin of the Testimonium Slavianum and the other expansion about the disciples of Jesus suggests itself on the basis of the observations collected under 1–3? How is the relationship to the Testimonium Flavianum to be defined? What objections are there to Bienert's reconstruction which assumed that the Testamentum Slavianum is the Christian revision of an authentic text of Josephus that depicted Jesus as a political rebel?

---

[75]References to the extra-canonical comparative material are in the solution and you can compare it with the apocryphal letter of Pilate, which is printed in the tasks for §14 (see pp. 472f. below).

4

The Evaluation of the Sources:
Historical Scepticism and the Study of Jesus

M.E. Boring, 'The Influence of Christian Prophecy on the Johannine Portrayal of the Paraclete and Jesus', *NTS* 25, 1978, 113–23; id., *Sayings of the Risen Christ. Christian Prophecy in the Synoptic Tradition*, SNTS MS 46, Cambridge 1982; F. Buri, 'Entmythologisierung oder Entkerygmatisierung der Theologie', in H.-W. Bartsch (ed.), *Kerygma und Mythos* 2, Hamburg 1954, 85–101; E. Fuchs, *Studies of the Historical Jesus*, London 1964; B. Gerhardsson, *Memory and Manuscript. Oral Tradition and Written Transmission in Rabbinic Judaism and Early Christianity*, ASNU 22, 1961; M. Hengel, *Acts and the History of Earliest Christianity*, London and Philadelphia 1979; G. Hölscher, 'Der Ursprung der Apokalypse Mrk 13', *ThBl* 12, 1933, 193–202; J. Jeremias, 'The Present Position in the Controversy Concerning the Problem of the Historical Jesus', *ExpT* 69, 1958, 333–9; M. Kähler, *The So-Called Historical Jesus and the Historic, Biblical Christ* (1892), Philadelphia 1964; S.J. Patterson, *The Gospel of Thomas and Jesus*, Sonoma, CA 1993; H. Riesenfeld, 'The Gospel Tradition and its Beginnings', *Studia Evangelica* 73, 1959, 43–65 [= id., *The Gospel Tradition*, Oxford 1970, 1–29]; J.A.T. Robinson, *Redating the New Testament*, London 1976; J. Roloff, *Das Kerygma und der irdische Jesus*, Göttingen 1970; H. Schürmann, *Jesus – Gestalt und Geheimnis*, Paderborn 1994, 420–34; G. Theissen, 'Wandering Radicals*'.

Introduction

Time and again the study of Jesus has been swamped by waves of radical scepticism – to the point of a denial of the historicity of Jesus. Three names may be mentioned as examples.[1] Bruno Bauer (1809–1882), who once lectured in theology at Bonn, regarded the earliest Gospel as a literary work of art: history is produced in it, not described.[2] Albert Kalthoff (1850–1906) understood Jesus as a product of the religious needs of a social movement which had come into contact with the Jewish messianic expectation.[3] Arthur Drews, who was professor of philosophy in Karlsruhe, declared Jesus to be the concretization of a myth which already existed before Christianity.[4] Here we find three motives for scepticism

---

[1]Cf. Schweitzer, *Quest**, 137–60 (on B. Bauer), 314–18 (on A. Kalthoff). A contemporary advocate of the thesis that Jesus never lived is discussed in Task 2 on pp. 122ff.

[2]*Kritik der evangelischen Geschichte der Synoptiker* (3 vols), 1841–42; *Kritik der Evangelien*, 1850–51.

[3]*Das Christusproblem. Grundlinien einer Sozialtheologie*, 1902.

[4]*The Christ Myth*, London 1910.

which are also operative where there is no dispute over the historicity of Jesus: Jesus is understood as a product of literary imagination, social needs or mythical traditions. Here historical scepticism appears within or outside theology, often with a great ethical solemnity, and foists on its critics the ungrateful role of apologists driven by their wishes. This is quite wrong. In discussion of the historical Jesus nothing is free from wishes and interests, not even scepticism. Outside theology scepticism wants to rob Christianity of its legitimation. Inside theology it is employed for purposes of legitimation. For example, people say: since we only have sources about Jesus which are coloured by faith, an approach to Jesus governed by faith is the only legitimate one; the only alternative is unbelief. Quiet historical work should rule out such pressure imposed by a single alternative – for the sake of the freedom to be able to come to terms critically with Jesus without having to legitimate one's faith or unbelief by the results of scholarship. But any scholarly discussion of Jesus begins with the problem of the appropriate historical evaluation of the sources (most of them Christian), which report about Jesus.

To bring out the problem of method in all its acuteness, here are thirteen objections made by historical scepticism which, taken together, suggest that any historical evaluation of existing Christian sources is an impossible enterprise. Of course this is an extremely one–sided standpoint, which is seldom put forward in this form, but it has been adopted here to demonstrate the reservations of historical scepticism.

Task

Attempt – not least against the background of what has been worked out in the previous chapters – to discuss the objections as they relate to research and theology, and to formulate possible counter-arguments.

1. *The 'silence' of non-Christian sources.* The contemporary non-Christian sources (e.g. Philo of Alexandria) are silent about Jesus even where one would expect a note about him.

2. *The 'mythical' Christ of the letters of Paul.* The earliest Christian writings, the letters of Paul, depict Jesus as an almost mythical being, whose earthly existence seems to be only the intermediate stage between pre-existence and exaltation. In view of this the question arises whether there was a Synoptic tradition about Jesus at all in Paul's time.

3. *The unhistorical Johannine picture of Christ.* There are irresolvable contradictions (chronology, belief in pre-existence, style of the revelation discourses) between the Synoptic picture of Jesus and the Johannine Christ.

4. *The Easter gulf.* The Easter faith has so reshaped the pre-Easter tradition that post-Easter worship and historical reminiscence have become indissolubly fused.

5. *The chronological distance of the Synoptic Gospels.* The Synoptics were composed at a considerable distance from the historical Jesus, between forty and seventy years after his death, outside Palestine and in Greek, i.e. not in the mother tongue of Jesus and his first followers.

6. *The intention of the Jesus tradition.* In its intention the Jesus tradition is kerygmatic, i.e. it speaks to the present (has an interest in preaching) and is not interested in preserving historical reminiscences.

7. *Shaping by the 'Sitz im Leben'.* The Jesus tradition is primarily governed by the situation in which it was used (the *'Sitz im Leben'*). Community needs have reshaped the picture of Jesus in the tradition to the point that it becomes unrecognizable.

8. *The productive power of the proof from scripture.* The first Christians not only interpreted memories of Jesus in the light of the Old Testament but often produced them on this basis in the first place. The holy scriptures of Israel were more reliable for them as God's testimony than the testimony of human eyewitnesses.

9. *The formation of analogies.* New community formations came into being along the lines of the existing Jesus tradition, which was in the form of small units. These display the same structures of genre and can therefore can hardly be distinguished from authentic traditions about Jesus.

10. *The sayings tradition as the fruit of primitive Christian prophecy.* The logia tradition contains early Christian prophetic sayings which were spoken in the name of the exalted Christ and in Q can no longer be distinguished from the words of the earthly Jesus.

11. *Miracle stories.* The narrative tradition contains miracle stories in which the typical motifs of ancient belief in miracle have transformed historical recollection. Possibly whole miracle stories have been transferred to Jesus without having any concrete basis in his life.

12. *Mythical elements.* The framework of the story of Jesus (birth, temptation, transfiguration and resurrection) has been transformed with mythical motives. That shows that the historical Jesus was swallowed up by his myth.

13. *The one-sided criteria of research into the historical Jesus.* The criteria developed in research to define historical Jesus material cannot fulfil their purpose reliably.

The *criterion of difference* chooses as its starting point the impossibility of deriving Jesus material from Judaism and earliest Christianity. Thus it presupposes the possibility of a negative historical generalization. In view of our limited sources, such statements are not reliable material for historians and can be falsified at any time by the discovery of new sources (Qumran!).

The *criterion of coherence* is problematical because authentic material which contradicts the general picture of Jesus can be contained precisely in isolated Jesus traditions which are hard to find a place for.

1. Thirteen objections by historical sceptics to the historical evaluation of the Jesus tradition and arguments against them

1. The 'silence' of non-Christian sources

> The contemporary non-Christian sources are largely silent about Jesus. Even where we would expect a note about Jesus, we do not find any report about him.

Philo of Alexandria (died 42/50 CE), a contemporary of Jesus, reports on Pilate: 'Here one might impeach him in respect of his corruption, and his acts of insolence, and his rapine, and his habit of insulting people, and his cruelty, and his continued murders of people untried and uncondemned, and his never ending, and gratuitous, and most grievous inhumanity' (*LegGai*, 302). There is nothing about Jesus.

Justus of Tiberias, a contemporary of Flavius Josephus, composed a 'Chronicle of the Jewish Kings' and a 'History of the Jewish War'. According to a statement by Photius of Constantinople (c.820–886 CE), who knew the work which is now lost, he does not mention Jesus either (Photius, cod.13).

Counter arguments

> 1.1 Ancient sources are silent about many people whose historicity cannot be doubted.

John the Baptist is mentioned by Josephus (*Antt.* 18, 116–19) and in Mandaean texts, but not by Philo, Paul and in rabbinic writings.

Paul of Tarsus is attested by authentic letters but is not mentioned either in Josephus or in other non-Christian authors.

The Teacher of Righteousness is known only from the Qumran writings, and there is no account of him in the ancient reports on the Essenes which have come down to us (Josephus, Philo, Pliny the Elder).

Rabbi Hillel, the founder of the school of Hillelites, is never mentioned by Josephus, although Josephus is an avowed Pharisee.

Bar Kochba, the messianic leader of the Jewish revolt against the Romans in 132–5, is passed over in silence by Dio Cassius in his account of this revolt.

> 1.2 The mentions of Jesus in ancient historians allay doubt about his historicity.

The notices about Jesus in Jewish and pagan writers in §3 above – especially those in Josephus, the letter of Sarapion and Tacitus – indicate that in antiquity the historicity of Jesus was taken for granted, and rightly so, as two observations on the above-mentioned sources show:

- The notices about Jesus are independent of one another. Three authors from different backgrounds utilize information about Jesus independently: a Jewish aristocrat and historian, a Syrian philosopher, and a Roman statesman and historian.
- All three know of the execution of Jesus, but in different ways: Tacitus puts the responsibility on Pontius Pilate, Mara bar Sarapion on the Jewish people, and the Testimonium Flavianum (probably) on a co-operation between the Jewish aristocracy and the Roman governor. The execution was offensive for any worship of Jesus. As a 'scandal' it cannot have been invented (cf. I Cor.1.18ff.).

2. The 'mythical' Christ of the letters of Paul

> *The earliest Christian writings, the letters of Paul, depict Jesus as an almost mythical being, whose earthly existence seems to be only the intermediate stage between pre-existence and exaltation.*

As the Synoptics are later than the letters of Paul, given the fact that Paul cites hardly any traditions about Jesus, the suspicion arises that a good deal of the Jesus tradition did not yet exist in the time of Paul.

Counter arguments

> 2.1 Paul attests the existence of some Synoptic traditions for the forties and fifties. As he quotes them explicitly only on particular occasions, he could have known far more traditions about Jesus.

Paul cites the following sayings of the Lord on particular occasions. The saying about the question of marriage in I Cor. 7.10f. is a response to an enquiry from the Corinthians; the logion on the question of earning one's own living in I Cor. 9.14 is a reaction to criticism in the Corinthian community; the words of institution in I Cor. 11.23–25 indicate a standpoint on the dispute over the eucharist; the text about the parousia in I Thess. 4.16f. clarifies a problem in the community, namely the dying of Christians before the parousia.[5]

---

[5]For the question whether I Thess. 4.16f. is a saying of the Lord see p. 55 above.

Traditions of Jesus possibly cited anonymously by Paul could take up two main commandments of the Sermon in the Plain.

- The command to love one's enemy (Luke 6.27–36) in Rom. 12.14, 17: 'Bless those who persecute you; bless and do not curse them . . . Recompense no one evil for evil.'
- The prohibition against judging (Luke 6.37ff.) in Rom. 14.13: 'Then let us no more pass judgment on one another.'

Paul above all emphasizes the crucifixion of Jesus (I Cor. 1.18ff.). By introducing the words of institution with the words 'In the night that he was betrayed . . .' (I Cor. 11.23), he shows that he knew more about the passion of Jesus, the night before the execution and the betrayal than he writes.

> 2.2 Personal factors – the Easter appearance which he had and the 'rivalry' with other apostles – lead Paul to concentrate on cross and resurrection.

That in Paul the 'exalted one' shapes the picture is biographically understandable: Christ encountered him in an appearance. The tension between this 'exalted' heavenly being and the crucified Jesus becomes the basic theme of Pauline christology.

As Paul had to defend his apostolate against other apostles who had known the earthly Jesus and therefore could cite traditions about Jesus to legitimate them, in II Cor. 5.16 he can even dismiss in principle a reference to the historical Jesus: εἰ καὶ ἐγνώκαμεν κατὰ σάρκα Χριστόν, ἀλλὰ νῦν οὐκέτι γινώσκομεν (even if we knew Christ from a human point of view, we no longer know him in this way).

> 2.3 Theological convictions prevent Paul from enhancing the earthly Jesus. Jewish monotheism could worship a heavenly being who owed his status solely to God – but not an earthly man who was given divine dignity on the basis of his own words and actions.

In the time of earliest Christianity Jews could recognize heavenly figures alongside God (e.g. the 'Son of Man', wisdom or the Logos). They could conceive of God exalting a human being (like Enoch) to himself. However, they protest against a human being making himself God (John 5.18; 10.33) and being worshipped in the cult (cf. Acts 12.21–23; 14.8–18). The faith of the Jew Paul is therefore concentrated on the cross and resurrection: God has exalted the crucified Christ to himself solely through his action. Traditions which already seemed to surround the words and actions of the earthly Christ with the splendour of the exalted one must have been alien to him.

> 2.4 Form-critical and sociological reasons are behind the sparseness of the Jesus tradition in Paul, since this tradition fades into the background throughout the earliest Christian epistolary literature.

The letters of John probably presuppose the Gospel of John, but do not quote it anywhere: even the commandment to love, which has a central place in the Gospel as a καινὴ ἐντολή (new commandment) of Jesus, does not appear in them as Jesus tradition. One cannot conclude from the silence of the Johannine letters about the Johannine Jesus that there were no Jesus traditions in the Johannine community – any more than one can draw similar conclusions from the 'silence' of the Pauline letters.

The rest of earliest Christian epistolary literature up to the Apostolic Fathers also quotes amazingly few Jesus traditions. Possibly the ethical radicalism of the Synoptic tradition did not fit the life of settled Christians well. Was there a sociological threshold of tradition here? The Jesus tradition spread throughout earliest Christianity only in the framework of a retrospective narrative, i.e. in the form of Gospels.

3. The unhistorical Johannine picture of Christ

> *There are irresolvable contradictions between the Synoptic picture of Jesus and the Johannine Christ.*

The contradictions relate, among other things, to the following spheres:

- Chronology: according to John, Jesus' public ministry was at least three years (three Passovers) and he was crucified before the feast. The Synoptics seem to presuppose a year's public activity on the part of Jesus and report the crucifixion of Jesus at the Passover.
- Pre-existence: in the Gospel of John Jesus is a divine being walking over the earth, the creator of all things who is even aware of his pre-existence. By contrast the Synoptics do not know the idea of pre-existence.
- Style of the revelation discourses: The long revelation discourses with parabolic 'I am' sayings contradict the short sayings and parables of the Synoptic Gospels.

Counter arguments

> 3.1 The picture of Christ in the Gospel of John is the result of a special develop-
> ment which is limited to the Johannine circle, whereas traditional material with a
> Synoptic stamp occurs in different spheres of tradition.

Traditions with a Synoptic stamp appear in a number of sources independent of
one another: Matt[s], Q, Mark, Luke[s], Thomas. The parables handed down in all
spheres of the tradition fit one another well in content (cf. e.g. the lost sheep, Q;
lost son, Luke[s]; contrasting sons, Matt.[s]). The specifically Johannine features in
the picture of Christ can therefore be understood as a 'deviation' from a broadly
attested Jesus tradition, a deviation which is present only in the sphere of the
Johannine tradition (Matt. 11.27 is an exception). The historical value of the
Synoptics is clearly to be rated higher than that of the Gospel of John. Here the
sayings and the narrative tradition can be treated separately.

> 3.2 The Gospel of Thomas allows a limited check on the Synoptic sayings
> tradition: although here too a one-sided picture of Jesus is at work, the Synoptic
> stamp of the sayings of Jesus is still recognizable.

The Gospel of John also has a series of sayings of Jesus with a Synoptic stamp.[6] Its
long revelation discourses, which show a certain proximity to Gnosticism, deviate
stylistically from these short sayings. The short sayings with a Gnostic colouring
in the Gospel of Thomas also diverge from the traditions with a Synoptic stamp,
but in a different way from the long revelation discourses in John. Where the two
Gospels which are close to Gnosticism follow their 'Gnostic' tendencies most
strongly, they therefore adopt different stylistic forms; where they correspond in
style to the Synoptics they also agree stylistically with one another. That indicates
that there was already a sayings tradition with a Synoptic stamp.

> 3.3 The Gospel of John could have preserved historically accurate information in
> its narrative sections, where the specifically Johannine stylization of the picture of
> Jesus has not been at work.

Thus for example the dating of the crucifixion of Jesus before the Passover agrees
with Mark 14.1f. The high priests and scribes discuss the timing of the execution

---

[6]Cf. John 2.19 = Mark 14.58 par.; 3.3 = Matt. 18.3; 4.44 = Mark 6.4 par.; 13.20 = Luke
10.16/Matt. 10.40; 13.16 and 15.20 = Matt. 10.24; 15.7b = Mark 11.24 par.; 16.32 = Mark
14.27 par.; 18.11 = Mark 14.36 par.; 20.23 = Matt. 18.18.

of Jesus and say, 'Not during the feast, lest there be a tumult of the people' (Mark 14.2).

Political motives sometimes appear in John more clearly than in the Synoptic Gospels:

- John 6.14f.: messianic expectations are transferred to Jesus. The crowd want to make him βασιλεύς (king). But Jesus evades them.
- John 11.45–53: the decision of the Sanhedrin to kill Jesus is politically motivated: 'If we let him go on thus, every one will believe in him, and the Romans will come and destroy both our place and our people' (11.48).
- John 19.12: Pilate is put under pressure by the suggestion of disloyalty to Rome: 'If you let this man free, you are not Caesar's friend.'

4. The Easter gulf

> The Easter gulf has so reshaped the pre-Easter tradition that post-Easter worship and historical reminiscence have become indissolubly fused.

There is no doubt that the disciples looked on their pre-Easter memory of Jesus afresh in the light of the Easter experience. According to the Gospel of John the Spirit given with the Easter experience recalls all that Jesus taught (John 14.26). Only after Easter did the disciples understand the words of Jesus (cf. John 2.22; 12.16). Motives and statements associated with Easter are also shifted back into the life of Jesus in the Synoptic Gospels:

- The story of the miraculous catch appears in John 21.1–14 (and presumably in the Gospel of Peter) as an Easter story, but in Luke 5.1ff. as a pre-Easter call story.
- At an Easter appearance of Jesus the disciples fear that they are seeing a 'ghost' (Luke 24.36–43). Mark offers the same motif in the miraculous walking on the water – perhaps originally an Easter appearance (Mark 6.45–52).
- According to Rom. 1.3f. Jesus was revered as 'Son of God' with authority after (or on the basis of) the resurrection of the dead. In Matt. 11.27 (= Q), by contrast the earthly Jesus already speaks of himself as son of God to whom everything has been given by the Father.
- In Acts 13.33, Ps. 2.7 ('You are my son, today I have begotten you') is quoted as Old Testament evidence for the resurrection. The same verse of scripture appears in the Gospels as a heavenly voice at the baptism (cf. Mark 1.11 par.).
- According to John 20.23 the authority to forgive sins is given to the disciples by the Risen Christ, but according to Matt. 18.18 by the earthly Jesus.

- According to John 20.21 the sending out of the disciples is done by the risen Christ, 'As my Father has sent me, so I send you.' A logion with a similar statement appears as a saying of the earthly Jesus in Matt. 10.40; Mark 9.37b.; Luke 10.16.
- According to the Easter stories Jesus is a being who is not bound to space and time. He goes through closed doors to be with the disciples (cf. John 20.19ff.). In Matt. 18.20 the earthly Jesus already promises such omnipresence: 'Where two or three are gathered together in my name, there am I in the midst of them.'

Counter arguments

4.1 Back-projections from the period after Easter were clearly also partly occasioned by situations before Easter. Today the two cannot be separated.

- According to Mark 1.16ff. the call of Peter took place while he was fishing. Only for that reason could this call story attract to itself the motif of the 'miraculous catch' (Luke 5.1ff.).
- Jesus certainly often crossed Lake Gennesaret in a boat with his disciples, who were also fishermen. Only for that reason could Easter experiences be projected back as walking on the water.
- During his life Jesus already practised the forgiveness of sins. The baptism of John took place 'for the forgiveness of sins' (Mark 1.4). Jesus' friendship with toll collectors and sinners put this into practice. Only for that reason could the authority to forgive sins already be attributed to the earthly Jesus in Matt. 18.18.

4.2 Back-projections from the period after Easter have not been able to overlay and suppress attitudes to Jesus from before Easter.

- The accusation of Jesus' family that he was mad (Mark 3.20ff.) is certainly no projection backwards, given the great significance of the family of Jesus after Easter.
- The charge that Jesus was a glutton and a wine-bibber, a friend of publicans and sinners (Matt. 11.19), cannot possibly refer to the exalted Christ.
- The charge that Jesus is in league with Beelzebul can only refer to the exorcisms of the earthly Jesus (Matt. 12.22ff.).
- The rumour that Jesus is John the Baptist *redivivus* (Mark 6.14) presupposes that the birth and origin of Jesus of Nazareth are still unknown.

Doubtless the Easter faith has influenced our traditions. However, this influence has to be demonstrated in detail; it cannot be sweepingly asserted. The 'Easter gulf' has not transformed the traditions into an undifferentiated ahistorical whole. Pre-Easter recollection stubbornly persists.

> 4.3 Back-projections from the period after Easter are particularly concentrated on the person of Jesus and on giving meaning to his death. So they can be limited to particular points and be relativized by the demonstration of pre-Easter 'relics' even in these spheres.

Post-Easter faith is introduced into pre-Easter life when in it Jesus is already proclaimed as 'Son of God' (Mark 1.9–11; Matt. 11.27; but cf. Rom. 1.3f.) and is thought to be omnipotent (Matt. 11.27) and omnipresent (Matt. 18.20). Nevertheless pre-Easter elements have been preserved in the tradition: Jesus refuses to be called 'good', because only God is good (Mark 10.18). He has himself baptized for the forgiveness of sins (Mark 1.9 with 1.4). He cannot always heal (Mark 6.5).

The scandal of his humiliating execution provoked interpretations of its meaning after Easter (like Mark 10.45) and prophecies of suffering (like Mark 8.31 etc.). But in Luke 13.34 there is still a hint that Jesus expected to be stoned as a prophet – not to be crucified as a royal pretender.

5. *The chronological distance of the Synoptic Gospels*

> *The Synoptics were composed at a considerable distance from the historical Jesus, between forty and seventy years after his death, outside Palestine and in Greek, i.e. not in the mother tongue of Jesus and his first followers.*

Counter arguments

> 5.1 Individual traditions and complexes of tradition can be dated back far beyond the time of the composition of the Synoptic Gospels.

Not only 'small'[7] but also 'large units', possibly in written form – go back to the 40s and 50s.

- The 'Synoptic Apocalypse' (Mark 13) was composed in 39/40 CE in the Caligula crisis.[8]

---

[7]For example the traditions handed down by both Mark and Q are 'small' units, which can be traced back over quite a long period of time.

[8]Thus already Hölscher, 'Ursprung'. Also Theissen, *Gospels**, 124–65.

- The passion narrative can probably similarly be traced back into the 40s; this is shown by various indications like the protection of people still alive by anonymity. Although the persons in the passion narrative are usually named, the two figures who come into conflict with the 'police' are anonymous: the one who drew his sword on the arrest of Jesus and the young man who fled naked after a scuffle (Mark 14.47, 51f.).[9]
- Finally, in its account of the temptation of Jesus the Logia source reflects the surmounting of the Caligula crisis. The picture of the Pharisees as drawn in it fits Palestinian Jewish Christianity before 58/62 CE better than later times.[10]

> 5.2 Individual traditions (and complexes of tradition) contain so much 'local colouring' and 'indications of familiarity' that they must have originated in Palestine.

Matt. 11.7–9: the 'quivering reed' mentioned in the logion is probably an ironic allusion to coins of Herod Antipas on which a reed was depicted, and which were in circulation only in his realm.[11]

Mark 7.24–30: the story of the Syro-Phoenician woman is stamped by the tensions in the border region between Galilee and Tyre.[12]

Mark 1.4: the paradoxical 'baptism in the wilderness' only becomes conceivable if one knows that before entering the Dead Sea the Jordan flows through a wilderness (and there has only a very narrow channel).

> 5.3 The transition from the Aramaic- to the Greek-speaking world was not an abrupt break because Syria was largely bilingual.

There is much to suggest that the very first followers of Jesus had an elementary knowledge of Greek. A toll collector like Levi could hardly have practised his profession without such linguistic knowledge. In other respects, too, crossing linguistic barriers need not necessarily have led to a loss of the original meaning. The Gospel of Thomas was originally written in Greek, but even in its Coptic translation the Synoptic sayings in it are still clearly recognizable.

5.4 Postscript. Often other ways are adopted in New Testament scholarship to reduce the chronological, territorial and linguistic distance between Jesus and the Gospels.

---

[9]Cf. in detail Theissen, *Gospels**, 165–99.   [10]Cf. in detail ibid., 203–34.
[11]Cf. in detail ibid., 26–43.   [12]Cf. in detail ibid., 61–80.

The theory of a 'cultivated tradition' begins from the assumption that Jesus made his disciples learn traditions by heart. The tradition was controlled by 'known authorities' so that it has been handed down to us in a largely authentic way (Scandinavian school).[13]

The early dating of the Gospels (J.A.T. Robinson[14]) or their attribution to known authorities in earliest Christianity (M. Hengel[15]) in accord with the tradition of the early church (Luke the physician is the author of the Gospel of Luke; John Mark is the author of the Gospel of Mark) is another attempt to reduce the distance.

The way taken in 'local colouring and contemporary history' continues the work of form criticism and tradition criticism (Bultmann and Dibelius) and extends it by the evaluation of 'external evidence' (country, contemporary history, archaeology). The thesis of a 'cultivated tradition' cannot be verified; many results of historical criticism tell against the defence of the tradition of the early church: it cannot be carried through at all with the Gospel of Matthew, and with the Gospel of John only with compromises.

6. The intention of the Jesus tradition

> The Jesus tradition speaks kerygmatically to the present and is not interested in preserving historical reminiscences.

In his *From Tradition to Gospel*, Dibelius presents the thesis 'that the primitive Christian missionaries did not relate the life of Jesus, but proclaimed the salvation which had come about in Jesus Christ'.[16] Here relating and proclaiming almost become opposites. In this view the primitive Christian tradition about Jesus owes its existence and its form exclusively to a 'preaching interest'[17] orientated on the present.

Counter arguments

> 6.1 Jesus traditions are explicitly called 'memory'.

---

[13]Representatives of this school are Riesenfeld, *Gospel Tradition*; Gerhardsson, *Memory*. Similarly in Germany R. Riesner, *Jesus als Lehrer. Eine Untersuchung zum Ursprung der Evangelien-Überlieferung*, WUNT 2/7, Tübingen 1981.

[14]Robinson, *Redating*.

[15]Hengel, *Acts and the History of Earliest Christianity*.

[16]Dibelius, *Tradition**, 15.

[17]The primitive Christian preaching is 'propaganda' for the faith (ibid., 37).

In *Apology* I, 67, Justin explicitly designates the reading of scripture in worship as the reading aloud of the ἀπομνημονευμάτα τῶν ἀποστόλων (recollections of the apostles).

Papias (in Eusebius, *HE* 3, 39, 15) described the evangelist Mark as ἑρμηνευτῆς Πέτρου (translator of Peter), who wrote down the words and actions of Peter ὅσα ἐμνημόνευσεν (as he remembered them).

In Acts 11.16 Peter remembers a saying of the Lord: 'And I remembered (ἐμνήσθην) the word of the Lord, how he said, 'John baptized with water, but you shall be baptized with the Holy Spirit' (cf. similarly Acts 20.35).

This intention of remembering, clearly attested in the sources, certainly does not prove that authentic Jesus material was indeed 'remembered' – as is shown by Acts 11.26, where a saying of John the Baptist (cf. Mark 1.8) is transferred to Jesus. However, it does demonstrate an interest in keeping the story of Jesus in mind.

6.2 Jesus traditions have been shaped in the Gospel as memory: as biographical narrative with historicizing elements and offers of identification.

The Gospels belong to the biographical tradition of antiquity: 'The Hellenistic biography . . . takes so many forms that even the Gospels could have a place in it.'[18] The genre implies the claim to be reporting about a historical figure.

All the Gospels contain 'historicizing elements' which serve as distancing signals and through which past and present are distinguished (cf. Mark 2.20).[19] In the Gospel of Mark it is above all the motif of secrecy that is missing after Easter (cf. Mark 9.9f.). The Gospel of Matthew makes Jesus order the mission to Israel, which after Easter is extended to a mission to the Gentiles (cf. Matt. 10.5f., 23 with 28.19f.). Finally, in the Gospel of Luke there is an ethical radicalism in the mission speech in Luke 10 which is removed for the period after Easter (Luke 22.35f.).[20]

At the same time all the Gospels contain 'offers of identification': Jesus and his disciples are depicted in such a way that readers can enter into their 'role'. The disciples are models of discipleship, but also of failure. Jesus provides the model of the ἐξουσία (authority) of every Christian and moreover is a model of suffering. The 'roles' offered contain a great tension between exaltation and lowliness, success and failure.[21]

---

[18]K. Berger, *Formgeschichte des Neuen Testaments*, Heidelberg 1984.

[19]In addition, traditions which historically are clearly 'outdated' have been handed down, e.g. Jesus' saying about swearing by the temple (Matt. 23.16ff.).

[20]Roloff, *Kerygma*, investigates the historicizing elements in the Synoptic Gospels.

[21]Ancient historians deliberately set out to offer readers possibilities of identifying with their characters: cf. Plutarch in his introduction to the story of Alexander: 'I am not writing history but painting pictures of life, and prominent bravery or reprehensibility is not always revealed in striking deeds' (*Alex.*1).

Thus we may not play off the interest in preaching, which is present in the Gospels as a matter of course, against their intention to remember. The Gospels are biographical narratives with distancing signals and offers of identification. They seek to remember in order to make Christian identity in the present possible.

> 6.3 The Jesus tradition is combined in the Gospels with statements about other figures in whose case the intention of historical reminiscence and facticity is indisputable: with John the Baptist, Herod Antipas, Pontius Pilate. Analogies can be drawn from traditions about them to the historical reliability of the Jesus tradition.

The Gospels report about John the Baptist, Antipas and Pilate, doubtless in the awareness and with the intention of referring to figures in real history. Josephus also reports on all three in Book 18 of the *Antiquities*, and Dio Cassius reports about Antipas (55, 27, 6; 59, 8, 2), Philo (*Leg Gai* 302, quoted above, p. 93) and Tacitus (*Ann.* 15.44, above, p. 82) on Pilate. Coins and inscriptions have been preserved from the first two. Now the interests of the evangelists in describing these figures are certainly different from their interests in the case of Jesus, But the close interweaving of the memory of Jesus with these historical figures on the one hand documents the historical intention which is woven into all the kerygmatic narration about Jesus; on the other hand, to the degree that in the case of John the Baptist, Antipas and Paul we can reckon with the historicity of the Gospel tradition, we can also presuppose a historical background to the Jesus tradition.

7. Shaping by the 'Sitz im Leben'

> As oral tradition the Jesus tradition is primarily governed by community needs and only secondarily by the historical Jesus. It is not Jesus but a social movement which speaks to us from the sources.

The form-critical scepticism about the possibility of evaluating the tradition about Jesus historically is grounded in the knowledge that the texts have been strongly governed by the situation in which they have been used (their so-called 'Sitz im Leben').[22] Now if the tradition is shaped by the social group which handed it down, it is only a short step from there to assume that it is a creation of this group, a community formation.

---

[22]However, 'scepticism about scepticism' is called for, in so far as we cannot define these situations of use as clearly as we would like.

Counter arguments

> 7.1 Not all the community needs demonstrable between the thirties and sixties
> have found expression in the Synoptic Gospels.

The question of circumcision, which according to Galatians and Acts 15 was
disputed in the 40s, is not addressed at all in the Synoptic Gospels (only Thomas
53 has a saying of Jesus about it).

Structures of authority are not legitimated. Nowhere is there a saying of Jesus to
reinforce the *presbyteroi* or the *episkopoi* and *diakonoi* (presbyters, bishops and
deacons), although that would have been appropriate enough: there had been
presbyters in Jerusalem since the 40s (cf. Acts 11.30; 15.6).

After Easter, the family of Jesus belonged to the Christian community (Acts
1.14) and occupied leading positions, especially James the brother of the Lord
(Gal. 1.19; 2.9; Acts 15.13; 21.18ff.). This special position of the family of Jesus
has not found any echo in the canonical Gospels. On the contrary, the Synoptic
Gospels report tensions between Jesus and his family (Mark 3.20ff.); the Gospel
of John knows of the unbelief of Jesus' brothers (John 7.5). Only in the Gospel of
Thomas is James promised pre-eminence (Thomas 12); in the Gospel of the
Hebrews his Easter appearance is mentioned (frag.7; cf. I Cor. 15.7).

> 7.2 The Jesus movement is comparable to chiliastic movements which it has been
> possible to observe in the nineteenth and twentieth centuries in the former
> European colonies in Africa and Asia. At the centre of all these social movements is
> a prophetic individual who shaped them.

Certainly a trans-cultural comparison between the Jesus movement and other
chiliastic (or 'millenarian' movements) is possible only to a limited degree.[23] However, in both instances it is possible to compare the clash between an imperialistic
culture and an indigenous culture which reacts to it with visions of an imminent great
turning point. These movements are sparked off and formed by charismatic
prophetic figures. The prophetic figures shape these movements far more strongly
than these movements shape the picture of the charismatic. Something similar may
also have been the case with the relationship between Jesus and the Jesus movement.
At this point the sociological approach which has contributed so much to historical
scepticism about the Jesus tradition encourages questions about the historical Jesus.
That is also shown by the following consideration:

---

[23]For these movements see N. Cohn, *The Pursuit of the Millennium*, London 1957.

> 7.3 Part of the Synoptic sayings tradition does not correspond to the needs of local communities, but comes from primitive Christian itinerant charismatics who continued the life-style of Jesus and in his Spirit handed down sayings and reshaped them.

The break between the historical Jesus and earliest Christianity has been accentuated in New Testament research by the tacit assumption that the *Sitz im Leben* of Jesus as a wandering 'itinerant preacher' and that of the earliest Christian 'local communities' were totally different.

By contrast, the thesis of 'itinerant charismatics' brings out a sociological continuity between Jesus and earliest Christianity.[24] These itinerant charismatics in particular lie behind the collections of sayings in the Logia source and in the Gospel of Thomas, whereas the Synoptic Gospels work over these radical traditions so that they can be used in local communities.

8. *The productive power of the proof from scripture*

> *The first Christians not only interpreted memories of Jesus in the light of the Old Testament but often produced them on this basis in the first place. The holy scriptures of Israel were more reliable for them as God's testimony than the testimony of human eye-witnesses.*

The productive power of the proof from scripture can be demonstrated by the misunderstandings of *parallelismus membrorum*. What in Hebrew poetry is a varying description of the same process is sometimes in the New Testament divided into two actions:

- Zechariah 9.9 describes the entry of the messianic king 'on an ass, on a foal, the colt of an ass'. Only one animal is meant (thus also in John 12.13f.). Matthew makes it two; in 21.7 he speaks of 'an ass and a foal', on which the disciples lay their clothes. The animals are spoken of in the plural (ἐπ' αὐτῶν).
- In Ps. 22.19 the suffering righteous man laments: 'They divide my garments among them and cast lots for my clothing.' What is meant (as in Mark 15.24) is a process. The Gospel of Peter clearly turns it into two acts (Gospel of Peter 12); the Gospel of John relates it to different objects: the clothes are divided; lots are cast for the robe. That is explained (secondarily) by the statement that the robe was seamless and therefore could not be divided (John 19.23f.).

---

[24]Cf. Theissen, 'Wandering Radicals'*; Patterson, *Gospel*.

If the evaluation of Old Testament passages has demonstrably helped to shape the subject-matter of the narrative, we must reckon with the possibility that the Old Testament has often not only produced details of the event but even the event itself.

Counter arguments

> 8.1 The Old Testament was exploited productively by the first Christians because it helped them to give meaning to existing (and often offensive) facts: the execution of Jesus, the flight of the disciples, but also the cleansing of the temple and the origin of Jesus in Galilee. Here the Old Testament interpretation presupposes an event to be interpreted.

Here is a list of scriptural quotations which have not produced the event interpreted, but show it in a new light:

- Zech. 13.7: 'I will smite the shepherd and the sheep I shall scatter' is interpreted in Mark 14.27f. in terms of the flight of the disciples. The flight of the disciples puts them in a bad light and is therefore certainly not invented, but is historical.
- Isa. 53.12 is quoted in Luke 22.37: 'He was numbered among the transgressors.' But that does not mean that the crucifixion of Jesus between two 'robbers' is unhistorical; nor are the suspicions about him which wanted to see him as a violent transgressor. Rather, the proximity to such evildoers was offensive. The quotation helps to tone down this offence.
- Isa. 56.7 interprets the cleansing of the temple: 'My house shall be a house of prayer for all nations . . .' The cleansing of the temple and the violent action of Jesus against the merchants there which is presupposed in it has certainly not been developed from this. It contradicts the picture of the 'peaceful and gentle' Jesus and is therefore historical.
- Isa. 8.23–9.1 prophesies that a light will dawn for Galilee of the Gentiles and legitimates the origin of Jesus from Galilee in this way – in the exegesis of Matt. 4.12–16. It was not a recommendation (cf. John 7.52; 1.46). The origin of Jesus has certainly not been read out of this scriptural quotation.

Conversely, we are sometimes astonished that some Old Testament motives have not been exploited. Psalm 22 runs through the passion narrative (cf. Mark 15.25 = Ps. 22.19; Mark 15.29 = Ps. 22.8; Mark 15.34 = Ps. 22.2). Verse 17 says, 'They pierced (LXX they dug through) my hands and feet.' Although at a very early stage the crucifixion of Jesus was imagined as a piercing of hands and feet (the earliest example is John 20.25 for the hands, and Luke 24.39f. indirectly perhaps for the hands and feet), Ps. 22.17 is applied to the interpretation of the crucifixion only very much later (see Justin, *Dial.* 97.3). Moreover, the discovery of the crucified man in Giv'at ha-Mivtar in 1968 has made it historically probable that Jesus was nailed to the cross.

> 8.2 Jesus and the disciples lived in their Bible. We cannot rule out the possibility that agreements between the Old Testament and the history which has been handed down came about through a deliberate 'fulfilment' of scripture on the part of Jesus himself.

- It will never be possible to clarify completely whether Zech. 9.9 is a subsequent interpretation of the entry of Jesus into Jerusalem or whether the historical Jesus himself was governed by the picture of a king riding in on an ass (who in Zech. 9.9 is not called 'Messiah').
- In the case of John the Baptist it is probable that Isa. 40.3 is not only a subsequent interpretation of his life in the wilderness but also motivated this. For in Qumran, too, Isa. 40.3 is the reason for the community to live in the wilderness (cf. 1QS VIII, 12–14).
- So far nothing comparable has yet been demonstrated for Jesus. The view is often put forward that he understood himself to be the fulfilment of the prophecies of Isaiah – as the eschatological messenger of peace.[25]

> 8.3 A clear distinction can be made between the reinterpreting power of the proof from scripture in the passion narrative and its productive power in the infancy narratives (especially in Matthew): a 'deficit of information' had to be supplied for the infancy of Jesus and a 'deficit of meaning' at his execution.

The productive power of the proof from scripture is unmistakable in the infancy narratives of Matthew. The virgin birth is developed from Isa. 7.14 LXX (Matt. 1.23), and the birth in Bethlehem from Micah 5.1ff. (Matt. 2.6); the time in Egypt (Matt. 2.15) is developed from Hos. 11.1 and so on. All this is grouped around a few existing facts: his birth towards the end of Herod's reign, the name of his parents, his origin in Nazareth.

In the passion narrative, by contrast, the proof from scripture is working on 'scandalous' (I Cor. 1.23) historical facts. I Cor. 15.3ff. at first relates the postulate of being in accord with scripture only to the passion (cf. similarly Luke 24.26f., 44). The fact of the execution was already there, and only the further circumstances could be 'filled out' here by the Old Testament. So we cannot draw conclusions for the whole of the Jesus tradition from the indisputably productive power of the proof from scripture.

---

[25]Cf. W. Grimm, *Die Verkündigung Jesu und Deuterojesaja*, Frankfurt and Bern ²1981.

9. *The formation of analogies*

> *The Jesus tradition exists in the typical form of small units. The structures of genres that can be recognized in them make analogous formations possible, so that it is almost impossible to distinguish between authentic and secondary traditions.*

Classical form criticism closely combined the recognition of the structures of typical genres with an inference to a particular *Sitz im Leben*. However, there is no clear connection between a genre and the social situation in which it was used. Paul uses the words of institution afresh in I Cor. 11 within the framework of a community paraenesis. Conversely, different genres can have the same *Sitz im Leben*. The productive force of genres can therefore be distinguished conceptually from the productive power of 'community', even if the two belong closely together. Doubtless there were analogous formations to the Jesus tradition. Do they make the historical Jesus unrecognizable for us?

Counter arguments

> 9.1 Even if it must remain uncertain whether individual sayings are to be attributed to Jesus, we know the 'form' of Jesus' language with a high degree of probability.[26]

In most forms of the Jesus tradition there is at least one saying which can be regarded as authentic – and that demonstrates the whole 'form' for Jesus.[27] Jesus quite certainly uttered wisdom-type admonitions and proverbs, prophetic beatitudes and cries of woe, sayings about the kingdom of God and the judgment, commands to the disciples (call to discipleship), legal statements, and probably also antitheses. In addition there are different kinds of parables. There are disputes above all over sayings n the first person.[28]

> 9.2 Many forms of Jesus tradition take up existing literary forms, but Jesus gives them a new emphasis which can only go back to him.

- Admonitions are predominantly formulated in the plural (elsewhere only in the wooing of wisdom).[29]
- Beatitudes are shaped as anti-Beatitudes (Blessed are the poor).

---

[26]We know, to use Saussure's terminology, the *langue* of Jesus but not his always his *parole*.

[27]Even Bultmann, a scholar who is so sceptical about the authenticity of traditions, comes to this conclusion, *HST**, passim.

[28]See below under objection 10.

[29]Cf. D. Zeller, *Die weisheitliche Mahnsprüche bei den Synoptikern*, Würzburg 1977, esp. 77–143, 170–2.

- Parables are not told to illustrate scriptural sayings but are self-evident.
- In prophetic sayings there is no 'I' to identify the prophet, with which he takes the place of Yahweh.[30]

So we can not only attribute individual forms to Jesus: we recognize his power to shape in their form.

> 9.3 The combination of the forms present in the Jesus tradition is singular, though there may also be some analogies which illuminate individual genres and forms. The totality of the form of Jesus' language shows his individuality clearly.

Singularity is very difficult to demonstrate in history. The more complex something is, the greater the chance there is of finding singular features. There are improbable combinations of forms in the Jesus tradition, especially the combination of miracle stories (in the narrative tradition) with prophetic-apocalyptic sayings (in the sayings tradition). The dawning of the kingdom of God (βασιλεία) is thus realized in healings and exorcisms in the present.

In what follows we shall treat the sayings tradition and the narrative tradition separately. An important distinction is that narratives about Jesus are always narratives of others about him. The structures of the genres derive from the disciples, the communities or the people. But the structures of the genres in the sayings tradition could derive from Jesus himself.

10. *The sayings tradition as the fruit of primitive Christian prophecy*

> *The sayings tradition contains primitive Christian prophetic sayings which were spoken in the name of the exalted Christ and can no longer be distinguished form the words of the earthly Jesus.*[31]

Counter arguments

> 10.1 The primitive Christian prophetic sayings which have been identified can be distinguished from the sayings of Jesus by an identifying divine ἐγώ.

The divine 'I' is common above all from the OT, e.g. Amos 3.1: 'Hear this word

---

[30]See below under objection 10.
[31]This theory is advanced above all by Boring, 'Sayings'.

that the Lord has spoken against you, O people of Israel, against the whole family which I brought up out of the land of Egypt: "You only have I known of all the families of the earth; therefore I will punish you for all your iniquities." ' This 'I' in which a divine subject not bound by human limitations is speaking is rare in the Synoptic tradition, e.g.:

- In an OT quotation: 'Behold, I send my messenger before you . . .' (Matt. 11.10 = Ex. 23.20/Mal. 3.1).
- In a Sophia saying: 'Therefore also the Wisdom of God said, "I will send them prophets and apostles, some of whom they will kill and persecute"' (Luke 11.49 par. Matt. 23.34).
- In a promise: 'For where two or three are gathered together in my name, there I am in the midst of them' (Matt. 18.20).

But this divine ἐγώ is regarded as characteristic of earliest Christian prophecy.

- False prophets claim authority by appearing with the words ἐγώ εἰμι (I am, Mark 13.6).
- The letters in the book of Revelation use it frequently, e.g. 'I know your works, your toil and your patient endurance . . . But I have this against you . . .' (2.2, 4).
- Montanist prophets appeared with the claim: 'Neither angel nor messenger but I the Lord, God the Father, am come' (Epiphanus, *Pan.* 48, 11, 9).
- This linguistic form has also been handed down by (perhaps) non-Christian prophets. Celsus reports one such: 'It is our practice and customary for each to say, "I am God or a child of God or a divine Spirit. But I have come; for already the world is passing away . . . But I wish to save you and you will see me coming again with heavenly power." '[32]

The specific 'I' style of the Johannine revelation discourses can be explained as the earliest Christian prophets speaking in the name of the exalted Christ.[33]

As this 'I' style, which is characteristic of earliest Christian prophecy, is present in the Synoptic Gospels, but only to a limited degree, we may suppose that the influence of the earliest Christian prophets is not of decisive significance in the sayings tradition. There is no disputing the fact that it is present in some passages, e.g. in the mission charge of the Risen Christ in Matt. 28.18–20: 'To me is given all power in heaven and on earth', and in the promise in Matt. 18.20 already mentioned: 'Where two or three are gathered in my name . . .'

---

[32]Origen, *Celsus* VII, 9, ed. H. Chadwick, *Contra Celsum*, Cambridge 1953, 402.
[33]Cf. Boring, 'Influence'

11. *Miracle stories*

> *In the narrative tradition miraculous motifs have overgrown historical recollection.*

According to a widespread view, the 'wild and profuse jungle of ancient belief in miracles'[34] has also overgrown the picture of Jesus; it is coloured with the 'golden glow' of the miracle worker, which conceals the original colours. There are many analogies for the motifs and themes of the miracle stories;[35] the stories about Jesus used the same formal patterns as those about other miracle workers and similar motifs.

Counter arguments

> 11.1 The earliest Christian miracle stories are partly popular traditions which have been subject to other conditions of transmission than the Jesus tradition, which was handed on within the community.

Miracle stories as popular traditions are narratives about Jesus which were also told outside the circle of disciples and the first local communities. This was especially true of those which Dibelius called 'novellas', with their secular motifs.[36] Thus already during Jesus' lifetime the miracles were the first to attract interest everywhere – regardless of whether people were interested in his ethical and eschatological message. This *'Sitz im Leben'* of the miracle stories explains two phenomena:

First the 'popular shift' of the picture of Jesus in the miracle stories: they contain no specific features of the proclamation of Jesus:

- βασιλεία preaching (preaching about the dawn of the kingdom of God), despite the combination of βασιλεία and exorcisms in Matt. 12.28f.;
- Discipleship ethics – ἀκολουθεῖν (follow) occurs only in Mark 10.52, where it is possibly redactional; instead of being called to discipleship, people are often sent home;
- The use of the metaphor of father for God – it only occurs in the Johannine miracle stories (John 5.17; 6.32; 11.41);
- The *amen* formula, which is elsewhere characteristic of the Jesus tradition.

---

[34]G. Klein, 'Wunderglaube und Neues Testament', in *Ärgernisse*, Munich 1970, 13–57: 28.
[35]Depicted in detail in Theissen, *Miracle Stories**. Cf. §10 below.
[36]Cf. Theissen, *Gospels**, 103–18.

Secondly, miracles transferred from elsewhere or which surpass miracles done elsewhere: miracles are related of Jesus in order to transcend the miraculous deeds of rival 'deities' or semi-deities (this is demonstrable in the Gospel of John):

- John 2.1ff.: this goes beyond a miracle by Dionysus; miracles with wine were also related in temples of Dionysus.
- John 5.1ff.: this exceeds healing cults (Asclepius, Serapis). The story takes place at the Sheep's Pool – a cultic place dedicated to Asclepius has been excavated next door.

So it is probable that in the Synoptics, too, whole stories have either been transferred to Jesus or related with the help of motifs which derive from other ancient miracle traditions. But that does not mean that here was no historical nucleus around which the tradition was grouped:

> 11.2 The miracle tradition about Jesus would not have arisen had not Jesus done miracles.

Miracle stories are concentrated in antiquity on a few figures; not every itinerant preacher attracted miracle traditions. In the New Testament period we know of Hanina ben Dosa (c. 70 CE), Eliezer ben Hyrcanus (c.90 CE) and the exorcist Eleazar, who in 68/69 CE carried out an exorcism in the presence of Josephus and Vespasian which is reported by Josephus around twenty-five years later (*Antt.* 8, 45f.). Finally, mention should be made of Apollonius of Tyana (c.4–96 CE), of whom nine great miracles are narrated. More miracle traditions are concentrated on Jesus than on any other individual in antiquity.

Furthermore, there is twofold attestation to the miracle tradition in the sayings tradition and in the narrative tradition,[37] and it was already used in the NT by opponents (!) to make accusations against Jesus (Mark 3.22f. par.). There is no disputing the fact that Jesus was a charismatic exorcist and had the art of healing.

12. *Mythical elements*

> *In particular the framework of the story of Jesus (birth, temptation, transfiguration and resurrection) has been transformed with 'mythical motifs'. That shows that the historical Jesus was swallowed up by his myth.*

---

[37]In the sayings tradition Matt. 12.28 is about exorcisms; Matt. 11.2ff. about miracles.

Counter arguments

> 12.1 Ancient biographical texts similarly contain mythical elements in their framework: the influence of the gods is shown in signs, dreams, etc. Such a mythical framework does not justify our disputing in principle the historicity of the traditions handed down within this framework.

Here are two examples from many:

Plutarch reports about Alexander the Great[38] that Alexander's mother Olympia dreamed on her bridal night that 'it thundered and lightning struck her body; a fierce fire was kindled by the lightning, flickering in many flames and spreading on all sides'. This dream is an indication of conception by Jupiter: on the basis of this and other signs Philip sent an envoy to Delphi. The oracle commanded him to sacrifice to Ammon and to show special reverence to this god.[39] This legend is probably not pure fiction. The historical nucleus may be that Alexander was later welcomed by the priest in the desert sanctuary in the temple of Ammon as 'son of Ammon'. This divine sonship is backdated in legendary and mythical form: it must have led to the story of the miraculous conception.

Suetonius depicts the cremation of Augustus on the field of Mars:[40] 'an ex-praetor actually swore that he had seen Augustus's spirit soaring up to heaven through the flames.' Previously Tiberius had given a funeral oration before the temple of the Caesar, who had already been taken up to the gods. In an analogous fashion now Augustus, too, had to be 'divinized'. The expectation of divinization produced traditions to match!

> 12.2 The mythical elements in the Gospels have their real ground in the Easter appearances. The exalted state of Jesus is recognized in these appearances and is time and again backdated.

The Easter appearances are attested in two ways, in the traditional formula (I Cor. 15.3–5) and in the appearance narratives.[41] This tradition is old, as I Cor. 15.3–5 is pre-Pauline tradition (and thus goes back to the 30s/40s). In addition, Paul himself gives an eyewitness report of an appearance of Christ to him. Doubt in the subjective authenticity of the appearances is unfounded.

The divine sonship grounded in Easter (Rom. 1.3f.) is backdated in different ways: transfiguration and baptism (Mark), birth (Matt./Luke), pre-existence

---

[38]Plutarch, *Alexander* 2.   [39]Ibid., 3.
[40]Suetonius, *Augustus* 100.   [41]Cf below §15.2 for details.

(John/Paul). The one who appears is seen as a divine being and increasingly interpreted as a 'deity'.

13. *The one-sided criteria of research into the historical Jesus*

> *There are no reliable criteria for separating authentic from inauthentic Jesus tradition. Neither the criterion of difference or the criterion of coherence can fulfil this task.*

In the process of the quest for the historical Jesus exegesis has orientated itself on the following three criteria:

The criterion of difference: What cannot be derived from Judaism and earliest Christianity or what cannot be fitted either 'into Jewish thought or the views of the later church' can be regarded as authentic Jesus material.[42] By this method of exclusion it was thought possible to arrive at a critically guaranteed minimum.

The criterion of coherence: What agrees in content with the traditions gained on the basis of the criterion of difference is authentic Jesus material (even if it fits with Jewish and primitive Christian thought).

The criterion of multiple attestation: multiple attestations of a tradition which are independent of one another heighten the probability of being able to identify authentic Jesus material.

These criteria are now rightly being criticized:

The criterion of difference is dogmatics disguised: Jesus' uniqueness and originality are posited *a priori*. This prior assumption leads to a distortion of history: what connects Jesus with Judaism and primitive Christianity is suppressed or underestimated. The criterion of difference thus favours, for example, the rise of an anti-Jewish picture of Jesus.

The criterion of difference is not practicable: negative historical generalizations can hardly be verified, as we do not know all the sources, but have only a random selection. We can certainly 'derive' something positively in history, but it is almost impossible to establish complete originality.

The criterion of coherence is not a certain 'guideline': it is based on the criterion of difference and therefore continues its false assumptions. Furthermore, it underestimates possible contradictions and developments in Jesus and overlooks the possibility that authentic material could be contained precisely in alien, unwieldy Jesus traditions.

The criterion of multiple attestation cannot be criticized, but can always be used only in connection with other indicators.

---

[42]Thus the formulation of H. Conzelmann, *Jesus*, Philadelphia 1973, 16, which has become classic.

Counter arguments

> 13.1 The criterion of difference needs to be replaced with the criterion of historical plausibility, which reckons with influences of Jesus on early Christianity and his involvement in a Jewish context. Whatever helps to explain the influence of Jesus and at the same time can only have come into being in a Jewish context is historical in the sources.

The criterion of difference was the methodological basis for the 'new quest' of the historical Jesus. The altered presuppositions of the 'third quest' require a re-formulation of method: a historical form differs from a fictitious novellistic form by being imaginable only in a particular historical context (13.3), and can be recognized from its historical effects, namely the sources which attest it (13.2).[43]

> 13.2 Jesus traditions have a historically plausible influence when they can be explained as the influence of the life of Jesus – partly because independent sources correspond, and partly because elements in these sources go against the tendency. Coherence and opposition to the tendency are complementary criteria for the plausibility of historical influence.

In principle, what can be interpreted coherently in independent traditions despite all the differences can have a historical basis – regardless of whether it corresponds to something that is singular in religious terms or not. Whereas in the methodology of the 'new quest' the criterion of coherence was applied only in connection with the criterion of difference (see above), now the criterion of coherence is to be used independently. What is attested often in sources independently of one another can be an influence of the historical Jesus. It is possible to go on to draw distinctions:

- Multiple attestation of the same tradition in independent sources means that the tradition must be older than the earliest of the sources in which it occurs.
- Such multiple attestation of the same tradition is to be distinguished from a correspondence in content: two clearly different sayings can fit together well in terms of content, but each may only be attested once. Multiple attestations of substantial motifs and subjects in independent streams of tradition (in Q, Mark, Matt.[s], Luke[s], Thomas and John) are therefore an important criterion. Some scholars talk here of 'cross-section proof'.[44]

---

[43]These remarks are based on D. Winter, *Das Differenzkriterium in der Jesusforschung*, Heidelberg theological dissertation 1995.

[44]Cf. H. Schürmann, 'Kritische Jesuserkenntnis. Zur kritischen Handhabung des "Unähnlichkeitskriteriums"', in id., *Jesus – Gestalt und Geheimnis*, Paderborn 1994, 420–34: 425.

- Finally, motifs, subject-matter and traditions with multiple attestation can be explained in particular as the effect of the historical Jesus on the sources, if they cannot be explained from known tendencies of primitive Christianity- or are explicitly 'recalcitrant'.[45]
- Multiple attestations of motifs, subject-matter and traditions in the sources can be shown to be plausibly the effect of the historical Jesus when they cannot be explained from known tendencies of earliest Christianity – or are even explicitly 'recalcitrant tendencies'.

> An example: the concept of the kingdom of God occurs in all streams of tradition (from Matt[s] to Thomas). A cross-section demonstration can be made. In addition, many sayings about the kingdom of God have been handed down several times (e.g. Mark 10.15; Matt. 18.3; John 3.3, 5; Thomas 22). The kingdom of God is mentioned in several genres: in parables (Luke 13.18–21), admonitions (Matt. 6.33), beatitudes (Matt. 5.3), in prayer (Matt. 6.10), in didactic dialogues (Mark 12.34) and in the passion narrative (Mark 15.43). A specifically Christian tendency cannot be recognized: talk of the kingdom of God has almost been suppressed in some spheres of Christianity (e.g. in Paul).

In addition to the correspondences between different traditions, elements which do not agree with the general picture of Jesus (even if they occur in only one tradition) can also be evaluated. For some inconsistencies are historical relics which have been preserved despite powerful tendencies to revere Jesus (e.g. his baptism by John, his conflict with his family, the charge of being in league with the devil, the betrayal and flight of the disciples, the crucifixion). A complementary addition to the criterion of coherence is the criterion of 'resistance to the tradition'. The apparent contradiction that makes it possible to evaluate both the consistent and the inconsistent in the sources as the influence of Jesus is resolved by using yet another criterion: what can be interpreted as plausible in the context also goes back to the historical Jesus.

13.3 Traditions of Jesus have a plausible historical context when they fit into the Jewish context of the activity of Jesus and are recognizable as individual phenomena within this context. Contextual correspondence and contextual individuality are complementary criteria for the plausibility of the historical context.

Whereas the criterion of difference requires that it should not be possible to derive Jesus traditions from Judaism, something which can never be demonstrated strictly, the criterion of a plausible historical context requires only a demonstration of positive connections between the Jesus tradition and the Jewish context,

---

[45]This criterion occurs as a postulate in Fuchs: where Jesus' sayings and behaviour correspond, they are historical. Cf. Fuchs, *Studies*, 21.

i.e. between Jesus and the land, the groups, the traditions and the mentalities of the Judaism of that time. Such a demonstration is possible in individual cases. But here what is required is the opposite of what the old criterion of difference sought: what cannot be 'derived' from the Judaism of the time is probably not historical. In other words, Jesus can only have said and done what a first-century Jewish charismatic could have said and done. Obviously here he can come into conflict with his environment. Judaism is full of sharp criticism of individual charismatic figures and of polemic between Jewish groups. But it must be possible to follow this criticism in the context.

Against the background of a positive setting in the environment it is possible to demonstrate the individuality of Jesus. Here individuality does not mean total originality, but the possibility of distinguishing him in a common context. Here Jesus is not against Judaism, but stands out from it. His individuality is not an originality which is independent of the context, but a peculiarity which is bound up with the context.

> Here is an example: the *Assumptio Mosis,* which is to be put not too far in time and space from the historical Jesus, shows (in its present form) that there was a lively expectation of the kingdom of God in the first half of the first century. It appears here in a non-militant form. The pious await the kingdom of God by suffering willingly undertaken and retreat into a cave (*AssMos* 9). In addition to the enemies of Israel, Satan above all is an opponent of the kingdom of God (*AssMos* 10.1). Jesus stands out all the more against the background of these associations and similarities: for him the kingdom of God is beginning already. It is not being established against the enemies outside Israel, but allows marginal groups among the people who have not had their due to regain their rights.

This gives us in all four partial criteria into which the criterion of historical plausibility can be divided:

	Coherence and agreement	Incoherence and disagreement
Plausibility of influence	Plausible coherence of influence	Plausible influence contrary to the tendency
Plausibility of context	Correspondence of context	Individuality of context

2. Hermeneutical reflections

Despite the best historical methodology, all historical knowledge remains hypothetical, burdened with the proviso that things could also be (somewhat) different. By contrast, faith is unconditional. Between historical hypothesis and unconditional trust there is an abyss which since Lessing has been called an 'ugly broad ditch'.[46] What steps has theology taken to bridge this ditch with arguments? Here are four of them:

1. *Orientation on the biblical picture of Jesus.* All historical reconstructions of Jesus are surrounded with an aura of hypothesis. Why should we not prefer the biblical picture of Jesus to these constructs of scholarly imagination, confident that it is an effect of the historical Jesus? Do we not have the 'real Jesus' in the picture which he has produced? Is the real Jesus the effective Jesus? Martin Kähler argued for this 'biblicist' solution in 1892 in his classical work *The So-Called Historical Jesus and the Historic, Biblical Christ.*

2. *The historical safeguarding of the picture of Jesus.* Time and again the need arises to safeguard this biblical picture of Jesus by historical research. This concern of 'positive-critical' scholars researching into Jesus has been made a programme by Joachim Jeremias, Leonhard Goppelt and Werner Georg Kümmel. Assured results are expected from historical research – in the midst of a wealth of hypotheses and uncertainties: 'Only the Son of Man himself and his word can give authority to preaching.'[47]

3. *The reduction of the picture of Jesus in keygmatic theology.* Those who have little trust in those results of historical research which are capable of gaining a consensus and do not want to make the Christian faith dependent on the changing hypotheses of scholars, can follow Bultmann's kerygma theology in reducing the reference of Christian faith to the formal 'that' of the coming of Jesus: in preaching and faith one indeed refers to the biblical picture of Jesus, but in theological argument and reflection to an invisible point of reference.

4. *The symbolic understanding of the picture of Jesus* detaches itself even more consistently from history. Poetical and metaphorical texts (like the parables of Jesus) have their own intrinsic truth, independent of their historicity and authenticity. Why should the New Testament testimony to Jesus not be interpreted as an image and parable of timeless truths, for example, by finding here the insight that human beings in their existence and freedom live from a grace which they do not have at their disposal? In this way the picture of Jesus is not just 'demythologized' but 'dekerygmatized'. It thus becomes a timeless cipher instead of a message rooted in a particular historical situation. F. Buri – following the philosopher Karl Jaspers – argues for this solution.[48]

However one decides, there is no disputing the fact that despite the hypothetical character of all our statements, there are certainties in the historical sphere. No

---

[46]Cf. G.E. Lessing, 'On the Proof of the Spirit and of Power' (1777), in *Theological Writings*, ed. H. Chadwick, London 1956, 51–6.

[47]Jeremias, *ExpT* 69, 1958, 338.   [48]Cf. Buri, 'Entmythologisierung'.

one disputes that Caesar and Luther lived, that the former extended the Roman empire over Gaul and the latter introduced the Reformation. It would seem more important to make the certainty we have understandable than to construct certainty that we do not have. In that case the question is: is the certainty possible in the historical sphere also attainable in the case of Jesus?[49]

In answering this question it is decisive to be clear that certainty arises neither solely from external data nor solely from convictions which have an a prioristic effect. Certainty arises through the correspondence between axiomatic convictions which we already have before encountering the sources and external data in the sources. In particular the three axiomatic ideas of the historical consciousness – the idea of human capacity for error, historical relativity and hermeneutical distance – form the basis both for historical scepticism and for the historical certainty that we can have in dealing with the sources. For all three contain an internal dialectic:

(a) If all the sources derive from imperfect human beings who are capable of error, this is a strong reason for being sceptical about them. But we may also be confident that just as people are not perfect enough to hand on the pure truth, so they are not perfect enough to distort it totally. Even the most powerful committee for misleading later historians in Palestine could not have controlled all the chance sources which attest past events and persons to us. It could not have persuaded Josephus, Tacitus and the evangelists to distribute different information about Pilate at the same time. It could not have hidden its coins in Palestine and at the same time provided an inscription which was later used in the theatre of Caesarea as building material, and so on. The random nature of the historical sources persuades us that we are making contact with a historical figure and not just with the imagination of former times.

(b) If all history is relative, i.e. can be derived from previous traditions and events, then the uniqueness of Jesus is also markedly relativized. He too must be found a place in developments, and analogies must also be produced to him. But again the idea of historical relativism has a strange dialectic: if everything has to be fitted into lines of development, it must be possible to distinguish the earlier from the later and create an order which is not arbitrary. Now this is possible only if the individual elements of the process of development have 'individuality', i.e. can be clearly distinguished from other elements in the same development. Thus the axiomatic idea of development implies the individuality of the particular phenomena, which we connect by a line of development. We already introduce the notion of individuality when we investigate development. Both heuristic historical ideas were formulated at the same time during the last century.

---

[49]The following remarks are developed in G. Theissen, 'Historical Scepticism and the Criteria of Jesus Research or My Attempts to Jump over Lessing's Ugly Ditch', *SJT* 1995/6.

(c) The axiomatic conviction of the alien hermeneutical nature of the past is perhaps the latest idea of the historical consciousness. However, once it has arisen, one can no longer approach the past without a deep antipathy to judging it by models and criteria of the present. Now if everything in history were merely alien, no figure in it could become relevant to the present without having violence done to him or her. However, here too the heuristic idea of historical conscious- ness contains a dialectic. Let us try an intellectual experiment. If in the past we encountered only the world in which we ourselves live, we would never arrive at the notion that it is historical. We would regard it as nature, unchangeable and pre-existing. Only by confrontation with other worlds do we recognize what binds us together more than anything else over the centuries: the powerful activity of human beings in giving meaning, with which we build up the various worlds in which we live. Only now do we recognize that to label some mental and physical disturbances as 'possession' contains an interpretation of human activity. Only now do we understand that apocalyptic expectations of judgment are images sketched out by human beings.

The conclusion remains that it is humanly possible to be certain in dealing with the historical Jesus that we are not engaging in 'dialogue' with a product of our imagination, but with a concrete historical phenomenon. All the individual concrete statements within a description of Jesus have different degrees of probability. A permanent aura of hypothesis necessarily hangs over any picture of Jesus. Therefore we should be reconciled to the hypothetical character of our knowledge. For not only our pictures of Jesus but our whole lives can be regarded as hypotheses, as an attempt to correspond to an unconditional reality. The whole stream of living and being can be understood as a chain of trial and error. If the hypothetical is so deeply rooted in the structure of reality, why should we take offence at it? Should we not accept it? Three arguments can help here.

An ethical argument: we are bound to all creatures through hypothetical knowledge. We distance ourselves from them through illusions of unconditional knowledge.

An aesthetic argument: hypothetical knowledge can convincingly be given an aesthetic shape. An aesthetically attractive depiction of Jesus has a value even when its hypotheses are superseded.

A religious argument: Christian faith consists in the conviction that God accepts our failed attempts. Will not God also accept our hypotheses about Jesus if we develop them to the best of our knowledge and certainty?

3. Tasks

3.1 'Taking the kingdom by storm' – an authentic logion of Jesus?

The interpretation of a logion of Jesus which talks of 'taking the kingdom by storm' is much disputed; the logion has been handed down in three variants: Matt. 11.12f.; Luke 16.16; Justin, *Dial.* 51.3.[50] Once specifically Matthaean and Lukan redaction has been removed, an original version of the saying appears for Q which is almost identical with Justin's logion:

ὁ νόμος καὶ οἱ προφῆται ἕως	The law and the prophets (extend) to
Ἰωάννου	John;
ἀπὸ τότε ἡ βασιλεία τοῦ θεοῦ	from then on the kingdom of God
βιάζεται	suffers violence,
καὶ βιασταὶ ἁρπάζουσιν αὐτήν.	and men of violence take it by storm.

The 'men of violence' probably refers to Jesus and his disciples (the dating 'since John' fits only them and the fact that they are successfully taking hold of the kingdom of God – as the verb probably presupposes). So this is an extremely negative metaphor to describe the conduct of Jesus and his disciples, although it is about a positive entity (the kingdom of God).

Compile arguments which could form the basis for a judgment about the authenticity of the logion:

1. Can the logion be understood in the context of the life and preaching of Jesus (plausibility of historical effect)?
– How good is the attestation?
– Are there parallels in content to other traditions in independent streams of tradition, if possible also in various genres? Distinguish here the levels of content (proclamation of the kingdom of God) from the linguistic version (the negative metaphor of violence).
– Are there elements (in respect of both content and form) which make it improbable that the saying arose after Easter?

2. What is the plausibility of the historical context? Can the logion be understood in the Jewish context of Jesus and does it have a distinctive profile by comparison with it?

3.2 Is Jesus an invention of the third Christian generation?

The thesis that Jesus never lived has recently been put forward by G.A. Wells in

---

[50]As a basis for the exegetical decisions see G. Theissen, 'Jünger als Gewalttäter (Mt 11, 12f.; Lk 16, 16). Der Stürmerspruch als Selbststigmatisierung einer Minorität', in *Mighty Minorities? (FS J. Jervell)*, Studia Theologica 49, 1995, 183–200.

a number of books.[51] He thinks that the whole history of Jesus, his miracles, teaching and crucifixion under Pilate were only invented by Christians after 70 CE. Before that Jesus Christ was proclaimed as incarnate wisdom, which had been crucified for the sins of men in unknown circumstances and had risen again. This thesis is based on three strands of argument:

(a) The evidence for the existence of Jesus outside Christianity is too late for it to be accepted as proof independent of the Christian tradition (Wells does not accept that any mention of Jesus by Josephus is authentic).

(b) The Gospels are not sources from which historically reliable facts can be reconstructed, because they were written too late – after the year 70, which represented a total break in any possible Palestinian traditions – because over large stretches they are independent of one another and therefore there is no multiple attestation of the story of Jesus in them, and because they are largely legendary and steeped in the theological ideas of their authors, who were not Jews and therefore wrote outside Palestine.

(c) The letters of Paul are certainly early Christian evidence, but they are silent about the life of Jesus, especially his miracles, his teaching and the closer circumstances of his death. From this Wells concludes that they knew nothing about all this. Rather, the letters of Paul portray Jesus Christ as a pre-existent incarnate redeemer who as the suffering righteous man had been crucified at an unknown time for the sins of his people. According to Wells, this myth is the expanded myth of the pre-existent wisdom which took up its dwelling in Israel (became flesh); here statements about the shameful death of the just man (the representative of wisdom, Wisdom 2.20), enriched by passages from the prophets (the servant songs, Zech. 12.10), were interpreted in terms of a crucifixion. Peter, Paul and the other apostles proclaimed this myth on the basis of appearances (I Cor. 15.3ff.) in which the risen crucified Christ had made himself known to them.

1. You can apply most of the historical and methodological insights communicated in pp. 2–4 above to this sketch in answering the questions. What objections are there to G.A. Wells' view (no solution, cf. pp. 2–4)?

2. By comparison with other grounds for extreme historical scepticism, it is interesting that Wells regards the Pauline letters as authentic and early, but disputes that Jesus is recognizable in them as the contemporary of Peter, James, Paul, etc. Of course he has to explain how in Gal. 1.19 James is called 'the brother of the Lord' and (married) 'brothers of the Lord' also appear in I Cor. 9.5. His answer is that 'brother of the κύριος' does not mean (physical) brother of Jesus but 'member of the brotherhood of the exalted κύριος'. The Risen Christ

---

[51]The above account is based on the summary article 'The Historicity of Jesus', in *Jesus in History and Myth*, ed. R.J. Hoffmann and G.A. Larue, Buffalo, NY 1986, 27–45.

spoke of those who followed him as 'my brothers' in this sense in Matt. 28.9f. and John 20.17.

(a) What objections are there to understanding 'brother' in Gal. 1.19 and I Cor. 9.5 in a transferred sense? Note the other groups and persons named in the immediate context!

(b) Investigate all the relevant Christian and extra-Christian traditions relating to the question whether Jesus had brothers. Note the distribution of the tradition (multiple attestation, invariable genres), the coherence of the traditions and their plausible effect, and the way in which they resist the tendency.

Part Two: The Framework of the History of Jesus

5

The Historical and Religious Framework of the Life of Jesus

R.W. Barnett, 'The Jewish Sign Prophets – A.D. 40–70. Their Intentions and Origins', *NTS* 27, 1981, 679–97; A.I. Baumgarten, 'The Name of the Pharisees', *JBL* 102, 1983, 411–28; P.R. Callaway, *The History of the Qumran Community*, Sheffield 1988; P. Davies, 'Hasidim in the Maccabean Period', *JJS* 28, 1977, 27–140; M. Hengel and R. Deines, 'E.P. Sanders' "Common Judaism", Jesus and the Pharisees', *JTS* 46, 1995, 1–70; R.A. Horsley and J.S. Hanson, *Bandits, Prophets, and Messiahs*, San Francisco, etc. 1985; A.J. Saldarini, *Pharisees, Scribes and Sadducees in Palestinian Society*, Edinburgh 1989; E.P. Sanders, *Judaism. Practice and Belief 63 BCE–66 CE*, London and Philadelphia 1992; H. Stegemann, *Essener**; G. Stemberger, *Pharisäer, Sadduzäer, Essener*, SBS 144, Stuttgart 1990 (cf. also bibliography on §7).

Introduction

Any historical figure is to be understood in its historical context. This principle of historical study is often ignored in research into Jesus. Many accounts of Jesus want to understand Jesus *against* his Jewish context. The Judaism of his time serves as a negative background against which Jesus can be made to stand out all the more brightly. But even where the relationship of Jesus to Judaism is not seen as a contrast but in positive terms, we find distortions of perspective: Jesus often appears as the secret centre of Judaism, as if all lines ran to him. However, viewed from outside Jesus is a 'marginal phenomenon'.[1] His movement is part of a Judaism in upheaval, which despite some constants – faith in the one God, obligation to the Torah and the sanctity of the temple – consists of many trends and currents. In what follows, after a sketch of the basic convictions common to

---

[1] Cf. the characterization of Jesus as a 'marginal Jew' in the title of J.P. Meier's three-volume monograph on Jesus.

all Jews, Jesus will be given a place in this multiplicity of Jewish trends and currents.

Reading the sources and a task

Read Josephus, *BJ* 2, 117f., 119ff., 137–42, 152, 162–66. To which of the 'religious parties' is Jesus closest?

1. Features of 'common Judaism' in Hellenistic and Roman times

Despite its internal multiplicity, Judaism in the time of Jesus had some common basic convictions and forms of expression: monotheism and God's covenant with Israel, temple and synagogues, sacrifices and liturgy of the word, and holy scriptures and traditions (oral and written). Jesus shared the basic convictions and forms of expression in Judaism, i.e. what is called 'common Judaism'.[2]

- *Monotheism*: twice a day Jews said the *sh^ema Israel*, the confession of the one and only God (Deut. 6.4ff.). Certainly Greek philosophers had also progressed to belief in the one God, but they had allowed it to coexist with the polytheistic practice of the people. According to Josephus, only Moses had dared to commit a whole people to this faith (*Apion* 2, 168f.). This Jewish monotheism means a renunciation of all other gods. It is not a 'synthetic' monotheism, which has intimations of one and the same God behind different deities, but an exclusive monotheism. Furthermore it is an ethical monotheism. Immoral stories are told of many pagan gods: 'Our lawgiver showed that God possesses virtue (ἀρετήν) in purity and thought that people should strive to participate in it' (*Antt.* 1, 23). In Judaism God is the embodiment of ethical will. In short, Jewish faith is exclusive and ethical monotheism.
- '*Covenantal nomism*':[3] there is a special relationship between this one and only God and Israel, namely the covenant. By election, God has made the people his own possession – in the fundamental acts of the making of the covenant, the call of Abraham, the exodus and the lawgiving on Sinai. The Torah was given so that the people could remain in this covenant – not to create it by fulfilling the commandments.

Here the Torah comprises 1. both demands on people and ways of preserv-

---

[2]E.P. Sanders, *Judaism*, 1992, gives a sympathetic picture of this 'common Judaism'.
[3]The term 'covenantal nomism' was coined by Sanders to denote the basic structure of Jewish faith. Cf. id., *Paul and Palestinian Judaism*, London and Philadelphia 1977.

ing the covenant when the commandments are transgressed: through possibilities of atonement, conversion and the assurance of the mercy of God. It comprises 2. both cultic and ethical commandments, including important and less important norms. The whole way of life, including what among other peoples was only custom and morality, is thus put under the authority of God. The higher valuation of the ethical commandments which is the result of this needs to be emphasized. These commandments are rooted at the centre of faith. Judaism did not put, say, cultic and ritual commandments on the same level as ethical commandments. Rather, it was the other way round: the ethical commandments were thought to be as 'holy' as everything else that makes it possible to approach God.

All religions have forms of expression in material objects, actions and verbal statements. We find characteristic forms of these in Judaism:

- The *temple and synagogues* are the material objects which give form to Jewish religion. Judaism in the time of Jesus was a temple religion with two special features: God allows himself to be worshipped only in one place, namely in Jerusalem, and in a temple without an image of God. The high esteem for the temple had an intrinsic connection with monotheism: the more transcendent, invisible and aniconic the one and only God was, the more piety was directed towards that one place in which God had made 'his name' dwell (cf. Deut. 12.5 etc.). Alongside this, synagogues came into being everywhere. In our time in Palestine, as a rule these were private rooms which were put at the disposal of the community. Whereas the priest ruled in the temple, here a lay religion developed: here Jesus could teach and find a hearing (cf. Mark 1.21, 39 etc.). However, it was equally natural for him to go to Jerusalem for the Passover; when there was a conflict with the temple and its priesthood there, it was a conflict at the centre of the Judaism of the time.
- *Sacrifice and a liturgy of the word of God* were the performative forms of expression of the Judaism of the time. At the centre of the sacrificial cult at the Jerusalem temple stood the Day of Atonement. Only on this day once a year did the high priest enter the Holy of Holies to accomplish atonement for the people. Alongside the sacrificial cult (as the form of worship which was taken for granted throughout antiquity), the Jews developed a form of worship without sacrifice: synagogue worship, at the centre of which scripture was read aloud and interpreted – one of the most momentous religious innovations which we owe to Judaism. Reading scripture aloud in a way which was accessible to anyone was a strong motive for learning to read (and write), at the least to acquire a certain 'learning in scripture'. Therefore Jews often appeared

to ancient observers to be a 'philosophical people':[4] a whole people was striving to live its whole life consistently in accordance with a teaching which it continually studied and which had been summed up in a book.

- Thus *holy scriptures and traditions* are the linguistic form in which Judaism was expressed. The canon consisted of law, prophets and writings and in the time of Jesus was *de facto* complete, though Ecclesiastes and the Song of Solomon were generally accepted only at the end of the first century. Alongside this there were other (apocryphal) writings and oral traditions. The various currents in Judaism were distinguished by these.

As we saw above, the penetration of the whole of life by divine commandments was characteristic of Judaism. This applied to ethical commandments, most of which were also shared by other peoples (like prohibitions against murder, adultery and theft). But it also applied to the ritual commandments through which they differed from all other peoples. The most important elements of this ritual symbolic language were circumcision, the hallowing of the sabbath, food laws and regulations about purity. This ritual symbolic language had the function of protecting monotheism: faith in the one and only God was a deviant conviction in a polytheistic world. This deviant minority could preserve and hand down its conviction only if marriage between Jews and non-Jews did not bring the worship of other gods into families and their own convictions were not denied by taking part in alien cults. The many commandments were thus a protective hedge around the Torah. After characterizing Jews as people who all their life contemplate the rule (of the one and only God), the Letter of Aristeas continues: 'So, to prevent our being perverted by contact with others or by mixing with bad influences, he hedged us in on all sides with strict observances (lit. purities or purifications), connected with meat and drink and touch and hearing and sight' (Aristeas 142). The ritual sign language of the Torah thus became the hallmark of Judaism, which distinguished it from the surrounding world in a recognizable way.

From around c.200 CE this Judaism was in the grip of a chain of renewal movements which as a rule moved within the framework of these common basic convictions, but which now and then put some forms of expression in question. Jesus stands at the centre of one of these renewal movements within Judaism. All these movements ultimately go back to the challenge posed to Judaism by Hellenistic culture. Here two phases in the Hellenizing of Palestinian Judaism need to be distinguished. We shall first of all characterize them in summary form before describing the renewal movement which appeared in them more closely.

---

[4]Theophrastus (Porphyry, *Abst* II.26 = *GLAJJ* no.4); Megasthenes (Clement of Alexandria, *Strom.* I, 15, 72 = *GLAJJ* no.14); Clearchus of Soloi (Josephus, *Apion* 1, 176–83 = *GLAJJ* no.15).

1. With the Macedonian conquerors, Greek culture penetrated as far as the East and there – in an exchange with the indigenous cultures – turned into 'Hellenism'. In 322 Alexander the Great conquered Palestine. The country experienced a foreign power which was superior in military, economic and cultural terms; this exercised a great attraction for the upper classes, which assimilated to it. However, with the change of rule over Palestine from the Ptolemies to the Seleucids (from 200 BCE on), the Hellenization of the East came to a standstill. On the one hand Rome, which had risen to become a 'world power' by its victory over Carthage (201 BCE), weakened the Hellenistic kingdoms from outside, and on the other the indigenous Eastern cultures underwent a renaissance (not without support from Rome). In reaction to Hellenism at that time a vital resistance movement developed in Palestine and an independent Jewish state was formed with 'anti-Hellenistic features' (from c.140–63 BCE). Judaism re-formed in this time of crisis during the first phase of Hellenism. The old aristocratic upper classes split into rival parties; the fundamentalist rebellion of the Maccabees brought a new ruling class to power, which allied itself with the remains of the old aristocracy (the Sadducees), driving the religious movement of the people originally allied with it (the Pharisees) into opposition and forcing the parts of the old aristocracy which it had kicked out into an alliance with new religious forces; this took form in the Essenes. Thus all three 'classic' religious parties among the Jews came into being in the course of the second century BCE. But they continued to exist in the next phase of Hellenization. They shaped Judaism at the time of Jesus.

2. In the time of crisis for Hellenism in the second/first century BCE, for a while it looked as if Hellenistic culture would disappear from the East. That changed with the intervention of the Romans in the East. A second, now more lasting impulse towards Hellenization began with them. In 63 BCE Pompey conquered Palestine. The Jewish commonwealth lost the independence which it had laboriously achieved. In this second phase of Hellenization, too, we can see an initially relatively successful advance in Palestine, which came to a climax in the rule of Herod I (40–4 BCE). The Hellenization which he imposed provoked opposing forces. A period of crisis began with the unrest after his death, which culminated in the three wars between the Jews and Rome, in 66–74, 115–117 and 132–135 CE. In contrast to the first phase of Hellenization, this time the resistance movement had no success. Political independence could not be restored. Judaism experienced a chain of catastrophes, of which the destruction of the temple in 70 CE was the greatest.

The Jesus movement belongs at the beginning of this time of crisis. It was preceded by messianic resistance movements after the death of Herod I, and the radical-theocratic protest movement of Judas the Galilean after the deposition of his successor Archelaus in Judaea in 6 CE. A series of prophetic protest movements then begins with John the Baptist; among these Jesus also belongs.

The dream of all these movements, a shift of history in favour of Israel, did not come about. The Romans remained the rulers of the land. But one of these protest movements gave rise to Christianity, which in the course of several centuries was to overthrow the Roman empire from within.

2. The earlier renewal movements within Judaism in the second century BCE

After the conquest of Palestine by the Macedonian armies, a continuous Hellenization of Palestine began under the Ptolemies in the third century BCE. The book of Jesus Sirach, which was written about 200 BCE – the last document of a culture which had not yet split into different currents – shows a self-confident Judaism which, while influenced by Hellenistic culture, opposes to it an autochthonous culture by the further development of an indigenous wisdom tradition.[5] A Zadokide high priest still stood unchallenged at the head of the Jewish commonwealth. However, the change from Ptolemaic to Seleucid rule caused latent tensions in the aristocracy to break out: it split into a conservative pro-Ptolemaic wing centred on the high-priestly family of the Oniads and a modernistic pro-Seleucid wing to which most members of the rival Tobiad family belonged. This split in the leading elite gave the fundamentalist Maccabaean revolt, deeply rooted in the people (and the 'Hasidim', i.e. the pious allied with it), a chance.

2.1 The split in the traditional aristocracy at the time of the Hellenistic reform

1. *The Hellenistic reformers.* With the support of the Seleucid king, under the high priest Jason, in 175 BCE the wing of the priestly aristocracy orientated on modernity began an attempt at reform: Jerusalem was to be incorporated into the network of international Hellenistic culture as a *polis* with a Hellenistic organization. The aristocracy adopted a Hellenistic life-style, in part ostentatiously. The reformers represented a typical Jewish conversion movement. They called for a return to the true origins. Their opponents present their programme with the words, 'Let us go out and make a covenant with the Gentiles round about us, for since we separated from them many evils have come upon us' (I Macc. 1.11). Probably they had the notion of a pure Mosaic cult – with a spiritual, aniconic

---

[5]Cf. O. Wischmeyer, *Die Kultur des Buches Jesus Sirach*, BZNW 77, Berlin and New York 1995.

notion of God, but also without the separatist rites like circumcision, the sabbath commandment and the food laws. They probably regarded these as a later addition to the Law of Moses. At least such a picture of history has been preserved for us in Strabo's account of the Jews (*Geogr.* XVI, 2, 34–46 = *GLAJJ* no.115). The Hellenistic reformers were very soon weakened by a split into a moderate wing around the (Zadokide) high priest Jason and a radical wing around the high priest Menelaus (who was not legitimated by any Zadokide descent). The radical wing attempted to get the better of the others with the help of the Syrian king, but was hopelessly compromised when the king claimed the temple treasure for himself (to pay contributions to the Romans) and entered the sanctuary in the presence of Menelaus (I Macc. 1.20–28). When the moderate wing around Jason subsequently got the better of the radical wing and for the moment took over power in Jerusalem, as a counter-measure in 168 (or 167 BCE) the Syrian king Antiochus IV Epiphanes prohibited the practice of the Jewish religion: circumcision and the hallowing of the sabbath. He had Torah scrolls burned, and a cult of Zeus Olympius or Baal ha-Shamayim was introduced in the Jerusalem temple. We may assume that these measures were suggested to him by parts of the radical reform movement, but not by the moderate reformers. On the contrary, the religious edict of Antiochus IV was (also) directed against the moderate reformers, the majority of whom were priests; the basis of their existence was removed with the abolition of the traditional cult. Such a compulsory reform had to fail. In 164 the Maccabees conquered Jerusalem and dedicated the temple anew. Their opponents withdrew into a fortress in Jerusalem erected by the Seleucids, the Acra; this was only captured by their opponents in 141 BCE. We know very little about these reformers, and that little usually comes from sources of their opponents, who branded them wicked men. Historical scholarship may not take over these verdicts. Rather, we must note that this was a first attempt to extend Jewish identity. In its moderate form it was not a surrender of Jewish identity or assimilation, but a limited acculturation to Hellenism. It was a reform from above, supported by part of the upper class. Primitive Christianity was the first to make a new attempt – but this time from the centre of the people, 'from below', and without any compulsion. But again this was an attempt to form a universalist Judaism without separatist rites. It must have reminded many Jews of the failed Hellenistic reform and therefore provoked bitter resistance (as with the pre-Christian Paul).

2. *The conservative Oniads.* Nor could the opponents of the Hellenistic reformers in the aristocracy gain the upper hand. When the Maccabaean Jonathan became high priest in 152, it was clear that the Oniads had lost the battle for the high priesthood. As partisans of the Ptolemaeans, around 150 BCE they withdrew to Egypt, where they established a second Jewish temple in Leontopolis. This was a rival sanctuary to that in Jerusalem, which existed until 73 CE and was only destroyed by Vespasian in the Jewish–Roman war.

Not only the Oniads were forced out at that time. Possibly in 152 BCE the high priest Jonathan forced out of office a Zadokide high priest whose name we do not know, the 'Teacher of Righteousness' in the Qumran writings. Thereupon this high priest made the Essene 'covenant' with other traditionalist circles – as an opposition alliance against what in his views was the wicked temple cult, the leadership of which had been usurped by the Maccabees.

2.2 The revolt against the Hellenistic reformers and the Seleucid rulers

As has already been mentioned, the reform supported by the Seleucid king provoked a rebellion in the country. It began in Modein, the home town of the Maccabees. They are also called 'Hasmonaeans' after their ancestor Hasmon. As a priestly family, they had every reason to rebel against the profanation of the temple and the loss of their social and economic status. They formed the political and military wing of the resistance movement, but allied themselves with groups with a strongly religious motivation, the so-called 'Hasidim'.

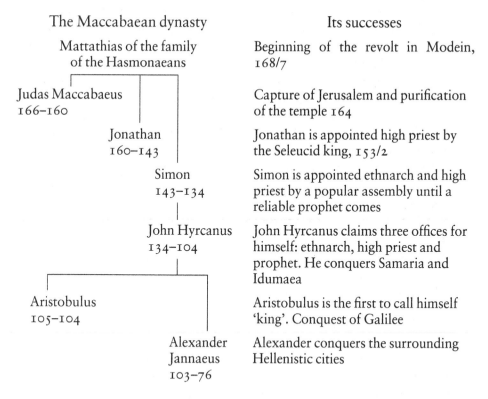

The Maccabaean dynasty	Its successes
Mattathias of the family of the Hasmonaeans	Beginning of the revolt in Modein, 168/7
Judas Maccabaeus 166–160	Capture of Jerusalem and purification of the temple 164
Jonathan 160–143	Jonathan is appointed high priest by the Seleucid king, 153/2
Simon 143–134	Simon is appointed ethnarch and high priest by a popular assembly until a reliable prophet comes
John Hyrcanus 134–104	John Hyrcanus claims three offices for himself: ethnarch, high priest and prophet. He conquers Samaria and Idumaea
Aristobulus 105–104	Aristobulus is the first to call himself 'king'. Conquest of Galilee
Alexander Jannaeus 103–76	Alexander conquers the surrounding Hellenistic cities

1. The *Maccabees*. When a royal official required the performance of pagan sacrifices in Modein he was killed by Mattathias, the father of the Maccabees. In

168/7 that was the sign to revolt (I Macc. 2.15–30). Mattathias's sons and descendants took over the leadership of the revolt in succession. With varying success they succeeded, step by step, in restoring an autonomous, indeed later politically independent, Jewish state. The most important stages of this development are depicted in the diagram above. The course of the Maccabees shows that they increasingly moved away from their power base, the Jewish people and its pious circles. Their revolt led to a state which saw itself in analogy to the Hellenistic kingdoms, although originally it had emerged from an anti-Hellenistic revolt.

2. The *Hasidim*. The Hasidim (I Macc. 2.42) appear alongside the Maccabees as their allies. They are mentioned only three times in the books of Maccabees – which is not surprising, since these seek to glorify the Maccabees, who in the meanwhile had parted company with their erstwhile allies. Nevertheless, these Hasidim are called the backbone of the resistance: they are said to be the real warriors (II Macc. 14.6). On the other hand they are the first to be ready for peace once their religious aims – the restoration of temple worship and the appointment of a legitimate high priest, Alkimus – have been achieved (I Macc. 7.13f.). By contrast the Maccabees fought on. According to the traditional view these Hasidim are the forerunners of Pharisees and Essenes who branched off from them. Recently it has been doubted whether the three brief mentions of the Hasidim provide relevant information about the prehistory of Pharisees and Essenes.[6] At all events, however, they belong to a revitalizing of Jewish culture which is also evident e.g. in the Pharisees and Essenes.

2.3 The rise of the three traditional religious parties in the Maccabaean period

1. The *Essenes*: even if the origin of the Essenes (and the Qumran community, which was probably their centre) is surrounded by many historical riddles,[7] the following traditional view is still the most probable. In the second century a Zadokide high priest was forced out of office by a Maccabaean high priest (the 'Wicked Priest' of the Qumran writings). This deposed high priest thereupon allied himself with fundamentalist groups which had already existed previously independently of him (as Hasidim, cf. CD I, 9). As the 'Teacher of Righteousness' he transformed this community into a substitute temple for the Jerusalem cult, which in his eyes had been profaned. The 'sons of Zadok', i.e. members of legitimate high-priestly families, dominated in this cultic community. Questions of priestly purity therefore assumed a central role. Along with questions about the

---

[6] Cf. Stemberger, *Pharisäer*, 91ff.

[7] P.R. Callaway, *History,* reports and discusses various theories about the history of the Qumran community.

calendar and individual ritual norms they became marks of social identity which set the group apart (cf. the letter of the Teacher of Righteousness in 4QMMT). The new community celebrated heavenly worship in communion with the angels and had the function of atoning for the whole land. As the archaeological evidence in Qumran indicates that the settlement began in 100 BCE at the latest (according to others, 125 BCE), only one of three Maccabees, Jonathan, Simon or John Hyrcanus, could be regarded as the Wicked Priest (i.e. as a high priest who has come to power illegitimately). The identification with Jonathan (see above) is most probable. Moreover the Damascus Document (CD I, 5–11) dates the refounding of the community at 390 + 20 years after the fall of Jerusalem (587 BCE). This is a 'round' number, but it too points to the second century. Attempts to identify the Teacher of Righteousness with later figures (e.g. John the Baptist or even James the brother of the Lord) are therefore untenable.[8]

2. The *Sadducees*: the intrinsic unity of the remainder of the Zadokides was restored by the splitting off of the Oniads on the one hand and the Teacher of Righteousness on the other (with substitute temples in Leontopolis or the Essene community respectively). As the more conservative priests had parted company with the Jerusalem sanctuary, the temple was left with those priests who had once been supporters of the moderate Hellenistic reform. The 'Sadducees' probably emerged from these 'Zadokides'; John Hyrcanus made an alliance with them, in so doing driving his former allies, the Pharisees, into opposition. Both domestic and foreign policy determined his change of course.

- As far as *domestic policy* was concerned, John Hyrcanus (134–104 BCE) laid claim to three offices, as ethnarch, high priest and prophet. By laying claim to the prophetic office he demonstratively invalidated the 'eschatological' proviso which had still been made in appointing Simon ethnarch and high priest: 'until a trustworthy prophet should arise' (I Macc. 14.41). He could not hope for support for such a claim to power in the fundamentalist circles, but he could do so among the traditional priestly circles which were concerned with the position of the temple (and their own status). The Pharisees went into opposition against him. They criticized the union of political and priestly office – above all with the argument that the mother of John Hyrcanus had been a prisoner of war, and so her descendants were no longer qualified to hold priestly office (since sexual abuse by the victors was assumed in the case of women who had been taken prisoner in war, his 'pure' priestly descent was uncertain, cf. Josephus, *Antt.* 13, 288–292).
- In *foreign policy*, John Hyrcanus's programme was to gather all Jews and the ethnic groups of Palestine akin to them in a Jewish state. He conquered

---

[8]See below, pp. 148ff. (Task 2 on the 'Teacher of Righteousness').

Samaria, which had separated itself cultically from the other Jews under Alexander the Great, and destroyed the Samaritan temple on Gerizim. He also had the Edomites, who were akin to the Jews, forcibly circumcised (probably reviving a custom traditional there). For this programme he needed a theology which was minimalist: the Sadducees recognized only the Torah of Moses and the Samaritans only the (Samaritan) Pentateuch. In addition they rejected new religious notions (eschatology, belief in demons). The kind of religious 'in-novations' advocated by the Pharisees were likely to 'split' the Jewish nation (extended by the kindred Samaritans and Edomites), since these had not shared in the special religious developments of the Jews in Judaea.

As Josephus associates criticism of the legitimacy of the Hasmonaeans both with John Hyrcanus (*Antt.* 13, 288–296) and with Alexander Jannaeus (*Antt.* 13, 372, cf. bKidd. 66a), some scholars assume that open conflict between Sadducees and Pharisees is to be dated only to the time of Alexander Jannaeus.[9] But it is more probable that Alexander Jannaeus, who is regarded as a notorious villain in the tradition, drew upon himself the criticism made of his father. In coming to a judgment about Jesus it is important to note that Galilee was conquered by the Maccabees under Aristobulus (105/4), i.e. it again came under intensified Jewish influence at a time when the Sadducees were at the peak of their power. The 'Pharisees' came to power here only later. Possibly criticism of them with a Sadducean colouring found more of an echo in Galilee than elsewhere.

3. The *Pharisees* appear in Josephus in the early period as political opposition to the ruling Hasmonaeans – having originally been allied with them. Connections with the 'Hasidim' are more than probable, for these too were originally allied with the Maccabees (I Macc. 2.42) and like the Pharisees were sceptical about a purely military and political development of power. But when were they given the name 'Pharisee'? Perhaps they called themselves פָּרוֹשִׁים (*pārōshīm*), i.e. 'those who distinguish precisely'. That fits their characterization by Josephus, who keeps emphasizing their ἀκρίβεια (preciseness). פְּרוּשִׁים (*p^erūshīm*), i.e. 'splitter', could be a derogatory epithet applied by others (thus Baumgarten, 'Name'). In the Qumran texts they probably appear as the community of the Liar and as 'those who teach smooth things' (דוֹרְשֵׁי חֲלָקוֹת, *dōr^eshē h^alāqōt*, cf. 4QpNah I, 2). This last designation similarly seems to go back to a word-play; it characterizes the interest of the Pharisees in the establishment and precise observance of the rules of everyday religious practice, the *h^alākōt* (הֲלָכוֹת). According to the Nahum commentary, this opposition group can be identified with the opponents of Alexander Jannaeus who summoned the Seleucid king

---

[9]Cf. Stemberger, *Pharisäer*, 98–102.

Hellenistic reformers   *Anti-Hellenistic opposition*
Reform 175

Radical reformers   *Moderate*
Menelaus, high   *reformers*
priest without   Jason, high priest
Zadokide   with Zadokide
legitimation   legitimation
172–63   175–72

The religious   The religious   *Revolt of the Maccabees*, i.e. country
edict of Antiochus edict is (also)   priests, leads to the rededication of the
IV in 168/7   directed against   temple in 164. After that the opposition
(inspired by him?) the moderate   splits:
leads to the   reformers
profanation of the
temple

Hasmonaeans,   The Aaronide   *Hasidim*, who are   Conservative
who fight for   high priest   content with the   Zadokide priestly
political   Alkimus   restoration of the   circles, who
independence   (164–160)   cult and the   remain in
from the Syrian   appointment of   opposition
king   Alkimus as high
                                        priest

Usurpation of the   The *Teacher of*
high priestly   *Righteousness* a
office by   high priest driven
Jonathan (=   out in 152(?)
Wicked Priest?)   founds the

Development of   *Sadducees*   *Pharisees*   *Essenes*,
the Hasmonaeans   support the   initially allied   an opposition
into a Hellenistic Hasmonaeans   with the   alliance of
monarchy,   and their   Hasmonaeans,   Hasidim and
especially after   development   from John   Zadokide priests
John Hyrcanus   towards the   Hyrcanus on are   against the
134–104   Hellenistic   in opposition   Hasmonaeans
                    monarchy

Demetrius to their aid (cf. *Antt.* 13, 376). Alexander Jannaeus had 800 of these opponents crucified (4QpNah I,7; *Antt.* 13, 380f.). Even if Josephus does not call the opponents of Jannaeus who were executed Pharisees, there are connections with them: after the death of Alexander Jannaeus the Pharisees came to power under Queen Alexandra Salome (76–67). They unleashed a bloody persecution on those responsible for the mass execution (*BJ* 1, 113; *Antt.* 13, 410). So from the time of Alexander Salome the Pharisees, representatives of what was originally an opposition movement, were bound up with the power elite through an alliance. From this time on they had a seat in the 'Sanhedrin'. King Herod probably strengthened their power further, since he deliberately weakened the Sadducees as allies of the Hasmonaeans in the Sanhedrin. Perhaps the blood-bath which Herod perpetrated among the members of the Sanhedrin was directed above all against Sadducees (cf. *Antt.* 14, 175; 15, 6). At all events the two parties which were formerly at odds, Sadducees and Pharisees, were represented in the Sanhedrin.

The diagram on the opposite page is meant to illustrate in summary form the complicated origin of the three classical 'religious parties' in Judaism.

2.4 The differences between Sadducees, Pharisees and Essenes according to Josephus (in the first century BCE)

Josephus compares the three most important 'religious parties' of the Jews several times: *Antt.* 13, 171–173, 297f.; 18, 11–25; *BJ* 2, 118–166. He describes them for his readers, who have a Hellenistic education, as analogous to the philosophical schools of the Greeks: the Essenes as Pythagoreans (*Antt.* 15, 371), the Pharisees as Stoics (*Vita* 12); for the Sadducees he suggests an identification with the Epicureans but does not make this explicitly. His most important points of comparison are: attitudes towards εἱμαρμένη (fate, behind which of course is God), free will and the question of the immortality of the soul. In addition further differences can be inferred from him. They will apply to the time of Josephus, i.e. to the first century CE:

	Sadducees	Pharisees	Essenes
Determinism and free will (*Antt.* 13, 171–173; *BJ* 2, 162–166)	*Indeterminism*: human beings are the cause of their destiny	*Synergism*: God (εἱμαρμένη) and human beings work together	*Determinism*: everything is determined by God (εἱμαρμένη)
Eschatology and the doctrine of souls	*Denial of another world*: the ongoing existence of the soul and eternal punishment and reward are denied (*BJ* 2, 165; *Antt.* 18, 16)	*Resurrection of the righteous*: the soul is immortal, but only among the good does it go into a new body. The wicked are punished eternally (*BJ* 2, 163)	*Immortality of the soul* (*BJ* 2, 15off.): freed from the body the good enjoy a life in joy, the wicked suffer punishment.
Scripture and tradition	*'Scriptural principle'*: Sadducees observe only the written laws and reject the (oral) tradition of the fathers (*Antt.* 13, 297).	*Scripture and tradition*: Pharisees add laws from the tradition of the fathers to the written laws of Moses (*Antt.* 13, 297).	*Secret literature*: Essenes have secret books (*BJ* 2, 142): they are concerned intensively with the writings of the ancients (*BJ* 2, 136).
Sitz im Leben	*Link with the upper class*: Sadducees have the well-to-do on their side (*Antt.* 13, 298), but in office follow the teachings of the Pharisees (*Antt.* 18, 17).	*Closeness to the lower class*: the Pharisees give the people their laws and have them on their side (*Antt.* 13, 297f.; 18.15).	*Separate community*: divided into strict and moderate Essenes (*BJ* 2, 16of.). They keep their teachings secret (*BJ* 2, 141).
Modes of behaviour	*'Culture of conflict'*: Sadducees contradict their teachers (*Antt.* 18, 16) and are rude to one another (*BJ* 2, 166).	*Principle of authority*: Pharisees venerate the old (*Antt.* 18, 12) and prize mutual harmony (*BJ* 2, 166).	*Ideal of community*: they live in a model community (sharing possessions), for the most part unmarried (*BJ* 2, 119ff.; 16of.).

2.5 The development in the course of the first century CE and the relationship of Jesus to the old 'religious parties'

None of the three traditional 'religious parties' of the Jews survived the Jewish War unchanged. The Sadducees were closely associated with the temple. Its destruction in 70 CE deprived them of their material and spiritual foundations. At that time the Essenes probably also disappeared from history: their centre in Qumran was destroyed in the Jewish War, probably by the Romans (or by rebels). There is now vigorous argument over the significance of the Pharisees for first-century CE Judaism. Three discussions are sketched out here:

1. Are the Pharisees of central or marginal significance?

- The traditional view is put forward by M. Hengel (e.g. in his review of E.P. Sanders' *Judaism*): according to this the Pharisees decisively shaped first-century Judaism. They are more than the 6,000 who refused to swear an oath to Herod (*Antt.* 17, 42). Above all they want to have a deliberate influence on the people and have many supporters among the people (*Antt.* 13, 297f.). The fact that a four-person delegation to Galilee from the leaders of the revolt in Jerusalem contains three Pharisees (cf. *Vita* 197) corresponds to the general balance of power.
- An alternative view is put forward e.g. by E.P. Sanders (*Judaism*). At the time of the second temple the leaders of Judaism were its priests. What was put forward by the priests and accepted by the people forms a 'common Judaism', the significance of which is to be reckoned far more important than the influence of small 'religious parties'. The Synoptic Gospels present a false picture because of the discussion in them between Jesus and the Pharisees (which is largely unhistorical).

2. Are the Pharisees political or religious in character?

- J. Neusner has developed the thesis that the Pharisees in the Hasmonaean period had been a political opposition party, but in the first century were a movement of religious piety. They had undergone a change 'from politics to piety'.[10]
- Against this it can be objected that the Pharisees did indeed shape the private sphere in the first century CE, but this was that free space which even a subject people had. This is the sign of a political will for self-preservation (Saldarini, *Pharisees*, 213). Furthermore the question of the relationship with the Gentiles led to vigorous debates and conflicts: a Pharisee founded the resistance movement along with Judas of Galilee (*Antt.* 18, 4). Hillelites and Shammaites – two schools of Pharisees – carried on a bitter controversy over the eighteen *halakhot*, rules for marking the Jews off from the pagans.[11]

---

[10]Cf. J. Neusner, *From Politics to Piety*, New York 1973, ²1979.
[11]Cf. Hengel, *Zealots**, 202ff.

3. *Continuity or discontinuity between the Pharisees and rabbinic Judaism?*

- The traditional view says that of the various religious parties only Pharisaism survived the first Jewish War and thus became the foundation of rabbinic Judaism. The Pharisees could assimilate the loss of the temple theologically better than others because of their intrinsic presuppositions. A characteristic of their piety is an extension of the priestly notion of holiness to the whole of life. Thus Jewish identity became possible independently of the temple. The study of the Torah could take the place of the sacrificial cult.
- An alternative view says that the Pharisees appear in the rabbinic texts only as a special ascetic group, and nowhere as the group from which the rabbis originated, their erstwhile home. So there is no evidence for the thesis of a continuity between the Pharisees before 70 CE and the rabbinic movement after 70 CE. Judaism after 70 CE has a broader base than just the Pharisees. According to Stegemann (*Essener**, 361ff.), the priestly Essenes could also bring their heritage into the rabbinic movment; that would explain the intensive interest of the rabbis in the Jerusalem cult (which meanwhile had ceased to exist).

How does Jesus relate to the three 'religious parties'?

- The Synoptic tradition says nothing about the *Essenes*. Either there were no Essenes in Galilee, in which case this striking silence would reflect the limited Galilean world in which Jesus lived. Or they appear in the Synoptic tradition under the name of Pharisees. The Teacher of Righteousness says in his letter (4QMMT) that he 'separated' along with his followers; here the verb פרשׁ is used, which is contained in פְּרוּשִׁים (= Pharisees). It is more probable that unlike the Pharisees, the Essenes did not seek to influence the whole people. They kept their teachings secret (*BJ* 2, 141; 1QS VII, 11f.) and avoided arguments with outsiders (1QS IX, 16). Therefore in the Jesus tradition we find debates with Pharisees but not with Essenes. In fact in any cases there are clear distinctions between them and Jesus: certainly in both cases we find an intensification of the Torah, but we find a corresponding relaxation of the Torah only with Jesus. The separation from the sinners and the unclean among the Essenes goes against the concern for sinners that we find with Jesus.
- The difference from the *Sadducees* is even emphasized in the Jesus tradition: like the Pharisees, Jesus hoped for the resurrection of the dead and on this point contradicted the Sadducean doctrine (Mark 12.18ff.). The Sadducean part of the Sanhedrin was probably more hostile to him than the Pharisaic part. This is the only explanation of the traditions about the Pharisees Nicodemus (cf. John 7.45–52), Joseph of Arimathea (who waited for the kingdom of God, Mark 15. 43), and Gamaliel (Acts 5.33ff.). Here the Pharisees (or people close to them)

always show greater understanding of Jesus than the other members of the Sanhedrin. But at the same time Jesus could also have learned from the Sadducees: his criticism of the Pharisees' principle of tradition (Mark 7.1ff.) could have been a new use of Sadducean arguments against the Pharisees.

• Doubtless the closest proximity is that of Jesus to the *Pharisees*. Their criticism of Jesus shows that they measure him by special criteria – as though he is a teacher standing close to them. K. Berger, 'Jesus als Pharisäer und frühe Christen als Pharisäer', *NT* 30, 1988, 231–62, has reduced the opposition and the nearness to the formula: the Pharisees advocate a defensive notion of cleanness. They are thus concerned to avoid infection through uncleanness. By contrast, Jesus advocates an offensive notion of cleanness: it is not uncleanness but cleanness which infects. But the fundamental motive is the same. Both want to hallow everyday life in the light of God's will.

3. The origin of the later renewal movements within Judaism in the first century CE

The Jesus movement does not belong in the context of the earlier 'religious parties' but in a series of renewal movements which only came into being after the Romans took over power. At first the Romans had a stabilizing influence. Herod I, their client king, succeeded in keeping the country under control, but only with unusual repression and equally unusual competence. After his death in 4 BCE the suppressed tensions came to the surface.

3.1 The messianic movements in the 'Robber War' of 4 BCE

The first wave of open opposition was expressed in uncoordinated revolts. Nicolaus of Damascus saw in them a revolt with an anti-Hellenistic aim: 'Then people revolted against his [= Herod's] sons and against the Greeks' (*De vita sua*, *GLAJJ* no.97). The danger was so great that the Syrian legate Quintilius Varus (6–3 BCE) had to intervene. It took the deployment of several legions to restore order. The rebellious groups had been motivated by a messianic longing, i.e. the longing for an indigenous political liberator with a charismatic aura. Two figures certainly had such a messianic aura:

• *Simon*, a former slave of Herod, put the diadem on his head at that time and was proclaimed king (*Antt.* 17, 273f.). Joseph can explain this only by the longing of the people for an 'indigenous king' (*Antt.* 17, 277). The rule of the Idumaean Herod, who had distanced himself from Jewish traditions (even if he observed them for political reasons in the presence of Jews), had provoked this longing.

- *Athronges*, a shepherd, styled himself a new David. He too put the diadem on his head (*Antt.* 17, 287–80) and treated his brothers as satraps and generals. Apart from physical strength and a certain charismatic aura he did not have much to offer to make his claim plausible.
- By contrast, *Judas*, the son of Hezekiah (who is not identified by Josephus with Judas of Galilee), was another figure. In *Antt.* 17, 272 Josephus suggests that he too was aiming at the kingdom, but nowhere does he assert that Judas made himself king. Rather, *BJ* 2.56 says that he contested all those who sought for the rule. Possibly royal ambitions are attributed to him in *Antt.* 17, 272 only because of the association with Simon and Athronges. Probably he advocated radical theocratic ideas, i.e. the repudiation of any rule but the rule of God.

Royal pretenders are attested later in the Jewish War. In it Menahem appears in royal garb (*BJ* 2, 433f.). Simon ben Giora was a claimant to royal dignity. He was treated as such by the Romans – and executed in Rome after the triumphal procession (*BJ* 4, 510, 575; 7, 26–31, 118, 154f.). It is possible that there were further royal pretenders.[12] However, it is decisive for the understanding of the history of Jesus that expectations of a messianic king were alive among the people at that time – and these expectations were politically explosive. It would be improbable for Jesus not to have been confronted with such messianic expectations during his lifetime.

3.2 The radical theocratic teaching of Judas of Galilee (6 CE)

A violent revolt was replaced in the second wave of resistance by a teaching which had far greater consequences than any direct revolt. After the deposition of Archelaus in 6 CE, Judaea and Samaria came under direct Roman administration. From now on the taxes had to be paid directly to Rome. A tax assessment by Quirinius created the basis for this payment. A 'teacher', Judas of Galilee, engaged in polemic against it with two theses. The first was the sole rule of God; from this it followed that one might recognize no other ruler alongside God. To this was added the thesis of a revolutionary synergism: human beings were obliged actively to collaborate in the establishment of the sole rule of God. In practice this amounted to a refusal to pay tax. Josephus makes this teaching, which he introduces as a 'fourth philosophy' alongside the three traditional 'philosophies of the Jews', responsible for the outbreak of the Jewish revolt of 66–74 CE (*BJ* 2, 117f.; *Antt.* 18, 4ff., 23–25). It must in fact have been this teaching which later

---

[12]Evans, *Jesus**, 53–81, also lists in his survey of all 'messianic claimants' Judas son of Hezekiah, Judas of Galilee and John of Gischala. From the period after 70 CE he discusses Lukuas of Cyrene (115 CE) and Simon bar Kochba (132–135 CE).

motivated parts of the (younger) aristocracy to rebel. Even if Judas of Galilee did not create any organized resistance movement (and this is disputed), he laid the ideological foundation for many groups of the resistance movement. And he was thought to be dangerous. At all events, according to Acts 5.37 he perished by violence.

His teaching became acute again after 44 CE. At that time – after the death of Agrippa I – Galilee too came under direct Roman administration, with the unavoidable consequence that now in Galilee, too, the taxes had to be paid directly to Rome. It cannot be a coincidence that at that time two sons of Judas of Galilee created disturbances, presumably with the same teaching as their father: the rejection of any payment of tax to the Romans. Both were crucified by the Roman procurator Tiberius Alexander (c.46–48, *Antt.* 20, 102). In Acts 5.36–37 the real revolt of Judas of Galilee is seen in their 'revolt'. That explains why Judas of Galilee is there put chronologically after the revolt of 'Theudas' (immediately after 44 CE).

But the teaching of Judas of Galilee was also influential in the interim: Jesus is asked whether it is lawful or not to pay tax to the emperor (Mark 12.13–17). It makes sense that he was asked about this by the Herodians, since the Herodian client princes commended themselves to the Roman administration because they blunted the problem of the payment of tax. If they collected the taxes and then in turn paid a tribute to the Romans, no Jew need pay taxes directly to the emperor. To this degree the Herodians had a 'secret' interest in the radical theocratic refusal to pay tax. According to Mark 12.13–17 Jesus clearly rejected the teaching of Judas of Galilee: belief in the one and only God did not carry with it an obligation to resist the emperor. But in Jesus, too, there is a radical theocratic alternative: between God and Mammon there is only an abrupt either-or. In this sphere one cannot serve two masters at the same time (Matt. 6.24/Luke 16.13). As the emperor ultimately stands behind the money, in Jesus, too, a political tension remains.

In earlier scholarship the supporters of Judas of Galilee were usually called 'Zealots'. However, there is no evidence for this in Josephus. In him 'Zealots' appear as a group only after the outbreak of the Jewish War in 66 CE, in connection with the temple. It has been concluded from this that the 'Zealots' did not exist as a group before the Jewish War and remained a group limited to Jerusalem. However, there is an important piece of evidence to the contrary: among the twelve disciples of Jesus there is a 'Simon the Zealot' (Luke 6.15). Here a 'Zealot' is already attested for the first half of the first century – and moreover for Galilee!

3.3 The prophetic opposition: the movements of John the Baptist and other prophets

3.3.1 *John the Baptist*

A third wave of opposition emerged in the 20s. This time it was not directed against the Romans, but against their client princes, the Herodians. The preaching of John the Baptist[13] articulates a widespread criticism of the life of the ruling house. We can note among the Herodians a cultural alienation from the norms of the Jewish people.

- Herod Antipas transgressed the commandments relating to cleanness in founding his new capital, Tiberias, when he built the city on a cemetery (*Antt.* 18, 37f.). Among other things the attractiveness of John the Baptist's conversion movement was based on that and on the sense of being 'endangered' culturally by the Hellenistic life-style of the upper class. The requirement of baptism presupposes a sense of the threat from uncleanness.
- Herod Antipas transgressed against the prohibition of images in his palace. At the beginning of the Jewish War, various rebel groups competed in destroying the pictures of animals in his palace (*Vita* 65ff.). We find no criticism of this in John the Baptist, but in Matt. 11.8ff. Jesus contrasts John's ascetic life generally with the court life of the Herodian rulers (cf. Theissen, 'Local Colouring'*, 26–44).
- Herod Antipas offended against the traditional marriage laws when he married Herodias. The direct criticism of John the Baptist is directed against this, and according to Mark 6.17–29 it cost him his life.

There is no mistaking the fact that the Baptist's movement, too, belongs in the series of renewal movements within Judaism which sought to preserve and redefine Jewish identity in the face of the Hellenistic pressure towards assimilation.

3.3.2 *The later Jewish prophets after John the Baptist*

John the Baptist and Jesus are only the beginning of a series of prophets who reactivate the eschatological hope. It is characteristic of these prophets, of whom we often have only brief pieces of information, that they prophesy a great miracle which motivates followers to go to the place where it is expected. As a rule they are regarded by the political authorities as a danger and put down by force. The following summary gives a survey of these so-called 'sign prophets'.[14]

---

[13] John the Baptist is discussed thoroughly in 8.4. Here he is only introduced under one aspect: that of the political opposition movement.

[14] Barnett, 'Sign Prophets'; R. Meyer, *Der Prophet aus Galiläa*, Leipzig 1940, esp. 82ff., 108ff.

- Around 36 CE a *Samaritan prophet* promised a crowd of people that he would point out on Gerizim the vanished vessels of the temple that Moses had buried there. He collected his followers to go to Gerizim, but Pilate intervened and had the crowd massacred. He was deposed because of the protests against his brutal action (*Antt.* 18, 85–87).
- Under the procurator Cuspius Fadus (44–46 CE) a certain *Theudas* persuaded a crowd of people to 'follow' him with their possessions to the Jordan. He promised that the Jordan would divide there, so that they could pass over with dry feet. Again the procurator intervened and ended this attempt at a new 'conquest' with a blood bath (*Antt.* 20, 97–99; cf. Acts 5.36).
- Under the procurator Antonius Felix (52–60 CE), a number of *anonymous prophets* appeared who called on their supporters to 'follow' them into the wilderness. There they would see signs and wonders (or signs of freedom). This start of a new exodus was again bloodily suppressed (*Antt.* 20, 167f.; *BJ* 2, 258–60).
- At the same time an *Egyptian* appeared who led his followers to the Mount of Olives. He promised that the walls of Jerusalem would fall down at his command. So the miracle at the walls of Jericho was to repeat itself in Jerusalem (*Antt.* 20, 169–172; *BJ* 2, 261–263 [quoted above p. 89]; cf. Acts 21.38).
- Under the procurator Porcius Festus (60–62 CE) a *prophet* promised 'redemption' and an end to the evils if people followed him into the wilderness. The Romans put down this movement violently (*Antt.* 20, 188).
- Under Albinus (62–64?) a prophet called *Jesus son of Ananias* came from the country to Jerusalem with a message of judgment upon Jerusalem, the temple and the people. His cry of woe led to his being arrested by the Jewish aristocracy, who handed him over to the procurator. At the interrogation the procurator came to the conclusion that the man was mad and freed him. Jesus continued his prophecy of misfortune until the destruction of Jerusalem; he perished in the siege (*BJ* 6, 300–309 [quoted below, p. 470]).
- Again in the last days of the siege of Jerusalem prophets appeared who promised salvation. One of them proclaimed that God commanded him to go into the temple and await the signs of redemption. Josephus blames him for the deaths of so many people when the temple was burned (*BJ* 6, 285f.).

Jesus of Nazareth also displays some features which recall such Jewish 'sign prophets'. He promises the miraculous destruction and restoration of the temple in Jerusalem (Mark 14.57f.). Here, like the other sign prophets, he refers back to memories of the history of salvation, whether to the exodus, the conquest or the building of the temple. Like the other prophets, Jesus goes to the place of the promised miracle; like them, he calls for 'discipleship'. As in other cases, the

Romans intervene. The prophet (usually with many of his followers) perishes. Most prophets have a message which is in fact directed against the alien 'occupying power'. Anyone who promises a new exodus sees the people as oppressed. Only in the case of John the Baptist, Jesus of Nazareth and Jesus the son of Ananias, who was perhaps influenced by Jesus' prophecy about the temple, do we find a message of judgment which is directed against their own people.

4. Summary and hermeneutical reflections

Jesus shares the basic convictions of Judaism: faith in the one and only God who has made a special covenant with Israel. These basic convictions had to be reformulated in the age of Hellenism. Jesus and his movement belong in a long chain of renewal movements within Judaism which in view of the great pressure for change that emanated from the over-powerful Hellenistic culture attempted to preserve Jewish identity or to redefine it. In the case of Jesus this identity is defined in a comparatively 'open' way.

- Whereas other renewal and protest movements usually associate the expectation of a victory of Israel over the pagans with the eschatological hope for a fundamental change, in the Jesus tradition the rule of God is open to the influx of pagans. Against tendencies towards segregation, Jesus activates the universalistic Jewish tradition of the pilgrimage of the nations to Zion (Matt. 8.10f.).
- Whereas other renewal movements usually intensify specifically Jewish norms, in Jesus we find an intensification of the Torah in the case of universal ethical norms and at the same time a relaxation of norms which bring separation (the sabbath commandment and the laws relating to cleanness).
- Whereas many renewal movement 'separated' themselves from the people, in the Jesus movement we find a deliberate approach to all those who do not correspond to the traditional norms and stand on the periphery. Here Jesus activates the Jewish belief in a merciful and gracious God against other tendencies.
- Whereas many renewal movements express a direct protest against the foreign rulers with their military superiority and are part of the resistance against the foreigners, the Jesus movement avoids a direct confrontation: it formulates Jewish identity in such a way that in principle it avoids clashing with the legions.

A strong tendency towards integration, both inwardly and outwardly, is characteristic of the Jesus movement. What was possibly the aim of some radical Hellenistic reforms in the aristocracy at the beginning of our era, a Judaism which opened itself up, and which activated its integrative and universalistic traditions in the face of tendencies towards segregation, is realized in Jesus in another way: not against the ordinary people but from their midst. It is generally characteristic of the Jesus movement that we find in it aristocratic features in a non-aristocratic milieu.

After the death of Jesus, his renewal movement within Judaism first of all became a Jewish sect. In the first generation the hope was still alive that the separation from the other Jews was only provisional (cf. Rom. 11.26ff.). This Jewish 'sect' was one of the few sects which distinguished itself from the majority by greater openness and not by greater strictness. From around 70 CE the 'sect' became a final schism – caused by the destruction of the temple and the further internal development of both Judaism and primitive Christianity. As most primitive Christian texts were formulated in this period (after 70), they have a tendency to project that separation between Jews and Christians, which only became a reality in their time, back on to the time of Jesus. Conflicts of Jesus with other Jewish groups are therefore often depicted in them as conflicts between Jesus and Judaism. Historical criticism has the task of making clear this tendency in the sources. It is recognizing increasingly clearly – sometimes against its own tradition of research – that Jesus belongs within Judaism.

This historical insight has two hermeneutical consequences for the knowledge and assessment of the historical Jesus. All reconstructions of the historical Jesus are dependent on our picture of Judaism at the time of the Second Temple. Even a verdict on what in the Jesus traditions is historical and what is not depends on it, regardless of whether we base conclusions on the criterion of difference or its new version, the criterion of historical plausibility. Knowledge of Judaism and knowledge of Jesus are interdependent. The relativizing of knowledge has consequences for the assessment of Jesus. At first sight, for Jesus to be put wholly within Judaism and its renewal movements may have a markedly relativizing effect. But only at first sight: the estimation of Jesus is not lessened by showing that he was a Jew. Rather, one can only evaluate Jesus if one includes Judaism in this evaluation. And that should not be difficult for an unprejudiced approach: throughout its history, but certainly at the time of Jesus, Judaism shows itself to be a fascinating entity with a great inner liveliness. So for Christianity the relationship with the historical Jesus is an abiding approach to Judaism.

5. Tasks

5.1 Jesus in the framework of the prophets of the first century CE

	Content of preaching	Procurator/client prince	Mention in NT
John the Baptist			
Jesus of Nazareth			
The Samaritan prophet			
Theudas			
An anonymous prophet			
The 'Egyptian'			
Jesus son of Ananias			
Prophets at the siege of Jerusalem			

Here are various first century CE prophets. In each case give the most important content of their preaching or the miracle that they announce, the client prince or procurator under which they appeared and, if relevant, the passage(s) in the New Testament where they are mentioned (no solution).

5.2 The 'Teacher of Righteousness' and the 'Wicked Priest'

On the Qumran debate: O. Betz and R. Riesner, *Jesus, Qumran and the Vatican*, London and New York 1994; R. Eisenman, *The Dead Sea Scrolls and the First Christians*, Shaftesbury 1997; J. Fitzmyer, *Responses to 101 Questions on the Dead Sea Scrolls*, New York and London 1993; N. Golb, *Who Wrote the Dead Sea Scrolls?*, London 1995; H. Stegemann, *Essener**. For the Teacher of Righteousness, G. Jeremias, *Der Lehrer der Gerechtigkeit*, StUNT 2, Göttingen 1963; G. Vermes, *The Complete Dead Sea Scrolls in English*, London 1997.

Books which connect the Qumran community with Jesus and early Christianity are particularly popular at present. In particular the founder of the community, the 'Teacher of Righteousness', and his opponents, the 'Liar' and the 'Wicked Priest', stir peoples' imagination. For these are doubtless historical figures of great significance, although their names are never given. Popular (often also pseudo-scholarly) books in recent years have identified John the Baptist or James, the brother of Jesus, who was nicknamed 'the Just', with the 'Teacher of Righteousness'. Jesus and/or Paul are given the roles of 'the Liar' or the 'Wicked

Priest'.[15] A refutation of these untenable theses is impossible and indeed unnecessary within the framework of this book, since in the meanwhile a number of well-founded accounts have appeared (see above). But one should at least have some idea of the texts on which theses of this kind are based. so some extracts from the Habakkuk Commentary (1QpHab) are given below.[16] This work contains the most information about the 'Teacher of Righteousness' and is the most important source for reconstructing the history of the community because of its numerous, though ambiguous, references to contemporary history. The leather scroll, which is very well preserved, is to be dated palaeographically to around 50 BCE. This is a so-called *pesher* (= commentary), a form of interpretation of scripture so far only attested in Qumran, in which a work (usually a prophetic book) is quoted verse by verse and interpreted in terms of the most recent past, the present and the future.

I.16 [. . . Behold the nations and see, marvel and be astonished; for I accomplish a deed in your days, but you will not believe it when] II, 1 (Hab. 1.5). [Interpreted, this concerns] those who were unfaithful together with the Liar, in that they [did] not [listen to the word received by] the Teacher of Righteousness from the mouth of God. And it concerns the unfaithful of the New [Covenant] in that they have not believed in the Covenant of God [and have profaned] His holy Name. And likewise, this saying is to be interpreted [as concerning those who] will be unfaithful at the end of days. They, the men of violence and the breakers of the Covenant, will not believe when they hear all that [is to happen to] the final generation from the Priest [in whose heart] God set [understanding] that he might interpret all the words of His servants the prophets, through whom He foretold all that would happen to His people and [His land . . .

Cf. VII. 4–5 (The) Teacher of Righteousness, to whom God made known all the mysteries of the words of His servants the Prophets.

---

1. What does this tell us about the 'Teacher of Righteousness'?

IX. 8 Because of the blood of men and the violence done to the land, to the city, and to all its inhabitants (Hab. 2.8b).
Interpreted, this concerns the Wicked Priest whom God delivered into the hands of his enemies because of the iniquity committed against the Teacher of Righteous-

---

[15]To quote just two examples: M. Baigent and R. Leigh, *The Dead Sea Scrolls Deception*, London 1991 (for the identification of James with the 'Teacher of Righteousness' and of Paul with the 'Wicked Priest' they refer above all to publications of R. Eisenman); B. Thiering, *Jesus the Man*, New York 1992 (John the Baptist = Teacher of Righteousness'; Jesus = 'Liar' and 'Wicked Priest').

[16]Quoted from Vermes*, 478ff.

ness and the men of his Council, that he might be humbled by means of a destroying scourge, in bitterness of soul, because he had done wickedly to His elect.

XI. 2 Woe to him who causes his neighbours to drink; who pours out his venom to make them drunk that he may gaze on their feasts (Hab. 2.15).

Interpreted, this concerns the Wicked Priest who pursued the Teacher of Righteousness to the house of his exile that he might confuse him with his venomous fury. And at the time appointed for rest, for the Day of Atonement, he appeared before them to confuse them, and to cause them to stumble on the Day of Fasting, their Sabbath of repose . . .

XII. 6 And as for that which He said, *because of the blood of the city and the violence done to the land (Hab. 2.17),* interpreted, *the city* is Jerusalem where the Wicked Priest committed abominable deeds and defiled the Temple of God. *The violence done to the land:* these are the cities of Judah where he robbed the Poor of their possessions . . .

2. (a) What does this tell us about the 'Wicked Priest'? Whom could this be about?

(b) What does the text say about the encounter between the 'Teacher of Righteousness' and the 'Wicked Priest' (what was its purpose, when and where did it take place, what can be concluded from the circumstances)?

3. Because of the vagueness of the information, scholars are still not agreed on the precise time and place of the events and the identity of the two people involved. However, we can exclude the possibility that the 'Teacher of Righteousness' was John the Baptist or James the brother of the Lord. Nor is either Paul or Jesus identical with the 'Liar' and/or the 'Wicked Priest'. On the basis of information given in this section and this task, give arguments!

6

The Chronological Framework
of the Life of Jesus

J. Blinzler, 'Chronologie des NT', *LThK²*, 1958, 422–24; id., *The Trial of Jesus*, Cork 1959; J. Finegan, *Handbook of Biblical Chronology*, Princeton 1964; U. Instinsky, *Das Jahr der Geburt Christi*, Munich 1957; A. Jaubert, *La date de la Cène*, Paris 1957; J. Jeremias, *The Eucharistic Words of Jesus*, London 1966; J.P Meier, *Marginal Jew* 1*, 372–433 (with bibliography); E. Ruckstuhl, *Die Chronologie des letzten Mahles und des Leidens Jesu*, Biblische Beiträge NF 4, Einsiedeln 1963; A.N. Sherwin-White, *Roman Society and Roman Law in the New Testament*, Oxford 1963, 162–71; F.X. Steinmetzer, 'Census', *RAC* 2, 1954, 969–72; A. Strobel, *Ursprung und Geschichte des frühchristlichen Osterkalenders*, TU 121, Berlin 1977; id., 'Weltenjahr, grosse Konjunktion und Messiasstern. Ein themageschichtlicher Überblick', *ANRW* II 20.2, 1987, 988–1187; W. Trilling, *Fragen zur Geschichtlichkeit Jesu*, Düsseldorf 1969.

Introduction

Hardly anything clarifies the rise of Christianity from a minority religion, standing on the periphery of power and history and suspected of superstition, to a state religion and finally a world religion better than the fact that today the Christian reckoning of time is used in wide areas of the world.[1] Its beginning lies in a confessional formula, which Christian accounts of martyrdom hand down with recognizable polemic against ways in which their tormentors reckoned time: 'The blessed Apollonius the ascetic suffered three times according to Roman calculation on the eleventh day before the Calends of May, but according to Asian reckoning in the eighth month, according to our reckoning of time under the Lordship of Jesus Christ, to whom be honour for all eternity.'[2] The Scythian abbot Dionysius Exiguus (sixth century), on whose calculation of the Easter cycles our present reckoning of time rests, based his orientation on the birth of Christ (against Diocletian's era) among other things by saying that the memory of a

---

[1] For all the relevant aspects see H. Maier, *Die christliche Zeitrechnung*, Freiburg, Basel and Vienna 1991.

[2] Quoted from ibid., 17.

godless persecutor of Christians should no longer be preserved. After numerous calendar reforms in the Middle Ages, a uniform Christian calendar was established shortly before the French Revolution. Already at that time one could rightly ask whether this was not the expression of a Christian claim to absoluteness which had become obsolete. But we need not share this claim to regard the established reckoning of time as practical. As we now know, in any case the year zero is a basically arbitrary point: Dionysius miscalculated for some years, and even apart from that, the dates of the life of Jesus can always be defined only approximately, since he does not belong among the rulers in accordance with whose periods in office time was calculated in antiquity. The statement of faith that Jesus Christ is the true Lord of space and time must always be thought of along with the historical fact that he was born, appeared and died so much in the shadow of world history that not a single date in his life can be calculated exactly.

Task and suggested reading

The most important chronological information about the life of Jesus appears in the infancy narratives of Luke and Matthew (Luke 1.5; 2.1f.; Matt. 2.1ff., 19ff.) and in the passion narratives (Mark 14.1f., 12, 17, 26; 15.1, 25, 33, 42; John 13.1f., 30; 18.1, 12f., 28; 19.14, 31–36, 42); further information is contained in Luke 3.1f., 23; John 2.20. What indications do these texts contain for a relative and an absolute chronology of the life of Jesus?

For further help, consult commentaries on the passages concerned.

1. The framework of the history of Jesus (relative chronology)

Before we investigate absolute dates in the life of Jesus (2–4), this first section will bring together what we can determine about the chronological framework of Jesus' activity. The result is largely negative: the Gospels do not allow us to draw any reliable conclusions about the dates which would be needed to establish a relative chronology:

1. The duration of Jesus' activity is unknown; the possibilities extend from a few months to several years. This already led to vigorous discussions in the early church.

- The Synoptic Gospels give no information about the duration of the public activity of Jesus.[3]
- The Gospel of John mentions at least three Passovers (John 2.13; 6.4; 11.55);

---

[3]Some scholars want to infer indirectly that the traditions quoted presuppose at least an overall period of rather more than a year (e.g. the pericope Mark 2.23ff. takes place at harvest time, but probably not directly before the Passover at which Jesus died; Luke 13.1ff. might be referring to a riot among pilgrims to the Passover).

perhaps there is a fourth in John 5.1. This gives the impression that Jesus taught for two or three years. However, the historical value of this Johannine chronology of feasts is very questionable, as it could be a form imposed by the redactor.[4]

2. The chronological presentation of some actions of Jesus is similarly subjected to the theological concerns of the evangelists in shaping their works, and is historically unreliable. Two examples:

- According to the Synoptics, Jesus begins his public activity *after* the imprisonment of John the Baptist (Mark 1.14 par.); according to John, however, the two worked *side by side* for some time (John 3.22f.).
- The cleansing of the temple is put at quite different periods in the activity of Jesus: John puts it at the beginning (John 2.13ff.) and the Synoptic Gospels at the end of his appearance (Mark 11.15ff. par.).

3. Result: only the approximate chronological and geographical outline of the life of Jesus can be established. His public activity began in Galilee and ended in Jerusalem. In the following sections we shall attempt to establish some absolute dates in his life. Here too it will prove that every individual date that is debated is vague, and may be out a few years either way.

2. The year of Jesus' birth

1. Jesus was born under the emperor Augustus (27 BCE–14 CE: Luke 2.1), in all probability in Nazareth (see below 7.1). There is no certain indication of the precise year of his birth. Certainly Matthew and Luke agree in attesting that Jesus was born in the lifetime of Herod the Great (Matt. 2.1ff.; Luke 1.5), i.e. according to Josephus (*Antt.* 17, 167, 213; *BJ* 2, 10) before the spring of 4 BCE. This *terminus ante quem* is certainly probable, but there is some dispute over it, as doubts about the reliability of the chronological information in both the Matthaean and Lukan infancy narratives is justified.

2. In Luke, the way in which the birth of Jesus under Herod (Luke 1.5) is made parallel to the census of Quirinius (2.1f.) causes some difficulties. According to Luke's account, the emperor Augustus ordered a first empire-wide census shortly before Jesus' birth, at the time when Quirinius was governor of Syria. These two pieces of information cannot be harmonized:[5]

---

[4]J. Blinzler, 'Eine Bemerkung zum Geschichtsrahmen des Johannesevangeliums', *Bib* 36, 1955, 20–35, argues for the historical reliability of the Johannine framework.
[5]For the census see F.X. Steinmetzer, 'Census'; H. Braunert, 'Der römische Provinzialzensus und der Schätzungsbericht des Lukas-Evangeliums', *Historia* 6, 1957, 192–241, and the commentaries on Luke 2.1ff.

- Nothing is known from non-Christian sources of an empire-wide levy of taxation under Augustus. Certainly there was a universal tax assessment in the years 74/75 CE. Probably the evangelist transferred this experience to a local census.
- Quirinius was governor of Syria only from 6 CE onwards. So the information that Jesus was born both under his rule *and* under Herod involves a gap of at least ten years![6]
- Quirinius made what was evidently the first Roman census in the course of the incorporation of Judaea into the province of Syria. This was felt by the Jews to be a massive restriction of their freedom and provoked the revolt of Judas of Galilee (5.3.2), which Quirinius probably put down by military force[7] (Josephus, *BJ* 2, 117f.; 7, 253; *Antt*. 17, 355; 18.1ff.).[8]

    Two reactions are possible to this situation in the sources:

- One can reckon that Luke deliberately and falsely harmonized two chronological details which were not compatible.[9]
- One can construct hypotheses to make it possible for the information in Luke to be essentially accurate, i.e. by maintaining that there was a Roman census in the Judaea of Herod the Great in which Quirinius played a role. Here one must always operate with factors which are only postulated and not attested by non-Christian sources. Attempts at a solution vary considerably in detail: we shall report just one. According to Tertullian, the census took place under the governor Sentius Saturnus (9/8–4 BCE)[10] (*Marc*.4,19). Quirinius could have organized this as a special commissioner of the emperor.[11] The lack of any clear evidence is suspicious,[12] and there is the question whether such a restriction by

---

[6]Those holding office during the last years of Herod's reign (10–4 BCE) are known by name, so the possibility that Quirinius was governor earlier can be ruled out.

[7]Luke refers to this rebellion in connection with the census (ἀπογραφή) in Acts 5.37; evidently the same event as in Luke 2.1f. is meant.

[8]Furthermore it would not be usual for each person to have to travel to 'his city' for a census (such a thing happened only in Egypt). Nor was it necessary for women to appear before the officials; they were represented by fathers or husbands. The description of the journey from Nazareth to Bethlehem for the census (Luke 2.3–6) obviously serves to explain why Jesus was born in the city of David.

[9]Schürer, *History*, I*, ii, 138, points to similar grave errors on Luke's part, e.g. that Theudas, whom Luke introduces before Judas the Galilean (Acts 5.36ff.), lived around forty years later (cf. *Antt*. 20, 97f.). But cf. the comments on p. 143 above.

[10]Josephus, *Antt*. 12, 277; 17.89, confirms the governorship (no census).

[11]At any rate epigraphic evidence for a census made by Quirinius as legate of Syria has been found on a tombstone in the free city of Apamea on the Orontes (the so-called Titulus Venutus, *CIL Suppl*. 6687). The conclusion that Quirinius ruled in the East as an oriental chief 'like a vice-emperor' and carried out all the censuses is hardly justified (against Stauffer, *Jesus and His Story*, London 1960, 27–36).

[12]One might ask whether Tertullian's note is an apologetic construction prompted by the inconsistencies in Luke.

the Romans of the political autonomy of the client king Herod in levying taxes is probable.[13]

3. Views on the possibility of evaluating the Matthaean infancy narrative chronologically diverge widely. May we conclude from the report that Herod had all the children under two years of age killed that Jesus must have been born in the year 6 BCE at the latest? Moreover, time and again attempts have been made to identify and date the magi's star (Matt. 2.2, 9f.) with the help of astronomical calculations. There are three possible positions here:

- The possibility of evaluating the Matthaean infancy narrative chronologically is disputed on the basis of form criticism: the narratives of the massacre of the innocents and the wise men are legends the historicity of which cannot be evaluated directly. In Matt. 2 we have a miraculous travelling star, a phenomenon which cannot be described in astronomical categories. Since moreover there are many parallels in the history of religion to a star as the sign of a king's birth, to the persecution of a new-born king and even to the offering of gifts to honour a god who is born of a virgin mother,[14] many exegetes think it absurd to look for a historical nucleus behind Matt. 2.
- The possibility of a historical recollection is considered, as astronomical and astrological speculations were demonstrably widespread in antiquity and we are to assume that real observations underlie the astral prodigies of Hellenistic figures. In that case it is thought possible that there was an approximate coincidence between an unusual stellar phenomenon and the birth of Jesus. Two possibilities above all are discussed: a great conjunction of Jupiter and Saturn in the sign of Pisces observed three times in the year 7 BCE, or a comet which was visible for a lengthy period of time; according to the indications of Chinese astronomers, this was seen in March 5 BCE and in April 4 BCE.[15]
- An exact calculation of the year of Jesus' birth (and if possible the day of his birth) on the basis of astronomical and calendar dates. Such calculations, often made with much perceptiveness, confuse historical possibilities with facts and overestimate what the sources can tell us.

4. Result: it is impossible to discover the year in which Jesus was born, but the last years of the reign of Herod the Great are a possibility.

---

[13]Other hypotheses suggest that Josephus' information should be preferred to that in Luke and that Quirinius's census should be dated to 4 BCE, assuming that Qurinius carried out two censuses, or that a census lasted over several years, from 4 to 6 CE.

[14]Cf. Bultmann, *HST**, 292–4, and the commentaries.

[15]Details are given by Strobel, 'Weltenjahr'; Finegan, *Handbook*, 238–48; and the commentaries.

3. Jesus' public activity

It has already been demonstrated above that no certain statements can be made about the duration of Jesus' public activity. Can we at least date individual episodes? There are some chronological details in the Gospels which sound precise:

1. The synchronism of Luke 3.1 by which the appearance of John the Baptist (and probably also Jesus) is dated is the most precise indication of time in the Gospels: 'In the fifteenth year of the reign of Tiberius Caesar, Pontius Pilate being governor of Judaea . . .' But even it leaves questions open:

- The origin of this information remains unclear; some scholars suppose that it is based on the evangelist's own calculation.
- The period in question cannot be discovered with certainty, since 'the fifteenth year of the reign of Tiberius Caesar' is an ambiguous statement. Initially Tiberius was co-regent for three years with Augustus in the east of the empire (probably from October 12 CE); his sole rule begins in September of the year 14 CE. It is not certain whether the three years of the co-regency in the provinces is included by Luke. Taking various calendars into account, there is a possible time span of from January 26 to April 30.[16] It seems most plausible that Luke is thinking of the year August 28–August 29, but October 27–October 28 is also possible[17] and, by adding the period of the co-regency, 26/27.[18]

2. According to Luke 3.23 Jesus was around thirty years old (ὡσεὶ ἐτῶν τριάκοντα) when he began his public activity. This information is vague in two respects: it contains the indeterminate particle ὡσεί/around and probably alludes to biblical figures like David (II Sam. 5.3), Joseph (Gen. 41.46) and Ezekiel (Ezek. 1.1), who began their public career at the ideal age of thirty. So we must reckon with considerably leeway above and below.

3. In the framework of the cleansing of the temple, which in John occurs at the beginning of Jesus' activity, the Jews state that the temple has now been built forty-six years. According to Josephus (*Antt.* 15, 380), Herod began to build the temple in his eighteenth year, i.e. 20/19 BCE. In that case the Passover mentioned in John 2.13ff. fell in the spring of 27 or 28 CE.[19]

---

[16]Cf. Finegan, *Handbook*, 259–73; on pp.262–9 Finegan gives sixteen different possible datings of the fifteenth year of Tiberius, some of which differ only by a few months, others even by a few years.

[17]Thus, on the basis of the Syrian numbering of regnal years, see C. Cichorius, 'Chronologisches'.

[18]Thus e.g. A. Strobel, *Ursprung*, 84–92.

[19]Unfortunately Josephus gives yet another date: in *BJ* 1, 401, the fifteenth year of Herod is mentioned as the beginning of building; this is often said to be the result of a copyist's error.

4. Result: Jesus' first public appearance falls in the period between 26 and 29 CE.

4. The death of Jesus

4.1 The day of Jesus' death (week and month)

1. All four Gospels agree in saying that Jesus died on a Friday.[20] However, it is disputed whether this Friday was the day of rest of the Passover feast (14 Nisan), as the Gospel of John presupposes, on the 'afternoon' of which the Passover lambs were slaughtered (John 18.28; 19.31) before the Passover feast began with the onset of darkness, or whether the Friday of Jesus' death fell on the first day of the Passover feast (15 Nisan), as the Synoptics report.

2. According to the Synoptic account, Jesus died on the first day of the Passover feast (15 Nisan). The last supper of Jesus and his disciples was a Passover meal, which was held in the night of 14/15 Nisan.[21] Joachim Jeremias above all argued for this chronology (*Eucharistic Words*, 15–88):

- The Gospels agree in attesting that Jesus' last meal took place in Jerusalem (Mark 14.13 par.; John 18.1) and therefore was held in the night (I Cor. 11.23; John 13.10; Mark 14.17). Both these features are unusual, since at the time of the feast the city was so over-full that Jesus had to spend the night outside it, in Bethany,[22] and the main meal was eaten in the late afternoon. Only the Passover meal had to be eaten at night and within the city walls of Jerusalem.
- Wine was drunk at this last meal. That, too, was customary only at ceremonial meals and was prescribed for the Passover meal.
- According to Jeremias the words of interpretation can only be derived from the Passover celebration which is presupposed, at which the elements of the meal were interpreted.

3. According to Johannine chronology, which many exegetes think is historically accurate, the Friday on which Jesus died was the day of rest of the Passover, so in this year the Passover fell on a sabbath (John 19.14, 31).[23] Accordingly the meal

---

[20]Mark 15.42; Matt. 27.62; Luke 23.54; John 19.31, 42.

[21]For full details of the interpretation of Jesus' last supper as a Passover meal see §13.3. In all considerations it should be noted that according to the Jewish division of the day, the new day always begins at sunset.

[22]Mark 11.11, 19; 14.3/Matt. 21.17; 26.6 (Bethany); Luke 21.37 (Mount of Olives).

[23]The Gospel of Peter (2.5) and the Tannaitic tradition bSanh43a similarly attest that Jesus was executed on the eve of the Passover; cf. also Dalman, *Jesus Christ in the Talmud*, 85.

and the foot-washing the evening before did not take place within the framework of a Passover meal (cf. John 13.1). The following factors support this chronology:

- The Passover amnesty attested by all the Gospels makes sense only if the person set free could share in eating the Passover meal.
- Relics of this chronology seem to have been preserved in the Markan introduction to the account of the passion, Mark 14.1f., where it is reported that the high priests and scribes had not wanted to seize and kill Jesus 'at the feast', in case there was a rebellion.
- One may attribute the same consideration to Pilate: an execution at the Passover feast endangered the preservation of public order.

4. In John and the Synoptics theological interests are combined with the chronology presented.

- In the Johannine account Jesus dies at the time when the Passover lambs are being slaughtered in the temple. Probably this is meant to show Jesus as the true Passover lamb (cf. I Cor. 5.7). For the fact that the soldiers do not break Jesus' legs, as they do the legs of those who have been crucified with him, because he is already dead, is understood as a fulfilment of the scriptural saying about the Passover lamb, which requires: 'Not a bone of him shall be broken' (John 19.36; cf. Ex. 12.46, 10 LXX).
- It seems to be a main theological interest of the Synoptic chronology to depict the supper, the memorial meal of the new covenant, as a legitimate replacement of the Passover meal. Thus here Jesus to some degree takes over the function of the new Passover lamb.

5. Of the numerous attempts to harmonize the Johannine and the Synoptic passion chronology, reference will be made here only to that of A. Jaubert (*La date de la Cène*, 1957).[24] She attempted to demonstrate that the apparent contradictions between John and the Synoptics are to be attributed to the use of different calendars. Whereas all the evangelists used the official lunar calendar as a basis, Jesus went by the Essene solar calendar.[25]

- According to the solar calendar of Qumran, the Passover meal always fell on a Tuesday afternoon. According to Jaubert, Jesus will have celebrated the Essene

---

[24]Finegan, *Handbook*, 288–91, documents further attempts at harmonization.
[25]Examples of this calendar are offered by Jubilees, Ethiopian Enoch, CD, 1QS and the calendar fragments from 4Q.

Passover; the Synoptics wrongly transposed this meal to the Thursday because they were going by the official calendar.

- As John rightly reports, Jesus died on the day of rest of the official Passover.
- According to this theory, the chronology of the passion is spread over three days from Tuesday evening to Friday evening; this is supported by some early church sources[26] and allows more time for the hearings and negotiations before the Sanhedrin and Pilate than the compressed Synoptic sequence of supper and arrest in the night and crucifixion as early as the next morning at the third hour.

Against this theory of two calendars and a chronology involving three days it can be argued:[27]

- It is improbable that Jesus would have gone by the Essene calendar. The Jesus tradition shows no interest in questions of the calendar; Jesus seems to have joined in celebrating the official Jewish feasts and to have taught in Jerusalem in the temple, which can hardly be made to agree with the distance which the Essenes kept from the temple in principle.
- All the Gospels agree in a chronology of one day, according to which Jesus was arrested in the night and executed already the next day. This is also easy to conceive of historically, as the Jewish authorities probably did not carry out any formal proceedings against Jesus but merely interrogated him and then denounced him to Pilate, who can hardly have spent long on the case.[28]
- The early church sources which support the three-day chronology are pursuing a quite special interest, namely to provide a historical foundation for Christian fasting on Wednesdays and Fridays.

6. Result: the differences between John and the Synoptics cannot be reconciled. It is hardly possible to make a decision, but the arguments for the Johannine chronology are weightier.

4.2 The year of Jesus' death

1. The chronological framework is marked out by Pilate's time in office: Jesus must have died between 26 and 36 CE (cf. *Antt.* 18, 35, 89). If we add the shortest or longest possible period of Jesus' activity to the earliest or latest possible time of his appearance (26 or 29), we get a time span of between around 27 and 34 CE.

---

[26]SyrDidaskalia 21; Epiphanius, *Pan.* 51.26; Victorinus of Pettau, *de fabr mundi* 3f.
[27]There is an extensive refutation in Blinzler, *Trial*, 149–57.
[28]For full details see §14.

2. A further limitation is possible by calendrical and astronomic calculations, though these cannot give ultimate certainty.[29] In view of what was worked out under 4.1, the question must be: when did the 14 or 15 Nisan fall on a Friday?[30]

- In the years 27 and 34 CE the 15 Nisan was a Friday; these years would thus fit the Synoptic chronology; the same is also true, with less probability, for the year 31.
- The circumstances in the years 30 and 33, on which the 14 Nisan, the Passover day of rest, was a Friday, fit the Johannine christology.

3. Result: the year 30 CE seems most probable as the year in which Jesus died, but other years can by no means be excluded.

5. Summary and hermeneutical reflections

Jesus was born in c.6/4 BCE, probably before the death of Herod I; his public appearance only lasted for a short time at the beginning of Pontius Pilate's period in office (26–36 CE) and he was probably executed at Passover 30 CE. None of his judges could have dreamed that one day time would be calculated according to him. The message that with the figure of Jesus a turning point in history has come about contains this (chronologically inaccurate) calculation of time. It is independent of the question whether Jesus was born in 4 or 6 BCE, and moreover is also independent of the interpretation of him by those who in his lifetime expected everything of him. Jesus' message and the hopes of his contemporaries were eschatological. They longed for the end of time. The Christian reckoning of time which makes Jesus the 'middle of time' is a shift from the significance that Jesus himself gave to his activity. Possibly this new interpretation of Jesus already began in primitive Christianity. The evangelist Luke already follows up his portrayal of Jesus with an account of early church history. As a result Jesus appears as the 'middle of time', as an element of history that can be described historiographically. However, the original interpretation is preserved where something is perceived in Jesus that runs contrary to any time and cannot be calculated chronologically.

---

[29]One factor of uncertainty which present-day, absolutely accurate, astronomical calculations cannot remove is the weather. In antiquity the beginning of the month was fixed by the sighting of the new moon; if it was cloudy, this date could shift.

[30]Cf. Jeremias, *Eucharistic Words*, 37–41; Finegan, *Handbook*, 291–8; Strobel, *Ursprung*, 70–8.

6. Tasks

6.1 The day of Jesus' death

In the discussion about the day of Jesus' death the Johannine chronology (Jesus died on the Passover day of rest) was weighed up against the Synoptic chronology (Jesus died on the first day of the Passover feast). Now it could be claimed that it is just as possible that neither the Gospel of John nor the Synoptic Gospels offer the correct chronology. Jesus could have died on any day in the time before, during or after the festival. What are the objections to this – in terms of method and content?

7

The Geographical and Social Framework
of the Life of Jesus

S. Applebaum, 'Judea as a Roman Province: The Countryside as a Political and Economic Factor', *ANRW* II 8, 1977, 355–96; R.A. Batey, *Jesus and the Forgotten City. New Light on Sepphoris and the Urban World of Jesus*, Grand Rapids 1991; J.R. Charlesworth, *Jesus within Judaism. New Light from Exciting Archaeological Discoveries*, New York, etc. 1988, 103–30; V.C. Corbo, 'Capernaum', *ABD* 1, 866–9; id., *The House of Saint Peter at Capharnaum*, Jerusalem 1969; J.A. Fitzmyer, 'The Languages of Palestine in the First Century A.D.', *CBQ* 32, 1970, 501–31; G. Dalman, *Jesus-Jeshua*, London 1929; id., *Sacred Sites and Ways: Studies in the Topography of the Gospels*, London 1935; D. Fiensy, *The Social History of Palestine in the Herodian Period*, Queenston 1991; S. Freyne, *Galilee from Alexander the Great to Hadrian*, Notre Dame 1980; id., *Galilee, Jesus and the Gospels*, Philadelphia 1988; id., 'Hellenistic/Roman Galilee', *ABD* 2, 895–9; id., 'The Geography, Politics, and Economics of Galilee and the Quest for the Historical Jesus', in *Studying**, 75–121; J. Jeremias, *Jerusalem in the Time of Jesus*, London 1969; L. Levine (ed.), *Ancient Synagogues Revealed*, Jerusalem 1981; id. (ed.), *The Galilee in Late Antiquity*, New York/Jerusalem 1992; R.H. Lightfoot, *Locality and Doctrine in the Gospels*, London 1938; S. Loffreda and V. Tsaferis, 'Capernaum', *NEAEHL* 1, 291–6; E.M. Meyers, E. Netzer and C.L. Meyers, *Sepphoris*, Winona Lake 1992; E.M. Meyers and J.F. Strange, *Archaeology, the Rabbis and Early Christianity*, London 1981; D.E. Oakman, *Jesus and the Economic Questions of His Day*, Lewiston and Queenston 1986; J.J. Rousseau and R. Arav, *Jesus and his World*, Minneapolis and London 1995; S.E. Porter, 'Jesus and the Use of Greek in Galilee', in *Studying**, 123–54; J. McRay, *Archeology and the New Testament*, Grand Rapids 1991; id, 'Gabbatha', *ABD* 2, 861f.; S. Safrai and M. Stern (eds.), *The Jewish People in the First Century. Historical Geography, Political History, Social, Cultural and Religious Life and Institutions*, Compendia Rerum Iudaicarum ad Novum Testamentum 1/1–2, Assen 1974, 1976; J.E. Stambaugh and D.L. Balch, *The Social World of the First Christians*, Philadelphia and London 1986; J.F. Strange, 'Archaeology and the Religion of Judaism in Palestine', *ANRW* II 19.1, 1979, 646–85; id., 'Sepphoris', *ABD* 5, 1090–3; J.F Strange and H. Shanks, 'Has the House Where Jesus Stayed in Capernaum Been Found?', *BAR* 8, 1982, 26–37; id., 'Synagogue Where Jesus Preached Found at Capernaum', *BAR* 9, 1983, 25–31; D. Urman and P V.M. Flesher (eds.), *Ancient Synagogues. Historical Analysis and Archaeological Discovery*, Leiden 1995; Z. Weiss, 'Sepphoris', *NEAEHL* 4, 1324–8; P. Welten, 'Jerusalem I', *TRE* 16, 1987, 590–609.

Introduction

Jesus came from Nazareth in Galilee. When he is emphatically called 'the

Galilean', the term denotes more than mere origin. Thus in modern Jesus research, as a 'Galilean' Jesus is often removed from Judaea, indeed from Judaism generally. This has happened (and still happens) in three variants: ethnic, cultural and sociological.

Jesus the Galilean once meant the 'Aryan Jesus'. In Isa. 8.23 Galilee is called 'Galilee of the Gentiles' – occasion enough for asking whether it was a purely Jewish land. In the time of the National Socialists there was a search for a Jesus who could pass the Aryan regulations: Jesus, the Galilean, was said to have been descended from a non-Jew. This is the thesis of N. Grundmann in his book *Jesus der Galiläer und das Judentum* (1940). This dark antisemitic chapter also belongs to the history of the study of Jesus.

But 'Jesus the Galilean' often also means the Jew who was open to the world, open to Hellenistic influences. Independently of the racist theories sketched out above, one could ask: because of pagan cities in its neighbourhood and within it, was not Galilee much more under Hellenistic influence than Judaea? The assumption of such influence leads to W. Bauer's thesis: 'The Galilean Jesus represented Judaism in a form directed towards the universally human or, if you like, a syncretistically weakened form' ('Jesus der Galiläer' (1927), in *Aufsätze und Kleine Schriften*, Tübingen 1967, 104). Nowadays there is a discussion as to whether Jesus was a kind of Jewish Cynic who was moved by the same motives as the Hellenistic environment of Galilee.[1]

Jesus the Galilean, finally, can mean a prophet untouched by political and social conflicts. According to W.Bauer, there was little explosive material in Galilee for a revolution. 'Therefore Jesus' grandiose self-awareness did not clothe itself in political forms. He in no way felt himself to be a messianic king who would shatter the heathen, but to be the heavenly "Son of Man"' (ibid., 105). S. Freyne in particular has argued that Galilee was structurally different from Judaea (see pp. 173–5 below). In his writing Galilee appears as a pacified world. The consequence is obvious: Jesus must not be interpreted in terms of the social conflict of his time. A sociological interpretation of the crisis of the Jesus movement would be inadmissible.

However, already at this stage it should be emphasized that there are also other approaches to assessing Jesus' Galilean origin and home. Ethnic groups in a threatened marginal situation often attach themselves to the centre of their culture with especial intensity. They have to preserve their identity in the face of the overwhelming presence of foreigners. At the same time they are judged disparagingly at the 'centre': 'No prophet comes from Galilee', argues the Sanhedrin in John 7.52. So was the Galilean origin of Jesus a 'stigma' for the prophet from Nazareth?[2] It is worth asking what the significance of Jesus' Galilean origin and home is for his preaching and his fate.

---

[1] Cf. B. Mack, *The Lost Gospel*, San Francisco 1993.
[2] M.N. Ebertz, *Das Charisma des Gekreuzigten*, Tübingen 1987.

Tasks

Galilee can be divided into three districts: Upper Galilee (with mountains between 600 and 1200 metres high); hilly Lower Galilee (with heights between 100 and 600 metres); and the land around the Sea of Galilee. Here different political territories adjoin one another. By means of the place names mentioned in the Synoptic Gospels and a map determine: 1. in which districts Jesus was active, and 2. which political territories he touched on in so doing (according to the information in the Synoptics).[3]

Suggested reading

The *New Encyclopedia of Archeological Excavations in the Holy Land* (*NEAHL*), published by the Israel Exploration Society in 1993, contains admirable articles on the present state of archaeological investigation of biblical places.

1. Jesus' birthplace: Nazareth

1. Throughout the Gospel tradition *Nazareth* is regarded as Jesus' home town.[4] Mark and John implicitly presuppose that Jesus was also born there.

- In Mark, Jesus is emphatically called 'the Nazarene' (ὁ Ναζαρηνός, Mark 1.24; 10.47; 14.67; 16.6), and Nazareth itself is referred to with the designation 'his ancestral city' (πατρὶς αὐτοῦ, Mark 6.1). Luke avoids the obvious association that he was also born there by calling Nazareth the city in which Jesus grew up (οὗ ἦν τεθραμμένος, Luke 4.16).
- John still indicates that Jesus' origin from Nazareth in Galilee, which was known to all, made the Christian message of his messiahship unbelievable. When Philip told Nathanael that Jesus of Nazareth, the son of Joseph, was the one of whom Moses and the prophets had written, the latter replied, 'Can any good come out of Nazareth?' (John 1.45f.). Nicodemus had to be reprimanded in a similar way: 'Search and you will see that no prophet is to rise from Galilee' (John 7.52).

2. By contrast, the independent traditions Matt. 2 and Luke 2 report that Jesus

---

[3]W. Bösen, *Galiläa als Lebensraum und Wirkungsfeld Jesu*, Freiburg ²1990, provides information on the name Galilee, the extent of the area and the lines of its frontiers, its climate and geophysical conditions.

[4]Cf. Mark 1.9, 24; 10.47; 14.67; 16.6; Matt. 21.11; John 1.45f.; 18.5, 7, etc.

was born in the city of David, in Bethlehem. In both cases the tradition is steeped in belief in the Davidic sonship of Jesus as the Messiah.

- The birth narrative in Luke is shaped with motifs from the Davidic tradition. Joseph comes from the house and family of David (2.4). Because of a tax assessment ordered by the emperor, he went with Mary to the city of David, in which according to the promise of Micah 5.1 the Messiah was to be born (cf. Luke 2.11). Thus the evangelist achieves a close connection between world history and salvation history and at the same time explains how it was that Jesus was not born in Galilee. The shepherd motif also recalls David.
- Matthew also offers elements of the Davidic tradition in the narrative about the veneration by the Magi: the motif of the star perhaps comes from the messianic prophecy in Num. 24.17. As the Magi do not find the 'newborn king of the Jews' at the court of Herod, the scribes investigate where the Messiah was to be born; they come upon Micah 5.1 and send the wise men to the city of David.

Our conclusion must be that Jesus came from Nazareth. The shift of his birthplace to Bethlehem is a result of religious fantasy and imagination: because according to scripture the messiah had to be born in Bethlehem, Jesus' birth is transferred there.

3. In the first century CE Nazareth was a Jewish settlement in the hill country of southern Galilee remote from the trade routes, of so little political and economic importance that it is not mentioned anywhere in ancient sources (OT, Josephus, Talmud). However, archaeological excavations attest a settlement from around 2,000 BCE. At the time of Jesus the inhabitants (estimated at between 50 and 2000), who were predominantly engaged in agriculture, lived in wretched caves, partly natural and partly dug in the chalk; some of these had been extended by a roofed structure at the front. So far there are no archaeological traces of the synagogue mentioned in the Gospels (Mark 6.1; Matt. 13.54; Luke 4.16).

4. Nazareth is only about six kilometres from Sepphoris, a city which had been completely destroyed in 4 BCE by the Syrian legate Quintilius Varus. Herod Antipas (4 BCE–39 BCE) initially constructed it as his capital before he founded Tiberias as a new capital of Galilee around 19 CE. Excavations show that Sepphoris was a flourishing city with a Hellenistic Jewish stamp. Whether the great theatre, which contained 5,000 people, was built under Antipas is disputed. At all events, in his youth Jesus grew up within the sphere of influence of a Hellenistic city.[5] As he was a τέκτων, a craftsman (like his father), he possibly

---

[5]Cf. Batey, *Jesus and the Forgotten City*. Strange, 'Sepphoris'; Meyers et al., *Sepphoris*; and Weiss, 'Sepphoris', provide information about the most recent excavations in Sepphoris.

took part in the construction of Sepphoris. However, that remains a conjecture. Some imagery in his parables and sayings points to an urban world:

- Jesus attacks dishonest piety as 'play-acting' (ὑπόκρισις: Matt. 6.2, 5, 16; Mark 7.6; Luke 13.15).
- The parable of the talents shows familiarity with banking practices (Luke 19.11ff. par.).
- Matt. 5.25f. presupposes that debtors and creditors must be taken a certain distance to judgment. Gabinius (57–77 BCE) set up the court with jurisdiction over Galilee in Sepphoris (*Antt.* 14, 91).

However, this must not be overestimated. The more archaeology demonstrates the significance of Sepphoris, the more eloquent is the silence of the Jesus tradition about this city: Jesus must have known it. But he was not active in it any more than he was active in Tiberias. He turned to country people. It was among them that he found a response.

2. The centre of Jesus' activity: Capernaum

The centre of Jesus' public activity lay on the north shore of the Sea of Galilee: he called his first disciples in Capernaum (Mark 1.16ff.). There he found a welcome in Peter's house (Mark 1.29; 9.33) and probably also a base for an itinerant activity which began from there. Even the Logia source, which contains very few place names, mentions the place twice: in the story of the centurion from Capernaum (Luke 7.1ff.) and in the threat against the cities of Galilee (Luke 10.13–15 par.). According to Matt. 4.12f., Jesus of Nazareth moved to Capernaum. Therefore in this Gospel Capernaum can be called Jesus' 'own city' (Matt. 9.1).

Territorial history and archaeology can illuminate the Jesus traditions associated with Capernaum in a suprising way.

1. Geographically, Capernaum lay on the frontier between the territory of Herod Antipas and that of Philip. That perhaps explains the presence of a detachment of troops (Luke 7.11ff. par.) and a toll station (Mark 2.14) there. However, this toll station would only have made sense for a limited period:[6] there was a frontier here only from 4 to 39 CE. After the deposition of Herod Antipas, his land was divided into other territories. So the tradition of the call of a toll-collector in Capernaum goes back to the earliest period. Possibly Capernaum later lost political significance when it lost its position on the frontier. Josephus

---

[6]For what follows cf. Theissen, *Gospels**, 119f. It should be noted that toll stations were not just on frontiers. Toll collectors collected many taxes, and not just tolls. However, Mark 2.13f. clearly envisages a station on the road outside the town, to collect road and frontier tolls.

mentions the place only twice: once because he was thrown by his horse nearby and broke some bones (*Vita* 403), and the other time as the name of a spring in connection with a description of the countryside (*BJ* 3, 516–524). Although he organized the defence against the Romans in Galilee, for him Capernaum was totally insignificant at that time (i.e. c.66–68). Now and then it is conjectured that this frontier situation was welcome to Jesus because he could escape politically explosive situations so rapidly by moving to another territory. That is possible (cf. Luke 13.31ff.), but cannot be demonstrated.

2. The archaeological discoveries in Capernaum are striking. We hear from the Jesus tradition of a synagogue and a house of Peter's. Possibly both have been located by excavations.[7]

- The *synagogue*, which according to Luke 7.5 was founded by the centurion of Capernaum, is not identical with the fourth/fifth-century synagogue, the remains of which we can now admire in Capernaum. In the first century CE the 'synagogues' (συναγωγαί means assemblies) probably took place largely in rooms in private houses. For of the few first-century synagogues excavated in Palestine (in Gamla, Herodion and Massada), at least two (Herodion and Massada) are secondary, undedicated rooms without specific synagogue architecture.[8] However, it could be that the remains of synagogues visible today stand where there was already a synagogue in the first century (the so-called law of the constancy of holy places). The excavators at least are convinced that they have demonstrated remains of this New Testament synagogue.[9]
- The so-called *house of Peter* is even more important. Remains of dwellings have been found under a splendid octagonal church from the Byzantine period – miserable houses which go back to the first century BCE. Hooks found there indicate that they were lived in by fishermen, between 50 and 100 CE. One of these wretched houses was obviously 'restored'. Its crude walls were decorated and its floor covered with several layers of limestone. In the debris that has fallen down there are symbols and inscriptions which indicate an early Christian house church. Jesus is often mentioned with honorific titles, and the name of Peter also possibly occurs. All this suggests that the house of Peter was located here as early as the first century – possible on the basis of an accurate local tradition. So have we found Peter's house?[10]

---

[7]See Loffreda and Tsaferis, 'Capernaum'.

[8]For the history of the synagogues in Palestine on the basis of literary evidence and archaeological excavations cf. Levine (ed.), *Ancient Synagogues*, and Urman and Flesher, *Ancient Synagogues* (1995), especially the contributions by L.L. Grabbe, 17–26, and P.V.M. Flesher, 27–39.

[9]Cf. Corbo, 'Capernaum', 866–9, and Strange and Shanks, *Synagogue*.

[10]Cf. Corbo, 'House', and the summary in Charlesworth, *Jesus*, 109–15.

3. Jesus' travels: Galilee and the surrounding district

Jesus was an itinerant preacher. The places in which he was active and the routes by which he travelled can no longer be reconstructed. K.L. Schmidt has demonstrated that topographical and chronological information in the Gospels often form part of the redactional framework which the evangelists created when they adopted individual traditions and which is governed by theological, not historiographical interests (*Rahmen**).

- The Markan scheme of an activity initially concentrated completely on Galilee and adjacent areas and a single journey to Jerusalem to the passion is just as governed by theological criteria[11] as is the conception of the Gospel of John, which has several journeys by Jesus to Jerusalem for festivals.[12] It is impossible to be certain whether Jesus was in Jerusalem often, or only once.
- Certainly traditional topographical information is attached to some pericopes, but it is impossible to produce an itinerary of Jesus' journeys from these remains, nor in individual cases can it be decided with certainty whether in the detail of a place there is an accurate historical reminiscence or a local tradition which grew up very early. However, centres of Jesus' preaching can be established: Capernaum (see above) and the countryside around the Lake Gennesaret stand out. Apart from Nazareth and Cana, which lie in Lower Galilee, and Nain, which is as far away as the plain of Jezreel, all the places in the Jesus tradition point to the area around the Sea of Galilee: Capernaum, Magdala, Chorazim, Bethsaida – or the immediate environs of Galilee: to Tyre and Sidon, Caesarea Philippi (Mark 8.27ff.) and the Decapolis (Mark 5.1ff.).

How one estimates conditions in Galilee – especially possible tensions between Gentiles and Jews, town and country, rich and poor, rulers and ruled, is of great importance for an understanding of the preaching of Jesus. Our picture of Jesus changes considerably depending on whether we imagine him in a relatively stable and pacified world or in a society stamped by latent and manifest conflicts.[13]

3.1 Ethnic and cultural tensions between Jews and Gentiles

In Isa. 8.23 (quoted in Matt. 4.14), Galilee is called 'Galilee of the Gentiles'. Isaiah is probably referring to the fact that after the Assyrian conquest of the Northern

---

[11]Cf. Bultmann, *HST**, 337–50; W. Marxsen, *Mark the Evangelist*, Nashville 1969, 54–116.

[12]Most exegetes regard these journeys as a means of redactional shaping.

[13]For more detail on what follows see Theissen, *First Followers**, 31–95.

Kingdom (721 BCE), foreign people were settled there. That is well attested for Samaria, but it can only be inferred for Galilee. At all events the name Galilee of the foreigners (Γαλιλαία ἀλλοφύλων) occurs again during the Maccabean revolt in the second century BCE: the Jewish minority there asks the Jews in Judaea for help (cf. I Macc. 5.14f.). One of the sons of Judas Maccabaeus, Simon, thereupon moves this Jewish minority from Galilee to Judaea (I Macc. 5.21ff.). Galilee was conquered under one of his successors, Aristobulus I (104–103 BCE), and united with Judaea. The land again became Jewish: Ituraeans who had penetrated it could remain, provided that they had themselves circumcised (*Antt.* 13, 318f.). This policy of re-Judaizing must have been successful. When Pompey reorganized Palestine in 63 BCE and 'liberated' the Hellenistic city states which existed there from their Jewish rulers, the Jewish high priest was left with only those areas whose inhabitants were adherents of the temple cult in Jerusalem: only Galilee in addition to Judaea and Peraea. In the time of Jesus, Galilee was without doubt a land with a Jewish stamp.

The vernacular in Palestine was Aramaic, and in Galilee a dialect of Aramaic was spoken. It betrays Peter as a Galilean (Matt. 26.73). In the Talmud the story is told of a Galilean who wanted to buy something in the market in Jerusalem which he calls *amar*. He was mocked: 'You stupid Galilean, do you want something to ride on (donkey = *hamar*). Or something to drink (wine = *hamar*)? Or something for clothing (wool = *'amar*)? Or something for a sacrifice (lamb = *immar*)' (bEr53b, quoted from Vermes, *Jesus**, 52). Evidently the Galileans could not differentiate between the various gutturals of Aramaic. Some Galileans will also have spoken Greek – at least in the two largest cities, Sepphoris and Tiberias. The fact that there was a large theatre in Sepphoris probably presupposes a public with a knowledge of Greek. A toll-collector like Levi must have known a few scraps of Greek in order to be able to exercise his profession. Numerous epigraphical testimonies (coins with Greek inscriptions, papyri, epitaphs and other in- scriptions) attest the wide dissemination of Greek in Palestine. Hebrew was also written in the time of Jesus (Qumran texts, ossuary inscriptions, the Bar Kochba archive) and probably also spoken in certain religious circles.[14]

In what language(s) did Jesus preach? Whereas only a minority believes that he presented his teaching wholly or partly in Hebrew, there is a lively discussion as to whether we should suppose that Jesus spoke Greek. In view of the clearly recognizable way in which Jesus turned to the simple population of the villages and small towns of Galilee (see below 3.2), that seems more improbable.

Only a minority of Gentiles lived in the land. In Tiberias this minority was

---

[14]For the question of the languages of Palestine cf. J.A. Fitzmyer, 'The Languages of Palestine in the First Century AD', *CBQ* 32, 1970, 501–31; Schürer, *History* II*, 20–8, 74–80; Porter, *Use of Greek*; Meyers and Strange, *Archaeology*, 62–91.

murdered at the beginning of the Jewish War (*Vita*, 67) – just as conversely the Jewish minorities were massacred in the neighbouring city republics (e.g. *BJ* 2, 457f., 466ff., 477f., 559ff.). The relationship between Jews and Gentiles has never been totally free of tension. The two stories of an encounter of Jesus with Gentiles, with the Syro-Phoenician woman (cf. Theissen, 'Local Colouring*', 61–80) and the centurion of Capernaum indicate tension between Jews and Gentiles. In both cases we have healings at a distance. A difference always had to be overcome.

3.2 Social and ecological tensions between city and country

In New Testament times Galilee was surrounded by Hellenistic city republics. On the Mediterranean coast it bordered on the cities of Sidon, Tyre and Ptolemais, to the east on the Decapolis, an alliance of around ten Hellenistic city states. In the south, Samaria separated the whole territory from Judaea. Sebaste, the centre of Samaria, was a city with a Hellenistic stamp. In other words, Galilee was a Jewish enclave.

However, Hellenistic culture did not spread only in the region around Galilee. Herod Antipas encouraged this culture in the centre of Galilee itself.[15] He made Sepphoris a flourishing Jewish-Hellenistic city. Tiberias competed with it. The very founding of the city, around 19 CE, was disputed. Two offences against Jewish norms are attested. First of all there was an offence against the commandment regarding cleanness: Tiberias was built on a cemetery (*Antt.* 18, 37ff.). There was also a transgression of the prohibition against images. Herod had his palace in Tiberias decorated with pictures of animals. At the beginning of the Jewish war they were destroyed by rebel groups from Tiberias and by Galileans from the surrounding area, who not least hoped to be able to plunder great treasures (*Vita*, 65f.). Sepphoris, which was supported by the Romans and in the meantime had been conquered by Josephus for the rebels, felt the destructive force of the Galilean country population (*Vita*, 375–80). These events show that the cities with a Hellenistic stamp were in tension with the surrounding Jewish countryside because of their Hellenized culture and the wealth concentrated in them. There were differences of mentality: in times of peace these did not necessarily prevent a lively economic exchange (which is attested by archaeology), but in times of crisis they could lead to quite different reactions. Thus in contrast to the surrounding country, in the Jewish War Sepphoris remained loyal to the Romans and because of this for a while called itself 'city of peace' (Eirenopolis). Given this difference of mentality between the city and the surrounding coun-

---

[15]S. Freyne, 'Geography', 104–21, illuminates the social changes which took place with the flourishing of two Hellenized centres, which concentrated the market, finances and administration there.

tryside, it is quite improbable that in his youth Jesus was decisively stamped by influences from Hellenistic culture through Sepphoris, though there may also be points of contact with e.g. Cynicism (cf. 8.5.3).

So it is not by chance that the Synoptic Jesus tradition is silent about the two largest Galilean cities. Sepphoris, only six kilometres from Nazareth, is no more mentioned than Tiberias, which is only sixteen kilometres from Capernaum. Neither city seems to exist. From this we may conclude that Jesus above all addressed the country population, which lived in the many smaller places.

His journeys into neighbouring Gentile territory are interpreted by Mark and Matthew as an anticipation of the course of the gospel to the Gentiles. Here post-Easter developments are projected into the time before Easter, but not without a basis in the life of the historical Jesus. For Jesus in fact touched on the rural territories of the neighbouring Hellenistic city states, though not to gain Gentiles for his message. Rather, he turned to the Jewish minorities living there. The religious and cultural identity of these minorities had been just as much put in question by the domination of the Hellenistic city culture as the Jewish rural population in Galilee. The social milieu in which Jesus was active can therefore be defined as follows: it is the Jewish population in and around Galilee – above all where the influence of urban Hellenistic culture put Jewish identity in question. Here Jesus found openness to his preaching, whereas he had a distant relationship to the cities.

3.3 Social and economic tensions between rich and poor

As land was the primary source of employment, the social stratification was closely connected with ownership of land. In Galilee in the time of Jesus large landowners and smallholders lived side by side. There is conclusive evidence of large estates on the plain of Jezreel: Queen Berenice had estates in the Kishon defile, where Galilee borders on the city territory of Ptolemais (*Vita*, 119). It is also possible to infer from the Zeno papyri that there were great estates on the plains north of Sepphoris. Josephus attests that the village around Gischala had to pay a contribution from their harvest to the emperor (*Vita*, 71). Further domains are conjectured for the fertile north and north-west shore of the Sea of Galilee.[16]

There is evidence that there were smallholders in Jesus' family. Hegesippus reports on them (in Eusebius, *HE* 3, 20,1–6):

'But there still survived of the family of the Lord the grandsons of Jude, his brother after the flesh, as he was called. These they informed against, as being of the family of David; and the *evocatus* brought them before Domitian Caesar. For he feared the

---

[16]Cf. J. Herz, 'Grossgrundbesitz im Palästina im Zeitalter Jesu', *PJ* 24, 1928, 98–113; Applebaum, 'Judea', 355–96; Bösen, *Galiläa* (n.3), 183ff., and Fiensy, *Social History*, 21–73.

coming of the Christ, as did also Herod. And he asked them if they were of David's line, and they acknowledged it. Then he asked them what possessions they had or what fortune they owned. And they said that between the two of them they had only nine thousand denarii, half belonging to each of them; and this they asserted they had not in money, but only in thirty-nine plethra of land, so valued, from which by their own labours they both paid the taxes and supported themselves. And (he adds) that then they showed also their hands, and put forward the hardness of their bodies and the callosities formed on their hands from continual working, as a proof of personal labour. And that when asked about Christ and the kingdom, its nature and the place and time of its appearing, they tendered the reply that it was not of the world nor earthly, but heavenly and angelic; that it would appear at the end of the world, when he should come in glory and judge the quick and the dead, and render unto every man according to his conduct. And (he says) that after this Domitian in no way condemned them, but despised them as men of no account, let them go free, and by an injunction caused the persecution against the church to cease. And that when released they ruled the churches, inasmuch as they were both martyrs and of the Lord's family; and, when peace was established remained alive until [the time of] Trajan.'

Like these members of Jesus' family, most of his followers will have been active in agriculture. Fishermen and craftsman are the exceptions: that is the reason why we hear of them. Like his father, Jesus was a τέκτων. According to Justin (*Dial.* 88), that is someone who makes ploughs and yokes. Other evidence suggests work with wood and stone, i.e. a craftsman; that will especially come to mind in the case of Palestine, a country short of wood.

Social and economic tensions between poor and rich emerge from the parables. The large landowners were sometimes 'absentee' landowners, and (probably) lived in the city. For them the land was a source of exploitation. The leaseholders who were dependent on them handed over their produce with inner resentment. The parable of the wicked husbandmen documents the rebellious mood among them (Mark 12.1ff.). The Zeno papyri from the third century BCE indicate that conflicts indeed occurred when the produce was collected. The hired labourers with no possessions were in an even worse situation than the leaseholders; they were recruited for the harvest by the hour and the day. Matthew 20.1–16 depicts their situation. They could only 'murmur' against unjust treatment. They were dependent on the favours of the rich.[17] The conditions in which the free small-holders mentioned above lived were also grim. They were always threatened with debt if a scant harvest was insufficient to provide for the taxes, the support of the

---

[17]Cf. C. Hezser, *Lohnmetaphorik und Arbeitswelt in Mt 20, 1–16. Das Gleichnis von den Arbeitern im Weinberg im Rahmen rabbinischer Lohngleichnisse*, NTOA 15, Fribourg, CH and Göttingen 1990, 50–97.

family and the seed for the next year. Two parables presuppose imprisonment for debt (Matt. 5.25f.; 18.23ff.) – an indication that Palestine had come under the influence of alien law, since Jewish law knew no imprisonment for debt, but only temporary slavery for debt. Smallholders who lost their land sank to becoming leaseholders, emigrated, or swelled the ranks of the hired labourers, beggars and robbers at the bottom of the social hierarchy.

Given the difficulty of finding meaningful comparative economic data in antiquity, it is hard to judge whether all this is 'normal' or whether an especially oppressive situation had developed in Palestine at that time. Certainly the message 'Blessed are you poor, for yours is the kingdom of God!' found ready ears – those of people who were indeed poor and longed for a revolution in their situation.

3.4 Social and political tensions between rulers and ruled

Herodian client princes reigned in Galilee in the first century. The Romans resorted to this indirect form of rule where developments did not yet allow them to entrust the land to semi-autonomous city republics and put them under Roman administration. After the death of Herod I, the land was divided out between his three sons. Archelaus (4 BCE–6 CE) received the territory of Judaea and Samaria, which belonged together geographically but was disparate in religious terms; Philip (4 BCE–34 CE) received a territory in the north-east of Palestine which was predominantly settled by non-Jews (Gaulanitis, Trachonitis and Batanaea). Only Herod Antipas (4 BCE–39 CE) ruled over two ethnically homogenous territories, though they were geographically separate, Galilee and Peraea. The division of the land was a model application of the slogan 'Divide and rule'. However, this plan failed in Judaea and Samaria. After only ten years Archelaus was deposed because of complaints from the Samaritans and the Jews. After that Roman prefects, including Pontius Pilate, ruled his territory, from 26 to 36 CE.

Sean Freyne has put forward the thesis that Galilee was essentially freer from tension than Judaea.[18] He claims that this is shown, among other things, by the unusually long reign of Herod Antipas (4 BCE–39 CE). He argues that the resistance movement developed above all in Judaea, where the Romans ruled directly. By contrast, in Galilee and Peraea the Herodian client princes could mitigate the worst effects of Roman oppression. Here we shall go on to mention the indications that the political situation was unstable in Galilee also – despite the long reign of Antipas.

---

[18]Most pointedly in the *Anchor Bible Dictionary* article 'Hellenistic Roman Galilee', 89ff., cf. in more detail *Galilee*, 1980, 68–71, 208–47; *Galilee*, 1988, 135–75, 190–8. However, Freyne reckons with increasing tensions in Galilee, at times especially in the economic sphere. These he sees closely connected with the links between town and country, which became greater as a result of the construction of the centres of Sepphoris and Tiberias ('Geography', 104ff.).

- In the so-called Robber War after the death of Herod I, Galilee was one of the centres of unrest in Palestine. A Judas, son of Hezekiah, from Gamala, captured the arsenal in Sepphoris at that time. The city was drawn into the rebellion. The Syrian legate Quintilius Varus had it destroyed completely, and the inhabitants sold into slavery (*BJ* 2, 56, 68; *Antt.* 17, 271f., 289). No other Jewish city was treated with such cruelty at that time. Did not the tetrarch Antipas, who had been appointed by the Romans, *a priori* encounter opposition here?
- According to Strabo (*Geogr.* XVI 2, 46 = *GLAJJ* no.115), Antipas and Philip, the two sons of Herod, were put in danger when Archelaus was deposed in 6 CE. They had considerable difficulty in returning home and preserving their tetrarchies.
- When Judaea and Samaria went over to direct Roman administration after the deposition of Archelaus, a Judas who came from Galilee (and who is perhaps identical with the Judas of Gamala mentioned above) agitated against the payment of tax to the Romans (*BJ* 2, 118; *Antt.* 18, 4–10, 23).[19] Granted, the area of unrest is not Galilee, but the roots of the unrest point in that direction. That is shown by the following events: a generation later, after 44 CE, Galilee, too, was brought under direct Roman rule. Now two sons of Judas of Galilee appeared, Simon and Jacob, and were crucified by the Roman procurator Tiberius Alexander (*Antt.* 20, 102). If they delivered the same message as their father – namely that tax must not be paid to the Romans – after 44 CE, this message was topical only in Galilee. For only there was there a move to the direct payment of tax to the Romans. Furthermore, Luke wrongly regards this unrest under the sons of Judas as the real 'revolt' of Judas of Galilee. Therefore he can date him after Theudas, who appeared c.44/45 (Acts 5.36f.).
- In the period between 6 CE and c.30 CE there was an (a new) edition of the apocalyptic writing *Assumptio Mosis* in Palestine. Part of it which goes back to this time prophesies that the sons of Herod will rule for a shorter time than their fathers (*AssMos* 6, 7). As Archelaus had already been deposed, and Philip was ruling in remote areas, the interest of the work is focussed entirely on Herod Antipas: if prophecies throughout the land are fulfilled, he will soon disappear, and it would certainly not be possible to describe the political situation as 'stable'.
- Such expectations were fostered not only by writings but also by an influential prophet. In the 20s, in the territory of Herod Antipas, John the Baptist appeared and criticized the marital policy of the ruler. According to Josephus, Antipas had him executed in order to prevent an open revolt (*Antt.* 18,118).
- We do not know what lay behind the bloodbath caused, according to Luke

---

[19]See above, p. 154 and §5.3.2.

13.1ff., by Pilate among the Galilean pilgrims. But we may presuppose that Pilate was convinced that they threatened public order.

- Among the resistance fighters in the Jewish War two groups in particular emerged: on the one hand were the 'Galileans' around John of Gischala, who defended the outermost precinct of the temple, and on the other hand were the Zealots, who occupied the temple itself. As has rightly been emphasized for some time, these 'Zealots' appeared only with the Jewish War (i.e. from 66 CE) – and only in Jerusalem itself. But they were already in existence. For the period before 66 CE there is certain evidence only of one 'Zealot' : Simon the Zealot, a follower of Jesus, who went around with him through Galilee (cf. Luke 6.15; Acts 1.13). He probably came from Galilee. Possibly there is epigraphical evidence for a 'Zealot' buried in Rome: his home town is given as Sepphoris in Galilee (*CIJ*, no.362). So the prehistory of the most radical resistance groups leads to Galilee.
- Herod Antipas probably did not feel secure. This is indicated by his transfer of the capital from Sepphoris to Tiberias: the foundation of Tiberias is associated with the attempt to settle a population there which was loyal to him (*Antt.* 18, 37f.). Probably he also gathered there the armed force for which he was later denounced to the Romans and as a result of which he lost his kingdom: it is improbable that he needed these weapons only as a protection against external enemies (cf. *Antt.* 18, 240–256).

All in all, it can hardly be said that the political situation in Galilee was peaceful. Even the long reign of Herod Antipas is no evidence for this. His father Herod I had reigned just as long. Nevertheless, during his reign powerful tensions built up which exploded powerfully immediately after his death.

The conclusion must be that Galilee was riven by deep structural tensions, by tensions between Jews and Gentiles, town and country, rich and poor, rulers and ruled. When Jesus proclaimed here a turning point in everything, one which was beginning in the present, he found an audience which had reasons to long for a change. Nevertheless, the interpretation of the emergence of Jesus as a response to a structurally conditioned crisis is only one side of the coin. It is also true that in the midst of a period characterized crises (from the unrest after the death of Herod to the Jewish War), the time of Jesus was relatively peaceful. Tacitus' verdict on Palestine at that time was *sub Tiberio quies* ('There was peace under Tiberius', *Hist.* 5, 9, 2). The situation in Judaea could have been relatively free of tension by comparison with that in Galilee. But that mainly explains why Jesus' response to the crises of his time could be so 'peaceful'. The rule of God which he was proclaimed was already a hidden reality in the present: i.e. it could (for the moment) co-exist with the rule of the Romans and the Herodians.

3.5 The religious character of Galilee

The situation of Galilee as an enclave within non-Jewish territory, its geographical separation from the religious centre of Jerusalem and its various forms of government by contrast with Judaea up to 44 CE, could hardly fail to have consequences for the religious institutions of the Galileans. However, it is difficult to produce an adequate picture of the religious mentality in Galilee, not least because of the perspective of the sources with their one-sidedly Judaean stamp. The rabbinic literature, composed by Judaean scholars who after 135 – the defeat in the third Jewish War – had been forcibly resettled in Galilee, depicts the Galileans as uneducated in religion, as ignorant in ritual questions, indeed as despisers of the Torah. This view is already evident in the exclamation attributed to Johanan ben Zakkai (c.70), 'Galilee, Galilee, you hate the Torah!',[20] which was handed down by the teachers of the second century. It expresses the frustration of the rabbinic movement, which was emerging with an increasing claim to absoluteness, in the face of the resistance of the Galilean population to assimilation with it. However, a similar attitude to Galilee is already attested for the first century in the Gospel of John. The Jewish leaders react with annoyance to Jesus' public proclamation in Jerusalem. It is impossible for the Christ to come from Galilee; only the accursed people 'which knows nothing of the law' can believe that (John 7.41–49). When Nicodemus, himself a scribe, offers protection to Jesus, he is asked, 'Are you perhaps also from Galilee?' (John 7.52). Here too it is clear that this is an outsider's perspective, that of members of the religious elite in the capital, which had an interest in preserving their moral and religious superiority.

Unfortunately there are only a few sources which allow insights into the religious self-understanding of the Jews of Galilee. Their relationship to the central religious entities of temple, land and Torah can only be sketched out – with diminishing degrees of clarity.

1. *The temple.* A marked temple piety on the part of the Galileans, a close tie between the inhabitants of the periphery and the centre of the Jewish cult together with the institutions affiliated with it, can be clearly inferred from the sources. Even the critical attitudes towards the temple expressed by individuals (see below 4.1) are based on this foundation of intensive commitment to the temple (since they show the opposite of indifference towards it). The payment of the annual temple tax of half a shekel, which was collected centrally in places in Galilee, though evidently on a voluntary basis (cf. Matt. 17.24–27), in keeping with the Sadducean halakah against the Pharisaic tradition, and the colllection of tithes were external expressions of this. In addition there were the regular pilgrimages to one of the three annual pilgrimage festivals (cf. Luke 2.41f.).[21] In times of crisis

---

[20] jShab 15d, quoted in Vermes, *Jesus**, 57.
[21] For pilgrimage see S. Safrai, in S. Safrai and M. Stern (eds.), *Jewish People* I/1, 1291–201; I/2, 898–904; S. Freyne, *Galilee* (1980), 259–304; Jeremias, *Jerusalem*, 58–84.

people remained loyal to the temple: in 39 CE, Judaeans and Galileans in Tiberias protested *en masse* against the threat of the desecration of their capital by the erection of a statue of Caligula in the temple (*Antt.* 18, 269ff., see pp. 181f. below). When Josephus organized resistance in Galilee at the beginning of the Jewish War, he referred successfully to his priestly descent, as his account in the *Vita* shows throughout, and appealed to the loyalty of the population to Jerusalem, which he calls 'our all-powerful city', and the temple, 'the sanctuary which is common to us all'. The refusal of help by Sepphoris remained a notable exception (*Vita,* 348).

2. *The land.* The Galilean love of freedom is emphasized both by Josephus (e.g. *BJ* 3,41) and by the rabbis (jKet 29b); the resistance fighters from Galilee have already been mentioned above (3.4). The theological foundation of this attitude lies in the traditional faith that God alone is the owner of the land, which his people occupy. Therefore it is a religious concern that they should occupy it in the way required by God and without any 'pollution' by alien peoples, their customs and their gods. This concern was possibly felt particularly strongly because of the proximity of Gentile territories to Galilee. Nor can a certain 'nationalism' even on the part of Jesus be overlooked, as is shown by the comparison of a Gentile child with a dog (Mark 7.27); statements like Matt. 10.5; or the vivid symbolic action attributed to Jesus in Mark 5.11–13 – the drowning of a herd of swine. Although the kingdom of God which Jesus proclaimed has universalistic features, as a matter of course it is to constitute itself in the Promised Land as a restoration of the people of twelve tribes.

3. *The Torah.* The majority of the population in Galilee was Jewish, and Jewish life in all its forms is based on the Torah. The question was not whether, but how, this should be implemented. The Pharisaic halakah (which had stricter and more liberal expressions) was hardly predominant in Galilee in the time of Jesus. It seems, rather, that the Pharisaic movement in the first century spread only slowly, with powerful support from Jerusalem, in this area which had been reconquered at one point from the domination of the Sadducees. Nothing is known of any Essenes in Galilee. So what was the teaching of the leaders of the synagogues and the scribes who read the Torah aloud, translated it and interpreted it on the sabbath in the numerous synagogues of Galilee? Apart from Jesus of Nazareth, only isolated names of Galilean scribes have been handed down from the first century. They include Judas of Galilee (see above, 5.3.2), whose teaching had radical political consequences. In addition mention might be made of a certain Eleazar, who taught at the court of Izates, the king of Adiabene (*Antt.* 20, 43), and Joses the Galilean among the scholars of Jabneh. Generally speaking, virtually nothing is known about the Galilean halakah. May we assume that it was adapted to the requirements of agricultural life (just as the Pharisaic halakah corresponded more to an urban milieu)? The sources only give us isolated insights: thus Josephus, *Vita,* 74–76, relates that during a food shortage the

Jewish inhabitants of Caesarea Philippi were prepared to pay a quite excessive price for oil from Gischala prepared by Jews, 'so that they did not need to transgress their precepts by using Greek oil in an emergency'. As already mentioned, the country people in Tiberias destroyed pictures of animals in Herod's palace, and the protests of John the Baptist against the liberal manipulation of the marriage laws by the Herodians met with a response among the people. All this points to the fact that in Galilee, which had the bad reputation of being lawless, there was a great concern to observe the Torah. On the other hand, Josephus accuses the Zealot leader John of Gischala of having eaten food prohibited by the Law, and having violated the traditional rules of cleanness (*BJ* 7, 264). Perhaps this only means that he followed other (Galilean) halakoth. The rabbis, too, accused Galilean sages of laxity over the laws relating to cleanness (Vermes, *Jesus**, 54). This is possibly also an explanation of the liberal attitude of Jesus towards the food laws and questions of cleanness.

Unfortunately the Galilean context of the teaching of Jesus has largely been concealed by the later transformation of Galilean piety by the rabbis on the one hand and Christianity on the other. However, there is no doubt that at the time of Jesus Galilee was an area with a Jewish stamp, that its inhabitants were dependent on the temple, were interested in the distinction between the peoples and followed the precepts of the Torah in their oral and written form, presumably in specifically local versions.

4. The place of the passion: Jerusalem

At the end of his life, Jesus and his disciples went to Jerusalem for the Passover feast. They went there through Peraea (Mark 10.1). We can only understand Luke to imagine a direct way through Samaria (Luke 9.51f.). But because Jesus is rejected in a Samaritan village, Luke too only speaks of a journey 'between Samaria and Galilee' (Luke 17.11). If by 'Galilee' Luke means the territory under the rule of Herod Antipas (including Peraea), he could have envisaged a route along the frontiers of Samaria through Peraea. In fact a route through Peraea is more probable. That was the only way of avoiding setting foot on non-Jewish land.

4.1 The structural opposition of city and country in the passion narrative

Jesus made an appearance in Jerusalem with a prophecy against the temple which he underlined by the typically prophetic symbolic action of the cleansing of the temple. This prophecy and the fate of Jesus become more understandable if we reckon with an opposition between capital and country, between Jerusalem and Galilee (cf. Theissen, 'Tempelweissagung').

- A comparable opposition to the temple is also rooted elsewhere in the country. The Old Testament prophets who prophesied against the temple came from the country: Micah from Moresheth (1.1), Uriah from Kiriath-jearim (Jer. 26.20), Jeremiah from Anathoth (1.1). In the New Testament period Jesus comes from Nazareth in Galilee. After him another Jesus, son of Ananias, prophesied against Jerusalem and the temple before the Jewish war (c.62–60, *BJ* 6, 300ff., quoted p. 470 below). He too came from the country (τῶν ἰδιωτῶν ἄγροικος = one of the uneducated country people). Furthermore, in 35 CE a prophet appeared in Samaria who claimed to have found the vanished temple vessels on Mount Gerizim, doubtless to demonstrate the sanctity of this place over against the Jerusalem temple. He gathered his followers in a small village (*Antt.* 18, 85–9).
- Jesus made a public appearance with his prophecy against the temple during a pilgrimage festival, i.e. while the city of Jerusalem was full of country people. We know that in this situation there were often tensions between the people of Jerusalem and the country population (e.g. *Antt.* 20, 106f., 225). That is why the Roman prefect was in Jerusalem during such festivals. It should be noted that Jesus was greeted with 'Hosianna' not by the population of the city but by the pilgrims who went to Jerusalem with him (Mark 11.8f.). The population of the city was more provoked by his prophecy against the temple. Its own economic existence was too closely connected with the temple: criticism of the temple had necessarily to be understood as criticism of the foundation of its existence. The temple aristocracy will not have found it difficult to stir up part of the ordinary population of the city against Jesus. Thus the change from 'Hosianna' to 'Crucify him!' could be more understandable if there was a historical recollection behind the Barabbas scene.

4.2   Places and routes in the passion narrative

It is not only the major structural tensions which play a role in the passion. The passion narrative gives us more indication than other traditions of the routes taken by Jesus and the places where he was. Even for K.L. Schmidt, the details of place in it had to be evaluated differently from the preceding pericopes. Only here did he find (rightly) an old consecutive account. Doubtless specific memories were associated with place names like Bethphage and Bethany (Mark 11.1), the Mount of Olives (13.3), Gethsemane (14.32), Pilate's Praetorium (15.16), Golgotha (15.22), and probably also the tomb of Jesus. Now and again we can bring to life what has been handed down to us by literary sources through archaeological insights.

(a) The *Praetorium* was the seat of office of the Roman prefects. It was often sought in the citadel Antonia, directly adjoining the north-east corner of the temple. However, the prefect probably resided in Herod's palace, which lies in the west of the Jerusalem of that time (near the present-day Jaffa Gate, cf. Philo, *LegGai* 299; Josephus, *BJ* 2, 301). This palace was at a higher level than the temple. From it one could check what was going on there. The *lithostroton* (something like marble floor) before the Praetorium is called Gabbatha in Aramaic (John 19.13), which means 'height', 'high place'.[22] As the whole of the former west city was called the 'upper city' (cf. *BJ* 1, 402; *Antt.* 15, 318) and a stone platform was found there in the 1970s, the 'high place' should probably also be located in it.[23] From there Jesus was led to the place of execution after his condemnation – and therefore not by what is now called the Via Dolorosa.

(b) According to the unanimous report of all the Gospels the place of execution, *Golgotha*, lay outside the city. Such an unclean place was only conceivable there. However, in Byzantine times the present-day Church of the Sepulchre, within which Golgotha and the tomb of Jesus[24] have traditionally been located, clearly lay in the centre of the city. Still, there is much to indicate that in the 30s the land lay outside the city walls. Josephus reports that Jerusalem had three walls (*BJ* 5, 136, 142ff.). The latest, so-called third, wall was only begun by Herod Agrippa I between 41 and 44, and then had to be left incomplete because of Roman intervention. So the course of the second wall, which in the time of Jesus was the outer city wall, is decisive. However, this is difficult to reconstruct. If the Church of the Sepulchre proves to lie outside it, the location of Golgotha within it could preserve an old tradition going back to the time before 70. If, however, the Church of the Sepulchre proves to lie within this wall, this is a later localization – say from the period after the Jewish War, when Jerusalem had been destroyed. Today archaeologists tend to put Golgotha outside the second wall.[25] In that case, in New Testament times Golgotha would have been a rock towering around thirteen metres above the rocky ground – the remains of an abandoned quarry from the pre-exilic period. Jesus could have been crucified there.

5. Hermeneutical reflections

Jesus' way led from Nazareth in Lower Galilee to the Sea of Galilee, from the northern bank of which he began his lively activity as an itinerant preacher. The centre of his itinerant activity was Capernaum. From here he addressed the Jewish countryfolk in and around Galilee who had been made unsure of their identity by

---

[22]Unfortunately this interpretation is not completely certain. Scholars have also thought of *gabbaḥta* ('bald forehead', thus Dalman, *Jesus-Jeshua*, 14).

[23]Cf. McRay, 'Gabbatha'; id., *Archeology*, 114–19.

[24]For the tomb of Jesus see below §15.2.5.3.

[25]Cf. Charlesworth, *Jesus*, 123f.; E. Otto, *Jerusalem – die Geschichte der heiligen Stadt von den Anfängen bis zur Kreuzfahrerzeit*, Stuttgart 1980, 153–9; P. Welten, 'Jerusalem I', *TRE* 16, 1987, 598.

Hellenistic city culture. His preaching addressed a world full of social, economic and political tensions. When he went up to Jerusalem he became a victim of these tensions. Traces of his way can be illuminated by territorial history. Sometimes they also become tangible in archaeological remains: Peter's house in Capernaum, the Praetorium in Jerusalem, and Golgotha as a place of execution could derive from traditions extending back into the first century with which remains visible today were possibly originally associated.

The connection of the historical Jesus with archaeological discoveries and the material reality of the land of Israel which is still tangible today continue to exert a special fascination. Archaeological material preserved by chance is more authentic than sources written from a particular perspective. However, when it comes to the archaeology of the New Testament we also have the human, all-too-human longing for 'a tangible form of transcendence'. Therefore it is impossible to emphasize enough how provisional all our conclusions are. New datings, new discoveries and new interpretations can put in question at any time the picture which has been formed. We must expect that a very early stage the places and routes of Jesus were identified with particular places and remains – probably as early as the first century C E. Such identifications need not be accurate – but they need not necessarily be false either.

Historical criticism of the Gospels and the story of Jesus has long neglected archaeology and territorial history (at least in Germany). Both have often been left to conservative scholars – or American exegetes. This is a regrettable development, since neither archaeology or territorial history are the problem, but the uncritical evaluation of them. The fascination exerted by Galilee and Jerusalem is quite untouched by this: whether the supposed 'traces' of the history of Jesus that we come across are spurious or authentic, he certainly worked somewhere in this small area. Somewhere on the north shore of the 'Sea of Galilee' he called people to follow him. Somewhere in Jerusalem he was condemned. Somewhere – not just in a place invented by religious fantasy – he was tortured and executed. The word was made flesh. That means it was located, was dated, and was in the thick of the conflicts and tensions of its time. But who was this Jesus? So far we have described only the context of his activity. In the next section we shall turn to his person.

6. Tasks

6.1 Petronius and the resistance against the statue of the emperor

In the year 39 Gaius Caligula ordered that his statue was to be set up in the Jerusalem temple and instructed Petronius, the legate of Syria, to implement this, if need be by armed force. After a first unsuccessful intervention by the

Jews in Ptolemais, Petronius established himself in Tiberias (*Antt.* 18, 261–268).

'The Jews, though they regarded the risk involved in war with the Romans as great, yet adjudged the risk of transgressing the law to be far greater. As before, many tens of thousands faced Petronius on his arrival at Tiberias. They brought him by no means to put them under such constraint nor to pollute the city by setting up a statue . . . And falling on their faces and baring their throats they declared that they were ready to be slain. They continued to make their supplications for forty days. Furthermore, they neglected their fields, and that, too, though it was time to sow the seed. For they showed a stubborn determination and readiness to die rather than to see the image erected. At this juncture Aristobulus, the brother of king Agrippa, together with Helkias the Elder and other most powerful members of this house, together with the civic leaders, appeared before Petronius and appealed to him, since he saw the deep feeling of the people, not to incite them to desperation but to write to Gaius telling how incurable was their opposition to receiving the statue and how they had left their fields to sit protesting, and that they did not choose war, since they could not fight a way, but would be glad to die sooner than transgress their customs. Let him point out that, since the land was unsown, there would be a harvest of banditry, because the requirement of tribute could not be met. Petronius dismissed the assembly of the Jews and requested those in authority to attend to agricultural matters and to conciliate the people with optimistic propaganda' (*Antt.*18, 269–274, 284).

Which of the structural tensions in Galilee discussed above are suggested by this account of events in Tiberias in 39 CE?

6.2 *Jesus and Sepphoris*

Discuss the two following attempts at an explanation by W. Bösen and S. Freyne for the silence of the Jesus tradition on Sepphoris, the 'glory of all Galilee' (*Antt.* 18, 27):

W. Bösen justifies his thesis that 'the Gospels are silent because Jesus was active in Sepphoris but without success' (*Galiläa als Lebensraum und Wirkungsfeld Jesu*, Freiburg [2]1990, 74) as follows:

Geographical and theological considerations suggest that Jesus was active in Sepphoris. Galilee is a small area, which can be crossed from any point in two or three days . . . There was no real reason for keeping away from [the former capital]. On the contrary, if he [Jesus] wanted to remain faithful . . . to himself and his programme, he could not by-pass it. Certainly at that time the countryside was full of the 'lost', the poor and the sick, the social and religious outcasts; but the majority of them gathered . . . in the cities. So Sepphoris too . . . was overwhelmed by the poor in the broadest sense. To by-pass them without having confronted them with the new offer of salvation robbed Jesus of credibility – and not just in the eyes of the people of Sepphoris (74). In view of the failures of Jesus that are reported in Nazareth (Mark 6.1–6a), Capernaum, Chorazim and Bethsaida (Matt. 11.20ff./Luke 10.12ff.), Bösen states: 'Thus a failure of Jesus in Sepphoris would not be out of the ordinary; given its proximity to Nazareth it was a probability' (75).

By contrast, S.Freyne, *Galilee,* 1988, 139f., thinks that Jesus deliberately avoided Sepphoris and Tiberias:

It is quite unlikely that Jesus' avoidance of either place [Sepphoris or Tiberias] was due to religious attitudes, in view of his apparent disregard for the purity laws and his openness to the Gentiles, even to the point of travelling in their territory – something that is well attested in all the narratives. His avoidance of the main Herodian centres of Galilee is best explained, therefore, in the light of a conscious decision not to become directly embroiled in a confrontation with Herodian power. The fate of the Baptist must surely have been a salutary warning (see Matt.14.13). It was possible to conduct an itinerant ministry adopting the strategy of avoiding open confrontation.

Task on 5–7: Chronological survey[26]

Put the following names in the spaces in the table on the next page: Agrippa I, Archelaus, Claudius, Gaius Caligula, Herod I (the Great), Herod Antipas, Octavian Augustus, Philip, Pilate, Quintilius Varus, Quirinius, Tiberius.

---

[26]Cf. Bösen, *Galiläa* (n.3), 150.

Roman emperors	Rulers in Palestine			Syrian legates
	(5) .... (37–4)			– – – – – – –
				(11) ....
(1)	Judaea	Galilee and	Gaulanitis +	(6–3)
(−27 – +14)	and	Peraea	Trachonitis	– – – – – – –
	Samaria		+ Batanaea	
	(6)	(9)	(10)	
	(−4 – +6)	(−4 – +39)	(−4 – +34)	
	Roman			– – – – – – –
	prefects			(12) ....
				(6–11)
(2)				– – – – – – –
(14–37)				
	(7)			
	(26–36)			
(3)				
(37–41)				
(4)		(8)		
(41–54)		(39/41–44)		

Part Three: The Activity and Preaching of Jesus

8

Jesus as a Charismatic: Jesus and his Social Relationships

A.I. Baumgarten, 'The Name of the Pharisees', *JBL* 102, 1983, 411–28; M.J. Borg, *Conflict, Holiness and Politics in the Teaching of Jesus*, New York and Toronto 1984; M. Hengel, *The Charismatic Leader and His Followers*, Edinburgh 1981; B.L. Mack, *A Myth of Innocence*, Philadelphia 1988, 172–207; J. Neusner, *The Rabbinic Traditions about the Pharisees before 70* (3 vols.), Leiden 1971; id., *From Politics to Piety. The Emergence of Pharisaic Judaism*, New York 1973, ²1979; R. Otto, *The Idea of the Holy*, Oxford 1923; id., *The Kingdom of God and the Son of Man*, London ²1943; A.J. Saldarini, *Pharisees, Scribes and Sadducees in Palestinian Society*, Edinburgh 1989; G. Theissen, 'Die Erforschung der synoptischen Tradition seit R. Bultmann', in R. Bultmann, *Geschichte der Synoptischen Tradition*, FRLANT 21, ¹⁰1995, 409–52; G. Vermes, *Jesus**; M.Weber, *Economy and Society*, London 1956.

Introduction

The question 'Who was Jesus?' has often been put by New Testament scholars as a question of Jesus' messianic self-awareness. They have asked whether he understood himself as Messiah, Son of Man or Son of God. Only gradually has Jesus research detached itself from the question of Jesus' self-awareness. It has become more important to describe the nature of his authority. Here the term 'charisma', taken from the history of religion, has been used; it is independent of christological titles, and its application to Jesus does not presuppose any Christian confession, but can be accepted by the Christian confession. For it corresponds to biblical statements: Jesus' 'charisma' is none other than the 'authority' (ἐξουσία) attributed to him, which is evident in his teaching and his miracles (Mark 1.21ff.).[1] Charisma is an irrational power of attracting other persons. A

---

[1] The word χάρισμα itself appears only in Paul; there it denotes the supernatural competence of human beings, e.g. in prophecy, the power to perform miracles and teaching (cf. Rom. 12.6; I Cor. 12.30).

charismatic is dependent on the expectations, hopes and assent of the persons around him. Charisma always develops in interactions. So Jesus' charisma is also evident in his relation to his family, to his teachers, to his disciples, male and female, to the crowd and to his opponents. Through these relationships the sources indicate a mass of things. They are a key to understanding Jesus.

Tasks: 1. The term 'charisma'

Taking up distinctions made by the church lawyer Rudolf Sohm, Max Weber introduced 'charisma' and 'charismatic authority' into sociology as categories of analysis. The orientation of his definition on earliest Christian history can in part be clearly recognized. Illustrate individual elements of Max Weber's definition below by means of the story of Jesus which can be seen in the Gospels, and his relations to his disciples and followers among the people.

> 'The term "charisma" will be applied to a certain quality of an individual personality by virtue of which he is considered extraordinary and treated as endowed with supernatural, superhuman, or a least specifically exceptional powers and qualities. These are such as are not accessible to the ordinary person, but are regarded as of divine origin or as exemplary, and on the basis of them the individual concerned is treated as a "leader" . . . It is recognition on the part of those subject to authority which is decisive for the validity of charisma. This recognition is freely given and guaranteed by what is held to be a proof, originally always a miracle, and consists in devotion to the corresponding revelation, hero worship, or absolute trust in the leader . . . Psychologically this recognition is a matter of complete personal devotion to the possessor of the quality, arising out of enthusiasm, or of despair and hope . . . The administrative staff of a charismatic leader does not consist of "officials" . . . It is rather chosen in terms of the charismatic qualities of its members. The prophet has his disciples; the warlord his bodyguard; the leader, generally, his agents. There is no such thing as appointment or dismissal . . . only a call at the instance of the leader on the basis of the charismatic qualification of those he summons . . . There is no such thing as a salary or a benefice. Disciples or followers tend to live primarily in a communistic relationship with their leader on means which have been provided by voluntary gifts. There are no established administrative organs. In their place are agents who have been provided with charismatic authority by their chief or who possess charisma of their own. There is no system of formal rules, of abstract legal principles, and hence no process of rational judicial deicison oriented to them. But equally there is no legal wisdom oriented to judicial precedent. Formally concrete judgments are newly created from case to case and are originally regarded as divine judgments and revelations. From a substantive point of view, every charismatic authority would have to subscribe to the proposition, "It is written.. but I say unto you . . ."' (*Economy and Society*, 241–3).

2. John the Baptist (Antt. 18, 116–119)

Jesus' public appearance begins with his baptism by John the Baptist. In addition to the Christian accounts there is also a report on this by Josephus (*Antt.* 18, 116–19).

Τισὶ δὲ τῶν Ἰουδαίων ἐδόκει ὀλωλέναι τὸν Ἡρώδου στρατὸν ὑπὸ τοῦ θεοῦ καὶ μάλα δικαίως τιννυμένου κατὰ ποινὴν Ἰωάννου τοῦ ἐπικαλουμένου βαπτιστοῦ.

κτείνει γὰρ δὴ τοῦτον Ἡρώδης ἀγαθὸν ἄνδρα καὶ τοῖς Ἰουδαίοις κελεύοντα ἀρετὴν ἐπασκοῦσιν καὶ τὰ πρὸς ἀλλήλους δικαιοσύνῃ καὶ πρὸς τὸν θεὸν εὐσεβείᾳ χρωμένοις βαπτισμῷ συνιέναι·

οὕτω γὰρ δὴ καὶ τὴν βάπτισιν ἀποδεκτὴν αὐτῷ φανεῖσθαι μὴ ἐπί τινων ἁμαρτάδων παραιτήσει χρωμένων, ἀλλ᾽ ἐφ᾽ ἁγνείᾳ τοῦ σώματος, ἅτε δὴ καὶ τῆς ψυχῆς δικαιοσύνῃ προεκκεκαθαρμένης.

καὶ τῶν ἄλλων συστρεφομένων, καὶ γὰρ ἤρθησαν ἐπὶ πλεῖστον τῇ ἀκροάσει τῶν λόγων, δείσας Ἡρώδης τὸ ἐπὶ τοσόνδε πιθανὸν αὐτοῦ τοῖς ἀνθρώποις μὴ ἐπὶ στάσει τινὶ φέροι, πάντα γὰρ ἐῴκεσαν συμβουλῇ τῇ ἐκείνου πράξοντες, πολὺ κρεῖττον ἡγεῖται πρίν τι νεώτερον ἐξ αὐτοῦ γενέσθαι προλαβὼν ἀνελεῖν τοῦ μεταβολῆς γενομένης [μὴ] εἰς πράγματα ἐμπεσὼν μετανοεῖν.

καὶ ὁ μὲν ὑποψίᾳ τῇ Ἡρώδου δέσμιος εἰς τὸν Μαχαιροῦντα πεμφθεὶς τὸ προειρημένον φρούριον ταύτῃ κτίννυται. τοῖς δὲ Ἰουδαίοις δόξα ἐπὶ τιμωρίᾳ τῇ ἐκείνου τὸν ὄλεθρον ἐπὶ τῷ στρατεύματι γενέσθαι τοῦ θεοῦ κακῶσαι Ἡρώδην θέλοντος.

But to some of the Jews the destruction of Herod's army seemed to be divine vengeance, and certainly a just vengeance, for his treatment of John, surnamed the Baptist.

For Herod had put him to death, though he was a good man and had exhorted the Jews to lead righteous lives, to practise justice towards their fellows and piety towards God, and so doing to join in baptism.[2]

In his view this was a necessary preliminary if baptism was to be acceptable to God. They must not employ it to gain pardon for whatever sins they committed, but as a consecration of the body implying that the soul was already thoroughly cleansed by right behaviour.

When others[3] too joined the crowds about him, because they were aroused to the highest degree by his sermons, Herod became alarmed. Eloquence that had so great an effect on mankind might lead to some form of sedition, for it looked as if they would be guided by John in everything that they did. Herod decided therefore that it would be much better to strike first and be rid of him before his work led to an upheaval, get involved in a difficult situation and see his mistake.

John, because of Herod's suspicions, was brought in chains to Machaerus, the stronghold we have previously mentioned, and there put to death, yet the verdict of the Jews was that the destruction visited upon Herod's army was a vindication of John, since God saw fit to inflict such a blow on Herod.

Collect common features and differences between this and the earliest Christian accounts of John the Baptist (esp. Mark 1.2–9; Matt. 3.1–12; Luke 3.1–18; Mark 6.14–29).

1. Phases in the history of research

1.1 The description of Jesus as a charismatic in the phenomenology of religion

When at the beginning of this century the quest for the historical Jesus found itself at a dead end and Jesus' messianic self-awareness was exposed to doubts (W. Wrede, see p. 6 above), Rudolf Otto sought a new approach to the mystery of his person (an approach which today is forgotten): he attributed the figure of Jesus to a widespread religious 'type'. In his book *The Idea of the Holy*, which appeared in 1917, he defined Jesus as 'holiness made manifest', which can be affirmed with inner evidence on the basis of a religious *a priori* in human beings (ibid., 159). In his *The Kingdom of God and the Son of Man* he reconstructed Jesus' self-understanding in the light of eschatology, and by it understood the presence of the kingdom of God in Jesus as his charisma: 'The kingdom of God, as already at hand, is δύναμις, the inbreaking miraculous power of the transcendent. As such, it is operative in the exorcistic δύναμις of its messenger, and equally in the ἐξουσία

---

[2]The syntax of this sentence allows different interpretations and translations: only the infinitive construction βαπτισμῷ συνιέναι is directly dependent on the participle κελεύοντα ('. . .a good man who asked the Jews to come to baptism'). The two participial constructions which have been inserted, ἀρετὴν ἐπασκοῦσιν and τὰ πρὸς ἀλλήλους . . . χρωμένοις, relate to τοῖς Ἰουδαίοις and there is a dispute as to their meaning. Does Josephus mean that only the Jews who (always) practised virtue, justice and piety should come to baptism? J.P. Meier, 'John the Baptist in Josephus: Philology and Exegesis', *JBL* 111, 1992, 225–37, also argues, from the analogy with the following sentence, in which the participial construction with the same verb χράομαι is clearly a qualification, that the particples are conditional: 'he was a good man and [simply] bade the Jews to join in baptism, PROVIDED THAT they were cultivating virute and practising justice toward one another and piety toward God' (233). But can one think an interpretation intended which only follows retrospectively from the next clause? A purely paratactical solution is also grammatically possible, thus e.g. J. Ernst, *Johannes der Täufer und Jesus von Nazareth*, BSt 63, Neukirchen 1972, 253 n.1: 'He admonished the Jews to be assiduous in virtue and to practise justice to one another and piety towards God and to come to baptism.'

[3]It is not clear precisely whom Josephus means here. Possibly he wants to say that while the preaching of John the Baptist first of all addressed only people who practised justice and piety, soon others (with less good motives) also flocked to him.

and the χαρίς of his preaching. He himself is "charisma"' (334). For Otto, Jesus is himself 'primarily charismatic' (ibid., 344).[4]

1.2 The search for an 'implicit christology' in kerygma theology

In the kerygma theology of Rudolf Bultmann, Otto's question about the authority of the historical Jesus was initially suppressed. The significance of Jesus for (primitive) Christian belief was said to be based entirely on what God had done in Jesus, not in what Jesus might have said and done. Only with Bultmann's pupils did the question of a pre-dogmatic interpretation of Jesus' authority return as the question of an 'implicit christology'. In contrast to the phenomenological approach, however, no attempt was made to find this 'authority' of the historical Jesus by giving him a place in the history of religion (and understanding him as the representative of a generally widespread type). Rather, his claim to authority was worked out by a historical contrast with Judaism. The way in which Günther Bornkamm defines Jesus' 'immediacy' by a threefold comparison with the surrounding world is characteristic of this approach.[5]

- The first comparison relates to the understanding of history: the Judaism of the time looked back on a great past in which God had acted and expected a new action of God in the end-time. Thus it lived in a 'world between past and future . . . so strongly identified with the one and with the other that, according to Jewish faith, the immediate present is practically non-existent' (*Jesus**, 54). By contrast, for Jesus God is again directly at work, and the expected end-time already begins now with him.
- The second comparison relates to the foundation of authority: Jewish scribes appealed to their exegesis of scripture. 'Jesus' teaching, on the other hand, never consists merely in the interpretation of an authoritatively given sacred text . . . The reality of God and the authority of his will are always directly present, and are fulfilled in him. There is nothing in contemporary Judaism which corresponds to the immediacy with which he teaches' (ibid., 57).
- Closely connected with this is a third comparison in the understanding of the law: the rabbis had put a 'hedge round the Torah' in order to protect it by casuistic individual definitions. But such casuistry gives the law an equlibrium. It threatens to detach itself from God and 'has become man's real authority. It no longer leads to a meeting with God but rather threatens to frustrate it' (ibid.,

---

[4]H. Windisch, 'Jesus und der Geist nach synoptischer Überlieferung' (1928), in S.J. Case (ed.), *Studies in Early Christianity*, New York and London 1928, 209–36, similarly already saw in the accounts of Jesus' authority a 'pre-dogmatic interpretation of Jesus' (226) and in it a 'continuity' with post-Easter belief in Christ (236).

[5]Cf. Theissen, 'Theologie'*, 319–25.

104). By contrast, Jesus speaks of God's will in wisdom-style admonitions, which are directly evident.

With his central interpretative category of immediacy, Bornkamm grasped an important point, namely Jesus' charisma. Charisma is characterized by being able to gain direct influence without mediation and support from authorities, institutions and traditions that have already been recognized. The contrast with Judaism is problematical. Of course the Judaism of the time also knew experiences of a direct presence of God – in particular in the Torah, in the Temple or in creation.[6] Of course there were Jewish charismatics before, alongside and after Jesus.

1.3 Jesus as a charismatic within the 'third quest'

With the retreat of kerygma theology at the end of the 1960s, the interpretative category of 'charisma' also returned to the study of Jesus, often enriched by the sociological recognition that charismatic rule is a special form alongside traditionalist and bureaucratic rule (M. Weber).[7] It is based on the presence of a quality in the person of the charismatic which goes beyond the everyday, and which shows itself among other things in miracles and revelations. Three characteristics of the charismatic in particular play a role in the new Jesus research: his authority, his miracles and his readiness for conflict.

1. First of all the relationship of Jesus to his disciples was investigated as a form of charismatic authority. In his 1968 book on *The Charismatic Leader and his Followers*, Martin Hengel showed that despite all the analogies, say, with the sign prophets, the authority of Jesus breaks through the most elementary norms like piety towards one dead father (cf. Matt. 8.21). In his 'Wandering Radicals' (1973) and *The First Followers of Jesus* (1977), G. Theissen put Jesus in a circle of 'itinerant charismatics' who practised a deviant life-style, but gained influence in the communities precisely with this radical life-style.

2. At the same time, in *Jesus the Jew* (1973), the Jewish historian G. Vermes interpreted Jesus as a charismatic miraculous healer. He put him in a charismatic milieu in the Judaism of the time which he saw represented by Honi the Circle-Drawer in the first century BCE and the Galilean Hanina ben Dosa in the first century CE. Hanina ben Dosa also combined miracles and wisdom teaching – at the same time being uninterested in legal regulations. That makes him comparable to Jesus.

3. Jesus' conflict with his environment became a separate theme. In *Conflict, Holiness and Politics in the Teaching of Jesus* (1984), M.J. Borg speaks of Jesus as a 'holy man'. Jesus used his holiness to replace the fundamental paradigm of

---

[6]For further forms of the quest for an 'implicit christology' see above, § 1.1.4.
[7]Cf. Weber, *Economy and Society*, 241–8.

Jewish life, that of a holiness orientated on Torah and temple (an exclusive holiness), with the paradigm of a mercy which includes the sinner. M.N. Ebertz went one stage further in his book on 'The Charisma of the Crucified' which was published in 1987: he sees that charisma does not lead to conflict but arises through the voluntary acceptance of conflicts. Precisely by self-stigmatizing, i.e. by the demonstrative adoption of outsider roles scorned by social morality, new values and orientations are established in society. Here he depicts Jesus in sharp contrast with his environment. Helmut Mödritzer corrected this view with his investigation 'Stigma and Charisma in the New Testament and its Environment', by pointing to the phenomenon of self-stigmatization not only in Jesus but also in John the Baptist, in Paul and Ignatius and attributing it to his Jewish environment (including the Jewish martyr theology).

2. The sources: the apophthegms

Certainly the whole of the Jesus tradition attests that Jesus was a charismatic, but this is true in a particular way for the apophthegms. We find these in two variants: one the one hand as sayings of Jesus within a narrative framework and on the other as didactic sayings and disputes. They show Jesus interacting with followers and opponents. Here they bring out his charisma, for charisma is a relational phenomenon: an irrational power of attraction which fascinates followers and provokes opponents.

Other terms have been proposed as a replacement for 'apophthegms' (literally statements).[8] One is 'chria' (from $\chi\rho\epsilon\acute{\iota}\alpha$ = usage) – a statement which can be 'used' in life and which is depicted in particular 'usage situations'. Alongside this one can find the term 'paradigm', from the presumed function in primitive Christian preaching, and the general term 'pronouncement story'. The established term apophthegm has the advantage that in contrast to sentences, apophthegms are always attributed only to particular persons and thus the connection between the saying and the person of Jesus is emphasized. Moreover apophthegms occur with and without narrative frameworks. That too fits the earliest Christian tradition, in which for example the saying about the prophet in his fatherland occurs in Mark 6.1–5 with a narrative framework but in Thomas 31 without.

Three considerations tell against a direct historical use of the apophthegms: 1. the possibility that some of Jesus' conversation partners were made specific, e.g. as 'Pharisees', only at a secondary stage; 2. that some situations narrated represent 'ideal scenes' – thus at best are typical situations from the life of Jesus;

---

[8]Cf. Theissen, 'Erforschung', 433–5.

and finally, 3. that of these some scenes and debates had their place in the post-Easter community. Its discussions and conflicts with the world around have possibly been projected back on to the life of Jesus, especially where the criticism is not of the conduct of Jesus but that of his disciples (Mark 2.23ff.; 7.1ff.).

However, there is no doubt that the apopthegms in particular contain something of Jesus' character. The very appearance of this form suggests that. There is no earlier evidence of it in Judaism. Its closest analogies are pagan Hellenistic apophthegms and chrias. Through the stimulus of these, at that time an analogous form arose in Judaism which we later also find in the rabbinic writings and in the early church (in the so-called *Apophthegmata Patrum*).[9] Here we always have the literary shaping of the impression made by charismatic figures. Even if some of the apophthegms should not prove to come from Jesus, it is significant that the historical Jesus also attracted these statements and points – furthermore, that his appearance was an impulse also to relate apophthegms in Judaism, short anecdotal narratives about people who differed pointedly from their environment and had an unmistakable profile.

The content of many apophthegms also suggests a historical background. In the earliest Gospel we find them collected in three groups: Mark 2.1–3.6 in Galilee, 10.1–45 on a journey from Galilee to Jerusalem, 12.13–44 in Jerusalem. In the first cycle we are struck by general images by which Jesus illustrates his authority: he is like a 'physician' (2.17), comparable to a 'bridegroom' (2.19). As 'Son of Man' he is an example of any human being who has authority over the sabbath (2.27f.): here the term Son of Man is hardly an honorific title. Granted, the authority of Jesus is meant to be shown everywhere, but the post-Easter christology is not yet activated for it.

In the disputes and didactic sayings on the way to Jerusalem the free way in which 'scripture' is handled is noteworthy. In the pericope about divorce, two biblical passages (Deut. 24.1ff. and the creation account) are played off against each other. In the story of the rich young man Jesus goes beyond the commandments of the Decalogue. The young man is to do even more than they require. On the other hand, in the same pericope Jesus does not allow himself to be called 'good', because no one is good but God: this juxtaposition of the relativization of the person of Jesus with his distance from God and a demand by Jesus which goes beyond God's commandment has hardly been invented as a secondary development.

In the disputes in Jerusalem, the theocentric argumentation is striking: the requirement to pay tax to Caesar is contrasted only with God's demand; the hope of resurrection is grounded only in faith in God: in faith in the God of Abraham,

---

[9]Cf. C. Hezser, 'Die Verwendung der hellenistischen Gattung Chrie im frühen Christentum und Judentum', *JSJ* 27.4, 1996, 371–439.

Isaac and Jacob; the supreme commandment is seen in the way in which love of God and neighbour is put above the cult. Here nothing is said and thought which could not be thought in Judaism, nor is there anything which could not have provoked a dispute in it.

The apophthegms certainly tell us something about the historical Jesus – and about Jesus in his relationships. Here five different relationships can be distinguished, each of which will be investigated independently in the following sections; here statements which are not contained in apophthegms will also be evaluated.

1. The relation to his family
   The kinsfolk of Jesus and the 'family of God' (Mark 3.20f., 31–35 par.)
   The rejection in Nazareth (Mark 6.1–6a par.)
   The beatitude on Jesus' mother (Luke 11.27f.).
2. The relationship to John the Baptist
   John the Baptist's question (Matt. 11.2–6 par.)
   Jesus on John the Baptist (Matt. 11.7–15 par.)
   The peevish children (Matt. 11.16–19 par.)
   The question of authority (Mark 11.27–33).
3. The relations to his disciples and settled followers
   The call narratives (Mark 1.16–18, 19–20; 2.14ff.)
   The unsuccessful call of the rich man (Mark 10.17–27 par.)
   The reward of discipleship (Mark 10.28–31 par.)
   The sending out of the disciples (Mark 6.7–13 par.)
   Peter's messianic confession (Mark 8.27–33 par.)
   The conversation with the sons of Zebedee (Mark 10.35–45 par.)
   Traditions about the 'family of God'.
4. The relations to women in his environment
   The anointing at Bethany (Mark 14.3–9 par.)
   Mary and Martha (Luke 10.38–42)
   The women who followed Jesus (Luke 8.1–3; Mark 15.40f.: summary notices)
   The anointing by a woman in Simon's house (Luke 7.36–50).
5. The relations of Jesus with his opponents:
   with Pharisees (Mark 2.23–3.6; 7.1ff.; 10.2–9; 12.13–17 par.)
   with Sadducees (Mark 12.18–27 par.)
   with the scribes (Mark 12.28–34, 35–37, 38–40 par.)
   with the Herodians (Mark 3.4–6; 12.13–17).

3. Jesus and his family

Charisma is the presence of something extraordinary: by contrast, the family controls everyday life. No wonder that charismatics come into conflict with their families. According to Mark 3.20f., 31–35 Jesus' relatives thought that he was mad; according to John 7.5, his brothers did not believe in him. Nevertheless, later many members of the family appear in the Christian community. Jesus' mother was a member of the earliest community in Jerusalem (Acts 1.14). James was one of the witnesses to the resurrection (I Cor. 15.7; Gospel of the Hebrews, frag.7). In the 40s he became leader of the Jerusalem community. Other brothers of the Lord (cf. Acts 1.14; I Cor. 9.5) were similarly Christians.

We cannot say much about the religious stamp of the family. The nomenclature is orientated on the biblical history, cf. Joseph, Mary (= Miriam), Jacob, Joses (= Joseph), Judah, Simon (Mark 6.3). Jesus (another form of Joshua) also fits this. That indicates a pious family. Some scholars think that it was close to Pharisaism, since later James the brother of the Lord achieved such a reputation among the strict observers of the Law that they protested against his execution (62 CE) by a Sadducean high priest (*Antt.* 20, 200, quoted on p. 470 below).

For an assessment of Jesus as a charismatic the decisive question would be whether his family claimed to be descended from David or not – in other words whether as well as his personal charisma Jesus had a 'Gentile charisma' by virtue of dynastic origin, which played a role in the expectations attached to him. Two possibilities are conceivable; it is impossible to decide between them with certainty.

3.1 Jesus as a member of the house of David

If Jesus' family claimed descent from David, it would be understandable why in Rom. 1.3f. Paul takes Jesus' Davidic descent for granted. There he quotes a formula that he has taken over, which is earlier than the period of the composition of Romans (c. 55 CE). Paul knew members of Jesus' family personally (Gal. 1.19). Moreover it would be understandable why many members of the family joined the Christian community (and quickly enjoyed great respect in it): it must have been plausible that the Messiah should have come from their family. It is also hard to imagine how they could have claimed an inappropriate descent, although this could bring them into difficulties, as is shown by the interrogation of the descendants of Jesus by Domitian (Eusebius, *HE* 3, 20, 1–6, quoted above, pp. 171f.). But how are we then to explain the two passages which deny any Davidic sonship for Jesus?

- In Mark 12.35–37 par., reference is made to the contradiction that in Ps.110.1

David calls the Messiah his 'Lord'. Thus the Messiah cannot be Son of David (for David is regarded as the author of the psalm). If this pericope has a historical nucleus, Jesus – presupposing his Davidic descent – would have declined the title Messiah for himself. As a member of the house of David according to Mark 12.35ff. he could not be the Messiah expected by the scribes.

- In John 7.42 it is objected to the messiahship of Jesus that the Messiah has to be a descendant of David and come from Bethlehem. It is presupposed that Jesus fills neither of these two conditions. Anyone who wants to defend the Davidic consciousness of the family of Jesus as historical must presuppose that it was largely unknown or deliberately denied by the family. There would be reasons for this: as long as other dynasties ruled, it was certainly not opportune to emphasize one's membership of a royal house. That would have meant danger, especially in the Jewish War.

The divergent genealogies of Jesus (Matt. 1.1ff.; Luke 3.23ff.) need not be an argument against a Davidic family consciousness. They only show that it was not derived from such genealogies, but is already presupposed by them. There were correctly kept genealogies only in the circles of priests and levites. But non-priestly families also had their family traditions (cf. the lists of those returning from the exile in Ezra. 2.1ff.; 8.1ff.; Neh. 7.6ff.; 11.3ff.; also Phil.3.5).

3.2 Jesus' Davidic sonship as a messianic postulate

Another theory says that Jesus was not a member of the house of David.[10] Only when he was venerated as Messiah after Easter was it postulated that he must also be a member of the house of David. John 7.42 and Mark 12.35–37 would then be echoes of the awareness that this was not the case: John 7.42 as an echo of Jewish criticism, which played off the lack of Davidic sonship against the messiahship of Jesus; Mark 12.35ff. as a Christian answer to this criticism: according to Ps. 110.1 the Messiah need not be a son of David. The criticism collapsed.

The weak point of this theory lies in the fact that it has to explain how already in the first generation after Jesus, the family could develop a Davidic consciousness without this encountering contradiction. Could it have taken over this conviction with the post-Easter belief in Jesus as Messiah? This assumption, too, causes some difficulties:

- As PsSol 17 shows, the expectation of a transcendent earthly Messiah is associated with the term 'Son of David'. But after the cross and resurrection

---

[10]This view has been given the most thorough grounding by C. Burger, *Jesus als Davidssohn,* FRLANT 98, Göttingen 1970.

[11]For details see Theissen, *Gospels**, 81–96.

this expectation could be taken up only in transformed and broken form and be regarded as fulfilled in Jesus.

- The postulate that the Messiah has to be a son of David was not insuperable: other messianic pretenders from the New Testament period were not required to be members of the house of David. Bar Kochba, the messiah of the Third Jewish War in 132–135 CE, was not a member of the house of David.
- The moment that belief in the virgin birth became established, the belief that Joseph came from the house of David (Luke 1.27; 2.4) was superseded. It is doubtless older: it already occurs in Paul (Rom. 1.3f.) and in the earliest Gospel (Mark 10.47f.).

So we must reckon with the possibility that the family of Jesus in fact claimed Davidic descent. The expectation that the Messiah must come from a Davidic family could have played a role in the environment of Jesus and in the origin of his 'charisma'.

4. Jesus and his teacher: John the Baptist

J.D. Crossan, *Jesus**, 227–64; P.W. Hollenbach, 'The Conversion of Jesus: From Jesus the Baptizer to Jesus the Healer', *ANR W* II 25.1, 1982, 196–219; C.H. Kraeling, *John the Baptist*, New York 1951; J.P. Meier, *Marginal Jew 2**, 19–233; C.H.H. Scobie, *John the Baptist*, London 1964; R.L. Webb, *John the Baptizer and Prophet: A Socio-Historical Study*, JSNT SS 62, Sheffield 1991; id., 'John the Baptist and His Relationship to Jesus', in *Studying**, 179–229; W. Wink, *John the Baptist in the Gospel Tradition*, Cambridge 1968.

The primitive Christian tradition combines the bestowal of a personal charisma on Jesus with baptism. This is one of the most certain pieces of information in the life of Jesus. It shows that Jesus assented to John the Baptist's preaching – i.e. to belief in the imminent judgment and the need for conversion and baptism for the forgiveness of sins. However, in his own preaching he sets different accents from those of John. This requires a historical explanation. We shall discuss in succession the life, teaching and self-understanding of John the Baptist as this can be reconstructed from the sources about him (4.1) and the primitive Christian tradition of the baptism of Jesus (4.2), compare John the Baptist with Jesus (4.3), and attempt to explain the 'development' of Jesus beyond his beginnings as a follower of John (4.4).

4.1 The sources about John the Baptist and their evaluation

Various independent sources report on John the Baptist. The picture of John the Baptist in the Gospels and Acts has many facets – in individual points these are even contradictory – and draws on a variety of currents of tradition (Mark, Q,

Matt⁵, Luke⁵, John and Thomas). Common to the Christian sources is the fact that they are interested in John the Baptist only in the context of the history of Jesus and therefore depict him markedly in relation to Jesus. They start from the superiority of Jesus even where an unprejudiced assessment of the facts seems to exclude it (e.g. in the baptism of Jesus by John). The account by Josephus in *Antt.* 18, 116–119 (quoted above, p.187) is completely free of this tendency, but by the use of key words which derive from the Hellenistic Roman philosophical discussion it arouses the suspicion that Josephus could have tailored his account of John the Baptist heavily to the values and expectations of his time. Accordingly, we can arrive at a reliable picture only through the critical interpretation of all the sources at our disposal. Therefore we shall first go on to list the source material in a table and then discuss what historical conclusions can be drawn from them.

4.1.1   *The place of John the Baptist in history*

	Josephus, *Antt.* 18, 116–19	Earliest Christian sources
1. Origin	Josephus is silent about the origin and background of John the Baptist	Luke 1: priestly origin
2. Date of appearance and death	Execution at the fortress of Machaerus (in Peraea) an indefinite time before the defeat of Herod Antipas by the Nabataean king Aretas in 36 CE.	Luke 3.1: John the Baptist appeared in the fifteenth year of the emperor Tiberius = c.28 CE. Execution in Galilee (probably Tiberias) during the time that Jesus was still working there (Mark 6.14–16, 17ff.) = probably before spring 30 CE.
3. The motive for the execution	*Political motive*: the execution takes place on the orders of Herod Antipas for fear of a rebellion caused by John the Baptist on the basis of pure suspicion. It remains unclear to what these fears in fact related.	*Private motive*: according to Mark 6.17ff., the execution of John the Baptist takes place on the instructions of Herodias and is a reaction to John's criticism of her marriage to Herod Antipas. The political context of the execution remains unclear.

On the basis of these sources the contemporary framework can be reconstructed as follows.

1. Only the birth legend in Luke 1 relates the *birth and family background* of John the Baptist; the evangelist has skilfully composed this as a parallel to the miraculous conception and birth of Jesus and interwoven it with that. It is meant to show John as a messenger of God and forerunner of the Messiah from his mother's womb. It has little historical value – regardless of the origin of the traditions from the circle of John the Baptist's disciples which are used; such an origin has often been conjectured but can hardly be demonstrated with certainty.

• The *origin from a priestly family* could be historical. The distance from the temple and the rivalry with it, which in any case are indicated by the baptism, would then have to be interpreted as a deliberate break by a member of the priesthood with the rites of purification and forgiveness of sins rooted there.
• The note about John's *life in the wilderness* to the day of his appearance before Israel (Luke 1.80) is a redactional link by the evangelist. For want of further information he makes John grow up where he finally made his public appearance, namely in the wilderness (cf. Mark 1.4/Luke 3.2). This literary function and the vagueness of the verse do not allow us to conjecture that John was brought up among the Essenes.

Certainly points of contact between John and the Essenes cannot be denied: their distance from the temple and life in the wilderness (with reference to Isa. 40.3); conversion as the central theological category in connection with immersions. But all this points more towards a rival prophetic claim with sometimes comparable basic convictions. It was not life in accordance with the Torah and following the strict rules of the Essenes in the 'covenant of conversion' (CD XIX, 16) with daily baths for purification, but the one baptism by the prophet John, that promised deliverance from the judgment.

2. The *chronological data* in the Gospels according to which John appeared around 28 CE and was executed soon afterwards, even before Jesus, make the less accurate statements of Josephus (in the years before 36 CE) more precise.

3. The *circumstances of the execution of John the Baptist* cannot be reconstructed in detail, as Josephus indicates political motives but does not specify them, and the court legend which has been worked over in Mark 6.17ff. hands down historical facts, places and names inaccurately or wrongly.[11]

• As with Josephus, Herod Antipas is responsible for the execution: the motif of the request at the banquet and the negative depiction of the Herodian women in Mark are part of a popular elaboration.

---

[11]For details see Theissen, *Gospels**, 81–96.

- Josephus also hands down the place of execution correctly: the fortress of Machaerus lay in Peraea, near the place east of the Jordan where John baptized and the frontier with the Nabateans.
- Probably territorial disputes with the neighbouring Nabataeans (*Antt.* 18, 113) form the political context of the execution of John the Baptist. This is already indicated by the popular view that the military defeat of Antipas by the Nabataean king Aretas was a divine punishment for the death of John. The enmity, which for the moment was stilled, had flared up again after Antipas dissolved his marriage with a Nabataean princess in order to marry Herodias, as Josephus reports in the immediate context (*Antt.* 18, 109ff.), though without making any connections with the story of John. This puts John's criticism of the marriage, reported by Mark 6.18, in a new light: it not only showed up Antipas and Herodias as lawbreakers[12] and undermined their reputation among the people, but could also be understood as support for the hostile neighbours and their territorial claims.

4.1.2 *The teaching of John the Baptist*

Josephus, *Antt.* 18, 116–119	Earliest Christian sources
1. The preaching	
Ethical preaching dominates	*Eschatological and messianic preaching dominates*
John the Baptist is described as a Hellenistic 'philosopher' who teaches virtue (ἀρετή), especially the two cardinal virtues	The Baptist is depicted as a Jewish prophet who issues a summons to conversion (μετάνοια, Mark Q), because
• Justice to one another (δικαιοσύνη πρὸς ἀλλήλους), i.e. virtue in interpersonal relationships, and	• God's wrathful judgment is imminent (μέλλουσα ὀργή: Matt. 3.7/Luke 3.7 Q); • a 'stronger' (ἰσχυρότερος) is coming after him (Mark 1.7; Matt. 3.11/Luke 3.16 Q, cf. John 1.27; Acts 13.25),
• Piety towards God (εὐσέβεια πρὸς τὸν θεόν) i.e. virtue in relationship to God.	• who will baptize with holy spirit (Mark 1.7; John 1.33) or with the holy spirit and with fire (Matt. 3.11/Luke 3.16 Q), • and who performs judgment and ushers in the dawn of salvation (Matt. 3.12/ Luke 3.12 Q).
[The eschatological and messianic preaching of John the Baptist is not mentioned]	John's ethical preaching fades into the background. There is mention of: • criticism of the marriage between Antipas and Herodias which offends against the Law (Mark 6.17f.);

[12]Mark 6.18 is not very precise. The offence (Lev. 18.16; 20.21) lay in the fact that Herodias abandoned her first husband while he was still alive in order to marry his step-brother (*Antt.* 18, 136); the marriage of the widowed childless sister-in-law could even have been forbidden (cf. Deut. 25.5).

• John's preaching addressed to different professions (Luke[s] 3.10–14), which cannot be shown to originate from him.

2. The baptism

The baptism is *a rite of cleansing, not a sacrament* Baptism which is acceptable [to God] is claimed to be not for the forgiveness of sins (μὴ ἐπί τινων ἁμαρτάδων παραιτήσει χρωμένων), but for the cleansing of the body (ἐφ᾽ ἁγνεία τοῦ σώματος); here it is presupposed that the soul has already been cleansed previously by righteousness (τῆς ψυχῆς δικαιοσύνη προεκκεκαθαρμένης).	The baptism is *an eschatological sacrament* which saves from the wrathful judgment of God: Through John God offers a baptism of repentance for the forgiveness of sins (βάπτισμα μετανοίας εἰς ἄφεσιν ἁμαρτιῶν: Mark 1.4), which presupposes a confession of sins (Mark 1.5) and calls for (subsequent) 'fruits of repentance' (Matt. 3.8/Luke 3.8).

1. *Ethical or eschatological preaching?* In a few strokes Josephus depicts John as a Hellenistic teacher of virtue, in accordance with his custom of depicting Jewish groups in analogy to Hellenistic schools of philosophers. However, it is striking that he does not give any details of John's teaching, especially in view of the 'precautionary' execution of the successful preacher and by comparison with the Christian sources, which depict John as a prophet with an eschatological and messianic message. Since Josephus also tends elsewhere to keep quiet about the eschatological features in Judaism which were suspect in the eyes of the Romans, there is a suspicion that he is deliberately suppressing such traditions. So we are left only with the Christian sources to reconstruct them.

(a) Mark and Q agree that John is a preacher of repentance, who calls all Israel to μετάνοια (repentance). He finds a great response among the people, not least among groups which are regarded as particularly 'sinful' (toll collectors, prostitutes, soldiers), but comes up against resistance; here members of religious elites are particularly emphasized (cf. Matt. 11.18/Luke 7.33; Matt. 21.31f./Luke 7.29f.; Luke 3.10–14).

(b) John the Baptist's real preaching of judgment, which has many points of contact with the prophecy of judgment in the Old Testament and apocalyptic, has been handed down only in Q (Matt. 3.7–10, 12/Luke 3.7–9, 17), and hardly seems to have been subjected to a Christian revision.[13] Under the image of the axe already laid to the fruit of the tree there is an announcement of the imminent wrathful judgment on all Israel, from which being a child of Abraham cannot bring deliverance. Only baptism for the forgiveness of sins (see below) and the 'fruits worthy of repentance' will preserve those addressed from being cast into the fire as barren trees. Whereas in Matt. 3.10 par. judgment is spoken of in passive formulations, i.e. God is presented as judge, according to Matt. 3.12/Luke 3.17 the 'stronger one' announced in the previous verse will sweep the threshing floor and gather the fruit, but burn the chaff with unquenchable fire. This verse shows that beyond the judgment salvation awaits those who have been saved – John's dark preaching serves to preserve and restore Israel. But who is the figure who ushers in judgment and salvation?

(c) John's 'messianic' preaching: the announcement of someone coming after John who is stronger than he is attested in different forms in all the Christian sources. So this will be a very old tradition, though there is much dispute as to its original form[14] and meaning.

The debate is over whether the 'stronger one' or 'the coming one' is God or a messianic intermediary, and what task this figure has in the final event.

Initially there seem to be good arguments for identifying the 'stronger one' with God:

- God is already implied as judge in Matt. 3.7–10 Q. In Matt. 3.12 Q the possessive pronoun ('his threshing floor', 'his wheat'; Luke 'his barns') can only refer to God. ὁ ἰσχυρός (the strong one) is a divine name which is frequent in the LXX, and what the stronger one does is traditionally God's work: Isa. 27.12f.; Jer. 13.24; 15.7; Mal. 3.19.
- The baptism with fire by the stronger one, which is sometimes the only feature to be regarded as original, must refer back to the fiery judgment to be performed in 3.10 (by God).
- The eschatological baptism with holy spirit – if it is regarded as original at all and not as a Christian addition – has models in the Old Testament and in contemporary Jewish literature only in God's eschatological action (Ezek. 36.25–27; Joel 3.1–5; Jub. 1.23; 1QS IV, 21).

---

[13]At any rate, that is the dominant view at present (cf. e.g. Meier, *Marginal Jew* 2*, 29, 71f.), the main argument in which is that no specific Christian features can be recognized. E.g. Bultmann, *HST**, 117, differs; he thinks that threats by Jesus have been attributed to John the Baptist.

[14]The present Mark–Q overlap in Matt. 3.11/Mark 1.7f./ Luke 3.16f. makes it difficult to reconstruct the various underlying traditions. Compare e.g. Mark 1.7a/Luke 3.16c: 'One comes who is stronger than me [after me (only Mark)], ἔρχεται ὁ ἰσχυρότερός μου [ὀπίσω μου] with Matt. 3.11b (cf. John 1.27): 'He who comes after me is stronger than me: ὁ δὲ ὀπίσω μου

But against these arguments are set others which clearly indicate an inter-mediary distinguished from God:

- John's comparative relationship to another who is 'stronger' and brings an even more effective baptism assigns both figures to a sphere of only gradual differences.
- The anthropomorphism of 'wearing shoes' (Matt. 3.11) or 'unloosing thongs' (Mark 1.7) is hardly tolerable as an image for God – despite all the bold biblical anthropomorphisms.
- The pericope about John's question to Jesus, 'Are you he who should come . . .?,' (Matt. 11.2ff.) presupposes an intermediary who is active on earth.

How is this contrary evidence to be assessed? One way which is frequently chosen is to deny John the Baptist any messianic expectation. He understood himself as God's forerunner; the references to a messianic figure are to be seen as a Christian interpretation and originally referred to God or are in any case later Christian expansions.

> Thus an absolute use of ὁ ἰσχυρότερος (without the comparative μου) is postulated for Q (or the historical John), which would replace a superlative in the vernacular: 'the strongest one', 'the very strong one' – and thus the offensive comparison between John and God would be eliminated. The saying about wearing sandals is regarded as secondary; nor does the Baptist's enquiry have any historical nucleus. Or Mark 1.7; Matt. 3.11b, c Q are all reckoned to be a Christian formation.[15]

Against this is the fact that John's expectation as reported by the Synoptists by no means reproduces the christological notions of the earliest community. Neither ἰσχυρότερος (the stronger) nor ἐρχόμενος (the coming one) are attested as messianic titles before Christianity. That the one who is announced is to be Jesus Christ does not follow from John's words, which are so indefinite that they could be applied to a whole series of eschatological judgment figures known at that time,

---

ἐρχόμενος ἰσχυρότερός μου ἐστιν. Did Q have the participial form ὁ ἐρχόμενος as subject of the sentence, which would correspond to Matt. 11.3/Luke 7.19Q? Or did Matt. insert it redac-tionally with a christological interest (cf. Matt. 21.9 par.)? The verbal form ἔρχεται (one who is stronger is coming . . .), which is given by Mark (and Luke: Q or an assimilation to Mark?), is regarded as more original, because it has less christological significance. But the participle ἐρχόμενος in Matt. 11.3/Luke 7.19 by no means points clearly to Jesus of Nazareth. Originally its point of reference was open.

[15]Thus e.g. J. Gnilka, EKK II/1, 47; P. Hoffmann, *Studien zur Theologie der Logienquelle*, NTA 3, ²1972, 24.

but only through the overall account in the Gospels. Luke even thought it necessary to clarify the title Christ directly before introducing the saying about the stronger one (Luke 3.15).

The content of John's saying about the one who is to come and the juxtaposition of features which point to God and to a messianic figure as agents in the eschatological event can be interpreted within the framework of Jewish messianic expectations without reference to Christian ideas: R.L. Webb investigated several 'judgment/restoration figures' expected in Judaism (the royal and priestly Messiah, the archangel Michael/Melchizedek, the Son of Man and Elijah *redivivus*) and their relationship to Yahweh. It always proves that God as a heavenly entity stands behind his earthly plenipotentiaries. Alternating references to Yahweh and his agents in messianic texts are not unusual, but rather the rule. Accordingly, John announces God's imminent action in judgment and salvation, which will be accomplished by a plenipotentiary who is coming soon (*John the Baptizer*, 254–8, 284–8). Before John's function as one who baptizes with spirit and/or with fire can be investigated, first we need to discuss the significance of his baptism.

2. The Christian sources indicate the following understanding of the baptism of John: as a 'baptism of repentance for the forgiveness of sins' (Mark 1.4), it is a sacrament which communicates the forgiveness of sins; here repentance and a readiness for conversion which have been demonstrated by a confession of sins (Mark 1.5) were presupposed, along with the will for subsequent good works ('fruits of repentance', Q). Accordingly it did not have a 'magical' effect – through the mere performance of it. However, it represented an extraordinary divine offer of grace because it made it possible access to salvation in the face of the judgment which was an immediate threat for sinners, who otherwise would no longer have had a chance to withstand the judgment by the performance of other penitential rites, acts of mercy, etc.

According to Josephus' account baptism in no way served for the forgiveness of any sins, but merely for the cleansing of the body. The soul had already been purified previously by just actions. Josephus obviously knows the sacramental interpretation of baptism and rejects it. Perhaps it seemed to him to be too 'superstitious' – especially as he suppresses the eschatological context in which it becomes understandable as a last-minute offer. What remains amounts to an ordinary Jewish bath of immersion. There is no explanation for the two aspects which characterize the baptism of John in contrast to the other repeated rites of cleansing: the fact that the act of baptism is performed once and the function of John as intermediary in the performance of it, which was so extraordinary that it gave him the title 'the Baptist' – which is also attested by Josephus.

The power of baptism in forgiving sins was not just offensive to Josephus.

Among the Christian sources, only Mark and Luke report it (Mark 1.4; Luke 3.3). Matthew omits the formula εἰς ἄφεσιν ἁμαρτιῶν (for the forgiveness of sins) in the context of the baptism of John and characteristically presents it in the context of the last supper, to describe the effect of Jesus' death (26.28). The Gospel of John makes John the Baptist say of Jesus that he is the lamb of God who takes away the sins of the world. In view of these numerous attempts at relativization, we can assume that John did in fact attribute the effect of forgiving sins to his baptism.

In what relationship does the baptism of John stand to the baptism with the spirit which is announced (Mark) or the baptism with spirit and fire (Q) by the stronger one? Three of the numerous interpretations may be emphasized:

• None of our sources has preserved the original form: John the Baptist announces only a baptism with fire, namely the judgment which is also portrayed by fire in Matt. 3.10, 12 Q. Baptism by water and fire are related to each other antithetically: the former saves from the latter. The promise of baptism with the spirit has been put in John's mouth by Christians, in order to show the superiority of Christian baptism.
• Mark has preserved the oldest form: John the Baptist announced baptism with holy spirit: here he is taking up prophetic announcements which promise the pouring out of the holy spirit for the time of salvation (Ezek. 36.26f.; Joel. 3.1–5; Jub 1.23; 1QS IV, 20–22). In this case baptism by water symbolizes and anticipates what baptism with the spirit will bring about: the two are related to each other comparatively (Meier, *Marginal Jew* 2*, 35–40, 81–4).
• Q hands down the original announcement by John the Baptist of a baptism with holy spirit and fire, in which salvation and judgment – in the sense of the first two interpretations – are put side by side; this is confirmed by the verse which follows directly under the images of bringing forth fruit and burning chaff.

As Mark is largely silent about John the Baptist's preaching of judgment, his account of an exclusively salvific function of the stronger one and his baptism is coherent, but not historically reliable. The pure baptism by fire is a reconstruction without support in the sources, which moreover could lead to the paradoxical conclusion that the baptism of John which preserves for eternal life would in the last resort be superior to the baptism of the stronger one, which destroys those who have not repented! Q might have preserved John's preaching best: his own activity, which combined the announcement of judgment and the offer of salvation, is said to be surpassed by the divine plenipotentiary in that he performs the final judgment (the baptism with fire) and pours out the spirit on those who have been baptized by John.

4.1.3 The place of John the Baptist in the history of salvation: the Christian picture of John and John's understanding of himself

Josephus still indicates that the Jewish contemporaries of John the Baptist regarded him as a legitimate emissary of God, on whose execution God took vengeance by destroying Antipas's army. Josephus says nothing about how John understood himself. This can only be ascertained by inferences from the earliest Christian sources, but first after removing all the features which serve to incorporate John the Baptist into the saving history which points towards Christ.

1. The Christian take-over of John the Baptist has gone furthest in the Gospel of John. John is the witness to Jesus, the Son of God (1.7f., 15, 29–34). He rejects all titles – even 'prophet' – for himself (1.19ff.). The baptism of John merely serves to reveal Jesus before Israel (1.31) and to identify him as the one who baptizes with spirit (1.31). John is several times contrasted antithetically with Jesus (cf. 1.7f.; 3.30f.; 10.41 etc.). Whether there is an actual situation of rivalry between the Christian community and the disciples of Jesus who venerated John as Messiah behind this is disputed. However, on the basis of all the sources it is historically clear that John never bore direct witness to Jesus. On the contrary, John's enquiry (Matt. 11.2–6/Luke 7.18–23 Q), the only text in which he speaks about Jesus that can lay claim to a historical nucleus, reveals that in prison John, doubting his own announcement of judgment by a heavenly judge which has not yet taken place, considers the possibility that Jesus is the coming one, whom he has announced in a quite different way. The doubting character of the question, Jesus' indirect answer and the diplomatic warning clad in a beatitude ('Blessed is he who does not take offence at me'), together with the fact that no positive reaction is reported on the part of John, fit the historical situation presupposed better than the post-Easter proclamation of the church.[16] John was not a witness to Jesus.

2. The account in the Synoptic Gospels possibly brings us closer to the way in which John understood himself if we take away specifically Christian elements. They portray John as a prophetic forerunner who prepares the way for Jesus:

- The scriptural quotations Ex. 23.20; Mal. 3.1; Isa. 40.3 are related to the person and preaching of the Baptist – partly as narrative commentary, partly on the lips of Jesus. He is the messenger sent by God who prepares the way of the Lord (κύριος = Jesus) in the wilderness (Mark 1.2f.; Matt. 3.3; Luke 3.4–6; Matt. 11.10 par. Q).
- The Elijah typology also interprets him as a forerunner. John is identified with

---

[16]Meier, *Marginal Jew 2**, 131–7, 198–204, presents a careful argument.

the Elijah redivivus (cf. Mal. 3.1,23f.) who is expected before the end: the veiled reference on the lips of Jesus (Mark 9.13) is interpreted in terms of Elijah in Matt. 17.13; 11.14. Luke deletes these passages, but provides clear references to Mal. 3.1, 23; Isa. 40.3 in the infancy narrative on the lips of the angel and the spirit-filled Zechariah (Luke 1.17,76).

- The parallelism between John and Jesus is achieved in several ways: Matthew puts teaching which is sometimes identical word for word on the lips of John the Baptist and Jesus (3.2/4.17; 3.10/7.19; 12.33ff.; 21.32/5.20). Mark interprets the death of John the Baptist, like the death of Jesus, as a divine necessity prophesied in scripture (9.9–13). Finally Luke puts the birth narratives in parallel.

The fundamental christological tendency of this depiction is unmistakable, and of course does not indicate how John the Baptist understood himself. But the Christian narrators could take up the point that John understood himself to be the last messenger of God and the heavenly judgment figure who acted on God's behalf before the final judgment and the restoration of Israel (cf. above 4.1.2).

- So in the case of the scriptural citations we can imagine that John the Baptist already related Isa. 40.3 to his mission. Its central role in the writings of the Qumran community also indicates that this text was understood as a task for the end-time, namely to prepare for God's coming in the wilderness (1QS VIII, 13–16; IX.19f.).
- The Elijah typology also has some support in the historical John: there is no disputing the fact that he understood himself to be a prophet.[17] Jesus and his other audience shared this view (Matt. 11.9 Q). Since John regarded himself as the last prophet before the final judgment, it is natural to assume that he regarded himself as the Elijah *redivivus* announced in Mal. 3.1, 23f.; however, this cannot be proved conclusively.[18]

---

[17]M. Tilly, *Johannes der Täufer und die Biographie der Propheten*, BWANT 137, Stuttgart, etc. 1994, lists numerous features which indicate that against the background of the image of the prophet in Palestinian Judaism John the Baptist was a typical prophet.

[18]According to Stegemann (*Essener**, 298–301), John deliberately provoked memories of Elijah, by his clothing (cf. Mark 1.6 with II Kings 1.8; also Zech. 13.4), by the choice of the place where he baptized, at the spot where Elijah had been transported to heaven in a chariot of fire (II Kings 2.1–11), and by the echoes in his preaching of Mal. 3.1ff.: 3.1 fuses Ex. 23.20 and Isa 40.3; 3.2f. announces a firery judgment; 3.7 calls for repentance; 3.19 uses the imagery of the burning of straw and trees. As counter-arguments it may be said: 1. John's clothing is sometimes identified as merely the usual clothing of those who live in the wilderness or as a prophet's garb, without any special reference to Elijah. 2. The place where John baptized cannot be identified with complete certainty. 3. The allusions to Mal. 3 are present, but not very specific (the individual elements also occur elsewhere in the prophets). They become evocative only on the presupposition that Mal. 3.1, 23f. (and only secondarily Isa. 40.3) stood at the centre of John's self-understanding – and it is precisely this that cannot be demonstrated with certainty.

- The way in which the life of the forerunner and Christ are put in parallel is of course a retrospective creation on the part of the evangelist. But there were also points of reference for this: we are to presuppose agreements between the teaching of John the Baptist and that of Jesus (see below), and indeed common features in the life-style of the two; the group of disciples which surrounded them, their opposition to religious elites and their great following among the people. The two figures evoked similar expectations and reactions. It was not fortuitous that they suffered a similar fate at the hands of the rulers. However, historically we should interpret these parallels as continuities between Jesus and his teacher John rather than as an indication of John's function as a forerunner.

The process in which the original teacher–pupil relationship between John and Jesus became that of forerunner and Messiah probably already began in Jesus' lifetime. We shall be investigating this in the following sections.

4.2 The primitive Christian tradition about Jesus' baptism

The recollection of Jesus' baptism by John visibly caused problems for the earliest Christian tradition, on the one hand because of John's apparent superiority to Jesus, and on the other because of the forgiveness of sins associated with the baptism, which indicated an awareness of sin on the part of Jesus. Precisely for that reason the baptism can be regarded as a basic historical fact:

- In Matt. 3.13–17 John declines to baptize Jesus. Jesus must rather baptize him. Nevertheless, Jesus has himself baptized 'in order to fulfil all righteousness' (3.15). This makes it clear that he receives baptism as a just man, not as a sinner.
- The Gospel of the Ebionites (frag.3) extends these apologetic motifs: John hears the heavenly voice, kneels before Jesus and asks to be baptized by him. Here no doubt remains as to who is superior.
- According to John 1.29ff., Jesus comes to John burdened with sins, but he does not bear his own sins. He is rather the lamb of God who bears (or takes away) 'the sins of the world' (1.29). There is no account of a baptism. The task of John and his baptismal activity is simply to identify Jesus as the one who baptizes with the spirit.
- In Luke 3.21–22 this distancing of John from Jesus has progressed even further. There is the account of a baptism without John the Baptist. According to Luke 3.20 John had in fact already been imprisoned.
- In the Gospel of the Nazarenes (frag.2), Jesus is invited by his mother and his brothers to be baptized for the forgiveness of sins. He replies, 'Wherein have I sinned that I should go and be baptized by him? Unless what I have said is ignorance (a sin of ignorance).' Jesus himself gives the lie to the fact that he has sought baptism for the forgiveness of his sins.

These apologetic features make plausible the conjecture that the same apologetic tendency was already at work in the earliest literary account of the baptism. In it the baptism is combined with the mythical motif of the voice from heaven (Mark 1.9–11). If Jesus is God's beloved son, he is more than John. Precisely what this apologetic tendency attempts to deny will be historical: for a while Jesus recognized John as a superior 'master' and underwent baptism by him for the forgiveness of his sins. He knew himself to be one of many in Israel who wanted to repent in order to escape the imminent judgment of God.

Possibly we may even presuppose that Jesus belonged to the closer circle of John's disciples. Some texts presuppose that John had such disciples in the narrower sense in addition to the numerous people who were baptized and immediately returned to their everyday life. These disciples addressed their teacher as 'rabbi' (John 3.26) and were at his disposal as personal servants (Matt. 11.2; Mark 6.29). They shared common religious rites and traditions like fasting (Mark 2.18) and prayers (Luke[s] 11.1). According to John 1.35ff. some of the later disciples of Jesus came from the circle of John the Baptist's disciples. John 3.22ff. even presupposes that Jesus and some disciples baptized (on behalf of John?, but cf. 4.2).[19]

Because the sources are so contradictory, just how intensive Jesus' contact with John the Baptist in fact was must remain open. It is certain that although Jesus had great respect for John all his life (cf. Matt. 11.7–15 Q; Mark 9.9–13; 11.27–33 par.; Matt.[s] 21.28–32; Thomas 46), he went his own way in his teaching. That is shown by a comparison between the two figures.

4.3 Jesus and John the Baptist – a comparison

The following table gives a survey of the most important differences between teacher and disciples (for Jesus, reference should be made each time to the more detailed account in the following sections):

John the Baptist	Jesus
Preaching of judgment	
John threatens with the μέλλουσα ὀργή (wrath to come, Matt. 3.7/Luke 3.7), which will also strike the pious. He criticizes an illusory certainty of salvation which trusts in being a child of Abraham.	Jesus continues John's preaching of judgment. But he seems to have put more emphasis on the offer of salvation (even to sinners) bound up with the preaching of the βασιλεία.

---

[19]Cf. also Acts 18.24–26; 19.1–7.

Messianic preaching

John expects the ἰσχυρότερος (the stronger one) by whom he understands either • God himself or • a judge figure (like the Son of Man)	Jesus speaks of the future Son of Man as if he is another figure – possibly he identified himself with this figure or claimed that he already represented him on earth.

Imminent futurist eschatology

For John, the end of the world is imminent: the axe has already been laid to the roots.	Jesus shares this imminent eschatology, but already looks back on a decisive turning point which has begun with John (Matt. 11.12/Luke 16.16; Matt. 11.11/Luke 7.28; Thomas 46) There is a present eschatology in his writings as well as the future eschatology.

The baptism

The baptism is an eschatological sacrament administered by John: through public self-accusation (the confession of sins) and baptism, it brings salvation in judgment if those who are baptized bring forth 'fruits of repentance'.	Jesus detaches the notion of repentance from baptism. He himself does not baptize (John 3.22 is corrected in 4.2), but he recognizes John's baptism. The notion of purity which he puts forward (Mark 7.15) is in tension with the sacrament of baptism.

Asceticism

John acts in a demonstratively ascetic way by • Ascetic clothing (a coat of camel hair) • Ascetic food (locusts and wild honey); • An ascetic abode (living in the desert in accordance with Isa. 40.3). The asceticism is part of his message: society is criticized by his demonstrative self-stigmatization.	Jesus does not have an ascetic life-style and in this respect is distinguished from John • by being called a 'glutton and wine-bibber' (Matt. 11.19) • by living in populated areas of Galilee. Ascetic regulations are to be found above all in the mission rules: here asceticism appears as a means of mission.

Some differences call for more detailed comment:

1. In *eschatology* John the Baptist expresses his imminent expectation with the images both of the tree and its fruit and the seed and the harvest:[20] the axe is

---

[20]Cf. P. von Gemünden, *Vegetationsmetaphorik im Neuen Testament und seiner Umwelt*, NTOA 18, Fribourg CH and Göttingen 1993, 122ff., 182ff.

already laid to the roots of the barren tree (Matt. 3.10). The judge is ready with the winnowing fan to separate the chaff and the wheat (Matt. 3.12). Both images recur in Jesus, but are used in such a way as to give people time: in the parable of the barren fig tree (Luke 13.6–9), the tree gets a reprieve. The clear deadline indicated by John becomes the certainty of gaining time to repent. Similarly, in the image of the seed and harvest the accent does not lies on the judgment. In the parable of the 'seed which grows by itself' the point is rather the spontaneous growth of the seed and the way in which it bears fruit. Only after that does the harvest, the judgment, follow.

It is worth considering whether Jesus came to terms with a first 'delay in the parousia': John's imminent expectation had not been fulfilled, since he had been arrested and killed. Any moment in the world which continues to exist is now interpreted as an expression of the grace of God. God delays his judgment in order to give people a chance to repent. A blunt preaching of judgment (with the offer of the grace of baptism at the last moment) turns into a preaching of grace with the offer of repentance in the face of the judgment which threatens. The mere existence of the world, the mere fact that the sun rises upon the good and the bad, can now become a sign of the love of God (Matt. 5.45).

2. This changed eschatology has important consequences in the *understanding of baptism*. In the face of the threat of an immediate end, baptism was an eschatological sacrament, i.e. a symbolic action which God accepted instead of actions for which there was not enough time. But if time had been gained for repentance, there was also time to prove repentance by good deeds. So Jesus did not baptize. He called for repentance without baptism (cf. Luke 13.1f.) and (probably) promised the forgiveness of sins (Mark 2.5). At the same time he drew a conclusion which was latent in John's baptism: the forgiveness of sins by baptism is a vote of no confidence in the temple as the place where sins are forgiven, whether through individual sacrifice or through the rites of the Day of Atonement. This latent aspect of baptism which is critical of the temple becomes manifest in Jesus. After the cleansing of the temple, the aristocracy ask him by what authority he does this. Jesus asks a counter-question about the divine legitimation of the baptism of John. Here he explicitly combines the objective right to cleanse the temple with the recognition of baptism (Mark 11.27–33). Behind this lies the unexpressed notion that anyone who seeks the forgiveness of sins in baptism cannot regard the temple cult in its present form as effective.

3. Jesus' present eschatology presupposes the experience of a shift in the ages marked by John's person and with it at the same time a sense of superiority to him. Matthew 11.11/Luke 7.28/ Thomas 46 describe John the Baptist as one of the greatest of those born of a woman. However, the least of those in the kingdom of God is greater than he – how much more then is Jesus, whose task is to proclaim the good news of the dawn of the βασιλεία. In his *messianic preaching*, John the

Baptist had announced a 'stronger one' or 'coming one', whose shoes he was not worthy to bear and who would perform the final judgment through a baptism of spirit and fire and bring in the harvest, i.e. salvation. This mediator figure bore none of the usual messianic titles. Since the salvation announced by Jesus is depicted as superior to John the Baptist and at the same time is bound up in time and substance with his person (cf. also Matt. 11.12/Luke 16.16; Matt. 11.16–19 par.), one can assume that Jesus identified himself with the mediator figure announced by John.[21]

4.4 The development from John the Baptist to Jesus

Even if we avoid seeing John the Baptist and Jesus as contrasting figures, a shift in accent can be noted. The Jewish understanding of God comprises both the strict and the merciful, the righteous and the loving God. John puts more emphasis on the aspect of strictness and justice; Jesus puts more emphasis on love and mercy. The certainty of salvation (with a constant expectation of judgment in the background) replaces fear of judgment (with the offer of salvation in baptism). How did that come about? Two explanations are discussed: either Jesus received his new certainty of salvation in the experience of a call or he based it on his miracles. The two explanations need not be exclusive.

4.4.1 Jesus' experience of a call?

The New Testament narrative tradition attributes Jesus' personal charisma to a visionary experience at his baptism. Jesus sees the heavens open. A voice declares him to be 'son of God'. Here Easter faith may have been projected back on to the life of Jesus: according to Rom. 1.3f. Jesus is Son of God only from Easter. Moreover the combination with the baptism could derive from an apologetic tendency (see above). On the other hand, like many other prophets, Jesus, too, may have had the experience of a call. The echo of this is often seen in Luke 10.18. There Jesus tells the disciples, who are delighting in their authority to perform exorcisms, 'I saw Satan fallen from heaven like lightning'. At that time the defeat of Satan was an expectation for the future. *AssMos* 10.1 says: 'And then his [God's] kingdom shall appear throughout his creation, and then Satan will be no more, and sorrow shall depart with him.' This writing was in circulation shortly before the appearance of Jesus in Palestine. Jesus now asserts that what is expected has already taken place in heaven. Evil has already been conquered. He states this as a visionary seer. Later, primitive Christianity attributed the victory over Satan to Jesus himself (cf. John 12.31; Rev. 12.7). It is quite conceivable that a visionary

---

[21]There are further comments on the self-understanding of Jesus and the relationship between Jesus and the Son of Man below, §16b.

experience of Jesus led him to be able to replace John the Baptist's fear of judgment in his preaching with the certainty of salvation.[22] But that does not explain everything.

4.4.2 *Jesus' experience of miracle*

According to Luke 10.18 the fall of Satan is the objective ground for the authority of the disciples to perform exorcisms: 'Behold, I have given you authority to tread upon serpents and scorpions, and over all the power of the enemy, and nothing shall hurt you.' Regardless of whether Jesus had a vision and a call or not, his charisma to perform miracles could have given or reinforced a certainty that Satan had been overcome and that a time of salvation was beginning.[23] The pericope about John the Baptist's question indicates this (Matt. 11.2f.). John enquires of Jesus whether he is the 'coming one'. Jesus replies with references to miracles and preaching. Here he does not say '*I* give sight to the blind and make the lame walk . . . and bring the good news', although echoes of Isa. 61.1f. could suggest the first person. For there we read: 'He has sent *me* to bring good news to the poor . . .' Rather, Jesus is referring to the miracles which are taking place around him without saying that he himself is their author. The miracles performed in his presence by God, by the disciples or by himself convinced him that the time of salvation had already begun now, that Satan had been conquered and that he himself was perhaps the 'coming one' announced by John. This too corresponded to expectations in Judaism: according to 4Q 521 the miracles announced in Isa. 35.3–5 and 61.1–2 will take place in the time of the Messiah.[24] Both passages are echoed in Matt. 11.2–6.

   To sum up, one can say on the relationship between John the Baptist and Jesus that Jesus owes to his teacher basic features of his preaching and his understanding of himself. He is both associated with John and in conflict with him. John was convinced that God was in the process of making a final intervention in history through a 'messianic intermediary' (without a title) in order to execute his

---

[22]Cf. U.B. Müller, 'Vision und Botschaft. Erwägungen zur prophetischen Struktur der Verkündigung Jesu', *ZThK* 74, 1977, 416–48.

[23]According to Hollenbach, the experience of miracle led to a regular 'conversion' of Jesus 'from Jesus the Baptizer to Jesus the Healer', cf. also above all Stegemann, *Essener**, 316–30, esp. 323ff. Similarly, Otto, *Kingdom of God and Son of Man*, 104, 114, already argued that the recognition of the dawnings of the kingdom in Jesus arose in and with the stirrings of his charismatic powers.

[24]Cf. the text, translation and short commentary in Evans, *Jesus**, 127–30. By contrast, Stegemann, *Essener**, 50f., 341, disputes on the basis of his different translation that 4Q 521 has any messianic character: he argues that the text does not speak of 'his anointed' (singular = the Messiah), but of 'his anointed' (plural = the prophets), since the plural 'the holy ones' occurs in the next half-verse, in synonymous parallelism.

judgment. His baptism was an offer of salvation at the last minute: a symbolic action to prove the earnestness of the repentance which God would accept – even if there was no longer much time to live a life stamped by repentance. In Jesus this future imminent expectation becomes the certainty that God's final intervention had already begun – not for an annihilating judgment but for salvation. Mythical evil had already been conquered and Satan had been removed from the centre of reality. The miracles of the end-time were already taking place now. People still had time: God was giving them the opportunity to overcome moral evil by repentance. Perhaps Jesus also imagined the judgment as the conclusion of a development in which evil would be overcome;[25] for the harvest which John the Baptist expected as the breaking-in of the penal judgment was already taking place in the preaching of Jesus and his disciples (Matt. 9.37f.). The question necessarily arose: was Jesus himself the expected coming one? Jesus had to grapple with it. It might be the key to his self-understanding. It was probably marked consistently by two characteristics. On the one hand the 'coming one' was a mediator figure without a christological title. There is much to suggest that Jesus had reservations about any honorific titles. That would be understandable, given his close connection with John. On the other hand, in his public appearance Jesus was anything but the coming one who had been announced. He did not appear as a judge but as a charismatic who performed miracles with a message of salvation for the poor and the marginalized. So must it not have been stamped deeply on his consciousness that salvation does not come as expected? And therefore did not the 'messianic intermediary', too, have to be different from any messianic expectations?

5. Jesus and his disciples

Just as Jesus owes his charisma to his teacher John the Baptist, so he handed it on to his disciples, men and women. According to all the Gospels, the calling of disciples was one of his first acts.

5.1 The call narratives in the Gospels

In the Gospels we find three types of call narratives. All are stylized, and none covers the historical reality without seeing it in a particular light.

---

[25]Thus especially Stegemann, *Essener**, 330ff.; cf. id., *Der lehrende Jesus. Der sogenannte biblischer Christus und die geschichtliche Botschaft von der Gottesherrschaft*, NZSTh 24, 1982, 3–20.

- *The Markan type*: Jesus calls his disciples directly by his authoritative word from their work as fishermen or toll collectors (Mark 1.16–18, 19f.; 2.13f.).
- *The Logia source type*: followers come to Jesus on the basis of their own decision, but Jesus tests their commitment (Matt. 8.19–22/Luke 9.59–62).
- *The Johannine type*: people follow Jesus by means of intermediaries. Andrew brings his brother Peter and Philip Nathanael (John 1.35ff.).

It is always presupposed that the disciples followed Jesus in the literal sense. They accompanied him on his journeys through Palestine. What analogies are there to such a relationship between master and disciples?

5.2 Analogies to discipleship in the world of the time

Two analogies above all are discussed: the rabbinic teacher–pupil relationship and the relationship between the prophet and his followers (cf. Hengel, *Charismatic Leader*):

1. The *rabbinic teacher–pupil relationship* displays great differences to discipleship in the Jesus tradition. The following table sums it up in key words:

Rabbinic teacher–pupil relationship	Relationship of Jesus to his disciples
Stable abode in a house of study	Itinerant life in Galilee and its environs
Limited period of time: a change of teacher is possible	Discipleship is a permanent relationship
Conscious forming of tradition by memories	Free formation of tradition (exceptions, e.g. in the case of the 'Our Father', are conceivable)
Discipleship is reserved for men	There are also women among followers and hearers

2. The relationship between *prophets and their disciples*: the nearest analogy to the calling of the disciples is the calling of Elisha by Elijah (I Kings 19.19–21). Elijah is called straight from his work. Before becoming a disciple he wants to say farewell to his father and mother but is allowed to do so only in the LXX and *Antt.* 8, 254. After slaughtering his cattle and using his yoke as wood to cook the meat, he follows Elijah. It is important that the key word 'follow' also occurs with the sign prophets of the first century CE. Their adherents follow (ἔπεσθαι) them to

the Jordan (*Antt.* 20, 97) or into the wilderness (*Antt.* 20, 167). ἀκολουθεῖν, the New Testament technical term for 'become a disciple', appears once (*Antt.* 20, 188). However, no particular 'staff' (like the twelve disciples) can be recognized with these sign prophets.

3. There is no doubt that the calls of the prophets offer the nearest analogy to discipleship of Jesus. In the case of Elijah and Elisha we have the calling of a prophet of equal status: a primary charismatic communicates his authority to a secondary charismatic; Jesus promises his disciples a high status. They are basically more than just 'disciples'.

5.3 Characteristics of discipleship

Three characteristics are associated with discipleship: disciples, both men and women, share in Jesus' role as an outsider, i.e. their discipleship is voluntary self-stigmatization. At the same time it is participation in Jesus' charisma, i.e. it means participation in his mission and his authority. Finally, discipleship means the promise to achieve a lofty position in Israel with Jesus.

1. *Discipleship as self-stigmatization*: anyone who becomes a disciple of Jesus must be ready to do more than share his homelessness (Matt. 8.19). He or she must also put their tie to Jesus above piety towards the family: even burying one's dead father is unimportant (Matt. 8.21). Anyone who was capable of such provocative acts – always a gross offence against the fourth commandment – was not to be surprised if he or she was hated as much as their master: 'A disciple is not above his teacher . . . if they have called the master of the house Beelzebul, how much more will they malign those of his household' (Matt. 10.24f.).

2. *Discipleship as participation in a charisma*: the disciples, male and female, participate in Jesus' mission and authority; they have received from Jesus the gift to heal and the authority to drive out demons (Mark 3.14; Luke 10.9). They have been sent like Jesus by God into the harvest (Matt. 9.37f.). They disseminate an aura of eschatological salvation and judgment: their blessing is communicated like a magical protection to the houses in which they find a welcome (Luke 10.5f.), and likewise their curse: if they are rejected in a city, things will go badly with it in the last judgment (Luke 10.10).

The rules about what they are to take with them are striking: the disciples are to practise a demonstrative asceticism in their mission. It is part of their message. With this 'missionary asceticism' they surpass what are doubtless analogous rules for equipment in the world of the time. A comparison might be made with the 'travel rules' of the Essenes attested by Josephus (*BJ* 2, 125f.) and the typical equipment of itinerant Cynic philosophers:[26]

---

[26]Cf. the collection of texts in F.G. Downing, *Christ and the Cynics. Jesus and the Other Radical Preachers in First-Century Tradition*, Sheffield 1988.

Rules for equipment in the Jesus tradition	Essene rules for travelling	Typical characteristics of itinerant Cynic philosophers
No shoes [Q] (conceded in Mark)	Shoes are worn out	Frequently bare-footed
No staff [Q] (conceded in Mark)	Weapons for self-defence against robbers	Staff as a weapon
No bag for provisions (πήρα)	No bag	A bag for provisions (πήρα) as a characteristic
Only one shirt	Worn out clothes	Cloak folded twice

So Jesus is not a Jewish Cynic: he and his disciples are not demonstrating their self-sufficiency but the imminence of the kingdom of God and their trust in God's providence. To the degree that there is a relationship to Cynicism (and that is possible), it is more one of contrast. The disciples of Jesus are to distinguish themselves emphatically from it and surpass its 'asceticism'.

3. Finally, discipleship is *participation in the promise*. In the logion about the 'Twelve', the disciples are promised a high position in the end-time. They will 'sit on (twelve) thrones and judge the twelve tribes of Israel' (Matt. 19.28/Luke 22.30). According to PsSol 17.26 that is the task of the Messiah: 'He judges the tribes of the people whom God has hallowed.' The disciples are here promised messianic authority. They are to form a messianic collective. Jesus transforms the traditional messianism into a group messianism (cf. G. Theissen, 'Gruppenmessianismus'*).

The emphasis on a group of twelve disciples (cf. Mark 3.13–19 par. and the talk of 'the Twelve') needs explanation. There have been attempts to derive it from the Easter experience.[27] Paul reports a vision by the 'Twelve' (I Cor. 15.5). However, more probably Peter gathered together 'the Twelve' on the basis of his vision – as a fixed entity which need not necessarily have been identical with 'twelve disciples'; Judas was lacking. The reassembled 'Twelve' then shared an appearance of the risen Christ. It is harder to imagine how the promise of messianic dignity to the Twelve could have arisen only after Easter: here Judas would certainly not have been included in the group of the twelve bearers of authority.[28] The number

---

[27]Thus e.g. Bultmann, *Theology**, 37, 58; H.W. Kuhn, 'Nachfolge nach Ostern', in D. Lührmann and G. Strecker (eds.), *Kirche (FS G. Bornkamm)*, Tübingen 1980, 105–32.

[28]The saying about the Twelve and the fact that there were twelve disciples is defended in particular by Sanders, *Jesus**, 98ff., as being authentic and historical.

twelve can only be interpreted to mean that Jesus knows himself to be sent to the twelve tribes of Israel; not just to the remnant which lived in Palestine but to the whole scattered Diaspora. With the help of the twelve disciples he wants to gather Israel and bring it together again. The group of twelve already represents the restored people of twelve tribes and has a special promise over against it.[29] However, not only the Twelve but all disciples participate in Jesus' mission. Here they share both the stigmatizing outsider role of the itinerant preacher Jesus of Nazareth and his charismatic authority in the present and the future. Both stigma and charisma belong closely together: the power for social deviant behaviour in the service of a new vision of life can become the charisma with which this new vision is established over against the existing form of life.

6. Jesus and his followers among the people

The charismatic power of attraction shows itself in being able to gain sympathizers and move larger crowds of people beyond the narrower circle of followers. Thus three concentric circles form around the primary charismatics: at first a small staff of secondary charismatics, consisting of the followers of Jesus (especially from the circle of the Twelve); then the wider circle of sympathizers without whose support no charismatic movement can exist, i.e. the circle of people who did not leave house and home like Jesus' closest disciples, but continued to lead their lives externally as before. Such tertiary charismatics in turn stand out from the people as a whole – from all those who listened to Jesus and were perhaps attracted by him without becoming his sympathizers and active supporters.

6.1 Jesus and the crowd

Crowds of people had already flocked to John the Baptist (Mark 1.5; Luke 3.7 Q; 7.24; Josephus, *Antt.* 18.118). A stereotyped feature of the picture of Jesus in the Gospel of Mark is that a crowd (ὄχλος) surrounds Jesus. Usually it is neutral or positively disposed towards Jesus (cf. 3.7–12; 3.20; 4.1f.; 6.34, etc.). The term 'crowd', which often has negative connotations (e.g. in the term ochlocracy), is used positively in Mark. Things only change in the passion narrative: here we have the term which is used on the one hand for a military 'division' (Mark 14.43) and on the other for the crowd which can be led astray by demagogues and calls for Jesus' death (15.6–14). Perhaps this is an indication that the passion narrative in fact formed an independent complex over against the other traditions. Mark's

---

[29]The promise of taking part in the judgment also occurs in I Cor.6.2, addressed to all the 'saints', and in Rev. 3.21; 20.4, restricted to martyrs.

picture of Jesus cannot be completely unhistorical. Q could have contained references to the crowd (Luke 6.20 Q?, 7.24 Q); however, above all the double saying about Jonah and the Queen of the South presupposes that Jesus has a large audience (Luke 11.31f. Q). As John also knows the motif of Jesus' great success with the crowd (cf. John 6.5, 14f.; 7.48, etc.), and the proceedings of the San-hedrin presuppose such success, this view could not have arisen without some support in the life of Jesus.

6.2   Jesus and the 'family of God'

People stand out from this larger crowd. In addition to 'discipleship' in the closer sense Jesus knew a second form of a positive relationship to him: membership of the *familia dei*, the 'family of God'.[30] In the strict sense this can be clearly distinguished from disciples, male and female. For we encounter this 'family of God' above all as 'hearers of the word' and as supporters of itinerant charismatics. In some traditions there is a contrast here between the natural family and the 'family of God'.

- The *relatives of Jesus* (Mark 3.20f., 31–35): Jesus' mother, brothers and sisters come to Jesus to bring him back because they think him crazy. But Jesus distances himself from his family by redefining the concept of family: 'Whoever does the will of God is my brother and my sister and my mother' (3.35). The fact that the role of father remains unoccupied is in part explained biographic-ally by the (postulated) early death of Joseph and in part theologically by the exclusiveness of the heavenly Father. At all events it contains a repudiation of 'paternal power', just as the altered sequence of members of the family (brothers, sisters, mother) expresses a change in status (cf. 3.35 with 32, 33, 34).
- The *beatitude on the mother of Jesus* (Luke 11.27f.) contains a comparable notion: what is decisive is not the natural relationship to the mother; it is decisive 'to hear the *word of God and to keep it*'.
- The *reward of discipleship* (Mark 10.28–30): this pericope brings out the social background of the idea of the 'family of God': anyone who has left house and home along with his family will receive everything back one hundred fold. He or she will find acceptance among brothers and sisters in faith, into which the 'family of God' constituted by sympathizers was incorporated. Here too the retreat of the father's role is striking: the disciple finds in the new 'family of God' all that he has left behind – with the exception of new 'fathers'.

---

[30]For this we refer to a Heidelberg dissertation in preparation by T. Roh, *Die familia dei in den synoptischen Evangelien.*

- The *warning against the recognition of earthly authority* (Matt. 23.8–10) supplements these traditions: none of Jesus' followers is ever to be called 'father' among themselves, because they have only one father in heaven. None of them is to be called 'rabbi', because they are all brothers and sisters (literally brothers).[31] This pericope is formulated with a view to the (post-Easter) community, but it goes back to the conception of the family of God which we may already presuppose with the historical Jesus.

For the notion of the 'family of God' is attested in many complexes of tradition, in Mark and in Lukan and Matthaean special material. However, in Q we find only traces of it, in so far as God is addressed as 'Father' and other human beings are addressed as 'brothers' (cf. Luke 6.36; 11.2; 11.11ff.; 12.30 Q and Luke 6.41f.; 17.3 Q). Instead, the tension with the natural family is brought out all the more abruptly (cf. Luke 9.59f.; 12.51–53; 14.26 Q). The Gospel of Thomas contains many of the 'family of God' traditions (cf. 99; 79), including criticism of the natural family (cf. 101; 55; 16). The wide dispersion of this tradition guarantees that it originates with the historical Jesus: Jesus himself already called those who heard his words 'family of God', but within this circle there is emphasis once again on the bearers of the word: his disciples, men and women, with whom he shared his mission.

In the sayings about the 'family of God' the emphasis on the women is striking: the mothers are more important than the fathers, the sisters are sometimes mentioned alongside the brothers. By contrast there is only sparse mention of women disciples. No clear historical conclusions can be drawn from this. For in the reconstruction of the role of women in the beginnings of the Jesus movement, too, first of all the tendencies in the sources need to be noted.

7. Jesus and the women around him

B. Brooten, 'Junia . . . Outstanding among the Apostles (Romans 16:7)', in L. and A. Swidler (eds.), *Women Priests*, New York 1977, 141–4; K.B. Corley, *Private Women, Public Meals: Social Conflict in the Synoptic Tradition*, Peabody, Mass. 1993; M.R. D'Angelo, 'Women Partners in the New Testament', *JFSR* 6, 1990, 65–86; M. Fander, 'Frauen im Urchristentum am Beispiel Palästinas'. *JBTh* 7, 1992, 165–85; Amy-Jill Levine, 'Second Temple Judaism, Jesus, and Women. Yeast of Eden', *Biblnt* 2, 1994, 8–33; L. Schottroff, *Let the Oppressed Go Free*, Louisville 1993; ead., *Lydia's Impatient Sisters. A Feminist Social History of Early Christianity*, Louisville and London 1995; E. Schüssler Fiorenza, *In Memory of Her. A Feminist Reconstruction of Christian Origins*, New York and London

---

[31]The explicit addressees (the disciples and the crowd, Matt. 23.1), like the implicit readers of the Gospel of Matthew (the Christian communtiy), are not a purely masculine group, so that the ἀδελφοί (brothers) addressed here are to be understood in an inclusive sense.

[2]1993; L. Siegele–Wenschkewitz (ed.), *Verdrängte Vergangenheit die uns bedrängt. Feministische Theologie in der Verantwortung für die Geschichte*, KT 29, Munich 1988; G. Theissen, *Frauen im Umfeld Jesu*, Sexauer Gemeindepreis for Theologie 11, Sexau 1993; B. Witherington III, *Women in the Ministry of Jesus. A Study of Jesus' Attitude to Women and Their Roles as Reflected in His Earthly Life*, MSSNTS 51, Cambridge etc. 1984.

The fact that in this section the relations of the charismatic Jesus with the women in his environment must once again be treated separately, although as members of families, disciples and followers from among the people women were already explicitly or implicitly in view, arises from the androcentric character of the Jesus tradition and its ambivalent attitude to women. On the one hand it is largely governed by androcentric language and unbroken patriarchalism, and on the other both the sayings and the narrative tradition indicate a remarkably varied inclusion of women and their world.

Examples of a basic patriarchal attitude include, for example, the choice of twelve male disciples as representatives of the renewed Israel, mentioned in the last section, or sayings in which women appear as the objects of male action who are e.g. coveted by (Matt. 5.28) or married or given in marriage (Matt. 24.37–39) to men. It is in the nature of androcentric language to make women invisible, so that they can or cannot be meant in statements relating to men. In addition there is often a restricted androcentric perception of texts in the history of exegesis. Whereas, for example, no one doubts that the grammatically male sinners, poor and sick to whom Jesus was sent were both women and men, a vigorous dispute arises over the question whether there were also women among the disciples, whether we also have to imagine married couples or pairs of women among the 'labourers in the harvest' sent out in twos by Jesus (Luke 10.1ff.), or whether women were among the itinerant charismatics.

Over against the patriarchal features stand the inclusive elements in the Jesus tradition. A strikingly large number of women appear in the narrative tradition, sometimes in roles which are not typical of their sex. The anointing of the Messiah by a woman in Mark 14.3–9 might be mentioned as an example. The sayings tradition is shot through by 'gender-symmetrical pairs', double sayings in which male and female protagonists and/or their specific spheres of life are set side by side. Mention should be made of the double parables of the grain of mustard seed and the leaven (Luke 13.18f., 20f. par.) and the lost sheep and the lost coin (Luke[s] 15.3–7, 8–10); the parables of the importunate friend and the importunate widow (Luke[s] 11.5–8, 18.1–8) are also comparable, though they are not combined in the same context. Gender-symmetrical examples from the history of Israel are named in Matt. 12.41f. (Jonah and the Ninevites/Solomon and the Queen of the South) and Luke[s] 4.25–27 (Elijah and the widow of Zarephath/Elisha and Naaman the leper). The working worlds of men and women are mentioned side by side in Matt. 24.40f. (work in the fields/grinding at the mill); Mark 2.21

(textile work, wine-making) and Matt. 6.26, 28 (spinning/working in the fields).

This form of preaching typical of Jesus, which is apparently not attested in literary form[32] in the world of his time, must be explained in terms of his audience. Jesus deliberately addressed men and women. In the following sections we shall sum up what can be inferred from the sources about the almost exclusively Jewish women to whom the message of Jesus was addressed, who were healed by him and who belonged to the Jesus movement as itinerant charismatics or as settled sympathizers. Here we must also take note of the metaphors which come from a woman's world. In this connection it emerges that in Jesus' preaching on the one hand the everyday world of women was capable of being a parable of the reality of God, and on the other hand the everyday world of women and the roles assigned to them are relativized in the face of the message of the kingdom of God.

A pattern of explanation widespread in scholarship, according to which Jesus with his friendly attitude towards women was an exception among his patriarchal Jewish contemporaries, and women, if they accepted his message, were at the same time liberated from a Jewish law which despised women, is more nourished by triumphalist and anti-Jewish motives than supported by the sources.[33] Rather, we must note that the Jesus movement was a movement within Judaism. The tension recognizable in its attitude towards women between unbroken patriarchal and emancipatory tendencies reflects a process of discussion within Palestinian society which increased under Hellenistic influence. Moreover, a warning should be issued against the over-hasty assumption that women always or indeed exclusively heard and judged Jesus' message in relation to their gender.

7.1 Women around Jesus

1. Women appear in the Jesus tradition as those addressed by the message of Jesus and thus as religious subjects in their own right.

- The crowd which gathers when Jesus arrives in a village or follows him consists of men and women. Thus the Synoptic sources do not confirm the picture of the restriction of Jewish women to the home, as other sources seem to presuppose (or to require?). In the impoverished, rural areas of Palestine this could not be realized merely for economic reasons: anyone capable of working was required outside.

---

[32]Indeed, there are parallels in epigraphy: Schottroff, *Sisters*, 81, mentions an altar at a grave in Este from the first century CE on the side of which the tools of both the man (anvil, tongs) and the woman (wool basket, spindle) are depicted.

[33]Cf. Levine, 'Judaism', who among other things refers critically to Witherington, *Women*, and the articles in Siegele-Wenschkewitz (ed.), *Verdrängte Vergangenheit*.

- The double saying about the women turning the mill and sleeping or eating peacefully (Luke 17.34f.) or the men working in the field (Matt. 24.40f.) shows that in the face of the message of Jesus, women and men are themselves responsible for their actions and their eschatological consequences.
- Jesus' message is deliberately also addressed to the women who are poorest economically and most despised socially: the prostitutes. Matthew 21.31f. promises entry into the kingdom of God to them and to the toll collectors. According to Luke 7.36–50 Jesus accepts the touch and kiss of a prostitute, interprets it as an expression of her love, and assures the woman of God's forgiveness.

2. Jesus healed numerous women. Through them the kingdom of God is shown to be a healing power which restores the bodily integrity of women and incorporates them into the community of those grasped by the kingdom of God. The charisma of Jesus by which he performs miracles thus does not make women objects of his action but rather involves them in an event in which they take an active part.

- Mary from the Galilean city of Magdala 'from whom seven demons had gone out' (Luke[s] 8.2) followed Jesus to Jerusalem, and for a strand of the tradition was the first witness to Easter (John 20.11ff.; Mark 16.9)[34] and Peter's rival (Thomas 114; Gospel of Mary).
- The woman who according to Luke[s] 13.10–17 is healed on the sabbath is described by Jesus in religious terms as 'daughter of Abraham'. After the healing she praises God publicly in the synagogue.
- The Syro-Phoenician woman overcomes Jesus' resistance, shaped by a sense of national superiority, for the sake of her sick daughter. Mark 7.24–30 is the only apophthegm in the NT in which Jesus does not dominate the argument but allows himself to be convinced.
- The woman with an issue of blood (Mark 5.25–34) suffers not only from her illness but from the social and cultic stigma which her permanent state of uncleanness brings, a heightened form of the exclusion which affects all menstruating women. She breaks the taboo of contact; this is made public by Jesus and interpreted as an expression of faith.

3. There were women among the followers who went around with Jesus (their number and composition probably changed), some of whom accompanied him to Jerusalem and remained itinerant preachers even after his death.

---

[34]See below §15: 2. 5. 2.

- The admonition not to be anxious (Matt. 6.25ff./Luke 12.22ff.) compares those addressed with birds and lilies which do not spin, sow or reap. Evidently the reference is to the itinerant followers, men and women, who did not engage in the usual male and female occupations.
- The earliest logia mention as members of the family left behind by the itinerant radicals brothers, sisters, mothers, fathers and children (Mark 10.29, cf. Matt. 10.37). Those left behind can also be men and women; only Luke redactionally inserts the wife among those who are left behind (Luke 14.26; 18.29b).
- Mark 15.40f. and Luke 8.1–3 hand down divergent lists of followers of Jesus who went around with him in Galilee and accompanied him to Jerusalem. These summaries have certainly undergone heavy redactional revision, but their nucleus goes back to reliable tradition.
- It emerges from I Cor. 9.5 that after the death of Jesus some of his women followers ('sisters')[35] engaged in mission with their husbands, say in the area of Palestine and Syria.[36] The androcentric sources only allow an indirect inference that women also went around on mission alone or in pairs. Perhaps the pairs of women active in preaching according to Rom. 16.12 and Phil. 4.2f. (Tryphaena and Tryphosa, Euodia and Syntyche) were itinerant missionaries.[37]

4. The itinerant charismatics, both men and women, depended on settled followers of Jesus for support (Mark 6.10; Matt. 10.11–13; Luke 10.5–9). Although they cannot be taken to be the direct account of historical facts, some Synoptic narratives and notices indicate that these included women whose houses became centres of the developing local communities (cf. Mark 1.29–31; Luke 10.38–42; Acts 12.12; John 4.4–42).

5. Both settled and itinerant followers of Jesus, men and women, saw themselves as taking part in the dawning kingdom of God which would turn the systems of rule in this world upside down. Although the different forms of life necessarily entailed differences in self-understanding and ethos, in both groups the patriarchal model of the family was put in question in favour of the new family of God, in which God alone is father and human beings are brothers and sisters.

- In order to announce the kingdom of God, the men and women who lived an

---

[35]'Sister' (ἀδελφή) in this passage might be the title of a woman missionary in analogy to Sosthenes and Timothy, the mission partners of Paul, who are designated ἀδελφοί (I Cor. 1.1; II Cor. 1.1, Philemon 1, etc.); cf. D'Angelo, 'Women Partners', 74–8, and Schüssler Fiorenza, *In Memory of Her*, 177–82.

[36]Further missionary couples are mentioned in Rom. 16.3f., 7 (15?). Here quite by chance, 16.7 discloses that the masculine title ἀπόστολος (apostle) can also denote a woman, as the Junia greeted there can conceal a woman, cf. B. Brooten, 'Junia'.

[37]Cf. M.R. D'Angelo, 'Women Partners'.

ascetic life as itinerant charismatics repudiated basic family obligations like collaboration in supporting the family, care of children and even burial of parents (Mark 10.29f.; Matt. 10.37 par.; Matt. 8.21f.).

- The tensions between the old family order and the obligations of discipleship also led to massive conflicts among the settled followers of Jesus, even leading to the break-up of families; here women are explicitly mentioned as being involved (Matt. 10.34–36).
- Those living as itinerant charismatics and the believers in Jesus who accepted them together formed the new family of mothers, sisters, brothers and children – a family of God which shared houses and fields, but got by without a human father (Mark 10.29f.; 3.31–35; cf. also Matt. 23.9). Patriarchal hierarchies were not to count in this society; rather, those who were traditionally privileged were required radically to renounce their status (Mark 10.42–45; 9.33–37, etc.).
- On occasion the effects of this community of discipleship on the role of women becomes a specific theme: according to Luke 11.27f. (and Thomas 79), followers of Jesus are not governed by motherhood but by doing the will of God, i.e. discipleship. Whether feminine duties are done (Luke 17.35) or not (Matt. 6.28) is incidental in the face of the kingdom of God. In Luke 10.38–42 Mary puts learning before Martha's housework.[38]

7.2 The world of women as a sphere which provided images for the preaching of Jesus

1. The occasional mention of women's work and the world of women in Jesus' sayings is significant, because it is an exception in an androcentric culture. As a rule women's work is made invisible in what is said, in that the father of the house who gives the children bread (Matt. 7.9) is the focus of attention, and the woman who has baked it is not mentioned. Any explicit mention makes women visible and as result necessarily raises the question of their value – both contrary to implicit basic dogmas of patriarchal culture. The incorporation of the woman's world into the language of preaching will have to be attributed to a heightened sensitivity on the part of Jesus and his followers to the interests of the marginalized, to whom the message of the coming kingdom of God is first addressed, and to the active participation of women in the Jesus movement.

2. The choice of women as protagonists in parables and similitudes makes

---

[38]However, the story of Mary and Martha also shows the limitations of this reflection. A woman (Mary) may indeed take over the privileged role of the woman disciple who is learning, but the men (including the Lukan Jesus) seem unwilling to renounce their patriarchal privileges (being looked after). Therefore the hostess (Martha) is burdened with conflicting claims (learning and housekeeping).

them figures with whom both women and men can identify. The fact that the parable of the widow tenaciously fighting for her rights (Luke 18.1) is set alongside the parable of the importunate friend's request (Luke 11.5–8) means that a woman represents the appropriate behaviour of human beings before God. The use of such imagery is an implicit protest against the identification of human being and male inherent in language and patriarchal thought.

3. Jesus' parables of the leaven (Luke 13.20f./Thomas 96) and the lost coin (Luke 15.8–10) use women and their world as an image for God's action. The women who searches and finds the coin which is important for buying essentials, the hands of the women which prepare the bread needed for life, become transparent to God's care for human beings and the abundance of the promised kingdom.[39] The use of such imagery is an implicit protest against the symbolizing of God in male categories which is often dominant in religion.[40]

8. Jesus and his opponents

Every charismatic has opponents. His power of attraction must often establish itself in the face of stigmatizations from the world around. The conflicts of Jesus with his opponents handed down by the Synoptic Gospels therefore have a historical nucleus. However, the contrast between Jesus and his opponents might subsequently have been sharpened, and differentiations between various groups of opponents smoothed out, at a secondary stage, partly in order to interpret the execution of Jesus and partly in order to cope with post-Easter experiences of persecution. Conversely, where representatives of typical groups of opponents are depicted positively and in a differentiated way, historical recollections could be an influence.

8.1 The scribes

The word 'scribe' (γραμματεύς) denotes in Greek an official who can draw up a document – from the village scribe to the scribe at the royal court. Only in Judaism did the notion of the 'scribe' as a religious teacher develop, on the basis of the high importance of 'holy scripture'.

---

[39]There is a detailed analysis of the parables in L. Schottroff, *Sisters*, 79–100.

[40]Moreover it is striking that in the preaching of Jesus the image of the father has particularly gentle features (cf. Luke 11.11–13; 12.29–32; 15.11–32). By contrast, Wisdom, which traditionally is a more feminine aspect of God, is associated with conflicts leading to death and judgment (cf. Luke 7.31–35 par.; Luke 11.49–51 par.; Luke 13.34–35). Cf. Theissen, *Frauen*, 20–3.

8.1.1   *The history of the 'scribes'*

The archetype of the scribe is Ezra, who is regarded as 'skilful in the law of Moses' (Ezra 7.6). Jesus Sirach sings the praise of such a scribe in Sir. 38.24ff; he can imagine him only in the upper class. At around the same time (c.200 BCE), a group of privileged 'scribes' at the Jerusalem temple appears in a document (Josephus, *Antt.* 12, 138–144). But nowhere in the Jewish sources do scribes appear so clearly as a closed group as in the Synoptics. The rabbinic writings certainly refer occasionally to the teachings of the scribes. But neither their teaching nor their group form a unity (Saldarini, *Pharisees*, 241–76, esp. 268ff.).

8.1.2   *Jesus and the 'scribes'*

The unity suggested in the New Testament derives partly from the contrast between the charismatic Jesus and the scribes: 'And they were astonished at his teaching, for he taught them as one who had authority, and not as the scribes' (Mark 1.22); nevertheless, differentations can be recognized even in the earliest Jesus tradition.

- *The differentiation between scribes of different tendencies.* Mark speaks explicitly of the 'scribes of the Pharisees' (2.16). The presupposition is that not all Pharisees are scribes (cf. 7.1) and not all scribes are Pharisees. The 'reasonable' scribes of Mark 12.28ff. are not assigned to any tendency![41] The Markan Jesus discusses above all doctrinal questions with the scribes. His teaching authority and theirs are at issue (cf. 9.11ff.; 12.28ff.; 12.35ff.). He argues over concrete questions of behaviour with the Pharisees: his table-fellowship with sinners (2.13ff.), the commandments about cleanness (7.1ff.) and divorce (10.2ff.) – questions which of course are also doctrinal questions.[42]
- The distinction between sympathetic and hostile scribes: the scribe who asks Jesus about the greatest commandment is depicted as a sympathizer with Jesus (Mark 12.28ff.). Only Matthew and Luke attribute a hostile intention to him (cf. Matt. 22.35; Luke 12.25). The pericope originally aims to maintain a consensus between Jesus and a scribe that the twofold love commandment is the most important. Matthew even knows a 'scribe' who wants to follow Jesus (Matt. 8.19 diff. Q?). He presupposes Christian scribes (Matt. 13.52; 23.34).
- The differentiation between Jerusalem and Galilean scribes. Twice Mark makes scribes come to Galilee from Jerusalem as enemies of Jesus (3.22; 7.1). Is he reflecting a historical situation, namely that at that time some forms of

---

[41]Because it is delighted at the prompt 'dismissal' of the Sadducees, the Gospel of Mark could have seen him as a Pharisee. But that is not necessarily the case.

[42]Cf. D. Lührmann, 'Die Pharisäer und die Schriftgelehrten im Markusevangelium', *ZNW* 78, 1987, 169–85.

scribal learning spread from the capital to the 'province'? Or does he want to bring the Galilean conflicts into close connection with the passion? The 'scribes' have a firm place in the passion narrative as one of the three groups represented in the Sanhedrin (cf. Mark 8.31; 10.33; 11.18, 27; 14.1, 43, etc.). Possibly they have found their way into other traditions from the passion narrative. In Q, where there is no passion narrative, 'scribes' are nowhere mentioned, but rather 'teachers of the law' (νομικοί: Luke 11.45ff. Q), who correspond to them.

The differentiated view of the 'scribes' is based not least on the fact that in a broader sense Jesus himself was a 'scribe': John the Baptist and Jesus are the first Jewish teachers for whom the form of address 'rabbi' or 'rabboni' is attested (cf. John 3.26; Mark 9.5; 10.51; 11.21; 14.45). Later, all the scribes have themselves addressed in this way. John the Baptist and Jesus gathered disciples around them (for John see Mark 6.29; John 1.35; cf. Acts 19.1). Nevertheless, they did not work like other scribes.[43]

In what did Jesus differ from most other scribes? According to Mark 1.22 by the nature of his teaching. This is only peripherally the exegesis of scripture. Rather, it is a 'new teaching with authority' (Mark 1.27), partly wisdom teaching which relies on the inner evidence of image and thought – like the teaching of Solomon (Matt. 12.42); partly prophetic discourse which conveys a divine message – like the message of Jonah (Matt. 12.41); partly teaching which is reinforced by miracles (Mark 1.27; 6.2). All in all it is a charismatic teaching which establishes itself independently of existing authorities: where it refers to scripture it does so very freely. In Mark 10.22ff., for example, two biblical passages are played off against each other: the statements about man and woman in the creation account against the institution of divorce according to Deut. 24.1ff. In the antitheses (Matt. 5.21ff.), the Torah of Moses is re-interpreted or given a new original formulation by a self-confident 'But I say to you'. In rabbinic discussions the formula 'But I say to you' probably served to distinguish the teaching of one scribe from another, and never to distinguish the teaching of a scribe from the Torah of Moses.

8.2 The Pharisees

Some of the scribes who came into conflict with Jesus belonged to the Pharisaic movement. The name 'Pharisee' means either 'splitter' or 'the separate ones' (פְּרוּשִׁים, p⁽ᵉ⁾rūshīm). This could be a derogatory term used of them, which became one that they used of themselves: 'those who make precise distinctions (פְּרוֹשִׁים,

---

[43]See below, §12.2.

pārōshīm, A.I. Baumgarten, 'Name'). Both Josephus (*Vita*, 191) and the New Testament (Acts 22.3; 26.5) characterize the Pharisees by their preciseness (ἀκρίβεια).

8.2.1 The history of the Pharisees

According to J. Neusner, the Pharisees, whose origin lies in the Hasmonean period, underwent a transformation from a political party to a pious movement: 'From Politics to Piety'.[44] It is correct that the religious character of the Pharisaic movement emerges more clearly in the first century CE. Josephus describes their convictions among other things as belief in the resurrection and emphasis on 'the traditions of the fathers'. One can draw only indirect inferences about the content of these traditions from Josephus: as a Pharisee he accompanied captured priests to Rome, and was amazed that even in this situation they observed the food laws (*Vita* 13f.). At the beginning of the Jewish War he and other Pharisees were part of a delegation which collected the tithes in Galilee (*Vita*, 28f., 63).

The picture given by Josephus is confirmed by the New Testament. Belief in the resurrection separates Pharisees from Sadducees (Acts 23.6–8). Pharisees emphasize 'the traditions of the fathers' (Gal. 1.14; Mark 7.1ff.). They observe the sabbath commandments (cf. Mark 2.23–3.6) and the purity commandments (Mark 7.1ff.) strictly and tithe even the most trivial agricultural produce (Matt. 23.23f.; Luke 18.12).

This picture of the Pharisees finds indirect confirmation in later rabbinic writings. Neusner has worked out from them the traditions, laws and controversies which can be traced back to the time before 70 CE.[45] His finding is that at that time norms of cleanness, tithes and festivals had a central place. Even if these traditions and laws are not specifically attributed to Pharisees, they are characteristic of the forerunners of the rabbi before 70 CE – and therefore also of the Pharisees, who presumably embodied a mentality and piety which was widespread beyond their circle.

However, this piety was in no way unpolitical. Rules for cleanness are strategies of social segregation. In the first century CE they were concentrated in that sphere which even a politically subject people could shape: private life with its norms for eating, sexuality, and rest on festivals (A.J. Saldarini, *Pharisees*, 213). The Pharisees whom we meet in the Hasmonaean period as a political and religious

---

[44]Cf. J. Neusner, *From Politics to Piety*, New York 1973, ²1979. For the Phariseees see above §5.2.3–2.5 and E.P. Sanders. *Judaism: Practice and Belief 63 BCE–66 CE*, London and Philadelphia 1992, 380–451.

[45]J. Neusner, *The Rabbinic Traditions about the Pharisees before 70*. The title of the book is misleading in that only a few of the traditions investigated are explicitly attributed to Pharisees. We learn something about the period before 70 CE, but not necessarily anything about the Pharisees.

group which goes on to the offensive, now adopt a defensive strategy to protect Jewish identity against the political and cultural supremacy of foreigners. So they do not make a change 'from politics to piety' but rather alter their strategy. They are always both a religious and a political factor at the same time.

Josephus associates the Pharisees above all with Jerusalem and Judaea. However, the Synoptic Gospels (with the exception of Matt. 27.62; Mark 12.13 and Luke 19.3) never have them appearing in Jerusalem. In them the Pharisees appear in Galilee. They are located in Jerusalem only indirectly as (a part of the) scribes (which is not emphasized). One possible explanation for this is that the Pharisaic movement only spread to Galilee at the beginning of the Common Era. Scribes coming from Jerusalem supported them there (cf. Mark 7.1). But they did not find a response everywhere in Galilee: Jesus could have been the spokesman of a local resistance to their programme – despite his indisputable closeness to the Pharisees.

8.2.2 Jesus and the Pharisees

Jesus' attitude to the Pharisees is ambivalent. As well as great closeness to their convictions we find a fundamental conflict, and alongside references to a positive attitude to Pharisees indications of hostility.

- Jesus shared the basic religious convictions of the Pharisees: belief in the resurrection (cf. Mark 12.18–27; Matt. 12.41f.), even if it faded into the background alongside the expectation of the imminent kingdom of God. Like them he believed in demons (cf. Acts 23.8), though he hoped that these would disappear with the kingdom of God. Like them he advocated a (naive) synergy between God and human beings: the two co-operate, just as a countryman must 'work with' the earth for fruit to grow (Mark 4.26–29).[46]
- However, Jesus collided with the practical rules put forward by the Pharisees. He transgressed against the commandments relating to the sabbath and purity. For him the 'traditions of the elders' were not a sacrosanct criterion but were subject to criticism (Mark 7.1ff.). The obligation to pay tithes was unimportant to him – by comparison with the fundamental ethical demands of justice, mercy and faithfulness (Matt. 23.23). In other words, he did not share the Pharisees' strategy of demarcation from all that was alien, based on ritual commandments. Against their defensive notions he put forward the notion of an 'offensive' purity (Berger, *Jesus*). Purity, not impurity, was infectious. Therefore he could approach sick people who were unclean, could eat with

---

[46]Cf. G. Theissen, 'Der Bauer und die von selbst Frucht bringende Erde. Naiver Synergismus in Mk 4, 26–29?', *ZNW* 85, 1994, 167–82.

sinners, make contact with aliens and in Mark 7.15 fundamentally relativize the notion of ritual cleanness: he embodied a purity with a charismatic aura.

This notion of a purity with a charismatic aura is best attested in what he says when he sends out his disciples: the disciples bring a 'peace' with an almost magical effect into the houses which welcome them (Luke 10.5f. Q). They may eat everything set before them there – without heeding the food regulations (10.7f.) and have the power to heal the sick (10.9). The Gospel of Thomas even quotes the logion about cleanness in this connection (14).

- According to the tradition, Jesus' personal relation to Pharisees was equally ambivalent. As well as vigorous polemic against the Pharisees (Luke 11.37ff. Q) we find – especially in Luke – references to a friendly relationship: Pharisees warn Jesus about Herod Antipas (Luke 13.31ff.). Pharisees repeatedly invite him to meals (Luke 7.36ff.; 11.37ff.; 14.1ff.). However, Luke regards Christianity generally as a continuation of Pharisaic belief: the Lukan Paul appeals to the fact that he is a Pharisee even when he is a Christian (Acts 23.6ff.; 26.4ff.).

8.3 The Sadducees

The term 'Sadducees' (Σαδδουκαῖοι) is probably derived from 'Zadok', the tribal ancestor of the high-priestly family of the 'Zadokites' (I Chron 5.27ff.; 24.1ff.). The change from 'Zadok' to 'Zadduk' is also attested in the LXX (e.g. Ezra 7.2) and in Josephus. The derivation from Hebrew צַדִּיק (tsadīq = righteous) is less likely.

8.3.1 The history of the Sadducees

The Sadducees[47] appear for the first time under John Hyrcanus (134–104 BCE) after his break with the Pharisees, who had criticized his lack of dynastic legitimacy. Perhaps he had succeeded in gaining support for his (questionable) claims from the representatives of the sole legitimate high-priestly family. According to Josephus their teaching was dominant in the Hasmonean period until Queen Alexandra Salome (76–67 BCE) again made the Pharisees powerful and influential. In other words, this was precisely the time of that Hasmonean policy of expansion which led to the reunion of Idumaea, Samaria and Galilee with the Jewish tribal territory. Because the Sadducees rejected special religious developments in Judaism as contained in the 'traditions of the fathers' which went beyond

---

[47]See also §5.2.3–2.5.

the Torah, their theology was most suitable as the foundation for an expanded Judaism. As representatives of the sole legitimate high-priestly family they could support the destruction of the rival sanctuary on Gerizim by John Hyrcanus and the orientation of all Jews on the one temple. We may assume that they also found a response in Galilee; after all, they represented the piety of those circles responsible for the reintegration of Galilee into the Jewish territorial state. They had passed the peak of their power at the end of Hasmonean rule (i.e. 40/36 BCE). But even after that they remained a religious tendency associated with the Jewish upper class.

In the first century CE they appear beside the circle of high-priestly families in the Sanhedrin. According to Acts 5.17 they are the party which supports the proceedings of the high priest against the Christians, whereas the Pharisee Gamaliel counsels moderation (Acts 5.33ff.). On the arrest of Paul (c.58/60 CE) this constellation is repeated: Paul succeeds in getting the Pharisees on his side, whereas he stirs up the Sadducees against him. With the Pharisees he shares an eschatologizing of thought and life – belief in the resurrection, which is rejected by the Sadducees. This constellation appears a third time in Josephus: in 62 CE the Sadducean high priest has James the brother of the Lord and some other Christians executed, but is deposed on the urging of circles loyal to the law (probably the Pharisees, *Antt.* 20, 200).[48] With the destruction of the temple the Sadducees lost their base, Jerusalem temple worship.

8.3.2 *Jesus and the Sadducees*

The relationship between Jesus and the Sadducees is ambivalent. Certainly he is closer to the Pharisees than he is to them. In the dispute with the Sadducees he defends the 'Pharisaic' belief in the resurrection against them and in so doing refers to Ex. 3.6, i.e. to a part of the Bible which had the highest authority both for the Sadducees and for all other Jews. The dispute might have a historical nucleus: nowhere is there a hint of a legitimation of belief in the resurrection by the Easter faith.

There is much to suggest that the constellation of power between Pharisees, Sadducees and Christians attested above for the first century is already to be presupposed for Jesus' passion. It cannot be a coincidence that precisely this constellation appears in a source independent of Acts and Josephus: in the Gospel of John, the Pharisee Nicodemus is the only one to intercede for Jesus in the Sanhedrin (John 7.45ff.; cf. 19.38ff.). We might compare Joseph of Arimathea, who as a 'councillor' was probably a member of the Sanhedrin: according to Mark 15.43 he expected the kingdom of God, and with his eschatological expectation was closer to the Pharisees than to the Sadducees. According to Luke

---

[48]Quoted on p. 470 below.

23.51 he did not assent to the execution of Jesus. All these are indications that it was not the Pharisees but the Sadducees who were Jesus' real enemies in the Sanhedrin. In fact the Sadducees must have felt attacked by Jesus' criticism of the temple. Their interests were wholly bound up with the temple. If the Sadducean members of the Sanhedrin were Jesus' real enemies, that would explain why the passion narrative nowhere mentions Jesus' 'typical' enemies, the Pharisees – although they, too, were represented in the Sanhedrin. The narrators of the passion did not attribute the proceedings against Jesus to Pharisaic motives, but even knew of a certain sympathy on the part of some Pharisees for Jesus. The connection between the Pharisees and the decision to kill Jesus which is made in Mark 3.6 only arose when the disputes with Galilean Pharisees were combined with the passion narrative and a connection was sought between the conflict in which Jesus was engaged and his death. Perhaps Mark was the first to relate Mark 3.6 to the passion.

Despite this enmity to the death between Jesus and the Sadducees, in some respects we find an amazing affinity between their convictions. Jesus could have borrowed some of his arguments against the Pharisees from the arsenal of Sadducean criticism of them, and some striking 'aristocratic' features in his activity could be explained as the adoption of Sadducean attitudes. The following comparison makes the similarities clear:

Sadducees	Jesus
In contrast to the Pharisees, the Sadducees reject 'the tradition of the fathers' (*Antt.* 13, 408f., cf. 13,297f.)	Jesus rejects the 'traditions of the fathers', especially where they run contrary to the original will of God (Mark 7.9–13).
The Sadducees cultivate disputes: they deliberately contradict the wisdom of their teachers (*Antt.* 18, 16f.)	Jesus makes a public appearance in disputations. He contradicts religious authorities (Mark 2.1–3.6; Mark 10.1ff., etc.)
The Sadducees regard the present as the place of salvation and damnation and reject the eschatologizing of thought and life (*BJ* 2, 162ff., etc.).	Jesus modifies the future eschatology by a 'present eschatology': the present is fulfilled time, the beginning of the final salvation (Mark 1.14f.; 2.18ff., etc.).
The Sadducees deviate in private from their public conduct (*Antt.* 18, 17).	Jesus removes private piety from public control (Matt. 6.1ff.; cf. Matt. 17.24ff.).

This produces the following picture: Jesus' charisma also consists in his adoption of arguments and modes of behaviour from the upper class. He confronted the temple aristocracy with an attitude which necessarily challenged them all the more, since here a simple Galilean was claiming 'authority': in view of his lowly origin this could only be felt to be arrogance. After the cleansing of the temple, the temple aristocracy rightly asked Jesus, 'By what authority do you do this?' (Mark 11.28).

8.4 The Herodians

The term, which appears only in Mark 3.6 and 12.13, derives from the Latin formation *Herodiani,* which (in analogy to *Caesariani, Pompeiani,* etc.) denotes the political adherents of a leader. The name could have been coined by the Romans in Palestine. In Josephus (*BJ* I, 319), the Graecized form 'Herodaeans' ('Ηρωδεῖοι) appears, along with a periphrasis for Herod's supporters: οἱ τὰ 'Ηρώδου φρονοῦντες (something like 'those who represent Herod's cause', thus *Antt.* 14, 450; cf.15, 2).

8.4.1 *The history of the Herodians*

The Herodians were client princes who ruled the land on behalf of the Romans from 40 or 36 BCE on. Such client princes were tolerated where direct Roman rule provided too much material for conflict. The life-style of the Jews differed in many points from that of other peoples. Nevertheless, the Romans did not hesitate to take control of Judaea and Samaria after bad experiences with Archelaus son of Herod, though they respected a certain remnant of Jewish autonomy under the Jewish high priests. Only in the north of the land were the two other sons of Herod, Herod Antipas and Philip, ruling at the time of Jesus. They had their brother's fate before their eyes. They had to legitimate themselves by maintaining internal law and order. If the Roman prefects in the south had difficulty in ruling, that could be all right for them. So it is credible that there was some tension between Pontius Pilate and Herod (cf. Luke 23.12). The Herodian client princes were able to remain in power with fluctuating success throughout the first century. Only with the death of Agrippa II in the 90s did their rule cease. So it was based entirely on their finding followers and supporters among the people – and thus appearing more advantageous for the Romans than direct rule. In other words, without 'Herodians' there would have been no Herodian client princes.

8.4.2 *Jesus and the Herodians*

That the Herodians appear only in connection with a sabbath healing (Mark 3.6) and the question of tax (12.13)[49] and are deleted by Matthew and Luke (except in Matt. 22.16) suggests a historical deposit in these mentions. For only the quite special circumstances of Palestine explain their appearance at these two particular points.

1. The question of taxation was controversial in Jewish Palestine if tax was paid directly to the Romans. Therefore the transition from indirect to direct rule in Judaea had led to a regular campaign of refusal to pay tax under Judas of Galilee. He saw the payment of tax to the emperor as an offence against the first commandment. By contrast, the payment of tax to a Jewish client prince was less problematical: he then paid a tribute to the Romans from his own income. The Herodians thus functioned as a kind of religiously neutral 'money launderers' and in so doing profited from the religious reservations about the direct payment of tax. It is credible for them to have wanted to seduce Jesus into taking a position on the tax question (Mark 12.13–17). The Pharisees who appear with them probably put forward the standpoint of Judas of Galilee, that any payment to the emperor was idolatry. At least a Pharisee was with Judas of Galilee when he propagated refusal to pay tax (*Antt.* 18, 1ff.).

2. The appearance of Herodians in Mark 3.1–6 is also well motivated: the question there is the observance of the Jewish sabbath commandment. But at the same time there is the echo of a political debate. Jesus asks: 'Is it lawful on the sabbath to do good or to do harm, to save life or to kill?' (Mark 3.4). The question 'Kill or heal' is not under discussion. Here Jesus is alluding to the debate about a violation of the sabbath commandment in war. After pious Jews had allowed themselves to be massacred without resistance during the Maccabean revolt (I Macc. 2.41), it had become the rule to allow military actions in self-defence on the sabbath (cf. *Antt.* 12, 272–277). Representatives of the ruling class presuppose an allusion to this debate: only they can wage war.

3. It is not fortuitous that the Herodians appear only in two pericopes about the exercise of political power, whether this is the power to exact payments (called 'taxes') or the control of deadly military force. They show that Jesus is far removed from this sphere of the exercise of compulsion.

People from the circles around Herod Antipas seem to have found their way to Jesus. Among his women followers mention is made of a Joanna, wife of a Herodian administrative official (Luke 8.3). Later in Antioch we find Menahem, a close friend of Herod, as a member of the community there (Acts 13.1). In respect of the Herodians, too, the sources do not just paint things in black and white. Here, too, the more complex historical reality glimmers through.

---

[49]Otherwise only in a reading on Mark 8.15.

9. Summary and hermeneutical reflections

Who was Jesus? The question is often thought to be unanswerable. Rudolf
Bultmann thought that one could 'know no virtually nothing' about his person
and life (*Jesus**, 14). But quite apart from the fact that we know a good deal about
Jesus' preaching and life (and thus indirectly also something about the preacher
and teacher), this sceptical view is correct only in one respect: we know nothing
about Jesus' development from his childhood up to the time when he made a
public appearance. Here Jesus is no different from most historical figures of
antiquity. Nevertheless, we know his person. For who someone is becomes
evident not only in the sequence of different stages of life but to an equal degree in
inter-personal relations. We are what we are in our relationships. And the sources
about Jesus show a whole mass of these; some of the most certain pieces of
information about Jesus involve his relationships. These gives us a relatively
precise profile of his person – though only for a short section of his life, the time of
his public activity.

Jesus was a charismatic who had an almost inexplicable aura: fascinating to
followers, provocative to opponents. He already provoked his family to such a
degree that they thought him 'mad' (Mark 3.21). His conflict with them is
reflected in some sayings which are generally critical of the family, e.g. about the
inevitability of family disputes in the end-time (Luke 12.51–53) and the renunciation of the family as a presupposition for discipleship (Luke 14.26). Nevertheless,
he owes perhaps part of his charisma to his family: they may have considered
themselves descendants of David and thus – willy-nilly – encouraged the expectation that Jesus could be the expected son of David who would restore Israel.
Granted, that is not certain. Jesus was probably reserved about this expectation.

Jesus owes decisive stimuli to John the Baptist. He had himself baptized by John
as a sinner. He took over from John the images, themes and problems of his
preaching, probably to a greater degree than we can recognize today, so that there
could be some unknown sayings of John the Baptist among the sayings of Jesus
which have been handed down. But soon Jesus showed his own profile everywhere, most clearly in the priority of grace over judgment in his preaching. This
had important consequences: people had a 'reprieve', baptism was relativized and
Jesus diverged from the strict protest asceticism of the Baptist. Probably John's
expectation that someone stronger would come after him aroused in Jesus the
belief that he was this stronger one – an understanding of himself which dispensed
with any title.

Jesus passed on to his disciples the charisma that the Baptist had aroused in him.
The choice of twelve disciples was to be the beginning of the restoration of Israel –
not as a messianic monarchy but as a kind of representative popular rule. The
Twelve, simple fishermen and farmers, were to rule united Israel as a messianic

collective. He sent them out as messengers of the kingdom of God and gave them strict ascetic rules. Their missionary asceticism had a different function from the protest asceticism of John the Baptist. It did not promote retreat into the wilderness but a mission into the world to win people over by demonstrative self-stigmatization.

Here charisma proves to be the capacity to advocate unconventional values and modes of behaviour. That also becomes clear in Jesus' relationship with the women around him. It was unusual at that time for a teacher to count women among his disciples. It was also unusual that Jesus often took note of them in his preaching (alongside men), so that they had their own images and statements. Finally, it was unusual for some of them to go round the country with him, not only giving him material support as sympathizers with a fixed abode, but belonging to the group of disciples in the narrowest sense.

A charismatic has opponents. His charisma consists in being able to reinterpret dismissal by the world around in a positive way – and possibly even in being able to gain followers among opponents. Jesus' attitude to his opponents is in fact ambivalent. He is set over against the 'scribes', but at a central point (love of God and neighbour) he is at one with a scribe (Mark 12.28ff.). Pharisees are his notorious critics in particular questions of behaviour and are the target of his polemic, but he shares their religious convictions and seems to have had positive relations with some Pharisees. Possibly he advocated a local Galilean mentality over against their Jerusalem-based piety. There may have been some elements of Sadducean thought in Jesus' views: the arguments with which he attacks the high esteem that the Pharisees had for the 'traditions of the fathers' could come from the arsenal of Sadducean theology. Although Jesus was remote from the Sadducees as representatives of a theology associated with the upper class, despite some differences in substance there are some structural affinities between his thought and theirs: in Jesus we find characteristics of an aristocratic way of thinking, modified for a popular milieu.

It is striking that in the traditions before redaction no connection is made between Jesus' conflicts and controversies and the passion. Conversely, most of the previous debates cease to play a role in the passion narrative. Jesus' real opponents were the temple aristocracy in Jerusalem, especially the high priest and the Sadducees (including priests and laity). The Pharisees fade completely into the background as opponents.

The first answer to the question 'Who was Jesus?' is therefore that he was a Jewish charismatic. Both a sociologist of religion and a theologian can give this answer. Precisely for that reason, the hermeneutical question arises as to whether each does not mean something completely different by it. In theology, is not charisma always a gift of God to be evaluated positively, whereas the sociologist can also speak of 'charismatics' in the case of leaders of Fascist movements? But primitive Christianity already knows that along with the Messiah is the pseudo-Messiah, and along with the prophet the false prophet! Or does the contrast consist in the fact that theology emphasizes the vertical dimension of the charisma, the relationship to God, whereas sociology emphasizes the horizontal dimension, the relationship between people? But in primitive Christianity, too, the charismatic's 'nearness to God' proves to be based on his capacity to influence people and found a community. Or is the contrast that for theologians there is no control over the emergence of charismatics and they have no explicable derivation, whereas sociologists attempt to define the probability of the appearance of charisma as a universal human possibility? But in the end, time and again just the one significant difference remains: that theology presupposes a religious system of reference and sociology a sociological one. There are overlaps between the two, but they do not coincide. If one shifts from one to the other, a process of translation is necessary, but it is possible. The term 'charisma' is accessible from both sides. However, it must be defined more closely. According to Paul, charisma shows itself in extraordinary human gifts, above all in prophecy, miracle-working and teaching (cf. Rom. 12.6; I Cor. 12.30). In the following sections we shall be discussing these various aspects of Jesus' activity one after the other. To this degree they all relate to Jesus' charisma.

10. Tasks

10.1 John the Baptist and Jesus: lasting parallels

Jesus made his first public appearance as a candidate for the baptism of John, and one of his logia attests his abiding respect for John. Despite the clear shifts of accent which have been discussed in this chapter, a whole series of abiding parallels can be observed between John the Baptist and Jesus: 1. in their appearance and teaching; 2. in the perception of them by outsiders; and 3. in their fates. Sum these up.

10.2 John the Baptist and Jesus: incompatible?

Comment – on the basis of what has been worked out so far – on the following text by Ernst Haenchen which, starting from the incompatibility of the pictures of God held by John the Baptist and Jesus, doubts that Jesus was baptized by John.

Why did Jesus – if this tradition about his baptism by John is really accurate – go to John? In order to recognize correctly the difficulty here we must first of all make clear the deep differences between the preaching of Jesus and that of the Baptist, which in turn are based on the similarly deep (sic!) differences in the belief in God held by the two figures.

In his preaching John referred with great emphasis to the 'coming one' who would perform God's judgment. To the degree that John spoke of deliverance from the judgment, he attributed it exclusively to penitence and the sacrament of baptism associated with it. That was the only possibility of pardon . . . Today we can hardly have any idea of the force that was released in the imminent expectation of the judgment.

But none of that prevents this God who had made himself known to John from showing precisely those features and that form which God had in the eyes of pious Jews. God was the jealous God, the God of retribution, who is not content with bits and pieces, but requires total obedience and therefore, because the Jews did not give this, calls for total repentance . . .

We can infer what John's picture of God was like from his own way of life: he was an ascetic . . . Such apparently different things as John's baptism and his fasting have one and the same root: the will to lead a life of penitence. Only someone who lives like that can confidently look towards the great day of God . . .

[Jesus' God is not a 'nice' God who can be understood in an inoffensive way:] the sayings Matt. 5.21f., 27f., 33f., 38ff., 43f. show that Jesus' God radically accentuated God's demands as they were understood by Judaism. As Jesus sees him, rather, God's demands have a hardness which no human good will can satisfy. Only if we reflect on that do we hear Jesus' preaching of grace rightly. God is incomprehensibly gracious to those who can no longer achieve anything by themselves . . . Because the toll collector . . . [in Luke 18.10ff.] confesses himself a sinner and asks for pardon, he and the 'prodigal son' (Luke 15.1ff.) are models for the behaviour of human beings towards God – not because they have atoned but because they are no longer trapped in the delusion that they can put their own merit in the scales.

[The twofold error of the Baptist consists in] his presupposition that human beings can decide from now on to make the contribution that has been missing by changing themselves and becoming fundamentally obedient, and secondly in his association of God's forgiveness not only with this moral radicalization (which is nevertheless sought within human possibilities) but with a sacrament which was permanently in danger of becoming a magical means instead of a sign of divine grace, a means that a human being can use successfully to establish his own aims . . .

Now what does that mean for the tradition about the baptism of Jesus? . . . [If it is historical,] there would be a change of extraordinary depth between Jesus' image of God, which makes him go to the Baptist, and the one underlying his own activity . . . [It is more likely that the 'fact' of Jesus' baptism was only invented later:] contrary to the activity of Jesus, the primitive community made baptism the condition of entry into the Christian community. It also, on the basis of its own experiences, connected baptism with the receiving of the spirit. This suggested the presupposition that Jesus too received baptism. So what led to the composition of this narrative was not old historical tradition but a projection of the earliest Christian experience back into the life of Jesus (E. Haenchen, *Der Weg Jesu*, Berlin 1966, 57–62, extracts).

The argument put forward here draws essentially on polemical stereotypes which have their original *Sitz im Leben* in the dispute between Judaism and Christianity on the one hand and Christian confessions on the other. Identify these stereotypes and judge their heuristic value for understanding the relationship between Jesus and the Baptist. Sum up briefly what supports the historicity of the baptism of Jesus. What other objections can be made to Haenchen's theory of the origin of the story of the baptism?

10.3 *Jesus and his opponents: the Pharisees*

The relationship between Jesus and the Jesus movement and the Pharisees was said above to be a close one in terms of convictions and aims. This explains the intensive arguments over the controversial questions of religious practice which were also there and the fluctuation between recognition and repudiation on both sides. This initial situation encouraged the development of hardly compatible views about the Pharisees in various primitive Christian traditions. Thus on the one hand there are texts which do not put in question the righteousness of the Pharisees before God, but which emphasize Jesus' special mission to those who cannot live up to the Pharisaic criteria of righteousness.[50] Over against them there are traditions which dispute that the Pharisees could achieve their aim – obedience to the Torah, righteousness and holiness – along the line which they followed.

Attribute the following eight texts to the two basic views sketched out above: Matt. 5.20; Mark 2.16/Luke 5.30–32; Mark 7.1–15 par.; Luke 7.36, 41–43; 11.37, 44; 15.(2,) 7; 15. (2,) 29–32; 18.10–14.

---

[50]Cf. K. Berger, 'Jesus als Pharisäer und frühe Christen als Pharisäer', *NT* 30, 1988, 248–51 (4. The Recognition of Pharisaic Righteousness by Jesus).

9

Jesus as Prophet: Jesus' Eschatology

B.D. Chilton (ed.), *The Kingdom of God*, London and Philadelphia 1984; C.H. Dodd, *The Parables of the Kingdom*, London 1935; J.G. Gager, *Kingdom and Community. The Social World of Early Christianity*, New Jersey 1975; W.G.Kümmel, *Promise and Fulfilment*, London 1957; J.P. Meier, *Marginal Jew 2**, 237–506; N. Perrin, *The Kingdom of God in the Teaching of Jesus*, London 1963; id., *Jesus and the Language of the Kingdom. Symbol and Metaphor in New Testament Interpretation*, London 1976; O. Plöger, *Theocracy and Eschatology*, Oxford 1968; A. Ritschl, *Instruction in the Christian Religion* (1875), New York 1901; M. Reiser, *Jesus and Judgment*, Minneapolis 1997; E.P. Sanders, *Jesus and Judaism*, London and Philadelphia 1985; A. Schweitzer, *The Mystery of the Kingdom of God*, London 1914, ²1925.

Introduction

At the centre of Jesus' eschatological preaching stands the saving message of the kingly rule of God (βασιλεία τοῦ θεοῦ) which is proclaimed on the one hand as already having come and on the other as imminent. The two earliest sources agree in summing up the message of Jesus and the messengers that he sent out in the formula: ἤγγικεν (ἐφ᾽ ὑμᾶς) ἡ βασιλεία τοῦ θεοῦ (Mark 1.15/Luke 10.9 Q: the kingdom of God has come near [to you]). The kingly rule of God or the kingdom of God[1] is also the theme of numerous parables, many logia from all strata of the Synoptics and the Gospel of Thomas. Otherwise talk of the kingly rule of God occurs only rarely in primitive Christianity: in the Johannine sphere John 3.3, 5 is a relic, and the few logia about the βασιλεία are not constitutive of Pauline eschatology. Outside Palestine the term was evidently not suitable as a summary of salvation. However, Jesus spoke of the βασιλεία τοῦ θεοῦ without having to explain the term. He could assume that it was familiar to his hearers: from the scriptures of the Hebrew Bible, from contemporary apocalyptic traditions, and from prayer and liturgy. However, it seems that only Jesus put the kingly rule of God at the centre of his eschatological message. Also characteristic of him is a concentration on the saving side of God's eschatological action, but without omitting its correlate, judgment. Although there is now a consensus that the kingdom of God forms the centre of Jesus' preaching, there is a controversy over how to interpret it. The following problems are discussed:

---

[1] מלכות יהוה; LXX/NT: βασιλεία τοῦ θεοῦ/τῶν οὐρανῶν.

1. Is the 'kingdom of God' present or future or both?[2]
2. In it, is the expectation of salvation or judgment dominant, and how do the two relate?
3. Is it to be understood dynamically (as God's rule) or spatially (as God's realm)?[3]
4. Is it realized only by God or with the participation of human beings?
5. Is it realized theocentrically or messianically (without or with a messianic intermediary)?
6. Is it a political or a purely religious entity?
7. Does Jesus promise his followers rule in it or that they will become the people in it?
8. Is the term 'kingdom of God' a symbol, which presupposes a pre-existing myth, or a metaphor, which allows us to discover new things?
9. Is the preaching of the kingdom of God exclusively an apocalyptic tradition or is it also stamped by the wisdom tradition?
10. Does Jesus only continue Jewish traditions with it or does he depart from Jewish convictions here?

At the end of this section we shall attempt to answer these questions.

Suggested reading and task

Norman Perrin, *The Kingdom of God in the Teaching of Jesus*, offers a good survey of the material.

Look at the central statements of Jesus about the βασιλεία by reading the following passages and dividing them into present and future eschatological sayings:

Mark 1.14–15; 4.26–29; 10.14–15; 10.23–25; 14.25; Matt. 11.12f.; Luke 11.2; 11.20; 17.20f.

Collect the social groups which are positively associated with the βασιλεία in Jesus' preaching:

Matt. 5.3ff.; 8.11f.; 11.12f.; 19.12; 21.31; Mark 9.43–47; 10.14f.

---

[2]The permanent problem in the exegesis of Jesus' βασιλεία τοῦ θεοῦ preaching is how to explain the juxtaposition of present and future statements about the kingdom of God: 'Jesus talked . . . of the present kingly rule of God as if nothing more was to follow and of the rule to come as if it had not yet arrived' (Burchard, 'Jesus'*, 29).

[3]The expression βασιλεία τοῦ θεοῦ embraces both the accomplishment of the rule of God and the spatial notion of a sphere of rule. The former is better expressed by the translation '(kingly) rule of God', the latter by the rendering 'kingdom of God'.

1. The understanding of Jesus' eschatology from Ritschl to the present day: six phases of research

1.1 The understanding of the kingdom of God in A. Ritschl (1822–1889): an ethical interpretation

According to Albrecht Ritschl,[4] the kingdom of God is the loving community of human beings as the highest good. It begins within human beings (cf. Luke 17.20f.: the kingdom of God is ἐντὸς ὑμῶν/in you) and establishes itself in a development within history. Ritschl used the parables of growth for this understanding: the seed which has been sown grows and spreads with human collaboration.[5] In so far as Jesus speaks of future, cosmic catastrophes, he takes over Jewish apocalyptic notions, but he has no interest in these. As a systematic theologian Ritschl thus continues the tradition of Kant,[6] according to whom the kingdom of God organizes human beings in accordance with laws of virtue.[7] However, he 'Lutheranizes' this Enlightenment tradition in so far as love (and not virtue) is the central value, and acceptance into the kingdom of God comes about through the justification of the sinner.

Around the turn of the century, New Testament scholars, who recognized the significance of apocalyptic for Jesus, protested against the interpretation of the kingdom of God in liberal theology which saw it as being within history and involving human collaboration. A leading figure here was Ritschl's son-in-law Johannes Weiss, a member of the 'history of religions school', in which Jesus and primitive Christianity were deliberately interpreted from the context of ancient religion, Jewish and pagan, and not from the 'context' of modern theology.

1.2 'Consistent eschatology' in J. Weiss (1863–1914) and A. Schweitzer (1875–1965): a future interpretation

In his book *Jesus' Proclamation of the Kingdom of God*, which appeared in 1892, Johannes Weiss interpreted Jesus consistently in an apocalyptic context. He

---

[4]A. Ritschl, *Instruction in the Christian Religion*, 1901, especially §§ 5–10.

[5]Cf. the formulation in § 5 of the *Instruction*, that the images of 'fruit always indicate a human product which issues from human activity'. This interpretation of the parables of growth, according to which they describe a process to be encouraged by human beings through work, is now usually rejected. According to the understanding which predominates today, the focus of the parables of growth is in fact a sudden change which is not at the disposal of human beings. The contrast between the initial stage and the final stage is emphasized under the images of the seed and fruit, mustard seed and tree, etc.; so the phrase used is 'parables of contrast'. But see in § 12.4.3, p. 376, on Mark 4.26–29.

[6]For Kant's views of the kingdom of God see J. Weiss, *Die Idee des Reiches Gottes in der Theologie*, Giessen 1901, 82–9.

[7]Cf. I. Kant, *Religion Within the Limits of Reason Alone* (1792), reissued New York 1960, Part 3.

argued that Jesus expected a new world which would break in after cosmic catastrophes, a world which would be brought in by God alone (cf. Mark 4.28: αὐτομάτη ἡ γῆ καρποφορεῖ/the earth brings forth fruit of itself). Palestine will be the centre of the new kingdom, in which Jesus along with his followers will rule over the restored people of the twelve tribes and the pagans who will stream there from all over the world. The kingdom of God is by nature future, and statements relating to the present are the expression of a prophetic elation on the part of Jesus. Jesus' ethical demands are the conditions for entering the kingdom.

Albert Schweitzer[8] made this view quite precise with his assumption that Jesus expected the rule of God to break in in the immediate future and that he sent his disciples out in this hope. He was convinced that they would not finish going round the cities of Israel before the Son of Man came (Matt.10.23!). After the return of the disciples (a first 'delay of the parousia'[9]), the resolve grew in Jesus that he would force the end to come by voluntary acceptance of the messianic woes which, according to a general conviction of apocalyptic, would precede the downfall of the world. Therefore he went to Jerusalem to suffer there. Jesus' ethic is an 'interim ethic' which applies to the exceptional situation shortly before the dawn of the kingdom of God.[10] This consistent eschatological interpretation inevitably provoked a counter-scheme, that of C.H. Dodd.

1.3 'Realized eschatology' in C.H. Dodd (1884–1973): a present interpretation

According to C.H. Dodd,[11] Jesus' real message was the statement that all eschatological expectations were fulfilled in his person ('realized eschatology'). The kingdom of God has already come: ἤγγικεν ἡ βασιλεία τοῦ θεοῦ (the kingdom of God is at hand, Mark 1.15) was synonymous with ἔφθασεν ἐφ' ὑμᾶς ἡ βασιλεία τοῦ θεοῦ (The kingdom of God has already come upon you, Matt. 12.28/Luke 11.20). Accordingly, Jesus' parables of judgment (parables of crisis) are not about the last judgment but about the division among people in the face of God's kingly rule which is already taking place in the present: according to Dodd this was later misunderstood in terms of the future.[12]

The juxtaposition of a future interpretation by Weiss and a present interpretation by Dodd, who did not attach any significance to the sayings about the future, called for a synthesis.

---

[8]Schweitzer, *Quest**, 348–95.   [9]Ibid., 357.
[10]A. Schweitzer, *The Mystery of the Kingdom of God*, London 1914, 87–99.
[11]Cf. Dodd, *Parables*.   [12]Ibid., 154–74.

1.4 Double eschatology in W.G. Kümmel: the beginnings of an interpretation in terms of salvation history

Werner Georg Kümmel[13] demonstrated by an analysis of the whole tradition that in all probability Jesus made both present and future statements about the βασιλεία. This finding can nowadays be regarded as a consensus. However, there are many possible ways of explaining the juxtaposition. According to Kümmel, the person of Jesus is the basis for continuity between present and future: in Jesus what the future kingdom will bring is already present. Jesus was reckoning with a (short) time between his death and the coming of the kingdom of God. Here was the beginning of a 'theology of salvation history' in which this brief interim period (caused by the delay of the parousia) was extended into an independent era. By contrast, existentialist theology offered a completely different way of interpreting the tension between present and future.

1.5 The existentialist interpretation of eschatology in the Bultmann school

Rudolf Bultmann[14] put forward the conviction (in terms of consistent eschatology) that Jesus himself lived in the apocalyptic myth, i.e. the expectation of a change in the world in the very near future. However, this future myth had an existential meaning for the present: it confronted every individual with a last decision here and now. 'The consciousness that man's relation toward God decides his fate and that the hour of decision is of limited duration clothes itself in the consciousness that the hour of decision is here for the world, too.'[15] However, this present (existential) significance of future eschatology was only worked out conceptually by modern exegetes (after Bultmann).

Bultmann's pupils went further and attributed this transformation of myth into an existential reality to Jesus himself: Jesus already 'demythologized' the future expectation and interpreted it as an experience of the pressing nearness of God.[16] That was the explanation of the sayings in the present: the changes which the future kingdom of God already brings about in the present are decisive.

In a last focus of this approach, in his book on 'The Present and God's Kingly Rule. Reflections on the Understanding of Time in Jesus and the Early Community', which appeared in 1993, H. Weder argued that it was fruitless to concentrate on the chronological question and predominantly used spatial metaphors to describe the eschatology of Jesus. The decisive aspect of the βασιλεία was not time but power, its 'new extension to the here as well as the now', as opposed

---

[13]Kümmel, *Promise and Fulfilment.*
[14]Bultmann, *Jesus* *; id., *Theology I* *.   [15]*Theology I* *, 22.
[16]This is true in different ways for H. Conzelmann, E. Käsemann, E. Fuchs and E. Jüngel; cf. L. Goppelt, *Theology of the New Testament*, Grand Rapids 1981, 53.

to apocalyptic. Through Jesus' preaching and conduct the present becomes 'the place where true time flashes out', and the kingly rule of God enters 'the sphere of human experience'.[17]

1.6 New approaches in present-day exegesis: metaphor theory, social history and the 'non-eschatological Jesus'

Norman Perrin[18] begins with the linguistic form of Jesus' preaching: Jesus' eschatology is articulated in symbolic language at the basis of which lies, in particular, the Old Testament myth of the battle with chaos and the tradition of an accession feast of YHWH. The kingdom of God is a 'symbol' with many levels, which resists being translated into non-symbolic language – in emphatic opposition to Bultmann, Perrin has a positive view of the term myth.

J.G. Gager[19] sees a parallel between the eschatological expectation of Jesus (and of early Christianity) and the chiliastic ('millenarian')[20] expectations which can often be noted in the confrontation between an imperialistic and an indigenous culture. The failure of the parousia to materialize is overcome by a heightened missionary activity along the lines of the theory of cognitive dissonance.[21]

In most recent North American exegesis, future eschatology is denied. It is said to be based on the Son of Man sayings (which are not authentic). The sayings about the kingdom of God did not contain any note of time and are to be understood in terms of the kingdom of the wise man – an expression for a form of life but not an expectation of a future change in the world (thus, in different ways, e.g. J.D. Crossan, M.J. Borg).[22]

---

[17]H. Weder, *Gegenwart und Gottesherrschaft. Überlegungen zum Zeitverständnis bei Jesus und im frühen Christentum*, BThSt, Neukirchen 1993, 11–64: quotations 33, 37, 40 (our italics).

[18]N. Perrin, *Jesus and the Language of the Kingdom*.

[19]Gager, *Kingdom and Community*.

[20]Chiliasm, from *chilia* = 1000, is originally the expectation of the thousand-year kingdom according to Rev. 20. Today it is used to denote any charismatic movement which expects the miraculous break-through of a new world. Similarly *millennium*, Latin = 1000 years.

[21]Gager, *Kingdom and Community*, 37–49. The theory of cognitive dissonance put forward by L.Festinger states among other things that the reduction of cognitive dissonance (which arises, for example, through incompatible convictions, facts etc.) is an important factor in motivating action. In Gager's view, in primitive Christianity the failure of the expected parousia to arrive led to 'rationalization' (e.g. Mark 13.10: 'first the gospel must be proclaimed among all nations') and as a result to missionary activity, in order to be able to maintain the eschatological conviction despite the facts.

[22]Cf. Crossan, *Jesus**, passim; M.J. Borg, 'A Temperate Case for a Non-Eschatological Jesus', in id., *Jesus in Contemporary Scholarship*, Valley Forge 1994, 47–68.

2. The metaphor of the kingdom of God as a (first) historical presupposition of the eschatological preaching of Jesus

In his preaching of the kingly rule of God, Jesus revitalizes the traditional Israelite metaphor of the king in the framework of a modified eschatological expectation. 'The metaphor of the king' and 'apocalyptic' are the two presuppositions for the eschatological preaching of Jesus. Therefore we shall first devote a section to each (2 and 3), before describing the characteristic features of Jesus' eschatological preaching.

2.1 The origin of the notion of the kingdom of God

Worship of YHWH as king was added to belief in YHWH only at a relatively late point – along with the rise of (earthly) kingship.

1. Historically, the complex of ideas related to God's kingship comes from the Canaanite world. Here in Israel the static kingship of El (God is king) could have been fused with the dynamic kingship of Baal (God becomes king) and both could have been transferred to YHWH.[23] At all events, from the beginning we find 'timeless' and 'dynamic' statements about God's kingship side by side in Old Testament texts.

2. The *Sitz im Leben* is temple worship in Jerusalem (perhaps an ancient Jebusite[24] heritage). The connection with the temple cult which persists down to the Qumran sabbath hymns is attested by:

- Isaiah's vision in the temple at his call: 'I have seen the king, YHWH Sabaoth, with my eyes' (Isa. 6.5: the earliest instance which can be dated with certainty).
- The divine predicate of the cherubic thrones: 'YHWH, God of Israel, you who are enthroned above the cherubim . . .' (II Kings 19.14f. = Isa. 37.14–16; cf. Ps. 47.9; 99.1). Accordingly, the cherubim in the temple of Solomon were regarded as YHWH's throne.
- Numerous allusions in the Psalms attest the close connection between the title of king, the temple and Zion (cf. e.g. Pss. 24.7–10; 29.9f.; 68.17f., 25 etc., and especially the psalms of Zion and the 'YHWH is king' psalms (see below).[25]

3. Sociologically, a connection between the emergence of the new picture of God and the introduction of the monarchy as a state form in Israel is probable; here the notion of the kingship of God can and did serve both to confirm the earthly kingship and to exercise a critical function towards it.[26]

---

[23]Thus W.H. Schmidt's classical thesis in *Königtum Gottes in Ugarit und Israel*, BZAW 80, Giessen 1960.

[24]The 'Jebusites' are the original Canaanite population of Jerusalem. After the conquest of the city by David, the Jerusalem temple became the centre of the fusion of the ancient Israelite and Canaanite heritage. Probably the pre-Israelite city god Zedeq was already worshipped as god-king, cf. the name of the priest-king in pre-Israelite Jerusalem handed down in Gen.14.18ff. [Melchizedek]: מלכי־צדק (= my king is [the god] צדק).

In Old Testament texts from the exilic and post-exilic period, generally speaking a distinction can be made between a theocratic (2.2) and an eschatological (2.3) notion of the kingdom of God. Theocracy means the acknowledgment of the present rule of God, as distinct from eschatology, which expects the establishment of God's rule in the end-time.[27]

2.2 The theocratic notion of the kingdom of God in the post-exilic period

The cultic community in post-exilic Jerusalem was regarded as the realization of the kingly rule of God already in the present. Examples of this notion are the 'YHWH is king' psalms, Chronicles and Josephus.

- The post-exilic (?) 'YHWH is king' psalms (47; 93; 96–99): the rule of God over the world is celebrated in the sanctuary in Jerusalem (cf. Ps.93). However, this notion may be older, even if we assume that the psalms were composed after the exile.
- I and II Chronicles were conceived as an aetiology of the cult community of Jerusalem with its theocratic constitution. For example, Solomon sits on 'YHWH's throne' (II Chron. 9.8). There are no tensions between his kingship and that of God.
- Josephus sees the Jerusalem community as a 'theocracy'; here he himself probably coined the term (Ap 2, 164–166). By it he means a constitution in which God himself rules, through his laws and a priestly aristocracy. 'Aristocracy is the best . . . in which you have the laws as rulers and do everything in accord with them. For God shall be sufficient ruler for you' (thus Moses to the people according to Antt. 4, 223).

2.3 The eschatological expectation of the kingdom of God in the exilic/post-exilic period

In Deutero-Isaiah (Isa. 52.7), Obadiah (21) and Zephaniah (3.15), the kingly rule of God becomes the expectation of salvation after the catastrophe of the exile. According to Deutero-Isaiah the content of the 'good news' (LXX: εὐαγγελιζόμενος) is the proclamation 'Your God has become king' (52.7). Additions to the

---

[25]Cf J. Jeremias, *Das Königtum Gottes in den Psalmen*, FRLANT 141, Göttingen 1987; B. Janowski, 'Das Königtum Gottes in den Psalmen', *ZThK* 86, 1989, 389–454; H. Spieckermann, *Heilsgegenwart. Eine Theologie der Psalmen*, FRLANT 148, Göttingen 1989.

[26]Cf. N. Lohfink, 'Der Begriff des Gottesreiches vom Alten Testament her gesehen', in J. Schreiner (ed.), *Unterwegs zur Kirche. Alttestamentliche Konzeptionen*, QD 110, Freiburg etc. 1987, 33–86.

[27]This distinction is made following O. Plöger, *Theocracy and Eschatology*, Oxford 1968, 106–17.

prophetic books show the transformation of this expectation by apocalyptic notions into a growing dualism between this world and a future one.

- The so-called 'little apocalypse' (Isa. 33): God becomes king through judgment on foreign powers and his entry into Zion (Isa. 33.17–22).
- The Isaiah apocalypse (Isa. 24–27) proclaims: 'YHWH Sabaoth has become king on Mount Zion and in Jerusalem' (24.23) – not least by conquering the kings of the earth (24.21f.). But he will give all peoples a feast on Zion. Death will be destroyed (25.6–8).
- Trito-Zechariah (12–14) promises after a judgment on all hostile peoples: 'And YHWH will be king over the whole earth' (Zech. 14.9).
- The Daniel apocalypse (Dan. 2 and 7): the kingdom of God replaces the kingdoms of the world symbolized by beasts! This kingdom of God comes without human collaboration.

In the time of Jesus all these statements stood in what by that time were already canonized scriptures of the Bible. The phrase 'kingdom of God' could therefore arouse expectations of a victory over the Gentiles and the establishment of an eternal kingdom of Israel.

3. Apocalyptic as a (second) historical presupposition of the eschato logical preaching of Jesus

The notion of the kingdom of God is transformed by apocalyptic in the intertesta-mental period (as had already been the case in the Old Testament texts last discussed). The further development of prophecy into apocalyptic is presupposed by Jesus. But in addition to apocalyptic 'kingdom of God sayings', there are still non- apocalyptic statements about the eternal kingship of God over this world. Both are taken up in liturgical passages, e.g. prayers, and are familiar to Jesus and his contemporaries from this context.

3.1 Prophecy and apocalyptic: a comparison

'Apocalyptic' is the expectation in writings containing a secret revelation of a new world in which God consummates his plan for Israel and the creation – against the resistance of evil powers which dominate this world. This new world had been accessible to a few seers and visions in 'primal' prehistory in visions and raptures, and they wrote down their knowledge in books. In the present these books, 'sealed' for the end-time, which have now been opened for privileged circles, communicate secret knowledge about this world, whereas obedience to the Torah to the point of martyrdom bestows the right to belong to it through the resurrection of the dead.

Despite many transitions, ideally prophecy and apocalyptic can be distinguished:

Prophecy	Apocalyptic
Immanent eschatology: Prophecy predicts the consummation of this history by God's action	*Transcendent eschatology*: Apocalyptic forecasts a new world after this world (the dualism of two ages) in which the just will take part through the resurrection of the dead
Open expectation of history: Prophecy proclaims the will of God which can be revised at any time as a result of the conversion of human beings (cf. Jonah)	*Historical determinism*: Apocalyptic reconstructs a determined plan (δεῖ γενέσθαι/it *must* take place, Dan. 2.28f.; Mark 13.7)
Individual prophetic figures proclaim God's will under their own name – supplemented by the (pseudonymous) prophecy of disciples	*Pseudonymous secret writings* by authors allegedly from prehistory (Adam, Enoch, Moses, etc.) come to light in the present

In substance Jesus presents a variant of apocalyptic expectation, but formally it appears as prophecy – not in the form of an esoteric secret writing from dim prehistory but as a proclamation (in oral form) tied to his person. His preaching is a revitalization of apocalyptic in prophetic form.

3.2 Apocalyptic statements about the kingdom of God in the intertestamental period

The statements about the 'kingdom of God' in the extra-canonical apocalyptic writings of Judaism accentuate the eschatological sayings in the canonical scriptures (see above §2.3) by a dualism between God and Satan.

- TestDan 5.10–13 (the Testaments of the Twelve Patriarchs were written between the second century BCE and the first century CE) intensifies the dualism. God establishes himself against Satan (= Beliar): 'and he himself will wage war against Beliar and give victorious vengeance over his enemies . . . for the Lord will be in their midst and the holy one will be king over them' (5.10,13).
- 1QM VI, 6 (c. first century BCE): in a final battle against the enemies of Israel the 'sons of light'[28] will be victorious. 'And sovereignty shall be to the God of

---

[28]The term that members of the Qumran community used of themselves in contrast to the 'sons of darkness', cf. 1QM 1,1,3 etc.

Israel. He shall accomplish mighty deeds by the saints of his people.' The battle against Belial runs parallel to the battle against the Gentiles.[29]

- *AssMos.* 10.1ff. (final version, beginning of the first century CE): after a great religious persecution comes the decisive turning-point: 'And then his (God's) kingdom shall appear throughout all his creation, and then Satan shall be no more, and sorrow shall depart with him' (10.1). There follows a description of the bloody judgment on the Gentiles, accompanied by cosmic signs and the exaltation of Israel in heaven, in God's immediate presence.[30]

- Sib 3, 767 (second century BCE): in contrast to the expectations supported by nationalistic thoughts, in the third book of the Sibylline Oracles there is also a universalistic conception of the rule of God. After a terrible war there will be a turning point which favours the good: 'And then indeed, he will raise up a kingdom for all ages among men, he who once gave the holy Law to the pious . . .'[31] The centre of this divine universal kingdom is Jerusalem, and all people will be united by God's law, interpreted by the prophets. A world-wide kingdom of peace is sketched out in utopian fashion. Here, too, cosmic revolutions are indicated as a sign.

- A common characteristic of the apocalyptic statements about the kingdom of God is the dualistic opposition between the kingdom of God on the one hand and the Gentiles and Satan on the other. The apocalyptic background of Jesus' βασιλεία preaching is evident in the contrast between the βασιλεία and the demons (with Satan at their head) as this appears e.g. in Matt. 12.28; Mark 3.23–27. By contrast, in Jesus there is no opposition to the Gentiles.

3.3 Non-apocalyptic sayings about the kingdom of God in the intertestamental period

If Jesus can also speak of the present kingdom of God without further explanation, this will have been familiar to his hearers, as the notion of a timeless kingdom of God in many writings shows.

- Ps. 145.1, 11, 13: this late Old Testament psalm is a prototype of non-apocalyptic statements about a timeless kingdom of God which is evident in God's care for his creatures. The one who gives food to all his creatures in due season (145.15f.) is praised with the words: 'Your kingdom is an everlasting kingdom, and your dominion endures throughout all generations' (145.13).

- Wisdom 6.4; 10.10: all kings are 'servants of his kingly rule' and are subject to God's will and judgment. Wisdom shows the righteous (Jacob) God's kingdom

---

[29]Quoted from Vermes, 169.   [30]Quoted from Barrett, 331.
[31]Quoted from Charlesworth 1, 379.

in a dream at Bethel (exegesis of Gen. 28): 'She showed him the kingdom of God and gave him knowledge of the saints' (Wisdom 10.10).

- PsSol. 17.1–3, 46: in the framework of this messianic psalm there is mention of a timeless rule of God: '. . .and the kingdom of our God is for ever over the Gentiles with judgment' (17.3). 'The Lord himself is our king for ever and ever' (17.46).
- Jesus' βασιλεία preaching cannot be understood solely in terms of these 'timeless' statements about the kingdom of God. At all events, in Matt. 6.33 ('Seek first the kingdom of God . . . and all this (clothing and food) will be added to you') statements about the kingdom of God as care for God's creatures could be fused with the apocalyptic notion of the kingdom of God.[32]

3.4 The juxtaposition of future and present/timeless statements about the kingdom of God in prayer and liturgy

At the time of Jesus the notion of God's present and at the same time future kingly rule was anchored in prayer and liturgy, and in contest to the esoteric apocalyptic writings it was known to broad strata of the population.

1. In these contexts cultic-present statements often occur about the eternal, heavenly kingdom of YHWH in which a share can be gained through participation in the cult:

- A *berakah* formula (formula of praise or blessing) already customary in the liturgy of the Second Temple as a response to the mention of the name of YHWH ran: 'Blessed be the name of the glory of his kingdom for ever and ever (ברוך שם כבוד מלכותו לעולם ועד).[33]
- In the Book of Jubilees (c.150 BCE), the sabbath is called a 'day of the holy kingdom' (50.9); here observance of the sabbath is to be understood as a confession of this kingdom and a place in the heavenly court.[34]
- In the Qumran sabbath liturgies (c.150–50 BCE), the glory of the kingly rule of YHWH is praised by believers who thus join in the choirs of angels and take part in the heavenly worship. The kingly rule (מלכות) praised here is exclusively located in the heavenly divine sphere. The seventh hymn which forms the

---

[32]Thus M. Hengel and A.M. Schwemer (ed.), *Königsherrschaft Gottes und himmlischer Kult im Judentum, im Urchristentum und in der Hellenistischen Welt*, WUNT 55, Tübingen 1991, 12.

[33]Quoted from A.M. Schwemer, 'Gott als König in den Sabbatliedern', in *Königsherrschaft* (n.32), 46 n.3; cf. also 62f. The fixed liturgical connection between the hallowing of God's name and the rule of God which occurs here (see also in the Kaddish) also governs the first two petitions in the Our Father (Matt. 6.9f./Luke 11.2).

[34]Quoted from Charlesworth 2, 142. There are further indications about interpretation in Schwemer, 'Gott' (n.33), 52–4.

climax of the thirteen hymns begins with the invitation: 'Let the holy ones of the "gods" sanctify the King of glory . . . for in the splendour of praises is the glory of his kingship. In it are (contained) the praises of all the "gods" together with the splendour of all [his] king[ship].'[35] However, these sabbath liturgies were known only to the members of the Qumran community.

• According to Pharisaic and rabbinic understanding the confession of monotheism and especially the recitation of the *sh[e]ma* were known as taking upon oneself the 'yoke of the *malkuth*'.[36]

2. The petition for the establishment of the kingdom of God in the future appears in two prayers which were possibly already spoken in the time of Jesus. This would suggest that this notion was widely known:

• In the Eighteen Benedictions: 'Restore our judges as before . . . and be king over us, you alone' (Eleventh petition).
• In the Kaddish: 'Magnified and sanctified be His great name in the world . . . may His kingdom be established during your life and during your days, and during the life of all the whole house of Israel, even speedily and at a near time.'[37]

3. It can be inferred from the examples given that in a liturgical context Jews in the time of Jesus could equally praise the present rule of God and ask for its coming without seeing an irresolvable contradiction here. Evidently the eternal kingdom of God must be regarded as a presupposition and basis for the future realization of the kingdom.[38] In doxological language what has still to come in reality is experienced and believed in as already present. The characteristic feature of Jesus' preaching does not then lie in an unresolved juxtaposition of present and future sayings about God's rule, but in the fact that he believed that the *future* βασιλεία had already dawned.

4. The relationship between present and future in the preaching of Jesus

The Jesus tradition contains both future and present statements about the kingdom of God. Those who regard a 'non-eschatological Jesus' as historical

---

[35]4Q403 frag.I, 1, 31,33, quoted from Vermes, 325. For the interpretation see Schwemer, 'Gott', esp.94–103.

[36]Cf. L. Jacobs, 'Herrschaft Gottes/Reich Gottes III', *TRE* 15, 1986, 192f.

[37]Quoted from Barrett, 206.

[38]Cf. Schwemer, 'Gott' (n.33), 117: 'In heaven what on earth is expected in the future salvation is eternally present.'

must dispute the future statements; those who accept only the 'apocalyptic Jesus' must dispute the present statements. Nowadays both series of sayings are usually accepted as authentic.

4.1 The future rule of God

Sayings about the future rule of God appear in (almost) all currents of tradition: in Mark (e.g. 10.15, 23; 14.25), Q (Luke 6.20; 11.2; 13.28f.; etc.), Matt.^{s} (cf. 21.31) and Luke^s (cf. 14.15). In the Gospel of Thomas the future eschatology is put on the lips of the disciples and is explicitly corrected by Jesus: 'His disciples said to him, "When will the repose of the dead come about, and when will the new world come?" He said to them, "What you look forward to has already come, but you do not recognize it"' (51; cf. 3, 113). Here too a future eschatology is presupposed historically, but it is replaced by the Gnostic identification of the kingdom of God with the true self. In view of this broad attestation we can hardly deny Jesus a future expectation, especially as his forerunner, John the Baptist, similarly put it forward, as did his followers, the first Christians, who lived in it. Some of the examples cited below are certainly authentic.

1. *The petition for the coming of the kingdom of God* (Luke 11.2/Matt. 6.10). The second petition of the Our Father, 'Your kingdom come', is focussed on a future kingdom. The phrase about the 'coming' of the kingdom is new in Jesus. It takes the place of talk of the coming of God (cf. Isa. 35.4; 40.9f., etc.). The primitive Christian expectation is orientated on the coming of the 'Lord' (cf. I Cor. 11.26; 16.22). Therefore this petition of the Our Father can hardly be derived from primitive Christianity. Also in support of the authenticity of the logion is the fact that the New Testament knows a wealth of songs and confessional formulations, but attributes only this one prayer to Jesus and depicts it as having been ordained by him. Had it been usual to attribute primitive Christian prayers to Jesus, we would necessarily have found that in texts much more closely related to the liturgy. Furthermore, had the Our Father not been 'protected' by the authority of Jesus in a special way, it would surely have been assimilated much more markedly to the post-Easter faith of the Christians[39] (there is more on the Our Father at 4.3 below).

2. The *three oldest beatitudes* (Luke 6.20f.; Matt. 5.3f., 6). The beatitudes on the poor, the hungry, the sorrowing and the persecuted were in the Logia source. Whereas the last of them could reflect the experiences of post-Easter persecutions, the first may be original in the following form:

> Blessed are the poor,
> for theirs is the kingdom of God.

---

[39]For a detailed discussion of the authenticity of the Our Father see Meier, *Marginal Jew 2**, 294.

> Blessed are those who hunger (now),
> for they shall be satisfied.
> Blessed are those who weep (now),
> for they shall be comforted.

Poverty, hunger and sorrow are not positive qualities. Rather, in accordance with an ideal of kingship widespread in the ancient Near East (cf. Ps. 72), God intervenes on behalf of the poor and weak, so that their fortunes soon change for the better. Just as there is a request for food in the Our Father, so here the coming kingdom is associated with the prospect of a (festal?) meal. The 'spiritualizing' of the beatitudes which soon began, and which in Matthew leads to the 'poor in spirit' and 'hunger and thirst for righteousness', shows that in primitive Christianity there was a tendency to understand the specific material promises in a 'spiritual' way. That supports the authenticity of the original beatitudes understood in a concrete way.

3. *The expectation of the pilgrimage of the peoples* (Luke 13.28f./Matt. 8.11). A banquet with the patriarchs also stands at the centre of the future pilgrimage of the peoples to the kingdom of God. Here the Jesus tradition takes up expectations from the pilgrimage of the peoples to Zion (Isa. 2.2ff.; Micah 4.1ff.) with which the expectations of the return from the Diaspora were bound up (cf. Isa. 43.1ff.; Bar. 4.36ff., etc.), except that, contrary to the tradition, neither Jerusalem nor Zion appear as the goal. This logion cannot come from primitive Christianity. There the notion was very soon established that the Gentiles do not find access to salvation only in the future end-time (beyond the frontier of death, as the appearance of Abraham, Isaac and Jacob shows), but already in the present. At a very early stage there was no longer an expectation that God would bring the Gentiles from the ends of the earth in a miraculous fashion; rather, they were canvassed by active mission.

4. *The eschatological eucharistic saying* (Mark 14.25). An authentic saying of Jesus has also been handed down to us from the context of the Last Supper – one of the few sayings of Jesus the original situation of which can be defined:

> 'Truly, I say to you,
> I shall not drink again of the fruit of the vine
> until that day
> when I drink it new in the kingdom of God.'

The saying can be understood as a prophecy of death: Jesus is drinking for the last time before he takes part in the meal in the kingdom of God. But possibly he hopes that the kingdom of God will break in so soon that it will spare him the way through death. At all events, this logion hardly came into being in primitive Christianity: Jesus has no special role at the eschatological meal. It is not his person but the future kingdom of God that stands at the centre.

5. *The sayings about admission.* Sayings about admission like Matt. 7.21;

Mark 9.43ff.; 10.15, 23 etc. formulate conditions for future entry into the kingdom of God: 'Not every one who says to me, "Lord, Lord," shall enter the kingdom of heaven, but he who does the will of my Father who is in heaven' (Matt. 7.21). In structure they are suited to formulating ethical conditions which justify entry into the kingdom of God. The paradoxical character of these conditions for entry is characteristic of Jesus: the rich have little chance of entering the kingdom of God (Mark 10.23 par.). Instead, it is open to those who receive it like a child (Mark 10.15), to those who would prefer to enter it crippled, with one foot and one eye, rather than offending against God's will (Mark 9.43ff.). The toll collectors and prostitutes will be admitted before the pious who are unwilling to repent (Matt. 21.31f.). A secondary analogy (by the evangelist Matthew?) might serve as a title for the antitheses in the Sermon on the Mount: 'Unless your righteousness exceeds that of the scribes and Pharisees, you will never enter the kingdom of heaven' (Matt. 5.20). But where paradoxical conditions for entry are formulated, everything suggests that they come from Jesus: whereas he sees an opportunity in the kingdom of heaven for prostitutes (πόρνοι), Paul already wants to exclude whoremongers (πόρνοι) apodeictically from it (I Cor. 6.9f.).[40]

6. *Sayings about a date* (Mark 9.1; 13.30; Matt. 10.23). By contrast, the authenticity of the sayings relating to a date is rightly disputed. They promise the advent of the kingdom of God (or the Son of Man) still in the lifetime of the hearers. Probably they were a comfort, since the coming of the kingdom of God was delayed. Initially it was said that everything would be fulfilled in this generation (Mark 13.30). Then the coming of the Son of Man was promised before the mission to Israel had ended. Finally, there were still a few of the first generation left. To them the promise was given: 'There are some standing here who shall not taste of death until they see the kingdom of God coming with power' (Mark 9.1). But in the end the expectation of the parousia was attached to the last survivor of the first generation, a disciple who had grown very old – the 'Beloved Disciple' of the Gospel of John. A saying of Jesus is handed down about him which promises that he will not die before Jesus comes (cf. John 21.22f.). Anyone who attributes the stimulus towards composing such sayings about a date to Jesus himself is thus arguing that these sayings caused perplexity in primitive Christianity, since they had not been fulfilled. They could only have been preserved because they were associated with the authority of Jesus.

We learn only a little from the sayings about the future kingdom of God about life in it. It is striking what is missing. National needs are not addressed, nor are there any liturgical dreams of worship in the eternal presence of God. The Torah is

---

[40]Matt. 21.31f. and I Cor. 6.9f. can be logically harmonized. The two sayings promise salvation to the sinner who is ready to repent. But the form and basic attitude are different: in the former we hear a saying about admission, in the latter a saying which threatens exclusion.

not studied by enlightened scholars. The fulfilment of the longing is a good meal –
not as a sacrificial meal in the temple but as a festal meal in the circle of the
patriarchs.[41] The ritual separation of Gentiles and Jews no longer plays a role
here. Indeed, 'the kingdom of God is not an empire, but a village'.[42] The most
natural explanation for this may be Jesus' origin in Galilee. He drew his imagery
from a world which lay on the periphery, far removed from the centres of power,
education and religion.

4.2   The present rule of God

Whereas the existence of a future eschatology in Jesus can be disputed only if one
quite violently denies Jesus clearly future sayings, the authenticity of sayings
about the present is undisputed. However, it is open whether there is really talk of
a kingly rule of God in the present, since this notion would be new in Judaism:
Jesus 'is the only Jew of antiquity known to us who proclaimed not only that
people were on the edge of the end-time, but at the same time that the new time of
salvation has already begun' (Flusser, *Jesus*, 91). However, it should be remembered that the notion of a present kingly rule of God over the world and creation
was also known in Judaism. Jesus did not need to give his contemporaries any
complicated explanations as to why he spoke of the rule of God in the present. But
he filled familiar images with new content: for he did not mean the presence of the
rule of God over the world which had always existed, but the presence of the rule
of God which was expected in the future – that state of affairs in which God would
establish himself completely against all enemies and against evil. That was a bold
statement. Was not Israel still dominated by foreign powers? Was not the world
full of evil? How is the proclamation of this present rule of God, contrary to the
facts, to be understood? The relevant statements can be divided into three groups:
into sayings which express a consciousness of fulfilment; sayings which speak of a
struggle between the powers of the old world and of the new; and sayings which
contain an awareness of a new dawn: the certainty of the beginning of the new
world in the midst of the old

4.2.1   Fulfilment sayings

In the summary characterization of the preaching of Jesus in Mark 1.15f.
(sketched out from a post-Easter perspective), his eschatological message is
summed up in two statements. The first is, 'The time is fulfilled.' That does not
mean that it is fulfilling itself but that it has fulfilled itself (in the perfect). And
secondly, 'The kingdom of God is at hand.' Here too the statement is not that the

---

[41]Paul sees this, too, quite differently: 'For the kingdom of God does not mean food and
drink, but righteousness and peace and joy in the Holy Spirit' (Rom. 14.17).

[42]Burchard, 'Jesus'*, 42.

kingdom of God is approaching (ἐγγίζει) but that it has approached (in the perfect, ἤγγικεν). Here too the focus is on a process which is already complete, which is making a mark on the present. The rule of God is dawning. Now whereas there is no argument about Jesus' sense of fulfilment, his consciousness of a dawning needs to be interpreted. So we shall begin with the certain statements about his consciousness of fulfilment.

1. *The beatitude on eye-witnesses* (Matt. 13.16f./Luke 10.23f.) says more than that the eye-witnesses are seeing the signs of salvation. That is shown by Jewish parallels in PsSol. 18.6: 'Blessed are those born in those days to see the good things of the Lord which he will do for the coming generation (which will be) under the rod of discipline of the Lord Messiah . . .' (cf. also PsSol. 17.44). The future generation expected here is present for Jesus. Prophets and other figures of the past have not just waited for further signs of the time of salvation but for that time itself. The logion can hardly derive from primitive Christianity, since there those are called blessed who believe without seeing (John 20.29).

2. In its original version the *saying about taking the kingdom of God by storm* (Matt. 11.12f./Luke 16.16) probably ran: 'The law and the prophets (are) until John. From then on violence is done to the rule of God, and men of violence seize it.' Regardless of the way in which this saying is interpreted, at all events the kingdom of God is a present entity, which has been there since the days of John the Baptist. That is the only reason why it can be 'seized' in the present. It leads beyond the law and prophets – probably as their fulfilment. There is a dispute as to whether those who seize the rule of God are its opponents or its supporters. If we note that they have only been at work since John the Baptist, we will think more of supporters: all possible opponents – politicians, demons, religious groups – were already in existence beforehand. Only Jesus and his followers appeared with and after John the Baptist. Matthew 11.11/Luke 7.28 also contains this view that John the Baptist represents a turning point: he is the greatest of all human beings hitherto, but the least in the kingdom of God is superior to him. Precisely because John is given such a central position in both sayings, they can hardly come from primitive Christianity. Here John as a forerunner is related directly to Jesus – but not to a group of anonymous 'men of violence' or to the least in the kingdom of God!

3. Even the *sayings about there being something 'greater than'* attest a consciousness of fulfilment in Jesus: John is more than a prophet (Matt. 11.9). Already with him, history enters a stage which surpasses anything hitherto – and even more in the time after him, in which Jesus is active. His preaching about wisdom and repentance surpasses the wisdom of Solomon and the preaching of Jonah (Matt. 12.41 par.).

4. *The question of fasting* (Mark 2.18ff.) is focussed on a statement about fulfilment in the present. Because the bridegroom is now there, the disciples – in contrast to John the Baptist's followers – cannot fast. The role of fasting which derives from first-century CE Pharisaic circles illuminates the implicit presup-

positions: in it days of joy are introduced, recollections of positive events in Israel's history, on which fasting and mourning are forbidden. In the presence of Jesus this impossibility of fasting becomes a permanent state. This pericope, too, cannot be derived from primitive Christianity, as the custom to fast existed in it – and the pericope itself alludes to the return to the practice of fasting after Jesus' death: 'The days will come when the bridegroom is taken away from them, and then they will fast on that day' (Mark 2.20).

4.2.2 Sayings about struggle

Positively, the present consists in the fulfilment of age-old promises. This fulfilment is shown most clearly in a negative certainty: in principle, evil has been conquered. Some apocalyptic statements about the kingdom of God knew the dualism of God and Satan presupposed by Jesus (cf. TestDan. 5.10ff.; 1QM VI, 6; AssMos. 10.1ff.; see above 3.2). They expected a victory over Satan. Only Jesus is certain that this victory has already been won.

    1. *The vision of a fall of Satan* (Luke 10.18) may have only been handed down in the Lukan special material, but there is a legendary echo of it in the tradition in the temptation story. Perhaps a reference to a vision of Jesus at his call has been preserved in Luke 10.18. Primitive Christianity later associated the overcoming of Satan with the cross and resurrection (cf. John 12.31; 16.11; Rev. 12.5ff.). But already in his earthly activity Jesus presupposes a fall of Satan. It becomes a certainty to him as a result of his exorcisms: if the demons flee, that is a sign that the power of evil has fundamentally been broken.

    2. *The saying about exorcism* (Matt. 12.28/Luke 11.20) has rightly been cited as the main evidence for a present eschatology. If the demons are being driven out, the rule of God has already arrived. The verb 'arrive' (φθάνειν), here in the aorist, means more than 'come close'. It can mean 'catch up with' or 'overtake'. Other New Testament instances confirm this: the term means more than a sign announcing the kingdom of God in advance, namely the rule of God itself (cf. φθάνειν in I Thess. 4.15; 2.16). At all events, one could assume a prophetic saying which describes the future as already having taken place – in the certainty that it is coming. But that is contradicted by the connection with the exorcisms of Jesus, since these have already taken place in the present. By contrast, there is no dispute about the connection with the exorcisms of Jesus' opponents. The logion is often isolated from its immediate context – despite parallel notions in Matt. 12.27f. and Luke 11.20, which confirm the connection with the context for Q:

> 'And if I cast out demons by Beelzebul,
> by whom do your sons cast them out?
> Therefore they shall be your judges.
> But if it is by the "finger (Matt. spirit) of God" that I cast out demons,
> then the kingdom of God has come upon you.'

The 'finger of God' (thus Luke) is more original than the 'spirit of God' to which Matthew refers in the context (cf. Matt. 12.18 = Isa. 42.1; 12.32). In view of the significance of the 'spirit' in Luke–Acts, one cannot imagine Luke having deleted it. Now the 'finger of God' is an allusion to Ex. 8.15 – to Moses' miracles before the exodus from Egypt. The Egyptian magicians fail to make gnats out of dust. They recognize the superiority of Moses with the words, 'That is the finger of God.' So the key word in the Old Testament derives from a controversy over the origin of miracle-working power in rival miracles. Just as there the Egyptian miracle workers stand over against Moses, so here opponents of Jesus and the exorcisms of their 'sons' stand over against Jesus. It can hardly be said that in Matt. 12.27 quite a different audience is in view from that in 12.18: certainly, in the former Jesus is taking an argument of his opponents ironically *ad absurdum*. By contrast, in the latter he is addressing people who have been reached by the kingly rule of God (in the positive sense). But the advent of the rule of God always also has a negative aspect: it is judgment for those who reject it. So this advent of the rule of God always also has a threatening accent. Further exegesis would take us too far afield here. The only important thing to note is that the separation of the exorcisms of Jesus from the exorcisms of others is not as obvious as is often assumed. Either these other exorcisms contrast with Jesus' exorcisms, in which case the double logion would mean: whereas in my exorcisms God's power is certainly at work, according to your logic something quite different must be at work in the exorcisms of your sons (on the presupposition that the two are really as fundamentally different as you think). Or the two sets of exorcisms are related in a positive analogy: if the exorcisms of your sons do not themselves stem from Satan (which is obviously your assumption), how much more do my exorcisms show the power of the rule of God! But the analogy could also be meant in a negative sense: if you accuse me of being in league with Satan, how much more must you accuse your sons of the same thing!

3. The kingdom of God and the kingdom of Satan are opposed throughout *the Beelzebul debate* (Matt. 12.22ff./Luke 11.14ff.). The image of the stronger one is illuminating for Jesus' eschatological consciousness: in Mark 3.27 (and Matt. 12.29) we have the plundering of a house. In Luke 11.21f. (= Q?) this has become a military clash between armed forces. But at all events the statement is that a stronger one must be conquered and bound before one can plunder his house or palace. Satan has to be conquered before one can drive out the demons.

4.2.3 *Sayings about the dawn of the rule of God*

The sayings of Jesus unmistakably talk of the fulfilment of old expectations and the overcoming of evil. But the sayings about the dawn of the rule of God are much vaguer and more enigmatic. We have already discussed some sayings, which include the one about taking the kingdom by force. If the kingdom of God can be 'seized' or 'robbed', it must already exist in the present – at least since the days of John the Baptist. The saying about exorcism also contains a positive statement about the dawn of the rule of God. The allusion to Ex. 8.15 possibly shows how it is to be understood: just as at that time there was a prelude to the exodus in the miracles of Moses, so in the exorcisms today there is a prelude to the liberation of Israel through the kingdom of God. Other sayings about a dawning of the kingdom are more enigmatic.

1. The statement about the *'kingdom of God in your midst'* (Luke 17.21) may be attested in the New Testament only in the Lukan special material, but it appears twice in the Gospel of Thomas, in such different versions that it cannot be regarded as a redactional reworking of the same Lukan original (cf. 3; 113). The statement in Logion 113 that the kingdom of God, among other things, is 'spread over the earth' is hardly a characteristically Gnostic reinterpretation of the 'kingdom of God in you'. As elsewhere, doublets indicate variants in the history of tradition rather than literary dependence. Like the saying about exorcism (Luke 11.20), the saying about the 'kingdom of God in your midst' (Luke 17.21) is also addressed to Pharisees – in other words to the opponents of Jesus. Jesus' reply to the question when the kingdom of God is coming is:

'The kingdom of God is not coming with signs to be observed;
nor will they say,
"Lo, here it is!" or "There!"'
For behold, the kingdom of God is in the midst of you (ἐντὸς ὑμῶν).'

The translation and meaning of ἐντός are disputed. Is it to be understood in a spiritual sense, 'The kingdom of God is internally in you' – as in Gospel of Thomas 3, 'The kingdom of God is within you and outside' – so that it is at the same time the self of the redeemed and his heavenly home? Or is ἐντός to be understood spatially, 'in your midst'? That is the most widespread translation. In fact the Greek translation of the Old Testament by Aquila knows an ἐντός with this meaning as a rendering of the Hebrew 'in our midst' (בְּקִרְבֵּנוּ), cf. Aquila on Ex. 17.7; 34.9. But as a rule ἐντός means 'within'. That is shown by the only parallel in the New Testament in the noun form: 'the interior' (τὸ ἐντός) in Matt. 23.26. Moreover Luke has the clear 'in the middle of' in the form of ἐν μέσῳ (cf. Luke 2.46; 8.7; 21.21 etc.). If we add that the repudiation of a spatial localization of the kingdom of God – it is neither 'here' nor 'there' – hardly suggests a spatial view which seeks the kingdom of God in the midst of those addressed (say in the form of the person of Jesus), Luke himself could have understood the logion spiritually: the previous pericope ends in 17.19 with the promise: 'Your faith has saved you'. The kingdom of God could begin within human beings as faith. Luke can imagine Pharisees as believing Christians, as is shown by Acts 15.5. But this Lukan interpretation (which is only a possible one) would not do away with the original sense. In addition to the spiritual and local sense Luke also knows a dynamic interpretation in the sense of 'the kingdom of God is at your disposal' or 'in your sphere of experience'. That is a possible meaning of the word. In that case the logion would have to be understood as an invitation to put oneself in possession of the rule of God. At all events there is a present eschatology. For the future interpretation, the kingdom of God is suddenly in your midst, is quite improbable. The suddenness of the coming of God is introduced by the following context. The saying remains a riddle.

2. The *parables of growth* attest the hidden beginning of the rule of God. However, not all parables were originally images of the rule of God. Only in some cases is this confirmed by an old introduction. The instances of this are the 'parable of the seed growing by itself' (Mark 4.26–29) and the double parable of the 'mustard seed' and the 'leaven' (Luke 13.18f., 20f.). The point is always that something great grows from a small beginning. The decisive thing, the sowing, has already taken place. The mustard seed is already growing. The leaven is already permeating the dough. Even if we may not 'translate' parables like allegories, the 'naive' listener is doubtless directed to a reality which is already beginning imperceptibly in the present.

Thus the statements about the present rule of God have both clear and enigmatic aspects. It is clear that the expectations of history so far are now being fulfilled: it is also clear that evil has decisively been conquered. But in parables and paradoxical phrases it is enigmatically stated that the dawn of the rule of God has already taken place.

4.3 The combination of present and future in the Our Father

If we regard both the future and the present statements as authentic, we are faced with the almost insoluble task of how to interpret their relationship. Or should we console ourselves with the fact that the logical coherence of our expectations is inappropriate for Jesus? Did not the whole of primitive Christianity express this tension between 'already' and 'not yet' without ever feeling the need to balance them intellectually? But at all events we have an evocative text from Jesus which combines future and present in a remarkable way: the Our Father. Just as we find present and future statements side by side in Jewish prayers (see above, pp. 251f.), so too we find them in this prayer of Jesus. There is a fairly broad consensus as to which is the earliest version: the longer Matthaean version has come about by expansions at the beginning (after the address), in the middle (after the petitions in the second person singular), and at the end (after the petitions in the first person plural).The expansions emphasize the transcendence of God in heaven, give the eschatological orientation of the first petitions an ethical emphasis, 'Your will be done . . .' (Matt. 6.10b), and set the everyday ethic of the petitions in the first person plural against an eschatological horizon: 'And deliver us from evil!' For this deliverance can only come about with the establishment of the rule of God.[43] However, the combination of eschatology and everyday ethics is characteristic not only of the additions in the Matthaean version but already of primitive Christian prayer. Therefore to the present day, almost necessarily, exegesis fluctuates between an eschatological interpretation and one related to everyday life.

The eschatological interpretation of the Our Father	The ethical interpretation of the Our Father related to everyday life

OUR FATHER

IN HEAVEN (= an expansion of the form of address)

I. HALLOWED BE YOUR NAME The hallowing of the name is God's eschatological revelation of himself: God shows his power and glory.	The petition is focussed on the acknowledgment of the one and only God among human beings: they are the ones who hallow the name.
2. YOUR KINGDOM COME The coming of the kingdom is the eschatological realization of the salvation that God alone ushers in.	The petition (at the same time) is focussed on the universal obedience of all people: God's kingdom is realized through this obedience.

3. YOUR WILL BE DONE
AS IN HEAVEN SO ON EARTH (= expansion of the petitions in the second person singular)

God's will is his plan of salvation which he wills to implement everywhere, also on earth.	The petition is focussed on the fulfilment of the will of God by human action.

4. OUR DAILY BREAD GIVE US TODAY

ἐπιούσιος (= future) means the bread of the eschatological meal, a share of which people already ask for today.	ἐπιούσιος means the bread that is needed or 'bread for tomorrow', the possession of which already brings relief today from everyday anxiety.

---

[43] Jesus assumed that Satan had already fallen in the present. But here the removal of evil is expected in the future.

5. AND FORGIVE US OUR DEBT AS WE ALSO FORGIVE OUR
DEBTORS

The petition is for the remission of debt in the final eschatological judgment.	Just as those who pray already forgive their debtors now, so now already they hope for the forgiveness of their sins by God.

6. AND LEAD US NOT INTO TEMPTATION

BUT DELIVER US FROM EVIL (= an expansion of the petitions in the first person plural)

Temptation is the eschatological temptation which must be endured before the final change to salvation.	The petition is focussed on everyday temptations. Those who pray want to be protected from their own sins.

The two types of exegesis[44] must probably be combined. Both petitions in the second person singular are to be understood eschatologically. The Kaddish (see above 3.4) combines the petition for the hallowing of the name and the realization of the kingdom and relates both to the near future. The three petitions in the first person plural are to be related to everyday life and the present. The petition for daily bread means everyday bread. Forgiveness of sins is asked for the present, since the forgiveness of the sins of others is not first promised for the future. In the great eschatological temptation the petition must run, 'Preserve us in this temptation (which must necessarily come)'. But the Our Father meaningfully prays for preservation *from* temptation. Nevertheless, the eschatological interpretation also has a correct insight here: the rule of God which is dawning puts a tremendous emphasis on everyday life. Jesus can already see everyday meals as a sign pointing to the eschatological meal. The great readiness of God to forgive at the end is already at work in every mutual act of forgiveness. In every little temptation the great temptation is mastered. The additions to the Matthaean version are an appropriate interpretation of the prayer: the end-time is seen in the light of the ethical will of God, and everyday life is illuminated by the light of an eschatological liberation from disaster. But both these things happen in a prayer which is addressed to God. In the last resort future and present are combined in the understanding of God. That is shown by the two metaphors for God which are combined in the Lord's Prayer. The present God is addressed as 'Father' just as elsewhere God as 'Father' is associated with care in the present (Matt. 6.25ff.).

---

[44]Those who support an eschatological interpretation are E. Lohmeyer, *Our Father*, London and New York 1965; J. Jeremias, 'The Lord's Prayer in the Light of Recent Research', in *The Prayers of Jesus*, London 1967, 82–107; Meier, *Marginal Jew* 2*, 291–302. For the interpretation related to everyday life see U. Luz, *Matthew 1–7*, Minneapolis and Edinburgh 1989, 367–89.

But the future coming of God is denoted with the metaphor of God's kingship, i.e. God's will to establish salvation for human beings in this world. Accordingly the 'kingly rule of God' is the expression of a powerful ethical energy. To go into this more deeply we must discuss the second tension between salvation and judgment in Jesus' eschatology. But first, here is a diagram which sums up our results so far on the 'temporal structure' of the eschatology of Jesus.

> The two overlapping ellipses depict the old and the new ages. Sayings about struggle conjure up the conflict between the powers of the old world and the new. Sayings about fulfilment illuminate the present as the realization of age-old expectations. Sayings about the future announce the dawn of the new world. Sayings about the dawning of the kingdom confirm that it is already beginning now in a hidden way. And in prayer to God, present and future are combined: the Father's concern in the present with the coming of his kingly rule in the future.

Sayings about struggle

Satan ⟷ God

Sayings about fulfilment

Sayings about the dawning of the kingdom

Future sayings

Prayer:
Father . . . your kingdom come

5. The relationship between judgment and salvation in the preaching of Jesus

In Judaism, God's eschatological action always has an aspect of judgment and an aspect of salvation.[45] The advent of salvation, of a new world under God's rule, presupposes that evil is overcome, both the mythical personification of evil in the figure of Satan and his demons, and historical evil in the form of those among the Gentiles and in the people of God who are dominated by them. Jesus shares this dialectical connection between salvation and disaster with all contemporary Jewish currents: with apocalyptic visionaries who triumph over the downfall of the ungodly, preachers of repentance like John the Baptist who threatened judgment

---

[45]For the judgment in the eschatological conceptions of Judaism around the turn of the ages see M. Reiser, *Judgment*, 1–163.

and the salvation of a remnant, and with Zealots who wanted to root out the evil embodied in the Romans in order to hasten the establishment of the sole rule of God. Despite the common assumption that initially evil must triumph and the eschatological separation take place before salvation can be fulfilled, Jesus puts the announcement of salvation at the centre of his preaching. Above all in the βασιλεία preaching, the aspect of judgment remarkably fades into the background, but without being completely absent. Jesus invites people to take part in the rule of God – but those who do not accept the salvation he offers in words and deeds incur the judgment which is depicted in the sayings and parables about judgment.

5.1 Jesus' preaching of judgment

Here we shall describe Jesus' preaching of judgment by raising four questions. We shall investigate: 1. the responsibility for salvation and damnation in judgment; 2. the images and metaphors for judgment; 3. the time of judgment; and 4. those to whom the preaching of judgment is addressed.

5.1.1 The responsibility for salvation and damnation in the judgment

Jesus' preaching and conduct brought the eschatological salvation, the rule of God, into the everyday life of his hearers. As an appropriate reaction, they were to accept this gift in sheer joy like an treasure discovered unexpectedly or a pearl (Matt. 13.44–46); they were to celebrate the present as an eschatological time of salvation, instead of fasting as though God was still always distant (Mark 2.18ff.), and lead a life in keeping with Jesus' preaching. In a word (cf. Mark 1.15f.), the arrival of the kingdom of God which brought salvation was to produce repentance (μετάνοια). However, for those who did not accept salvation the preaching of salvation became the preaching of judgment. The following passages show that Jesus understood the judgment as a self-chosen or deserved exclusion from the salvation which he brought near in word and deed.

- The *sayings about admission* presuppose that only those who fulfil certain conditions will enter into the kingdom of heaven. In Matt. 7.21 those who do the will of the Father, or Matt. 19.23f.: those who are ready to part with their riches.
- Especially in the Matthaean version, the saying about the *pilgrimage of the peoples* (Matt. 8.11f./Luke 13.28f.) is a vivid threat against the Israelites, the υἱοὶ τῆς βασιλείας (the sons of the kingdom), to whom the saving promise of the eschatological meal was originally given. If they do not believe, they will be cast out, while the Gentiles stream in. The Lukan version, which is probably more original, does not concern all Israel, but contains the same abrupt notion of judgment.
- In the *parable of the marriage feast* (Luke 14.16–24/Matt. 22.1–14/Thomas

64), those who are first invited exclude themselves from participation in the βασιλεία. There is a dispute about who is addressed at the earliest level of the tradition: the pious of Israel – so that the promises then apply to the toll collectors, sinners etc. – or Israel generally – in which case, as in Matt. 8.11f., Israel and the Gentiles are contrasted.

- The *woe on the Galilean cities* (Luke 10.13–15/Matt. 11.21–24) announces judgment on Chorazim, Bethsaida and Capernaum because they have not repented (μετενόησαν) in the face of the miracles of Jesus (δυνάμεις) that have been done in them. The guilt of the Israelites who reject the kingdom of God present in the miracles is regarded as more serious than that of the accursed cities of Tyre and Sidon, for which things will be more tolerable in the judgment.
- In the double saying in Q about the *Queen of the South and the Ninevites* (Matt. 12.41f./Luke 11.31f.), the attitude to Jesus' preaching of wisdom and repentance becomes the criterion for 'this generation'. Since there is 'more than Solomon' and 'more than Jonah' in Jesus, the Queen of the South who heard Solomon's wisdom and the men of Nineveh who repented after the preaching of Jonah will take part in the final judgment as witnesses in the condemnation of 'this generation'.
- In Mark and Q the rejection of the preaching of the kingdom of God and the miracles that are done in its wake also becomes the judgment when *Jesus' disciples* preach and heal. If they are rejected, they are to shake the dust off their feet, i.e. perform a symbolic action which characterizes the place concerned as being under judgment (Mark 6.7–13; Matt. 20.14/Luke 9.5; Luke 10.10f.).
- The parable of the *merciless* creditor (Matt. 18.23ff.) shows that the salvation offered becomes disaster if people do not hand on the forgiveness shown them by God.

In essentials, Jesus' preaching of judgment is a preaching of repentance, i.e. it seeks to prevent damnation by announcing it, to save those on whom it announces judgment. It is no coincidence that Jesus explicitly compares himself with the prophet Jonah (Matt. 12.41f.) – a prophet whose message of judgment led to the conversion of Nineveh. This announcement of judgment is not final. Only in the woe on the Galilean cities (Luke 10.13–15/Matt. 11.21–24) does Jesus seem to have anticipated God's final verdict ('Capernaum, you will be cast down into hell'), just as final salvation is already promised now in its positive counterpart, the beatitude on the eye-witnesses (Luke 10.23f.). Both logia presuppose that the present, Jesus' accomplishment of the βασιλεία τοῦ θεοῦ in preaching and signs of power, is the time of decision, whether for salvation or damnation.

5.1.2 *Images and metaphors for judgment*

In his preaching of judgment Jesus made use of metaphors which also occur elsewhere in the eschatological notions of contemporary Judaism.

1. The *kingly rule of God* also embraces the activity of God as judge. This activity as judge is indicated by the metaphor of 'king'. The 'judgment' can thus be imagined as a formal legal process (as in Matt. 18.23ff.) or as a punitive military action (thus secondarily in Matt. 22.1ff., cf. v.7). It is all the more striking that these notions of judgment are only very rarely connected with the kingdom of God. The judgment that comes with the 'kingdom' of God consists above all in the self-exclusion of those who do not repent and do not meet the conditions of entry into the βασιλεία (see above, 5.1.1).

2. A sphere which more frequently provides images is the *judgment* (ἡ κρίσις). The end of the world comes as forensic judgment, and the course of the proceedings corresponds to the customs of the time (e.g. the appearance of witnesses, Matt. 12.41f.; imprisonment for debt, Matt. 18.23ff.). The judge is usually God, but can be God's representative. Thus the Son of Man is often imagined as the one who delivers judgment on God's behalf. In Matt. 19.28 the authority to judge has possibly been delegated to the twelve disciples (the twelve thrones, taking up Dan. 7.9f.).[46] κρίσις can also denote the execution of the verdict (thus in Luke 10.14).

3. Closely related to the metaphor of judgment is the notion of an eschatological *reckoning*, an image from the world of business. It occurs for example in the parables of the unjust steward (Luke 16.1ff.) and the talents (Luke 19.15–24/Matt. 25.19–28).

4. The image of the *harvest* can depict both sides of the eschatological event, salvation or disaster. For Jesus, in the parables of growth (Mark 4.29 etc.) and the logion about the lord of the harvest and his workers (Luke 10.2/Matt. 9.37f.), the harvest symbolizes the final establishment of the kingdom of God, but this also brings judgment with it (Matt. 13.30, 41f.: the tares among the wheat will be destroyed).

5. The image of *exclusion from the eschatological meal* occurs particularly frequently within the preaching of the kingdom of God (Matt. 8.11f. par.; Luke 14.16–24 par.; Matt. 25.1–13).

6. Frequently *catastrophes which occur unexpectedly* serve as metaphors for the last judgment: the coming of the flood upon a carefree humankind is compared in Luke 17.26f./Matt. 24.37–39 with the coming of the Son of Man; Luke 13.1–5 uses a massacre of Galilean festival pilgrims under Pilate and a tragic accident, the collapse of the tower of Siloam in which eighteen people lost their lives, as a comparison; the closing parable of the Sermon on the Mount (Luke 6.47–49/Matt.

---

[46]A Tannaitic midrash on this passage says that 'the great of Israel' sat on the thrones (cf. Reiser, *Judgment*, 258–62. Matthew 19.28 might be interpreted similarly. But it also remains conceivable that there is no thought of the office of a judge and that κρίνειν means 'rule'.

7.24–27) uses a violent cloudburst which sweeps away a house with bad foundations as an image of the judgment. The images of catastrophe come both from mythical recollection (the flood) and the world of present experience.

5.1.3   The time of the last judgment

Given the close connection between the preaching of the kingdom of God and the preaching of judgment, it is not surprising that both display the same structure. Jesus' announcement of judgment also displays present and future features: just as salvation is already present, so too is the disaster which results from its rejection. Matt. 5.25f. illustrates the close connection between present and future judgment in an image: like any individual, Israel is on the way to court. But as long as creditors and debtors are still on the way, agreement is possible, and the slavery of debt, eternal destruction, can still be averted. The judgment already begins in the present as a consequence of the presence of salvation in three forms:

- As *judgment on Satan* and the demons (cf. Luke 10.18; Matt. 12.28 par.; Mark 3.22ff. par.).
- As the beginning of an *eschatological division* in the face of Jesus' miracles and his preaching of the kingdom of God (see above, 4.2.1). The logia according to which the intercession of the Son of Man in the judgment is made dependent on people's present confession of Jesus can also be mentioned (in so far as they are regarded as having an authentic nucleus): Mark 8.38/Luke 9.26; Luke 12.8/Matt. 10.32f.
- In isolated instances this present division even leads to an *anticipation of God's eschatological verdict* by Jesus himself (woes on the Galilean cities: Luke 10.13–15/Matt. 11.21–24).

5.1.4   Those to whom the preaching of judgment is addressed

As Jesus' preaching of judgment is focussed on repentance, the final judgment contains no attack on collectives: every individual has an opportunity to detach himself from the 'collective of damnation' by repentance. Nevertheless, it is illuminating to see which groups and entities Jesus attacked and which he did not.

1. The threats of judgment against *'this generation'* (cf. Luke 11.49–51 par.; Luke 11.29ff. par.) come under suspicion of being reactions to negative experiences of the mission to Israel. Such experiences are introduced in Matt. 23.34–36 when the persecution of the prophets, wise men and scribes sent by Jesus is mentioned. But on the whole the attacks on 'this generation' probably go back to Jesus. He thus continues John the Baptist's preaching of judgment. When here in Luke 11.29ff. he contrasts Gentiles (the Queen of the South and the Ninevites) with 'this generation', there is no doubt that all Israelites living at the time are meant.

2. The threats of judgment against *individual places*, against Chorazim, Bethsaida and Capernaum (Luke 10.13ff.) and some cities which rejected Jesus' preaching (Luke 10.10ff.), only make sense if other places had a chance of being spared in the judgment. That already excludes a collective judgment of destruction upon 'this whole generation'. The discourse when Jesus sends out the disciples shows that anyone who accepts Jesus and his messengers receives protection in the judgment which has an almost magical effect (cf. Luke 10.5ff. par.).

3. Other threats of judgment are directed against the *leaders of Israel*: Pharisees and teachers of the law are attacked in the woes (Luke 11.37ff.). The announcement of judgment is absent from these woes. The basic statement 'Woe to you . . . for . . .' mentions only the crime and not the punishment (cf. by contrast the woes in Ethiopic Enoch, e.g. 95.4–7; 96.4–8). That is not a final destruction. The rich are attacked as well as the educated religious élite – regardless of whether the woe against the rich, which is handed down only by Luke (6.24), is authentic or not. For the saying 'It is easier for a camel to go through the eye of a needle than for a rich man to enter the kingdom of God' (Mark 10.25) is clear enough. It is striking that while the powerful are sharply criticized (Mark 10.41ff.), unlike the scribes and the rich they are spared eschatological threats of damnation. Particularly those in power are the preferential object of fantasies of punishment in other apocalyptic pictures of judgment (cf. EthEn 62.3ff.; Dan. 7).

4. The threat of judgment as an *individual separation* between people who are extremely close is especially characteristic of Jesus' preaching of judgment:

'I tell you,
in that night there will be two men in one bed;
one will be taken
and the other left.
There will be two women grinding together;
one will be taken
and the other left' (Luke 17.34/Matt. 24.40f.).

Since here no specifically 'Christian' criterion (like 'faith') is mentioned for the separation in the last judgment, this logion may go back to the historical Jesus. Only at first glance is there a contradiction between the sweeping attack on 'this generation' and this individualizing judgment. Both have the same focus: no one is certain of withstanding the judgment. All are called to repentance, the 'whole generation' and each individual in it.

All in all, there is no reason to deny that Jesus preached judgment. The tradition of this is too broad. Moreover, with it Jesus is merely continuing the Baptist's preaching of judgment. Rather, we must reckon that now and again sayings of John the Baptist have found their way into the sayings of Jesus – or (even more probably) that Jesus adopted sayings of John the Baptist as his own words in his preaching.

5.2 Jesus' preaching of salvation

Jesus' preaching of judgment aims to make his audience uncertain: salvation and damnation are not distributed as they think. The Israelites and their religious leaders who believe that they are safe are threatened with damnation in the judgment. But the Gentiles and sinners who saw themselves threatened with damnation are given a chance in the kingdom of God. In this way the traditional expectation of salvation is fundamentally changed: according to Ps.Sol 17, salvation means that the Gentiles will be conquered and driven out. The land will be freed from all that is unclean. No sinner, no alien and foreigner may dwell in it (Ps.Sol 17.28). But then all peoples will acknowledge the God of Zion and stream there to submit to Israel and its Messiah. With Jesus the poles of this expectation are reversed. The kingdom of God is not a victory over the Gentiles, but Gentiles are admitted into it – and Israelites who are unwilling to repent are excluded. No victories over foreigners are to be expected here. In fact a kind of 'internal revolution' is taking place: groups which hitherto had been underprivileged now come into their own.

5.2.1 *Salvation for the Gentiles outside Israel*

Most sayings about the kingdom of God in the prophetic and apocalyptic texts contain a contrast between Israel and the Gentiles. In apocalyptic texts it is even intensified so that it becomes a mythical dualism of God and Satan. In parallel, heavenly and demonic powers fight in heaven, and Israel and the Gentiles or the children of light fight against the children of darkness on earth. Such a social mythical parallelism appears, say, in Daniel and in 1QM. Jesus preserves the mythical dualism. For him, too, the kingdom of God establishes itself against the rule of Satan. But no corresponding battle against the Gentiles takes place on earth. On the contrary, the kingdom of God is open to the Gentiles: Gentiles and Jews will eat in it along with the patriarchs (Matt. 8.10f.). The food laws no longer have any divisive role. We hear nothing of a subjection of the Gentiles to Israel, and there is not even any mention of their conversion to the God of Israel. The socio-mythical parallelism is transcended and abolished: the victory of Satan in heaven does not result in the victory over alien rule on earth. It leads to the healing of the possessed.

5.2.2 *Salvation for outcast groups within Israel*

The kingdom of God at the same time brings a revaluation of stigmatized groups within Israel. Groups which have social, physical or moral defects are brought particularly close to it.

　　1. *Groups with social defects.* The poor, the hungry, those who weep, the

persecuted and children are called blessed because the kingdom of God is theirs (Matt. 5.33ff./Luke 6.20ff.; Mark 10.14f.). According to biblical tradition the 'poor' are the poor both in the real sense and in the transferred religious sense: people who (on the basis of their external poverty or other defects) have a special relationship of protection from and trust in God. The real and the transferred sense may not be played off against each other, even if the (secondary?) Matthaean phrase the 'poor in Spirit' emphasizes the religious significance. With the 'real' significance, too, there is more in the biblical tradition than the absence of wealth: anyone is 'poor' whose rights are infringed and who is oppressed by the powerful. The element of a lack of power is contained in the term. So in the first beatitude Jesus calls the poor blessed, not because they will become rich but because they will participate in God's power: theirs is the kingdom of God. Their defect is a lack of power to resist injustice. The hope for a new distribution of power may also play a role in the statement that the kingdom of God belongs to children (Mark 10.14).

2. *Groups with physical defects.* Eunuchs, who could not take part in the Israelite cult (Matt. 19.12), and those who have mutilated themselves so as not to become an offence (Mark 9.43–47), are also brought near to the kingdom. Here, too, we need to distinguish between the literal and the transferred meaning. The saying about eunuchs probably plays on both meanings. For according to it there are those who are born castrated or are castrated by force – and others who are eunuchs for the sake of the kingdom of God. Possibly the disciples were taunted with being 'eunuchs' because they avoided marriage and having families. The logion would then mean that even such interests fade into the background for the sake of the kingdom of God. Even the obscure saying about the 'offence' (Mark 9.43ff.) could also be meant to be understood in a transferred sense: an offence is what leads to apostasy from God. Measured by that, physical integrity is unimportant – far less everything else.

3. *Groups with moral defects.* The parable of the two sons together with its application in Matt. 21.28–32 says that the toll collectors and prostitutes have more chance of entering the kingdom of God than the pious who say yes to God's will and then do not do it. Repentance is decisive. The sinner who repents is ahead of the pious person who is unwilling to repent. In another passage we find expressions which are probably to be understood in a metaphorical sense: in Jesus' remark that 'men of violence' seize the kingdom of God, an accusation against Jesus and his followers could have been reshaped positively. Here is a demonstrative assertion that precisely those who do violence to some norms are the ones who truly possess the kingdom of God (Matt. 11.12f.). We also have a reshaping of an originally negative term when Jesus calls the disciples to be 'fishers of men' (Mark 1.17). Anyone who leaves his 'ordinary work' to take up the offensive trade of dealing in and hunting people exposes himself to criticism.

5.2.3 Salvation as a new legal and social order in the kingdom of God

A new legal order prevails in the βασιλεία which is shaped by God's unconditional readiness to forgive, as is shown above all by Jesus' parables (e.g. the merciless creditor in Matt. 18.23ff.; the prodigal son in Luke 15.11ff.). The citizenship of the kingdom of God is made up of forgiven sinners. In return, God expects them also to forgive one another and not to judge (Matt. 6.12; 7.1). What in earthly legal circumstances is embezzlement – an arbitrary reduction of the debts of others – is a positive act in the legal order of the kingdom of God. In it, the immoral and disloyal steward becomes a moral hero (cf. Luke 16.1ff.)

Rank and hierarchy are also known in the βασιλεία. At least people reflected on it, as is shown by sayings of Jesus (authentic and inauthentic): people asked who was the 'greatest' and the 'least' in the kingdom of God (cf. Matt. 5.19; 11.11; 18.4). They argued over places of honour in the future world (Mark 10.37). They dreamed of 'judging' the twelve tribes of Israel in it (Matt. 19.28 par.). The longing for rank, respect and status even extends to peoples' eschatological dreams. Precisely for that reason, it is striking that Jesus gives substance to the kingdom of God in only one image. He depicts the eschatological salvation as a great feast. Certainly there were places of honour and problems of rank even at feasts (cf. Luke 14.1ff.), but all those who have been invited and take part in the meal share in the rank of the host. It is the 'social' image which even now forces power and status into the background. Here 'whoever would be great among you must be your servant, and whoever would be first among you must be slave of all' (Mark 10.43f.).

5.3 The unity of the preaching of salvation and judgment, of future and present eschatology

The two basic tensions in the eschatology of Jesus – the tensions between judgment and salvation, present and future can be understood in terms of the Israelite understanding of God. In the time of the exile Israel had been forced into a consistent monotheism. Deutero-Isaiah had proclaimed the bold message of the one and only God, thus formulating the problem that any consistent monotheistic faith entails: the one and only God becomes responsible for everything, for good and evil. According to Deutero-Isaiah, this God creates light and darkness, salvation and disaster (Isa. 45.6f.). In Deutero-Isaiah this problem could be overcome because his preaching says that God already caused disaster in past catastrophes; now he has finally decided on salvation for Israel. This salvation already begins in the present: 'Behold, I am doing a new thing, now it spreads forth, do you not perceive it?' (43.19). But it will only be fulfilled in a new exodus in the future (40.1ff.). The tension between 'already' and 'not yet' makes it possible for Deutero-Isaiah to understand the God who establishes himself in the future as the will for salvation. The same is true of Jesus. The monotheistic problem is sharpened for him, because he can identify God with the good. 'No one is good but the one God' (Mark 10.18). Given the ethical irrationality of the world in which the good must often suffer and the villain triumphs, this notion of the goodness of God now and again has to be maintained by reinterpretation: God makes his sun rise on good and bad – but not because he is ethically indifferent. Rather, this shows his boundless goodness towards the wicked (Matt. 5.43ff.). However, God does not give the recompense which would be 'just' by abstract measures: rather, those who work for a short time receive the same subsistence wage as those who work for a long time. That is not injustice, but an expression of the goodness of God (Matt. 20.1ff.). However, not everything can be coped with in this way. In addition to such reinterpretations, a monotheistic faith has three possibilites of coping with evil,which are usually combined. One accepts the dark side in God – a will which is incomprehensible for human beings, which they cannot discern any more than a clay vessel can discern the will of the potter. Or evil is attributed to human guilt and sin. Or a quality is attributed to the 'world' which makes evil comprehensible: this third entity is Satan, the embodiment of the numinous hostility of this world which cannot be attributed either to God's will or to human guilt. In the case of Jesus – as a continuation of Jewish traditions – we find all these ways of dealing with evil, but all on the premise that God will soon establish himself as the power of the good.

- Jesus, too, knows the dark side of God. His preaching of judgment brings it out in a threatening way. But in it God's punitive and lethal energy is here concentrated as the power to punish sinners. Thus it has an ethical orientation – and in the last resort is distanced from God, because human sin comes into the centre.
- Evil is rooted in human beings. Whereas God is *the* good (Mark 10.18), human beings are identified with evil: 'If you who are evil can give your children good gifts . . .' (Matt. 7.11). But this evil loses its terror because repentance is offered to everyone, unconditionally.
- There remains Satan as the embodiment of the hostile world which is working against God and human beings. It is Jesus' conviction that the victory has already been won, that Satan has already fallen. His demons flee at the sight of the activity of Jesus.

Because God appears as the unconditional will for good, he is presented as a God who is coming. For the present world is marked by evil. But whatever causes this evil – God's dark side, human sin and Satan's activity – is overcome and can be overcome in the face of the intervention of the will for the good. This understanding of God is deeply rooted in the traditions of Judaism. Wellhausen depicted it like this in connection with the preaching of Amos:

> 'What Yahweh requires is righteousness, nothing else; what he hates is injustice. Insult to the deity, sin, is always of a moral nature. That had never been stressed before with such tremendous emphasis. It is morality alone through which all human beings have existence, which is the only essential thing in the world. It is not a postulate or an idea but at the same time both a necessity and a fact, the most lively personal power – Yahweh the God of powers. Angry and destructive, the holy reality makes itself felt; it destroys all appearance and all that is vain.'[47]

The God of Jesus is the God of Israel: a blazing fire of ethical energy which seeks to change people in order to kindle the love of neighbour in them; but which becomes the devastating fire of hell for those who exclude themselves from salvation. So it is characteristic of Jesus' understanding of God that God will soon also come to power as the unconditional will for the good. One can best understand this peculiarity of Jesus' understanding of God through the basic metaphors which he uses to speak of God. He combines two images which come from Judaism, those of the father and the king. Occasionally the two were combined before him. According to Wisdom 11.10 God tested the Israelites 'like a father who chastizes', but he punished the Gentiles 'like a strict king' after he had condemned them. Tobit's hymn of praise celebrates him as king (Tobit 13.6, 7,15) and as father (13.4). Here, too, the metaphor of father expresses the gracious side of God: 'He chastizes us because of our unrighteousness but he again has mercy on us . . .' (13.5).

The new thing in the preaching of Jesus is not the combination of the metaphors of father and king but something which is not obvious at first sight: Jesus never speaks of God as 'king'. The few instances are secondary: Matt. 5.35 is special material and a secondary extension of the antithesis on swearing. The parable Matt. 22.1ff. has a parallel in Luke 14.16ff., which does not speak of a 'king'. Two further instances are Matthaean special material: 18.23ff.; 25.34ff. As a rule Jesus speaks only of the 'kingdom' of God. In other Jewish writings we usually find a juxtaposition of 'king' and 'kingdom' (cf. e.g. AssMos. 4.2; 10.1; Ps.Sol 17.1, 3; 1QM XII, 7f.; TestBenj. 9.1; 10.7; Sib. 3, 46, 55; Wisdom 3.8; 6.4). This juxtaposition is absent from the words of Jesus. This can be interpreted to mean that for Jesus, God's nature is expressed as goodness in his fatherhood. And as father he will come to power. For Jesus 'power' is not a value in itself but serves to make God's goodness break through universally.

---

[47]J. Wellhausen, *Israelitische und jüdische Geschichte*, Berlin [7]1914, 106.

6. Summary and hermeneutical reflections

Jesus' proclamation of the kingdom of God is governed by the Jewish understanding of God. God is the unconditional will for the good. Jesus spreads the certainty that this will is soon going to establish itself in the world. God will help the weak to secure their rights, give power to the poor, satisfy the hungry, and offer the sinner a chance of repentance. This unconditional ethical will is already active in the present. What opposes it – Satan, sin and a 'dark side' in God – has already been overcome. Satan has fallen. Sin is forgiven. God's punitive action is directed only against those who reject the unconditional offer of salvation. To conclude, we shall attempt to answer the ten questions about the understanding of the eschatological preaching of Jesus which were formulated at the beginning. The alternatives formulated there are each time indicated by key words:

1. *Present or future?* The kingdom of God is both present and future. The time of fulfilment is already here, and Satan has already been conquered. Sayings about fulfilment and struggle (the conflict between the realms of Satan and God) express a present eschatology. The sayings about the dawn of the kingdom also have a present sense; they indicate in paradoxical formulations and images that a new world is beginning in the midst of the old. But only the future will bring the full realization of the kingdom of God.

2. *Expectation of salvation and expectation of judgment.* The two belong together. John the Baptist preaches judgment, but opens a way to salvation through baptism. Jesus proclaims salvation, but in the background threatens with judgment. The greater the salvation offered in the present, the more inexorable the judgment on all those who exclude themselves from salvation. The greater the judgment which threatens, the more overwhelming the salvation that is promised to all.

3. *Rule or kingdom?* In so far as God's kingdom is the establishment of his ethical will, the kingdom of God is to be understood dynamically as rule. But the 'kingdom of God' is not an end in itself. God's power serves to realize his goodness. God is 'father' by nature. His 'kingdom' is his instrument. Therefore this kingdom can become independent as the 'kingdom of God' and can be spoken of as a realm differentiated by God which a person can enter.

4. *God alone at work or human participation?* If the 'kingdom of God' is an image for the establishment of God's ethical will, there is even more of a demand on the human ethical will. The expectation of the kingdom of God activates in human beings that concern for the weak, sick and marginalized which God realizes in his eschatological action. If human beings are enabled to perform exorcisms, they are taking part in the victory over Satan; when they forgive one another's sins, they are taking part in God's forgiveness of sins; when they move others to accept salvation, they are taking part in the establishment of God's saving will (see further below, §12.4.3, p. 376 on Mark 4.26–29).

5. *Theocentric or with a messianic intermediary?* Jesus presents a theocentric expectation. The lack of a messianic mediator figure in some sayings about the kingdom of God is an indication of their authenticity. However, at the same time Jesus probably spoke of the 'Son of Man'. If this was not an honorific messianic title, that would be compatible with a theocentric expectation of the kingdom of God. If it was an honorific title, there would be a tension here in Jesus' eschatological preaching (for more see on the 'Son of Man' in §16.4, pp. 541–53).

6. *A political or religious factor?* The kingdom of God is not as spiritual as it is often portrayed as being: there is eating and drinking in it. It is localized in Palestine. The Gentiles stream there. But beyond that it also extends into a realm beyond the frontier of death: the dead patriarchs appear alive in it. To this degree it is certainly not a 'political kingdom', but a religious expectation with political relevance. The legal and social structure hoped for in it stands in contradiction to the basic elements of existing rule. It delegitimizes the present distribution of power and possessions.

7. *Rulers or people in the kingdom of God?* The disciples can be promised a share of rule in the new world (Matt. 19.28 par.). If it is the kingdom of those whom the followers of Jesus call 'father', as the 'family of God' they *a priori* have a privileged relationship to the ruler of this kingdom. It is symbolized by participation in the eschatological meal – i.e. with an image in which status and rank fade into the background. All participants share in the dignity of the host.

8. *Symbol or metaphor?* The term 'kingdom of God' did not evoke any well-defined myth among hearers at that time, so according to the alternatives formulated here it would not be a 'symbol'. But it had associations: hope for the overcoming of the Gentiles, the gathering of the dispersed tribes, the realization of a pure theocracy. If the hearers of Jesus' preaching had such associations, Jesus led them to a new view of the kingdom of God. The Gentiles belong to the kingdom of God. The kingdom of God is not what was expected. With Jesus, the term again becomes a living metaphor.

9. *Apocalyptic and wisdom traditions.* Jesus stands in apocalyptic traditions – but not in that scribal and esoteric apocalyptic which we find in many writings. Jesus' preaching has the form of oral prophecy. In its temporal dimensions it remains limited to the near future, as oral preaching would suggest: only something meant to apply to far later generations had to be set down in writing. Sometimes wisdom features are combined with this apocalyptic expectation. So one is to 'seek' the kingdom of God – just as one is to seek wisdom (Matt. 6.25ff.).

10. *Jewish tradition or an abandonment of Jewish convictions?* The kingly rule of God which stands at the centre of the preaching of Jesus can only be understood in terms of the centre of Jewish belief in God. Jesus is not a 'marginal Jew' in his eschatological preaching. Rather, in it he responds to basic problems of Jewish monotheism – problems which cannot be understood outside this frame of reference.

If the description of Jesus' preaching of the kingdom of God given above is correct, the hermeneutical problem of the rule of God would be the hermeneutical problem of monotheistic belief in God generally: how does the one and only God establish his will in this world? The most important comments on this have already been made in 5.3. Here we shall concentrate on the problem of Jesus' erroneous expectation of an imminent end. Regardless of how one interprets the perspective implied by his preaching, the problem remains: Jesus proclaimed an imminent kingdom of God, but a Christianity came which was often far removed from the 'kingdom of God'. Jesus did not reckon that the world would continue to exist for so long a time. In principle there are three approaches to a solution, which can only be sketched out briefly here:

1. *The salvation-historical solution*: Jesus expected his death, and an intermediate period which would follow it until the kingdom of God came. Anyone who shares this view can say that while Jesus was perhaps wrong about the time-span, he was not wrong about the structure, i.e. the sequence of different phases. After his death the 'intermediate period' has been extended, but his eschatology has been preserved in principle. Similarly, today his eschatology has been preserved – with new indications of time. This solution, which is fond of referring to Luke–Acts, is represented, among others, by W.G. Kümmel.

2. *The existential solution* distinguishes between obsolete 'objectivizing notions' about the end of the world and a 'real intention' behind these notions which are first worked out by the exegete. This approach can be developed further alongside the solution offered by existentialist interpretation in the narrower sense.

- The kerygmatic call of Jesus can be regarded as a real intention which confronts every individual with God and eternity and is a summons to an existential decision. The consciousness of the interval which has been given for decision has (erroneously) been clad in the awareness of an interval in time for the whole world (Bultmann, cf. 1.5 above).
- The ethical will can also be regarded as the real intention which is expressed in time-conditioned 'notions'. Here the important thing is not to connect this ethical will with more appropriate notions about the world but in principle to recognize how it is intrinsically independent of any 'world-view'. It is based on[48] an inner affirmation of the will to life in each individual, not in statements about the external world.[49]

---

[48] Cf. Kümmel, *Promise and Fulfilment*; id., 'Eschatological Expectation in the Proclamation of Jesus' (1964), in B.D. Chilton (ed.), *The Kingdom of God*, Minneapolis and London 1984, 36–51.

[49] A. Schweitzer, *Civilization and Ethics* (1923), London 1946.

- What apocalyptic notions really mean to convey can also be interpreted as an internal transformation of human beings: the unconscious inner world (along with its archetypes) is reorganized in a far-reaching way. This transformation of the unconscious sparks off anxiety and hope, and is projected on to the world as an expectation of a cosmic change.[50]

3. *The evolutionary solution*: religious images and language are the result of a long process of assimilation to the objective structures of reality – long before people see through this assimilation. The wisdom which is hidden in them precedes the recognition of it. Jewish apocalyptic (including Jesus) expresses an objective reality, namely that human beings live in the transition between two worlds, between biological and cultural evolution. They are subject to the biological laws of mutation and selection, but have already taken a step into a phase of evolution in which culture is an opportunity to reduce selection. Like the whole of the Bible, the preaching of Jesus articulates a direct protest against the principle of selection which gives opportunities in life to those who are better adapted and 'fitter' at the expense of the weaker. The transition between the two phases of evolution takes place throughout history. It is consciously articulated in the Bible. Here religious symbols and images decode the secret programme of culture.[51]

Jesus' erroneous expectation of an imminent end (which was shared by the first Christians) did not spark off a great crisis in primitive Christianity. However, the problem was registered, as is shown by Luke–Acts; II Thessalonians; II Peter; I Clem. 23ff.; II Clem. 11f.; the Apocalypse of Peter; and Justin, I *Apol.* 28, 2. Yet even that did not lead to a fundamental restructuring of eschatology.[52] Understandably. Whereas human consciousness can always shape its relationship to the past rationally, that is only possible to a limited degree in relation to the future. The past is increasingly brought into an understandable context through written sources and historiographical accounts. The 'beginnings' go further and further back in the consciousness. By contrast, the mythical consciousness allows the beginnings, i.e. the archetypal primal time, to move with us like a horizon. They begin where recalled time ceases – in oral tradition often after a few generations. In respect of the future, in our experience we remain tied to such mythical structures: the future moves like a horizon (occupied by anxieties and hopes) and always remains the same distance away. Therefore today we still have a quasi-mythical relation to it. The expectation of the kingdom of God could also move with the whole of the history of Christianity as a constant horizon.

---

[50]K. Niederwimmer, *Jesus*, Göttingen 1968.

[51]G. Theissen, *Biblical Faith*, London and Philadelphia 1984.

[52]Cf. K. Erlemann, *Naherwartungen und Parusieverzögerung im Neuen Testament*, Tübingen and Basel 1995.

7. Tasks

7.1 *The history of research*

Indicate in the following table the way in which the various interpretations of eschatology interpret and evaluate the present and future sayings:

	Present sayings	Future sayings
1. Ethical eschatology (A. Ritschl)		
2. Thoroughgoing eschatology (J. Weiss/ A. Schweitzer)		
3. Realized eschatology (C.H. Dodd)		
4. Double eschatology (W.G. Kümmel)		
5. Existential eschatology (R. Bultmann and pupils)		

7.2 *Does Jesus' notion of judgment leave the process of judging behind?*

The following extracts from a book on the Sermon of the Mount which appeared in 1985 show an understanding of the rule of God and the place of judgment in Jesus preaching which differs from the account given above.

> [on Matt. 5.25f. 'the accuser'] 'This parabolic saying refers metaphorically to the coming judgment. It works with the notion of the penal judgment of God . . . It does not speak about the then but to the now. The theme is not the judgment, but being on the way. The parabolic saying recalls the future judgment in order to give the correct dimensions to being on the way in the present. That Is characteristic of Jesus' understanding of time as it is also expressed specifically in the Sermon on the Mount. Jesus makes the future rule of God a topic in such a way that he brings it into the here and now. His real theme is being on the way in life as the place where people can adopt an attitude to the rule of God.'
> 'Judge not that you be not judged' [Matt. 7.1] . . . Here any form of judging is

rejected.. here there is not simply a prohibition of human judging with an eye to the sole divine judge . . . Far more is given up here: here the *notion* or the *process* of judging is itself given up, both for human beings and for God. For anyone who judges is drawn into the maelstrom of being judged. The one who judges will not be able to imagine God otherwise than as the judge, at best as a righteous judge. The one who judges is prepared for the Last Judgment . . . This abrupt rejection of judging by Jesus can best be explained if we think in terms of his message of the kingdom of God. The kingdom of God is the rule of that God who does justice to all human beings by making all human beings just. The kingly rule of God is that rule in which human beings are not corrected by judgment but by love. This kingly rule of God is on the way . . . One has to imagine what such statements meant at the time when they were first made. In both Jewish and Hellenistic–Greek thought the notion of God was dominated by the notion of judgment. God is the judge, his verdict is incorruptible and just . . . God in his eschatological coming is presented as judge. This is the context in which Jesus issues his clear and unmistakable invitation to dissociate oneself from any judging, even from gracious judging, and even from the judging which brings those above down and raises those below up. That is a breathtaking notion, which shakes the basic foundations of the notion of God. It is not surprising that this notion shines out only here and there in the New Testament, breaks through only here and there, whereas in many other passages the old status of judging is kept in new wineskins.'

[On Matt. 7.19f., 21–23:]: 'Is not precisely the notion of judging which Jesus had bidden farewell to in Matt. 7.1f. reintroduced here? . . . In v.21 entry into the kingdom of God is unmistakably made dependent on doing the will of the Father . . . The debate is about righteousness by works . . . It is indisputable that the notion that the person is made by his or her works was taken for granted in contemporary Judaism. But may a Christian community which only exists at all because of the grace which is embodied in Christ assume such a thing as a matter of course? Did not Jesus stake everything on convincing people of the unsurpassable nearness of God? . . . Can my works undo God, destroy his creation of my person? In the sphere of Christian theology there is only one answer to this question: No. All other answers are unbaptized.'

1. Characterize in your own words the understanding of the kingdom of God expressed here. Where is it to be located in the history of research? Who could be the author of this text?

2. In particular, the interpretation that while Jesus conjured up God metaphorically as a judge he did not expect a final judgment because this could not be reconciled with his understanding of God and his βασιλεία contradicts the reflections above on the relation of salvation to damnation in Jesus' eschatological preaching. What do you think of that?

10

Jesus as Healer: The Miracles of Jesus

G. Ebeling, 'Jesus and Faith', in id., *Word and Faith*, Philadelphia and London 1963, 201–46; H.-J. Held, 'Matthew as Interpreter of the Miracle Stories' , in G. Bornkamm, G. Barth and H.-J. Held, *Tradition and Interpretation in Matthew*, London 1963, ²1972, 165–299; L.R Hogan, *Healing in the Second Temple Period*, NTOA 21, Fribourg CH and Göttingen 1992; E. and M.-L. Keller, *Miracles in Dispute*, London 1969; B. Mack, *A Myth of Innocence*, Philadelphia 1988, 'The Miracle Stories', 208–45; J.P. Meier, *Marginal Jew 2**, 509–1038; G. Theissen, *Miracle Stories**; G.H. Twelftree, *Jesus the Exorcist. A Contribution to the Study of the Historical Jesus*, WUNT 2/54, Tübingen 1993; T.J. Weeden, 'The Heresy That Necessitated Mark's Gospel', ZNW 59, 1968, 145–15, reprinted in W. Telford (ed.), *The Interpretation of Mark*, Edinburgh 1995, 89–164.

Introduction

Just as the kingdom of God stands at the centre of Jesus' preaching, so healings and exorcisms form the centre of his activity. Certainly Jesus did not just perform miracles. Equally characteristic of him are his symbolic actions: the choice of the Twelve, the sending out of the disciples, eating with toll collectors and sinners, the entry into Jerusalem, the cleansing of the temple and the last supper. But Jesus impressed and provoked his contemporaries above all by miracles. Provocation predominates among modern historical critics. On the one hand miracles are attested in so many old strata of tradition that there is no doubt about their historical background. On the other hand they seem to us to be an unhistorical 'gleam' born of longing and poetry which has attached itself to the historical figure of Jesus. Some argue that if incredible accounts appear so early (in Mark and the Logia source), the sources are incredible generally. Others argue the opposite: as the attestation of the miracles is comparable to the attestation of the sayings of Jesus, for them, too, a far greater degree of historicity must be assumed than is usually conceded.[1] In our view the historical challenge lies in differentiating in a convincing way – i.e. in explaining the relatively early rise of a miracle

---

[1]Meier, *Marginal Jew 2**, 617–45, makes a resounding plea for the historicity of the miracle tradition. He comes to the significant conclusion: 'Put dramatically but with not too much exaggeration: if the miracle tradition from Jesus' public ministry were to be rejected *in toto* as unhistorical, so should every other Gospel tradition about him' (630).

tradition with a great degree of wishful thinking and poetry without discrediting the whole Jesus tradition. Here the approach cannot be to regard the objectively probable as historical and the objectively improbable as unhistorical. Rather, it is necessary to explain how the two can lie so closely together in the tradition and can nevertheless be distinguished with good reason. An important step here is a historical comparison with other miracles and a form-critical analysis of the miracle stories with a view to discovering typical motifs. The two following tasks are an introduction to these questions.

1. Ancient parallels to New Testament miracle stories

Read the following miracle stories from antiquity and compare them with Synoptic and Old Testament miracle stories.

1. Exorcism of Eleazar, which Josephus reports as an eye-witness in *Antt.* 8, 46–48:

> 'I have seen (ἱστόρησα) a certain Eleazar, a countryman of mine, in the presence of Vespasian, his sons, tribunes and a number of other soliders, free men possessed by demons, and this was the manner of the cure: he put to the nose of the possessed man a ring which had under its seal one of the roots prescribed by Solomon and then, as the man smelled it, drew out the demon through his nostrils, and, when the man at once fell down, adjured the demon never to come back into him, speaking Solomon's name and reciting the incantations which he had composed. Then, wishing to convince the bystanders and prove to them that he had this power, Eleazar placed a cup or foot-basin full of water a little way off and commanded the demon, as it went out of the man, to overturn it and make known to the spectators that he had left that man.'

Compare this exorcism with Mark 5.1–20.

2. Raising of the dead by Apollonius of Tyana (Philostratus, *Vita Apollonii* IV, 45):

> 'Here too is a miracle which Apollonius worked. A girl had died just in the hour of her marriage, and the bridegroom was following her bier lamenting as was natural his marriage left unfulfilled, and the whole of Rome was mourning with him, for the maiden belonged to a consular family. Apollonius then witnessing their grief, said: "Put down the bier, for I will stay the tears that you are shedding for this maiden." And he asked what was her name. The crowd accordingly thought that he was about to deliver such an oration as is commonly delivered as much to grace the funeral as to stir up lamentation; but he did nothing of the kind, but merely touching her and whispering in secret some spell over her, at once

woke up the maiden from her seeming death; and the girl spoke out loud, and returned to her father's house, just as Alcestis did when she was brought back to life by Hercules. And the relations of the maiden wanted to present him with the sum of 150,000 sesterces, but he said that he would freely present the money to the young lady by way of a dowry. Now whether he detected some spark of life in her, which those who were nursing her had not noticed – for it is said that although it was raining at the time, a vapour went up from her face – or whether life was really extinct, and he restored it by the warmth of his touch, is a mysterious problem which neither I myself nor those who were present could decide.'

Compare this raising of the dead with I Kings 17.17–24 and Luke 7.11–17.

3. Miracle of bread performed for the wife of the penniless Rabbi Hanina ben Dosa according to bTaan 24b, 25a:

'His [Hanina ben Dosa's] wife used to heat the oven every sabbath eve and used to throw fuel in to make smoke because of the shame (that is, because she was ashamed before her neighbours). She had this spiteful neighbour. She (the neighbour) said, "This is odd, when I know they have nothing, nothing at all. What does all this mean?" She (the neighbour) went and knocked on the door [of Hanina's house]. She [Hanina's wife] was ashamed and went into the room. Then a miracle took place for her [Hanina's wife]; she saw the oven full of bread and the trough full of dough. Then she [the neighbour] said to her, "Bring a shovel. Your loaves are beginning to burn." And she [Hanina's wife] said to her, "That's why I went in"' (quoted from Theissen, *Miracle Stories** 104).

Compare this gift miracle with II Kings 4.1–7, 42–44 and Mark 6.34–44.

2. *The motifs in New Testament miracle stories*

The Synoptic miracle stories vary a particular set of motifs[2] in ever new combinations; each time the individual miracle story actualizes only a limited number of potentially possible motifs. The survey given below sums up all the motifs (from Theissen, *Miracle Stories**, 47–80) and at the same time indicates their (most usual) place in a composition (e.g. introduction) and their relationship to those involved.

---

[2]Here the smallest independent narrative units than can be defined are regarded as 'motifs'. The motifs also occur outside the miracle stories. They belong to the store of a narrative generally, as is shown by F.G. Downing, 'Words as Deeds and Deeds as Words', *BiblInt* 3, 1995, 129–43.

Introduction (introductory motifs)	1. The coming of the miracle-worker 2. The appearance of the crowd	
	The appearance of	3. The distressed person 4. Representatives[1] 5. Embassies 6. Opponents
	7. Reasons given for the appearance of 'opposite numbers'[2]	

Exposition (expositional motifs)	8. Description of the distress	
	Approach to the miracle-worker	9. Difficulties in the approach 10. Falling to the knees 11. Cries for help 12. Pleas and expressions of trust
	Holding back	13. Misunderstanding[3] 14. Scepticism and mockery 15. Criticism (from opponents) 16. Resistance of the demon
	Behaviour of the miracle-worker	17. Pneumatic excitement[4] 18. Assurance 19. Argument[5] 20. Withdrawal

Centre (central motifs)	21. Setting the scene[6]	
	Miraculous action	22. Touch 23. Healing substances 24. Miracle-working word 25. Prayer
	26. Recognition of the miracle	

Conclusion (final motifs)	Adversaries[7]	27. Demonstration 28. Dismissal
	Miracle-worker Other characters[7]	29. Command to secrecy 30. Wonder[8] 31. Acclamation 32. Rejection 33. Spread of the news

[1] *'Representatives' are people making requests on behalf of the sick, including those who carry or accompany them.*

[2] *'Reasons given for the appearance of "opposite numbers"'; in other words,why the sick come to the miracle workers. On 'opposite numbers' see below.[7]*

[3] *There is a 'misunderstanding' if people expect the help within the framework of normality or do not count on the miracle and therefore misunderstand words/actions of the miracle-worker.*

[4] *'Pneumatic excitement': statements about the emotional reaction of the miracle-worker in view of the distress (expresses its fulfilment with divine power).*

[5] *The 'argument' of the miracle-worker occurs as a reaction to the rejection of the miracle because of norms, e.g. in the case of miracles performed on the sabbath.*

[6] *'Setting the scene' comprises preparatory actions preceding the miracle, e.g. a change of place (the sick person comes, is put in the midst), the exclusion of the public, etc.*

[7] *'Opposite numbers' and 'intermediaries' do not denote concrete persons but roles over against the miracle-worker (who remains constant), which can be taken by different persons and which structure the narrative. Miracle-workers and 'opposite numbers' (very often the sick) form the two poles; all the other people who appear occupy the field of the 'intermediaries'.*

[8] *'Wonder' – 'acclamation': the motif of wonder embraces all the narrative elements which express astonishment, fear, dismay etc.; the acclamation is when a comment on the miracle is reported or quoted.*

With the help of this scheme, familiarize yourself with the structure of miracle stories by: 1. analysing the motifs of the healing of the leper in Mark 1.39–45 and the healing of the paralysed man in Mark 2.1–12, and 2. looking for one or two examples from the Synoptic miracle stories for each of the thirty-three motifs.

1. Six phases of the discussion of the miracles of Jesus

In church tradition before modern times the miracles were explained in 'super-natural' terms as interventions by God in the course of nature. Along with the fulfilment of prophecies, miracles were among the arguments with which people supported the truth of Christian faith. In modern times the miracles then changed from being a basic pillar of apologetics to being the subject of apologetics: modern theologians tend more to 'excuse' the existence of miracle stories in the Gospels. The miracles have become a problem.

1.1 The rationalist interpretation of miracles

Rationalistic theologians attempted to make the miracles plausible to modern understanding by interpreting the really miraculous element out of them. Thus the

Enlightenment theologian C.F. Bahrdt (1741–1792)[3] did not doubt the historicity of the accounts, but saw in the miraculous interpretation of what was narrated a time-conditioned interpretation which he sought to replace with a better one: Jesus' walking on the water, for example, was explained by the presence of logs of wood which were floating in the precise place in the Sea of Galilee where Jesus went over the water. In the stilling of the storm Jesus had said 'Be silent' to the anxious disciples, but they had related the command to wind and waves which by chance calmed down at the same time. Bahrdt's romance-like account often slips into the abstruse – thus he believed in a secret Essene society for whom Jesus functioned as the front man: it ensured the success of miracles behind the scenes, for example by putting large quantities of bread in remote caves.

The mature form of the rationalistic explanation of miracles lies in the work of the Heidelberg theologian H.E.G. Paulus (1761–1851).[4] He consistently looked for intermediate causes which were not mentioned in the text, the knowledge of which could bring a superficially miraculous event into harmony with reason. For example, he explained the miracle of the feedings by saying that the crowds had provisions with them, but the poorer ones had run out of them. To ensure a better distribution Jesus began to share his provisions and started a meal. In so doing he gave a positive example: others brought out their provisions, shared them, and all were satisfied.

1.2 The mythical interpretation of miracles by David Friedrich Strauss (1808–1874)

D.F. Strauss adopted a new way of interpreting the miracles over against the supernatural and rationalistic interpretations, both of which he found equally unsatisfying. He argued that the miracle stories are to be understood 'mythically', i.e. as poetic compositions which seek to express an idea, namely the messianic idea. Since a feeding miracle was narrated of the prophet Elijah (II Kings 4.42–44), the Messiah had to surpass the wonder. Jesus himself was somewhat reserved towards a belief in miracles. But 'it was supposed according to the mode of thought of the period and of his contemporaries, that miracles he must perform, whether he would or not. As soon as he was considered a prophet . . . miraculous powers were attributed to him; and when they were attributed to him they came of course into operation.'[5] The expectations of the people with their belief in miracles produced on the one hand miraculous healings which are to be explained psychosomatically, and on the other inventions of miracles which never

---

[3]C.F. Bahrdt, *Briefe über die Bibel im Volkston*, Halle 1782; id., *Ausführungen des Plans und Zwecks Jesu. In Briefen and Wahrheit suchende Leser*, Berlin 1784–1792; cf. E. and M.-L. Keller, *Miracles in Dispute*, 67–79; Schweitzer, *Quest*, 38–44.

[4]H.E.G. Paulus, *Das Leben Jesu als Grundlage einer reinen Geschichte des Urchristentums* (2 vols.), Heidelberg 1828; cf. Schweitzer, *Quest**, 48–57. W. Baird, *History of NT Research*, Vol.1, Minneapolis 1992, 201–8.

[5]D.F. Strauss, *A New Life of Jesus*, Vol.1, London 1879, 365.

happened. These were not deliberate deceptions, but the purposeless products of a collective consciousness. With this explanation of Strauss's the way was opened for disputing the historicity of miracles, while being able nevertheless to value their religious meaning.

1.3 The interpretation of the miracles in form criticism and the history of religions

Whereas Strauss explained the New Testament miracle traditions wholly from the biblical Old Testament traditions (as a product of messianic faith), at the beginning of the century in particular, form criticism and the history of religions represented a new approach in so far as they discovered a whole series of motifs shared by the miracle stories in antiquity and those in the New Testament.

- Rudolf Bultmann made a convincing collection of these in his *History of the Synoptic Tradition,* which appeared in 1921, though not in English until 1968 (218–38). Furthermore, he demonstrated the probability that not only individual motifs but whole miracle stories had been taken over from the Hellenistic world. Thus for example the transfer of the miracle at Cana was the transfer of a Dionysus miracle to Jesus (ibid., 238). 'Moreover the Hellenistic origin of the miracle stories may be taken to be overwhelmingly probable' (ibid., 240).
- In *From Tradition to Gospel* (1919, English translation 1934), Dibelius classified a large number of the miracle stories as 'novellas' in which he saw a 'profane' delight in story-telling at work. He judged them to be phenomena of assimilation to the (non-Christian) world.[6]
- In 1935/36, with his work on 'ΘΕΙΟΣ ΑΝΗΡ. The Image of the Divine Man in Late Antiquity and Early Christianity', L. Bieler put forward the thesis that in antiquity there was a clearly definable type of miracle-worker whom he called θεῖος ἀνήρ (divine man). In the primitive Christian tradition Jesus, too, had been formed in accordance with the model of such a θεῖος ἀνήρ.

Whereas D.F. Strauss had still explained the miracle tradition in terms of the messianic idea, i.e. the centre of Christian belief, the miracles now retreated to the periphery of the New Testament thought-world. A consensus was formed that the Christian message had merely 'made use of these miracle stories' to express the message of faith. The miracle stories were interpreted kerygmatically, 'from above'.[7]

---

[6]Dibelius, *Tradition**, 70–103.

[7]Cf. e.g. the following comment: 'The New Testament miracle stories only appear to report remarkable events from the life of the earthly Jesus. In truth they proclaim what God did through Jesus as the Christ, that is, through the crucified and risen Lord of the community, to this community and wills to do to the world' (W. Schmithals, *Wunder und Glaube*, BSt 59, Neukirchen 1970.

1.4 The redaction-critical relativization of the miracle stories

The redaction-critical interpretation of the miracle stories basically confirmed the thesis put forward in classic form criticism of a fundadamental use of the language of miracle for the Christian kerygma. The miracle stories were there in the tradition, and they were revised and relativized critically by the evangelists to convey their message.

- The tense relationship between the critical and the positive view of miracles in *Mark*[8] was explained within the framework of the messianic secret: Mark sought to relativize the miracles by inserting commandments to keep silent and the failure of the disciples to understand. The *theologia gloriae* of the miracles was corrected by a *theologia crucis* (for Jesus' person and work can be understood only in the light of the cross and resurrection, not in the light of the miracles). T.J. Weeden ('Heresy') even went so far as to assume that Mark wrote his Gospel to contest a heresy defined by belief in a θεῖος ἀνήρ.
- In 'Matthew as an Interpreter of the Miracle Stories' H.J. Held demonstrated that the miracle stories in *Matthew* are heavily abbreviated and like apophthegms are focussed on a theological point over against which miraculous features have been suppressed (cf. the omission of the miracle Mark 7.31–37; 8.22–26). As a result of the miracles, which are primarily concentrated in Matt. 8–9, Jesus proves himself to be the merciful 'Messiah of action' who takes upon himself the diseases of all by healing them (Isa. 53.4 in Matt. 8.17).
- According to U. Busse, the miracles in *Luke*, of which there are more than there are in Mark, illustrate the salvation present in the activity of Jesus. The miracles are interpreted in terms of salvation history; as the last eschatological prophet Jesus fulfils 'the biblical promise of Isa. 61.1f./58.6 to the poor, enslaved and sinners in Israel when, equipped with the spirit, as the salvation-historical instrument of God, in a benevolent way he heals them, liberates them and invites them to the messianic banquet.' In Luke the miracles are stories of the success of God's saving will (Die *Wunder des Propheten Jesu*, Stuttgart 1977, 384f.).
- In *John*, according to Bultmann the so-called σημεῖα (signs) source (a pre-Johannine collection of seven miracle stories) was reshaped by the evangelist in a far-reaching way by a symbolic interpretation of the miracles in order to correct the naive and massively intensified belief in miracles that it contained. Miracles are only σημεῖα (signs) which are meant to point to the real miracle: the person of Jesus as the one who brings true life. The δόξα (glory) of the miracle-worker is

---

[8]Mark's understanding of miracle is investigated by K. Kertelge, *Die Wunder Jesu im Markusevangelium*, StNT 23, Munich 1970; L.Schenke, *Die Wundererzählungen des Markusevangeliums*, SBB, Stuttgart 1974; D.-A. Koch, *Die Bedeutung der Wundererzählungen für die Christologie des Markusevangeliums*, BZNW 42, Berlin and New York 1975).

only a reflection of the divinity of the revealer who arouses authentic faith by his word, over against which belief in miracles is provisional.[9]

1.5 The place of Jesus in a typology of ancient miracle-workers

In the 1970s, two Jewish scholars attacked the one-sidedly theological interpretation of the miracle stories with a view to restoring Jesus' miracle-working to its concrete historical context. They represent two possibilities: Jesus appears either as a charismatic or as a magician.

- *Jesus as charismatic.* Geza Vermes puts Jesus' miracle-working in a Jewish charismatic milieu (he even speaks of 'Hasidic Judaism') which is characterized by charismatics like the Palestinian rain-maker Ḥoni (first century BCE) and the Galilean rabbi Ḥanina ben Dosa (first century CE), who performed miracles (*Jesus**, 58–82). In both cases a certain immediacy in the relationship to God – as in the case of Jesus – is striking: these charismatic miracle-workers have access to God independently of the Law and are therefore also judged critically by institutionalized Judaism or subsequently made Pharisees in the rabbinic tradition (see further below, pp. 307f.).
- *Jesus as magician.* Morton Smith sees the miracles of Jesus totally from the perspective of his opponents (Mark 3.20–30; John 8.48 etc.), and in *Jesus the Magician* (1978) puts forward the thesis that Jesus probably received a regular training as a magician in Egypt (91–3).[10] He had been possessed by the demon 'Beelzebub', had regained control of himself by conjuring up the spirit of John the Baptist from the dead (Mark 6.16!), and performed his miracles through both of them with the help of magical practices. He regarded himself as a 'son of God', i.e. a god in the sense of the magical papyri. Alongside the miracles Smith also sees numerous other features of Jesus' behaviour and way of speaking as indications that he was a magician: miraculous foreknowledge and sudden disappearance, the retreat of the one possessed into the wilderness, the knowledge of demons and spirits, the transmission of the authority to drive out demons to the disciples, the distribution of bewitched food for the purpose of uniting those who eat it in love (eucharist), etc.: Jesus even practised 'black magic' when he made Satan enter Judas through bewitched bread (for an assessment see below, pp. 306f.).
- *The juxtaposition of charismatic and ritual miracle-workers.* Nowadays it is usually assumed that charismatic and 'magical' miracle-workers were active in antiquity side by side. In 1993 G.H. Twelftree described Jesus by both

---

[9]R. Bultmann, *The Gospel of John*, Oxford 1971.
[10]This conjecture is based on a rabbinic tradition (bShab 104b) according to which Ben Stada (probably a cipher for Jesus) brought magical formulae from Egypt which were tattooed on his skin. Smith regards Matt. 2.12–21 as an apologetic Christian reworking of the same tradition.

categories in his *Jesus the Exorcist*. If one compares Jesus' exorcisms against the varied background of contemporary exorcisms, in most 'technical' aspects Jesus is to be described as a 'very ordinary exorcist' (173). But generally speaking he belongs in the group of exorcists who heal predominantly on the basis of their outstanding personality (like Old Testament prophets, Abraham in the Genesis Apocryphon [1QGenAp XX], Apollonius of Tyana), and not on the basis of magical conjurations and magical rituals. There is no parallel to Jesus' confidence that through his exorcisms God himself is acting and the kingdom of God is dawning.

D. Trunk, *Der messianische Heiler*, Freiburg 1994, arrives at a similar result on the basis of a survey of all the traditions of exorcism in antiquity:

> 'Exorcism of the charismatic type, in which the miracle-worker acts on his own authority and with the help of a power that dwells in him and cannot be derived further, appears in a pure form only in the Gospels and in the Life of Apollonius of Tyana. The second type attributes the success of the exorcisms to the effectiveness of the means used. The exorcisms in Acts (16.16–18; 19.13–16), in Josephus and Lucian, and the corresponding texts in the Apologists contain mixed forms and already elements of formalization and ritualizing. We must conclude from the fact that the second type is far more frequently attested that exorcisms like those performed by Eleazar (Josephus),[11] the Syrian from Palestine (Lucian) or the sons of Sceva (Acts 19) were far more common than those which corresponded to the phenomenon represented by Jesus and Apollonius' (426).

1.6 Sociological aspects of the belief in miracle and of the emergence of miracle-workers

The classification of the miracles of Jesus in a historically verifiable typology of miracle-workers does not tell us anything about the function and origin of belief in miracles. Contributions from sociology and social anthropology concern themselves with these aspects.

- *Sociology* objects to the notion of a timeless belief in miracles. G. Theissen showed that belief in miracles is also historically conditioned, in that in some periods it clearly increases and in others it declines. Primitive Christianity belongs in the forefront of an increasing belief in miracles in antiquity. Nowhere else are so many miracles reported of a single person as they are in the Gospels of Jesus. One factor in the increase of belief in miracles and the appearance of miracle-workers was the tension between country and city culture, between Jews and Gentiles, and between traditional and new cultural

---

[11]Quoted ibid., 257.

forms of life (which can be explained only in terms of charisma). Among other things the charismas to perform miracles and 'magic' can be distinguished by their social functions: protest movements and renewal movements are time and again legitimated by charismatic miracles. Independently of that, ordinary people pluck up courage in the face of concrete emergencies by telling miracle stories. These stories are therefore to be read not only kerygmatically 'from above' but also as the expression of human protest 'from below' (*Miracle Stories**, 231–302).

- *Social anthropologists* drew attention to a situation which is 'timeless'. Each time, what is regarded as sickness and health, as deviant and normal behaviour, is defined socially. Society's power of definition decides what is socially unacceptable as magic, and what is accepted as 'miracle'. The difference between magic and miracle is (at least also) a question of social labelling (Crossan, *Jesus**, 303ff.). More importantly, not only the evaluation of phenomena but also their existence and form are socially conditioned. Whether there 'are' demons or not depends on the social construction of reality: if there is generally a belief in them in a society, people can express their problems in 'demonological' forms and through this receive 'reinforcement' from the toleration of their deviant behaviour, through care and exorcistic therapy. One cannot explain either the sicknesses and possessions in the New Testament or the miraculous way in which they are overcome without taking into account the social power of definition and construction (cf. Trunk, *Heiler*, esp.7–39, 375ff.).

2. The primitive Christian miracle stories

In the narrative tradition about Jesus' miracles, characteristic features of his preaching like repentance and discipleship, God as father, the coming of the kingdom of God and concern for the poor strikingly fall into the background. Not even the formula 'amen' appears in them. In the miracles Jesus was perceived in a broken way through a 'popular shift', depending on the kind of the miracle, but from different aspects. In the following section we shall first survey the miracles under four form-critical sub-genres. Then we shall describe the individual sub-genres briefly and investigate their relationship to the historical Jesus (2.1–6).

1. Bultmann classed some miracle stories as apophthegms, since in them the saying of Jesus is the real point (e.g. healings on the sabbath). He divided the rest of the miracle stories into healings (including the exorcisms as a special group) on the one hand and nature miracles on the other (*HST**, 209–44).

2. Dibelius counted miracles with a clear theological point as paradigms. All the others are 'novellas', the interest of which is less in the message than in the miracle-

worker. They reflect the influence of a secular 'pleasure in the narrative itself' (*Tradition**, 37–103: 70).

3. Theissen distinguished between exorcisms and therapies, deliverance miracles and gift miracles, norm miracles and epiphanies, depending on which person from the inventory of persons in the miracle stories comes to stand at the centre of the narrative. In them the demon or the healed person, the disciple or the crowd, Jesus' opponents or the miracle-worker himself are central (*Miracle Stories**, 99–129).

4. Berger disputes the existence of a genre of 'miracle stories';[12] he argues that the miraculous element is a relic of an ancient understanding of reality which can occur in many genres. Berger speaks of the '*demonstratio*' of divine authority, with and without miracles (e.g. 'classic' therapies versus Mark 6.1–6); at the same time *mandatio* (texts on commissioning and obedience, e.g. the stilling of the storm versus the calls of the disciples); *petitio* before a powerful person with or without a desire for miracles (e.g. Mark 7.24ff.: Syrophoenician woman versus Matt. 27.62ff.: the request for a guard on the tomb).

2.1 Exorcisms

1. Exorcisms report the driving out of a demon from a 'possessed person'. We do not have an exorcism if a disease is attributed to a demonic cause (e.g. the bent back of the woman in Luke 13.10–17 to her having been bound by Satan). Rather, the characteristics are:

- The person is delivered over to the demon: the demon takes the place of the human subject.
- The battle between the demon and the exorcist, in which both sides use the same weapon (e.g. miraculous knowledge, foreign language, violence). The lack of exorcistic rituals is characteristic of the exorcisms of Jesus, as a comparison with Josephus (*Antt.* 8, 46–48, quoted above, p. 282) shows: the Jewish exorcist Eleazar uses conjurations, a ring and a root to drive out the demon.
- The destructive activity of the demon also outside human beings, among other things to demonstrate its departure (cf. the killing of the herd of swine in Mark 5.1ff.).

2. As exorcisms are also presupposed in the Logia tradition, were even the subject of controversies with Jesus' opponents (Matt. 12.22ff.), and are closely connected with the coming of the kingdom of God (Matt. 12.28 par.), we must assume not only that the historical Jesus was active as an exorcist but also that

---

[12]K. Berger, 'Hellenistische Gattungen im Neuen Testament', *ANRW* II 25.2, 1984, 1212–18; *Einführung in die Formgeschichte*, UTB 1444, Tübingen 1987, 76–84; *Formgeschichte des Neuen Testaments*, Heidelberg 1984, 305ff.

exorcism was of great importance for his understanding of himself. The exorcisms gave him (or confirmed for him) the awareness of standing on the threshold of a new world, in which evil had finally been overcome. Satan had already fallen from heaven (Luke 10.18). The strong one had already been fettered (Matt. 12.29). The kingdom of God had already arrived (Matt. 12.28). However, this eschatological interpretation of the exorcisms does not appear anywhere in the narrative tradition.[13]

2.2 Therapies

1. Therapies are healing miracles in which no struggle takes place but the healing is brought about by the transference of a miraculous energy from the miracle-worker to the sick person.

Typical features are:

- the notion of a healing power which can be activated by the 'woman with an issue of blood', even without Jesus' knowledge (Mark 5.21ff.);
- a healing touch (often the laying on of hands) by which this power is transferred;
- healing means which introduce the process of healing: in the New Testament only spittle (cf. Mark 8.22ff.).

2. The motive of faith occurs in therapies (but also in an exorcism, cf. Mark 9.14ff.). The promise 'Your faith has saved you' is without parallel in connection with miracles in antiquity. Ancient miracle stories always talk only of subsequent belief in the facticity of miracles which have already taken place; only in the case of Jesus does faith become a miracle-working power which precedes the miracle. The theme also occurs in the Logia tradition in the saying about the faith which can move mountains (Mark 11.22–24/Matt. 21.21) and may go back to the historical Jesus. Although great expectations of miracles attach to his person, ultimately he attributed the power of healing to the persons who sought help.

2.3 Norm miracles

1. Norm miracles serve to provide a basis for norms, to punish offences against them ('punitive miracles') or to reward their fulfilment.

2. Strikingly, the Jesus tradition does not contain any punitive miracles in connection with human beings (by contrast, in primitive Christianity see Acts 5.1ff.; in the Old Testament II Kings 2.23f.). The cursing of the fig tree is a punitive miracle which in the framework of Mark probably has a symbolic sense:

---

[13]In Matt. 8.29 the request of the demons not to be tormented 'before the time' is a redactional addition which is absent from the Synoptic parallels.

such a miracle in connection with a tree indicates a change of power (cf. Mark 11.12–14, 20ff.).[14] Even more importantly, norm miracles usually accentuate norms. But Jesus' norm miracles serve to tone down the Torah. He transgresses the sabbath commandments by healing on the sabbath. Here he certainly acts in accordance with a principle of Jewish scribes that emergencies allow the suspension of the sabbath commandments, but he interprets this principle in an extensive way. Plucking ears of grain on the sabbath and healing a paralysed hand (Mark 2.23ff.; 3.1ff.) are not connected with an acute, life-threatening emergency. So we may also see an effect of the historical Jesus on the history of norm miracles, especially as here, too, the sayings tradition points in the same direction of a liberal interpretation of the Law (for details see §12.3, 4, 2, pp. 367ff.).

2.4 Gift miracles

1. Gift miracles include the miraculous multiplication of loaves, the miraculous fishing trip (Luke 5.1ff.) or the miracle with the wine at Cana (John 2.1ff.). Here the issue is always that Jesus provides material goods in a miraculous way. Characteristic features are:

- The miracle takes place spontaneously: no one asks the miracle-worker for it. The miracle is so improbable that it is beyond the horizon of expectations of the people who appear in the story.[15]
- The process of the miracle is inconspicuous. Externally, everything seems to go 'normally'.
- By contrast, the demonstration of the miracle, i.e. the indication that a miracle has taken place, is developed broadly.

2. Thus we must assume that a miraculous feeding by Jesus was already narrated at an early stage. It has been handed down in Mark as a doublet (6.35ff.; 8.1ff.) and independently of this in John (6.5ff.). The origin of this miracle story can be explained only through a combination of different factors. On the one hand there is the expectation that a new prophet will surpass the miracle of feeding reported of Elisha (II Kings 4.42–44) – an expectation which is experienced by the longing of the people for the overcoming of material need. On the other hand there is Jesus' promise that in the new world which is beginning with him the hungry will be satisfied (Luke 6.21) and all 'citizens' of the kingdom of God will be gathered for a great feast (Matt. 8.11f.). If we add to this the

---

[14]Cf. P. von Gemünden, 'Die Verfluchung des Feigenbaums Mk 11, 13f., 209f.', *WuD* 22, 1993, 39–50.

[15]However, one could cite John 2.3 as evidence to the contrary. But is the remark of Jesus' mother, 'they have no wine', a request? Hardly!

amazement at how Jesus could 'feed' those who went around with him and the riddle of how he did it, the rise of stories of a miraculous feeding is understandable as poetry: The expectation he aroused of a miraculous feeding of all became the story of a multiplication of loaves which had already taken place – prompted by the meals which Jesus and his followers actually had together.

2.5 Deliverance miracles

1. The Jesus tradition contains two deliverance miracles:[16] the stilling of the storm (Mark 4.35–41) and the miraculous walking on the water (Mark 6.45ff.). Their typical features include:

- the description of the emergency to the point when the desperate people give up;
- either an epiphany which brings rescue from outside by the intervention of a divine figure,
- or deliverance through a protective passenger who is already present in the threatened ship.

2. The deliverance miracles in the Jesus tradition embody both variants: those of a deliverance through epiphany (in the walking on the water) and of the protective passenger (in the stilling of the storm). Here, too, poetic fantasy has caught hold of historical reminiscences. Certainly Jesus travelled over the Sea of Galilee with his disciples. People knew that. And once he was seen as a great miracle-worker, it was only a small step also to attribute to him divine power over the wind and the waves. This step was possible only after Easter. In antiquity the capacity to walk on water was regarded a sign of divine power. He is like the gods 'who can make the apparently impossible possible, who, if he wants, can walk on the sea . . .' (Dio Chrysostom 3, 30). Therefore in Matt. 14.33, after Jesus has walked on the water they recognize him as the 'Son of God'. So they are rebuked in Mark 6.52 because they do not have this insight. Now that means that the story as a whole already presupposes a belief in the divine character of Jesus which was possible only after and on the basis of Easter (cf. Rom. 1.3f.).

2.6 Epiphanies

Epiphanies, too, are related of Jesus; he appears to his disciples after Easter in divine glory. Here actual visionary experiences were shaped. One of these

---

[16]Outside the Gospels the freeing of prisoners (Acts 12.1ff.; 16.16ff.), in which the hostile power of the state is overcome, is included among the deliverance miracles.

appearances was probably projected back on to the life of Jesus in the form of the transfiguration (Mark 9.22ff.). It shows how Jesus has been received in the heavenly world: from now on his authority surpasses that of the Law and the Prophets (i.e. of Moses and Elijah). It is not bound to any place of worship (Peter may not build any booths at the place of the appearance). At the end there is a miraculous ἀφανισμός, i.e. a 'disappearance' of the divine figure, which in the present context is now understood as a restoration of the one who has been transfigured to his normal earthly form.

2.7 Survey and summary

The six types of miracle story can be depicted by means of the following diagram:

Effects of the historical Jesus	Presupposition of Easter faith
Exorcisms	Deliverance miracles
Therapies	Gift miracles
Norm miracles	Epiphanies

The exorcisms stand opposite deliverance miracles: on the one hand the power of a demon is broken; on the other the power of wind and waves. The therapies stand over against the gift miracles: on the one hand physical weakness is removed and on the other material want. The norm miracles stand opposite epiphanies: on the one hand the divine will is manifested and on the other a divine being. We can assume that exorcisms, therapies and norm miracles originate in the historical Jesus. Jesus himself performed these kinds of miracles: through exorcisms he had incurred the charge of being in league with the devil (Mark 3.22ff.); by norm miracles he had incurred the charge of breaking the sabbath (Mark 3.1ff.). By contrast, the Easter faith is the presupposition for deliverance and gift miracles and for epiphanies. Here capacities exceeding anything human are attributed to Jesus. Generally speaking these miracles are far less numerous. It should not be disputed that reminiscences of the historical Jesus have been woven into the deliverance and gift miracles and the epiphanies. The rescue from an emergency at sea derives from actual voyages undertaken by Jesus; the miraculous feeding from actual 'feedings'; and the transfiguration on the mountain from actual periods spent by Jesus on a mountain. But such 'relics' have been fused into stories of the revelation of a superhuman being. Nor did the miracle stories which arose on the presupposition of Easter faith form much of a genre. They certainly adopt the forms of ancient miracles, but within the primitive Christian tradition there are only a few examples – in contrast to the exorcisms, therapies and sabbath conflicts which are frequently attested.

So far we have not discussed the question of the historicity of the miracles for each sub-genre of miracle story. The provisional result can be examined once again by 1. comparing the miracle tradition in other genres (in summaries, apophthegms and logia), and 2. comparing Jesus with other types of miracle-workers of the time. These two sets of questions correspond to the two criteria of Jesus research. The criterion of plausible effect makes us ask whether the sources explain the influence of Jesus, and the criterion of plausible context whether Jesus traditions can be interpreted as individual phenomena incorporated into a context.

3. The primitive Christian miracle tradition as the effect of the historical Jesus: the multiplicity of testimonies

That Jesus performed miracles is widely attested. It is attested in the various traditions and genres and has found an echo in the testimony of 'witnesses' with various attitudes.

3.1 Witnesses to the miracle tradition with different interests

Witnesses with different attitudes report that Jesus performed miracles. Alongside the Christian witnesses mention should be made of the Testimonium Flavianum, in which Jesus is described as a wise man and miracle-worker: as one who performs παράδοξα ἔργα (wonderful works). However, there is no reference to miracle in Agapius' version of the Testimonium Flavianum (see above §3, pp. 72f.). Nevertheless, it hardly derives from a Christian reviser. The term παράδοξα ἔργα does not occur anywhere in the Jesus tradition, but Josephus does use it to describe the miracles of Elisha (*Antt.* 9, 182). In *Antt.* 18, 63 it also goes back to him. However, not all his contemporaries saw the miracles as the actions of a 'wise man', as he did. Some of Jesus' opponents inferred from the exorcisms that Jesus was in league with the devil (Mark 3.22ff.), a charge which was certainly not invented by Christians but is a historical reflection of the miracles of Jesus. The way in which exorcisms retreat in Matthew – for example, Mark 1.23ff. is omitted – and the complete absence of exorcisms from John shows that this aspect of Jesus' miracle-working activity also caused confusion to Christians. A third non-Christian reaction to the miracles has been preserved for us (indirectly) in Mark 6.14f.: there people say, ' "John the baptizer has been raised from the dead; that is why these powers are at work in him." But others said, "It is Elijah." And others said, "It is a prophet, like one of the prophets of old."' This is an old tradition; it presupposes that Jesus is unknown. Even if his origin from Nazareth is unknown, people do not know that he has a father, mother and brothers, and can regard him as John the Baptist *redivivus*. Moreover,. the attempt to understand him alternatively as Elijah *redivivus* does not fit the Christian picture of him: not he but John the Baptist is the new Elijah (cf. Mark 9.13; Matt. 11.14). So there is no reason to doubt that even those who were not followers of Jesus were impressed (or provoked) by his miracles. It is credible for the Gospels to report that the stories of miracles spread with tremendous speed (cf. Mark 1.28, 45; 5.20; 7.24f., 36f.) and even led to the use of the name of Jesus in exorcisms by alien miracle-workers (Mark 9.38f.): the miracle tradition was not limited to his followers.

3.2 The miracle tradition in different strata of the tradition

Various currents of tradition have preserved the memory of Jesus' miracles in primitive Christianity. Alongside Mark, mention should be made of Q. Although this is predominantly a collection of the sayings of Jesus, we find here the healing of a centurion's son (Luke 7.1ff. Q), an exorcism which provokes the Beelzebul conversation (Luke 11.14ff. Q). Furthermore, there are references to miracles in the sayings tradition, among which particular emphasis should be put on the summary of miracles in Jesus' answer to John the Baptist (Luke 7.18ff. Q). In addition to Mark and Q, the Lukan and Matthaean special material also contains miracles: the Lukan material a raising of the dead (Luke 7.11ff.), Peter's miraculous fishing trip (5.1ff.) and three healings (Luke 13.10ff.; 14.1ff.; 17.11ff.), the first two of which take place on the sabbath and are to be included among the norm miracles; the Matthaean material the healing of two blind men (Matt. 9.27ff.) and the miraculous discovery of a coin for the temple tax (Matt. 17.24ff.). There are no more exorcisms either in Luke or in Matthew. That corresponds to the situation in John: here exorcisms are completely lacking. Certainly Jesus carries on a controversy with Satan; however, this is not through miracles but through cross and resurrection: they are his victory over the 'prince of this world' (John 12.31; 16.11). John itself relates only seven great miracles, but it knows that Jesus performed very many more signs (John 20.30; 21.25). Parts of what for us is an 'apocryphal' miracle tradition appear in the fragments of the Egerton Gospel and in other extra-canonical Gospels. However, the miracle tradition was not cultivated in all spheres of primitive Christianity. Thus the Gospel of Thomas contains neither a miracle story nor references to miracles of Jesus. However, the disciples are commissioned to perform healings (14), though not exorcisms (in contrast to Luke 9.2; 10.17ff.; Matt. 10.8; cf. Mark 6.13). This may not be by chance. In the Gospel of Thomas the controversy with Satan plays no role (apart from 57). The 'opposite number' of the disciples of Jesus is not Satan but the world.

Therefore it is not so extraordinary that Paul makes no reference to the miracles of Jesus. It can be inferred only indirectly from his letters that he knows of healings performed by Jesus. Tormented by his own sickness, he asked the Lord (i.e. the exalted Christ) three times for healing – without success (II Cor. 12.8). Why is there no direct reference to the miracles of Jesus in Paul?

- In Syrian Christianity, where Paul got to know the Christian traditions, did he encounter a picture of Jesus close to that of the Gospel of Thomas? The Gospel of Thomas belongs in Syria. Preliminary stages of its picture of Jesus could already have existed in the time of Paul.[17]
- Could Paul as a monotheistic Jew have worshipped the one raised by God as a divine being – but not a man who was surrounded with a divine aura on the basis of his own gifts? Possibly the transfiguration of the earthly man Jesus would have been a problem for him: he understands Jesus' earthly life only as an 'emptying' of divine power (cf. Phil. 2.6ff.).
- Did Paul want to avoid getting into hopeless rivalry with other missionaries? He could not relate miracles at first hand,. The basis of his Christian faith was the encounter with the risen Christ. It was on this that he founded his theology.

Independently of this, Paul knows the charisma of healing (I Cor. 12.9). He himself claims to have performed signs, miracles and mighty acts in Corinth (II Cor. 12.12). He did not advocate a Christianity free of miracle.

Our conclusion is that the miracle tradition is widely attested. The retreat of exorcisms is striking – an indication that precisely this part of Jesus' activities caused difficulties and is historical. This is confirmed by the fact that the miracle tradition has also been transmitted in other genres than the 'miracle stories'.

3.3 The miracle tradition in various forms and genres

Different genres contain references to the miracles of Jesus: summaries, apophthegms and logia. They confirm the historicity of the healings and exorcisms of Jesus, but sometimes give a different picture of them from the narrative tradition.

1. *Summaries* bring together the typical features of Jesus' activity and in so doing offer a significant selection of his miracles.

- In the Synoptic summaries (cf. Mark 1.32–34; 3.7–12; 6.53–56 with parallels) only exorcisms and therapies are mentioned and not 'nature miracles' – in other words, there is no walking on the water and no multiplication of loaves.

---

[17]Thus S.J. Patterson, 'Paul and the Jesus Tradition. It is Time for Another Look', *HTR* 84, 1991, 23–41.

At an early period these were not regarded as typical miracles of Jesus but as exceptions. It is interesting that the exorcisms are also absent from the last summary of Mark (cf. 6.53ff.).

• The summaries in Acts mention the miracles of Jesus as 'mighty acts and wonders and signs' (Acts 2.23) and closely associated healings and exorcisms (as elsewhere in Luke): Jesus 'healed all that were oppressed by the devil' (Acts 10.38; cf. Luke 6.18; 13.16). The 'extrinsic' nature miracles are also absent here. There is a dispute as to whether these summaries contain an overall picture of Jesus independent of the individual Synoptic traditions; this is not impossible. It is striking that the summaries in Acts have points of contact with the Testimonium Flavianum (cf. also Acts 13.23ff.).

2. *Apophthegms* indicate the sceptical attitude of contemporaries to the miracles of Jesus:

• The inhabitants of Jesus' home town are amazed at Jesus' miracles, of which they can only have heard, but reject Jesus. He can do no miracles among them because of their unbelief – Mark adds, '. . . except that he laid his hands upon a few sick people and healed them' (Mark 6.5). The independence of miracle-working charismas from the milieu is aptly described. This feature is historical: it contradicts the picture of Jesus in the Gospels.
• Jesus' answer to the John the Baptist is also about scepticism towards him: is he the one who is to come or should one wait for another? In response, Jesus refers to the miracles which are taking place in the present: the healing of the blind, the lame, lepers and the deaf, and the resurrection of the dead. Here he uses the language of Old Testament prophecy (cf. Isa. 26.19; 29.18f.; 35.5ff.; 42.18; 61.1). He says nothing of exorcisms. Perhaps they do not appear because Jesus' miracles were meant to represent the fulfilment of age-old promises. Exorcisms are absent from the Old Testament. The apophthegm might have a historical background. The person of Jesus is hardly emphasized. It is decisive that miracles are taking place in the present – whether through Jesus or others remains open. There is no explicit christology, and the implicit christology is minimal: it is enough for salvation if one does not take offence at Jesus (Matt. 11.6).
• Finally, the 'request for a sign' shows how controversial the miracles were: Jesus is asked for a 'sign from heaven' to make it quite clear whether the miraculous powers in him derive from God or not (cf. Mark 8.1ff.; Matt. 12.38f. differs). What is meant is a cosmic sign which is less ambiguous than the earthly activity of Jesus.

3. *Logia* associate the miracles of Jesus with characteristic features of his message which are absent in particular from the narrative tradition: with the

kingdom of God, repentance and the preaching of salvation for the poor. In accordance with the narrative tradition the significance of faith is emphasized.

- The kingdom of God is already realized in the driving out of demons, as the saying about exorcism (Matt. 12.28/Luke 11.20) shows. Healings and eschatological preaching belong together in the mission discourse (Matt. 10.7f./Luke 10.9).
- The invitation to repent is linked with Jesus' miracles (δυνάμεις) in the woe on the unbelieving cities: the Gentiles in Tyre and Sidon would have converted long since after such miracles (Matt. 11.20–24).
- In the response to John the Baptist, the miracles appear as an expression of Jesus' concern for the 'poor'. For sick people to be made whole is good news for the poor (Matt. 11.2–6/Luke 7.18–23).
- Faith is understood as a miraculous power in the logion about the faith which moves mountains (Mark 11.22–24 par.).

3.4 The primitive Christian miracle tradition as an effect of the historical Jesus and as primitive Christian poetry

The analysis of all the references to the miracles of Jesus in miracle stories, summaries, apophthegms and logia makes possible a differentiated assessment of their historicity: exorcisms and healings form Jesus' real miracle-working activity. Only here is there a broadly attested formation of a genre; only these two types of miracle are mentioned in the summaries and presupposed in the logia. These historical miracles also include those exorcisms and healings which took place on the sabbath, i.e. norm miracles. The right to judge the other miracles – walking on the water, transfiguration, multiplication of loaves and miraculous fishing trip – differently arises out of the sources. At a very early stage they were not included among the 'typical' miracles of Jesus.

1. A comparison between the narrative and the sayings tradition makes this distinction even deeper: healings and exorcisms are attested in parallel in both forms of the tradition. In both instances the understanding of miracles is so different that the traditions must be independent. Only the understanding of miracles in the sayings tradition corresponds to Jesus' own self-understanding. Only here do we find his eschatology and ethics, his preaching of the kingdom of God and of repentance, his message of salvation for the poor and his consciousness of fulfilment. All these themes and motives are absent from the miracle stories proper, in which a 'popular shift'[18] has taken place. The Jesus of the miracle stories is therefore a different figure from the historical Jesus, just as the Paul of Acts is a different figure from the historical Paul – precisely as regards his attitude

---

[18]Cf. G. Theissen, Gospels*, 99–115.

to miracles. This popular shift – i.e. the smoothing out of motifs characteristic of Jesus – is again most easily explained if we note that the miracle stories were current throughout the people, as the Gospels indicate (cf. Mark 1.28 etc.) and the Testimonium Flavianum confirms: news of Jesus' miracles had even reached Josephus! It is already inherently probable that the miracle stories extended over a wide range of tradition. The sensational is the first to draw attention to itself. And if the miracle stories were known, handed down and related outside the circle of Jesus' followers, the characteristic feature of the preaching of Jesus would inevitably fade in the process. Indeed, in such an 'uncontrolled' process of tradition, stories about other miracle-workers could have been transferred to Jesus and have been mixed up with stories about miracles of Jesus, so that these coloured one another.[19]

So we have in the miracle stories a tradition which in contrast to all the other Jesus traditions has also been shaped by those standing further from it. Mark seems to have encountered miracle stories even outside the followers of Jesus. He acknowledges them as authentic Jesus tradition, but deliberately indicates that Jesus had not wanted them to be recounted everywhere (cf. Mark 7.36). He is aware that a certain 'adaptation' to the general belief in miracles in the world around took place in the miracle stories. Mark reintegrates texts in these traditions into the narrative store of the community, but combines them with a decision to follow Jesus even into suffering. This decision is alien to those miracle stories which had been narrated and shaped in wider circles.

2. The comparisons between exorcisms and healings on the one hand and miracle stories on the other can once again confirm this view of things. In the latter we find clear signs of a specifically Christian stamp:

- The miraculous feeding is narrated in such a way (especially in Mark 8.6f.) that primitive Christian listeners were involuntarily reminded of the words of institution in the eucharist:

And he took	He took
the seven loaves,	bread
and having given thanks	and blessed
he broke them	and broke it,
and gave them to his disciples	and gave it to them
(Mark 8.6).	(Mark 14.22).

---

[19]This view of the miracle tradition gives a new explanation of the 'worldly' character of the so-called novellas observed by Dibelius: their secular content is matched by the bearers of the tradition, who come from the people, or those addressed by the tradition, who are to be sought among ordinary people.

Only Christian tradents could have shaped the narrative in this way. Nevertheless, it is impossible for the miraculous feeding to be derived completely from the experience of the celebration of the eucharist: not bread and wine but bread and fish stand at the centre of Mark 6.35ff. par. But there was probably no version of this miracle which lacked such 'eucharistic echoes'. For they are present in all three versions (Mark 6.35ff.; 8.1ff.; John 6.5ff.).

- The miraculous walking on the water is described with motifs which could come from an Easter story. Compare the sections of text from the 'walking on the water' and an Easter appearance juxtaposed below:

But when they saw him	But they were startled
walking on the sea	and frightened
they thought	and supposed they saw
it was a ghost,	a ghost.
and cried out;	
for they all saw him	
and were terrified.	
But immediately he spoke to them	And he said to them,
and said,	'Why are you troubled . . .
'Take heart,	it is I myself'
it is I;	(Luke 24.37–39).
have no fear!'	
(Mark 6.49–50).	

Here, too, narrators who were familiar with the Easter faith have shaped the story – and they were certainly followers of Jesus. In content the whole story presupposes the Easter faith: only a divine being can walk on water.

- No detailed proof is needed to show that Easter experiences have been woven into the text of the miraculous fishing trip (Luke 5.1ff.). It also occurs as an Easter story (John 21.1ff.), but even in the Lukan version contains references to the Easter situation. Peter's denial of the Lord may be thought of in his confession that he is a sinful man. Strictly speaking, Jesus' forgiveness of this sinful man with the words 'Fear not, from now on you will catch men!' (5.10) was true only after Easter: from then on Peter engaged in independent mission.
- The Easter character of the transfiguration (Mark 9.2ff.) is easily seen. Matt. 28.16ff. also knows of an Easter appearance on a mountain. According to Rom. 1.3f. the worship of Jesus as 'Son of God' dates only from Easter. The commandment to keep silent after the Transfiguration until Jesus has risen from the dead shows that Mark is still aware of this Easter character of the story. Mark may not say that it took place after Easter, but does say that it only became known after Easter (cf. Mark 9.9).

It is therefore no modern whim to note that the 'nature miracles' which we find hard to understand – the multiplication of loaves, the miracle with the fishes and the walking on the water, along with the transfiguration – have a special character within the miracle tradition. They are demonstrably steeped in Easter motifs, which cannot be said of the exorcisms and therapies. In so far as a post-Easter perspective is adopted there (possibly in Mark 2.6–10), it can easily be recognized as a secondary elaboration.

3. So it is not possible sweepingly to attribute the miracle tradition to Jesus: exorcisms and therapies can in essence be traced back to the historical Jesus (after removing a popular shift and enrichment by general motifs relating to miracles). Other miracles have only an indirect connection with him: they are poems of primitive Christianity shaped by the Easter faith. But there should be no doubt of Jesus' activity in performing exorcisms and therapies. A last argument may underline that further: it was certainly not the case that in the world of the time of Jesus every charismatic attracted miracle traditions. No miracles were related of John the Baptist. Therefore in John 10.41 he is contrasted with Jesus: 'John did no signs . . .' It is even more remarkable that even James the brother of the Lord, with whom such a rich legendary tradition was connected, nowhere attracted miracle stories.[20] The same goes for Ignatius of Antioch. Paul was different. Some miracles by him are reported in Acts, but that was possible only because there was a basis for them in the historical Paul: he asserted to the Corinthians that 'the signs of an apostle' had happened among them – signs, wonders and mighty acts (II Cor. 12.12). But of no individual at that time were so many miracles related as they were of Jesus. That cannot be fortuitous. However, the question of comparable miracle workers already brings us to the subject of the next section.

4. Jesus as a miracle-worker compared with contemporary miracle-workers

Historical research has brought out three types of miracle-worker who can be applied to a history-of-religions comparison with Jesus: the Hellenistic (whose negative counterpart is the magician), the rabbinic charismatic miracle-worker, and the Jewish sign prophets. Jesus shows contacts with them all, but there are also important differences.

4.1 *Theios Aner*, the divine man

L. Bieler, ΘΕΙΟΣ ΑΝΗΡ. *Das Bild des 'Göttlichen Menschen' in Spätantike und Früh-christentum* (2 vols), Vienna 1935/1936, reprinted Darmstadt 1967; B. Blackburn, Theios Aner *and the Markan Miracle Traditions*, WUNT 40, Tübingen 1991; G.P. Corrington,

---

[20]See the survey of all the traditions about James in P.-A. Bernheim., *James, Brother of Jesus*, London 1997.

'The Divine Man'. His Origin and Function in Hellenistic Popular Religion, American University Studies VII/17, New York, Bern and Frankfurt 1986; C.R. Holladay, Theios Aner in Hellenistic Judaism, Missoula 1977; M. Smith, 'Prolegomena to a Discussion of Aretalogies, Divine Man, the Gospels and Jesus', JBL 90, 1971, 174–99; id., Jesus the Magician, New York 1978, 158–64; D.L. Tiede, The Charismatic Figure as Miracle Worker, Missoula 1972.

The θεῖος ἀνήρ is an ideal construct of a human being regarded as divine, in whom miraculous powers are at work – whether through healings or through oracles and foreknowledge. The best-known example is Apollonius of Tyana, who was active in the first century CE as an itinerant neo-Pythagorean philosopher (died c.96/97). His biography was written at the beginning of the third century by Philostratus. In his Vita Mosis, Philo possibly depicts Moses after the model of such a 'divine man'. However, it is disputed whether we have here a clearly definable type of miracle-worker or merely a collection of motifs.[21] It could be that the picture of Jesus in the tradition has been assimilated at a secondary stage to such motifs (or to a coherent structure of motifs). By means of them it was possible to express the fact that a human being was regarded as divine through his miraculous actions (and not just that a deity was manifested in its miracles). However, such a view of Jesus as a bearer of divine powers would be secondary to his own understanding of himself as being the beginning of a new world, even if it had points of contact with him.

4.2 Was Jesus a magician?

M. J. Hull, Hellenistic Magic and the Synoptic Tradition, London 1974; M. Smith, Jesus the Magician, New York 1978.

That Jesus was in league with the devil (Mark 3.22), a cheat (πλάνος, John 7.12; Matt. 27.63), a charlatan and a magician (γόης; μάγος) is primarily a comment made by his opponents, aimed at disparaging his miracles and the claim made for his preaching. But according to Morton Smith this often refers to historical reality, since Jesus not only performed magical practices and rites but also disseminated magical teachings and had a magical understanding of himself.[22] However, Smith's demonstration is not convincing, especially in con-

---

[21]For θεῖος ἀνήρ see Corrington, Crossan; against: Blackburn, Holladay.

[22]M. Smith (see above, pp. 45f. and 289) makes use of the ambiguity of the term magician (as already did ancient authors): usually magician is used pejoratively (charlatan) But alongside this there is the neutral use of 'magic' (as a correlate to 'cult') as the art of influencing the superhuman sphere of the spirits, demons, angels and gods, practised by an individual (magician, miracle worker, etc.). By contrast, although Smith recognizes that the picture of Jesus' opponents has been distorted polemically, he allows the negative connotations of the taunt-word 'magician' to echo in his analysis.

nection with the last two points. He does not see the 'Son of God' christology of the Gospels as dictated by Jesus' magical understanding of himself; Jesus regarded himself as a son of god (= god) in the sense of the Greek magical papyri. But it is more than improbable that Jesus (who himself avoided the Hellenistic cities of Galilee!) was at home in the Greek syncretistic milieu presupposed by the magical papyri. Jesus' understanding of himself was prophetic, not magical.[23] The magical manipulations in healings rooted in popular piety do not alter this. The promise to those who are healed, 'Your faith has saved you', which presumably goes back to Jesus, shows an awareness which is opposed to trust in magical manipulations. Nor does the repudiation of a miracle to provide authentication fit well with a magician; such people tended to have this kind of miracle in their repertoire. The similarities between Jesus and a Hellenistic magician claimed by Smith remain external, and do not do justice in particular to his understanding of the miracles as the dawn of the eschatological kingdom of God and his prophetic, wisdom-type preaching.[24] The Jewish charismatic miracle-workers we shall be discussing in the next section stand considerably closer to Jesus; among them we find the following triad: miracles (sometime through magic), immediacy to God (with the awareness of being a son), and a prophet's following.

Excursus: Magical and charismatic miracles

The provocative thesis that Jesus was a magician has provoked a discussion about magic and miracle. On one side Jesus' miracles are classified unreservedly as 'magic'. The distinction between magic and miracle is said merely to be a matter of labels in which we have the power of definition of society, or dominant circles in it: 'magic' is the miracle which it repudiates; 'miracle' is the magic that it accepts. In this sense J.D. Crossan (*Jesus**, 137–67) speaks of Jesus as a 'magician'; he sees this magic as a social protest which he evaluates positively. On the other side, magical and charismatic miracle can be regarded as two ends of a continuum between which there are many points of transition.[25] Put in simplified form, the most important distinctions are as follows:

---

[23]In an appendix (ibid., 268–75), M. Smith attributes all Jesus' prophetic features to the later tradition, which is hardly convincing. J.D. Crossan's heading 'Magician and Prophet' (*Jesus**, 137) is much more appropriate.

[24]M. Smith's magical interpretation of the teaching of Jesus (which is regarded quite inadequately as merely the 'consequence of his miracles') is based almost completely on the methodically questionable use of magical texts, omitting questions about the historicity of the tradition, Jewish parallels which are close in content and the overall framework of the preaching of Jesus. It would take us beyond the bounds of this chapter to demonstrate this. However, here is a random example: Jesus' saying that he has come to set people at odds with one another (Matt. 10.35f.) is assessed as evidence that he sowed hatred through magical conjurations (111, 197). For a more thorough discussion see H. Twelftree, *Exorcist*, 190–207.

[25]Meier, *Marginal Jew* 2*, 535–75; D. Trunk, *Heiler*, 375–80.

Magical miracles	Charismatic miracles
They do not presuppose a personal relationship between the magician and those to whom the magic is directed. They often take place without the knowledge and the will of the one to whom they are done.	They take place in the framework of a personal contact between the miracle worker and the one seeking help: without 'faith', confidence and positive expectations they are impossible (cf. Mark 6.5f.).
They serve individual purposes – independently of the community and often also against the community (as black magic and harmful magic).	They make community possible: miraculous healings restore normal life to people. Charismatic miracle workers often call a new community to life.
They are performed by ritualized practices (conjurations, stereotyped magical formulae, magical means). In extreme cases they are said to be effective *ex opere operato*, automatically.	They take place on the basis of the authority of individual miracle workers, often solely through their word and with a minimum of ritualized practices.

Where the borderline between magical and charismatic miracles is to be drawn is a matter of social convention. As this borderline is disputed, in fact the defining power of society has an effect: charismatic miracle-workers can be attacked as magicians and magicians recognized as charismatic miracle-workers. Thus Jesus was partly admired by his environment as a charismatic miracle-worker and partly attacked as being in league with the devil.

4.3 Rabbinic charismatic miracle-workers

C.A. Evans, *Noncanonical Writings**, 232–8; W.S. Green, 'Palestinian Holy Men: Charismatic Leadership and Rabbinic Tradition', *ANRW* 2.19, 1979, 619–47; G. Vermes, 'Hanina ben Dosa. A Controversial Galilean Saint from the First Century of the Christian Era', *JJS* 23, 1972, 28–50; 24, 1973, 51–64.

Rabbinic charismatic miracle-workers can be demonstrated for the period at the turn of the eras.[26] Vermes refers to Honi in the first century BCE, who was well known for his miracles with rain (performed by drawing a magic circle); the rabbinic tradition was somewhat critical of him (Taan III.8), but Josephus is

---

[26]Meier, *Marginal Jew* 2*, 581–8, is very critical of the attempt to bring Jesus near to Hanina ben Dosa.

more positive (*Antt.* 14, 22–24). Most interesting of all is Ḥanina ben Dosa in the first century CE, who like Jesus worked in Galilee. Granted, the tradition about him was only written down a long time after he was active. Therefore it is hardly possible to compare the historical Ḥanina ben Dosa with the historical Jesus. Traditions about Ḥanina ben Dosa describe a miraculous immunity to snake bites (bBer 33a), two healings at a distance through prayer (bBer 34b), and power over demons (bPes 112b). Like Jesus, he deliberately renounced possessions (bTaan 24b, 25a) and was indifferent to questions of ritual. Contemporaries and tradition connect him, like Ḥoni and also Jesus, with the prophet Elijah. No interpretation of the Law (halakah) is reported of him, any more than it is of Jesus. Three of his wisdom sayings have been preserved in the tractate Pirke Aboth (Ab III, 9–10). He could have come from the same milieu as Jesus. It is also striking that charismatic miracle-workers in the rabbinic tradition were given the status of sons of God: Ḥanina ben Dosa is designated 'my son' by God himself (b.Taan 24b; cf. Mark 1.11; 9.7 par.). It is said of Ḥoni that we was 'like a son of the house' before God (mTaan 3.8). Conversely, the address 'Abba' is used towards God only twice in rabbinic literature: on the lips of Ḥoni (bTaan 23a) and his grandson Ḥanan ha-Nehba (who was also active as a magician producing rain, bTaan 23b). The parallels to Jesus, who particularly in the context of miracles is regarded as 'son of God' and is known for addressing God as 'Abba', is obvious.[27] Differences to be mentioned are that the Jewish charismatic miracle-workers were active primarily through their prayer; it was not they but their God who performed miracles. There are no eschatological miracles whatsoever among the Jewish charismatic miracle workers. But they do occur among the sign prophets – albeit in a different form from those performed by Jesus.

4.4 Jewish sign prophets of the first century CE

P.W. Barnett, 'The Jewish Sign-Prophets – AD 40–47. Their Intentions and Origin', *NTS* 27, 1981, 679–97; R. Meyer, *Der Prophet aus Galiläa*, Leipzig 1940, esp. 82ff., 108ff.

According to Josephus' account, in the decades before the outbreak of the Jewish war several sign prophets appeared in Palestine.[28] They already include the Samaritan prophet, who around 36 CE promised his followers that he would discover the vanished temple vessels on Gerizim (Josephus, *Antt.* 18, 85–87). Shortly after 44 CE, Theudas announced the dividing of the Jordan (*Antt.* 20, 97–99), a repetition of the miracle at the Jordan reported of Joshua and Elijah in

---

[27]However, it is disputed whether the title 'Son of God' has an original foundation in the miracle stories. If one does assume that, then with Vermes (*Jesus**, 192–213), one should see the basis in the Jewish charismatic tradition (and not in the son deities of the magical papyri).

[28]For more detail see above, §5, 3, 3, 2.

the tradition (Josh. 3; II Kings. 2.8). Under the procurator Felix (52–60 CE), an anonymous prophet appeared who announced miracles and signs of freedom in the wilderness; in other words, he prophesied a new exodus (*Antt.* 20, 167–168; *BJ* 2, 259). Finally, mention should be made of the Egyptian who led his followers to the Mount of Olives and promised that the walls of Jerusalem would fall down at his command (*Antt.* 20, 168–172; *BJ* 2, 261–3 [quoted above, p. 89]; cf. Acts 21.38). There is a parallel in Jesus' activity to this miracle promised for the future, not in his present exorcisms and healing miracles, but in the promise of a miraculous new temple after the destruction of the old (cf. Mark 14.57f.; 15.29). None of these sign prophets performs any miracle himself; they only announce them. Acts 5.36 shows that Jesus' opponents compared him with the sign prophets. A later echo is the description of Jesus in the Testimonium Slavianum, which follows *BJ* 2,261–263 (see above, pp. 87f.).

4.5 The distinctive character of the miracles of Jesus

The uniqueness of the miracles of the historical Jesus lies in the fact that healings and exorcisms which take place in the present are accorded an eschatological significance. 'As an apocalyptic charismatic miracle-worker Jesus is unique in religious history. He combines two conceptual worlds which had never been combined in this way before, the apocalyptic expectation of universal salvation in the future and the episodic realization of salvation in the present through miracles' (Theissen, *Miracle Stories**, 278). Nowhere else do we find a charismatic miracle worker whose miraculous deeds are meant to be the end of an old world and the beginning of a new one. This puts a tremendous emphasis on the miracles (and it is unhistorical to relativize their significance for the historical Jesus). The present thus becomes a time of salvation in microcosm – contrary to an apocalyptic pessimism which sees in the present only the great crisis in which the new world is born in pain. Thus both are modified: belief in miracles by its eschatological revaluation, and the apocalyptic disparagement of the present through belief in miracles. The miracles are 'all already the microcosm of a new heaven and a new earth'.[29]

5. Summary and hermeneutical reflections

A miracle is an event which goes against normal expectations and has a religious significance: it is understood as the action of a god. Cosmic signs (like the star at

---

[29]E. Bloch, *The Principle of Hope*, Oxford 1986, Vol.3, 1306.

Jesus' birth or the eclipse at his death) also fall under this definition. But the miracles of Jesus all have an earthly agent: they are Jesus' miracles. Though the first Christians may have also reported 'signs from heaven' which surrounded his life, Jesus himself rejected such self-authenticating signs (Mark 8.11ff.). He (and his followers) performed all the miracles. They are all the expression of a saving power of deliverance; the punitive miracle in Mark 11.12ff. is an exception. So as a rule God does not appear in the miracle tradition (except in John 11.41f.); Jesus is the subject in the miracle stories. To the degree that the ancient mentality attributed miracles to a superhuman power (whether of God or Satan, cf. Matt. 12.22ff.), it necessarily had to suspect, recognize or reject a superhuman being in such miracles performed by Jesus.

Miracle only becomes a problem where one's own experience knows no analogies to miracles. We all judge historical reports on the principle of analogy: we tend to regard the elements in them that contradict our own experience as unhistorical. We cannot imagine anyone walking on the water or multiplying loaves in a miraculous way and are therefore rightly sceptical about these reports. But the same principle of analogy which is the basis of our scepticism obliges us to recognize the possibility of healings and exorcisms. For in many cultures there is an abundance of well-documented analogies to them – and even in the 'underground' of our culture, although that may be officially denied. In that case there is always an argument as to whether the tradition of a charismatic saviour is historically credible or not in the individual instance – and above all whether it is to be interpreted in religious or non-religious terms.

For Jesus the historical question is to be answered affirmatively. According to the criterion of 'plausible influence' the tradition about his miracles cannot be understood apart from his activity as a charismatic bringing salvation. The reports of his healings and exorcisms are formulated through a 'popular shift', but in the general language of the ancient belief in miracle: by contrast, the reports of such extraordinary 'nature miracles' as walking on the water and multiplying loaves have been shaped by motifs from the (post-) Easter Christian faith. So at all events we have to do with a modified and transformed tradition enriched by 'poetry'. However, because of the agreement in testimony between the sayings tradition and the narrative tradition there can be no dispute that it originates with Jesus. This is confirmed by the use of the second criterion. The miracles of Jesus fit into the context of analogous phenomena in antiquity, but in this connection display an individual stamp at two points: on the one hand in the attribution of miraculous power to the faith of those who seek help, and on the other in the eschatological interpretation of the miracles. The plausibility of influence and context support the historicity of the miracles of Jesus.

However, that does not yet indicate whether they are to be interpreted in religious or 'naturalistic' terms. Here scholarly research can only contribute towards a clarification to the degree that it can work out the historicity of any interpretation. Both the 'evil' that is overcome in the miracles and the power of those who perform them are seen differently, depending on the culture of the observer. Here the power of the particular society to define and create reality has an effect.

1. *Sickness as a fact and a social construct.* When there is mention of leprosy, blindness or possession in the New Testament, we must not simply think of modern leprosy, blindness or psychoses. Rather, sicknesses are defined differently in every society, and narratives about sickness and healing are stylized accordingly. In the New Testament 'leprosy' probably covered every possible kind of skin disease and blindness and impairment of sight. The so-called 'epileptic' (Mark 9.14ff.) is indeed depicted in accordance with experiences with epileptics, but his dumbness points to mutism, and his attacks could be an expression of a dissociative disturbance. The fact that he throws himself into water or fire indicates self-destructive tendencies. All of this does not follow simply from the picture of epilepsy as an illness. Much more has come together here. But the most unmistakable effect is the power of society to make definitions and establish realities in the case of 'possession'. Spirits and demons are part of the world of societies outside cultures with a European stamp. Belief in them is fed by anxiety about losing control – in other words by those situations in which we are no longer 'masters' in our own homes but experience ourselves as being under alien domination. Uncanny places are regarded as being occupied by demons because in panic attacks, in the face of the uncanny, people no longer feel in control of themselves. Strong emotions and dependencies are regarded as the effects of demons: the Testaments of the Twelve Patriarchs see demons at work in drunkenness, sex and anger! For in these 'vices' people lose control of themselves. Similarly, normal sicknesses can be attributed to demons, because they too force people out of their lives: great pain or handicaps rob them of their power to control themselves. And that is even more the case where because of psychologically deviant modes of behaviour people no longer appear as they once were – in other words, in the cases of 'possession' in the narrower sense, in which an alien subject displaces the subject of the sick person. Today we classify such behaviour as a disturbance in identity (part of a borderline syndrome), as dissociative disturbance, as 'multiple personality' or as a psychosis. A society which offers a demonological pattern of explanation for these disturbances will also produce corresponding symptoms in those of its members who are threatened, including symptoms which are not to be found in our society. In that case, in situations of crisis, 'possession' can spread to a greater degree than usual. In the time of Jesus it could possibly be found frequently among the ordinary people of Galilee. Therefore in our eyes belief in demons and possession is always also a 'social construct' which in some societies makes it possible for people to express their

hopeless situation in a language of symptoms which is publicly acceptable and claim the help of exorcists for themselves. Therefore possessions are not exclusively social constructs. The problems are already there. But the way in which they are labelled and explained and the symptoms that they produce are in part socially conditioned.

2. *Miraculous power as an existing fact and a social construct.* Perhaps the way in which we understand Jesus' extraordinary gift of healing (which in our view he undoubtedly had) is even more decisive for his miracles. We need not doubt that historical events underlie the healing of Peter's mother-in-law (Mark 1.29–31), the 'raising' of the fatally-ill daughter of Jairus (Mark 5.21–43) or the healing of the blind beggar Bartimaeus (Mark 10.46–52) – to mention only the three miracles in which the person healed is mentioned by name, directly or indirectly. The decisive question is: which power is expressed in these miracles? The traditional supernaturalist interpretation of the miracles assumes interventions by God. But there is less support for that in the texts than appears at first sight. According to the text it is Jesus who is acting, not God. He works 'through the finger of God', i.e. God's power is at work in him and through him. But Jesus is not active as a suppliant who prays to God to intervene. The naturalistic (or rationalistic) solution is just as unsatisfactory: here the miraculous power of the charismatic healer is derived from a knowledge of natural laws which is still inadequate. The 'mythical interpretation' *a priori* explains only the origin and form of the miracle traditions – and not the historical activity of the charismatic miracle-workers which underlie them. A further interpretation is possible in terms of the theology of creation, which is neither supernaturalistic or naturalistic: the charisma to perform miracles is a power which emerges spontaneously and which is present in the creation. It cannot be exploited technically, since its appearance cannot be calculated, but it is connected with charismatic figures and their interactions with others. No natural laws as yet unknown underlie it; rather, here leeway seems to open up in 'nature' which is not determined by natural laws in the usual sense. Such a miraculous charisma appears among many people. It can be used responsibly or irresponsibly. Because it appears spontaneously, and remains independent of interaction and trust, it is natural to interpret it in religious terms. Jesus had such 'paranormal' gifts to an extraordinary degree. He knew how to combine them with the centre of his message and give them a fascinating religious interpretation: he saw them as the dawn of the new world. In his miracles, possibilities were announced which people would have to a far greater degree if they took the step into the new world. For him they are the expression of the saving will of God which he himself embodies in his activity. Such a miracle-working charisma interpreted in religious terms is also socially conditioned. The Jesus tradition shows that now and again. The charismatic miracle-worker cannot act without the 'faith' of the world around (Mark 6.5f.). Just as social

expectations and patterns of explanation are a constitutive part of the sicknesses and infirmities, so too social expectations and interpretations play a part in the charisma of the miracle-worker.

But how are people of today to deal with the tradition about Jesus' miracles? Generally speaking, exegesis takes one of two ways. The first consists in interpreting the miracle stories symbolically. This already begins in the New Testament. At decisive points in the Gospel Mark embarks on miracle stories which 'symbolically' anticipate what is to follow: before Peter's confession of the Messiah there is the healing of a blind man which shows that the disciples who previously were chided as being 'blind' now have their eyes opened to the true status of Jesus (cf. Mark 8.22–26). After the entry into Jerusalem Mark relates the miracle of the withered fig tree to show that the leaders of Israel are no longer bringing forth the fruits expected of them (cf. Mark.11.12ff.; 12.1ff.). Matthew gave a symbolic meaning of the stilling to the storm: it shows the 'ship' of the church threatened by wind and waves but not sinking, despite all dangers (Matt. 8.23ff.). In Luke the miraculous fishing trip (Luke 5.1ff.) has a symbolic meaning: it describes mission. Finally, in John miracles basically have a deeper underlying meaning. The important thing is that only the miracles of Jesus are interpreted symbolically in antiquity. That does not lead to any diminution of them. Rather, it indicates the high esteem in which they were held: they become the vehicles of central theological insights. In the last resort the accentuation of their symbolic meaning lies with Jesus: in interpreting them as signs of the dawn of the end-time, he gave them a surplus symbolic value which then prompted many further interpretations of their meaning.

In such a symbolic interpretation the miracles are often inadmissibly 'spiritualized' by an interpretation 'from above'. The miracles of Jesus were initially meant to bring concrete, material, healing help. They contain a protest against human distress. They deny all previous experience its validity rather than denying the right for human distress to be removed. Wherever these stories are related, people are not content that there is too little bread for many, that there is no healing for many who are sick, and that there is no home in our world for many who are hurt. Wherever these miracles are related, people do not turn away from those who are hopelessly ill. The miracle stories need always to be read 'from below' as a protest against human suffering. How this desire relates to suffering, to destruction by hunger, sickness and distress that we have to accept, in unavoidable suffering and handicaps which cannot be removed, is a problem. There is a reason why in the New Testament alongside the miracles we have Paul – a 'charismatic miracle worker' whose charisma is not even enough to heal himself! He embodies the other side: despite all his protests against his suffering he was not freed from it but had to be content with the information that 'My power is sufficient in weakness (the weakness of the sick)' (II Cor.12.9).

6. Tasks

6.1 Belief and unbelief

Compare the motif of faith in the following miraculous healing from Epidaurus[30] and that in Mark 9.14ff. (esp.22–24).

> A man who could move only one finger of his hand came to the god as a suppliant. When he saw the votive tables in the sanctuary he did not believe in the cures and made fun of the inscriptions. In his sleep (in the sanctuary) he had a vision. It seemed to him that as he was playing dice in the room under the temple and was about to throw the god appeared, jumped on his hand and stretched out his fingers. When he had stepped off, he saw himself bend his hand and stretch out each finger on its own; when he had stretched them all out straight the god asked him whether he still did not believe the votive tablets, and he said no. 'Because before you had no faith in them, though they were worthy of belief, your name in future shall be Apistos,' said the god. When day came he emerged from the sanctuary cured (Epidaurus 3, quoted from Theissen, *Miracle Stories**, 131f.).

6.2 Miracle-workers and favourites of God

In *Histories* 4, 81 (written c.105/110), Tacitus reports how Vespasian unwillingly became a miracle-worker. The episode described takes place in the year 70. Vespasian had been acclaimed emperor by the troops but his power had not yet been confirmed:

> During the months while Vespasian was waiting at Alexandria for the regular season of the summer months and a settled sea, many marvels occurred to mark the favour of heaven and a certain partiality of the gods toward him. One of the common people of Alexandria, well known for his loss of sight, threw himself before Vespasian's knees, praying him with groans to cure his blindness, being so directed by the god Serapis, whom this most superstitious of nations worships before all others; and he besought the emperor to deign to moisten his cheeks and eyes with his spittle. Another, whose hand was useless, prompted by the same god, begged

---

[30]For Epidaurus the place of healing, the sanctuary of Asclepius there, and the accounts of miracles in inscriptions found there, see R. Herzog, *Die Wunderheilungen von Epidaurus*, Ph.S 22, 3, Leipzig 1931; H.-J. Klauck, *Die religiöse Umwelt des Urchristentums* I, Stuttgart 1995, 130–9; M. Wolter, 'Inschriftliche Heiligungsberichte und neutestamentliche Wundererzählungen. Überlieferungs- und formgeschichtliche Beobachtungen, in K. Berger et al., *Studien und Texte zur Formgeschichte*, TANZ 7, Tübingen and Basel 1992, 135–75.

Caesar to step and trample on it. Vespasian at first ridiculed these appeals and treated them with scorn, then, when the men persisted, he began at one moment to fear the discredit of failure, at another to be inspired with hopes of success by the appeals of the suppliants and the flattery of his courtiers: finally, he directed the physicians to give their opinion as to whether such blindness and infirmity could be overcome by human aid. Their reply treated the two cases differently: they said that in the first the power of sight had not been completely eaten away and it would return if the obstacles were removed; in the other, the joints had slipped and become displaced, but they could be restored if a healing pressure were applied to them. Such perhaps was the wish of the gods, and it might be that the emperor had been chosen for this divine service; in any case, if a cure were obtained, the glory would be Caesar's, but in the event of failure, ridicule would fall only on the poor suppliants. So Vespasian, believing that his good fortune was capable of anything and that nothing was any longer incredible, with a smiling countenance, and amid intense excitement on the part of the bystanders, did as he was asked to do. The hand was instantly restored to use, and the day again shone for the blind man. Both facts are told by eye-witnesses even now when) falsehood brings no reward.

Suetonius, *Vespasian* 7 (c.117/122 CE), offers a much briefer account of the two miracles in accordance with the essential facts, but according to this account the second sick man has a lame leg.

1. What does this account suggest about the relationship between deity, miracle-worker and sick person, and about the assessment of the possibility of miracles?

2. What differences between the perception of the representatives of the upper class and the ordinary people become clear?

3. What ideological function does miracle and the narration of miracle have?

4. How do you judge the historicity of Vespasian's miracle?

11

Jesus as Poet: The Parables of Jesus

M.A. Beavis, 'Parable and Fable', *CBQ* 52, 1990, 473–98; C.L. Blomberg, *Interpreting the Parables*, Leicester 1990; J.D. Crossan, *In Parables. The Challenge of the Historical Jesus*, New York, Evanston, San Francisco and London 1973; C.H. Dodd, *The Parables of the Kingdom*, London 1935, revised 1936; J.R. Donahue, *The Gospel in Parable*, Philadelphia 1988; J. Drury, *The Parables in the Gospels: History and Allegory*, London and New York 1985; P. Fiebig, *Die Gleichnisreden Jesu im Lichte der rabbinischen Gleichnisse des neutestamentlichen Zeitalters*, Tübingen 1912; A. Feldman, *The Parables and Similes of the Rabbis*, Cambridge 1924; D. Flusser, *Die rabbinischen Gleichnisse und der Gleichniser- zähler Jesus*, Judaica et Christiana 4, Bern 1981; R.W. Funk, *Language, Hermeneutic and the Word of God*, New York 1966; id., *Parables and Presence. Forms of the New Testament Tradition*, Philadelphia 1982; B. Gerhardsson, 'If We Do Not Cut the Parables out of Their Frames', *NTS* 37, 1991, 321–35; W. Harnisch (ed.), *Gleichnisse Jesu. Positionen der Auslegung von Adolf Jülicher bis zur Formgeschichte*, WdF 366, Darmstadt 1982; id. (ed.), *Die neutestamentliche Gleichnisforschung im Horizont von Hermeneutik und Literatur- wissenschaft*, WdF 575, Darmstadt 1982; C.W. Hedrick, *Parables as Poetic Fiction*, Peabody, Mass. 1994; J. Jeremias, *The Parables of Jesus*, London and New York 1954, ²1963, ³1972; A. Jülicher, *Die Gleichnisreden Jesu*, Tübingen 1888/98, ²1910; W.S. Kissinger, *The Parables of Jesus. A History of Interpretation and Bibliography*, ATLA 4, Metuchen, NJ 1979; H.J. Klauck, *Allegorie und Allegorese in synoptischen Gleichnistexten*, NTA NF 13, Münster 1978; J. Lambrecht, *Once More Astonished. The Parables of Jesus*, New York 1981; E. Linnemann, *Parables of Jesus*, London 1966; H.K. McArthur and R. M. Johnston, *They Also Taught in Parables. Rabbinic Parables from the First Centuries of the Christian Era*, Grand Rapids 1990; L. Schottroff, *Lydia's Impatient Sisters. A Feminist Social History of Early Christianity*, Louisville and London 1995; W. Schottroff and W. Stegemann (ed.), *Der Gott der kleinen Leute*, Vol. 2, Munich ²1979; B.B. Scott, *Hear Then the Parable*, Minneapolis 1989; D. Stern, *Parables in Midrash: Narrative and Exegesis in Rabbinic Literature*, Cambridge 1991; W.D. Stroker, 'Extracanonical Parables and the Historical Jesus', *Semeia* 44, 1988, 95–120; C. Thoma and M. Wyschogrod (ed.), *Parable and Story in Judaism and Christianity*, New York 1989; M.A. Tolbert, *Perspectives on the Parables*, Philadelphia 1979; D.O. Via, *The Parables. Their Literary and Exisential Dimension*, Philadelphia 1967; H. Weder, Die Gleichnisse Jesu als Metaphern, FRLANT 120, Göttingen 1978, ²1984; A. Wilder, *Jesus' Parables and the War of Myths*, Philadelphia 1982; B.H. Young, *Jesus and His Jewish Parables*, New York 1989.

Introduction

It is generally agreed that the parables are the characteristic form of Jesus' teaching. However, many Christians are not aware that parables first become evident historically in Judaism in large quantities with Jesus, though here he was taking up a form that was widespread in his time. For the later rabbinic writings similarly contain many parables. The perception of them from a Christian perspective has long been distorted by prejudices against Judaism. Clichés like 'only Jesus shows God as a gracious Father in his parables' or 'the rabbinic parables are aesthetically inferior to Jesus' parables' are the legacy of a basic triumphalistic attitude in the Christian use of Jewish sources which has no substantive foundation.[1] Rather, in recent years research has shown that Jesus and the rabbis drew on the same store of familiar fields of imagery and motifs and create basic narrative structures; while their parables differ in some respects, they are expressions of the same genre.

Tasks

The two following parables probably belong to the Tannaitic period (first to second century CE) and show a clear affinity to the parables of Jesus:[2]

R. Eliezer said: Repent one day before your death. His disciples asked him, Does then one know on what day he will die? Then all the more reason that he repent today, he replied, lest he die tomorrow, and thus his whole life is spent in repentance. And Solomon too said in his wisdom [Kohelet 9.8]: Let your garments be always white; and let not your head lack ointment. R. Johanan b. Zakkai [c.70 CE] said: This may be compared to a king who summoned his servants to a banquet without appointing a time. The wise ones adorned themselves and sat at the door of the palace, ['for,'] said they, 'is anything lacking in a royal palace?' The fools went about their work, saying, 'Can there be a banquet without preparations?' Suddenly the king desired [the presence of] his servants: the wise entered adorned, while the fools entered soiled. The king rejoiced at the wise but was angry with the fools. 'Those who adorned themselves for the banquet,' ordered he, 'let them sit, eat and drink. But those who did not adorn themselves for the banquet, let them stand and watch' (bShab 153a).

---

[1]Cf. e.g W. Bousset, *Jesus*, London 1906, who first states that Jesus 'had caught the form of his parabolic speech from the scribes in the synagogues', and then goes on to assert: 'This is not in any sense to disparage him. For it is precisely in comparing his parables with those that are most akin to them that the unexampled mastery with which Jesus handled this form of teaching is known . . . There the parables are designed to illustrate the distorted ideas of a dead learning, and therefore often – though by no means always – themselves become distorted and artificial. Here the parable was handled by one whose soul was set, clearly and simply and with nothing to impede the vision, upon the real' (43f.).

[2]McArthur and Johnston, *Parables*, provide a collection of 125 early rabbinic parables in an English translation.

Or, 'Return to the Eternal One, your God' [Deut. 4.30]. R. Samuel Pargerita said in the name of R. Meir (c.150 CE): To what is this matter to be likened? To a king's son who was misbehaving. The king sent his tutor to him with the message: Consider, my son! The son sent to his father, saying: With what countance can I return? I am ashamed before you. Thereupon his father sent the message to him: My son, is a son ashamed to return to his father? If you return, are you not returning to your father? Similarly, God sent Jeremiah to the Israelites when they had sinned. He said to him: Go and tell my children: Consider! From where can that be proved? From Jer. 3.12: 'Go and proclaim these words to the north . . .' Thereupon the Israelites replied to Jeremiah: With what countenance can we return to God? From what can that be proved? It is said in v.25 of the same: 'We lie in our shame and our sin covers us . . .' Thereupon God had it said to them: My children, if you return, are you not returning to your father? From what can that be proved? From Jer. 31.9: I am a father to Israel' (Midrash Debarim Rabba 2 [198d] = DeutR 2 on Deut. 4.30).[3]

Compare the first parable with the Matthaean parables of the royal marriage (Matt. 22.1–14) and the wise and foolish virgins (Matt. 25.1–13), and the second with the Lukan parable of the prodigal son.

Note the common features and differences in the imagery, the narrative structure, the persons and their roles, the function of the work and its theological statement.

Suggested reading

K. E. Bailey, *Poet and Peasant*, Grand Rapids [2]1983, 158–206; Blomberg, *Parables*, 172–97, 233–40; H. Hendrickx, *The Parables of Jesus*, London 1986, 108–69; Jeremias, *Parables*, [3]1972, 136–9, 180–98 ; Linnemann, *Parables*, 73–97, 124–8, 150–96.

1. Phases in the interpretation of the parables since Jülicher

1.1 The didactic understanding of the parable in A. Jülicher (1857–1938): parables as figurative depictions of universal truths

Modern research into the parables[4] begins with Adolf Jülicher (*Die Gleichnisreden Jesu*) and his repudiation of the allegorical exegesis which had been predominant until then. This had interpreted the parables point by point as an

---

[3]A. Wünsche, *Bibliotheca Rabbinica III, Der Midrasch Debarim Rabba*, 32f., cf. Bill. II, 216.

[4]The bibliography and history of research by Kissinger, *Parables*, 1–230, gives an extended survey of research into the parables from Irenaeus to the present day.

encipherment of theological mysteries (in analogy to Mark 4.3–9, 10–20). Jülicher showed that the parables were understood allegorically in primitive Christianity only at a secondary stage. With Jesus they originally focused on one point of comparison ('one-point approach'), by means of which a universal truth was expressed, e.g. that one was always to sacrifice a lesser good for a greater (the parables of the treasure and the pearl, Matt. 13.44–46).[5] The use of figurative language had a didactic purpose:[6] the image increased the probability of assent to what the parable said, though in principle this could also be expressed without an image.[7]

1.2 The 'historicizing' understanding of the parables: parables as a time-conditioned prophetic message

The objection made to the interpretation of the parables in terms of timeless truths was that the parables are to be understood in the context of Jesus' preaching. This context was defined either as the whole of Jesus' eschatological preaching (C.H. Dodd) or as a number of concrete biographical situations within the life of Jesus.

1.2.1 The eschatological message of Jesus as the historical context of the parables (C.H. Dodd, 1884–1973)

According to C.H. Dodd, *The Parables of the Kingdom* (1935), the parables proclaim the presence of the kingdom of God in the person of Jesus ('realized eschatology') and the crisis provoked by this realization of eschatological hopes. Thus the parables of the treasure in the field and the precious pearl (Matt. 13.44f.) seek to make it clear that the kingdom of God as salvation is now accessible in Jesus and confronts people with the decision to give up their life hitherto and follow him. With the help of parables Jesus is saying: 'You agree that the Kingdom of God is the highest good: it is within your power to possess it here and now, if, like the treasure-finder and the pearl-merchant you will throw caution to the winds: "Follow me!"' (113).

1.2.2 The biographical situation of Jesus as the historical context of the parables (J. Jeremias, 1900–1979)

J. Jeremias (*The Parables of Jesus* [1947], English 1954) took up Dodd's view that the parables of Jesus were conditioned by their time and made it more precise in three ways:

---

[5] Jülicher discusses the 'essence of the parables of Jesus', ibid., I, 25–118.

[6] For the 'purpose of the parables of Jesus', cf. ibid., 118–43, esp. 143–6.

[7] Nowadays a didactic understanding of the parables is put forward by exegetes who interpret Jesus' parables in the context of rabbinic parables (e.g. D. Flusser), see below §1.6.

- The imagery often derives from concrete events: the parable of the nocturnal burglar (Matt. 24.43f.) refers to 'some recently effected burglary', the Lukan version of the parable of the talents (Luke 19.12–27) refers to Archelaus' attempt to get the kingship for himself in Rome (*Parables*, ³1972, 49, 59).
- The content of the message is governed by Jesus' eschatological message, which Jeremias describes as 'eschatology in the process of realization', since (*pace* Dodd) Jesus cannot be said to have no future eschatology. After Easter the delay of the parousia was often introduced into the parables at a secondary stage.
- The parables were originally addressed to the public, including Jesus' opponents, against whom he defended his message of God's love (the so-called 'first setting in the life of Jesus'). After Easter the parables often became instructions for disciples through being readdressed (the so-called 'setting in the life and thought of the primitive church').

By 'detaching' the post-Easter stratum Jeremias hoped to get to the historical Jesus: for him parables are the 'original rock of the tradition' (13) and as such are normative.[8]

The contextualizing approaches share two basic problems: first, the reconstruction of the context always remains hypothetical. Secondly, the more firmly the parables are anchored in a particular historical context, the more difficult it is to derive significance from them beyond this unique situation. By contrast, the successive currents of a hermeneutical and aesthetic understanding of the parables concentrate on the parables as autonomous formations which bear their message in themselves and express it in a constantly new way.

1.3 The hermeneutical understanding of the parables: parables as speech-event

Ernst Fuchs,[9] Eberhard Jüngel[10] and Hans Weder[11] along with others interpret the parables primarily in terms of the word-event which takes place in the uttering of them. Parables are understood as a dynamic speech-event in which Jesus claims the love of God for sinners, makes the kingdom of God present and changes people so that they are open to God's reality.

---

[8]In the preface to the third English edition Jeremias writes that his analyses set out to provide 'a return, as well grounded as possible, to the very words of Jesus himself. Only the Son of Man and his word can invest our message with full authority' (9).

[9]E. Fuchs, *Gesammelte Aufsätze* I–III, Tübingen 1959/1960/1965, esp. I, 281ff.; II, 136ff., 143ff.; III, 402ff.; id., *Hermeneutik*, Tübingen ⁴1970, 126–34, 211–30; id., *Marburger Hermeneutik*, Tübingen 1968, 227–48.

[10]E. Jüngel, *Paulus und Jesus*, HUT 2, 1962, ⁵1979, 87–174, esp. 135–42, 173f.

[11]Cf. the survey of the hermeneutical approach to the interpretation of the parables in Weder, *Die Gleichnisse Jesu als Metaphern*, 321–45.

- The author Jesus is present in the parables with his authority (in the form of an implicit christology). His behaviour matches his words, e.g. his table-fellowship with sinners matches the parable of the prodigal son (E. Fuchs).
- Those who are addressed are 'changed' by the speech-event of the parables so that they become open to God's message. Thus the parables create the conditions for understanding them in the hearers themselves (E. Fuchs).
- The substance of the parables is present in them as a simile. Since it does not 'take place' outside the parables, the assumption of a *tertium comparationis* between image and substance is inappropriate: the substance takes place in the picture itself.
- The basis of the imagery of the parables is metaphor (not the comparison). Now metaphor is a linguistic form which cannot be translated, and as 'poiesis'[12] helps to create the reality which it expresses.

1.4 The aesthetic understanding of the parables: parables as autonomous aesthetic objects

More recent American research into the parables, the most important representatives of which are Robert W. Funk, Dan Otto Via, John Dominic Crossan and Bernard B. Scott, is indebted to existentialist hermeneutics and its understanding of the parables as speech-event based on metaphor which transforms existence. Its literary-critical and sometimes structuralist interests see the parables as closed literary works which usually contain a shocking message that contradicts established religious attitudes.

- Parables are autonomous aesthetic objects, which do not point to something outside themselves; rather, their meaning arises in the interplay of inter-related elements of the fictitious narrative. They can therefore be understood independently of their original situation and are even autonomous over against their author (Via).
- The parables contain an implicit understanding of existence in the configuration of their elements, which cannot be reduced. Aesthetic language thus has the power to confront those who hear it and leads to a decision for the mode of existence which is appropriate for faith.
- The original effect of a parable is to be rediscovered by a radical decontextualizing,[13] i.e. by ignoring the context in the Gospels and the history of interpreta-

---

[12]*Poiesis* comes from the Greek ποιεῖν (*poiein* = make, produce, create) and underlies our word 'poetry': the poet creates his or her own (fictitious) reality.

[13]B. Gerhardsson has firmly rejected the de-contextualization of the parables in his article 'If We Do Not Cut the Parables out of Their Frames'. Since 54 of the 55 'narrative *meshalim*' of the Gospels are handed down with frameworks, he argues that it is improbable that here the original sense has regularly been lost. Gerhardsson does not see parables as 'aesthetic objects' either, as they have clearly been stylized with a view to a particular, didactic, purpose.

tion, and by a literary analysis of the structures and relationships within the literary work of art. According to B.B. Scott, only through this does one encounter the originating structure of the parable which underlies individual performances.[14] The possibilities of reaction offered to the recipients in these basic structures can then be reconstructed by taking into account the cultural context, so that the result is a kind of re-contextualization.[15]

Read in this way, say the parable of the good Samaritan communicates an unconventional message: B.B. Scott (*Hear Then*, 189–202) begins with the expectations of the audience which are implied. After the failure of the priest and levite, a Jewish audience would expect that an upright Israelite would now appear as a hero who would help the oppressed man. They would expect someone with whom they could identify. Instead, the arch-enemy appears as a hero and the hearers once again find themselves forced into the role of the (Jewish) victim. Jesus disappointed all expectations in order to show that in the kingdom of God the barriers between people are done away with. Only a pagan audience/readership of the kind that Luke presupposes could identify directly with the Samaritan and read the parable as an example of what it means to be a neighbour.[16]

In contrast to the domination of theological and literary-critical interests in the last two currents, in the two following approaches of research into the parables the quest for the historical context again comes into the foreground – as a question either about the social context of the parables in the Judaism of the time or about the literary-critical context in the framework of Jewish parable literature. This links up with the early 'historicizing' understanding of the parables.

1.5 Social reality and the practice of the Jesus movement as the historical context of the parables (Luise Schottroff)

As a prominent representative of sociological exegesis, Luise Schottroff puts forward a carefully thought out feminist sociological theory of the parables focussed on liberation theology (*Lydia's Impatient Sisters*). In her view the parables of Jesus are bound up with their context in three respects:

---

[14]Here de Saussure's distinction between 'parole', the actual act of speaking, and 'langue', the underlying structures of language, is applied to the parables. In contrast to J. Jeremias, who wanted to reconstruct the *ipsissima verba* of Jesus, Scott's interest is in discovering the *ipsissima structura*.

[15]B.B. Scott is strongly influenced by W. Iser, cf. id., *The Implied Reader*, Baltimore and London 1974; id., *The Act of Reading*, Baltimore and London 1978.

[16]R.W. Funk (*Semeia* 2, 1974, 74–81) was a pioneer of this interpretation. In his view, from the beginning the narrative perspective in Luke 10.30ff. calls for identification with the one who had fallen among thieves. Jesus told a parable about the kingdom of God as grace which comes upon the oppressed in an unexpected form.

- The *imagery* derives from the socio-economic realities of the time of Jesus; these have to be reconstructed by a comparative analysis of the sources, so that the point which was immediately evident to contemporaries emerges.[17] Thus the intensity of God's care for human beings expressed in Luke 15.8–10 is only recognized fully if the value of a drachma for a wage-earner is taken into account. For a woman was underpaid even in relation to the worst-paid man (*Sisters*, 91–110).
- *The message of the parables* – God's present action towards the creation in wrath and mercy – is communicated in images which presuppose concrete social conditions and force people to see these in a new light. If Jesus chooses an employer who gives a full wage even to those who have worked only for a short time as an image of God's goodness, he is criticizing the working world of his time.
- *The practice of the Jesus movement* which Schottroff defines as a Jewish liberation movement within the *Pax Romana* must also be seen as the context of the parables, even if only the beginnings of this situation can be inferred.

1.6 The homiletical understanding of the parables: parables as a new form of the didactic poetry of Judaism

A growing interest in the rabbinic parables[18] led to a reassessment of the parable as a popular form of oral religious instruction which flourished in the time of Jesus. Accordingly, Jesus' parables have been interpreted in the context of related rabbinic parables.

- *A common narrative tradition*: all Jews who tell parables draw on the same fields of images and motifs, as is shown by countless stereotyped agents, metaphors, plots etc., which appear in ever-new combinations. The special character of a parable is disclosed against the background of these shared narrative traditions and the attitudes of expectation established in them. Thus only in the context of all the known rabbinic parables about recompense does Jesus' parable of the labourers in the vineyard (Matt. 20.1–16) take on its special emphasis: the association of the statement about

---

[17]M. Hengel, 'Das Gleichnis von den Weingärtnern Mc 12, 1–12 im Lichte der Zenonpapyri und der rabbinischen Gleichnisse', *ZNW* 59, 1968, 1–39, is a model example of how sociology can illuminate a parable: the rebellious mood among the husbandmen and their attack on messengers from the owner has by no means been constructed artifically, but corresponds to social reality.

[18]Cf. the works cited in the bibliography by Flusser, McArthur and Johnston, Stern, Thomas and Wyschgorod, and Young. Among the earlier investigations special mention should be made of those of Fiebig and Feldman.

God's goodness, which rabbinic parables sometimes emphasize even more strongly, with an appeal to inter-personal solidarity (see below 3.6, pp. 339ff.).

- *Sitz im Leben*: at the pre-written stage, parables composed *ad hoc* were probably part of the repertory of preachers and teachers, regardless of whether they went around to teach, like Jesus, or appeared in a fixed place, for example at synagogue worship.
- *Literary-critical context*: as parables appear in Jewish tradition almost only in the Gospels and the rabbinic writings, and we are to rule out any dependence of the rabbis on Jesus, we will have here a genre which had just arisen in Palestine but was already established at the time of Jesus. In it, the Jewish wisdom tradition has been combined with stimuli from the Greek tradition (fables, the Cynic–Stoic diatribe).
- *Tradition and redaction*: just as the parables of Jesus in the Synoptics have demonstrably been adapted to current needs of the community, so too the redactional interest of the authors of rabbinic writings has shaped their use of parables and has put these in particular at the service of interpretation of the Torah. Analytic comparisons which leave the redaction-critical question out of account therefore necessarily lead to anachronistic conclusions.

2. Forms of figurative speech

The Synoptics call all forms of Jesus' figurative discourse παραβολή, from proverbs (Luke 4.23) or logia which use imagery (Luke 6.39) to extended parables.[19] This corresponds to the terminology of the Septuagint, which renders the Hebrew term מָשָׁל (*mashal*), which has the same breadth of meaning, with παραβολή. Here we shall list the most important differences of genre within this comprehensive group as they have become established among scholars in their critical discussion of A. Jülicher's basic outline.

2.1 The differentiation between parable and allegory: the discovery of the 'one-point approach' and its relativization

2.1.1 *The contrast between parable and allegory according to A. Jülicher ('one-point approach')*

All investigations of parable and allegory refer to A. Jülicher's classic contrast, which draws a distinction in five important points (*Gleichnisreden I*, 25–118):

---

[19]In John, Jesus' figurative discourses are designated παροιμία (dark saying, John 10.6; 16.25, 29).

Parable	Allegory
1. There is only one *tertium comparationis* between the image and its referent, each of which is to be related wholly to the other (the so-called 'one-point approach').	1. There are many points of comparison between the image and its referent (cf. the point by point exegesis in Mark 4.13–20; Matt. 13.36–43).
2. The parable arose from a comparison in which image and referent stand side by side and are 'as it were' connected by the comparative particle.	2. The allegory arises out of the metaphor, in which the image replaces the referent. Allegories contain a chain of metaphors in which each link is translated independently.
3. The images used are realistic and correspond to everyday experience.	3. The images used are artificial and constructed. They contradict everyday experience (cf. the beast with seven horns from Daniel 7).
4. The substance of what is said is generally understandable; the pictorial form serves to make it vivid. Parables are communicable.	4. The content is understandable only to the initiated, who have a 'key' to understanding (cf. the parable theory in Mark 4.10–12). Allegories are esoteric and therefore exclusive.
5. The parables go back to the historical Jesus, who addressed all men and women.	5. The primitive community (and the whole of the later church) interpreted the parables as allegories.

2.1.2 *The relativization of the 'one-point approach' by significant individual features*

The discussion since Jülicher has shown that the strict one-point approach in the interpretation of the parables cannot be sustained. In many parables, alongside the one point there are 'significant individual features' without which the parable would become allegory.

1. *Fixed metaphors*: the parables are based on the traditional store of metaphors in Judaism. In the time of Jesus a 'king' was involuntarily understood as an image for God. A 'vineyard' was a fixed metaphor for Israel.

2. *Unusual features* occur above all in the parables, for example the fact that all the guests decline the invitation (Luke 14.16–24 par.) or that the farmer sows his

seed equally on good and bad ground (Mark 4.3–9). Deviations from probability indicate a special purpose.

3. *Interlockings*: parables contain roles with which the hearers should and could identify. This leads to an interlocking of the reality of the parable with the reality of the audience, especially where possible 'protest' against what is said in the parable is anticipated in the parable itself, for example in the murmuring of the workers who have worked for a whole day (Matt. 20.11f.), or in the older brother's criticism of the 'prodigal son' in Luke 15.25ff. (Linnemann, *Parables*).

2.1.3 *The integration of the 'significant individual features' into the 'one-point approach'*

After the discovery of the 'significant individual features' the distinction between allegory and parable must be reformulated.

1. An *allegory* consists in a chain of 'significant individual features' which do not form a coherent connection at the level of the image. Their coherence can only be *known at the 'level of content'*.

2. By contrast, a *parable* has only one point, but in addition it can display significant individual features, though these may not put in question the image as a closed unity.

This can be illustrated with a diagram:[20]

C = content I = image F = individual feature   + = coherent connection

$$C \rightarrow \qquad\qquad I \qquad\qquad\qquad\qquad\qquad\qquad\qquad I$$

$$\overbrace{F_1 + F_2 + F_3 + F_4 + F_5} \qquad\qquad \overbrace{F_1 \quad F_2 \quad F_3 \quad F_4 \quad F_5}$$

$$\uparrow \qquad\qquad \uparrow \qquad\qquad\qquad \uparrow \quad\; \uparrow \quad\; \uparrow \quad\; \uparrow \quad\; \uparrow$$

$$I_1 \qquad\qquad I_2 \qquad\qquad\qquad I_1 + I_2 + I_3 + I_4 + I_5$$

$$\text{Parable} \qquad\qquad\qquad\qquad\qquad\qquad \text{Allegory}$$

This evaluation of 'significant individual features' amounts to a certain rehabilitation of the allegory. However, a distinction needs to be made between different forms of allegorical texts.

2.1.4 *Differentiations between allegorical texts*

According to H.J. Klauck (*Allegorie und Allegorese*), the allegorical texts can further be differentiated in the following way:

1. Texts which an author has from the start conceived as allegories (e.g. Dan. 7) are authentic *allegories*.

2. By *allegorizing* is to be understood the secondary revision of non-allegorical texts (e.g. parables) by introducing allegorical details into the parables. Numerous parables of Jesus show signs of more or less extensive *allegorizing*.

3. An *allegorization* is an allegorical exegesis of a text which was not intrinsically intended to be allegorical. From Mark onwards (Mark 4.13–20) allegorization became the usual form of the interpretation of the parables in the early church.

In all these forms allegorical texts are by no means inferior forms of communication. Moreover they are not just accessible to initiates; they can be understood. For example, Quintilian (*Inst.* VIII, 6, 52) regarded obscure and incomprehensible allegories as writer's errors.

2.2 Differentiations within the general category of parable: figures of speech, parables (in the sense of similitudes), parables proper (narrative metaphors), and example stories

Research into the parables has been influenced not only by Jülicher's distinction between parable and allegory but also by his distinction of various sub-genres. With small modifications these are still valid.

2.2.1 *Figures of speech and comparisons*

Comparisons (which are relatively rare) and above all figures of speech without a comparative particle (like) count as a primitive form of parable.[21] The latter frequently have two members, the synonymous clauses being linked by καί (and) or οὐδέ (nor).

- For example, Matt. 10.16b, 'be wise as serpents and innocent as doves', is a *comparison.*
- Matt. 24.28, 'Where the body is, there the eagles will be gathered together', is *a simple figure of speech.*
- There is a *two-member figure of speech* in Luke 6.44b: 'For figs are not gathered from thorns, nor are grapes picked from a bramble bush.'

Figurative discourses are based on metaphors. Metaphors (e.g. Herod is a fox, cf. Luke 13.32) can be understood (as they were by Jülicher) as abbreviated comparisons (e.g. Herod behaves *like* a fox) or comparisons as metaphors which have been rationalized at a secondary stage (this is the dominant view today); here the metaphor did not originally reflect on a distinction between the one conveying the image and the one receiving it, but made the two transparent to each other. It is

---

[20]Somewhat simplified from Weder, *Gleichnisse*, 71.
[21]Cf. Bultmann, *HST**, 170ff.

the 'rational' act of comparison between separate entities which comes first, and in the second the 'intuitive' act of a perception which fuses them together.

2.2.2 Similitudes

Similitudes differ from comparisons and illustrations by the details in their imagery.[22] They depict a recurrent, typical event which is (usually) described in the present. In the argument they often pick up something that is a matter of course and with which everyone agrees. Classical examples are the parables of the mustard seed and the leaven (Mark 4.30–32).

2.2.3 Parables proper

By contrast, parables proper narrate (in the aorist) an unusual individual instance and argue against the consensus. They call for an attitude to the unusual behaviour that is reported and in so doing seek to produce a change of attitude and behaviour at the level of subject-matter. The boundaries between the various forms fluctuate. Thus in the parable of the seed which grows by itself we have a typical recurring event in the form of a narrative – Jülicher includes the pericope among the parables, while Bultmann classes it as a similitude.

2.2.4 Example stories

Similitudes and parables are genres of imagery in which the image and the subject-matter belong in different spheres of reality. By contrast, this characteristic tension between image and subject-matter is absent from the example story, and the situation which is intended is introduced by means of a concrete example. So an example story can end with an invitation which is to be understood quite literally: 'Go and do likewise' (Luke 10.37). In the New Testament, example stories occur only in Luke (10.29–37; 12.16–21; 16.19–31; 18.9–14).[23]

2.2.5 The system of co-ordinates in the forms of parables

G. Sellin ('Allegorie und Gleichnis', ZThK 75, 1978, 334f.) has summarized the various forms of parables (excluding allegory) in a system of co-ordinates under the main perspectives given above – general and specific statement, language with and without imagery).

---

[22]Thus Bultmann, *HST**, 174. Some authors (e.g. A. Jülicher) make no distinction at all between pictorial words and parables, but treat both under the category of parable.

[23]The identification of a special Lukan genre of 'example stories', made for the first time by Jülicher, has not remained unchallenged. Thus e.g. Harnisch and Crossan define the corresponding texts as parables. Cf. W. Harnisch, *Die Gleichniserzählungen Jesu. Eine hermeneutische Einführung*, UTB 1343, Göttingen 1985, 84ff; Crossan, *In Parables*, 55ff.; E. Baasland, 'Zum Beispiel der Beispielerzählungen', *NT* 28, 1986, 193–219.

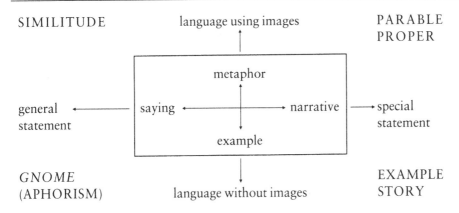

In addition to the forms already discussed, Sellin also includes the *gnome* or aphorism, which like an example story clarifies what is meant by means of an example. However, this does not happen in the form of a narrative but in a statement which is generally valid. Mark 7.15 is a typical aphorism: 'There is nothing outside a man which by going into him can defile him; but the things which come out of a man are what defile him.' In wisdom such proverbs fall under the designation מָשָׁל (*māshāl*), and a collection of aphorisms is also made in Luke 14.7ff. under the heading of parable (παραβολή).

3. Parables as narratives

3.1 The relationship between metaphor and narrative in the parable

Parables are metaphors developed as narrative. In the genre of the similitude whole stories appear as images. How can 'metaphors' become narratives? By what is their metaphorical character signalized to readers?

1. Traditional metaphors become narratives when the relationships to neighbouring images with related content which are suggested in the image are actualized, when the so-called 'field of images' is reactivated. Slaves, subjects, possessions and a kingdom, obedience and rebellion in fact go with 'king'. Potentially narrative tensions are contained in all these 'oppositions'.[24]

2. 'Image signals' – which make it possible to recognize a metaphor as such, arise in individual metaphors through the semantic tensions between two elements of the text: 'The stones cry out' cannot be meant literally, because the verb

---

[24]For the significance of research into semantic fields on exegesis see K. Berger, *Exegese des Neuen Testaments*, UTB 658, Heidelberg 1977, 137–59.

'cry out' presupposes a living being as a subject. So a metaphor can be defined as a 'word in a counter-determining context'.[25] In the case of parables, such semantic incongruities in the immediate context are replaced by the tension between framework and parable.[26]

Thus parables are more than 'images'. The term 'image' associates a static contrast of image and thing. But as narrative parables primarily communicate a story which is difficult to interpret in an abstract notion: 'The narrative continues to tell against the interpretations which the similitude (or parable) has been given' (C. Westermann, *Vergleiche und Gleichnisse im Alten und Neuen Testament*, CThM 14, Stuttgart 1984, 122).

3.2 The beginnings of the parables[27]

1. *Narrative beginning (= nominative beginning)*. The narrative begins immediately without an introductory formula, i.e. without an 'image signal'. Mark 4.3, 'A sower went out to sow . . .' is an example. Here the fact that this is an image is signalized by the wider framework ('he taught them in parables', Mark 4.2) and the theory and interpretation of parables which is attached (Mark 4.10ff.).

2. *Comparative beginning (= dative beginning)*. 'The kingdom of God is like . . .' (Matt. 13.24). This introduction corresponds to rabbinc introductions to parables which appear in two variants:

- *As a long form*: אמשל לך משל למה הדבר דמה ל (I will tell you a parable. With what can the thing be compared? It is with it as with . . .). In the NT, e.g. Mark 4.30f. offers the long form: 'With what can we compare the kingdom of God, or what parable shall we use for it? It is like . . .'[28]
- *As a short form*: משל ל (a parable. An X is comparable . . .). In the NT this is the more frequent introductory formula ('Ομοιώθη ἡ βασιλεία τῶν οὐρανῶν, the kingdom of heaven is like . . .', Matt. 13.24).

---

[25]H. Weinrich, 'Die Metapher. Bochumer Discussion', *Poetica* 2, 1968, 100–30; Berger, *Formgeschichte des Neuen Testaments*, Heidelberg 1984, 32f., offers a short summary of the results of more recent metaphor research which are relevant for exegesis.

[26]Without these contextual signals some parables would not be recognizable as parables at all: for example, the parable of the prodigal son could also be regarded as an example story about a father who was gracious in a model way, did not the context (cf. Luke 15.1–10) make it clear that it is about the place of people before God, so that the 'father' becomes recognizable as a standing metaphor for God.

[27]Cf. Jeremias, *Parables*,³ 1962, 97ff.

[28]Greek: Πῶς ὁμοιώσωμεν τὴν βασιλείαν τοῦ θεοῦ, ἢ ἐν τίνι αὐτὴν παραβολῇ θῶμεν; ὡς . . .

3. *Dialogue beginning*. 'Which of you has a friend . . .' (Luke 11.5). The hearers are addressed directly and invited to express an opinion.

Many parable beginnings are secondary. Especially in Matthew we find the stereotyped beginning 'The kingdom of heaven is like . . .' (Matt. 13.31, 33, 44, 45, 47). The thesis that all parables are about the kingdom of God has been encouraged by these secondary introductions. But the Logia source knows another initial comparison which mentions 'this generation' (ἡ γενεὰ αὕτη) as the theme of the parables: 'With what shall I compare this generation?' (Matt. 11.16/ Luke 7.31). The original theme of the parables is all of human life before God.

3.3 The narrative structure of the parables

Bultmann defined the narrative structure of the parables by means of a comparison with the structures of popular poetry[29] as follows:

- *The brevity of the narrative*: only the necessary persons appear. For example, the mother does not appear in the parable of the prodigal son.[30] The number of persons is usually limited to three main characters; where groups appear, these are treated as a unity.
- '*Law of scenic duality*': only two persons appear at the same time in speech or action.
- *Unilinear narrative*: the focus is never on two processes taking place at the same time. For example, we are not told how the father of the 'prodigal son' feels and what he thinks during his son's absence (Luke 15.11ff.).
- '*Law of repetition*': the 'prodigal son's' confession of sins is reported twice (Luke 15.18f., 21); three types of guest are invited to the royal wedding feast (Matt. 22.3, 4, 9); priest, levite and Samaritan go past the man who has been attacked, one after another (Luke 10.31, 32, 33). Here the emphasis is always on the one who is described last (the so-called '*law of concluding emphasis*').
- *The narrative breaks off after the point*: the conclusion of the narrative is absent. We are not told whether the rich farmer died that same night, as announced (Luke 12.16–21); whether the barren fig tree bore fruit again is not related (Luke 13.6–9); nor are we told whether the older son gave up his resistance to reconciliation with his 'prodigal' brother (Luke 15.11ff.).[31]

---

[29]*HST*, 166–205 *(esp. 170–5). Bultmann referred above all to A. Olrik, *Gesetze der Volksdichtung*.

[30]Of course this selection of 'necessary' persons reflects an androcentric perspective which a critical exegesis should mention. Cf. B. Wartenberg-Potter, 'Über die Frage, ob der Verlorene Sohn ein Halbwaise war', in D. Sölle (ed.), *Für Gerechtigkeit streiten (FS L. Schottroff)*, Gütersloh 1994, 304.

[31]Further typical stylistic characteristics collected by Bultmann are: brevity about motivation (emotions and motives are mentioned only where that is important for the action or point); the pallor of the incidental figures; a rich use of direct speech and soliloquy, etc.

Under the influence of structuralist narrative analysis, attempts have been made to understand the specific 'actant structure' of the parables beyond such general 'narrative laws'. By 'actants' are understood all those involved in the action: persons, animals, plants or things, i.e. all 'roles' which are involved in an action. So far no results capable of securing a consensus have been achieved. So we shall go on to sketch an attempt of our own.

Within the parables one can distinguish between complementary and contrasting roles (or 'actants'). In complementary roles, persons and things enter into a non-reversible relationship: a father cannot take over the role of his son, nor a farmer the 'role' of the seed. Contrasting roles result in opposite behaviour in opportunities which in principle are the same – as in the case of the foolish and wise virgins, the younger and older son. It is illuminating that antagonistic roles fade into the background in the parables – except in the parables of the king waging war (Luke 14.31–32), the burglar (Matt. 24.43 f.) and the wheat and the tares, in which an 'enemy' appears (Matt. 13.24–30). That is all the more remarkable, since outside the parables the kingdom of God has an antagonistic character: it establishes itself in the face of the rule of Satan. By contrast, the world of the parables is a civil society, in which militant hostility represents a disruption (Mark 12.1ff.). It might be mentioned in passing that all roles can be 'extended' by intermediary roles: messengers between the master and tenants can appear, etc.

1. *Structures of action with complementary roles.* In the case of complementary roles, either the fulfilment or the failure of an intention to act are described. Fulfilment is realized in many variants: in the parables of growth as the way from the seed to the harvest or to the completion of growth (cf. Mark 4.26ff., 30–32, etc.); in the parables of growth as a tension between the expectation and arrival of the lord (Mark 13.33ff.) or of the burglar (Matt. 24.43f.); in parables about finding as seeking and finding (Matt. 18.12–14; Luke 15.8–10) – here the discovery of treasure which has not been sought (Matt. 13.44) and of the pearl (Matt. 13.45f.) represent a special variant. Finally mention should be made of parables of asking and being heard (Luke 11.5–8; 18.1–8). Such parables are always concerned to spread courage and confidence: sowing, waiting, seeking and asking – all that is worth while. Other parables show the failure of intentions to act: a foolish rich man hopes to find security in his possessions; death thwarts his hopes (Luke 12.16–21). The building of a tower and the waging of a war need to be thought through carefully so that they do not end in a fiasco (Luke 14.28–32). A request for payment on a lease is not acceded to, but hindered by violent acts, extending to murder (Mark 12.1ff.). A trial does not take place because the opponents in the case come to an agreement while they are on the way to court (Matt. 5.25f.). All these parables contain a warning. Life is threatened by death and judgment. But there are possibilities of coming to terms in time and possibilities of conversion.

2. *Structures of action with contrasting roles.* Successful and failed intentions to act can not only be depicted in different parables but also be contrasted in one and the same parable. That makes the structure of the action more complex. The parables end up with a contrast either being intensified or being reduced or 'converted', so that it becomes a kind of exchange of roles. The contrast is sharpened with the wise and foolish virgins: all have the same starting situation; all sleep; all are waiting for the bridegroom. But then the expectation of the wise virgins is fulfilled and that of the foolish virgins goes wrong (Matt. 25.1–13). An accentuation of the contrast also stamps the action in the parable of the talents: the one who has a lot gets even more; the one who has a little loses even the little that he has neglected to increase (Matt. 25.14–30). It is the same with the parable of the different kinds of ground: the same seed falls on four kinds of ground, but only on the fertile soil does it grow and surpasses even the many losses (Mark 4.3–9). There is also an action which accentuates the contrast in the parable about building a house (Matt. 7.24–27). But the opposite kind of action structure is particularly characteristic of the preaching of Jesus: a contrast which exists at the beginning is reduced or even reversed; what seemed to have a positive evaluation at the beginning is there in negative form at the end (and *vice versa*). In the end those who have worked for a long time and those who have worked for a short time are treated equally – and those who have worked for a long time and grumble suddenly show themselves to be 'envious' (Matt. 20.11–16). The prodigal son and the older brother exchange roles: in the end the prodigal son acts more in accordance with his father's wishes than the older brother, who cannot rejoice over the return of the son who was believed dead (Luke 15.11ff.). The son who was originally disobedient takes the place of the son who was originally obedient, but does not keep his promise (Matt. 21.28–32). The rich man and poor Lazarus exchange their roles in the world to come (Luke 16.19–31). Pharisees and toll collectors have a different standing before God from their standing before their fellow human beings: the one who humiliates himself will be exalted and the one who exalts himself will be humiliated (Luke 18.9–14). Such structures of action are mixed up, enriched and varied in many parables – but time and again the same basic patterns can be recognized.

It is not difficult to recognize basic structures of the preaching of Jesus in these patterns of action. Preaching of salvation and judgment is clarified with the help of images from the everyday world. The preaching of judgment serves to arouse people. They have a chance to repent. But the preaching of salvation gives them courage to trust in God's goodness even against appearances. In the parables the present dawn of salvation in the parable event can be indicated with a complementary distribution of roles: the seed has already been sown, the harvest is certainly coming. The leaven already affects all the dough. The treasure in the field has already been found – now everything depends on acquiring it. The precious pearl is already within reach – now everything depends on possessing it. In the parables with a contrasting distribution of roles promise and warning are connected in 'didactic doses': the danger of failure is great. But there are alternatives of salvation. And they are often grasped by those who according to human judgment are failures and losers.

3.4 The conclusion of the parable (application)

After the conclusion of the narrative proper in the parable there follows either a short application,[32] often introduced with οὕτως (so), or a longer exegesis. In any case this emphasizes the imagery of the narrative (or the pre-imagery of the action narrated).

 1. The *epimythion* (or *moral*), e.g. Matt. 20.16: 'So (οὕτως) the first shall be last.' As in the ancient fables, these epimythia are often secondary and variable. As even those who originally handed it down were aware, the narrative in the parable contains more than a brief application can express. Therefore there are sometimes several applications one after the other (not wholly free from contradiction), e.g. in Luke 16.8–13: (*a*) Praise of the shrewdness of the steward (16.8); (*b*) an invitation to make friends by the social use of money (16.9); (*c*) an invitation to faithfulness in the administration of goods that have been entrusted, in things great and small (16.10–12); (*d*) the incompatibility of serving God and serving mammon (16.13).

 2. *Full allegorizations* (only Mark 4.13–20 and Matt. 13.36–43) appear in the New Testament only in the images of seed, growth and harvest, which are interpreted with reference to the Christian community. This metaphor was unknown earlier as an 'image of the community'. Here a new position in the field of images was taken up which had to be explained.

 3. The rabbinic parables are also usually concluded with an explicit application (the so-called *nimshal*). These are usually introduced with כן (corresponding to the Greek οὕτως), and unlike Jesus' parables are often dominated by scriptural references, quotations and interpretations; this can doubtless be explained by the exegetical interest of the rabbinic writings.

3.5 Classifying the parables by literary criticism

The history of the parables begins in the Old Testament. Here we find many comparisons, above all in the dialogical forms of speech in prophecy and the Psalms (Westermann). Only rarely, however, are such comparisons developed into parables.[33] These often contain allegorical features and anthropomorphisms

---

[32]Cf. Matt. 13.49; 18.14; 18.35; 20.16; Luke 12.21; 14.33; 15.10; 17.10; Mark 13.29.

[33]The Old Testament parables can be quickly listed: in addition to Jotham's fable (Judg. 9.7–21), mention should be made of Nathan's parable (II Sam. 12.1–4), the parable of the two brothers (II Sam. 14.5–7), the prisoner who escaped (I Kings 20.39–40), the thistle and the cedar (II Kings 14.9), the faithless vineyard (Isa. 5.1–7) and the allegories in Ezekiel (Ezek. 17.3–10; 19.2–9, 10–14; 21.1–5; 24.3–5).

which make animals and plants appear human and are characteristic of the 'fable'. There is no mistaking the fact that in the parable of the wicked husbandmen, the Jesus tradition is taking up Isaiah's song of the vineyard (Isa. 5.1–7). That makes it all the more notable that the form has been changed: it is not the vineyard but the husbandmen who work in it who come into conflict with the owner of the vineyard. There is a reversal of the anthropomorphizing of the vineyard. All in all, despite such links with the Old Testament in Jesus, a new phase of Jewish parable composition becomes visible.

The parables of Jesus are a form of wisdom. They appear in Judaism to a considerable extent first with Jesus. At the beginning of the second century BCE, Jesus Sirach could be active as a wisdom teacher from the Jewish upper class without incorporating this form into his book of wisdom. Certainly in his view the use of parables (παραβολαί) was one of the characteristics of the wisdom teacher (Sir. 39.3), but these are pointed sentences, riddles and reflections with images – not those short stories that we call 'parables'. With Jesus' appearance around 200 years later as a popular wisdom teacher who puts such parables at the centre of the forms he uses, the aristocratic education of Jesus Sirach, which excluded working men (Sir. 38.24ff.), has become a wisdom for ordinary people – possibly a consequence of Jewish schooling, which had arisen as a reaction to Hellenism.[34] Where one wants to make ordinary people and children understand, one needs illuminating short stories and images. The rabbis interpreted the Torah with such parables. For Jesus, they bore their message in themselves.

Thus the parable form (like other forms of the Synoptic tradition) emerged from the meeting of two cultures. Precisely as a result of this, a characteristic of the forms of language used by Jesus becomes significant. He does not use fables – those short narratives which were widespread in antiquity in both the Near Eastern and the Greek world. That is all the more striking. since at least one of Jesus' parables reworks traditional material from fables. Compare Luke 13.6–9 with the following fable from the Ahikar tradition:

> 'My son, you were to me like a palm which stood at the side of the road, but from which no one plucked fruit. The owner came and wanted to tear it up. Then the palm said to him: give me one more year and I will bring you cardamom (= saffron, i.e. a sweet–smelling crop). Its owner replied: "Unhappy tree! You did not bring forth your own fruit, how can you bring forth an alien fruit"?' (Syrian Ahikar 135).[35]

---

[34]For the origin of the Jewish school cf. R. Riesner, *Jesus als Lehrer. Eine Untersuchung zum Ursprung der Evangelienüberlieferung*, WUNT 2/7, Tübingen 1981, 97–245.

[35]For the text see M. Küchler, *Frühjüdische Weisheitstraditionen*, OBO 26, Fribourg CH and Göttingen 1979, 329. There is a detailed comparison of the various versions of the fable of Ahikar in P. von Gemünden, *Vegetationsmetaphorik im Neuen Testament und seiner Umwelt*, NTOA 18, Fribourg CH and Göttingen 1993, 135ff.

In the case of Jesus the tree which is threatened does not speak. It is given a human intercessor. The 'anthropomorphism' of the fable is lacking. However, as the Jesus tradition is familiar with animals (cf. the 'fox' in Luke 13.32) and plants (cf. the 'reed' in Matt. 11.7) from fables, a conscious concern for form may underlie the absence of animal and plant fables. The following contrast between animal or plant fables and the parables of Jesus makes clear the decisive points which the two have in common and the differences between them.

	Ancient animal and plant fables	Parables of the Jesus tradition
Social location	The fable is a genre which is accessible to all: whereas wisdom is often attributed to persons in high positions (Amenemope, Solomon, Ahikar), the fables are regarded as the work of the slave Aesop and the freeman Phaedrus.	The parables of Jesus are a genre accessible to all – in contrast to the allegories of apocalyptic secret literature. They become the revealed knowledge of a small group only a result of secondary allegorization.
Form and persons	Fables often make animals and plants act and speak anthropomorphically in order to depict human life.[36] The message is: human beings behave like animals. No change seems possible: a wolf remains a wolf; a fig tree cannot bring forth grapes.	The parables of Jesus deal with people (also in relation to animals and plants) in order to depict the relationship between God and human beings. The message is that God acts in a 'humane' way. He gives an opportunity for change. Human beings can repent and a 'barren tree' can become a 'fruitful person'.
Moral	The fables present a utilitarian and defensive morality: those who do not fit in are done down by those who are stronger. Generosity and mercy are not rewarded (one only nurtures the 'serpent in the bosom'). Joyful risk is folly. Here we find an everyday morality (especially that of ordinary people) which contrasts with the aristocratic ethos of the (heroic) epic and tragedy.	The parables of Jesus advocate a morality which delights in risk which is demanded and made possible by God: people must not hide their talents defensively but use them. One is to give everything for the treasure in the field. In the parables we find a popular literary form of an aristocratic morality of high responsibility and a way of life which is ready for risk.

This comparison between animal and plant fables on the one hand and the parables of Jesus on the other is confirmed by the 'hierarchy of genres' which is evident in Quintilian, the famous teacher of rhetoric. In *Inst.* V, 11, 1f., he discusses the different kinds of examples according to their degree of proof: historical examples rank above fictitious examples, and among the latter those close to reality rank above those which are remote from reality. The fables come at the end. They 'tend to work above all on the hearts of peasants and the uneducated' (*Inst.* V, 11, 9). D. Dormeyer has worked out the following 'hierarchy of genres' from Quintilian's remarks (the parallels from the Jesus tradition have been put in brackets):[37]

1. The *exemplum* as a historical example, often in the form of a series of examples (cf. the Old Testament typologies in Matt. 12.40–42).
2. The *similitudo* as a fictitious *exemplum* with less demonstrative power, graded by its nearness to the real case under discussion.
   2.1. The fictitious *exemplum* near to reality (narrative example)
   2.2 The fictitious *exemplum* remote from reality
       2.2.1 The figurative comparison (similitude)
       2.2.2 The story remote from reality (parable)
       2.2.3 The fable (with no parallel in Jesus).

This makes it possible for us to say that in the case of Jesus a 'high' self- understanding is communicated to ordinary people in a genre of which comparatively little was thought, in that they were confronted with God. Jesus makes use of this popular genre and is the first teacher of parables to appear in Jewish literary history. Alongside him and independently of him rabbis take up the same genre. However, among them, in most cases the parables remain subordinate to the interpretation of the Torah.

Excursus: The authenticity of the parables of Jesus

The parables of Jesus are generally regarded as authentic Jesus tradition. The reason for this is the special literary- and form-critical character of the parables which was sketched out above: although they can be explained fully from their Jewish context, the parables have an individual stamp. Above all, they can easily be distinguished from related text- forms in primitive Christianity.

* The pictorial discourses about the good shepherd and the vine (John 10.1ff.; 15.1ff.) and the parable of the olive tree (Rom. 11.17ff.) contain allegorical elements which have not been completely integrated into the context of the

---

[36]However, in the collections of fables there are also many fables without anthropomorph- ized plants and animals. They are partly parables and partly apophthegms.

[37]Cf. D. Dormeyer, *Das Neue Testament im Rahmen der antiken Literaturgeschichte*, Darmstadt 1993, 143–6.

imagery. For example, it seems artificial for a branch which has once been broken off to be stuck on again (Rom. 11.23). That is understandable only in terms of the subject-matter. Comparable allegorical elements can easily be removed from the parables of Jesus as a secondary stratum, e.g. the reference to the destruction of Jerusalem in Matt. 22.7. By contrast, they are a constitutive element of the (few) primitive Christian figurative discourses.

- The three figurative discourses mentioned, like those in the Shepherd of Hermas (I–IX), relate to the church. Now it cannot be a coincidence that the two (secondary) allegorical interpretations of parables of Jesus similarly interpret the parables with reference to the community (Mark 4.12–20; Matt. 13.36–43). Since in Old Testament-Jewish tradition images of seed and harvest were not related to the community, there was a need for an explanation here. It would have been much more natural to interpret images of the tree and its fruit or its branches in terms of the community, as happened in John 15.1ff.; Rom. 11.17ff. The tree itself symbolizes the lasting community; branches and fruit can depict the members and generations which succeed one another. The fact that for a while seed and harvest were used in primitive Christianity as images of the community was connected with the eschatological consciousness that the world would soon be coming to an end. There is no surviving 'stem'. There is only a once-for-all seed-time and harvest.

The plausibility of both context and impact thus suggest that the parables derive from the historical Jesus: they can be derived from Jewish tradition but have an individual stamp in their present context. Primitive Christianity soon went over to other forms of figurative discourse.

It could be objected to the view that the parable tradition is authentic that many parables have been preserved only in the tradition of special material. Of about forty parables of Jesus, eight have been preserved as Matthaean and seventeen as Lukan special material. If we regard the criterion of multiple attestation as decisive, a sceptical attitude about the authenticity of large parts of the parable tradition would be understandable. However, the following arguments need to be considered.

- The Gospel of Mark clearly betrays that Jesus spoke far more parables than it hands on. The generalization at the end of the discourse on parables indicates this: 'And by many such parables he spoke the word to them . . .' (Mark 4.33). In Mark. 12.1 the evangelist announces 'parables' (in the plural), but follows this with only one! The inclusion of only a few parables in the earliest Gospel is understandable, because they are not necessary for a consecutive narrative: they can very well be handed on as isolated stories. They are little works of art which contain their own point and can exist even without a wider literary context.
- The parables in the special material give many indications that they are not the compositions of the evangelists. The point in Matt. 20.16 – the first shall be last

and the last first – is in tension with the parable, in which all are treated in the same way. The admonition in Matt. 25.13, 'Watch therefore', does not fit the preceding parable in which all the virgins went to sleep, the wise as well as the foolish. In the two Lukan parables of the good Samaritan and the prodigal son the narrative shows a Jewish perspective: the Samaritans are aliens; the prodigal son almost comes to grief looking after (unclean) pigs; his family home lies in Jewish Palestine. It is improbable that the evangelist composed such parables with a Jewish perspective.

- The Gospel of Thomas offers parallels to eleven Synoptic parables – scattered over all the complexes of tradition but more 'densely' in the earliest sources Mark and Q. Three of the four Markan parables have parallels in Thomas (cf. 9; 20; 65). Four of the roughly ten parables from Q also appear in the Gospel of Thomas (cf. 64; 96; 103; 107). Furthermore there are three parallels with the Matthaean special material (57; 76; 109) and one with the Lukan special material (63). If we add the fact that the Gospel of Thomas contains parables of Jesus which throughout have a Synoptic stamp (cf. the parables of the fisherman, the jar and the assassin, 8; 97; 98) and that there are further parables with a partially Synoptic style in the Letter of James (NHC I, 7, 24–28; 8, 16–23; 12, 22–27, see below 2.3.3), we have evidence of a broad tradition of parables which also existed independently of the Synoptic Gospels.

With the criterion of multiple attestation we can usually judge the breadth and the age of a tradition. Even though we cannot apply the criterion to a large number of the parables, the breadth and age of the traditions in this case are assured by other indications. Of course we cannot exclude the possibility that the parables of Jesus which have been handed down to us contain compositions which Christians created imitating parables of Jesus which were already in existence. However, the individuality and uniqueness of most of the parables makes it very improbable that there are many such cases. Therefore it is still true that the parables of Jesus are 'the original rock of the tradition' (Jeremias, *Parables*, 11). The fact that multiple attestation is often lacking for the parables is no argument against their authenticity, but rather an argument that that this criterion should not be put at the head of all the criteria in a historical assessment of Jesus traditions.

3.6 The parable of the labourers in the vineyard (Matt. 20.1–16) within the framework of the rabbinic parables of recompense: an example

1. Jesus' parable of the generous employer is only one of numerous Jewish parables which use the field of images associated with recompense and show comparable narrative structures, persons and roles. An employer (a standing metaphor for God, who appears as a 'householder' or a 'king') is contrasted with

people (individuals or workers appearing in groups) who work for him for a shorter or longer period; they are competent or lazy and expect to get recompense which is agreed or held open. Here the actualizations differ widely, as do the theological questions which the parable is used on each occasion to answer.

2. If one begins with the metaphor of recompense, which is central to all the parables, two different basic theological interpretations can be demonstrated: reward as appropriate recompense ('just reward') and as unmerited gift ('gracious reward'). Significantly, it is above all the instances of the first type that are well known.

• *God's formal justice as the theological basis of parables about recompense.* In Sifra Bechuqqotai 2.5 on Lev. 26.9 a parable is cited in order to ground Israel's preferential position among the peoples in its special commitment to God.

'And I will have regard for you' (Lev. 26.9). A parable is told. What is the matter like? It is like a king who hired many workers. And there was a worker there and he worked for him many days. The workers entered to receive their recompense, and this worker entered with them. The king said to this worker: My son, I will have regard for you. I will give little recompense to these many who have done little work for me. But with you in future I shall reckon a great reckoning. Thus Israel was accustomed in this world to ask its recompense from God and the people of the world [also] asked for their recompense from God. And God said to Israel: My children, I will have regard for you. These peoples of the world have done little work for me and I will give them little recompense. But with you in the future I shall reckon a great reckoning. Therefore it is said: 'And I will have regard for you' (Lev. 26.9).[38]

The following parable is told without doing away with the principle of recompense, but clearly with the aim of excluding it as a primary motivation:

Similarly: 'Do not weigh up the way of life' (Prov. 5.6). R. Abba bar Kahana said: 'The Holy One, Blessed be He, says: Do not sit there and weigh up the commandments of the Torah . . .. Do not say, "Because this commandment is great I want to do it, for great is its recompense; because this commandment is easy I do not want to do it." What did the Holy One, Blessed be He, do? He did not inform the creatures of what was the recompense for each individual commandment, so that they would do each commandment in ignorance [of its recompense], as it says:

---

[38]Quoted from C. Heszer, *Lohnmetaphorik und Arbeitswelt in Mt 20, 1–16. Das Gleichnis von den Arbeitern im Weinberg im Rahmen rabbinischer Lohngleichnisse*, NTOA 15, Fribourg, CH and Göttingen 1990, 303.

"her ways wander, and she does not know it" (Prov. 5.6). To what is the matter like? A king who hired workers. And he immediately brought them into his garden and did not inform them what the recompense of the garden was, so that they would not leave aside the low-priced jobs and do [only] the high-priced jobs. In the evening he called each individual. He said to one: Under which tree did you work? That is a pepper tree; its recompense is a gold piece. He called another [and] said to him: Under which tree did you work? He said to him: Under this one. He said to him: Its recompense is half a gold piece; it is a caper tree. He called another [and] said to him: Under which tree did you work? He said to him: Under this one. He said to him: That is an olive tree, its recompense is 200 maneh. They said to him: Would it not have been appropriate to tell us which tree brings a great recompense, so that we could have worked under it? The king said to them: If I had told you which one, would the whole garden have been worked on?'[39]

Further parables of recompense with an underlying formal principle of justice are jBer 2, 8 (with parallels, which is mentioned most frequently, see below p. 346), Tan Ki Tissa 3, 151a; MidrPss 37, 3, 127a.

- *God's grace as the theological basis for parables of recompense*: in MidrPss 3, 3, 19a the following parable is cited to interpret Dan. 9.9:

According to the custom of the world. [if] a worker works honestly for the householder and he gives him his recompense, what thanks does he have for him? And when does he owe him thanks? In the hour in which he does not work honestly for him and [nevertheless] does not lose his wages. Therefore it is written: 'To the Lord our God belong mercy and forgiveness, although we have rebelled against him' (Dan. 9.9). R. Schmuel bar Nachmani said: Have you ever seen anyone rebel against a king and he [nevertheless] gives them food? R. Jonathan said: It is written 'They made a calf on Horeb' (Ps. 106.19), and [nevertheless] manna came down.[40]

The same parable appears often in modified form, sometimes also applied explicitly to learning and keeping the Torah.[41]

3. The special emphasis in Jesus' parables can be brought out only against the background of the rabbinic parallels. First of all, formally Jesus' parables have the most polished narrative structure (for example, only in them do we have so many individual scenes and dialogues, different groups of workers and a steward as an

---

[39]DeutR. 6.2 (Ki Teze) on Deut. 22.6, quoted from Heszer, *Lohnmetaphorik* (n.38), 303f. Similarly Tan Ki Teze 2, 330a and MidrPss 9, 3, 41a, ibid., 304–6.
[40]Quoted from Heszer, *Lohnmetaphorik* (n.38), 308.
[41]MidrPss 26.3, 109a; MidrPss 105.13, 227a (ibid., 307–9).

intermediary between workers and the master of the house).[42] On the side of the recipients of the images this is matched by a complex content for the metaphor of recompense which does not appear in the rabbinic texts. What is just (δίκαιον, Matt. 20.4) is defined on the one hand from the agreements over recompense (20.13), i.e. the promises and demands of the Torah, and on the other by God's goodness also towards the 'last', who have done only a fragment of what was really required of them (Matt. 20.4, 14b–15). So in the case of Jesus the two aspects of the metaphor of recompense, which always appear separately among the rabbis, are combined in one parable.

4. The difference in the appeal structures in the rabbis and in Jesus emerges from the fundamental content of the metaphor of recompense in each case, as formal justice, generosity, or a paradoxical combination of the two, and from the different audiences which are presupposed.

- The rabbinic parables which begin from a formal concept of justice usually call on the audience explicitly or implicitly to show God that they are 'good' workers, i.e. Jews faithful to the Torah (aware of the recompense, but without constantly keeping an eye on it). Rabbinic parables which put the graciousness of God at the centre are addressed to the same people, but now in an awareness of their faults (they are 'lazy' workers, neglect the Torah). They are assured that they will receive their recompense even if they do not deserve it. In reaction they are to respond with gratitude and praise of God (especially clearly MidrPss 105, 13, 227a). The appeal always refers to an appropriate human form of behaviour before God as a response to God's demand or generosity.
- The parables of Jesus presuppose both basic attitudes towards God: the need to labour in the face of God's formal justice, and gratitude for his generosity in the face of human fallibility. But they require the audience to differentiate between

---

[42]In the light of the rabbinic parallels the steward appears an enigmatic figure. In terms of the narrative it is unnecessary to delegate the payment of wages to him, since the householder does not leave the scene, as is shown by the following dialogue between him and the grumbling workers. One could see this as an insignificant reflection of the everyday world, but against this are first the strong stylization of the action without taking note of everyday customs (what employer would go five times to recruit labourers?), and secondly the fact that all rabbinic parables have the payment of wages made by the king (!) himself. Conversely, thirdly, the workers would also have been recruited by the steward if the parable were depicting everyday life. In general the parables contain no unnecessary persons and actions, and the juxtaposition of the master of the house who does the recruiting and the steward who makes a payment on his behalf will be a significant detail. As the householder who recruits labourers is God, who takes people into his service, the steward can only be the judge acting on God's behalf, i.e. in the framework of Matthew the Son of Man. Since the eschatological paymaster in the parable has a quite subordinate role and functions only as God's assistant, it cannot be thought impossible that Jesus depicted his own mission in the figure of the steward.

those to whom they are addressed and shifts the appeal to the interpersonal level. Whereas in the rabbinic parables all Israel is always on the side either of the workers who labour honestly (in contrast to the Gentiles) or the workers who fail, Jesus differentiates within his Jewish audience. Those who do their utmost to fulfil God's will (e.g. the Pharisees) receive their reward, but at the same time they are asked to react 'with a gracious eye' to God's goodness towards the less perfect (e.g. the toll collectors and prostitutes) and not be like the grumbling workers.

The conclusion must be that the kingdom of God proves to be the new community of Israel, made possible through God's justice and generosity, which again includes the marginalized groups and in which a new interpersonal perception is to be practised through *imitatio dei*. As has been shown, in all their individual and formal linguistic aspects the parables are rooted in Jewish traditions and at the same time, as a total poetic work of art, are an irreplaceable expression of the message of Jesus.

4. Summary account and hermeneutical reflections

The parables of Jesus are metaphors developed into stories and derive from the collective store of imagery in Judaism. Many of them have not lost their conventional significance as 'fixed metaphors'. Jesus develops some of them into brief descriptions, the similitudes; and some of them into longer narratives, the parables. The message expressed in the traditional store of images and motives, which on each occasion are repristinated, follows from the total picture and the narrative, which therefore has only one dominant point. Unusual features in the imagery and interlockings which draw the audience in can be interpreted along with the fixed metaphors as significant individual features, but they are subordinate to this dominant point. With the parables, Jesus chose a popular form which was accessible to everyone, but by confronting people with God communicated a high understanding of himself in it: an aristocratic ethic of responsibility and readiness for risk.

To the present day, Jesus' parables are rightly understood as a paradigm of religious discourse about God. For God can be spoken of appropriately only in images and similitudes. However, there is a dispute as to the way in which God relates to the verbal image.

A view of the parables as a sacrament of the word assumes a kind of real presence of God, with the eucharist as a model: 'Just as Christ is understood as the embodiment of the divine word (and not merely as information about its content), so the kingdom of God is embodied linguistically in the parable (and not merely described). The parable speaks as it were in the mode of the eucharist.'[43] The content would thus be as present in the image as (in some doctrines of the incarnation) the exalted one is really present in the elements of the eucharist.

This understanding of the parable in terms of the sacrament of the word can be contrasted with a poetic understanding of the parable in which the parables are regarded as symbolic pointers to God – as images which give people freedom to discover how far they disclose their content. In that case the parables do not make the rule of God really present in a way which creates reality, but change people by images which disclose reality, which show them something new in reality. A comparison can bring out the decisive differences between these two understandings of parables:

	The word-sacramental understanding of parables: parables as speech events which create reality	The poetic understanding of parables: parables as images which disclose reality
The relationship between image and content	The content (the kingdom of God = A) is present in the image of the parable (= B). It is incarnate in it: A is B.	The image points to a content which is identical with it, yet is not identical with it: A signifies B.
The theme of the parables	All parables speak of the kingdom of God. They have one theme and one content.	The multiplicity of images points to a multiplicity of content: parables speak of God and human beings in a variety of respects.
The possibility of translation	Parables are in principle incapable of being translated. The reality present in them comes into effect only through them.	Parables can initially be translated – by other images and ever new interpretations. But there remains a poetic surplus which cannot be translated.
Appeal to the audience	Parables are ultimately focussed on a christological confession; on the recognition of Jesus in whose word the kingdom of God is present.	Parables give a constantly new stimulus for thought and action: they make people sensitive to God's presence, which is not at their disposal.

---

[43]H. Weder, 'Wirksame Wahrheit. Zur metaphorischen Qualität der Gleichnisse Jesu', in id. (ed.), *Die Sprache der Bilder*, Gütersloh 1989, 110–27: 115.

Certainly there is a middle way between the two views of the parables. However, the understanding of parables as a sacrament of the word is in danger of failing to recognize the basic, metaphorical structure of the parable and deriving a mythical statement from it. It is as though there were a desire to turn the metaphor 'Achilles is a lion' into a story which says: 'In Achilles there is a little lion which at one time turned into Achilles and is now really present in him.' That would be a myth. It has the basic structure 'A is (literally) B'. By contrast, a metaphor always has the structure 'A is B' and at the same time 'A is not B'. God is a father and at the same time is not a 'real' father. Any metaphor is misunderstood if it is understood literally. A myth has to be understood literally; a metaphor allows poetic freedom to decide where image and content correspond and where they do not. It has an 'open referent' (a point of reference in reality). A myth does not allow this freedom. So it can express what has axiomatic validity in a group and is undisputed: its implicit and explicit dogmas. Beyond doubt Jesus also had mythical convictions. But he puts metaphorical sign language at the centre of his preaching: the parables, which are an undogmatic way of speaking of God. They do not seek to bear witness to the way in which people have always thought of God. Nor do they seek to prescribe how people should always think of God. They aim to give impulses towards thinking of God in constantly new and different ways.[44]

5. Tasks

5.1 Forms of figurative speech

1. In the parable of the wheat and the tares (Matt. 13.24–30), look for (possible) examples of each of the three forms of 'significant individual features' (fixed metaphors, unusual features, overlappings).

2. Assign the following Lukan parables to the sub-genres of similitudes, parables and example stories and explain your choice; Luke 6.43–45; 7.41–43; 10.30–37; 11.11–13; 11.34–36; 12.16–21; 15.8–10; 15.11–32; 16.19–31; 17.7–10; 18.1–8; 18.9–14.

3. Assign the following texts to the three allegorical forms (allegory, allegorization and allegorizing); Ezek. 17.3–10; Mark 12.1–11; Matt. 22.1–14; Matt. 13.36–43; Gal. 4.21–31; Rev. 17.1–6.

---

[44]Parables show a free way of dealing with the theological tradition: its hermeneutical development. Alternatives to them in the Judaism of the time were apocalyptic mystery writings which authorized new religious insights through visions, and allegorical scriptural exegesis which made secrets out of well-known texts – both forms which presuppose a certain degree of scriptural scholarship. By contrast, parables show a free hermeneutical way of dealing with the theological tradition, one which is not bound up with education and scribal learning.

4. Explain why Lessing's 'Parable of the Ring' in *Nathan the Wise* is not a parable as understood in New Testament scholarship. What should it be defined as?

5.2 The generous employer (Matt. 20.1–16): merit versus grace?

The clearness and simplicity with which our parable presents the Good News is thrown into sharp relief by comparison with a rabbinical parallel which has been preserved in the Jerusalem Talmud. A distinguished scholar, Rabbi Bun bar Ḥijja, died at an early age c.AD 325 . . . His former teachers, who had become his colleagues, assembled to pay him the last honours, and one of them, R. Z^e'era, pronounced his funeral oration in the form of a parable. He began by saying that the situation was like that of a king who had hired a great number of labourers. Two hours after the work began, the king inspected the labourers. He saw that one of them surpassed the others in industry and skill. He took him by the hand and walked up and down with him till the evening. When the labourers came to receive their wages, each of them received the same amount as all the others. Then they murmured and said: 'We have worked the whole day, and this man only two hours, yet you have paid him the full day's wages.' The king replied: 'I have not wronged you; this labourer has done more in two hours than you have done during the whole day.' So likewise, concluded the funeral oration, has Rabbi Bun bar Ḥijja accomplished more in his short life of twenty- eight years than many a grey-haired scholar in a hundred years [jBer 2, 8 (5c), freely related].

This raises the question whether Jesus had made use of a Jewish parable and recast it, or whether R. Z^e'era used a parable of Jesus, perhaps without being aware of its source. We can assert with a probability bordering on certainty that the priority belongs to Jesus, altogether apart from the fact that Z^e'era lived 300 years after Jesus. The reasons are that the rabbinical version shows secondary traits . . . and is artificial in character (the king walks with the industrious labourer from 8 a.m. till 6 p.m., that is, for ten hours); but most significant is the feature that only by Jesus is the murmuring of the discontented labourers made to arise naturally out of the actual situation which the parable depicts . . . In the rabbinical version the labourer who has only worked a short time has done more than all the rest; he is represented as having fully earned his wages, and the purpose of the parable is to extol his excellence. In the parable of Jesus, the labourers who were engaged last show nothing to warrant a claim to a full day's wages; that they receive it is entirely due to the goodness of their employer. Thus in this apparently trivial detail lies the difference between two worlds: the world of merit and the world of grace; the world of the law contrasted with the gospel.

What objections do you have to this interpretation in terms of method and content?

12

Jesus as Teacher: The Ethic of Jesus

G. Bornkamm, *Jesus**, ch.5; W.D. Davies, *The Sermon on the Mount*, Cambridge 1966; A.E. Harvey, *Strenuous Commands. The Ethic of Jesus*, London and Philadelphia 1990; R.B. Hays, *The Moral Vision of the New Testament*, San Francisco and Edinburgh 1996; R.H. Horsley, *Jesus and the Spiral of Violence*, San Francisco 1987; id., *Sociology and the Jesus Movement*, New York 1989; J. Jeremias, *New Testament Theology*, Vol.1, London and New York 1971; E. Lohse, *Theological Ethics of the New Testament*, Minneapolis 1991; W. Marxsen, *New Testament Foundations for Christian Ethics*, Edinburgh 1993; F. Matera, *New Testament Ethics*, Louisville 1976; H.K. McArthur, *Understanding the Sermon on the Mount*, London 1961; R. H. Merklein, *Die Gottesherrschaft als Handlungs-prinzip*, Würzburg 1978, ²1981; P. Minear, *The Commands of Christ*, Nashville 1972; E.P. Sanders, *Paul and Palestinian Judaism. A Comparison of Patterns of Religion*, Philadelphia and London 1977; id., *Jewish Law from Jesus to the Mishnah*, London and Philadelphia 1990; E.J. Schnabel, *Law and Wisdom from Ben Sira to Paul. A Tradition Historical Enquiry into the Relation of Law, Wisdom, and Ethics*, WUNT 16, Tübingen 1985; R. Schnackenburg, *The Moral Teaching of the New Testament*, London 1965; W. Schrage, *The Ethics of the New Testament*, Minneapolis and Edinburgh 1988; G. Theissen, ' "We Have Left Everything . . ." (Mark 10.28)', in *Social Reality**, 60–93.

1. Introduction

Jewish ethics is the interpretation of the will of God. This will of God is to be found in the Torah, in creation, and in God's future eschatological action. Here the Torah has a central position. In early Judaism it is on the one hand interpreted as cosmic law and identified with the wisdom of God in creation. On the other hand, it grants access to the eschaton, so that those who are faithful to it become citizens of the new world. Corresponding to the threefold dimension of the will of God, Jesus' ethic can be understood as a Torah ethic, a wisdom ethic and an eschatological ethic.

1. *Torah ethic*. The relationship between Jesus and the Torah is disputed. The traditional Protestant picture of Jesus sees him as the one who overcomes Jewish legalism. A pointed formulation of E. Stauffer's proves to be the basic tenor of many books about Jesus: Jesus is 'the one who announces a morality without legalism, which in principle is free of any tie to the Mosaic Torah and Jewish obedience to the Torah'.[1] This view fails to recognize the differentiations in Jesus'

---

[1]E. Stauffer, *Die Botschaft Jesu*, Bern 1959, 26.

attitude to the Torah. Alongside a relativizing of norms of the Torah we find an accentuation of them; alongside a 'liberal' generosity there is rigoristic strictness which bears witness to a great inner bond with the Torah. Therefore the first basic problem in interpreting the ethics of Jesus is how to indicate the tension between the intensification of the Torah and the relaxation of the Torah. In addition there is a second basic problem: the tension between wisdom and eschatological motivation. A wisdom ethic reckons that the world will continue to exist; an eschatological ethic expects it to change (soon). Jesus combines motifs from wisdom and eschatology in his ethics.

2. *Wisdom ethic.* In addition to what the Torah as handed down prescribed as binding on all Jews, wisdom teachers formulated ethical maxims by reflecting on creation and life in which they perceived God's will directly in the present. For God had created the world through his wisdom. So human wisdom could infer from creation instructions for behaviour which were elsewhere formulated by the Torah. In parts of Judaism, that led to belief in the Torah as a cosmic entity which became identical with God's wisdom and was present throughout creation (Sir. 24, Wisdom, Philo). Since we find in Jesus an inner freedom towards the traditional law combined with recourse to immediate experience, his ethic could be a development of the Jewish wisdom ethic.

3. *Eschatological ethic.* However, the radicalism of Jesus' ethic is explained more by his eschatological expectation than by the wisdom-type quest for a life in accordance with the present creation. The kingdom of God appears in the preaching of Jesus as an ethical power which transforms the world and involves human beings in this transformation. Here the human being is confronted with a divine will which leads beyond Torah and wisdom without being fundamentally in tension with them.

The tension between wisdom and eschatology could indicate that, like all Jews, Jesus centred his life on the Torah and that the wisdom and eschatological aspects formed only the framework of his ethics. The wisdom-type images drawn from creation (e.g. of the 'lilies of the field') and the eschatological expectation serve as motivation towards doing the will of God. But the content of the will of God arises out of the interpretation of the Torah. Such an interpretation of the ethic of Jesus in terms of the Torah still comes up against traditional prejudices which caricature the picture of Jewish Torah ethics in the Christian tradition. Here, briefly, are five such prejudices:

1. *The absolutizing of the Law*: after the exile the Law became a constitutive entity of the covenant instead of being a regulative factor within the covenant (thus M. Noth, G. von Rad).

2. *Casuistry*: the Law is interpreted casuistically, i.e. in terms of many individual cases. As a result the will of God which lays claim to the whole person is

split up (and thus the whole person is removed from the will of God).

3. *A morality of recompense*: obedience to the Law is motivated by the prospect of recompense. Therefore there is a concern to acquire superfluous merits.

4. *Formalism*: the Law is obeyed because it is commanded. Obedience to the law is 'heteronomous', i.e. it follows an alien law and not its own insight.

5. *Suffering under the Law*: life under the Law was felt to be a burden (cf. Matt. 23.4; Acts 15.10,28). The scribes burden people with unnecessary demands.

A large part of the work on revising our picture of Judaism over recent decades has consisted in correcting these prejudices.

Task and suggested reading

On the basis of your picture of Judaism, attempt to formulate counter-arguments to the five statements about the Jewish Torah.

1. Phases in the history of research

It is in research into Jesus' ethics that the normative bond of scholars with their subject has probably been influential for the longest time. However much of the teaching and life of Jesus has been relativized historically, it has been done with a feeling that in Jesus' ethic there is a standpoint removed from all relativism. Jesus' ethics was regarded as being universally and timelessly valid. This claim always had to be communicated in the recognition that Jesus lived and taught in a Jewish context. But there was a time lag before a consistent 'historicizing' of the ethic of Jesus began, i.e. before it was explained and interpreted in terms of its historical context. This historicizing went through three stages. In succession, Jewish apocalyptic, the interpretation of the Law and the wisdom tradition were applied to Jesus' ethics as their primary historical context. Only in most recent decades has it also been set in its sociological context.

1.1 The Jewish context of the teaching of Jesus and the timeless validity of his ethics

For the first time in H.S. Reimarus (1694–1768) we find the recognition that the life and teaching of Jesus remained wholly within the limits of Judaism. Jesus 'did not want to give any offence to Judaism, far less to abolish the written Law . . .' It was his disciples who had first detached themselves from the Law 'and buried Judaism'.[2] D.F. Strauss (1808–1874) also emphasized that Jesus' high esteem for the Law was not just an accommodation to his contemporaries. He was convinced of the validity of the Law of Moses. He interpreted the Law in a way which made an impact on people's natures and convictions. Strauss attached no fundamental significance to the criticism of the sabbath regulations, whatever these may have consisted in.[3]

By contrast, for Strauss's teacher F.C. Baur[4] (1792–1860)[5] the ethic of Jesus was 'pure morality'. The Sermon on the Mount contained the 'absolute significance of the moral idea'. For him 'a new principle essentially different from Mosaism' was formulated in the antitheses: '. . . the inner is opposed to the outer, the conviction to the action, the spirit to the letter'. Jesus was so certain of being different from Judaism in principle 'that although he himself still observed as many of the old traditional forms as possible, and thus put new wine in the old skins, he did so with the definite awareness that the new content would soon enough break the old form'. This happened later in the form of Paul's universalism.

In H.J. Holtzmann (1832–1910), despite a changed overall historical perspective, there is a comparable view. In the ethic of Jesus 'eternal moral truth is produced free from and devoid of historical limitations'.[6] In the period of theological liberalism this 'eternal moral truth' was not located in the concrete demands of Jesus (which often could not be put into practice) but in fundamental convictions: Jesus' ethic is an ethic of conviction.

1.2 Jesus' ethic as eschatological ethics: the first step towards historicizing the ethic of Jesus

The advocates of a thoroughgoing eschatological interpretation of Jesus were the first to understand his ethic consistently in terms of its historical context: as an exceptional eschatological ethic (J. Weiss)[7] or an interim ethic (A. Schweitzer),[8] it is bound up with the presuppositions of Jewish apocalyptic. Jesus did not proclaim timeless ethical maxims for a world which was to last, but the conditions

---

[2]*Reimarus: Fragments*, ed. C.H. Talbert, Philadelphia 1970 and London 1971, 72.
[3]D.F. Strauss, *The Life of Jesus Critically Examined* (1835), ed. P.C. Hodgson, Philadelphia 1972 and London 1973, 338f.
[4]F.C. Baur, *Kritische Untersuchungen über die kanonischen Evangelien, ihr Verhältnis zueinander, ihren Charakter und Ursprung*, Tübingen 1847, 585.
[5]F.C. Baur, *The Church History of the First Three Centuries* (1853), London 1878, 32.
[6]*Die synoptischen Evangelien*, Leipzig 1863, quoted by Kümmel, *NT**, 153.
[7]J. Weiss, *Jesus' Proclamation of the Kingdom of God* (1892), Philadelphia and London 1971, 105.
[8]Schweitzer, *Quest**, 352.

for entering the kingdom of God, which would apply only for a short intermediate period before the end. That explains the 'unworldly' radicalism of some of his commandments.

The eschatology discovered by liberal theologians was brought into the centre in dialectical theology. According to R. Bultmann, it means the confrontation of human beings with God. The same thing happens in the ethical preaching of Jesus. Both put human beings in a situation of final decision in which the question is that of success or failure in life. Its radical nature tears people from their 'worldly' relationships and sets them before eternity.[9] That is its real meaning. Therefore the concrete content of ethical preaching is less important.

The eschatological stamp of Jesus' ethic is also recognized in recent research. In his 1978 book on 'The Rule of God as a Principle of Action', H. Merklein sees eschatology on the one hand as the formal basis for the immediacy with which Jesus gives instructions for actions independently of the Torah and cult: Jesus starts from a new eschatological knowledge of God's action in election. On the other hand, the slant of Jesus' ethic follows from eschatology: the fact that God chooses the poor and sinners has consequences for human behaviour towards them.

1.3 Jesus' ethic as interpretation of the Law: the second step towards historicizing the ethic of Jesus

Already at an early stage the objection was made to the thoroughgoing eschatological interpretation of the Jesus' ethic that for Jesus, as for all Jews, the eternal will of God is first contained in the Torah. The characteristic feature of his ethic consists in a specific way of interpreting the Torah which can be illuminated by historical comparisons. This may be a comparison with the rabbinic exegesis of the Law (G. Kittel; C.G. Montefiore; E.P. Sanders); the understanding of the Torah in Qumran (H. Braun); or the understanding of the Torah in Hellenistic Judaism (K. Berger). Thus three approaches can be distinguished:

1.3.1 The comparison with rabbinic exegesis of the Law

G. Kittel[10] showed that there are analogies in rabbinic literature to all the individual demands in the Sermon on the Mount. All the ethical statements made by Jesus are in principle also conceivable in Judaism. He sees the special feature of

---

[9] This parallelism between the message of the kingdom of God and ethics is attested for example by the following remark of Bultmann's: 'Since, then, the message of the coming of the Kingdom and that of the will of God point men to the present moment as the final hour in the sense of the hour of decision, the two do form a unity, each is incomplete without the other' (*Jesus**, 96)

[10] G. Kittel, 'Die Bergpredigt und die Ethik des Judentums', *ZSTh* 2, 1924, 555–94.

Jesus' ethic as simply being the concentration of the ethical message (which among the rabbis is very dispersed and mixed in with ritualistic and other elements) and its intensity: the absolute demands convict human beings as sinners, so that they remain dependent on grace. Here Jesus is made the forerunner of Luther. The liberal Jewish scholar C.G. Montefiore objected to such tendencies in the Protestant picture of Jesus.[11] He argued that it was unhistorical to distinguish rabbinic ethics as a work ethic from an ethic of grace. The rabbis, too, know that the grace of God is part of the realization of the good. Jesus is not a forerunner of Protestant theology but a follower of Jewish prophecy under changed historical conditions.[12]

At the present time E.P. Sanders (*Jewish Law*, 1990) above all has put Jesus' ethics and conduct in the tradition of Jewish exposition of the Torah. Thus neither the breaches of the sabbath nor the antitheses leave the Jewish Torah behind.

1.3.2   *The comparison with the exegesis of the Law in Qumran*

The rabbinic texts often come from a much later time than the Synoptic Gospels and their sources. When the Qumran texts were discovered around 1945, however, contemporary texts were available for comparison. In his investigation into 'Late-Jewish Heretical and Early Christian Radicalism' (1957), H. Braun showed that there is an intensification of the Torah in Qumran and with Jesus: in Qumran it takes place as a matter of principle, since the concern is to obey all the commands of the Torah; by contrast, in Jesus it does not.[13] In Qumran, obedience to the Torah is grounded in scripture as this is understood on the basis of its authoritative interpretation by the Teacher of Righteousness. By contrast, Jesus can play off one passage of scripture against another (cf. Mark 10.1ff.). In Qumran, Torah piety is the way to salvation; for Jesus, Torah piety seems to be a danger. Therefore to the intensification of the Torah is added the radicalization of grace, which applies precisely to those who are not pious: to the radicalization of 'you shall' is added the radicalization of the 'you may'.

1.3.3   *The comparison with the understanding of the Law in Hellenistic Judaism*

K. Berger showed that at the time of Jesus there was an understanding of the Law in Hellenistic Judaism which merely embraced 'monotheism, combined with universal and social virtues', so that here in fact the Old Testament Law was

---

[11]Cf. *The Synoptic Gospels* I/II, London [2]1927; id., *Rabbinic Literature and Gospel Teachings*, London 1930. For his picture of Jesus cf. W. Vogler, *Jüdische Jesusinterpretationen in christlicher Sicht*, Weimar 1988, 35–40.

[12]*The Synoptic Gospels* I, cxvii–cxx.

[13]Matt. 5.17ff. is regarded by Braun as a community formation.

reduced.[14] Over against it stood a rabbinic-Jewish understanding of the Law in Judaism which was stamped by a reaction against Hellenism. As the latter became established in Judaism, the more open understanding of the Law became a characteristic of Christianity. What was originally a difference within Judaism thus subsequently became a distinguishing mark between Jews and Christians. Berger sees the Jewish tradition as being largely stamped by its more open understanding of the Law – with the result that he denies that many traditions go back to Jesus or leaves their origin open.

1.4 Jesus' ethic as wisdom teaching: the third step towards the historicizing of the ethic of Jesus

At a very early stage (with Bultmann), form critics recognized that many ethical traditions about Jesus are contained in wisdom-type genres. However, the consequence of this for understanding this ethic were drawn only at a late stage. In 1971, G. Bornkamm[15] drew attention to the understanding of law in Judaism, to which any casuistry is alien. He sees it as the historical prerequisite of the ethic of Jesus, which is not casuistic and aims at being internally self-evident. In 1977, D. Zeller[16] showed that within the wisdom tradition the sayings of Jesus have peculiarities of form and content; the frequency of admonitions in the plural is characteristic of their form and a concentration on inter-personal relations of their content. Finally, in his 'Wisdom Traditions of Early Judaism' (1979), M. Küchler put the special character of Jesus' wisdom under the heading of 'the self-intensification of wisdom'; elsewhere wisdom in Judaism becomes relevant only in connection with other entities (with the Torah or the Logos, etc.). But Jesus 'provokes wisdom in its most authentic form' (ibid., 583).

1.5 The sociological quest for the *Sitz im Leben* of the ethic of Jesus

For a long time the interpretation of the ethic of Jesus in the framework of his day was limited to making intellectual and tradition-historical connections. Since around 1970 this form of 'historicizing' the Jesus' ethic has been extended to sociological conditions. In 1973 G. Theissen interpreted the radicalism of the Synoptic tradition, especially the high importance it attaches to homelessness, dispensing with possessions and protection, and its dismissal of the family, as an expression of the situation of itinerant charismatics: independent of everyday ties and a 'normal' way of life, the disciples of Jesus could have practised a radical

---

[14]K. Berger, *Die Gesetzesauslegung Jesu* I, WMANT 40, Neukirchen 1972, 39.

[15]G. Bornkamm, 'Wandlungen im alt- und neutestamentlichen Gesetzesverständnis', in *Geschichte und Glaube II, Gesammelte Aufsätze 4*, BEvTh 53, Munich 1971, 73–119.

[16]D. Zeller, *Die weisheitlichen Mahnsprüche bei den Synoptikern*, Würzburg 1977.

ethos and preached norms in keeping with it without losing credibility ('Wandering Radicals'*). Their homelessness was an expression of a 'social uprooting'[17] which was conditioned by an all-embracing crisis of Jewish–Palestinian society (*First Followers**, 1978). The 'new' ethic was interpreted in 1989 as a 'revolution in values', i.e. an appropriation of the values of the upper class by the lower classes. Theissen sees the sayings about love of enemy, making peace, generosity with possessions, freedom from care and wisdom's summons to rest (Matt. 11.29f.) as fragments of upper-class ideals which are made accessible to all in the preaching of Jesus (*First Followers**). R.H. Horsley put forward an alternative sociological interpretation of the ethic of Jesus in *Jesus and the Spiral of Violence* (1987). He argued that this ethic did not have its *Sitz im Leben* among itinerant charismatics but in Palestinian village life, which Jesus wanted to renew by recourse to popular traditions: therefore he strengthened solidarity among people. Itinerant charismatics were merely the catalysts in this village renewal movement.[18]

Regardless of whether Jesus' ethic has its *Sitz im Leben* among marginal itinerant charismatics or at the centre of Palestinian village life, at all events one sociological condition is presupposed: Jesus disseminated his ethic in the social role of a teacher. What do we know about this role in the time of Jesus?

2. Jesus as teacher (rabbi)

B. Chilton and C. Evans, 'Jesus and Israel's Scriptures', in *Studying**, 281–335; R. Riesner, *Jesus als Lehrer*, WUNT 2/7, Tübingen 1981, [3]1988.

In a part of the Jesus tradition which has been preserved especially in Mark and John, Jesus (like John the Baptist) is addressed as 'Rabbi'.[19] Because it is improbable that a title which aligned the person who bore it with many others should have found its way into the tradition after Easter, this is generally thought to be reliable tradition. However, there is a dispute as to what the address 'rabbi' means.

There is a widespread view that in the case of Jesus, 'rabbi' was merely a respectful form of address for people in higher positions. This is based on the fact that the rabbinic writings use 'rabbi' only for scholars living after 70 CE and that there is little connection between Jesus and these scribes.[20] But the assumption of two

---

[17]Theissen, ' "We Have Left Everything" '.

[18]R.H. Horsley sharply criticizes Theissen's sociological view of the Jesus movement in *Sociology and the Jesus Movement*.

[19]Mark 9.5; 11.21; 14.45; John 1.38, 49; 3.2; 4.31; 6.25; 9.2; 11.8; Matt. 23.7f.; 26.25, 49; Rabbouni, Mark 10.51; John 20.16.

[20]Moreover epigraphical instances of the title cause confusion, since they do not seem to be given to rabbis faithful to the law, because the Jews honoured with it were buried near sarcophagi richly decorated with pictures, sometimes even with motifs from Greek mythology.

meanings of the title is hardly tenable. It stems from the *literary* definition of a rabbi in the rabbinic writings, which is imprisoned in the historical fiction of these circles that there was only a unified (rabbinic) Judaism after the assembly at Jabneh. The earlier Christian sources which go back before the year 70 attest that 'rabbi' was the Aramaic equivalent of διδάσκαλε (teacher, John 1.38; 3.2; Matt. 23.8), that the scribes and Pharisees – like John the Baptist and Jesus – responsible for the interpretation of the Mosaic Law had themselves called 'rabbi' (Matt. 23.2,7) and that there were Jewish Christian teachers who claimed this title (Matt. 23.8; cf. 13.52). An unpublished sociological evaluation of the Christian, epigraphical and rabbinic evidence by C. Hezser indicates that long beyond its beginnings in the first century the rabbinic movement formed more of a loose network of circles of scholars with heterogeneous convictions and without fixed rites of acceptance and exclusion. A scribe became a 'rabbi' as soon as others, and especially disciples, addressed him as such and asked him for advice.

In discussing with other scribes, gathering disciples (μαθηταί)[21] around him, teaching in synagogue worship and answering the theological enquiries of lay people, Jesus, the former disciple of the rabbi John, corresponded to the contemporary notions of a rabbi. Such activity as a scribe presupposes a certain degree of education – even if we can certainly exclude an education lasting over many years. Unfortunately we can no longer discover how Jesus acquired this.

2.1 Jesus' education

Granted, the apocryphal infancy Gospels relate stories from Jesus' schooldays, and the legend in Luke 2.41–51 can report the amazing learning of the twelve-year-old boy in the temple; however, these are not historically reliable reports about Jesus' education. We can sketch out only the general framework within which he acquired his knowledge.

1. *The home* was an educational institution of decisive significance. Here elementary religious education took place through telling stories, and learning central scriptural texts and passages of the liturgy by heart, and here the son learned his father's craft (cf. Mark 6.3 with Matt. 13.55). In the case of Jesus, there are some pointers – the biblical names of the sons, and his pious brother James – to a family firmly anchored in the traditions of Israel.

2. It must remain open whether Jesus went to an *elementary school* to learn to read and write. Certainly an efficient form of schooling arose in Palestine under Hellenistic influence, the development of which was completed by the rabbis (cf. Riesner, *Jesus*, 97–245). But it is impossible to say whether in the early first century an insignificant village like Nazareth had its own school.

---

[21]The usual translation 'disciples' is misleading.

3. However, there is literary evidence of a *synagogue* in Nazareth (Mark 6.2; Matt. 13.54; Luke 4.16). As such it possessed at least one Torah scroll, and in addition – depending on its wealth – most likely a scroll of Isaiah (cf. Luke 4.17), a Psalter and translations (Targums). The Torah and the Prophets were read aloud, translated and commented on every sabbath in synagogue worship; this was already the most natural way for children (cf. *Antt.* 14, 260) to gain knowledge of the scriptures. It was also possible to organize teaching for children in reading (and writing?) in the context of the synagogue, whether by father or mother,[22] synagogue officials, teachers or others who knew how to read.

4. A series of indications makes it very probable that Jesus could at least read:

- In a number of disputations the formula 'Have you not read . . .?' appears on Jesus' lips, which of course presupposes that he himself could read.[23]
- While Luke 4.16ff. certainly has a marked Lukan stamp, Jesus will have taught in the synagogues in the way described here: after the reading from the scriptures, which he himself may possibly have given sometimes. His teaching in synagogues is regarded as a typical feature of his activity (cf. Mark 1.39 etc.). It is hard to imagine that Jesus could have involved himself in teaching in an institution so markedly stamped by listening to the written word had he not been in a position to accept an invitation to read at the services.
- According to John 7.15, Jesus' hearers admire the way in which he teaches: 'How is it that this man knows letters (γράμματα οἶδεν) when he has never studied?' Here γράμματα οἶδεν refers to Jesus' capacity to comment on scripture and argue without having undergone a formal education with a well-known teacher (cf. also Mark 6.2/Matt. 13.54). However, this always presupposes a capacity to read.

5. We can only guess at how Jesus acquired further knowledge. Possibly his family went on pilgrimages to Jerusalem – at that time the centre of Jewish scribal learning – but despite Luke 2.41 that is not certain. Perhaps Jesus came to know the form and content of Jewish and Greek education as an itinerant craftsman in the synagogues and squares of the larger cities. Perhaps in the end John the Baptist

---

[22]That the Mishnah later explicitly forbids the appointment of women as elementary teachers (cf. Kidd. IV, 13 and Riesner, *Jesus als Lehrer*, 104f.) suggests that they were sometimes more intensively engaged in educating their own and others' children than might be expected from patriarchal tradition, which assigns this task to the father. The low age of marriage for girls (twelve to thirteen) which is regularly cited as an argument against the education of women is irrelevant this context, because the age at which elementary education was acquired is put between six or seven and thirteen.

[23]Mark 2.25 par.; Mark 12.10/Matt. 21.42; Mark 12.26/Matt. 22.31; Matt. 12.5; 19.4; 21.16.

– certainly carefully educated, since he was the son of a priest (?) – had more influence on Jesus' education than is often assumed.

2.2 The holy scriptures in Jesus' teaching

Before we investigate the role of the Torah in Jesus' ethic more closely in the next section, first of all, here is a general survey of Jesus' use of scripture. Here we must remember that where the Christian sources attribute clearly identifiable scriptural quotations or allusions to biblical traditions to Jesus, it is by no means certain that these go back to him. For the biblical scriptures depict a perception and interpretation of reality which was common to all Jews (and Christians). After Easter the story and message of Jesus was interpreted and continued to be told in the light of scripture. However, if reflections which clearly date from after Easter are excluded, the remaining material of the tradition indicates characteristics and tendencies which presumably go back to Jesus.

1. *The basis of Jesus' use of scripture*. It is impossible to say with certainty what writings were known to Jesus and were regarded as holy scripture. B. Chilton has demonstrated the probability that Isaiah was at least partially received in the popular form of the Aramaic Targum. We must also reckon with the possibility that Jesus knew writings which were later excluded as apocryphal and which have now perhaps been lost, and referred them to himself.

2. *Jesus' hermeneutic*. In his exposition of scripture Jesus shows familiarity with the hermeneutical principles of his time, which were later systematized by the rabbis (in the so-called Middoth). These include the inference from the smaller to the greater (*qal wāḥōmer*[24]): if God himself feeds the birds (cf. Ps. 147.9, etc.), the disciples certainly do not need to be anxious (Matt. 6.26/Luke 12.24 Q). Jesus' argument in the dispute over the resurrection (Mark 12.18–27) is based on a principle which was later called 'the foundation of a family' (בִּנְיָן אָב מִכָּתוּב אֶחָד). This states that one may infer an exegetical norm from a passage of scripture and transfer this to other passages, as a result of which the passages are to some degree bound together in a family. The basic conviction expressed in many texts that YHWH is a God of the living (Isa. 38.18f.; Ps. 6.5f., etc.) shows that in Ex. 3.15, where YHWH calls himself the God of Abraham, Isaac and Jacob, the resurrection of these patriarchs is presupposed. From this it is possible in turn to argue for the resurrection of all those whose God is YHWH.

3. *Jesus' use of scripture*. The small number of texts which have been handed

---

[24] קַל וְחוֹמֶר, literally easy and difficult. For the hermeneutical rules of the rabbis generally cf. G. Stemberger, *Einleitung in Talmud und Midrasch*, Munich [8]1992, 25–40. Chilton and Evans, 'Jesus and Israel's Scriptures', 284–99, compare Jesus' use of scripture with the seven middoth attributed to Rabbi Hillel and find at least one example for each middah. However, these include many texts the authenticity of which is hotly disputed.

down, at the centre of which there is a scriptural saying whose meaning is disputed, is striking. Unlike the Essenes and rabbis, Jesus did not see his task as being the exegesis of scripture for its own sake. For him an instrumental use of scripture is characteristic. Here scripture serves as a means for different ends: it expresses an awareness of fulfilment, provokes a new form of conduct, serves as an argument in polemic, and is a foundation of ethics.

- *Awareness of fulfilment.* Scripture communicates knowledge of God's eschatological action, which Jesus experiences as being fulfilled in the present and which he can interpret with its help. Thus he interprets the miracles which he performs as a fulfilment of prophetic statements about the time of salvation (Matt. 11.4f. Q). Possibly the depiction of Luke's 4.18–21, according to which Jesus claimed to fulfil the promise of Isa. 61.1f., similarly accords with his understanding of himself.
- *Provocative behaviour.* Frequently passages or motifs from scriptures are used by Jesus in a very provocative way in order to shock his hearers and to move them to a conduct appropriate to the new time. The confrontation of sceptical contemporaries with the biblical example of 'pious Gentiles' in connection with the eschatological awareness that the present goes beyond Solomon and Jonah is a use of scripture typical of Jesus (Matt. 12.41f. Q). The biblical motifs of the messianic banquet (Matt. 8.10f.) or the vineyard of Israel (Mark 12.1ff.) are used in a similarly provocative way. Similarly, Isa. 6.9f. (cf. Mark 4.12) could originally have been cited by Jesus as an accusation in order to move 'hardened' hearers to repentance.
- *Polemical argumentation.* Frequently the recourse to scripture occurs in polemical contexts aimed at safeguarding the advocate's own position. Sometimes there are reflections here of debates between the early Christian communities and their Jewish environment (cf. the sabbath question according to Matt. 12.1ff.); however, sometimes this form will go back to Jesus (cf. the debates on the resurrection in Mark 12.18–27). It could be characteristic of Jesus that in such debates he played off one passage of scripture against another (Mark 10.2ff.).
- *Ethical basis.* Finally, the Torah contains the will of God as a demand which puts obligations on people. Jesus (cf. Mark 10.17–19) shares this basic conviction with all currents in Judaism. Here no one gets anywhere without interpretation. Therefore it is above all in this sphere that we find exegesis of the Torah in the narrower sense that will be investigated in the following sections.

3. Jesus' ethic between intensification of the Torah and relaxation of the Torah

3.1 The Torah in Judaism

Christian theology often painted a distorted picture of Jewish ethics in order to make Jesus stand out from it in a positive light. The contrast thus constructed does not stand up to testing by the sources. These provide the following information, which can be set against the five prejudices about the ethics of Judaism which have already been mentioned in the introduction to this section:

Absolutizing of the Law: after the exile the Law became a constitutive entity of the covenant instead of being a regulative entity within the covenant (thus M. Noth, G. von Rad).	Even after the exile the religion of Judaism is to be described as 'covenantal nomism'; i.e. covenant and election precede the Law (E.P. Sanders).
Casuistry: the Law is interpreted in a casuistic way and as a result the will of God which makes a claim to the whole person is split up (and thus the whole person is removed from the will of God).	Casuistry (which moreover is first clearly attested for the period after the New Testament) serves to appropriate the everyday and to make a practical humanity possible: the Torah must be capable of being lived out.
Morality of recompense: obedience to the Law is motivated by the prospect of recompense. Therefore people make efforts to achieve superfluous merits.	Morality of reward is clearly rejected in the Pirke Abot: 'You shall not be like a servant who serves his master on condition that he gets a reward' (Ab I, 3). 'The reward of a commandment is a commandment' (Ab IV, 2).[25]
Formalism: the Law is obeyed because that is commanded. Obedience to the Law is not clear obedience, but is 'heteronomous'. Cf. e.g. the formal basis for ritual commandments: 'I, the Lord have made it a principle, and you have no right to reflect on the matter' (bYoma 67b).	There are also contrary voices which show that the Torah was appropriated personally; e.g.: 'After he has done what is pleasing to God's Torah, it becomes his own' (bAZ 19a).[26] Thus there is an identification with the will of God.
Suffering under the Law: life under the Law is experienced as a burden (cf. Matt. 23.4; Acts 15.10, 28). The scribes burden people with unnecessary demands.	'Joy in the Law' stamps Jewish piety (cf. Ps. 119). This joy is so great that learning the Torah is forbidden on the fast of 9 Ab, because it brings too much joy (bTaan 30a).

---

[25]Quoted according to J. Amir, 'Gesetz II (Judentum)', *TRE* 13, 1984, 54.
[26]Quoted according to ibid.

In principle, it may be said that Torah and temple are the two centres of Judaism at the time of the second temple. Only as a result of the destruction of the temple in 70 BCE did the Torah become the sole centre – but now not in the sense meant by the term 'law' in Christian theology. Rather, the Torah is the all-embracing revelation of the will of God. It encompasses the beginnings of the history of Israel as they are depicted in the Pentateuch, including the lawgiving on Sinai. The 'Law' is therefore embedded in a more comprehensive history of God with his people. In this history election precedes obligation. That is shown very vividly in the following rabbinic parable:

> I am the Lord thy God (Ex. 20.2). Why were the Ten Commandments not said at the beginning of the Torah? They (the sages) give a parable: To what may this be compared? To the following: A king who entered a province said to the people: May I be your king? But the people said to him: Have you done anything good for us that you should rule over us? What did he do then? He built the city wall for them, he brought in the water supply for them, and he fought their battles. Then when he said to them: May I be your king? They said to him: Yes, Yes. Likewise, God. He brought the Israelites out of Egypt, divided the sea for them, sent down the manna for them, brought up the well for them, brought the quails for them. He fought for them the battle with Amalek. Then he said to them: I am to be your king. And they said to him: Yes, Yes' (Mekhilta of R. Yishmael Bahodesh 5 on Ex. 20.2, quoted in E.P. Sanders, *Paul and Palestinian Judaism*, 86, cf. Bill. I, 174).

God only gives his commandments after he has won his people to himself by acts of grace. The covenant precedes the law, the indicative the imperative.

3.2 Basic statements on the Torah in the Jesus tradition: ambivalence towards the Torah

In the Jesus tradition there is a direct contradiction in the fundamental statements about the 'Torah'. On the one hand the eternity of the Torah is taught: 'Till heaven and earth pass away, not an iota, not a dot, will pass from the law until all is accomplished' (Matt. 5.18/Luke 16.17). On the other hand the saying about taking by force in the version reconstructed for Q speaks of the temporal limitation of the Torah: 'All the prophets and the law (apply) until John. From then on the kingdom of God suffers violence and men of violence take it by force' (Matt. 11.12/Luke 16.16).

Often the saying about the eternity of the Torah is attributed to the Jewish Christian community, which is said to have produced it as a reaction to tendencies in primitive Christianity critical of the law (cf. also Matt. 13.41); by contrast, the saying about the kingdom of God being taken by force is usually regarded as authentic. If one wants to attribute both passages to Jesus himself, one can harmonize them by arguing that the Torah has limited validity. According to Matt. 5.18, the Torah applies only until the eschatological upheaval. However, for Jesus this already begins in the present: Satan has already fallen from heaven (Luke 10.18).[27]

Regardless of the question of authenticity, both logia could be attributed to Jesus by virtue of their content, since his attitude to the Torah was in fact ambivalent. The combination of an intensification of norms and a relaxation of norms is characteristic of Jesus' attitude to the Torah.[28] Jesus intensified ethical norms (above all the love commandment) in which a tendency towards a universal ethic was clear. He relativized ritual norms (above all the commandment about cleanness) by which Judaism was separated from paganism – but without doing away with these norms completely. In the Judaism of his time we find analogies in the exegesis of the Torah to both the intensification of norms (Essenes, Pharisees, resistance movement) and the relaxation of norms (e.g. the radical allegorizers against whom Philo fights[29]), but hardly any comparable analogies for the combination of the two tendencies. At most they can still be found in the Pharisaic and later in the rabbinic exegesis of the Torah.

3.3 Intensification of norms in the Jesus tradition

1. *The first commandment.* Jesus shares the radical theocratic intensification of the first commandment. The resistance movement (Judas of Galilee) radicalized it to the point that loyalty to the emperor was regarded as treachery to God.[30] Jesus transfers this radical theocratic alternative from the political to the economic sphere. He does not call for any uncompromising choice between God and the emperor (cf. Mark 12.13–17), but he does call for a choice between worshipping God and serving mammon (Matt. 6.24/Luke 16.13).[31]

2. *The prohibition against killing and adultery* (from the second table of the Decalogue) is intensified (see below, 363f.). These intensifications are not formulated as a new imperative by Jesus in the first and second antitheses of the Sermon on the Mount but are 'assertions of guilt': 'Every one who is angry against his brother is liable to the judgment' (Matt. 5.22): 'Every one who looks at a woman lustfully has already committed adultery with her in his heart' (Matt. 5.28).

---

[27]Cf. above, §9.4.2.

[28]For the sociological interpretation of these tendencies cf. Theissen, *First Followers**, 75–95.

[29]In *Migr.* 89–92, Philo is polemical against Jews who understand the laws symbolically but completely neglect the concrete performance of them. He even mentions circumcision as a rite which was evidently understood only symbolically.

[30]Cf. *BJ* 2, 118; 7, 410, 418f.; *Antt.* 18.23.

[31]This alternative has influenced the story of the 'rich young man'. The confession of one God, εἷς ὁ θεός (who alone is good, Mark 10.18), is associated with the call to renounce possessions in favour of the poor.

3. In the Jesus tradition, *the command to love one's neighbour* (Lev. 19.18), which is discussed thoroughly in a separate section of this book (pp. 381ff.), is set alongside the command to love God (Mark 12.28–34) and is radicalized in three respects: as love of enemy (Matt. 5.43–48 par); as love of the stranger (Luke 10.25–37); and as love of sinners (Luke 7.36–50).

All the intensifications of norms mentioned so far are not halakic, i.e. Jesus is not formulating a new 'law' which is binding on all; rather, he is expounding laws in the style of paraenesis and wisdom. Jesus possibly formulates a new 'halakah'[32] only at two points – in accord with tendencies in Judaism.

4. *The prohibition against remarriage* (Mark 10.11f.) is usually called the prohibition against divorce, although it does not forbid divorce but remarriage after divorce, since for Jesus the marriage continues to exist despite the divorce of the partners.[33] Paul interprets this prohibition against remarriage as a command for reconciliation (I Cor. 7.10f.), but concedes divorce in marriages with non-Christians if the non-Christian partner wants it. Matthew interprets it as a restriction to make divorce harder; he allows divorce in cases of πορνεία (unchastity, Matt. 5.32; 19.9). The primitive Christian tradition thus deals with this commandment relatively freely – it understands it less as a legal than as an ethical norm.[34]

5. *The prohibition against swearing* (Matt. 5.3ff.; James 5.12). Here too the influence on primitive Christianity is very different. Paul swears openly to emphasize the truth of his statements (II Cor. 11.31; Gal. 1.20; Rom. 9.1); Matthew allows the duplication of formulae of assertion ('Yes, yes/No, no').[35]

---

[32]*Halakah* (הֲלָכָה = way of life, direction, from הלך = go, walk) denotes a fixed doctrine, law or principle which is a norm for religious practice.

[33]The understanding of remarriage as adultery is prepared for in Hellenistic Judaism, cf. K. Berger, *Gesetzesauslegung* (n.14), 518–20, 559–61. In Essene circles divorce was presumably forbidden (cf. 11Q Temple LVII, 17–19; CD IV, 21–V, 2).

[34]The 'prohibition against divorce' can be addressed one-sidedly only to the husband (Matt. 5.32; 19.9) or to both the husband and the wife (Mark 10.11f.; I Cor. 7.10f.). The form of address to both parties used to be regarded as a secondary adaptation to the Hellenistic milieu outside Palestine, because in Greece and Rome the wife, too, could take the initiative in divorce. That is why Paul is thought to have chosen the formula addressed to both parties. However, for Palestine and the East, too, a legal tradition diverging from the majority tradition has been demonstrated according to which women could also take the initiative in divorce; this may be attested in the Elephantine papyri, in the divorces of Herodian wives, and possibly in the letters of divorce from the Wadi Murabba'at (e.g. P. Mur 19), in PsPhilo, *Antt.* 42, 1 and in traces in the Talmud. See the extensive survey of research in M. Fander, *Die Stellung der Frau im Markusevangelium*, Münster 1989, 200–57. If such a legal tradition is to be presupposed, the form of prohibition of divorce addressed to both parties could also go back to Jesus.

[35]Criticism of swearing is widespread in Judaism at the time of Jesus, among the Essenes, Philo and in the wisdom literature, cf. the commentaries on Matt. 5.34f.

3.3.1   *The antitheses in the Sermon on the Mount*

W.D. Davies and D.C. Allison, *The Gospel According to Saint Matthew* I, ICC, Edinburgh 1988, 505–9; U. Luz, *Matthew 1–7. A Commentary*, Minneapolis and Edinburgh 1989, 273–352; H. Merklein, *Gottesherrschaft* (see above), 253–93.

The classical example of tendencies to accentuate the norm in the Jesus tradition are the antitheses in the Sermon on the Mount. Of the six antitheses, at most the first, second and (perhaps) the fourth on killing, adultery and swearing (Matt. 5.21, 27f., 33f.) have a claim to authenticity, since they have no parallels in a non-antithetical form and the other antitheses have possibly been formulated later, taking them as a model. However, there is as much of a dispute over this as there is over how to understand the antitheses: do they express a view on expositions of the Torah by other scribes? Or a view about the Torah itself – and here it is an open question whether this view is criticism, interpretation or a continuation of the Torah? Here are the most important arguments for the two positions:

The understanding of the antitheses related to expositions of the Torah	The understanding of the antitheses related to the Torah
The introduction to the antitheses in Matt. 5.20 is directed against the righteousness of the scribes and Pharisees and therefore has their understanding of the Law in view.	The introduction to the antitheses in Matt. 5.17, Jesus has 'not come to abolish the Torah but to fulfil it', leads us to expect a statement about the Torah.
The Old Testament commandments are not just quoted but supplemented, i.e. introduced in a particular interpretation. To the Old Testament commandment against killing is added, 'Whoever kills shall be liable to judgment' (5.21), and to the command to love one's neighbour the obligation to hate one's enemy, which is nowhere attested in the Old Testament (5.43).	The prohibition against adultery is quoted without any expansion. In any case, in Judaism Old Testament commandments are often expanded by further commandments which are not contained in the Torah.[36] These new commandments are also regarded as Torah.
The formula 'You have heard that it was said to the men of old time . . .' denotes a tradition handed down from antiquity.	The statement 'it was said to the men of old' contains a divine passive: God is presupposed as the one who speaks the commandments!

---

[36]Cf. the temple scroll in Qumran; Josephus, *Antt.* 4, 271–4; *Ap* 2, 190–219; Philo, *Hypothetica* 7, 1–9.

With 'But I say to you,' rabbis objected to the exegesis of other rabbis. Similarly, here Jesus is objecting to rival exegesis.	Nowhere is a 'But I say to you' in the rabbis directed against the scripture cited immediately beforehand; it is always directed against those who are expounding it. To that degree the form of the antitheses is unique (E. Lohse).
In terms of content the antitheses do not add anything to which there are not also parallels in Judaism. In wording, many of these parallels point just as much beyond the Torah as Jesus' antitheses.	Jesus does not just point beyond the Torah but makes this transcending of the Torah by his 'But I say to you' deliberate. There is no analogy to that.

In our view the antitheses are a view of the Torah. The meaning of the antithetical form is: 'You have heard that once (on Sinai) it was said (by God) to our forefathers: You shall not kill. But I say to you (going beyond that but not in contradiction to it) . . .' The Torah is not interpreted, not criticized, not done away with, but transcended. One can fulfil God's will only if one does not just fulfil his commandments by one's behaviour but also lets one's own will, down to the innermost emotions, be governed by them. If we see how in the Qumran Temple Scroll further commandments were added to Old Testament commandments in the first person as if spoken by God, an expansion and surpassing of the Torah in Judaism is by no means unthinkable. The special feature of Jesus' ethic is that the transcending of the Torah is deliberately articulated. It is not simply attributed to God but derived from Jesus by 'But I say to you' and thus distinguished from the revelation of God (in the tradition).

3.4 Relaxation of norms in the Jesus tradition

Where Jesus is critical of the Torah, as a rule this is in connection with ritual commandments. These are not done away with, but the social commandment (to provide help and show solidarity with one's fellow human beings) is set above them. Here Jesus stands in the prophetic tradition.

　　1. *The sabbath commandment.* The commandment to help is put before the sabbath commandment. Not only saving life but also furthering life robs the Sabbath commandments of their force. Saving life and self-defence in war generally had priority over the observance of the sabbath. Jesus picks this up: 'Is it permissible to do good on the sabbath or to do evil, to save a life or to kill?' (Mark 3.4). See below on §3.4.2.

　　2. *The command to give tithes.* Justice, mercy and faith, i.e. social obligations, are more important than the command to tithe: 'Woe to you, scribes and

Pharisees, hypocrites! For you tithe mint and dill and cummin, and have neglected the weightier matters of the Law (τὰ βαρύτερα τοῦ νόμου), justice and mercy and faith' (τὴν κρίσιν καὶ τὸ ἔλεος καὶ τὴν πίστιν) (Matt. 5.23f.). But it is expressly added that the one should be done and the other not rejected (Matt. 23.23).

3. *The commandment about sacrifice.* The commandment to be reconciled is set above the sacrifical cult: 'So if you are offering your gift at the altar, and there remember that your brother has something against you, leave your gift there before the altar and go; first be reconciled to your brother, and then come and offer your gift' (Matt. 5.23f.).

4. *The commandment about cleanness.* According to Matt. 23.25f., the content of the vessels should first be clean, i.e. not acquired by robbery and greed. Only then should care be taken that the outside is also clean. It can clearly be recognized that Jesus was accustomed to having contacts with groups of people who were regarded as unclean, like lepers, those possessed by unclean spirits, those afflicted with haemorrhages and those made unclean by sin (cf. Mark 1.21ff., 40ff.; 2.13–17; 5.25ff., etc.).

The logion about cleanness in Mark 7.15 and the conflicts over the sabbath in which Jesus was involved are generally regarded as test cases for the question how far Jesus came into conflict with the Torah, and therefore (along with the offence against the commandment to honour one's parents in Matt. 8.21f.) need to be discussed at length.

3.4.1 *Jesus and the commandment about cleanness*

R.P. Booth, *Jesus and the Laws of Purity*, JSNT SS 13, Sheffield 1986; H. Räisänen, *The Torah and the Christ*, Helsinki 1986, 209–18; id., 'Jesus and the Food Laws: Reflections on Mark 7.15', JSNT 16, 1982, 79–100 (*The Torah and the Christ*, 219–41).

For Käsemann it emerges clearly from Mark 7.15 that Jesus burst the bounds of Judaism: '. . . the man who denies that impurity from external sources can penetrate into man's essential being is striking at the presuppositions and the plain verbal sense of the Torah and at the authority of Moses himself' ('Problem', 39). Today the logion is either toned down in interpretation, in that it is seen as putting ethical purity above cultic purity, but not as repudiating cultic notions of purity; or it is understood as a criticism of the Torah, but then denied to Jesus and attributed to a post-Easter primitive Christianity which was 'critical of the law'. The following arguments come up here:

- *The inner logic of the logion.* 'There is nothing outside a man which by going into him can defile him; but the things which come out of a man are what defile him.' The contrast 'not . . . but' (οὐ . . . ἀλλά) is often understood by analogy with Mark 9.37: 'Whoever receives me, receives not me but him who sent me', i.e. as an intensification: not only Jesus is received, but God. Accordingly, Mark 7.15 would mean that defilement takes place not only by external things but very much more by what is within (R.P. Booth). However, this solution cannot be reconciled with the wording. It presupposes a different text, say: 'Not only what comes from outside makes unclean but (even more) what comes from inside.' Now the present text challenges quite fundamentally the view that external things are unclean: 'There is nothing . . . that can make unclean.' It certainly does not just say that external things do not in fact make unclean; it says that that in principle they cannot make unclean. The exclusive formulation, which states a matter of principle, does not allow any external uncleanness.

- *The situation.* Did Jesus think only of a limited situation? For example the washing of hands addressed in Mark 7.5, which was not a universal practice in Judaism? Rather, the context of radical discipleship comes in question: on their travels the disciples may accept any food that is offered them – regardless of whether it is clean or unclean, tithed or not tithed. That is probably how Luke 10.7,8 is to be understood. Gospel of Thomas logion 14, which is about cleanness, stands in the same context. Since Jesus can call for the Law to be broken in the context of radical discipleship – cf. the offending against the commandment to honour parents in Matt. 8.21 – a contradiction to the commandments about cleanness could be imagined in this context.

- *The Jewish analogies.* There is evidence of an internalized notion of cleanness in the Hellenistic Diaspora Judaism of Jesus' time. Pseudo-Phocylides 228 says: 'The purifications are healings of the soul and not of the body.' In *SpecLeg* III, 208f., Philo defines impurity primarily as injustice and godlessness. But at the same time he emphasizes the external ritual commandments! On the basis of such analogies, can one attribute an even more radical notion to the Galilean Jesus? At any rate in his portrait of John the Baptist, the Jerusalemite Josephus emphasizes that the baptism served only to sanctify the body, since the soul had already previously been purified by righteousness (*Antt.* 18.117). Thus radical thoughts on the question of purity are not inconceivable in Palestine – especially in the case of a follower of John the Baptist who continued John's preaching but dispensed with baptism.

- *The subsequent effect.* Had Jesus made a clear statement about the commandments relating to cleanness in Lev. 11, the dispute about them after Easter would be incomprehensible. That is an important argument against the authenticity of Mark 7.15 (H. Räisänen). However, the logion does not formulate any instructions about behaviour. It makes an indicative statement to the effect that whatever comes from outside cannot make unclean. One can share this conviction and nevertheless observe the commandments about cleanness, not because of the unclean and clean qualities of things and foods, but out of respect for a tradition or in order to avoid scandal. Thus in Mark 1.41ff. Jesus declares a leper clean, but nevertheless sends him to the priest for an official declaration of cleanness. In Matt. 17.23ff. he disputes in principle the obligation of the disciples to pay the temple tax – but pays it nevertheless! The fundamental reflection on the laws of cleanness in Mark 7.15 leaves it open how one should behave in particular instances. Mark 7.15 is therefore rightly regarded as an 'enigmatic saying' (as a παραβολή, 7.17), and there is controversy over its interpretation.

The logion about cleanness is a logion which makes a radical judgment. But we need not for that reason deny it to Jesus. Jesus was and remained a Jew when he uttered such thoughts. But he was a radical Jew.

3.4.2 Jesus and the sabbath commandment

S.O. Back, *Jesus of Nazareth and the Sabbath Commandment*, Abo 1995; E.P. Sanders, *Jewish Law from Jesus to the Mishnah*, London and Philadelphia 1990, 6–23.

In addition to the logion about cleanness in Mark 7.15, the sabbath conflicts are a test case for the disputed question whether or not Jesus went beyond the frontiers of Judaism (and its foundation, the Torah) in his preaching. The subject of the conflicts is plucking ears of corn and healing on the sabbath (Mark 2.23ff.; 3.1ff.). A comparison with other sabbath conflicts in primitive Christianity and Judaism shows that these conflicts are not just fictitious scenes.

1. *Jesus' sabbath conflicts and primitive Christianity*. The conflicts over the sabbath in the Jesus tradition are about how the sabbath is to be kept. The conflicts over the sabbath in primitive Christianity which can be inferred from Gal. 4.10f.; Rom. 14.5 and Col. 2.16 go beyond this, in that they put in question whether the sabbath was to be kept at all. In the former case the debates were within Judaism; in the latter they were between Jewish and Gentile Christians. Primitive Christianity handed down Jesus' conflicts over the sabbath in different currents of tradition without assimilating them to these later problems. In the parallel texts in Matthew and Luke, the pericope about the ears of corn (Mark 2.23ff.) has so many minor agreements over against the Markan version that a rival tradition will have been an influence here. The recollection of the healings on the sabbath (in Mark 3.1ff.) is generally confirmed by two traditions in the Lukan special material (Luke 13.10–17; 14.1–6) and is also an influence in the Johannine sphere (John 5.1ff.; 7.22f.). It is striking that in the traditions in the Lukan special material, the argument is each time built up from the help that may be given to animals on the sabbath to the disputed healing of human beings (Luke 13.15f., 14.5) – an argument which appears independently in Matt. 12.11f. and was probably used by Jesus. It is also striking that in no instance is the sick person in acute danger: all could have been healed the following day. The healing of them on the sabbath leads to controversies which are to be evaluated within the framework of other Jewish controversies over the sabbath.

2. *Jesus' conflicts over the sabbath and Judaism*. Precisely because the sabbath was an ideal characteristic of Jewish identity, how it was to be observed was controversial. The Essenes rejected any help for animals in distress on the sabbath (CD XI, 13f.) – in contrast to the other Jews, including Jesus (bShab 128b; Matt.

12.11f.). They reduced the 'sabbath mile' (cf. Acts 1.12), the maximum distance one could travel on the sabbath, from 2000 to 1000 ells (CD X, 21). By contrast, the Pharisees sought to extend it by allowing the formation of an 'erub' (literally 'mixing'). For example, they linked together a number of houses around a common courtyard to make them a single fictitious house within which the carrying of objects was allowed. The Sadducees firmly rejected this relaxation of the sabbath commandment (Erub VI, 2), as did the Essenes (CD XI, 4). Again, there was a dispute among the Pharisees as to whether it was permissible to begin before the sabbath work which would only be finished 'automatically' during it, like dyeing. The Hillelites allowed it, the Shammaites rejected it (Shab I, 4–5). Thus in the time of Jesus Jews put forward very different views about healing on the sabbath without forcing their views on others. Jesus represents a 'liberal' trend in this spectrum. He provoked those around him by it. That makes it all the more important for us to ask, 'What was this dispute about?'.

3. *The actual basis of the conflict.* There was a dispute between Jesus and his critics over whether exceptions to the prohibition of work on the sabbath could be extended from the generally recognized instances to some new cases. The two recognized exceptions were danger to one's own life and danger to the life of others. In these cases it was permissible to defend oneself, if necessary by killing one's enemy (cf. I Macc. 2.29–41) or to save other human beings and animals from deadly danger (Mekh. Ex. 31.13; cf. Bill. I, 633). It is hard to say how old further relaxations are; they are based on a wise interpretation of the Torah with a humane tendency. However, if they could be labelled as (permitted) eating and drinking and normal care of the body, they were admissible (Shab. XIV, 3–4). Moreover, healings were also allowed if there was some uncertainty as to whether or not the disease was life-threatening (Yoma VIII, 6). But such interpretations emphasize all the more the fact that in principle healings were forbidden because they were 'work' (מְלָאכָה). In our view, attempts to interpret Jesus' healings on the sabbath otherwise are mistaken: the fact that they took place only through words (as in Mark 3.1ff.) does not in itself make them a permissible action. Of course words were allowed on the sabbath. But so too was eating and drinking – however, not when both exclusively served a therapeutic purpose. Moreover the Jesus tradition clearly regards the healings as a breach of the sabbath. The discussion is not over whether they are a 'work' or not; the discussion is about whether it is permissible at all to heal in this way or not (Mark 3.4; Luke 14.3). The same goes for rubbing the ears of corn.[37] The reference to the example of David, who ate the shewbread reserved for the priests, shows that the discussion was over the right to break a rule, not about whether there was an offence. So does

---

[37]Philo writes of the sabbath: '. . . For it is not permitted to cut any shoot or branch, or even a leaf, or to pluck any fruit whatsoever' (*VitMos* II, 22).

that mean that with his conflicts over the sabbath Jesus falls out of the framework of the Judaism of the time? The following arguments tell against this:

- Jesus refers to a universal maxim which is also attested in Judaism, independently of him, for Rabbi Shim'on b.M^{e}nasya (c.180 CE): 'Behold, Ex. 31.14 says: "Observe the sabbath, for it is holy for you" (= for your benefit), i.e. the sabbath is given for you and you are not given for the sabbath' (Mekh Ex. 31.13; cf. Bill. II. 5). The terminology 'give' and 'hand down' suggests Sinai. In Mark 2.27 the thought could be more of creation: 'The sabbath was made (ἐγένετο) for human beings and not human beings for the sabbath.'
- Jesus refers to the two cases in which a transcending of the sabbath is recognized: the alternative of 'killing' or 'healing' on the sabbath possibly argues from the right to self-defence on the sabbath (and thus to killing) to the right to heal on the sabbath (Mark 3.4). The conclusion from the help allowed for animals to the disputed healing of human beings on the sabbath appeals to the permissibility of a breach of the sabbath if there is a danger which threatens the life of human beings or animals.
- Jesus follows a tendency to relativize the sabbath commandment for the sake of life which goes beyond these two recognized exceptions – except that he does not reinterpret this relativizing as a fulfilment of the sabbath commandment but depicts it as a breach of the sabbath. In principle that is only a short step beyond the tendencies which were already present in Judaism. Nevertheless it is important to ask: why did Jesus take this step?

4. *The motivation for the conflict over the sabbath.* One can assume three different motives behind Jesus' conflicts over the sabbath: (*a*) an ethical motive, a preference for helping people to other (ritual) commandments; (*b*) an eschatological motive, which is echoed, for example, when the fetters of Satan are loosened through a sabbath healing (Luke 13.16); or (*c*) a messianic motive: Jesus demonstrates his authority, which is comparable to that of David (Mark 2.25f.). As God's eschatological action is help for the weak and the poor, it has an intrinsically 'ethical' character. Since this ethical will of God also establishes itself against existing sabbath practice, it is bound up with charismatic authority – in short, the three motives do not contradict one another. In addition there is Jesus' concrete situation: rubbing ears of corn on the sabbath was not the regular custom of primitive Christian local communities, but it does fit in well with the situation of itinerant charismatics who could not always plan for their food on the sabbath. Healings of the chronically sick on the sabbath would be a provocation if they could just as well have been performed on the next day. But in the case of an itinerant preacher it would be 'natural' for him to heal a sick person on the day of their encounter – for the next day he might possibly already be somewhere else.

This situation of an itinerant charismatic also explains the requirement that a disciple should leave the burial of his father to the dead, i.e. not bother about it, and follow Jesus instead (Matt. 8.21f.; Luke 9.59f.). Being an itinerant charismatic presupposes a readiness to break with the family. Even an offence against the command to honour one's parents is tolerated: it is seen as a kind of prophetic symbolic action. Prophetic symbolic actions often offend against law and custom, for example when Isaiah goes round naked for three years (Isa. 20.1ff.) or Hosea marries a prostitute or adulteress (Hos. 1.2ff.; 3.1ff.). Neither Hosea nor Isaiah wanted to do away with law and custom here, but to emphasize a message by provocative behaviour. In the case of Jesus the message is that discipleship and the kingdom of God are more important than the most elementary family duties. The command to follow him in Matt. 8.21f., which is not a matter of principle, therefore does not allow us to assume that Jesus in principle abandoned the Torah.

The test cases, the way in which Jesus dealt with the commandments about purity, the sabbath and parents, therefore show that Jesus represents a very liberal view of the Torah within Judaism, but in no way a criticism of the Torah opposed to Judaism. In the question of cleanness he puts forward a general (indicative) maxim (Mark 7.15) which is in tension with the presuppositions of the Torah. In the sabbath question he puts forward a general indicative maxim (2.27) which corresponds with the Torah, using it to justify clear transgressions of the letter of the Torah. In both cases he shows a free attitude to the Torah – both to its spirit (in the question of cleanness) and its letter (in the sabbath question). In both cases, as in the offence against the command to honour one's parents, his life as a homeless itinerant preacher could explain the distance from the usual principles or norms, though without being able to explain these 'causally'. If we are to assess Jesus' attitude to the Torah correctly, in a further section we must look at the combination of the intensification of the Torah with the relaxation of it.

3.5 The relationship between intensification of norms and relaxation of norms in the ethic of Jesus

The secret of Jesus' ethic lies in the juxtaposition of texts which intensify the Torah and texts which relax it. Sometimes this tension can easily be reduced, as in the case of sexual morality. Here (predominantly in the Logia tradition) we find a tendency towards intensification: Jesus argues for the indissolubility of marriage (Mark 10.2ff), and sees adultery already being committed in sexual desires (Matt. 5.27f.); in his saying about eunuchs he praises a renunciation of sexuality for the sake of the kingdom of God (Matt. 19.12). These rigorous statements are addressed to males: the saying about erotic desire for a woman and adultery is as clearly addressed to them as is the saying about eunuchs. Moreover in a society in which predominantly men took the initiative in divorce, the insistence on the indissolubility of marriage is addressed primarily to them – especially as the statement in Mark 10.9, 'What God has joined together let no person (ἄνθρωπος) put asunder', is formulated in an ambiguous way and cannot be translated: 'What God has joined together the husband (ἄνθρωπος, as in Mark 10.8) should not put asunder.' By contrast, the tolerant statements about sexual morality appear above all in narrative traditions – often of disputed historicity, but hardly without any basis in the life of Jesus: Jesus demonstrates tolerance and humanity towards the 'woman who was a great sinner' and the woman taken in adultery (cf. Luke 7.36ff.; John 8.2ff.). His tolerance protects women from discrimination. This asymmetry of rigorism and permissiveness makes sense in a patriarchal society – and is coherent ethically: males are confronted with a rigorous sexual ethic, and women are protected by a tolerant and considerate sexual ethic.

But these observations on sexual ethics cannot be generalized for all spheres of life. All in all, it is rather the case that for Jesus an intensification of norms relates to ethical commands in the narrow sense, while a relaxation of norms relates to ritual and cultic norms. Ethical commandments tend to be universal. In all cultures, aggression and the striving for power and possessions have to be given a form that can be lived with, and that happens in comparable ways. Ritual commandments are far more the characteristic of specific cultures. In the ancient world, the sabbath and food commandments were distinguishing marks of Judaism, which differentiated it from other peoples and cultures.

May we conclude from this that Jesus forsook the limited world of Judaism by teaching a cosmopolitan ethic? Quite the contrary! Both tendencies of his ethics serve to preserve Jewish identity and make Jewish life possible.

From the time of its confrontation with the overwhelming power of Hellenistic culture, Judaism became caught up in a series of conversion and renewal movements. All in some way advocated 'intensifications of the Torah', i.e. an emphasis on the Jewish commandments which had been handed down. The fact that Jesus shows tendencies to intensify the Torah specifically in the case of universalistic commandments by no means points towards assimilation, as though Jews were to become open to a universal ethic. On the contrary, the Jewish followers of Jesus are to realize the universal norms formulated in an intensified way so consistently that in so doing they surpass the 'nations'. They are to be the 'salt of the earth' and the 'light of the world' (Matt. 5.13ff.)! The disciples are to distinguish themselves from the sinners and Gentiles (Luke 6.32ff.; Matt. 5.47) by loving their enemies. By renouncing the status of those who want to be first, they are to offer a contrasting posture to the life of the Gentiles (Mark 10.42–44). They are to differ from the 'Gentiles' by being free from care and first seeking the kingdom of God (cf. Matt. 6.32f./Luke 12.30f.). The universal ethical will of God is to be realized by the followers of Jesus in such a way that the identity of Jews as opposed to Gentiles can become visible precisely here.

The tendencies in Jesus' ethic to relax norms similarly have a social function.

Any rigorist ethics which intensifies norms is divisive. The stricter the norms, the fewer people can really observe them. The unity of the community requires not only preservation of its identity by demarcation from outsiders, but also preservation of its power to integrate within, so that groups are not marginalized and forced to the periphery. Such a motive underlies the relativizing of ritual commandments: the 'toll collectors and sinners' are also members of Israel; they too belong with the lost sheep who must be sought out. If one may breach the sabbath during war for self-defence (and, if need be, may even kill), how much more is there a right to breach it in order to restore a member of the people of Israel to social life! This is directly addressed in a pericope about the sabbath: 'And ought not this woman, a daughter of Abraham, to be loosed from this bond on the sabbath day?' (Luke 13.16).

So it cannot be said that in formulating his ethics Jesus did not have in view the social needs of a particular people. His ethic, which intensifies and relaxes the Torah, is a programme aimed at the restoration of Israel; it seeks to preserve the identity of Israel in relation to the Gentile environment and inwardly to make possible the integration of marginal groups. But this ethical programme has its *Sitz im Leben* in a group of itinerant charismatics around Jesus. who claimed to be renewing and representing Israel. Here one could formulate radical commandments and represent them credibly. Here one could avoid both daily necessities and ritual traditions. Here one could think and live in a way which was both rigorous and 'lax', intensifying and relaxing the Torah at the same time.

Jesus' programme presupposes an inner freedom towards the Torah. If we look for the spiritual foundation for this inner freedom in which norms were radicalized and relaxed, we come upon the wisdom and eschatological traditions in Judaism. The Torah could be relativized and transcended in the light of both these traditions.

4. The ethic of Jesus between motivations from wisdom and eschatology

Jesus' freedom towards the Torah is based in wisdom and eschatology. Here he combines two currents of tradition which had already been combined in many ways in Judaism before him. They seem to stand in insuperable tension as a motivation for ethical action. For an ethic grounded in wisdom counts on the world continuing, whereas an ethic grounded in eschatology counts on a radical transformation of it. Why they nevertheless belong together at a deeper level emerges from their history in Judaism.

4.1 Wisdom and eschatology in Judaism

The period of early Judaism was the heyday of wisdom. At this time Wisdom became a hypostasis of God, i.e. an independent aspect of God which opens up direct access to him. As Wisdom was at work in creation (Prov. 8; Sir. 24; Wisdom 6–8, especially 7.22), it can be recognized from creation. The great influence of the 'wise' on earth is grounded in the decisive significance attributed to wisdom 'in heaven'. New groups of 'scribes' and 'wise men' claimed to communicate direct access to God by virtue of their own competence (by virtue of Wisdom) – potentially independently of the priestly sacrificial cult and the Torah. However, usually there was a harmony: according to Sir. 24.9, Wisdom dwells in the temple; she is the Law which Moses commended to us (Sir. 24.23). This identification with Wisdom changed the way in which the Law was understood. The Torah became a cosmic entity which is pre-existent and through which God created the world.

The period of early Judaism was at the same time a heyday of apocalyptic literature. A wealth of revelation writings promised glimpses of a world beyond, in which the eschatological future of the world was being prepared and was already present. What had been communicated in them by revelations went beyond Torah and Prophets. These writings, too, document a dissatisfaction with the traditional mediators of revelation, with the cult and its priests. But they all referred back to the Torah (and the Prophets), since all the mediators of revelation were known from the scriptures: Enoch, Abraham, Moses, Ezra, Baruch, etc. This secret apocalyptic literature came into being in the context of penitential movements. The repentance called for in them (back to the Torah) was bound up with a hope of the (eschatological) transformation of history. Israel would become powerful again, although it was oppressed in the present. Martyrs gave their lives for the 'new world'. Resistance in this world was motivated by a hope of participation in the new world.

In the period of early Judaism, wisdom and eschatological traditions were combined. The Wisdom of Solomon presents an eschatologized wisdom: the wise and righteous who suffer tribulation in this world will rule in the new world. God will change the cosmos (cf. esp. Wisdom 1–5). The apocalyptic wisdom writings claim to be higher wisdom. Ethiopic Enoch 42 expresses this with a variant of the wisdom myth: wisdom found no abode among men and women on earth and returned to heaven. There it is now accessible to seers and visionaries – in the form of secret apocalyptic literature. What unites the two currents of tradition is the extension of the knowledge of revelation beyond the tradition: God become accessible through Wisdom and extra-normal visions independently of temple and Torah. Therefore both traditions were also available for Jesus in freely interpreting and transcending the Torah. Both traditions are equally original in him. Jesus claims to surpass on the one hand Old Testament wisdom, 'More than Solomon is here' (Luke 11.31/Matt. 12.42) and on the other the eschatological traditions of Judaism, 'More than Jonah is here' (Luke 11.29/Matt. 12.41).

4.2 Wisdom motives in the ethic of Jesus

Jesus largely formulates his ethic in wisdom-type admonitions and sentences. In form it is wisdom teaching. But in content too it has features from wisdom when it refers to the creation as a past primal time or as present nature. Reference to the past primal time of creation appears at three points in the Jesus tradition as an ethical argument – though with differing degrees of clarity:

1. *Marriage.* In the light of creation, marriage is meant to be indissoluble. Divorce was a concession by Moses to human imperfection (Mark 10.2–9). When Jesus again makes the indissolubility of marriage the norm – and wants at least to exclude the remarriage of those who have been divorced (Mark. 10.12) – he is renewing the original ordinance of creation in the present.

2. *The sabbath.* Such a reference to creation could also play a role in what Jesus says about the sabbath. In the logion 'The sabbath is made for man and not man for the sabbath' (Mark 2.27), there is perhaps an argument from the sequence of the creation of human beings (Gen. 1.26f.) and the sabbath (Gen. 2.1f.) to a priority in principle of human beings over the sabbath. However, that is by no means certain.

3. *Cleanness.* The saying about cleanness in Mark 7.15 which has been discussed above could have a background in the theology of creation. The distinction between 'clean and unclean' is introduced in the Torah only in Lev. 11, i.e. long after the creation. In a tradition with parallel content in Luke 11.40f., the distinction between outward and inner cleanness is explicitly criticized in the light of the notion of creation: 'You fool! Did not he who made the outside make the inside also?' In the light of creation, everything is clean.

A second group of wisdom motives is formed by the images from nature in the present, which occur as motivating arguments.

1. In Matt. 5.43ff., the *sun* becomes the model for love of enemy. Just as the sun shines upon good and evil, so the love of God is given to both good and evil. Therefore the followers of Jesus should love not only the good but also the evil, their enemies. Perhaps here an intrinsically pessimistic tradition of imagery is being reshaped: really it is part of the ethical irrationality of the world that good and evil fare equally well in this world and that the sun shines on both. But here this resigned insight becomes the motivation for a form of ethical behaviour which goes on the offensive, even from an inferior position. The thought-world is that of wisdom. But the reference to future reward links wisdom ideas with an eschatological motif.

2. In Luke 12.6f. the *sparrow* in God's hand becomes an argument for trust in God: 'Are not five sparrows sold for two pennies? And not one of them is forgotten before God. Why, even the hairs of your head are all numbered. Fear not; you are of more value than many sparrows.' Here too an image of nature from wisdom is combined with an eschatological outlook: one is not to fear human beings who take life, but God who has the power to 'cast into hell' (Luke 12.5).

3. The *birds* under the heavens and the lilies in the fields are probably the best-known examples of nature imagery drawn from wisdom (Matt. 6.25–34/Luke 12.22–32). They are to encourage an overcoming of anxiety about the where-withal to live and about clothing, so that all energy can be directed towards the one thing that is necessary: 'Seek first the kingdom of God (and his righteousness), and all these things will be added to you' (Matt. 6.33/Luke 12.31). Certainly it is sometimes disputed that the images of nature drawn from wisdom and eschato-logical admonitions form a unity. But comparable motives are already combined in the Jewish tradition. In the Letter of Aristeas we find a reflection on the difference between Gentiles and Jews. The Egyptians call the Jews 'men of God'. The Jewish sages think:

'This (designation) is ascribed exclusively to those who worship the true God, and not to those [i.e. non-Jewish men] who are concerned with meat and drink and clothes, their whole attitude being concentrated on these concerns. Such concerns are of no account among the people of our race, but throughout the whole of their lives their main objective is concerned with the sovereignty (δυναστεία) of God' (Aristeas 140f.).

In Jesus' saying, the concentration on the timeless 'sovereignty of God' has become a concern for the eschatological rule of God. The creator God who cares like a father for all his creatures is at the same time the God who is bringing in his eschatological kingdom.

The call not to be anxious also tells us something about the *Sitz im Leben* of the wisdom-eschatological ethic of Jesus: anyone who presents birds and lilies which do not work as a model of freedom from anxiety is addressing people who do not themselves work. With the traditional imagery it would have been possible to present at least the birds as an example of diligent work: birds build nests, feed their young, seek food. But none of that is mentioned. When it is said of them, 'They sow not, neither do they reap; they do not gather into barns', activities of human life are initially projected on to nature. Human beings are envisaged who do not sow and reap because they have given up their callings to follow Jesus. The fact that here one of the pictures focusses on the typical work of the man 'outside' in the field and the other on the typical work of women 'inside at home' (spinning) suggests that women, too, belonged among Jesus' itinerant followers. Certainly the logion is addressed to all men and women: that one cannot extend one's life by worrying, that every day has its own troubles (Matt. 6.27, 34), are universal human experiences. But its *Sitz im Leben* is the group of itinerant charismatics, both men and women, around Jesus.

4.3 Eschatological motives in the ethic of Jesus

We saw that the nature imagery from wisdom in particular is often combined with an eschatological perspective: reward and punishment in the new world or the coming kingdom of God. Eschatology provides the motivation. However, there are interpretations of the eschatology of Jesus which minimize its ethical significance. It is said that the rule of God breaks in as a supernatural event without any human contribution. It relativizes the significance of human action and is not that powerful stimulus to ethical conduct which appears in the preaching of Jesus. The classical proof text for this view is the so-called 'parable of the seed growing by itself' (Mark 4.26–29). According to this, the rule of God dawns 'of itself' (αὐτομάτη), without any human contribution. The term 'of itself' (αὐτόματος) is generally used of plants growing wild; here it is transferred to cultivated plants and strictly limited to the time between sowing and harvest. The parable has its point in the co-operation between the farmer and the earth in the bringing forth of fruit. Since the judge of the world stands behind the farmer at the end of the parable (4.29), the whole parable may be an image of the co-operation between God and human beings: God entrusts his seed to the earth, to human beings, so that these may bring forth fruit spontaneously, voluntarily and 'by themselves'.[38]

Mark 1.14ff. gives a summary description of the relationship between eschatology and ethics in the teaching of Jesus. The eschatological message, 'The time is fulfilled and the kingdom of God is at hand', is followed by three imperatives: 1. 'Repent!' The great cosmic turning-point is matched by the call to change one's behaviour, which is addressed to all. Jesus' eschatological ethic is an ethic of repentance. 2. 'Believe in the gospel!' According to the Logia source the good news (εὐαγγέλιον) is addressed particularly to the poor, the sick and the weak (cf. Luke 7.22, where the verb εὐαγγελίζεσθαι appears). As king, God shows a

---

[38]Cf. G. Theissen, 'Der Bauer und die von selbst Frucht bringende Erde. Naiver Synergismus in Mk 4, 26–29?', *ZNW* 85, 1994, 167–82.

preference for the disadvantaged. Jesus' eschatological ethic is an ethic of mercy.
3. 'Follow me!' (Mark 1.17). Immediately after the eschatological message with its call to repent and its promise of salvation, individuals are called as 'fishers of men' to 'discipleship'. Here they are voluntarily to take the role of outsiders ('fishers of men' has negative connotations). Jesus' eschatological ethic is an ethic of discipleship.

1. *Jesus' eschatological ethic as an ethic of repentance*: Jesus called on all to repent. This call to repentance is a legacy of John the Baptist. Characteristics of Jesus are:

- *The independence of repentance from baptism*: in all probability Jesus did not baptize. For him, ethical repentance is independent of a ritual act. Does that stem from his lack of any anxiety about uncleanness?
- *The gaining of time to demonstrate repentance ethically*: whereas John the Baptist lived in expectation of an imminent end (cf. the image of the axe laid to the roots, Luke 3.9), in which repentance could only be shown only by the symbolic action of baptism, for Jesus God grants time for an ethical proof (cf. the parable of the barren fig tree, Luke 13.6–9).
- *Confidence in the readiness of people to repent*: the prodigal son returns to his father of his own accord (Luke 15.11–32). Jesus is also confident that the Gentiles will repent; the people of Nineveh will condemn 'this generation' in the judgment because they repented (Matt. 12.41f.). The people of Tyre and Sidon would already have repented long since (Matt. 11.20–24). Even 'evil people' are capable of good: 'If you who are evil can give your children good gifts . . .' (Luke 11.11–13).

In contrast to Qumran (cf. 1QS V, 8f.; CD XV, 12), 'repentance' is repentance in the direction of strict obedience, not to the Torah, but to God's kingly rule. The cosmic change which is dawning finds its parallel in the changing of individual lives. Here God's eschatological action has an intrinsically ethical quality. It is an intervention in favour of the weak and poor. Therefore:

2. *Jesus' eschatological ethic is an ethic of mercy*. Whereas Jesus calls all to repentance (cf. Luke 13.1–5), he has a special message for the poor and weak. The promise of salvation is for them. This is shown by:

- *The beatitudes on the poor, the hungry and the thirsty*: in the face of the beginning of the rule of God these 'anti-beatitudes' call fortunate precisely those who by general standards are unfortunate (Luke 6.20b–21).
- *The sayings about admission*, which promise the kingdom of God to children (Mark 10.15), to toll collectors and prostitutes (Matt. 21.31), and to the mutilated (Mark 9.43–48).

• *John the Baptist's question* (Matt. 11.2ff.) whether Jesus is the one who should come, which is answered by the remark that the sick and the poor are receiving good news this very moment.

The preaching of the kingdom of God is opposed to selection. As Nietzsche already recognized, Christianity is a protest against the merciless mechanism of selection in this world.[39] This protest is articulated in the preaching of the kingdom of God – not only by Jesus but also by his followers. Certainly the sayings about discipleship only rarely combine discipleship and βασιλεία,[40] but those called to discipleship are messengers of the kingdom of God (Luke 10.9, 11). This leads to a third closer definition of the ethic of Jesus.

3. *Jesus' eschatological ethic as an ethic of discipleship*. The ethic of discipleship, too, is not a demand for all but only for those disciples who follow Jesus in the literal sense. The ethic of discipleship includes (as characteristics of 'itinerant radicalism'):[41]

• *The abandonment of a fixed abode*: the disciples follow Jesus (in the literal sense) on his travels through Palestine (cf. Matt. 18.19f.; Mark 10.28–30).
• *An ethic which has no connection with the family*: readiness for a break with the family (Mark 3.20f., 31–35), for the eschatological 'family war' (Matt. 10.34–36/Luke 12.51–53), for the hatred of members of the family (Matt. 10.37/Luke 14.26).
• *Freedom towards possessions*, whether this is giving up possessions for the poor (Mark 10.17–22) or leaving house and home (Mark 10.28–30).
• *A demonstrative lack of protection*: doing without a staff as a means of self-defence (Matt. 10.10; conceded by Mark 6.8), not fighting back (Matt. 5.38–42) to the point of being ready for martyrdom (Mark 8.34f.).

If we take all the eschatological motives in the ethic of Jesus together, it is striking that in them we once again find that tension between rigorism and acceptance which is characteristic of Jesus' interpretation of the Torah. The poor and the marginalized are given an accepting ethic of mercy; the disciples, both women and men, are given radical and rigorous commands to follow Jesus. But all are confronted with the call to repentance, a call which at the same time has both

---

[39]Cf. G. Theissen, *Biblical Faith*, London and Philadelphia 1984, esp. 140–62, and F. Nietzsche, *The Antichrist*, Complete Works, London 1911, 132: 'On the whole, pity thwarts the law of development which is the law of selection. It preserves that which is ripe for death and it fights in favour of the disinherited and the condemned of life.'

[40]But cf. Luke 9.59–62: '. . . but go and proclaim the kingdom of God' (9.60b); possibly this part of the verse is to be regarded as redactional.

[41]Cf. Theissen, *First Followers**, 8–16.

rigorous and accepting aspects: it compels them to change their behaviour radically in a painful way, but offers a chance specifically to those who had no chance according to traditional religious standards. Mark 2.17 is right in the way in which it sums up Jesus' preaching: 'Those who are well have no need of a physician, but those who are sick: I came not to call the righteous, but sinners.'

Basically, it needs to be emphasized that eschatology, i.e. the conviction of the coming of God's kingly rule and of judgment, does not just motivate the ethic of Jesus in the formal sense, by inculcating the doing of good. Rather, it offers substantive criteria for good behaviour. The reversal of criteria is characteristic of eschatology. Those who have no privileges here are given privileges by the eschatological transformation which is beginning in the present. God shows his kingdom by accepting the weak, even those who measured by the strict norms of the Torah are 'sinners'. Non-Jews, too, are accepted into his kingdom (Matt. 8.11f.), and tax collectors and prostitutes will also enter it (before the pious who refuse to repent, Matt. 21.32). Accordingly, good behaviour means supporting the weak, accepting sinners, welcoming foreigners, etc.

4.4 The relationship between wisdom and eschatological motives in the ethic of Jesus and the significance of the Torah

The tension between wisdom and eschatological motives is resolved in so far as the wisdom motives refer to the past and present, and the eschatological motives to the future. Like all Jewish ethics, Jesus' ethic is embedded in a biblical picture of history which he presupposes. His ethic does not correspond to the timeless structures of the cosmos which are accessible to human knowledge, as Greek-Hellenistic ethics does, but is an signpost on the way from the past to the future which challenges the human will. The will of God, which occurs as demand and promise and is to be found in the present, gives directions on this way. Here, too, is the centre of Jesus' ethic.

However, scholars often want to seek the nucleus of Jesus' ethic either in wisdom, which is potentially independent of the Torah, or in eschatology, which points beyond the Torah. But here in particular it is easy to succumb to false judgments. The Wisdom of Jesus Sirach is a testimony to upright Torah piety. Yet nowhere is the Torah directly quoted and expounded in it, although Jesus Sirach identifies Wisdom (and of course even more his own wisdom) with the Torah (Sir. 24.23). Compared with him, Jesus refers to concrete commands of the Torah far more frequently, e.g. in the antitheses, in the didactic sayings about the discipleship of the rich and about the greatest commandment. Compared with other wisdom writings, Jesus is clearly more orientated on the concrete Torah!

The same goes for eschatology: the apocalyptic writings of that time usually refer to the Torah in a cumulative and summary way. Individual problems of the Torah ethic are not discussed in them. Nevertheless, the Torah has a central role: it opens up the way to the new world. In Jesus (by comparison with some apocalypses), this way into the kingdom of God is related to the Torah, which he expounds in a much more concrete manner!

A comparison between the wisdom and the eschatological traditions of Judaism must also note that Jesus takes up themes from this tradition only in a characteristic selection and concentration. Jesus Sirach writes at length about the temple cult and the history of Israel. The apocalypses develop cosmological wisdom which has been gained in an esoteric way. There is none of this in Jesus. He takes from the wisdom and apocalyptic traditions only what is ethically relevant, whether for the action of God to human beings or for their response in their action. Thus wisdom and apocalyptic traditions are totally concentrated on ethical behaviour (of God and human beings). Underlying this is an image of God which is stamped by the Torah and the Prophets, or more precisely by the Torah read in a prophetic spirit: by nature God is ethical energy, is the will for the good. God's essence is this 'goodness' in such an exclusive way that Jesus can say, 'No one is good but the one (and only) God' (Mark 10.18). In the light of this understanding of God, the creation becomes transparent to the ethical will of God and human beings in parables and images. In the light of this understanding of God, at the same time the eschatological future is announced as the establishment of a justice which applies to the poor. This God has defined himself in the Torah as ethical will and has been interpreted by the prophets as ethical will. He is the God of the Jewish Bible (or, as Christians later called it, the Old Testament). From this centre wisdom and apocalyptic are remoulded.

An objection could be made to this interpretation of the ethic of Jesus in terms of a Torah expounded in the prophetic spirit: in the saying about taking the kingdom of God by force (Matt. 11.12f./Luke 16.16), Jesus himself clearly demonstrates that the time of 'Law and Prophets' is past. Now is the time of the kingdom of God, in which men of violence snatch it to themselves. One could easily reject the objection if one interprets the logion in a bad sense, i.e. understands the 'men of violence' as opponents of Jesus and the rule of God who offend against both the Law and the Prophets by 'taking by force' the kingdom of God. Jesus and his followers would then come to stand on the side of Law and Prophets. But it is more probable that the saying should be understood in a good sense: the men of violence are Jesus and his disciples. Perhaps here Jesus is rejecting an objection to his work, to the effect that with his liberal practice he is breaking with the Law and the Prophets and is therefore a sign of the dissolution of all order which according to the expectation of Jewish apocalyptic will take place before the end. Jesus is demonstratively acknowledging what in the eyes of others is a stigma: he and his disciples, who are supposed to be men of violence, are seizing the kingdom of God.

But that shows that God and his rule are on Jesus' side. The replacement of the Law and the Prophets must then be understood to mean that now the eschatological promises contained in the Law and the Prophets are being fulfilled – as in the rabbinic tradition: 'In the school of Elijah it is taught that the world will exist for 6,000 years, (namely) 2,000 years of chaos, 2,000 years of Torah and 2,000 years of messianic time; but because of our many sins, some of these have already passed' (bSanh 97a/b; bAZ 9a). Here the Torah is not abolished with the coming of the Messiah, but fulfilled. For it is only because of sins against the Torah that the coming of the Messiah has been delayed![42]

We can establish that the ethical preaching of Jesus corresponds precisely to the three sources of Jewish ethics: the Torah at the centre, with wisdom and eschatology alongside it. At its centre it is orientated on the Torah; however, it is orientated on a Torah read in the prophetic spirit. No scribe, but a charismatic, has interpreted the Torah here. From this centre Jesus appropriates ideas from wisdom and apocalyptic. That becomes particularly clear if we look at the centre of his ethic: the commandment to love.

5. The commandment to love as the centre of Jesus' ethic

V.P. Furnish, *The Love Command in the New Testament*, Nashville 1972 and London 1973; Pheme Perkins, *Love Commands in the New Testament*, New York 1982.

The commandment to love is often regarded as the distinctive feature of Christianity. In John 13.34 it is regarded as the 'new commandment' which Jesus left behind for his disciples. But an unprejudiced reading of the Synoptic texts will already show that Jesus agreed with a Jewish scribe over the commandment to love. So we shall begin with a careful analysis of the twofold commandment to love and the Jewish parallels to it. Then in this context we shall describe the distinctive way in which Jesus focusses the commandment to love on love of enemies, foreigners and the outcast.

5.1 The twofold commandment to love: a survey of the textual evidence and the tendencies in the Synoptic Gospels

Common features and deviations between the Synoptics in the account of Jesus' conversations about the greatest commandment emerge from the survey on the opposite page. In reconstructing the earliest tradition it should be noted:

---

[42]Cf. G. Theissen, 'Jünger als Gewalttäter (Mk 1, 12f.; Lk 16.16). Der Stürmerspruch als Selbst-stigmatisierung einer Minorität', in *Mighty Minorities? (FS J. Jervell)*, *Studia Theologica* 49, 1995, 183–200.

1. Probably a double Mark/Q tradition underlies this: Matthew and Luke agree in omitting the beginning of the *sh^ema* (Deut. 6.4) in Mark 12.29b, 32b and the statement in Mark 12.32d which is critical of the cult. Further minor agreements are that the question is put by a νομικός (Mark γραμματεύς) with the intention of 'tempting' Jesus (cf. [ἐκ]πειράζων αὐτόν). He addresses Jesus as διδάσκαλε. The phrase ἐν τῷ νόμῳ also occurs, but in a different context.

2. In its emphasis on monotheism and the accumulation of terms relating to reason,[43] the Markan version shows a marked Hellenistic stamp.

3. The Q version cannot be reconstructed with sufficient certainty, so that we can identify only the following common nucleus:

---

1. A supreme norm is extracted from the Law/the commandments are elevated to become a supreme norm.

2. In content it consists of the *combination of love of God* (quotation Deut. 6.5) *with love of neighbour* (quotation Lev. 19.18).

3. The nearness to or the *consensus with the Jewish conversation-partner* is demonstrated.

The synoptic table below which shows the differences in the pericope in Matthew, Mark and Luke indicates that each Gospel in its own way emphasizes the consensus with Judaism: Mark by the assent of the scribe, Luke by the scribe himself giving the decisive answer and Matthew by explicitly emphasizing the twofold commandment to love as the centre in which the Law and the Prophets are grounded.

Matt. 22.34–40	Mark 12.28–34	Luke 10.25–27, 28ff.
Question of a teacher of the law (νομικός) about the greatest commandment in the law (ἐντολὴ μεγάλη ἐν τῷ νόμῳ)	Question of a scribe (γραμματεύς) about the first/ greatest commandment of all (ἐντολὴ πρώτη πάντων)	Question of a teacher of the law (νομικός): What must I do to inherit eternal life (τί ποιήσας ζωὴν αἰώνιον κληρονομήσω)?

---

[43]Thus God is to be loved beyond MT and LXX at Deut 6.5 ἐξ ὅλης τῆς διανοίας or συνέσεως (with all reason/insight, Mark 12.30, 33). The scribe who agrees is called νουνεχῶς(reasonable) in the narrative commentary (12.34).

Matt. 22.34–40	Mark 12.28–34	Luke 10.25–27, 28ff.
Jesus' reply	Jesus' reply	Jesus' counter question
	1. Monotheism + Deut. 6.4) and love of God (ἀγαπήσεις κύριον τὸν θεόν σου + four strengths = Deut. 6.5) Second, along with this commandment, appears	What does it say in the Law (ἐν τῷ νόμῳ)?
1. Love of God (ἀγαπήσεις κύριον τὸν θεόν σου + three strengths = Deut. 6.5). This first and great commandment (μεγάλη κ. πρώτη ἐντολή) is like (ὁμοία)		
2. Love of neighbour (ἀγαπήσεις τὸν πλησίον σου ὡς σεαυτόν = Lev. 19.18) On these two hang the law and the prophets (νόμος καὶ προφῆται)	2. Love of neighbour (ἀγαπήσεις τὸν πλησίον σου ὡς σεαυτόν = Lev. 19.18) There is no commandment greater than these	

	Scribe's answer	Scribe's answer
	1. Monotheism (= Deut. 6.4 expanded by Deut. 4.35) 2. To love God (Deut. 6.5) and to love one's neighbour (Lev. 19.18) is more than all sacrifices	Love (ἀγαπήσεις): 1. God (κύριον τὸν θεόν σου + four strengths) and 2. your neighbour (καὶ τὸν πλησίον σου ὡς σεαυτόν = Deut. 6.5, Lev. 19.18)
	Jesus' endorsement: You are not far from the kingdom of God (οὐ μακράν εἶ ἀπὸ τῆς βασιλείας τοῦ θεοῦ)	Jesus' endorsement: Do that and you will live (τοῦτο ποίει καὶ ζήσῃ)! Counter question: Who is my neighbour? Parable of the Good Samaritan

Matt. 22.34–40	Mark 12.28–34	Luke 10.25–27, 28ff.
Dispute over the exposition of the Law: love of God and love of neighbour explicitly put on the same level; the twofold commandment as a summary of the Law and the Prophets without a focus which is critical of the cult.	Didactic conversation about the greatest commandment generally: priority of monotheism (even stronger in the answer!); subordination of the cultic law; closeness (or gradation? cf. οὐ μακράν) of the Jewish teacher to Jesus, of Judaism to Christianity.	Dispute over the action that leads to life: The scribe (!) gives the answer by a fusion of quotations; consensus between the scribe and Jesus; the parable of the Samaritan as an exposition, explicit extension to all human beings.

5.2 Jewish traditions on the twofold commandment to love

Given that Mark and Luke presuppose agreement between Jesus and his conversation partners in evaluating the twofold commandment to love as the heart of the Torah, Jewish parallels take on an important role.[44] Certainly so far no explicit combination of Deut. 6.5 and Lev. 19.18 has yet been found in a quotation, but there are three groups of statements which can be understood as analogies to the primitive Christian twofold commandment as an individual and characteristic new creation from a broad stream of other Jewish traditions:

---

1. Especially in Hellenistic Judaism, statements about *monotheism* as the first commandment are widespread (cf. Mark 12.28f., 32).

- Letter of Aristeas 132: 'First of all by demonstrating that God is one (προϋπέδειξε γὰρ πάντων πρῶτον ὅτι μόνος ὁ θεός ἐστι), that his power is shown in everything, every place being filled with his sovereignty . . .'
- Philo, *Decal.* 65: 'So we shall establish within ourselves the first and most holy commandment, one to observe and venerate for the Most High God . . . (πρῶτον μὲν οὖν παράγγελμα καὶ παραγγελμάτων ἱερώτατον στηλιτεύσωμεν ἐν ἑαυτοῖς, ἕνα τὸν ἀνωτάτω νομίζειν τε καὶ τιμᾶν θεόν).'
- Pseudo-Phocylides 8: 'Honour God foremost, and afterwards your parents' (πρῶτα θεὸν τιμᾶν, μετέπειτα δὲ σεῖο γονῆας).
- Josephus, *Ap.* 2, 190: 'The statement that God possesses the universe (πρώτη δ' ἡγεῖται ἡ περὶ θεοῦ λέγουσα ὅτι θεὸς ἔχει τὰ συμπάντα) is regarded as the first principle [of the Jewish people].'

---

2. Jewish traditions from Rabbi Hillel and Rabbi Akiba offer statements about showing *solidarity with other human beings as the heart of the Torah* – whether in the form of the Golden Rule (as Matt. 7.12) or as a commentary on Lev.19.18.

- bShab 31a reports how Shammai drove away a shameless non-Jew who wanted to become a proselyte if someone could teach him the whole Torah while he was standing on one leg. Thereupon he went to Rabbi Hillel (c.20 BCE), who made him a proselyte and said: 'What you would not want done to

---

[44]Converging Christian traditions of a supreme norm of the law are given by Matt. 7.12 – the Golden Rule, which is similarly called 'the Law and the Prophets' and represents a 'secular' version of Lev. 19.18 – and Matt. 23.23, where κρίσις (law/justice), ἔλεος (mercy) and πίστις (faith/trust) are regarded as the 'most important in the law'. However, both emphases derive from the First Evangelist himself, as the parallels Luke 6.31 and 11.42 show: the Golden Rule appears without further emphasis in the exegesis of the command to love one's enemy; in 11.42 the references (by Luke as redactor?) seems to be to the twofold commandment to love.

you, do not do to your neighbour. That is the whole teaching of the law [= Torah], all the rest is only explanation. Go and learn it.'

Too much emphasis is usually put on the difference between this apophthegm and the Jesus tradition. Certainly here the Golden Rule is thought of as a provisional summary for the purpose of instruction in the whole Torah and not as a replacement for it. But a summary which is intended as teaching is still a summary. Jesus, too, did not regard further explanations of individual questions in addition to the twofold commandment as being superfluous!

• According to SLev 19.18, Rabbi Akiba (died 135 CE) is said to have remarked on the command to love one's neighbour (Lev. 19.18): 'That is a great and comprehensive principle in the Torah' (Bill I, 357). According to ARN B 26 he similarly termed the Golden Rule the 'main rule' of the Torah (in a parallel version to the anecdote attributed above to Hillel).

Certainly R. Akiba probably understood the 'neighbour' to mean only one's fellow-Jew (see below on love of enemy), but there can be no doubting the emphasis on the command to love one's neighbour.

---

3. Finally, there is a series of traditions in which *the relationship to God and solidarity with one's fellow human beings* are combined and occupy an emphatic position in the framework of paraenetic series (Jubilees; Testament of the Twelve Patriarchs) or are even said to be basic teachings of the Torah (Philo).

• In the ethical admonitions handed down in the *book of Jubilees* (second century BCE) which Noah (Jub. 7.20), Abraham (20.2) and Jacob (36.7) entrust to their descendants, love/fear of God and love of neighbour stand side by side. Thus Jacob swears a great oath, the greatest (!): 'That you will fear and worship him [God] and (that) each one will love his brother with compassion and righteousness.'
• In the *Testaments of the Twelve Patriarchs* the twofold commandment to love occurs in paraenetic sequences. Unfortunately, so far the relevant Testaments have not appeared in the Qumran discoveries, so that while a pre-Christian origin of the traditions remains probable, it cannot be proved with certainty.

TestDan 5, 3: 'Throughout your life love the Lord, and one another with a true heart' ('Ἀγαπήσατε τὸν Κύριον ἐν πάσῃ τῇ ζωῇ ὑμῶν καὶ ἀλλήλους ἐν ἀληθινῇ καρδίᾳ).'
    Test Iss 5.1f.: 'Keep the Law of God, my children, achieve integrity; live without malice, not tinkering with God's commands or your neighbour's affairs. Love the

Lord and your neighbour (ἀλλὰ ἀγαπήσατε τὸν κύριον καὶ τὸν πλησίον); be compassionate towards poverty and sickness.' Cf. also TestZeb 5.1 with an explicit extension to all people.

The influence and interlocking of Deut. 6.5 and Lev. 19.18 is shown in the conclusion of the (ideal) biography in TestIss 7.6: 'The Lord I loved with all my strength; likewise, I loved every human being as I love my children (Τὸν Κύριον ἠγάπησα καὶ πάντα ἄνθρωπον ἐξ ὅλης τῆς ἰσχύος [v.l. καρδίας] μου). You do these as well.' Here enormous importance is attached to love of neighbour; they, too, are to be loved 'with all one's strength', like God.

TestJos 11.1 and Test Benj 3.3–5 command fear of God and love of neighbour. The (late) Hebrew TestNaph 1.6 offers a variant with the Golden Rule: 'Him [God] should all his creatures fear and none should do to his neighbour what he does not want to be done to him.'

- Philo, *SpecLeg* II, 63, reports on the 'philosophy' which is taught in synagogue worship on the sabbath: 'And there are so to speak two basic doctrines (δύα τὰ ἀνωτάτω κεφάλαια) to which the numerous individual doctrines and principles are subordinate: in respect of God the command to worship God and piety (τό τε πρὸς θεὸν δι' εὐσεβείας καὶ ὁσιότητος); in respect of human beings the command to love one's fellow men and justice (καὶ τὸ πρὸς ἀνθρώπους διὰ φιλανθρωπίας καὶ δικαιοσύνης). Each of these in turn falls into many, always praiseworthy, sub-divisions.'

The explicit characterization of 'worship of God and piety' alongside 'love of fellow men and justice' as 'two basic teachings of the law (δύα κεφάλαια [νόμου]) is the most carefully thought out adoption of the conception, common to antiquity, of two main groups of duties or virtues (towards God and one's fellow human beings) in Hellenistic Judaism.

- The following statement is attributed to Rabbi Meir (c.150 CE) in the Mishnah tractate Aboth: 'Anyone who occupies himself with the Law for its sake gains for himself many things . . .: he is called friend, beloved [viz. of God], one who loves God and loves the creatures (אוֹהֵב אֶת־הַמָּקוֹם אוֹהֵב אֶת־הַבְּרִיּוֹת), delights God and delights the creatures' (Ab VI, 1).

The creatures (בְּרִיּוֹת) are primarily human beings (cf. the analogous κτίσις in Mark 16.15 and the statement attributed to Hillel: 'Be a disciple of Aaron, loving peace and pursuing peace, loving the creatures and leading them to the Torah', Ab. I, 12). Granted, Ab. VI, 1 does not speak of commandments of the Torah but of the fruits which observing these commandments brings: above all else love of God and of one's fellow human beings!

5.3 The primitive Christian twofold commandment in the framework of Jewish traditions

Synoptic traditions	Jewish traditions
1. The commandments to love God and love one's neighbour are formulated as *direct quotations* from Deut. 6.5 and Lev. 19.18.	1. Admonitions to love God and one's neighbour only refer *indirectly* to Deut. 6.5 and Lev. 19.18.
2. Both quotations are fused only in the mouth of Jewish scribes (Mark; Luke); otherwise they are cited separately.	2. Usually the two commandments are fused and influence one another in wording, e.g. TestIss 5.2; 7.6.
3. The two commandments are numbered (Mark/Matt) and put on the same level (Matt.). Only Mark combines the command to love God with Jewish monotheism as the first commandment.	3. The 'first commandment' is always the obligation to Jewish monotheism. Love of God and love of neighbour appear alongside other commandments in paraenetic sequences.
4. Both commandments are regarded as summaries of the Law (and the Prophets, Matt.). Matthew explicitly emphasizes their summary character. However, for him the Golden Rule is also comparably a summary of Law and Prophets.	4. Summaries of the Torah are attested: • by the Golden Rule or the commandment to love one's neighbour for Palestinian Judaism; • by the two main commandments to worship God and love one's fellow human beings for Hellenistic Judaism (Philo).
5. Love of God and love of neighbour are polemically opposed to the cultic commandments (burnt offerings and whole offerings, Mark).	5. Cultic commandments also appear in paraenetic sequences. For example hearing Yahweh's word (I Sam. 15.22), doing what is just (Prov. 16.7 LXX); prayers and a perfect way of life (IQS IX, 3f.) are put higher than 'burnt offerings and whole offerings'.

As this summary survey shows, the primitive Christian twofold commandment to love is embedded in a broad current of Jewish analogies and yet has a distinct profile of its own. It would be only a small step beyond the different Jewish beginnings to quote the two commandments Deut. 6.(4,)5 and Lev. 19.18 verbally, and explicitly to set them above all other commandments. Here we have an actualizing and a development of what the Jewish traditions about love of God and neighbour already contain. However, as many parallels come from Diaspora Judaism, there is a dispute as to whether the twofold commandment to love can be attributed to Jesus (or the Jesus movement in Palestine) or whether it has been formed by a community in Hellenistic primitive Christianity. Two aspects in particular are ambiguous.

1. The Markan emphasis on monotheism as an answer to the question about the 'first commandment' points to writings from Diaspora Judaism, where it appears in the context of dissociation from a polytheistic environment. Matthew and Luke do not offer a quotation of Deut. 6.4. Is this an indication of a Q version without the *sh^ema* which is a more original tradition and can possibly be attributed to Jesus (thus G. Bornkamm)? Or is the Markan version (with the *sh^ema*) a more original tradition which arose within the sphere of Hellenistic Judaism, so that it cannot go back to Jesus (e.g. C. Burchard)? However, one should remember that first-century Palestine, too, was strongly influenced by Hellenistic culture and that there is good evidence of conflicts over the preservation of the sole rule of God. Thus there are analogous conditions to the situation of Diaspora Judaism, which could also have produced comparable traditions.

2. The consensus between Jesus and the scribe contradicts the typical picture in Mark. The Lukan version, in which the twofold commandment is cited by the Jewish conversation partner as a generally recognized rule, is even more remarkable. Is this an indication of debates over the Law between the historical Jesus and other scribes, of a kind which cannot be imagined later in primitive Christianity; in which agreement over the basic norms was arrived at; and the only issue was the extent of love of neighbour? Since there are numerous Jewish parallels, this is quite conceivable. Or does the assumed consensus point to the mission and apologetic of Hellenistic primitive Christianity, which emphasized the agreement of its teachings with the Jewish Law, rightly understood, and thus sought to attract Jews and their Gentile sympathizers?

3. At all events we should note that the twofold commandment fits well into the rest of Jesus' preaching. The radical theocratic message of the dawn of the kingdom of God does not allow obligations to other masters, and Jesus extended the concern for the neighbour which is called for to the limits of the possible (see below). So if the twofold commandment to love should be secondary, there was good reason for attributing it to Jesus. At all events, it is characteristic of the Jesus tradition that the commandment to love was extended and intensified, so that it explicitly applies to all human beings, especially foreigners, enemies and those

who are declassed and stigmatized as 'sinners' by their religion. There are also comparable approaches in Jewish writings, but the comprehensive opening up of the commandment to love in the Jesus tradition is without analogy.

5.4 The extension of the concept of the neighbour to the alien in the parable of the good Samaritan

The presumably Lukan redactional combination of the twofold commandment and the story of the Good Samaritan (Luke 10.25–28, 29–32) will give Jesus' interpretation of a doctrinal presupposition which is also shared by the Jewish scribe. With the parable of the Good Samaritan, the evangelist wants to depict what is specifically Christian and in so doing is referring back to what is perhaps an authentic parable of Jesus.

1. The composition is distinguished by a striking change of perspective: a question which is appropriate in the context of a Jewish discussion (see 3. below), namely what people are to be regarded as the neighbours who are to be loved (10.29), is turned into the question of what person has proved to be the one who shows love to his neighbour (10.36). It is not enough simply to explain this in literary-critical terms as a consequence of the linking of different sources, since the ethical point evidently lies in this shift of perspective: people are not neighbours (say by being near by or belonging to a particular group); it is their action stamped by love that makes them neighbours.[45]

2. The narrative communicates this notion by deliberate disappointing expectations about a predictable series of figures: after two representatives of the religious élite of Israel have neglected to do their duty as neighbours to a fellow Jew, the logic of the action really requires an upright Jewish layman to take pity on his brother. But the Samaritan, a member of an alien people who were associated with the Jews in a bitter history of enmity, hatred and prejudice, appears in this role of the neighbour. This demonstrates that love of neighbour is conceived of universalistically; it also embraces foreigners or is also practised by foreigners.

3. The extension of the concept of neighbour in the Jesus tradition stands in the context of Jewish discussions about the scope of the term 'neighbour' in Lev.19.18, which there originally meant only members of the people of Israel.

- Leviticus 19.33f. already extends Lev. 19.18 to the alien (גֵּר) living in the land. However, by its translation of גֵּר as προσήλυτος, the LXX limits this to aliens who have come over to Judaism. The majority of the rabbinic examples do the

---

[45]The word-play present here with the expression γίνομαι πλησίον τινός = 'come near to someone [in a spatial sense]' in which πλησίον could also be understood as an adjective which has become a noun (become a *neighbour*) instead of the usual adverbial adjective (come *near*) is also conceivable in Aramaic (רע = next, neighbour; רעה = join oneself to).

same thing: only the 'righteous alien' (גֵּר צֶדֶק) is to be loved.[46]

- In Hellenistic Judaism (Philo, Testaments of the Twelve Patriarchs, etc.) the concept of neighbour and love of neighbour were interpreted universalistically by adopting the basic Stoic conviction of a nature common to all human beings. It follows from the order of creation that every human being loves or should love his neighbour by nature. Sirach 13.15 LXX: 'Every animal loves its like and every man his neighbour' (πᾶν ζῷον ἀγαπᾷ τὸ ὅμοιον αὐτῷ καὶ πᾶς ἄνθρωπος τὸν πλησίον αὐτοῦ).'

- There were probably also the beginnings of a universalistic understanding in rabbinic Judaism with reference to the creatureliness of all human beings, but this is disputed by scholars. The debate carried on between Rabbi Akiba and Ben Azzai about the status of Lev. 19.18 may serve as an example of the subordination of love of neighbour limited to fellow-Jews to a general love of others: whereas Akiba calls Lev. 19.18, which has already been mentioned, the basic rule of the Torah, Ben Azzai retorts that Gen. 5.1 (the creation of the human being in the image of God) is a greater basic rule.[47] According to A. Nissen (*Gott*, 400ff.), it may by no means be assumed that the two main rules are intended to interpret each other, so that Ben Azzai meant that each human being is to be loved as the image of God. However, the earliest rabbinic commentary on the debate understood it in precisely that way, by weaving the two principles together and subordinating respect for the image of God to the principle of mutuality: 'You shall not say: because I have been despised, my neighbour may also be despised like me.'[48] R. Tanchuma said: 'If you act like that, know that you despise the one who has been made in the image of God.'[49]

Reference might be made once again to the saying about love of creatures (= human beings including the Gentiles) mentioned on p. 386 above. So in Palestinian Judaism, too, there were the beginnings of a universalistic understanding which Jesus could have taken up.

5.5 The extension of love of neighbour in the commandment to love one's enemy

L. Schottroff, *Four Essays on the Love Command*, Philadelphia 1978; G. Theissen, 'Nonviolence and Love of Our Enemies' (1979), in *Social Reality**.

---

[46]Cf. A. Nissen, *Gott und der Nächste im antiken Judentum*, WUNT 15, Tübingen 1974, 278–304; Bill. I, 353ff.

[47]SLev 19.18 [89b] and par.; cf. Bill I, 358f.; Nissen, *Gott* (n.46), 400ff.

[48]The Golden Rule which glimmers through here was common among the rabbis as an interpretation of Lev. 19.18; cf. M. Hengel, 'Zur matthäischen Bergpredigt und ihrem jüdischen Hintergrund', *ThR* 52, 1987, 390–5.

[49]GenR 24, 7 on 5.1, quoted in Nissen, *Gott* (n.46), 402; cf. *Wünsche* I, 112.

Whereas there is still a dispute as to whether the parable of the Good Samaritan can be attributed to Jesus, the Q tradition worked on in Matt. 5.38–48 and Luke 6.27–36 about love of enemies is generally regarded as authentic. The common element in the tradition, which goes back to Q, includes an *admonition*, preserved in the plural imperative, to love one's enemies (plural) and to pray for persecutors (Matt. 5.44; Luke 6.27f.). Four reasons are given for this:

1. A *comparison* with an attitude of mutuality which is practised by toll collectors and Gentiles or sinners and from which it is important to differentiate oneself (Matt. 5.46f.; Luke 6.32–34).

2. The *promise* of being a child of God, a status traditionally reserved for kings and wise men, which will be gained through the practice of love of enemies (in a way corresponding to the concept of the son of God in wisdom, Matt. 5.45) or as an eschatological reward (Luke 6.35).

3. A *foundation* in the behaviour of God, who gives his good things (like sun and rain) to all human beings (Matt. 5.45), or is gracious even towards the ungrateful and the wicked (Luke 6.35).

4. A direct *call* to imitate God, to be perfect or merciful 'like your Father' (Matt. 5.48; Luke 6.36).

The substance of the *logia about the renunciation of retribution*, which Luke cites as concrete examples of the love of enemies (6.29f.), was also already there in Q; by contrast Matthew has developed this into an antithesis which is sparked off by the Old Testament *ius talionis* and has inserted it before love of the enemy (5.38–42). In addition to suffering injustice without retaliation, they require a paradoxical reaction, namely to give the enemy more than he asks.

> The presentation in the form of antitheses by which the opposition to the Jewish tradition is emphasized is the most characteristic feature of the Matthaean redaction. By inserting the Golden Rule, which was widespread in antiquity (6.31), Luke emphasizes the universalistic feature of the command to love one's enemy and takes up current Hellenistic ethical terminology (καλῶς ποιεῖν, ἀγαθοποιεῖν/do good: 6.27, 33, 35; χάρις/gratitude: 6.32, 33, 34).

1. *The recipients of love of enemies*. Which enemies are to be loved? The requirement to love one's enemy does not apply just to the private enemy , but all enemies, including religious opponents and political oppressors:

- The double plural in the admonition 'love your enemies' sets groups against each other. This is striking, because the Old Testament-Jewish forerunners in casuistic law and wisdom are in the singular (cf. e.g. Ex. 23.4f.: If your enemy's ox or ass has strayed . . .; Prov. 25.21f.: If your enemy is hungry . . .).
- The means of persecuting and maltreating the supporters of Jesus lay with political and religious authorities like the temple aristocracy, the Roman authorities and the magistrates of the Hellenistic cities.

- Matt. 5.41 gives as a concrete political example the ἀγγαρεύειν, a technical term for the compulsory state service often exacted by soldiers (e.g. Mark 15.21!). Even in such an instance of state arbitrariness, to the mile which is forced on a person, a second mile should be willingly added.

2. *The subject of love of the enemy.* Who should love enemies? In non-Christian antiquity, admonitions to renounce retribution and calls to recompense evil with good and to further the prosperity even of enemies are addressed above all to three groups of persons. Accordingly three different settings should be emphasized:

- *Slaves* and other dependent persons are advised not to take vengeance for injustice with a reference to their lack of power (e.g. Seneca, *Ira* II 33, 2).
- The *powerful* should renounce vengeance, unexpectedly do good to opponents, and make their enemies their friends. *Clementia*/ἐπιείκεια(gentleness) is a ruler's virtue which is often propagated; it also served as a model in other asymmetrical relationships (e.g. that of the *paterfamilias* to the slaves and members of the family who were dependent on him). Here the graciousness of the king or others in power is explicitly evaluated as *imitatio dei.*

That is attested in Hellenistic Judaism by the Letter of Aristeas: because God rules the world graciously and without anger, the king too should rule his subjects without anger (254). Because God is gracious, the king should not punish the guilty harshly (188). He should be merciful, since God too is merciful (108).

   Seneca *On Benefits* IV, 26, 1; 28.1: '"If you are imitating the gods," you say, "then bestow benefits also upon the ungrateful. For the sun rises also upon the wicked, and the sea lies open also to pirates." "A king gives honours to those who are worthy and gifts to those who are unworthy; the thief and the perjurer and the adulterer alike receive the public distribution of grain . . ." '[50]

- It is reported and required of numerous *philosophers* (above all Socrates, cf. Plato, *Crito* 49Aff.) that in principle they refused to couter the injustice of others with injustice and showed benevolence towards the unworthy and their enemies. Epictetus says of the Cynic: 'He must needs be flogged like an ass and while he is being flogged he must love the man who flogs him, as though he were the father or brother of them all' (δέρεσθαι αὐτὸν δεῖ ὡς ὄνον καὶ δερόμενον φιλεῖν αὐτοὺς τοὺς δέροντας ὡς πατέρα πάντων, ὡς ἀδελφόν', *Discourses* 3, 22, 54).

3. *The distinctive feature of the Jesus tradition.* In the light of the contemporary parallels cited above, the distinctive feature of the Jesus tradition proves to be

---

[50]Quoted in M.E. Boring, K. Berger and C. Colpe (eds.), *Hellenistic Commentary to the NT*, Nashville 1995, 197.

that the imitation of God usually required of kings and the powerful is called for in the form of generosity and renunciation of power on the part of those who are powerless, persecuted and humiliated. The sovereignty which elsewhere is attributed only to philosophers is expected of all those who follow Jesus. Not only are they to suffer injustice without complaining; they are even to get used to loving it, and thus to break up the relationship between mutual utility and love characterized by group egotism, excluding all others. The values of the upper class are appropriated by little people and transformed. As sons and daughters of God they act with the self-confidence and autonomy of the rulers and the wise; not, however, as those who are dominated and isolated, but as members of the 'family of God' which is living in the dawn of the kingdom of God. The behaviour required by Jesus is not a passive surrender to evil, but an active, non-violent resistance of the powerless with the aim of showing up injustice and overcoming it. In the face of national enemies there is clearly an alternative to the Zealot concept of resistance and apocalyptic fantasies of the final battle, which was by no means unique. The non-violent resistance of the Jewish masses was successful in the face of Pilate's attempt to set up standards with effigies of the emperor in Jerusalem (*BJ* 2, 169–174) and in the conflict over the erection of a statue of Caligula in the temple in 39 CE (*Antt.* 18.271f., quoted above, p. 182).

5.6 The extension of love of neighbour in Jesus' encounter with the outcasts

An investigation of the scope of love of neighbour in the Jesus tradition would be incomplete without a dimension which markedly shaped his behaviour: his concern for those who were discounted by Jewish society, his friendship with 'toll collectors and sinners' which became proverbial at an early stage. Early traditions attest this behaviour and its potential for conflict (Luke 7.31–35; Matt. 11.16–19 Q; Mark 2.15–17); in Luke in particular there are further traditions which illustrate it convincingly (without necessarily being historical in every detail).

1. *Those to whom love is directed.* Just as the extension of love of neighbour to foreigners goes beyond the external limits of society, so the demonstrative concern of Jesus for 'sinners' goes beyond the devaluation and exclusion of particular groups of people within society (e.g. 'toll collectors and sinners', Luke 7.34 Q; 'toll collectors and prostitutes', Matt. 21.31; 'robbers, cheats, adulterers and toll collectors', Luke 18.11) to whom 'one' feels morally superior and social contacts with whom one avoids as far as possible. By contrast, when Jesus enters the house of a toll collector and eats with notorious sinners (Mark 2.15), or quite publicly tolerates bodily contact with a prostitute known throughout the city (Luke 7.37–39), this amounts to including in the community of neighbours these people who have been excluded.

2. *The subject of love.* The outcasts appear not only as those towards whom

love is directed but also as those who for their part practise love towards their neighbours on the basis of the love that is shown them: Jesus understands the anointing and contact by the woman as signs of love and gestures of hospitality (more generous than those of the real host, Luke 7.44–47); Zacchaeus – and not the rich ruler in Luke 18.18ff. who fulfils the Law perfectly in every respect – gives half his possessions to the poor (Luke 19.8).

3. As in the case of loving one's enemies, *the theological reason* for including sinners among the neighbours who are to be loved lies in God's example; it is the human response in keeping with God's forgiveness (Luke 7.41ff.).

6. Summary and hermeneutical reflections

Jesus' ethic is a Jewish ethic. It is an expression of that heightened 'ethical sensitivity' which we can trace in the writings of contemporary Judaism.[51] The centre of its content lies in the Torah, interpreted freely, and its motivating framework is that of wisdom and eschatology. Jesus presents it as a Jewish rabbi.

The Torah is its basis. As in any system of norms and regulations, one can distinguish between 'letter' and 'spirit' in it; i.e. on the one hand the concrete precepts for behaviour and on the other the axioms and maxims which underlie it – or, in the language of the Torah itself, the will of God. Jesus stands on the ground of the Torah by formulating ethical norms from the axioms and maxims of the Torah which are sometimes in tension with the literal statements of the Torah and its contemporary exegesis. He could use 'scripture' instrumentally – not because he was independent of it but because he took individual passages of scripture into 'service' in the light of its basic convictions. He could distinguish between what was important and what was unimportant. The commandment to love God and neighbour was the most important for him. The unimportant commandments included those relating to cleanness; here he did not even share the underlying 'maxim' that there was external uncleanness which brought ritual separation from God. Here he abrogates a maxim of the Torah by an even more important (implicit) axiom, which has the relationship to God governed by the will of God and human beings and not by reified qualities. But here, too, he does not draw any conclusions about an abolition of the concrete norms of purity. They are unimportant but valid; however, they can be broken in particular instances. Such offences against norms are sometimes connected with his existence as a homeless itinerant charismatic: as a rule the step into discipleship was a break with the parental home and could be combined with an offence against the

---

[51]D. Flusser, 'Neue Sensibilität im Judentum und Christliche Botschaft', in id., *Bemerkungen eines Juden zur christlichen Theologie*, Munich 1984, 350.

command to honour one's parents. The sabbath commandment could not always be observed consistently when travelling, as is shown by the incident of the disciples rubbing ears of corn. The distinction between clean and unclean foods was irrelevant to the hungry 'charismatic beggars'. Jesus did not elevate such minor transgressions of the Law into a universal norm for all (to 'halakah'). It is possible, but not completely certain, that he had such a halakah in mind with his prohibition against remarriage and oaths.

Two tensions run through this ethic of Jesus which is grounded in a free relationship to the Law. First is the tension between statements which intensify the Law and those which relax it, between rigorism and laxism, strictness and accept-ance. Radical ethical norms which were provocative for Jesus' contemporaries are formulated in both directions. Nevertheless, the intention of this radical ethic is one of integration. On the one hand, in an outward direction it seeks to safeguard Jewish identity by intensifying the norms of the Torah, and on the other, in an inward direction it seeks to integrate outcast and marginalized groups by relaxing the Torah. Therefore the commandment to love stands at the centre: in an outward direction, as love of enemies it is to distinguish the followers of Jesus from the 'Gentiles'; and at the same time, in an inward direction, it is to lead to the acceptance of the weak and sinners in a concern for the outcast. The will of God thus formulated is reinforced, and its content is expounded, with motives from wisdom and eschatology.

Here we find a second basic tension in the ethics of Jesus, the tension between a wisdom-type orientation on the abiding structures of creation and the eschato-logical expectation of a world which will soon be transformed. Wisdom-type images from creation and life – particularly in the parables – become an expression of the will of God. Experience becomes transparent to the human situation before the God of grace who makes demands. Here the issue is always that of the motivation of ethical conduct. The same is true of eschatology: through it the ethical behaviour of the individual becomes participation in the great transforma-tion of the world. By doing righteousness and showing love, people take the first step into the kingdom of God. The behaviour of the individual corresponds to the transformation of the cosmos on a large scale: by changing behaviour and changing criteria – especially towards the weak, the stigmatized and outcast. Thus through motives from wisdom and eschatology the whole of reality, creation, life and the goal of history, become the expression of the ethical will of God. The God of Jesus – like the God of the Old Testament – is a blazing fire of ethical energy which glows through all things and which either embraces and changes human beings as love or confronts them in the form of 'hell fire' with a life which has gone wrong for ever. Confrontation with this tremendous ethical energy in the words of Jesus in real life immediately raises the questions: Can this ethic be practised at all? Does it not ask too much of people?

The radical nature of Jesus' ethic has prompted a wealth of theories in the history of exegesis. Some are intended to make it 'livable' in some way and some to give it a sense which takes account of the impossibility of fulfilling it, but also often only to make it understandable in its historical context independently of any application to the present. The problem is usually discussed under the heading 'the hermeneutics of the Sermon the Mount', although the demands of the mission discourse (Matt. 10), the pericope about the rich young man (Matt. 19.16–30) and the saying about not being married (Matt. 19.10–12) play just as important a role in it as the Sermon on the Mount itself. The first of the interpretations sketched out below focus on the relativizing of the strict commandments.

1. *The distinction between* praecepta *and* consilia evangelica *in the mediaeval two-level ethics.* The *praecepta* (commandments), which consist largely of the Ten Commandments apply to all, but the *consilia evangelica* (gospel counsels) of poverty, chastity and obedience apply only to a few, to monks and nuns. By fulfilling the *consilia* one can acquire special merit (*opera superogatoria*). The two-level ethic has beginnings in the New Testament (cf. Matt. 19.21) and in the Didache: 'If you can bear the whole yoke of the Lord, you will be perfect. But if you cannot, observe what you can' (Did. 6.2). The classic form of this doctrine is to be found in Thomas Aquinas *(Summa Theologica* 1, 9; 107, 2; 108, 4).

2. *The distinction between an ethic of office and an ethic of person in Martin Luther.* According to this, the radical demands of Jesus do not apply to public and political life: as the representative of an office (as a politician, judge, teacher, etc.), the Christian must use power in the interest of others and establish justice in the face of resistance. But when it is a matter only of his own interests, if he is addressed as a private person, then the Christian is to renounce resistance, suffer injustice and practise unconditional love. Thus he acts differently within God's two realms. The fulfilling of radical and 'realistic' commandments is not divided into two groups here, but transferred to the individual – depending on the role in which he is acting.[52]

3. *The distinction between conviction and (time-conditioned) concretion in liberal theology.* A modern conception of this 'internalization' of the tension between the radical nature of an ethic and the possibility of living it out is the reduction of Jesus' ethic to a matter of conviction: only that which is done as the result of good convictions is good. So the commandments of Jesus are not meant to be fulfilled to the letter but in accordance with their inner spirit: they seek to shape the basic convictions by which we act. In this respect they are valid timelessly. By contrast, the concrete demands are historically conditioned. The classical representative of this position is W. Herrmann.[53] An existentialist variant

---

[52]The classical account of the distinction between an ethic of the office and an ethic of the person is Luther's *Secular Authority: To What Extent It Should Be Obeyed* (1523).

[53]Cf. W. Herrmann. 'Die sittlichen Weisungen Jesu. Ihr Missbrauch und ihr richtiger Gebrauch' (1904, ²1907), in id., *Schriften zur Grundlegung der Theologie* I, 1966, 200–41.

is Bultmann's view that the ethic of Jesus brings to light the 'absolute character of the divine demand' (*Jesus**, 74), which makes people face the existential decision whether or not they will put all their actions under the claim of love. This basic decision is more important than the concrete content of individual commandments.

The types of exegesis sketched out so far all start from the presupposition that the significance of Jesus' ethic lies in the fact that it is realized – at least by some monks, at least by Christians as private individuals, at least in convictions. Since the Reformation, alongside this, types of exegesis have arisen which attribute an 'indicative' sense to this ethic – despite the imperative form. It is argued that the 'Sermon on the Mount' focusses on statements about sinful human beings, about Christ and the new person.

4. *The radical ethic of Jesus as the accusing use of the Law*, which discloses the human need for redemption. Luther already regarded the Sermon on the Mount as a law which cannot be fulfilled. This line was continued in Lutheran orthodoxy. The demands of Jesus which cannot be fulfilled disclose human sin and create a longing for the gospel: 'For because the mere preaching of the Law without Christ either makes people who think that they can fulfil the law with outward works perplexed, or drives them utterly to despair, so Christ takes the Law into his own hands and interprets the same spiritually, in Matt. 5, Rom. 7, and thus reveals his "wrath from heaven" upon all sinners, however great they be, so that they are instructed in the law and from the same learn to know their sins even more . . .' (FC V, 10). M. Hengel stands in this tradition when he attributes to the Sermon on the Mount the significance of destroying 'any possibility of human self-righteousness'.[54]

5. *The radical ethic of Jesus as a christological statement about Jesus as the one who brings in the kingdom of God*. According to E. Thurneysen,[55] Christ is not only the author of the Sermon on the Mount but also its subject: only in him are the radical commandments of the Sermon on the Mount fulfilled: 'The christology of the Sermon on the Mount consists in the fact that in it Jesus is depicted as the one who brings the messianic kingdom with its new righteousness.' Thus the Sermon on the Mount becomes Jesus' pointer to himself. In contrast to the old Lutheran teaching that the Sermon on the Mount holds up a mirror to human sin, here the focus is not on a negative statement about the old person, but on a positive statement about the new person who has become reality in Christ. Therefore the interpretation of the Sermon on the Mount is related to indicative statements about the new person generally.

---

[54]M. Hengel, 'Leben in der Veränderung. Ein Beitrag zum Verständnis der Bergpredigt', *EK* 3, 1970, 647–61: 50.

[55]E. Thurneysen, *Die Bergpredigt*, TEH 46, Munich 1936; the quotation comes from p.14.

6. *The radical ethic of Jesus as an eschatological statement about life in the kingdom of God.* According to Dibelius, the sayings of Jesus are 'signs of the kingdom of God'.[56] They cannot all be fulfilled in this world, but they do point to a new world. An eschatological renewal of relations with God is promised for this world – above all that God's law will be written on human hearts (cf. Jer. 31.33; 32.40; Ezek. 36.26f.). Human beings will then do God's will spontaneously: 'The written Law with its character of compromise and its half-measures will then be superfluous, since then it will no longer be necessary to wring the minimum of social behaviour necessary for life in the community out of recalcitrant people by prohibitions and threats. Jesus is telling his disciples about these innovations. Their behaviour is to be a sign of the rule of God within the old world which is coming to an end.'[57]

In the case of the indicative (re-)interpretation of the Sermon on the Mount – as a hamartiological statement about the old person, as a christological statement about Jesus, or as an eschatological statement about the new person, doubtless 'reflection on the position in which the Sermon on the Mount places us has been confused here with the exposition of the words themselves' (Bornkamm, *Jesus**, 224). A series of expositions therefore attempts first to understand the radical quality of the sayings of Jesus in terms of their historical context – often with the consequence (which is not necessarily intended) that the obligation it places on the present seems to be put in question.

7. *The view of Jesus' ethic as an 'interim ethic' which is explicable in terms of the exceptional situation of the imminence of the end of the world.* J. Weiss interprets Jesus' ethic in the context of the imminent expectation. There is no thought of an ethical system which could regulate the interests of a community for centuries: 'Just as emergency laws come into force in a war which could not be enacted in times of peace, so too this part of the ethical preaching of Jesus has a special character. It demands tremendous, in part superhuman, things; it calls for things which would be simply impossible under ordinary circumstances.'[58] Schweitzer (*Quest**, 352) coined the term 'interim ethic' for this. He regarded the notion of an imminent end of the world combined with this ethic as time-conditioned; but the ethical will expressed in it was the basis of his Christianity.

8. *The view that Jesus' ethic can be explained as the expression of a radical itinerant charismatic life.* The 'thoroughgoing eschatological' interpretation of Jesus' ethic makes it appear as a series of demands alien to the world which have

---

[56]M. Dibelius, *The Sermon on the Mount*, New York 1940.

[57]J. Roloff, *Neues Testament*, Neukirchen ⁴1985, 115.

[58]Cf. *Jesus' Preaching of the Kingdom of God*, 105; however, the actual quotation comes from the untranslated second edition, *Die Predigt Jesus vom Reich Gottes*, Göttingen 1900, 139.

no 'Sitz im Leben' in this world. The question is whether this radical ethic could not have been represented credibly from the very beginning in marginal groups – just as in the course of church history it has been represented more credibly by religious orders, Anabaptists, Mennonites, Quakers and other special groups than by the mainstream churches. If we regard Jesus and his disciples as a group with socially deviant behaviour which went through Palestine without the ties and limitations of everyday professional and family life, the radical nature of Jesus' ethic seems capable of being lived out (thus Theissen, 'Wandering Radicals'*). It becomes irrelevant for today only if one thinks that minorities with deviant behaviour are 'irrelevant' to society as a whole.

There is an element of truth in all of these hermeneutical attempts at appropriation. Ethical statements usually have a concrete *Sitz im Leben*, a context into which they fit better than into other contexts, even if they are formulated in a universal and timeless way. A radical ethic is doubtless meant to be an exposition of the will of God which is valid timelessly. But it will always be a direct orientation for individuals, groups and persons who are ready to assume a marginal role in our society. However, precisely in that way indirectly it can become a guideline for all: it obliges everyone to create a society of such a kind that at least some have the chance of realizing such a radical ethic. To this degree it also has a political significance. The Defence Minister will hardly act in accordance with the slogan 'Do not resist evil', nor will the Finance Minister act in accordance with the slogan 'Take no thought . . .', or the Justice Minister in accordance with the slogan, 'Judge not, that you be not judged!' But all can be committed to and work for a society in which there is room for the conscientious objector, for those who adopt an ascetic life-style in protest against the consumer society, and for the 'meek' who renounce their rights to living space – indeed a society in which there is room for whole groups who want to put into practice the strict ethic of Jesus (or a comparable morality). It is correct to distinguish between an ethic of office and an ethic of person. That makes it possible to deal responsibility with compulsion – while at the same time maintaining an awareness of the ethical inadequacy of compulsion. But the use of compulsion and the implementation of the law is only part of the ethic of office – with it goes the responsibility to create spheres in life in which a demonstrative renunciation of compulsion, of precautions, of the implementation of the law becomes possible. Certainly at first only for individuals and minorities. But this has an effect on everyone: a society with space for radical ethical minorities is more humane than any other. And all are dependent on ethical minorities with divergent life-styles. For they are the ones who will re-establish the ethical norms which are compromised in everyday life and have sufficient sensitivity to the good not to be worn down by everyday cynicism. There remains the structural contradiction between the principles of such an ethic and concrete forms of behaviour which can be achieved by all. But such a contradiction, too, is ethically productive. The 'awareness of sins' which develops here on the one hand creates a sense of solidarity: all fail in what they affirm in their innermost depths. The awareness of falling fundamentally short of what one recognizes as an obligation is a presupposition for an understanding treatment of other people when they go wrong. And on the other hand, an awareness of sin is a moral pain which, like any physical pain, has an important function in life. It warns of the need for a change in behaviour – even where that is not possible at the moment. An awareness of sins is 'evolutionary pain', an indication that the world, too, must be structurally different if elementary norms are to be realized. That a fifth of the population of the world has more than four-fifths of its resources is a morally untenable position. The 'pain' at such a situation must be kept alive and must time and again lead to new programmes of action. For over and above what we can do, ethics is also an orientation of what we hope for: a sign of the future – just as in the case of Jesus it is a sign of the kingdom of God.

Thus in its radical nature, but also in its combination of radicalism with a readiness for reconciliation, the ethic of Jesus remains one of the ethical 'basic texts' of human culture.

7. Tasks

7.1 Jesus' education

The story of the twelve-year-old Jesus in the temple is usually regarded as a legend without a historical nucleus, because it is an example of a theme widespread in antiquity, that of the gifted hero who already shows amazing proofs of his knowledge in his youth. The story was told of famous generals, philosophers and religious leaders like Cyrus, Cambyses, Alexander, Epicurus, Apollonius, Moses, Solomon, Samuel and David.[59] Riesner, *Jesus*, 135, however, defends the historicity of the pericope, referring to the autobiography of Josephus (*Vita* 8–9, see below). Compare Luke 2.41–51 with the following two accounts of Moses' youth and Josephus's autobiographical account, and decide on the historical reliability of Luke 2.41ff. in the light of these parallels.

Philo on the young Moses (*VitMos* I, 21):

> 'Teachers at once arrived from different parts, some unbidden from the neighbouring countries and the provinces of Egypt, others summoned from Greece under promise of high reward. But in a short time he advanced beyond their capacities; his gifted nature forestalled their instruction, so that his seemed a case rather of recollection than of learning, and indeed he himself devised and propounded problems that they could not easily solve.'

---

[59]Cf. the commentaries on Luke 2.41ff. and H.J. de Jonge, 'Sonship, Wisdom, Infancy. Lk 2, 41–51a', *NTS* 24, 1977/78, 317–54, esp. 322–4, 339–42.

Josephus on Moses (*Antt.* 2, 230):

'His growth in understanding was not in line with his growth in stature, but far outran the measure of his years; its maturer excellence was displayed in his very games, and his actions then gave promise of the greater deeds to to be wrought by him on reaching manhood.'

Josephus on himself (*Vita*, 8–9):

'Brought up with Matthias, my own brother, by both parents, I made great progress with my education, gaining a reputation for an excellent memory and understanding. While still a mere boy, about fourteen years old, I won universal applause for my love of letters: in so much that the chief priest and the leading men used constantly to come to me for precise information on some particular in our ordinances.'

7.2 *Jesus' ethic as a protest against Jewish legalism?*

Make a critical comment on the following paragraph from Bultmann's *Theology* 1*, by identifying the stereotyped notions of 'Jewish legalism' which appear here and checking whether they are justified:

'As interpretation of the will, the demand, of God, Jesus' message is a great *protest against Jewish legalism – i.e.* against a form of piety which regards the will of God as expressed in the written Law and in the tradition which interprets it, a piety which endeavours to win God's favour by the toil of minutely fulfilling the Law's stipulations . . . The real result is that motivation to ethical conduct is vitiated. That is the result not only in the wide extent to which the idea of reward and punishment becomes the motivation, but also – and this is the characteristic thing for Judaism – that the obedience man owes to one, i.e. as an obedience which fulfils the letter of the law, obeying a law simply because it is commanded without asking the reason, the meaning, of its demand . . .

    The error of Jewish legalism reveals itself finally in the following. A statute, unlike an ethical demand, can never embrace every specific situation of life; instead there inevitably remain many cases unprovided for, cases for which there is no command or prohibition; that leaves room not only for every desire and passion that may arise but also – and that again is characteristic of Judaism – for works of supererogation. In principle, when a man's duties are conceived of as the committing or omitting of specific acts under legal requirement, he can completely discharge them and have room left over for extra deeds of merit. So there developed in Judaism the notion of "good works" that go beyond the required fulfilment of the Law (such as almsgiving.

> various acts of charity, voluntary fasting, and the like), establishing literal merits and hence also capable of atoning for transgressions of the Law. This indicates that here the idea of obedience is not taken radically' (11f.).

7.3 Religion and concern for one's daily bread

The Mishnah hands down the following saying of R. Simon b. Eleazar:

> 'Have you ever seen a wild animal or a bird practising a craft – yet they have their sustenance without care, and were they not created for nothing else but to serve me? But I was created to serve my Maker. How much more then ought I to have my sustenance without care' (Kidd. IV, 14). The Babylonian Talmud adds by way of explanation, 'as it is written: your sins hinder (Jer. 5.25)'.

Compare this argument with Matt. 6.24–34 and collect common features and differences. How can these be explained?

7.4 Jesus' ethic and the Essenes

So far there has been little mention of one Jewish group about whose relationship to Jesus there has recently been a good deal of discussion. So far no satisfactory explanation has been given of the silence of the primitive Christian sources about this group. Possibly there were no Essenes in Galilee. It could also be that they were seen as a group of scribes or Pharisees, or that they deliberately did not get entangled in discussions with outsiders. At all events, Essene traditions were known in Palestine in the time of Jesus. For some logia of Jesus show a closeness to texts which have (also) been found in Qumran and probably present originally Essene notions. Here are three examples relating to ethics.

> 'They shall be caught in fornication twice by taking a second wife while the first is alive, whereas the principle of creation is, Male and female created he them (Gen. 1.27). Also, those who entered the Ark went in two by two. And concerning the prince it is written, He shall not multiply wives to himself (Deut. 17.17)' (CD IV, 20 – V, 2).

Compare this text with Mark 10.2–12.

> 'Concerning the Sabbath to observe it according to its law: No man shall work on the sixth day . . . for this is what He said, Observe the sabbath day to keep it holy (Deut. 5.12) . . . No man shall walk in the field to do business on the sabbath. He shall not walk more than one thousand cubits beyond his town. No man shall eat on the sabbath day except that which is already prepared. He shall eat nothing lying in the fields . . . He shall

not drink except in the camp . . . No man shall carry perfumes [another translation is medicines] on himself whilst going and coming on the sabbath . . . No man shall assist a beast to give birth on the sabbath day. And if it should fall into a cistern or pit, he shall not lift it out on the sabbath . . . But should any man fall into water or fire, let him be pulled out with the aid of a ladder or rope or (some such) utensil . . . No man who strays so as to profane the sabbath and the feasts shall be put to death; it shall fall to men to keep him in custody. And if he is healed of his error, they shall keep him in custody for seven years and he shall afterwards approach the assembly' (CD X, 14f., 16f., 20–23; XI, 9f., 13f., 16f.; XII, 3–5).

Cf. also Josephus, *BJ* 2, 147: '. . . they abstain from seventh-day work more rigidly than any other Jews; for not only do they prepare their meals the previous day so as to avoid lighting a fire on the sabbath, but they do not venture to remove any utensil or to go and ease themselves.'

Compare these texts of Essene sabbath halakhah with Luke 14.1–6; Luke 13.10–17; Mark 3.1–6.

[The 'Community Rule' requires] 'that they may seek God . . . and do what is good and right before Him, as He commanded by the hand of Moses and all His servants the Prophets; that they may love all that He has chosen and hate all that he has rejected; that they may abstain from all evil and hold fast to all good; that they . . . admit into the Covenant of Grace all those who have freely devoted themselves to the observance of God's precepts, that they may be joined to the counsel of God and may live perfectly before Him in accordance with all that has been revealed concerning their appointed times, and that they may love all the sons of light, each according to his lot in God's design, and hate all the sons of darkness, each according to his guilt in God's vengeance' (1 QS I, 1–5, 7–11).

Cf. also Josephus, *BJ* 2, 139: on entering the order the Essenes swear terrible oaths, etc., 'always to hate the wicked and co-operate with the good'.

Compare these texts with Matt. 5.43–48/Luke 6.27–28, 32–36.

Part Four: Passion and Easter

13

Jesus as the Founder of a Cult: The Last Supper and the Primitive Christian Eucharist

C. Burchard, 'The Importance of Joseph and Aseneth for the Study of the New Testament: A General Survey and a Fresh Look at the Lord's Supper', *NTS* 33, 1987, 102–34; J.D. Crossan, *Jesus**; H. Gese, 'The Origin of the Lord's Supper', in *Essays on Biblical Theology*, Minneapolis 1981; J. Jeremias, *The Eucharistic Words of Jesus*, London and New York ²1966; D. Rensberger, *Overcoming the World*, Philadelphia 1988 and London 1989.

Introduction

The origin of religious rituals usually lies back in the mists of time. If one had asked ancient people why they offered sacrifices to God, they would have had only one answer: 'Because our ancestors have always done so.' By contrast, primitive Christianity developed new 'rituals'. With baptism it made a washing – which was usually merely a preparation for the ritual proper – the central rite of initiation. It replaced the centuries-old tradition of bloody sacrifices with the Lord's supper, a simple meal with a highly theological significance. Neither sacrament was derived from an age-old prehistory but from very recent history: baptism from John the Baptist and the Lord's supper from Jesus. Neither claimed legitimacy as tradition but as innovation. Both took on new significance by being related to the death of Jesus: baptism originally gave protection from the last judgment: it was an eschatological sacrament. It became baptism into the death of Jesus, being buried with Christ (Rom. 6.1ff.) in a new post-Easter interpretation. There is perhaps an analogous development with the eucharist: the meals which the historical Jesus held were a foretaste of the great eschatological meal. Possibly after the death of Jesus it was reinterpreted as a representation of his dying – but not everywhere. For in the Didache (chs.9–10) we find a sacramental meal with no reference to the death of Jesus and in John 13 a report of Jesus' last supper without the institution of a sacramental meal related to his death. The historical problem of Jesus' last supper lies in discovering the role it plays in this development. What contribution did it make to the origin of the primitive Christian 'sacrament'?

If we are to be able to understand this question we must define precisely what we mean by a 'sacrament'. Not every sacral meal is a sacramental meal, and not every presence is the sacramental presence of a deity. Rather, there are at least three forms of a 'presence' of the deity which are *pre-sacramental*:

1. *Personal presence*: the deity is present at the meal as host and guest – in a way comparable to the other participants.

2. *Presence in the memory*: the fate of the deity is represented by holding the meal. The deity is (mentally) present in the spirit of the participants.

3. *Symbolic presence*: the meal is a parable or a symbol of the fate of the deity or its (personal) presence.

One can speak of a *sacramental meal* only if natural elements of a meal are prepared in such a way that they have a supernatural saving effect which they would not have had without being shaped by ritual.[1] That is the case in the following three forms of a deity's presence:

4. *Social presence*: the community becomes identical with the deity in a mysterious way through the holding of the meal: for example, it becomes the 'body of Christ'.

5. *Causal presence*: as the one who provides the elements of the meal the deity gives them a supernatural character: they become 'spiritual food' which communicates salvation.

6. *Real presence*: the deity is itself present in the elements. The supernatural 'substance' of the deity is consumed in, with and under the substance of the meal.

Tasks: 1. Forms of the presence of Christ

Define the precise form of the 'presence' of Christ in the following texts on the eucharist. Here different versions of the forms of presence mentioned above can appear combined: I Cor. 10.3f.; I Cor. 10.16f.; I Cor. 11.25; John 6.51–58.

2. The eucharist in the Didache

Compare the text on the eucharist from the Didache quoted below with the Synoptic and Pauline texts on the eucharist and note at least three important differences:

---

[1]Cf. Burchard, 'Importance', 117: 'A sacrament is a special rite in which supernatural gifts are mediated through natural external means which are often prepared in a special way to have the power they lack in ordinary use.'

9. [1]And concerning the eucharist, hold eucharist thus:

[2]First, concerning the cup: We give thanks to you, our Father, for the holy vine of David your child, which you made known to us through Jesus your child. To you be glory for ever.

[3]And concerning the broken bread: We give you thanks, our Father, for the life and knowledge which you made known to us through Jesus your child. To you be glory for ever.

[4]As this broken bread was scattered upon the mountains, but was brought together and became one, so let your church be gathered together from the ends of the earth into your kingdom, for yours is the glory and the power through Jesus Christ for ever.

[5]And let no one eat or drink of your eucharist except those who have been baptized in the Lord's Name. Concerning this also the Lord said, 'Give not that which is holy to the dogs.'

10. [1]And after you are satisfied with food, thus give thanks: [2]We give thanks to you, O heavenly Father, for your Holy Name which you made to tabernacle in our hearts, and for the knowledge and faith and immortality which you made known to us through Jesus your child. To you be glory for ever.

[3]You, Lord Almighty, created all things for your Name's sake, and gave food and drink to men for their enjoyment, that they might give thanks to you, but you have blessed us with spiritual food and drink and eternal life through your Jesus, your servant.

[4]Above all we give thanks to you because you are mighty. To you be glory for ever.

[5]Remember Lord, your church, to deliver it from all evil and to make it perfect in your love, and gather it together in its holiness from the four winds to your kingdom which you have prepared for it. For yours is the power and the glory for ever.

[6]Let grace come and let this world pass away. Hosanna to the God of David. If any one is holy, let him come! If anyone is not, let him repent: Maran atha. Amen.

[7]But let the prophets hold eucharist as they will (Didache 9.1–10.7).

1. A history of research into the eucharist

Apart from the Reformed Churches, the theological tradition always understood Jesus' words of institution in the sense of a real presence of Christ. In D.F. Strauss[2] we find for the first time a symbolic interpretation of Jesus' last supper with a historical foundation: Strauss did not doubt its historicity. The growing hostility

---

[2]First in his book *The Life of Jesus Critically Examined* (1835), ed. P.C. Hodgson, Philadelphia 1972 and London 1973, but above all in the later version *A New Life of Jesus* (1864), London 1979.

of his environment prompted in Jesus the thought of his death. In the last (Passover) meal he 'steeped himself in the thought of his imminent death . . . he regarded this at the same time from the perspective of a sacrificial death, his blood as the consecration of a new covenant between God and humankind'.[3] The breaking of the bread brought home to him the image of his life consecrated to death, and the pouring of the wine the idea of blood soon to be shed.[4] Strauss regarded the Johannine account as secondary because of its date; he explained the detachment from the Passover meal by the need of Christianity to distance itself from Judaism as a new religion. Strauss's interpretation still preserves the continuity with the primitive Christian sacrament, for which the relationship with the death of Jesus is central. This changes only with the thoroughgoing-eschatological interpretation of the last supper: it is not the death of Jesus but entry into the imminent kingdom of God which now becomes the central meaning of the eucharist.

1.1 The thoroughgoing eschatological interpretation of the last supper

In his two-volume work on the last supper (*Das Abendmahl im Zusammenhang mit dem Leben Jesu und der Geschichte des Urchristentums*, 1901), Albert Schweitzer saw the last supper as the key to understanding the historical Jesus. Jesus' whole life had to be depicted in such a way 'that his solemn action at the last supper becomes understandable and comprehensible' (I, 62). Schweitzer argued that Jesus already anticipated the messianic feast of the end-time in the miraculous feeding in Galilee – in expectation of the universal tribulation and the kingdom of God. When the kingdom did not come he went to Jerusalem, to usher in this eschatological tribulation by his suffering. In expectation of his death he celebrated the meal once again with his disciples as an anticipation of the messianic feast. At the centre of his interpretation is the eschatological perspective in Mark 14.26, according to which Jesus will not drink wine again until the kingdom of God comes. Early primitive Christianity continued Jesus' practice: at the eucharist the first Christians were aware of being participants in the messianic feast and expected the parousia of the Messiah at such a meal. The eucharist (like baptism) was an eschatological sacrament. Paul simply continued this eschatological sacrament 'and gave the reference to the coming Christ a significance in connection with a communion with the transfigured one which was now already present and having its effect' (id., *Geschichte**, 612 [not in the English translation]). With

---

[3] *A New Life of Jesus* (n.2), 389.
[4] C. Weizsäcker, *The Apostolic Age of the Christian Church*, London 1894/5 (2 vols), II, 281, coined the formula: 'They are like a parable whose solution, however, he has not given' for this symbolic view of Jesus' words of interpretation.

the retreat of the hope for the parousia the eucharist then increasingly became 'the pledge of the resurrection and the medicine of immortality' (Ignatius, Eph. 20, φάρμακον άθανασίας, ibid.).

Schweitzer could demonstrate an eschatological promise in the text only in the saying over the cup (Mark 14.25). R. Otto found the missing promise in the saying over the bread in the Lukan account of the last supper.[5] So the original words of institution (Luke 22.17–19a, 29–30) would have run:

> 17 He took a cup, gave thanks and said, 'Take this and divide it among yourselves. 18 For I say unto you, Henceforth I will no more drink of the fruit of the vine, until the kingdom of God comes.'
> 19a And after he had taken bread and given thanks he broke it and gave it to them saying, 'This is my body (= this is I myself), 29 and I appoint unto you a kingdom in covenant, as my Father has appointed it unto me in covenant, 30 that you may eat and drink at my table in my kingdom, and sit upon thrones judging the twelve tribes of Israel' (*Kingdom of God*, 273).

He claimed that the significance of the last supper was 'the consecration of the disciples for entrance into the kingdom of God' (ibid., 263). Jesus performs this as the servant of God who is appointed a 'covenant' for Israel (cf. Isa. 49.8). As in Schweitzer, so here we find a derivation of the last supper from Jewish apocalyptic traditions combined with a defence of its historicity. However, at that time the history-of-religions school had already developed an alternative to both.

1.2 The history-of-religions derivation of the primitive Christian eucharist

This new direction in research was prompted by A. Eichhorn in articles on 'The Lord's Supper in the New Testament',[6] with two theses:

- The report of the Last Supper is so influenced by the 'dogma and the cult' of the community that the historical course of events remains unclear.
- The Pauline and primitive Christian view that the body and blood of Christ were eaten in the supper is to be explained in terms of the history of religion: the supper is a variant of the universally widespread 'theophagy', the primitive belief that one could appropriate the powers of a deity by eating and drinking.

His conclusion was: 'Whatever Jesus may have said and done that evening does not enable me to understand the cult meal of the church, with its sacramental

---

[5]R. Otto, *The Kingdom of God and the Son of Man*, London 1933, 265–329.
[6]Issues of *Christliche Welt* 36, Leipzig 1898.

eating and drinking of the body and blood of Christ' (quoted in Kümmel, *NT**, 254f.).

The Göttingen lecturer W.Heitmüller became even clearer in a lecture given to the Scholarly Preachers' Association in Hanover on 'Baptism and Lord's Supper in Paul. An Account and Elucidation in Terms of the History of Religion'; he argued that the primitive notion of feeding on the deity again came through in the Pauline view. Like baptism, it had a natural and mystical effect and was not a 'means of grace in the sense that the term is used in the Reformed tradition, that is, as means by which divine grace awakens faith, and thus identical in function with the gospel' (quoted ibid., 256).

R. Bultmann took over the view of his teacher Heitmüller and in his 1948 *Theology of the New Testament* summed it up like this. In primitive Christianity the last supper is a sacrament like the mysteries. Its significance is the 'sacramental communion' – namely that 'the participants by partaking of bread and wine take into themselves the body and blood of Jesus' (*Theology* 1*, 147); here the earthly body of Jesus is at the same time the body of the Risen Christ. For precisely that is characteristic of the mysteries: 'in them it is communion with a once dead and risen deity, in whose fate the partaker receives a share through the sacramental meal, as we know from the mysteries of Attis and Mithras' (ibid., 148). Evidence for this derivation from meals at the mysteries is:

- the contrast between the Lord's supper and pagan sacrificial meals in I Cor. 10.21, where the same effect is attributed to both (namely the creation of a fellowship);
- Justin's account of the eucharist, which is allegedly imitated by the demons in the mysteries of Mithras (Justin, *Apol.* I, 66).

Paul is said to have shared some of this magical view of the Lord's supper (when he attributes sickness in 11.29f. to an unworthy eating of the Lord's supper), but he himself is said to have understood the supper as 'proclaiming the death of Jesus' (I Cor. 11.26) and thus as a form of proclamation of the word. Moreover in I Cor. 10.1ff. he warns against false trust in the effect of the sacraments (in a magical way as in the mysteries). Paul is thus understood as having already been a critic of the Hellenistic primitive Christianity which he found in existence.

1.3 The synthesis of the thoroughgoing eschatological and history-of-religions explanation of the Lord's supper

In his study *Mass and Lord's Supper*,[7] which appeared in German in 1926, H.

---

[7]H. Lietzmann, *Mass and Lord's Supper*, Leiden, 1953–79 (published in fascicles).

Lietzmann started from the juxtaposition of eucharist and agape in the early church. He claimed that the eucharist was a sacramental meal in which the death of Jesus was presented, but that the agape was a communal meal without a sacramental character (which increasingly took on charitable features). He saw in both types of meal the influence of two primitive Christian forms of meal: on the one hand that of the eucharist of the earliest primitive community which went back to daily meals in the company of the historical Jesus, and on the other the last supper reinterpreted by Paul as a meal commemorating the death of Jesus. Here he combined a thoroughgoing-eschatological interpretation of the original Lord's supper with a history-of-religions explanation of the Pauline type. He claimed that Paul reinterpreted the Lord's supper as a memorial of Jesus' death on the analogy of pagan meals, on the basis of a revelation. Here are the two types of meal contrasted by Lietzmann:

The eucharist of the primitive community	The eucharist of Hellenistic primitive Christianity
It is celebrated in remembrance of Jesus' daily meals with his disciples and others.	It is celebrated in remembrance of the death of Jesus and goes back to the last supper.
It was 'created' by the historical Jesus or is a continuation of his everyday practice.	It stems from a personal revelation of the Lord to Paul, who reinterpreted the last supper as the institution of a meal commemorating Jesus' death. I Cor. 11.23 ('I have received from the Lord . . .') is interpreted as a revelation formula.
It is celebrated as an anticipation of the eschatological meal (cf. Matt. 8.10f.; Mark 14.25; Luke 22.30; Ethiopian Enoch 62.14). Therefore it is connected with eschatological jubilation (ἀγαλλίασις, Acts 2.46).	It is celebrated in analogy to the memorial meals for the dead held in the pagan Hellenistic environment. There in foundation documents for such meals the formula 'in memory/εἰς μνήμην' appears (cf. 'in memory of me'/εἰς τὴν ἐμὴν ἀνάμνησιν in I Cor. 11.24f.).
The agape developed out of it. This non-sacramental form of meal is preserved in Did. 9/10.	The eucharist or mass developed out of it.

Lietzmann's thesis of a new foundation of the eucharist by Paul did not gain acceptance. When Paul says, 'I received from the Lord what I also delivered to you' (I Cor. 11.23), he is not referring to revelation but (as in I Cor. 15.1ff.) to human tradition. So the understanding of the Lord's Supper which appears with him is older. The thesis of two original types of supper can therefore be put forward only in a modified form.

- E. Lohmeyer, *Vom urchristlichen Abendmahl* (1937/38), regarded both types as equally original: the joyful eschatological meal goes back to the Galilean community and the meal commemorating Jesus' death to the Jerusalem community.
- O. Cullmann, *Die Bedeutung des Abendmahls im Urchristentum* (1936), wanted to derive the supper with a reference to Jesus' death from the historical Jesus, whereas the joyful eschatological meal would go back to meals with the risen Christ.

Both maintained that the sacramental meal associated with the death of Jesus goes back beyond Paul. So can we draw conclusions for the last supper? In that case it would have to be explained from Jewish tradition.

1.4   The revision of the history-of-religions derivations of the Lord's Supper

1.4.1   *The explanation of the Lord's supper from Jewish analogies*

The possibility of deriving the sacramental Lord's supper from a last meal of Jesus grew as Jewish analogies to sacral, if not unconditionally sacramental, meals were evaluated.

1. *The Passover meal*. Most acceptance was found by the thesis of J. Jeremias, *The Eucharistic Words of Jesus* (1935), that Jesus' last meal was a Passover meal at which Jesus interpreted two parabolic actions by parabolic words: he interpreted the torn loaf of bread in terms of his death, and the juice of the grape in terms of his blood. This interpretation as a Passover meal will be discussed in detail below (pp. 423ff.).

2. *The Essene meal*. K.G. Kuhn was the first to refer to the meals of the Qumran community:[8] 1QS VI. 2–5 describes the community meal, at which bread and grape juice were blessed by the priest. This is matched in IQSa II, 17–27 by an eschatological meal at which the two Messiahs, the priestly and the royal

---

[8]K.G. Kuhn, 'Über den ursprünglichen Sinn des Abendmahls und sein Verhältnis zu den Gemeinschaftsmahlen der Sektenschrift', *EvTh* 10, 1950/1, 508–27.

Messiah, are present. Probably the present sacral meal is meant to anticipate the eschatological meal and replace the sacrificial cult, in which the Qumran community no longer took part because of the uncleanness of the present temple. However, Kuhn thought that this analogy did not determine Jesus' own action, but only the development of the celebration of the meal in primitive Christianity and the Synoptic accounts (apart from that of Luke) which bear witness to it.

3. *The* toda *sacrifical meal*. In his article 'Ps. 22 and the New Testament' (1968), H. Gese put forward an original thesis: in Ps. 22 there is a sudden change from lament and the distress of death to thanksgiving for deliverance. The one who is delivered is celebrating a sacrificial meal of thanksgiving, the *toda*, as a communal sacrifice: 'Those who were bowed down will eat and be satisfied' (Ps. 22.22). As Jesus went to his death with Ps. 22 on his lips, and the whole passion account is steeped in allusions to and quotations from Ps. 22, after Easter the disciples could respond to the unhoped-for deliverance of the crucified Jesus from death by celebrating the *toda* meal. The Lord's supper would then have come into being independently of any foundation by the historical Jesus, but in continuity with his activity.

1.4.2   *The re-evaluation of pagan Hellenistic analogies*

Just as Jewish analogies were seriously considered as a historical explanation, so too the pagan analogies were re-evaluated. On the one hand it became increasingly clear that the theology of the eucharist cannot be derived from them. On the other hand, the practice of holding a meal as the centre of community life was widespread.

1. Analogies to the *theology of the eucharist*. In *Herrenmahl und hellenistischer Kult*, Munich 1982, H.-J. Klauck showed that we do not have any real parallels to the notion of the real presence of a deity in the sacrament outside primitive Christianity. The closest we come to it is in statements about the cult of Dionysus, but there too it is only in ecstasy that the Bacchants think that they are eating the flesh of the deity. There is no mention of such ecstasy in connection with the eucharist. Nevertheless, in its fundamental conception the eucharist is very closely connected with the meal in the mysteries, which is a cultic act in the framework of an initiation concluded with a large meal. This 'has its basis in an act of foundation, an exemplary action on the part of the god of the cult which has been preserved in the narrative myth' (368), and is performed in imitation; here a communion between human beings and deity comes about and human beings gain a share in the indestructible divine life. However, clear differences remain (including the character of the fellowship and its public nature, and the understanding of time). These partly go back to

the influence of other forms of meals (association meals, meals to commemorate the dead), and in part cannot be derived from anywhere. According to Klauck, all in all the eucharist is a new creation which owes itself to the concrete historical event of Jesus' last supper.

2. *Analogies to the practice of a fellowship meal.* In *Gemeinschaftsmahl und Mahlgemeinschaft*, Heidelberg 1994, M. Klinghardt demonstrated that the existence of a fellowship meal did not need any special explanation. In antiquity the social life of associations took the form of shared meals. One does not need any prompting from Jesus' last supper to explain why the first Christians met for meals.

The provisional conclusion at present is that in primitive Christianity a 'normal' fellowship meal was combined with a highly theological interpretation which we cannot derive satisfactorily from the religion of the world of the time. It is still a riddle how this combination came about. Paul did not create it; Jesus could have prompted it. But that is not certain.

2. Texts about the eucharist and types of eucharist in primitive Christianity

Because the Christian eucharist is orientated on the Synoptic and Pauline texts, we often over-hastily come to believe that these texts represented the basic form of the eucharist from the beginning. The fact is that the eucharist was celebrated in many forms in primitive Christianity and interpreted in different ways. As the Pauline and Synoptic texts are the earliest in literary terms, it is natural to begin with them. As a second stage we shall then sketch out three further types of supper in primitive Christianity. Then, as a third step, we shall present attempts at reconstructing the last supper – first of all provisionally. Only by embedding them in the historical context of the life and death of Jesus can one define more closely what could have happened at the last supper.

2.1 The Synoptic and Pauline words of institution

The following synopsis simply brings out the most important differences between the four versions of the words of institution:

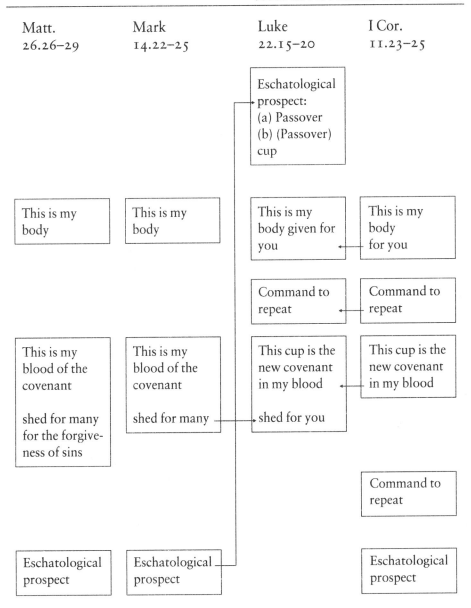

Matt. 26.26–29	Mark 14.22–25	Luke 22.15–20	I Cor. 11.23–25
		Eschatological prospect: (a) Passover (b) (Passover) cup	
This is my body	This is my body	This is my body given for you	This is my body for you
		Command to repeat	Command to repeat
This is my blood of the covenant	This is my blood of the covenant	This cup is the new covenant in my blood	This cup is the new covenant in my blood
shed for many for the forgiveness of sins	shed for many	shed for you	
			Command to repeat
Eschatological prospect	Eschatological prospect		Eschatological prospect

A comparison between the four versions of the words of institution shows that the Lukan version is a balance between the Markan and Matthaean words of institution and the Pauline type. As the Matthaean version depends on Mark, two ancient versions of the words of institution remain. The most important differences between them (including the differences which only emerge from the context) are set out below.

Mark (and Matthew)	Paul (and Luke)
The Lord's supper is depicted as a Passover meal – not, however, in the words of institution but in its narrative framework (cf. Mark 14.12–16).	The supper is not dated to Passover night in the narrative framework, but to the 'night in which he was betrayed' (I Cor. 11.23).
The two words of interpretation are formulated in strict parallel: 'This is my body' – 'This is my blood . . .'	The two words of interpretation are formulated asymmetrically: 'This is my body . . .' 'This cup is the new covenant . . .'
The blood is interpreted as 'blood of the covenant', in accordance with Ex. 24.8. There is no mention of a new covenant.	The cup is interpreted in accordance with Jer. 31.31 as a 'new covenant' which is concluded by the death of Jesus (i.e. by his blood).
The soteriological interpretation 'shed for many' appears only in the saying over the cup.	The soteriological interpretation '(given) for you' occurs only with the saying over the bread.
The text is stylized as a narrative of a single event: 'and they all drank from it'.	The text is stylized for repeated liturgical use by the command to repeat the action: 'Do this . . . in memory of me!'
An eschatological prospect of the future kingdom of God is attached to the word over the cup (Mark 14.25).	An eschatological prospect of the parousia of Jesus is attached to the saying over the cup: 'You proclaim the death of the Lord until he comes' (I Cor. 11.26).

Variations are offered on these two earliest versions of the eucharistic texts by Matthew and Luke, each independently:

  1. *Peculiarities of the Matthaean account of the institution*:

- The Matthaean text assimilates the Markan account more strongly to liturgical usage by changing the narrative 'They drank' into the invitation 'Drink you all of this' (in analogy to the preceding 'Take').
- Only in Matthew is the saying over the cup supplemented with a saying about the forgiveness of sins. This is, however, deleted at the baptism (cf. Matt. 3.6):

the forgiveness of sins is transferred from the once-for-all sacrament of baptism to the sacrament which is repeated; it also applies to sins committed after baptism.

2. Peculiarities of the Lukan account of the institution:

- The Lukan text assimilates the Markan account more strongly to liturgical usage by adding the command to repeat the action (as in the Pauline tradition) to the saying over the bread.
- In keeping with the Pauline tradition the saying over the cup is related to 'the new covenant in my blood'. According to Jer. 31.34 the new covenant is also associated with the forgiveness of sins.
- The eschatological vow of renunciation is put at the beginning and connected with the Passover meal. Only after the saying about the Passover (a festival which will not be repeated again) does Jesus institute the supper (with a command to repeat it): thus Luke depicts the replacement of the Jewish Passover meal by the Christian eucharist, which as the feast of the 'new covenant' is made to stand out from the Jewish tradition more strongly than in Mark and which from now on is to be celebrated in the community.[9]
- Only Luke has a soteriological interpretation both in the saying over the bread (with Paul) and also the saying over the cup (with Mark); he has also assimilated these to each other linguistically. Over the bread he says that it is 'given for you' (adding 'given') and over the blood that it is 'shed for you (here the second person plural 'for you' replaces the Markan 'for many').

2.2 Primitive Christian types of eucharist in addition to the Pauline-Synoptic type

We can establish three further forms of meal in primitive Christianity alongside the familiar Pauline/Synoptic type. Among other things they differ in the way in which they imagine the presence of Christ at the supper. John 13f. thinks in terms of a social presence of Christ at the meal, Didache 9 of a causal presence and John 6.51ff. of a real presence. Hypothetically, further texts from primitive Christianity can be connected with these three types.[10]

---

[9]The Lukan text is burdened with a problem relating to the text and the history of the tradition: 1. alongside the long version, D and it offer a short version which comprises vv.17–19a (up to 'my body'). It no longer contains the soteriological interpetation of the death, and to this degree would fit the Lukan theology well. However, it was probably composed at a secondary stage in order to avoid the duplication of the word over the cup. The deviations of the Lukan text from Mark are so great that many scholars think that this is a special tradition independent of Mark. Certainly a tradition close to Paul has influenced the Lukan version of the words of institution independently of the Markan text. Otherwise the divergences from Mark are redactional.

[10]Cf. B. Kollmann, *Ursprung und Gestalten der frühchristlichen Mahlfeier*, GTA 43, Göttingen 1990.

1. *The Johannine farewell meal. John* 13f. also depicts a farewell meal in the face of Jesus' death. Here, too, Jesus gives his disciples an abiding legacy: the commandment to love and the promise of the spirit. Jesus will continue to be present in their loving community. This is illustrated by the foot-washing, which is not just an ethical task but guarantees participation in salvation (John 13.8). To this degree it, too, has a 'sacramental' character. In the Johannine account of the supper, too, there is an allusion to the 'new covenant'.[11] Jesus gives his disciples a 'new commandment' (John 13.34). According to Jer. 31.31ff. (cf. Ezek. 36.26ff.; 37.26ff.), the new covenant consists in God's commandments being put in human hearts – a notion which was further developed in the direction of the Johannine Christ mysticism in the first farewell discourse: Jesus (John 14.21) and the Father (14.23) will take those who keep Jesus' commandments and love them and dwell in them. They will fill their innermost being. Jesus' presence is a social presence. The notion of this 'new covenant' does not imply any covenant ceremony with bloody sacrifices. There is no more mention of that in Jer. 31.31ff. than in the Johannine account of the last supper.

2. The commandments about the meal in the *Didache* (quoted above, p. 407) relate neither to a 'last meal' nor to Jesus' saying over the bread. Nevertheless they point to a sacrificial meal: God has given the community 'spiritual food and drink (πνευματικὴν τροφὴν καὶ ποτόν) and eternal life through Jesus your servant' (Did. 10.3). Jesus has revealed this miraculous food: the vine of David and the bread which gives life (Did. 9.2,3). Here we find the idea of a 'causal presence' of Jesus in the 'spiritual food' which he has given. There is a similar notion in I Cor. 10.3f.: here the elements of the eucharist are 'spiritual food' and 'spiritual drink' (πνευματικὸν βρῶμα . . . πνευματικὸν πόμα); Jesus is their origin, without being present in them. The 'breaking of the bread' in the primitive community is often classed as this type of eucharist (cf. Acts 2.42; 20.7).

3. In all probability the *eucharistic discourse* in John 6.51–58 refers to the Lord's supper. Food and drink are not just images of a revelation coming from heaven but elements in the Lord's supper which are called 'flesh' and 'blood'. Jesus is accessible as one who is really present: 'Whoever eats my flesh and drinks my blood abides in me and I in him' (John 6.56). For the first time in the Gospel of John a reciprocal immanence formula appears here – the next time is not until the first farewell discourse, a sign that notions in it associated with the Lord's supper have been theologically sublimated. The 'Christ mysticism' made possible by Jesus' commandment and love replaces the sacramental mysticism of the Lord's supper of John 6. But in contrast to John 13f., the supper presupposed in John 6 has no reference to the last supper. It is regarded as a deeper sense of the miracle

---

[11]For the 'covenant theology' in the first farewell discourse see J. Beutler, *Habt keine Angst. Die erste johanneische Abschiedsrede (Joh 14)*, SBS 116, Stuttgart 1984, 62ff.

with the bread and as a counter-image to the feeding with manna (6.58). A reference to Jesus' death is not completely absent: Jesus speaks of the bread of life as the 'flesh that I shall give for the life of the world' (6.51). Furthermore the statements about the Lord's supper in Ignatius stand close to the Gospel of John – strikingly above all through the terminology 'flesh and blood' instead of 'body and blood', which they have in common with John 6 (cf. Ignatius, Rom. 7.3; Smyrn. 7.1; Philad. 4) and the view of the eucharist as the 'medicine of immortality' (Ignatius, Eph. 20.2).[12]

2.3 Survey of eucharistic types and texts

Type of eucharist	Relationship to other types of meal	Presence of Jesus at the meal	Relationship to the life and death of Jesus
Pauline type: I Cor. 11.23–25	Meal of the new covenant – related to the covenant meal in Ex. 24.8.	Real presence or symbolic presence with the bread; no real presence with the wine.	Institution at the last supper in memory of his death for us.
Synoptic type	Covenant meal in the words of institution; Passover meal in the narrative framework.	Real presence or symbolic presence of Jesus in both elements.	Institution at the last (Passover) supper and interpretation of the death of Jesus as dying for many.
John 13	Farewell meal with 'new commandment' – allusion to the new covenant?	Social presence of Jesus in the loving fellowship of the disciples in the spirit.	Institution at the last supper; illustration of Jesus' loving devotion.

---

[12]Cf. L. Wehr, *Arznei der Unsterblichkeit. Die Eucharistie bei Ignatius von Antiochien und im Johannesevangelium*, NTA NF 18, Münster 1987.

Didache 9/10	Replacement for sacrifice (cf. Did. 14.1–3); here the thought is probably of prayers.	Causal presence of Jesus in the spiritual food which he gives.	No reference to the last supper and the death of Jesus.
I Cor. 10.3f.	Typological parallel to the manna in the wilderness and the water from the rock as a warning.	Causal presence of Jesus in the drink which he gives (*qua* rock).	No reference to the last supper and the death of Jesus.
John 6.51–58	Typological parallel to the manna in the wilderness as a contrast to the true bread of life.	Real presence of Jesus in the elements: flesh and blood.	Basis in the miraculous feeding. Reference to Jesus' surrender of his life.
I Cor. 10.16–18	Parallel to the Old sacrifices and contrast to the pagan sacrificial meal: the table of demons.	Real presence of Jesus in cup and bread: blood and body as the basis for his social presence in the community.	No explicit references to the last supper and the death 'for us'.

2.4 The reconstruction of the earliest eucharistic words

The starting point is the two earliest accounts of the last supper: the Pauline and Markan texts. The quest is for a version which is original not only in terms of the history of the tradition but also historically, one which can explain how a multiplicity of types of meal in primitive Christianity could come about.[13] The whole practice of meals held by Jesus and in his time needs to be noted.

---

[13]For a more intensive investigation see two different attempts at reconstruction in Kollmann, *Ursprung* (n.10), 171–4, and H.J. Klauck, *Herrenmahl und hellenistischer Kult. Eine religionsgeschichtliche Untersuchung zum ersten Korintherbrief*, NTA NF 15, Munich [2]1986, 304–14.

2.4.1 *The saying over the bread*

1. *The originality of the Pauline form.* Only in Paul does the saying over the bread have a soteriological interpretation of the meaning, 'for you'. That is absent from Mark, where instead the saying over the cup has the addition 'shed for many'. The Markan version of the saying over the bread can be understood as a secondary development: since in Mark the sayings over the bread and the cup are not separated by a meal proper, for him the two words of interpretation could be seen as a unity and the soteriological interpretation could be put at the end. The replacement of 'for you' with 'for many' could be explained by the influence of Isa. 53.12 (transmitted via Mark 10.45). The shift of the soteriological formula 'for you/for many' from the saying over the bread to the saying over the cup can also be explained by the fact that the notion of 'dying for others' can be associated much better with the shedding of blood than with the breaking of the bread. For 'shedding blood' and 'killing' are synonyms. Therefore the saying over the cup attracted the soteriological formula to itself at a secondary stage. The Pauline form of the saying over the bread is then the original one: 'This is my body for you.'

2. However, equally plausible arguments can be advanced for *the originality of the Markan form* 'This is my body'. In view of the general tendency to be observed in Mark to make the two words of interpretation symmetrical (the parallelism of body and blood), we might expect that both contain (or retain) an interpretative element: the saying over the bread the interpretation 'for you', and the saying over the cup the reference to the 'covenant'. However, as the Markan tendency to symmetry has not come through at this point in Mark, the saying over the bread without a soteriological interpretation could be original. In I Cor. 10.3f. and 17 Paul too refers to bread and wine without the further definition 'for us'. In I Cor. 11.24 it could have been added at a secondary stage. Would it not be harder to explain an abbreviation than an addition?

At this point it is difficult to make a well-founded decision between the Pauline and the Markan form, but there are important arguments in favour of the Pauline form.

2.4.2 *The saying over the cup*

1. *The originality of the Markan form.* The Pauline saying over the cup is often understood as a secondary simplification of the Markan version. Drinking blood was offensive to any Jew. Such offence is not caused by the Pauline version: 'This cup is the new covenant in my blood.' That simply states that the new covenant was founded by Jesus' violent death. The notion of drinking blood is quite remote. The substitution of 'new covenant' for 'covenant' would then have to be understood as an emphatic abrogation of the 'old covenant', i.e. in connection with a

growing demarcation from Judaism. However, there are better arguments for the opposite assumption.

2. *The originality of the Pauline form.*

- If drinking blood is unthinkable in Judaism, then Paul's formula, which corresponds more to Jewish sensibilities, might be more original. In the transition to a pagan Hellenistic milieu the 'new covenant in my violent death' (Paul) became the 'blood of the covenant' (Mark) which was drunk in the cup; for here, for example, the notion of the blood covenant was known![14]
- In most texts a tendency in the tradition to make the words of interpretation symmetrical in form can be detected. It comes to a climax in Justin, whose words of interpretation, 'That is my body' – 'That is my blood', are completely parallel in form (*Apol.* I, 66, 3). In that case, as an asymmetrical formulation ('body'/'new covenant') the Pauline saying over the cup would be more original than the Markan.

We may therefore conjecture that in their earliest form in the tradition the eucharistic words were like the Pauline form: 'This is my body for you. This cup is the new covenant in my blood.' Three arguments take us beyond the quest for the earliest version of the eucharistic words in the history of the tradition to the historical reconstruction of Jesus' last supper and the words he spoke at it:

- As the notion of the 'new covenant' has left behind a reminiscence in the 'new commandment' of the Johannine farewell meal, there could indeed have been mention of a 'new covenant' at Jesus' last meal. The motif of the 'new' also occurs in Mark: in an eschatological perspective Jesus promises that he will drink the fruit of the vine' new' in the kingdom of God. Could that also be an echo of the original words?
- In Jer. 31.31–34 the notion of the new covenant is not connected with bloody sacrifices. It appears in the Damascus Document (CD VI, 19; VIII, 21; XX, 12) as the self-designation of a group (a community which was the forerunner of Qumran?) which did not take part in the sacrificial cult in the temple. Where the notion of a future covenant occurs (Bar. 2.35; Jub. 1.17–23), the notion of sacrifice is remote. The origin of types of meals in primitive Christianity which had no reference to the death of Jesus would be easier to understand if the 'new covenant' is an old element. In that case, after Easter – because Jesus had meanwhile died – his death would have been interpreted as the sacrifice which

---

[14]Cf. Klauck, *Herrenmahl* (n.13), 52f.

according to Ex. 24.8 was the basis for a covenant. Originally, it was not said that the 'new covenant' was concluded 'in my blood'.

- The making of any covenant is a unique act.[15] If the 'new covenant' is made by drinking the cup, that is true only for the unique situation at the last supper. For Paul, an explicit command to repeat the action had to be added in order to provide the basis for a liturgical tradition: any further meal is not the making of a covenant but only a memorial of it. But the situation is different if one speaks of the 'blood of the covenant'. If it is present in a 'pneumatic way' in the form of the exalted Christ, it can be 'drunk' time and again as spiritual blood. That, too, would suggest the originality of the Pauline notion of the 'new covenant'.

The historical eucharistic words underlying the original form in the history of the tradition could have been: 'This is my (or 'the' [see below]) body for you. This is the new covenant.' In addition, the earliest form in the history of the tradition contains a reflection on the significance of the death of Jesus, on his 'blood'. Only after the execution of Jesus could one recognize in this death the 'sacrifice' that grounds and seals the new covenant (according to Ex. 24.8). That is expressed by the phrase 'This cup is the new covenant in my blood'. In a pagan milieu, where there was no abhorrence at drinking blood, by assimilation of the two words of interpretation and under the influence of Ex. 24.8 these words could become: 'This is my body for you. This is my blood of the covenant.' The soteriological formula 'for you' was probably later detached from the saying over the bread and at a secondary stage combined with the saying over the cup. But it cannot be emphasized enough that such reconstructions are only conjectures. Further indications of how we are to understand the last supper and the earliest tradition about it arise from its historical context.

3. Jesus' last supper in the context of the Passover

Texts are interpreted through their context. That also applies to the enigmatic texts about the eucharist. A historical context is indisputable: when Jesus went to Jerusalem, the feast of the Passover was imminent. The disciples must have expected to celebrate the Passover with him. But possibly Jesus was arrested and executed before it. That would at least correspond to the Johannine chronology. Or could Jesus have celebrated his last meal as a Passover meal? Jeremias in particular has put forward this thesis.

---

[15]Because it is a unique action, it is no wonder that 'covenant' is not a topic elsewhere in the preaching of Jesus. The 'isolation' of this term in the Jesus tradition is no argument against its authenticity.

3.1 Jesus' last supper – a Passover meal?

The Passover meal as we can reconstruct it from rabbinic texts (only codified in the post-New Testament period), comprises four parts:[16]

Before the meal proper	*First cup*: the kiddush cup, which is handed round by the father of the house with a blessing. *Food*: green herbs, bitter herbs and pieces of cooked fruit.
Passover liturgy	*Passover haggadah*, i.e. an explanation of the special features of the Passover meal by the father of the house for his children: – Why is the lamb roasted on the spit? – Why are bitter herbs eaten before it? – Why is unleavened bread eaten? *Passover hallel*, first part (= Pss. 113–114): a song of praise which in Ps. 114 celebrates the exodus. *Second cup*: the haggadah cup.
Main meal	*Grace* *Meal*, consisting of lamb, mazzoth, bitter herbs, cooked fruit and wine. *Third cup*: the cup of blessing, which was part of every festal meal, with grace.
Conclusion	*Passover hallel*, second part (= Pss. 115–116) with an individual song of thanksgiving for deliverance by the one who raises the cup of salvation (Ps. 116.13). *Fourth cup*: the *hallel* cup (cf. Ps. 116.13) with words of praise.

In an interpretation of the last supper as a Passover meal it must be presupposed that the course of the Passover meal is taken for granted the report. Only parts of the meal would be emphasized. What the Passover meal and the last supper have in common and where they differ emerges from the following survey:[17]

---

[16]Cf. Pes X; Jeremias, *Eucharistic Words*, 68–71; Bill IV. 1, 41–76.
[17]Cf. ibid., 41ff.

Common features	1. The Passover meal had to be celebrated in Jerusalem. Although Jesus had his lodgings in Bethany, he celebrated his last meal in Jerusalem. 2. The Passover meal was consumed at night, whereas at other times the main meal was usually eaten in the late afternoon. Jesus' last supper took place at night. 3. People were not to leave the city of Jerusalem on Passover night. Jesus, too, remained within the limits of the city (in Gethsemane) after his last supper.	
Differences	At the last supper Jesus interprets the bread and wine while they are being distributed.	The Passover liturgy interprets the event before the main meal.
	Jesus gives a general interpretation of both 'elements': he interprets bread and wine asa whole.	The Passover liturgy interprets only the special nature of the elements: not the bread but the *unleavened* bread.
	Jesus makes his disciples drink from one cup.	At the Passover meal each has his own cup.

We can follow Jeremias in interpreting the common features and differences as meaning that Jesus gives a Passover meal a new significance by a parabolic action: Jesus interpreted the tearing of the loaf of bread in terms of his violent death, and the red colour of the grape juice in terms of his blood which was to be shed. The tradition would have emphasized only those aspects of the Passover meal as a whole which gave this Passover meal a special significance as Jesus' last meal.

In addition to this, P. Stuhlmacher sees a wealth of biblical references already in Jesus' last supper (*Biblische Theologie* I, Göttingen 1992, 130ff.). The meal is:

- *A Passover meal* with reference to Ex. 12.1ff.: the supper brings Christians into the people of God;
- *A covenant meal* with reference to Ex. 24.1ff.: at this meal Israel's twelve tribes are represented. This happens at Jesus' last supper through his twelve disciples. The eschatological perspective on the kingdom of God is already suggested in Ex. 24.1ff.: the representatives of Israel see God;

- *A meal for the peoples* which was promised in Isa. 25.6–8 for the end-time. Moreover, in Isa. 24.23 the meal for the peoples is typologically combined with the covenant meal of Ex. 24.9–11;
- *The meal of the suffering servant*: Jesus celebrates the last supper in the awareness of fulfilling Isa. 53.11: 'by his suffering my servant will make many righteous, by taking their iniquities upon himself.'

According to this interpretation, the historical Jesus would have understood his imminent death as an expiation granted by God to all human beings, i.e. as the removal of an objective complex of guilt which separates human beings from God. Such an interpretation of the last supper can also be discussed independently of the historical Jesus. The biblical references are just as important whether they were first made by Jesus or whether the earliest Christians were the first to discover them. For there are solid reasons for doubting whether Jesus' last supper really was a Passover.

3.2 Criticism of the interpretation of the last supper as a Passover meal

An intrinsic improbability tells against the identification of the last supper as a Passover meal. The Passover is celebrated annually. Had Jesus celebrated his farewell meal as a Passover meal, it would have led to the origin of an emphatically annual meal. But all Christians celebrated the Lord's supper, which they derived from that last supper, every week (and even more often, cf. e.g. Did. 14.1; Pliny, *Ep.* X, 96, 7; Justin, *Apol.*, I, 67, 3, 7). And there are other difficulties: the Passover is celebrated in the family (with women and children), but Jesus (according to Mark) is alone with his twelve disciples. The women who followed him to Jerusalem are not present. The words of institution give no indication of a Passover meal. The interpretation in terms of a Passover arises only as a result of the context in which the words of institution stand in the Synoptic Gospels.

The external improbability of an identification of the last supper and Passover meal is grounded in chronology: in our view the Johannine chronology has the better arguments on its side. According to this Jesus died on Friday, 14 Nisan, before the beginning of the feast of the Passover (at sundown). This chronology is supported by Paul. His statement 'Christ is sacrificed as our Passover' (I Cor. 5.5) fits better Jesus' death before the Passover feast, at the time when the Passover lambs were being slaughtered in the temple. At least Paul's dating of the last supper to 'the night when Jesus was betrayed' does not tell against this chronology. Why does he not date it to Passover night? Granted, all these are only small indications. It is decisive that the (pre-Marcan) passion narrative can be understood very much better if Jesus (as also in Gospel of Peter 2.5 and in bSanh 43a) was already condemned and executed before the festival.

Mark 14.1f.: Jesus' opponents want him to be done away with before the festival. That would fit well with a report like John 18.1ff., according to which Jesus in fact died before the festival.

Mark 14.55: Legal proceedings on the Passover would be an offence against the commandment relating to festivals – especially a trial with a death sentence (cf. §14).

Mark 15.6: A Passover amnesty would make sense only if the person freed had an opportunity to take part in the Passover. Nowadays no one would proclaim an amnesty on Christmas Eve and not release those pardoned until 25 December. The narrators had another chronology in mind than the dating of the death of Jesus now put forward in the Synoptics.

Mark 15.21: Simon of Cyrene is coming from the field. Certainly it is not explicitly said that he is returning from work (which was forbidden at festivals), but that would be a natural way to understand the note – especially as he is then conscripted into abhorrent work: he has to bear Jesus' cross.

Mark 15.42: Here we find a dating of the crucifixion on a 'day of rest', i.e. the day before the sabbath. It is improbable that the Passover, one of the three great pilgrimage festivals, would be described only as a 'day of rest' for a sabbath following the Passover. Probably the day of rest originally referred to the Passover (since the Passover could coincide with a sabbath).

Mark 15.46: Joseph of Arimathea buys a linen cloth for burying Jesus. It is hard to imagine his finding a merchant to sell him such a thing on a high feast day.

If these reflections are correct, Jesus would have gone to Jerusalem for the Passover. But before he could celebrate the Passover there he was executed. In Luke Jesus begins the last supper with the words: 'I have earnestly desired to eat this Passover with you before I suffer' (Luke 22.15). The expression of longing (ἐπιθυμίᾳ ἐπεθύμησα) does not necessarily mean a longing which has been fulfilled. Luke uses the same expression in 17.22 when saying that the disciples will one day 'long' (ἐπιθυμεῖν) (in vain) to see one of the days of the Son of Man. If Jesus deliberately came to Jerusalem to celebrate the Passover, it would be understandable for the tradition to have made this intention an actual event – especially if there was a need for Christians to celebrate their own festival on the Jewish feast of the Passover. While their Jewish relations in faith were celebrating their Passover meal, they were celebrating the eucharist in remembrance of a last Passover meal of Jesus immediately before his death. Thus the redating of Jesus' last supper to the Passover feast could have taken place as an adaptation to liturgical usage.

4. Jesus' last supper in the context of his expectation of his death

Did Jesus foresee his death? Did he celebrate his last meal as a farewell meal – which need not mean that he referred bread and wine symbolically to his imminent death?

Even now, diametrically opposed views on this question are put forward. According to one view Jesus went to Jerusalem expecting that the kingdom of God would break in and without seeking his death there. His hopes (and those of his disciples) for this miraculous break-through of the rule of God failed, indeed, 'We may not veil from ourselves the possibility that he suffered a collapse.'[18]

According to the opposite view, Jesus foresaw his death. He affirmed it as a consequence of his messianic mission, in order to bring about reconciliation with God by atoning for the many (i.e. Israel and the nations) (thus P. Stuhlmacher, *Biblische Theologie* I, 154). Accordingly Jesus not only had an inkling of his death or foresaw it, but he deliberately wanted it, and saw it as a soteriological fulfilment of his mission.

The methodological difficulty of arriving here at statements which can be substantiated arises from the fact that all the statements about the death of Jesus, and in particular about interpretations of his death, can be read as if they already presupposed this death. All Jesus' prophecies of his death are under the suspicion of being prophecies after the event, and all soteriological interpretations of his death could have come into being after Easter to cope with his execution. Therefore all circumstances and statements which cannot be derived from a post-Easter perspective or which in addition are in tension with the actual course of the execution of Jesus are important in demonstrating that Jesus expected his death.[19]

4.1   The flight of the disciples

Regardless of whether Jesus deliberately went to his death or whether his death thwarted his expectations, it is certain that the death of Jesus thwarted the expectations of the disciples: they all fled (Mark 14.50). That fact cannot have been made up, especially as it is corrected in John: at least the Beloved Disciple does not flee (cf. John 19.26). We owe to this flight of the disciples the fact that the women who followed Jesus, who elsewhere remain invisible (or have been made invisible) in the tradition, come out more strongly at the end of the passion narrative. They show that not all the followers of Jesus shamefully left him in the lurch. The Emmaus story (Luke 24.13–35) illustrates very well from a post-Easter perspective what a catastrophe the execution of Jesus meant for the disciples: they had expected a redemption of Israel (understood in earthly terms, 24.21). With Jesus' death, their hopes had also been crucified. They had to be taught by the risen Christ that the Messiah had to suffer (Luke 24.26). There is much to suggest that this corresponds to the truth: insight into the need for suffering is a post-

---

[18]Bultmann, 'Kerygma'*, 24.
[19]Cf. H. Schürmann, *Jesu ureigener Tod*, Freiburg 1975; L. Oberlinner, *Todeserwartung und Todesgewissheit Jesu. Zum Problem einer historischen Begründung*, SBB 10, Stuttgart 1980.

Easter development. All the prophecies of the passion which already make the earthly Jesus state this necessity (cf. Mark 8.31f., etc.) might be later insights which were subsequently put on the lips of the earthly Jesus. They are prophecies after the event. However, the flight of the disciples tells us only a little. The hopes of the disciples and the expectations of Jesus need not have been the same. Did not Jesus realistically have to reckon with the possibility of his death?

4.2 The violent fate of the prophets[20]

Jesus clearly had the fate of a prophet before his eyes: that of John the Baptist. In the discussion about his authority to cleanse the temple Jesus associates this authority with that of John the Baptist (Mark 11.27–33). Did he not necessarily also have to see John's fate in parallel with his own? Moreover, John was only the last in a series of prophets.[21] The sayings which speak of the inevitable martyr death of the prophets could go back to the historical Jesus and be prompted by the fate of John the Baptist (cf. Luke 11.49–51 par.; Luke 13.34–35 par.). In these sayings there is a certain tension with a post-Easter perspective.

- *The multiplicity of prophets*: after Easter the death of Jesus could hardly have been put in the series of all the deaths of prophets without being emphasized. Paul, who knows this inclusion of the killing of Jesus in the killings of prophets, puts a special emphasis on his fate (cf. I Thess. 2.15).
- *The kind of death presupposed*: Luke 13.34 accuses Jerusalem of 'stoning' its prophets. In the so-called 'Sophia logion' (Luke 11.49–51/Matt. 23.34–36), Matthew is the first evangelist to make the general 'kill' more specific: 'crucify'.
- The *absence of a soteriological interpretation* of Jesus' death would be amazing in the period after Easter. In I Cor. 15.3ff. Paul presupposes it as the consensus of all the apostles. Of course one can also attribute the interpretation of the death of Jesus as the fate of a martyr prophet to the group which handed down Q.[22] But the picture of a prophet attested here could also already be presupposed for Jesus – especially as he had in view the fate of John the Baptist, which fully corresponded with it.

4.3 The parable of the wicked husbandmen (Mark 12.1–9 par.)

The tradition of the violent fate of the prophets also underlies the parable of the

---

[20]Cf. O.H. Steck, *Israel und das gewaltsame Geschick der Propheten*, WMANT 23, Neukirchen 1967.

[21]The Galilean charismatic and miracle-worker Honi had been stoned a few decades before Jesus after refusing to pray for the victory of one party over the other in a civil war; cf. Josephus, *Antt.* 14, 22.

[22]But that is possible only to a limited degree. The topic of the killed prophets also appears in the parable of the husbandmen in Mark 12.1ff. and Thomas 65; also in Paul, I Thess. 2.14–15.

wicked husbandmen. This could be a post-Easter construction: the killing of the 'son' in it is meant to explain the destruction of Jerusalem. The imagery itself is well attested for the world of Jesus.[23] It reflects the rebellious mood of the tenants against their absent landlord. What is decisive for us is that in two features the parable contradicts what actually happened. First, in it the tenants (i.e. the religious and political elite of Israel) kill the son, i.e. Jesus. But in fact Jesus was executed by the Romans. Secondly, the tenants kill the son in the vineyard and then throw his corpse out. However, Jesus was not put to death in Jerusalem but before the gates of the city.[24] His body was not 'cast out' unburied, but was given a burial. Would we not have to expect a greater agreement between the actual fate of Jesus and the parable if the killing of the son, who is sent last, were wholly a later allegorization? Despite some post-Easter allegorization, a feature from before Easter could have been preserved here.[25]

4.4 Mark 14.25: An expression of an eschatological imminent expectation or a prophecy of the death of Jesus?

The flight of the disciples and the collapse of their expectations because of the crucifixion of Jesus make it improbable that Jesus clearly prophesied his death. But prophecies which were ambiguous are quite possible, prophecies which expressed the possibility of dying but also the hope of soon being in the kingdom of God (without a violent death before that). Such a 'prophecy of death' could be contained in Mark 14.25: 'Truly, I say to you, I shall not drink again of the fruit of the vine until that day when I drink it new in the kingdom of God.' This saying can be understood as an expression of an intensive expectation of an imminent end: next time Jesus drinks wine, the kingdom of God will be there. It will begin in the next few days. Jesus himself will experience its breakthrough. But the saying can also mean that Jesus' death is imminent. Only after his death will he drink 'wine' again in the kingdom of God. Precisely this open view of the future could reproduce Jesus' expectations: he was aware of the danger that he might die a violent death. But he still hoped that God would intervene and that before his death the rule of God would begin and change everything.[26] But in any case the

---

[23]Cf. M. Hengel, 'Das Gleichnis von den Weingärtnern Mc 12, 1–12 im Licht der Zenonpapyri und der rabbinischen Gleichnisse', ZNW 59, 1968, 1–39.

[24]Matt. 21.39 therefore changes the text: 'They cast him out of the vineyard and killed him' (similarly Luke 20.15). Both adapt the parable to the fate of Jesus.

[25]Thus J.H. Charlesworth, *Jesus within Judaism*, New York 1988, 139ff.

[26]The Gethsemane prayer, 'Abba, Father, all things are possible for you, take this cup from me; yet not what I will but what you will' (Mark 14.36), is certainly not historical in that form. According to the narrative there are no witnesses to the scene. However, it could aptly recall Jesus' basic attitude in his last days – concentrated in an ideal scene: he reckoned with his death (the cup), but still hoped for the miraculous and saving intervention of God, the beginning of the kingdom of God.

meal on the eve of the Passover was a farewell meal for him. All the accounts agree that with it he left behind for the disciples something that was of abiding importance: in John this is the charge to create a loving community; in the Synoptics and Paul it is the institution of the primitive Christian sacrament of the Lord's supper. If the dating of the last supper argued for above is correct, the assumption of a consciousness of imminent death is almost unavoidable. Had Jesus been certain of being able to celebrate the Passover with his disciples, he would have been more likely to make this great festival the framework for his 'bequest'. In choosing a meal shortly beforehand he is indicating an awareness that his time is limited. It will be his last meal with his disciples. In a word, at the end Jesus lived in expectation of his possible death, but he was not certain of it.

But what was the origin of this expectation of a possibly limited time? The answer is obvious: Jesus' conflict with his opponents had escalated in the last week in Jerusalem. He had every reason to feel threatened.

5. Jesus' last supper in the context of his conflict with the temple

The last supper was a 'symbolic action': the Synoptic Gospels and Paul agree with John on that. It contained a message for those taking part which was expressed not with words but in actions. Other symbolic actions of Jesus are the choice and sending out of the twelve disciples, his eating with toll collectors and sinners, the entry into Jerusalem, and the cleansing of the temple. Such symbolic actions are also known to us from Old Testament prophets: Isaiah went naked for three years in order to announce the humiliation of Egypt and Ethiopia by the Assyrians (Isa. 20.1ff.). Jeremiah smashed a jar as a sign of the imminent destruction of the temple (Jer. 19.1ff.) and wore a yoke to call for subjection to Babylon (Jer. 27–28).

Jesus communicated his message in symbolic actions. It is illuminating that in part they interpret one another. His eating with toll collectors and sinners (Mark 2.15ff.; Matt. 11.19) shows that he was not afraid of being polluted by notorious outsiders, but trusted in the 'infectious' power of his charisma. What he says when he sends the disciples out shows the reason for his confidence: the disciples are to eat and drink what is set before them in strange houses (i.e. without asking whether it is clean or unclean). They bring an 'aura of peace' into the house which has a magical effect; it protects a house in the last judgment and even now permeates the house and its inhabitants with salvation as the power of the imminent rule of God (Luke 10.5ff.). Here we find an 'offensive purity' and 'inclusive holiness' that does not shrink from contact with the holy (K.Berger, 'Jesus als Pharisäer . . .', NT 30, 1988, 231–62). What applies to the symbolic actions in the Galilean phase of Jesus' activity could also apply to the symbolic actions in Jerusalem: the cleansing of the temple and the last supper interpret each other.

5.1 The cleansing of the temple as a symbolic action criticizing the cult

Jesus came to Jerusalem a week before the Passover feast. That was the usual practice. For one needed a week to perform the rites of purification necessary before taking part in the feast (cf. Num. 19 and John 11.55). Those who had become unclean were sprinkled with water for purification on the third and seventh days (Num. 19.19). Although we have many traditions from Jesus' last week in Jerusalem, nowhere do we find an indication that Jesus and his disciples had taken part in these rites. Were they taken for granted (thus E.P. Sanders)?[27] But how then could traditions have arisen which decidedly say the opposite? In a fragment of an unknown Gospel a Pharisaic chief priest criticizes Jesus: 'Who gave you leave to tread this place of purification and to look upon these holy utensils without having bathed yourself and even without your disciples having washed their feet?' (POx 840; cf. *NTApoc.* I, 94). Nor does the Gospel of John know anything of rites of purification undertaken by Jesus and his disciples, although it emphasizes the need for special cultic cleanness for the feast of the Passover (John 18.28). On the contrary, it reports Jesus' washing of his disciples' feet and explicitly declares this to be the fulfilment of all demands for cleanness: 'He who has bathed does not need to wash, except for his feet, but he is clean all over' (John 13.10). We may conclude from this that Jesus did not perform the necessary rites of purification. That shows a detachment from the temple.

This becomes even clearer in the symbolic cleansing of the temple, which is directed towards the money-changers and those who sold sacrificial animals in the forecourt of the temple (Mark 11.15–18 par.), and in Jesus' prophecy against the temple, which foretold a destruction of the temple and (probably) promised a new temple built by God himself.

The substance of Jesus' symbolic action against the temple cult and his prophecy against the temple belong together. However, only in the Gospel of John do both these occur in the same text (John 2.14–22). There the saying about the temple plays no role in the accusation against Jesus. By contrast, there is an allusion to it in the Markan passion narrative as 'false witness' against Jesus (Mark 14.58). There was an interest here in detaching it from the context of the cleansing of the temple which compromised Jesus, so as not to confirm the 'false' witness as truth. This saying about the temple is an authentic logion of Jesus. The different versions of it show what confusion it caused – partly because it had been

---

[27]E.P. Sanders, *The Historical Figure of Jesus*, London 1993, 250f.

fulfilled in a completely different way, and partly because it attributed a destructive message to Jesus:

- According to Mark 14.58 it has a negative and a positive part: Jesus will destroy the temple and in three days erect in its place a temple not made with hands. The false witness here is the suggestion that Jesus would destroy the temple himself (perhaps by arson). Jesus will have expected God to destroy it and in a marvellous way to put a new temple in its place – an expectation which is not without analogies (cf. Isa. 60.13; Ethiopian Enoch 90.28f.).
- Mark 13.1f. reformulates Jesus' prophecy about the temple so that it corresponds to the destruction of the temple in 70 CE. Only the negative part had been fulfilled then. So only the destruction of the temple was prophesied.
- John 2.19f. spiritualizes the temple logion and refers it to Jesus' life. Jesus invites his opponents, 'Destroy this temple, and in three days I will raise it up.' He means the temple of his body, which his opponents will kill, but which Jesus will restore again through divine authority (cf. John 10.17f.).
- Matthew chooses another way of blunting the temple prophecy. According to Matt. 26.61 Jesus did not say that he *would* destroy the temple but that he *could* destroy it (cf. John 10.17f.).
- Luke omits Jesus' prophecy about the temple, but Acts refers back to it in 6.14 and attributes it to Stephen: Stephen prophesied that Jesus of Nazareth would destroy this place and change the customs which Moses had handed down.
- Gospel of Thomas 71 knows the prophecy in the first person: 'Jesus said: I shall destroy this house, and no one will be able to build it (again).' Here the positive part of the prophecy is directly denied. It had not been fulfilled and had become a problem.

A prophecy which demonstrably caused so much perplexity and difficulty was not attributed to Jesus only at a later stage. It fits the historical context well: there is also evidence of opposition to the temple among other groups and individuals in the Palestine of the time.

The symbolic action of the so-called 'cleansing of the temple' is interpreted by the prophecy about the temple: the issue here is not a reform of the temple within present history, but its disappearance along with this transitory world. Such a prophecy would necessarily have been understood as a threat. It is plausible that it played a role in the trial of Jesus. But what did Jesus want to put in place of the temple? What was to happen in the kingdom of God? The last supper could have formulated an answer to this question – in a second symbolic action.

5.2   The last supper as a symbolic action founding a cult

The message of the prophecy about the temple and the 'cleansing of the temple' was: this temple is doomed to destruction. God will erect another in its place. Such a message must have not only caused concern to the temple aristocracy and provoked anxiety among the population of Jerusalem – after all, many of them were dependent on the temple for their livelihood – but also have made the disciples deeply uncertain. They could not have foreseen this critical focus on the temple from Jesus' previous preaching. One could hope for an eschatological turning-point in all things without directly criticizing present institutions and circumstances! But quite apart from that, Jesus' criticism of the temple must have been a tribulation for Jews. The temple was the centre of religious life. The more transcendent the notion of God was in Judaism, the more people were devoted to the place where this infinitely transcendent God became accessible. Blessing and prosperity were bound up with the temple. Salvation was communicated through it. By his criticism of the temple Jesus was *de facto* provisionally excluding himself from the cult (in a way which was eschatologically conditioned and transitory), and to many people that could seem as if he was excluding himself from salvation. It is hard to imagine Jesus taking a Passover lamb a few days later from the temple which he criticized so sharply, in order to eat it with the disciples. He probably hoped that the kingdom of God would have come by then: he would be eating and drinking in it in quite a different way.

The symbolic action against the temple cult was complemented by Jesus' symbolic action at the last supper in founding a cult, though he did not *intend* to found a cult which would last through time. He simply wanted to replace provisionally the temple cult which had become obsolete: Jesus offers the disciples a replacement for the official cult in which they could either no longer take part, or which would not bring them salvation – until a new temple came.[28] This 'substitute' is a simple meal. By a new interpretation, the last supper becomes a substitute for the temple cult – a pledge of the eating and drinking in the kingdom of God which is soon to dawn. The words of interpretation in the Pauline Synoptic tradition give the last supper the status of a cultic feast. Perhaps Jesus only said, 'This is the body for you',[29] meaning by that: this bread now replaces for you the sacrificial food which is otherwise consumed in the temple: it replaces the sacrifice animal. And over the cup he added: 'This cup which we drink together (i.e. which is passed round) is the new covenant' – namely a covenant without sacrifice, which according to Jer. 31.31–33 consists in the will of God being put in human hearts and God forgiving them their sins. Traces of this replacement of the official cult have also been preserved in the Johannine account of the last supper: the

---

[28] Anyone who follows the Synoptics in dating the 'last supper' to Passover night can bring out this 'substitute function' of the last supper even more strongly (as Luke among the evangelists already did).

[29] Here the word of interpretation would have been changed to 'This is *my* body for you' only after the cross and resurrection.

foot-washing replaces all the official ceremonies of purification in the temple as a complete cleansing. These ceremonies are obsolete.

The understanding of the last supper as a symbolic action which is the founding of a cult that is a substitute for the temple cult, now eschatologically devalued, could also explain Judas' action: he could have refused to follow Jesus from the moment that Jesus' message led to a dissociation from the existing temple cult. However, we do not know Judas' motives. The various traditions agree only in emphasizing two points.

- Judas betrays Jesus to the high priests – thus not to the whole Sanhedrin composed of high priests, elders and scribes (Mark 14.10f.; Matt. 25.14–16). Only in Luke is there the addition of 'officers' with whom Judas conspires (Luke 22.4). It is clear that only the group responsible for the cult is working with him.
- Judas leaves Jesus at or after his last meal. Only at this farewell meal does it become clear that Jesus is not only criticizing the temple theologically but replacing it with the beginnings of a new 'cult'. Judas could have recognized that the germ of a deep division could lie here.

Of course we should accept that all this is conjectural. But it is improbable that it was only for money that Judas betrayed Jesus, i.e. indicated where Jesus was to be found so that he could be arrested without attracting public attention. Traitors usually claim much more positive motives than those attributed to them by the group that they betray.

This interpretation which takes the cleansing of the temple and the last supper together is a hypothesis. Should it be correct, the question arises whether an exodus from Judaism did not begin with Jesus. Even now the development of new rites is one of the most important indications of processes which split churches. But in the context of the Judaism of Jesus' time we can say that Jesus' action was in line with a general tendency. After the loss of the temple in 70 CE the rabbinic movement completed what Jesus pioneered: it detached religious life from the temple. Everyday life and daily meals were hallowed afresh. The will of God to be found in the Torah became a witness to God's presence throughout everyday life. Jesus' conflict with the temple is also a conflict *in* Judaism – not a conflict *with* Judaism.

The reconstruction made here reckons with an ambivalence in the imminence of death and the expectation of the kingdom of God at Jesus' last supper: it would have been partly a farewell meal and partly an anticipation of the feast in the kingdom of God. This interpretation has to postulate that Jesus entertained the possibility of his death but was not certain of it, and therefore need not presuppose any relationship between the elements in the supper and the imminent death of Jesus. Thus it explains the various types of primitive Christian Lord's suppers, with and without the interpretation of the elements in terms of the death of Jesus. The state of research is open. Therefore we shall also sketch out a second possibility which is compatible with what has been said above. According to this, Jesus would have interpreted the elements not only as a substitute for the sacrifice at the temple but (additionally?) as a prior interpretation of his death. It was not the post-Easter community but Jesus himself who would first have understood his death as a sacrifice. The strongest argument for this is that the saying over the bread, 'This is my body' – with or without a soteriological interpretation – is probably to be interpreted in terms of Jesus' life: the breaking of the bread could be a symbol of the surrender of this life. By contrast, the interpretation sketched out above must presuppose an original saying over the bread which has nowhere been preserved in that form, something like 'That is the body', meaning, 'That is the body of the sacrificial animals for you.' However, the other interpretation would have to assume that shortly before his death Jesus became certain that he would die. It would be dishonest scholarship not to concede that we cannot reconstruct the course and significance of Jesus' last meal with any certainty.

6. Summary and hermeneutical reflections

John the Baptist and Jesus both prompted the origination of sacraments through symbolic actions. They did not found cults with the deliberate intention of providing a basis for a new tradition. Both expected the imminent transformation of the world and the end of all traditions. Their symbolic actions in founding cults are eschatological sacraments – an anticipation of the final judgment by baptism, and an anticipation of the eschatological meal by Jesus. But that does not yet comprise their whole function: baptism for the forgiveness of sins is *de facto* a ritual to rival the temple cult; for here the forgiveness of sins was really offered. The Lord's supper is *de facto* a ritual which is a substitute for the sacrificial cult. The origin of these new rites shows that there was dissatisfaction with traditional ritual forms.

Jesus probably celebrated a farewell meal with his disciples on the day before the Passover – in the awareness that his life was in danger, but also in the hope that the imminent breaking in of the kingdom of God would perhaps save it. In so doing he interpreted a simple meal (probably not a Passover meal) as the celebration of a 'new covenant' with God, aimed at impressing God's will directly on human hearts. For him and his disciples the meal was a substitute for the official cult which Jesus had radically devalued by an abrupt criticism (expressed by a symbolic action and a prophecy). After Jesus had been crucified and had appeared alive, the disciples interpreted his death as that bloody sacrifice through which the new covenant had been accomplished. Jesus probably already had this sacrifice in mind at the last supper when he spoke of the new covenant. With this new interpretation of the last supper after Easter, the foundation for the primitive Christian sacrament was laid.

The primitive Christian sacrament of the Lord's supper contains two great intrinsic tensions. It is a simple meal – but is associated with the most extreme of all sacrifices, human sacrifice. Whereas the external rite contains a repudiation of sacral violence – only bread is eaten and wine drunk; there is no bloody animal sacrifice – in the 'myth' which is its foundation we find an increase in violence through the reference to a human sacrifice. The 'progress' in the history of religions from bloody animal sacrifices to bloodless forms of worship is balanced out by a 'regression' into ideas of human sacrifice, believed long ago to have been superseded, which had provoked Jesus' violent death. It is precisely this tension which comprises the inner dynamic of the primitive Christian sacrament: it symbolizes both the inhuman fact that life lives at the expense of other human life, and also the promise that life is possible by sharing food, by eating and drinking together. Seldom has such an impressive rite been 'invented' which expresses the transformation of human beings from 'asocial' beings who live at the expense of other life to 'co-operative' human beings who share and give life in solidarity.

There is also a second tension: baptism and Lord's supper came into being in a very constricted space of time. Because there was no longer time to repent in face of the judgment, for those who were ready to repent John the Baptist preached 'baptism for the forgiveness of sins'. Because the old temple was to be replaced by a better one, Jesus already anticipated the eschatological meal as his farewell. In a paradoxical way, symbolic actions which did not reckon with a further period of time became sacraments which communicate salvation time and again. However, this very paradox remains in the sacrament: symbolic religious actions are an opportunity for moving from the inescapable stream of time into 'another time'. The confrontation with the end of all time from which the Christian sacraments emerged became forms of assurance of something which cannot be put in question by any passage of time.

7. Tasks

7.1 Forms of meals in primitive Christianity: conditions for taking part in the eucharist

The various forms of meals which were held in primitive Christianity are characterized, among other things, by different 'conditions for entry'. Collect the conditions that were imposed for taking part in the meal and the reasons given for them. Is there a connection with the presence of Christ in the eucharist which is dominant in each case? Note the following texts:

1. Paul: I Cor. 10.14–22; 11.17–22, 27–34.

2. Didache 9/10 (see p. 407 above) and Didache 14.1–3:

14 ¹On the each day of the Lord come together, break bread and hold eucharist, after confessing your transgressions, that your offering may be pure. ²But let not anyone who has a quarrel with his fellow join in your meeting until they are reconciled, that your sacrifice be not defiled. ³For this is that which was spoken by the Lord: At every place and time offer me a pure sacrifice, for I am a great king, says the Lord, and my name is wonderful among the nations (*Apostolic Fathers*, I, Loeb Classical Library, 331).

3. Ignatius arguing with opponents: Smyrnaeans 7.1; 8.1–2; Philadelphians 3.2, 4:

They abstain from eucharist and prayer, because they do not confess that the Eucharist is the flesh of our Saviour Jesus Christ who suffered for our sins, whom the Father raised up by his goodness. They then who deny the gift of God are perishing in their disputes; but it was better for them to have love, that they also may attain to the resurrection . . . See that you all follow the bishop, as Jesus Christ follows the Father, and the presbytery as if it were the apostles. And reverence the deacons as the command of God. Let no one do any of the things appertaining to the church without the bishop. Let that be considered a valid eucharist which is celebrated by the bishop, or by one whom he appoints. Wherever the bishop appears let the congregation be present, just as wherever Jesus Christ is, there is the catholic church. It is not lawful either to baptize or to hold an agape without the bishop, but whatever he approve, this is also pleasing to God, that everything which you do may be secure and valid (ibid., 259, 261).

    For as many as belong to God and Jesus Christ – these are with the bishop. And as many as repent and come to the unity of the church – these also shall be of God, to be living according to Jesus Christ. Be careful therefore to use one eucharist – for there is one flesh of our Lord Jesus Christ, and one cup for union with his blood, one altar, as there is one bishop with the presbytery and the deacons . . . (ibid., 241–3).

4. Justin, *Apol.* I, 66:

And this food is called among us 'eucharist', of which no one is allowed to partake but those who believe that the things which we teach are true, and who have been washed with the washing which is for the remission of sins, and unto regeneration, and who are so living as Christ has enjoined. For not as common bread and common drink do we receive these; but in like manner as Jesus Christ our Saviour, having been made flesh by the Word of God, had both flesh and blood for our salvation, so likewise we have been taught that the food which is blessed by the prayer of his word, and from which our blood and flesh by transmutation are nourished, is the flesh and blood of that Jesus who is made flesh (Ante-Nicene Fathers I, Edinburgh and Buffalo 1887, 185).

7.2 Jesus as critic of the cult?

The cleansing of the temple was interpreted above as a symbolic action critical of the cult, which Jesus performed in expectation of the dawn of the kingdom of God. However, the recollection of this prophetic symbolic action is not the only thing that the Jesus tradition has to say about Jesus' attitude towards the temple, the offerings to be made to it and the priests employed there. Group the following texts roughly according to whether their attitude to the cult is 1. friendly, 2. hostile, 3. critical and relativizing, though fundamentally acknowledging it. What conclusions can be drawn about Jesus' attitude to the temple (cult) on the basis of a critical evaluation of the tradition:

Mark 1.44f. par.; 7.6–13 par.; Mark^s 12.32–34;

Q: Matt. 23.23f./Luke 11.42; Matt. 23.35f./Luke 11.50f.;

Matt^s: 5.23f.; 9.13; 12.3–7; 17.24–27; 23.16–22;

Luke^s: Luke 2.21–52; 21.1–4; Acts 2.46–3.1ff.; 5.12–42 etc.;

Gospel of the Ebionites, frag. 6: He (Christ) says: 'I am come to do away with sacrifices, and if you do not cease from sacrificing, the wrath of God will not cease from you' (quoted in *NTApoc* 1, 1991, 170).

14

Jesus as Martyr: The Passion of Jesus

E. Bammel (ed.), *The Trial of Jesus*, London 1970; id. and C.F.D. Moule, *Jesus and the Politics of His Day*, Cambridge 1984; J. Blinzler, *The Trial of Jesus*, Cork 1959; S.G.F. Brandon, *Jesus and the Zealots*, Manchester 1967; id., *The Trial of Jesus of Nazareth*, London 1968; R.E. Brown, *The Death of the Messiah* (2 vols), New York and London 1993, 1994; D. Catchpole, *The Trial of Jesus*, Leiden 1971; O. Cullmann, *Jesus and the Revolutionaries of his Time*, New York 1970; M. Hengel, *Crucifixion*, London and Philadelphia 1977; id., *Was Jesus a Revolutionist?*, Philadelphia 1971; R.A. Horsley, 'The Death of Jesus', in *Studying**, 395–22; J. Juster, *Las Juifs dans l'Empire Romain* (2 vols), Paris 1914; W.H. Kelber (ed.), *The Passion in Mark*, Philadelphia 1976; K. Kertelge (ed.), *Der Prozess gegen Jesus. Historische Rückfrage und theologische Deutung*, QD 112, Freiburg et al. 1988; G.D. Kilpatrick, *The Trial of Jesus*, London 1953; H. Last, 'Coercitio', *RAC* 3, 1957, 235–43; S. Légasse, *The Trial of Jesus*, London 1997; E. Lohse, *The History of the Death and Suffering of Jesus Christ*, Philadelphia 1967; B. Mack, *A Myth of Innocence*, Philadelphia 1988; A.N. Sherwin-White, *Roman Society and Roman Law in the New Testament*, Oxford 1963; G. Theissen, 'Tempelweissagung'*; P. Winter, *On the Trial of Jesus*, SJ 1, Berlin and New York 1961, ²1974.

Introduction

Historians have a special obligation to elucidate the historical causes of the death of Jesus, because Christian anti-Judaism has time and again been nourished by the charge that 'the Jews' killed Jesus. At most, historically one could only claim that some Jews contributed to the death of Jesus, and it would be ethically intolerable to draw consequences from this for judging all Jews. But even in historical terms the situation is far more complicated. For example, Paul says not only that 'the Jews' killed Jesus (I Thess. 2.14f.) but also that 'the rulers of this world' had crucified him (I Cor. 2.8). Ultimately Paul explains the death of Jesus by saying that he gave himself up (Gal. 2.20) and that God gave him up (Rom. 8.32). None of these remarks is a neutral historical statement; each is full of interpretation. The same goes for the passion narratives in the four Gospels. One can get closer to historical reality only by a critical investigation and a historical reconstruction of the legal position. If what can be supposed probable after the removal of the bias in the sources matches what was historically possible in legal terms, we may be not far from the historical truth. Therefore to prepare for discussing this topic we must 1. work out the 'bias' in the sources and 2. identify the historical problems by asking more specific questions.

Task 1: The bias in the sources

In the following synopsis of the four passion narratives the boxes indicate special material from the particular Gospels. Describe with a few key words each set of special material and on the basis of this special material attempt to say something about the bias in the Matthaean, Lukan and Johannine passion narratives:

	Matthew	Mark	Luke	John
Trial of Jesus				
Arrest of Jesus	———	———	———	———
				18.12–14
Peter's denial	———	———	———	———
Jesus before the supreme council	———	———	———	———
Peter's denial	———	———		———
Handing over to Pilate	———	———	———	E ———
	27.3–10			
Hearing before Pilate	———	———	———	I ———
			23.6–12	
Passover amnesty /Barabbas	———	———	———	E ———
	27.19			I ———
				E 19.4–7
	27.24–25			I 19.8–12
Condemnation of Jesus	———	———	———	E ———
Mocking of Jesus	———	———		
Way to Golgotha	———	———	———	———
			23.27–31	
Crucifixion	———	———	———	———

Mockery of the
  crucified
  Jesus   _____   _____   _____   19.20–22

The two thieves   _____   _____   23.39–43

19.23–24

19.25–27

The death of
  Jesus   _____   _____   _____   _____

27.52f.

Witnesses
  beneath the
  cross

Centurion   _____   _____   _____   19.31–37

Burial of Jesus   _____   _____   _____   _____

27.62–66

E: External scene; I: Internal scene

2. The historical problems

Apart from the rarely doubted fact that Jesus was crucified under Pontius Pilate, there are no clear views about who provoked Jesus' condemnation and on what grounds he was executed. The alternatives listed below are not meant to offer any answers but to provide some structure to the problems. They begin from the three conflicting parties which were involved in Jesus' death (the Romans, the local aristocracy and the Jewish people), and each investigates the formal legal aspects, the substantive grounds and the motives of the proceedings against Jesus and their objective basis in his life.

2.1 The Romans

1. From the formal perspective we have to ask whether the Romans condemned Jesus on the basis of their own knowledge and interest or whether they merely confirmed a death sentence pronounced by the Sanhedrin, i.e. functioned as the 'executive organ' of the Sanhedrin *de facto* (but not *de jure*).
  2. For the Romans, the motive and the grounds for accusation can only have

been political: they assumed that Jesus was making or wanting to make a political claim to power by rebelling as 'king of the Jews' (βασιλεὺς τῶν Ἰουδαίων). In this connection the question arises whether or not the so-called *titulus* of the cross (the inscription on it, Mark 15.26 par.) is historical or not.

3. Did the historical Jesus claim the title Messiah for himself (in the sense of a 'king of the Jews')? Was this claim perhaps imputed to him? Was he a political rebel, as the Zealot theory claims? Or were the Romans utterly misguided when they crucified Jesus as a messianic pretender?

2.2 The Jewish local aristocracy

Historically the involvement of the Jewish authorities is disputed: the descriptions in Mark and Matthew report a trial before the Sanhedrin with a death sentence; it is an open question whether this trial was legal or illegal. By contrast, Luke and John describe only an interrogation before the Jewish body. There is a dispute over the historical question whether the Jews had the *ius gladii*, i.e. the competence to pass capital sentences.

2. The motives for the Sanhedrin would have been pragmatic reasons or theological convictions. They could have regarded Jesus as a political danger (thus explicitly John 11.48) which had to be removed as quickly as possible. However, most exegetes assume theological convictions as a motive. There is discussion as to whether Jesus' prophecy about the temple (according to Deut. 13) was interpreted as blasphemy or whether the conflicts over the sabbath and other laws or his claim to be Messiah were the catalyst.

3. The basis in the historical Jesus could be that Jesus was in fact a security risk and either sought to provoke those around him or unintentionally had a provocative effect through his behaviour and teaching.

2.3 The ὄχλος (the people)

1. Here the debate is whether or not there was such a thing as the Passover amnesty which is reported by all the Gospels (Mark 15.6–15).

2. The question is also raised as to the possible motives for the popular sympathy for Jesus on the one hand and the people's demand for his crucifixion in the Barabbas pericope on the other, as described in the Gospels. What historical situation is reflected by these contradictory statements?

3. Finally, we have to ask whether messianic expectations among parts of the people were directed towards Jesus, so that his opponents also saw him in the light of these expectations. Did Jesus identify himself with such expectations or at least did he not distance himself clearly from them? Or were there also anxieties among the people about messianic agitators (especially in Jerusalem)?

The following table sets out the basic historical questions or alternatives sketched out above.

	Formal and legal aspects and problems	Substantive grounds and motives	Basis with Jesus
Romans	In their own interest or as an executive organ of the San-hedrin?	Jesus as a potential/actual royal pretender? Is the *titulus* on the cross historical?	Political/unpolit-ical messianic consciousness in Jesus?
Local aristocracy	Legal/illegal trial with a death sen-tence or an interrogation? Could they pass a capital sentence?	Pragmatic motive: Jesus as a political danger? Theolog-ical reasons: criticism of the law? Messianic claim?	Unintended/inten-ded provocation?
People	Is the Passover amnesty historical?	Lively expectations of the Messiah or fear of their political consequences?	Attitude towards messianic expecta-tions among the people?

1. Phases and approaches in the history of research

1.1 The literary-critical quest for an old, historical source

The quest for earlier sources behind the present Gospel of Mark is usually governed by the wish to find texts which are closer to the events reported. That is shown by the title of book by E. Wendling, 'Ur-Mark. An Attempt to Rediscover the Earliest Reports of the Life of Jesus'.[1] Wendling's Ur-Mark, which he traces as far as the passion narrative, is vivid and historical, while the stratum overlaying it is much more poetical. The evangelist shaped his account on the basis of dogmatic preconceptions. Successors have made such divisions in the sources down to the present. Two attempts which are important for the passion narratives might be mentioned:

---

[1]E. Wendling, *Ur-Marcus. Versuch einer Wiederherstellung der ältesten Mitteilungen über das Leben Jesu*, Tübingen 1905; cf. id., *Die Entstehung des Marcus-Evangeliums*, Tübingen 1908.

- Vincent Taylor identified a source A, written in good Greek, which spoke of the 'Twelve'[2] and came from the community in Rome, the place where the Gospel of Mark was composed. The evangelist combined it with source B, a narrative with many semitisms which goes back to recollections of Peter.
- By contrast, W. Schenck wants to add together all the parts which are narrated in the historic present into a consecutive source which began with the account of the entry into Jerusalem. He argues that in Mark they have been combined with a later account of the passion steeped in apocalyptic motifs.[3]
- None of the numerous attempts at a literary-critical division has so far become established.[4]

1.2 The form-critical quest for the formative interests in the passion tradition and their 'Sitz im Leben'

In his book on 'The Framework of the Story of Jesus' (1919), K.L. Schmidt came to the conclusion that the passion narrative has a special position within the Synoptic tradition, which is composed of individual pericopes: only here do we have a narrative which was always consecutive. And just as later acts of martyrs are historically much more reliable than the martyr legends about the life and the work of the saints, so too the 'particularly high, immediately historical value' of the passion narrative is unmistakable (*Rahmen**, 306). Form critics, following Schmidt, therefore always also regarded the passion narrative as historical reminiscence, albeit interwoven with the current needs of the community. Here four overall conceptions can be distinguished: the passion narrative is interpreted as historical narrative, preaching, cult legend or paraenesis.

1. Bultmann regarded as *historical* the earlier passion narrative, which would have contained only the arrest, delivery to Pilate, condemnation and crucifixion. From this 'historical account' he excluded pericopes without eye-witnesses (e.g. the hearing before the Sanhedrin in Mark 14.55–64) and well-rounded pieces like the story of the anointing (Mark 14.3–9), Gethsemane (14.32–42), the Barabbas episode (15.6–14), or the mocking of Jesus on the cross (15.16–20a). The proof from prophecy along with apologetic and novellistic motifs will have reshaped the historical reminiscences throughout (*HST**, 275–84).

2. Dibelius interpreted the passion narrative as *preaching* (*Tradition**, 178–217). He excluded far fewer individual pieces (only the story of the anointing

---

[2]V. Taylor, *The Gospel according to St Mark*, London 1952.

[3]This goes back to a 'Twelve source' posited by E. Meyer, *Ursprung und Anfänge des Christentums* (3 vols), Berlin and Stuttgart 1921–23, I, 133ff.

[4]M.L. Soards, 'The Question of a Premarcan Passion Narrative', Appendix IX, in Brown, *Death* II, 1492–524, gives a survey (with a table) of thirty-five attempts at reconstruction.

in 14.3–9, the preparation of the last supper, 14.12–16, the three prayers in Gethsemane and the messianic confession before the Sanhedrin in 14.61–63). In his view the Easter appearance in Galilee announced in Mark 14.28 would have been part of the original account. Unlike Bultmann, Dibelius did not distinguish between an original 'historical' account and a secondary reshaping, but saw the passion narrative *a priori* as a sermon which interpreted the death of Jesus as a saving event in the light of the Easter faith.

3. G. Bertram (*Die Leidensgeschichte Jesu und der Christuskult*, FRLANT 32, Göttingen 1922) defined the passion narrative as a cultic legend. Here he based himself on the central position of the eucharistic tradition in it. However, he did not understand 'cult' only in the liturgical sense; he argued that any veneration of Jesus is 'cultic'. His somewhat vague remarks were taken further by G. Schille in 1955 in an article on 'The Suffering of the Lord' ('Das Leiden des Herrn', *ZThK* 52, 161–205). Schille discovered three liturgical units: in addition to the institution of the Lord's Supper (14.18–27, 30–54, 66–72), these were a recollection of Good Friday (15.2–41) and Easter texts (the legends connected with the tomb in 15.42–47; 16.1–6). L. Schenke (*Auferstehungsverkündigung und leeres Grab*, SBS 33, Stuttgart 1968) followed him in seeing 16.1–6 as a cult ideology for a celebration of Easter by the Jerusalem community at the tomb.

4. As is shown by the very title of his book, 'The Passion of Jesus as a Model for Behaviour', D. Dormeyer, *Die Passion Jesu als Verhaltensmodell*, Münster 1974, defined the passion narrative as paraenesis. He saw a combination of two forms from the tradition in it: on the one hand the Jewish account of the death of the martyr (cf. e.g. 1 Macc. 7.1ff.), and on the other the pagan Hellenistic acts of martyrs, in which the martyr withstands his trial; this is also known to us from the so-called 'pagan acts of martyrs' from Alexandria. The two are combined, extended and shaped so that Jesus becomes the model of the Christian martyr.

1.3 Redaction-critical and traditio-historical research into the passion narrative

In the period of redaction criticism, two opposed tendencies emerge in scholarship: Mark was regarded on the one hand as the *creator* of the passion narrative and on the other as a '*conservative redactor*', who handed on an existing account largely unchanged.

1. *Mark as creator of the passion narrative*. With the rise of redaction criticism, interest was directed to the text as it now is, and the tradition standing behind it disappeared from view. Two approaches are characteristic of this tendency:

- In her book *Studien zur Passionsgeschichte*, Göttingen 1970, E. Linnemann disputed that there was a consecutive passion narrative before Mark. She argued that the evangelist himself had created one from purely fragmentary traditions which had a kerygmatic, not a historical, character. The main interest of the composition was to correct the tendency towards glorification in the first part of the Gospel, dominated by miracle stories, by the *theologia crucis* of the passion narrative.
- As the very title of the book by D. Rhoads and D. Michie, *Mark as Story*, indicates, the two American writers investigate the passion narrative as an account by Mark, without any interest in the preliminary stages or the historical background of the texts.[5]

2. Mark as a *conservative redactor*: the opposite tendency is represented by R. Pesch in his commentary on Mark.[6] In his view, the evangelist took over an extensive account of the passion which will have already have begun with Peter's confession of Jesus as Messiah (Mark 8.27ff.), to which he made only a few changes. Pesch argues that this account had been written down before 37 CE, since the high priest who is introduced into it anonymously must still be the same as the high priest in the narrative; otherwise he would have to have been distinguished from the high priest who was currently in office. Caiaphas was deposed in 37 CE.

Stimulated by this observation, in 1989 G. Theissen systematically collected all the 'indications of familiarity' in the passion tradition (independently of any division into sources, 'Local Colouring*', 166–99). They indicate the probability that the narrator presupposes that those whom he addresses have prior knowledge of persons and events. Thus the two followers of Jesus who clashed with the soldiers at his arrest remain anonymous, although almost all the other individuals are mentioned by name (often even with their place of origin). If this is a 'protective anonymity', it would make sense only during the lifetime of the individuals concerned. In that case, the traditions in the passion narrative might already have been formulated in the first generation in Jerusalem.

1.4 Legal and sociological aspects of the passion tradition

Another approach to the passion narratives is to reconstruct on the basis of contemporary sources what was legally and actually possible at the time. If the passion tradition runs counter to this framework it is unhistorical – especially if

---

[5] Cf. also Kelber (ed.), *The Passion in Mark*.
[6] R. Pesch, *Das Markusevangelium*, HThK II/2, Freiburg 1977.

the contradictions to what was possible at the time can be explained by the bias in the history of the tradition. If it corresponds to this framework, it need not necessarily be historical, but it can be.

1. H. Lietzmann argued in 1931 against the historicity of the trial before the Sanhedrin in a study of the trial of Jesus. Basing himself on J. Juster, he argued that in the time of Jesus the Jerusalem Sanhedrin had the competence to condemn Jesus to death. But as the Romans were clearly responsible for his execution – Jesus suffered the Roman death penalty, crucifixion, and not the Jewish penalty of stoning – the involvement of the Jewish authorities in the death of Jesus is on the whole a legend. Moreover it presupposed the confession of Jesus' divine status: the confession of the earthly Messiah was not blasphemy but rather the confession of a human being who sits at the right hand of God, as is anachronistically presupposed in Mark 14.62 (cf. Acts 7.55f.), on the basis of the Easter faith. This theory was developed above all in P. Winter, *On the Trial of Jesus* (1961).

2. The argument for the historicity of the trial before the Sanhedrin was presented in most detail in J. Blinzler, *The Trial of Jesus*. According to the Jewish law codified in the Mishnah, this 'trial' involved a series of offences against the law,[7] but in the time of Jesus Sadducean law, which refers directly to the Torah, had applied in proceedings before the Sanhedrin, rather than the more humane Pharisaic law which we find in the Mishnah. So according to Blinzler Jesus was in fact condemned to death by the Sanhedrin, but the Sanhedrin was dependent on the Roman prefect Pilate to carry out the death penalty.

3. There is an argument in A.N. Sherwin White, *Roman Society* (1963), that the Sanhedrin and Pilate were the chief culprits. Representatives of the Sanhedrin appear only on the side of the prosecution. The nocturnal session of the Sanhedrin prepares the charge. Pilate gives Jesus a regular trial in the form of a *cognitio extra ordinem* (see below, p. 457). As in all Roman provinces, the authority to pass death sentences lay with the Romans; in this respect John 18.31 is historical. K. Müller makes a careful survey of the problems against the background of most recent scholarship in an article on the 'possibility and execution of a Jewish capital sentence in the trial of Jesus of Nazareth' (in Kertelge [ed.]), *Prozess*, 41–83.

4. Although all the legal investigations clearly attribute the main responsibility for the execution of Jesus to the Romans, some scholars still attempt to make the Sanhedrin the decisive factor. Here the main problem is: what charge could there have been against Jesus which according to Jewish law could have involved a death sentence? A. Strobel (*Die Stunde der Wahrheit*, Tübingen 1980) and O. Betz ('Probleme des Prozesses Jesu', *ANRW* II, 25.1, 1982, 565–647) agree that

---

[7]For this complex of problems see below, pp. 460ff.

this must have been a charge of leading the people astray and false prophecy, based on Deut. 13 and 18. But in the case of Jesus there can have been no question of leading the people astray to other gods!

1.5 The integration of literary and historical approaches

The comprehensive work by R.E. Brown, *The Death of the Messiah* (1993/94), presents an integration of existing approaches and a stocktaking of research into the passion narrative. Brown carefully interprets all the sources; he does not go so far as to reconstruct the text of a pre-redactional passion narrative, but contents himself with working out the elements which could have belonged to the early passion tradition by means of a comparison (above all of Mark and John). These in turn are evaluated through a contemporary, legal and sociological reconstruction. All the parties in the conflict are described in a differentiated way. In method and results the remarks which follow often agree with Brown's position.

2. The bias in the sources

The following tendencies can be demonstrated in the sources in connection with the three conflicting parties which appear in the Gospel passion narratives (the Romans, the Jerusalem local aristocracy and the crowd) and the description of Jesus and his disciples (§2.1–5).

2.1 The Romans in the sources

The special material in the Gospels is clearly concerned to *exonerate the Romans*.

1. In the *Matthaean special material* Pontius Pilate and is wife are two witnesses who confirm Jesus' innocence. Pilate is warned by his wife as the result of a dream (a divine revelation, as in Matt. 1.20; 2.13, 19) about 'this just man' (Matt.ˢ 27.19). Pilate washes his hands in innocence (Matt.ˢ 27.24f.).

2. In the *Lukan special material* two rulers are presented as witnesses to Jesus' innocence: Herod Antipas sends Jesus back to Pilate; Pilate explicitly declares that he and Herod have found no guilt in him (Lukeˢ 23.6–12).

3. In *John,* Jesus affirms in the second hearing before Pilate, 'He who delivered me to you has the greater sin' (John 19.11). The Jewish authorities who handed Jesus over (or is Judas meant?) are thus incriminated more than Pilate, though Pilate's share of responsibility is also maintained.

4. In the Gospel of Peter, after Pilate alone has washed his hands (cf. Matt. 27.24f.), Herod is handed over to the Jews for crucifixion. No guilt attaches to the Romans, as Pilate explicitly maintains after the resurrection: 'I am clean from the

blood of the Son of God, upon such a thing have you decided' (11.46). The increasing incrimination of the Jews can be noted in numerous later Christian sources (e.g. Justin, The Acts of Pilate).

Possibly the tendency to exonerate the Romans is already at work in Mark (thus Brandon, *Trial*).

2.2 The Jerusalem local aristocracy in the sources

The tradition fluctuates between depicting a *trial* (Matt./Mark) and an *interrogation* before the Sanhedrin (Luke) or the high priest (John).

1. The *nocturnal trial* before the Sanhedrin (Mark 14.55–65/Matt. 26.59–68) contains two charges:

- The prophecy against the temple. As the witnesses contradict one another in Mark (Matthew differs), this charge is not pursued further.
- Jesus attests his own messiahship. The combination of the three most important christological titles, 'Messiah' (Χριστός), 'Son' (υἱός), 'Son of Man' (υἱὸς τοῦ ἀνθρώπου) in Mark 14.61f. is striking. This makes Jesus the model for the Christian confessor.

The trial ends with the death sentence and the maltreatment of Jesus. Here he is mocked as a 'prophet'. Jesus' messiahship plays no further role.

2. In Luke the *interrogation* before the local aristocracy is depicted as a session of the Sanhedrin, in John as an interrogation in the house of the high priest.

- According to Luke 22.66–71, the Sanhedrin session takes place in the morning. The substance of the interrogation is the messiahship of Jesus. Before Pilate, that is turned into a charge of political agitation and a call to boycott the payment of taxes (Luke 23.2). No witnesses appear and no sentence is passed.[8]
- In John Jesus is interrogated about his 'teaching', by night, by the high priest Annas (John 18.19–24), and after that is sent to Caiaphas, the high priest in office that year.[9] The reader knows that Caiaphas wants Jesus' death for purely

---

[8]Elsewhere Luke/Acts contains clear references to a condemnation of Jesus by Jewish authorities (cf. Luke 24.20; Acts 13.27f.). Can one conclude from this that Luke wanted to depict the interrogation as a trial? Or is it a sign that the Lukan interrogation scene goes back to a pre-Lukan tradition which contradicts Luke's view elsewhere?

[9]According to John 11.49; 18.13, Caiaphas is the high priest of that year. But Annas, his son-in-law, is called *the* high priest in 18.19. The relationship between them in John remains unclear.

political and pragmatic motives (John 11.47–53). There is no mention of the Sanhedrin here. In John 11.47ff. it has already resolved to kill Jesus.

3. Inferences which go beyond the sources suggest the possibility that John and Luke have preserved an older recollection according to which the Jewish authorities only prepared a denunciation to Pilate. As the 'greater guilt' (John 19.11) is attributed to these Jewish authorities in John, the depiction of the nocturnal interrogation without the elaboration of this 'greater guilt' goes against the Johannine bias. It is also striking that political motives emerge more clearly in Luke/John.

2.3 The people (ὄχλος; λαός) in the sources

In Matthew/Mark the swing in popular sympathy (cf. also Mark 14.1f. par.), so that the people call for Jesus to be crucified, is attributed to the influence of the local aristocracy.

1. Matthew reinforces the involvement of the people by the curse that he makes them bring down upon themselves: τὸ αἷμα αὐτοῦ ἐφ᾿ ἡμᾶς καὶ ἐπὶ τὰ τέκνα ἡμῶν (his blood be upon us and upon our children, Matt. 27.25); here he is referring to the destruction of Jerusalem (cf. Matt. 22.7).

2. Luke partially exonerates the people. On the one hand it calls for the crucifixion (Luke 23.13ff.); on the other a large crowd of people (including many women) laments Jesus' execution. Jesus calls on the women to lament in view of their own fate (at the destruction of Jerusalem, Luke[s] 23.27–31). Just as a distinction is made within the people, so too a distinction is made between the two 'thieves': one insults Jesus, the other is converted to him (Luke 23.39–43 and – in connection with this? – Gospel of Peter 4.13f.).

3. John does not mention the people in the passion narrative. However, the high priest is identified with 'the Jews' (e.g. John 18.31,38).

4. The Gospel of Peter heightens the involvement of the people in the proceedings against Jesus. It is not the Roman soldiers but the people which mocks Jesus with a purple robe and a crown of thorns and crucifies him (Gospel of Peter 4.10–5.17). After Jesus' death, however, the people laments its sins and because of this expects judgment on Jerusalem (7.25).

2.4 The picture of Jesus in the sources

Whereas the Romans, the aristocracy and the people are incriminated and exonerated in the sources in various ways, Jesus appears as the suffering righteous man who goes to his death in a sovereign and prescient way. He is a model for Christians who follow him, and his innocence is elaborated in various ways. The following survey shows these three tendencies in the individual ways in which they are presented in the four canonical Gospels.

1. The suffering of Jesus is interpreted as the *martyrdom of the suffering righteous man* which is deliberately accepted, necessary and known in advance:

- In Mark Jesus knows the decisive events in advance: his death (14.9, 22, 25), the place of the last supper (14.14f.), but above all the failure and betrayal of those closest to him: Judas' betrayal (14.18), the flight of the disciples (14.27), Peter's denial (14.30), the coming of the traitor (14.41f.). There is a dispute as to whether the growing isolation of Jesus culminates in abandonment by God. Or is the cry 'My God, my God, why have you forsaken me?' (15.34 = Ps. 22.2), like the other words in Mark in a foreign language, a cry which works miracles, with which Jesus calls on God to make sense of his suffering (thus C. Burchard, 'Markus 15, 34')?
- In Matthew Jesus' suffering is an expression of his sovereign will. The passion narrative begins with a (redactional) prediction of events (26.1f.); the traitor is unmasked (26.25). Jesus has twelve legions at his disposal to defend him (26.53) and he can destroy the temple and rebuild it in three days (26.61). His suffering is a voluntary renunciation of power on the part of the one to whom all power in heaven and on earth has been given.
- In Luke. Jesus' suffering is accordance with a salvation-historical 'must'. What is written about Jesus must (δεῖ) be fulfilled in him (22.37: only in Luke). Only later does this divine necessity for suffering dawn on the disciples. First of all it dawns on the disciples on the Emmaus road, to whom Jesus expounds from the scriptures 'He had to suffer' (ἔδει παθεῖν, 24.25), and then on all the disciples: 'Everything has to be fulfilled as it is written' (δεῖ πληρωθῆναι, 24.44).
- In John the sovereignty of Jesus is heightened to an extreme degree: he has the power to lay down his life and to take it again (!); no one can take it from him against his will (10.17–18). Accordingly, the 'arrest' of Jesus is restyled: after his authoritative ἐγώ εἰμι (I am he), his enemies fall to the ground. Jesus gives himself up and obtains free passage for his disciples (18.1–9) to demonstrate his power. The crucifixion is interpreted as the hour of glorification and exaltation, as a staging post on the way back to the Father, which discloses access to eternal life for believers (12.23–33; 13.1; 17.1ff.).

2. In the passion Jesus is depicted as a *model* for the Christians who follow him:

- In Mark, Jesus' confession of himself (Mark 14.61f.) becomes the model for the confession of the disciples before others (cf. Mark 8.38). It contrasts with the denial of Peter, which in typically Markan fashion is put around the interrogation scene, and finds its first positive echo in the confession of the centurion under the cross (15.39): readers are to take their place alongside the centurion and repeat his confession – extended with the conviction of Jesus' resurrection.

- In Matthew, Jesus' exemplary conduct in the passion narrative is depicted with the colours of the Matthaean ethic: the prayer in Gethsamene is shaped in analogy to the petition in the Our Father, 'Your will be done' (26.42; cf. 6.10). Jesus' reaction to the attempt by one of his disciples to offer violent resistance recalls the renunciation of violence called for by the Sermon on the Mount (26.52; cf. 5.38ff.).
- In Luke, Jesus is a model martyr, who thinks of the salvation of his fellow human beings even when he is dying. On the way to the place of execution he is moved by compassion for the future catastrophe which will affect Jerusalem (23.22ff.). He prays for his executioners to be forgiven (23.34)[10] and promises salvation to the penitent sinner who is crucified with him (23.43). Confronted with this man, the people feels penitent (23.48).
- In John, Jesus' death is an expression of his love for his own, which he practises in exemplary form to the end (εἰς τέλος), and to which he obligates his disciples: he gives them an example in the foot-washing (13.1–17) and a new commandment as his last will with the commandment to love (13.34f.; 15.9–17; 17.20–26). To the end, he is concerned that none of his own should be lost (17.9–12; 18.9); he carries his own cross (19.17) and is anxious about the future of his mother who is standing under the cross (19.25–27).

3. In all the Gospels *Jesus' innocence* is confirmed by divine miracles and human testimony:

- In Mark, the miraculous events at the crucifixion demonstrate Jesus' innocence: earthquake, eclipse and the rending of the curtain of the temple convince the centurion that 'Truly this was a son of God' (Mark 15.39).
- In Matthew, this divine testimony is communicated by human beings: Jesus repents of his betrayal and attests Jesus' innocence to the high priests (27.3ff.). Pilate's wife is convinced of Jesus' innocence by a dream (given by God, 27.19), so that Pilate washes his hands in innocence and foists the guilt on the whole people (27.24f.). Many inhabitants of Jerusalem are confronted with God's action in Jesus by miraculous phenomena (27.52). In Matthew the demonstration of innocence is addressed to the Jewish world.

---

[10]Luke 23.34 probably found its way into the text at a secondary stage (cf. the apparatus in *NTG*[27]). Or did an earlier copyist delete the prayer for forgiveness because it was in tension with the fall of Jerusalem as a punishment for the crucifixion of Jesus?

- In Luke, Jesus' innocence is (also) attested by the joint testimony of two holders of 'official' mandates from the Roman empire, Antipas and Pilate (23.6–12). The centurion confirms Jesus' innocence along with the people (23.47). This demonstration of innocence is addressed far more to the pagan environment in which the evangelist lives.
- For John, the testimony to the truth contained in the accusation 'king of the Jews' is more important than the conviction of Jesus' innocence expressed by Pilate (18.38; 19.6, 12–16). Jesus personally confesses himself a king whose kingdom is not of this world and who bears witness to the truth (18.36–38). Pilate calls him 'king of the Jews' or 'your king' (18.39; 19.14f.) and refuses to change the inscription on the cross, which is formulated in such a way that it expresses the mere claim to be king of the Jews (19.19–22). Thus the unbelieving governor unwittingly becomes a witness to the truth before the unbelieving high priests ('we have no king but Caesar', 19.15).

2.5　The picture of the disciples in the sources

Mark and Matthew emphasize the failure of the disciples; in the other sources they are increasingly spared.

1. Throughout his Gospel Mark depicts the disciples as incomprehending followers of Jesus. They sleep in Gethsemane and flee when Jesus is arrested. Only the women observe the crucifixion 'from afar'.

2. Matthew accentuates this failure. All have confessed Jesus as 'son of God' (Matt. 14.33). Nevertheless they flee. Peter has confessed him as 'Messiah, the son of the living God' (16.16). Nevertheless he denies him at the very moment at which the high priest conjures Jesus by the 'living God' to say whether he is the 'Messiah, the son of God' (26.63).

3. By contrast, Luke emphasizes that the disciples have persisted with Jesus 'in his tribulations' (22.28) and consistently omits their flight (cf. 22.47–53). Peter is promised that Jesus has prayed for his conversion (22.32). When he denies Jesus, Jesus looks at him – a recollection of this promise (22.61). The crucifixion is observed not only by the women but by all the 'acquaintances' of Jesus (i.e. also by his disciples, 23.49).

4. The Gospel of John shows a comparable tendency. The disciples do not flee, but Jesus makes sure that they can depart unharmed (18.9). At least the Beloved Disciple stands – with the women – beneath (!) the cross (19,26f.).

5. In the Gospel of Peter the disciples hide because they are sought as 'incendiaries' of the temple. Before Easter they fast and mourn (7.26f.).

The tendencies which become visible in the sources in the pictures of the Romans, the local aristocracy, the people and Jesus must now be examined in the light of the legal situation and the historical context (§§ 3–5).

3. The role of the Romans in the proceedings against Jesus

Roman rule in Judaea was exercised by a 'prefect', who came from the class of the *equites*. Later (probably after 44 CE) this title, which derived from the military hierarchy, was replaced by the official designation 'procurator', derived from financial administration. Tacitus is therefore wrong when he writes that Jesus was crucified *per procuratorem Pontium Pilatum* (*Ann.* 15, 44). However, an inscription found in Caesarea in 1961 attests the title *praefectus Judaeae* for Pilate (who held office from 26 to 6 CE). Coins minted by Pilate show that he was the only one of the prefects or procurators to choose symbols which could offend Jewish religious sensibilities.[11] It is in keeping with this that he attempted to introduce images or symbols of the emperor into Jerusalem, but in so doing he came up against vigorous resistance (*BJ* 2, 169–174).[12]

3.1 Formal legal aspects

The legal circumstances and the form of execution clearly show that the Romans were those mainly responsible for the death of Jesus.[13]

    1. The *ius gladii* was reserved to the Romans:

- Analogies from other provinces show that the Romans did not let capital sentences out of their hands. For example in Cyrene the governor alone decided whether he would judge capital cases on the basis of his own knowledge or would appoint a sworn court, whose members he then alone determined (cf. K. Müller, 'Möglichkeit', in Kertelge [ed.], *Prozess*, 60f.). The involvement of other authorities is not *a priori* excluded. However, the Romans had the last word.
- Josephus emphasizes that the first prefect over Judaea, Coponius (6–9 CE), was given all powers including the *ius gladii* (*BJ* 2, 117).
- According to Talmudic tradition the right to hold trials on capital charges was withdrawn from the Jews forty years before the destruction of the temple (70 CE, jSanh 1.18a; 7.24b).[14] 'Forty years' is a round number. The reference is probably to the beginning of direct Roman rule of Judaea in 6 CE.

---

[11]A coin of Pilate from the year 29 CE shows on the reverse a drink-offering vessel, a *simpulum* (cf. Y. Meshorer, *Jewish Coins of the Second Temple Period*, Chicago 1967, no.229). Further coins from the years 20 and 31 have on the obverse the crooked staff of the augurs, the Roman soothsayers (cf. ibid., nos.230, 231). All the types of Pilate's coins that have been preserved thus bear a pagan symbol.

[12]For Pilate see Blinzler, *Trial of Jesus*, 177–86; Winter, *Trial of Jesus*, 51–61.

[13]K. Müller, 'Möglichkeit und Vollzug jüdischer Kapitalgerichtsbarkeit im Prozess gegen Jesus', in Kertelge (ed.), *Prozess*, gives detailed infomration about the legal situation in the Roman province of Judaea.

[14]Cf. Bill I, 1027.

- In primitive Christian literature, John reproduces the historical situation accurately. There 'the Jews' say, 'We are not allowed to execute anyone ('Ημῖν οὐκ ἔξεστιν ἀποκτεῖναι οὐδένα, John 18.31).

The cases in which Jewish authorities nevertheless passed or carried out death sentences in the first century CE can be explained as exceptions. They relate to the temple as a local 'legal enclave' and to 'interim periods' in which no holder of a Roman mandate was exercising power:

- 'Temple law' threatened any Gentile who penetrated the inner temple precinct that 'he will have himself to blame that his death ensues' (ἑαυτῷ αἴτιος ἔσται διὰ τὸ ἐξακολουθεῖν θάνατον).[15] Possibly there was a tendency to extend this community justice[16] which was allowed by law to other 'crimes'. Thus perhaps the death of Stephen is to be explained in this way (Acts 7.54–60).
- In an 'interim period' James the son of Zebedee was executed by the Jewish client king Agrippa I (41–44 CE, Acts 12.2). Similarly, the Sanhedrin condemned James the brother of the Lord in 62 CE during a vacancy between the death of the procurator Felix and the accession to office of his successor Albinus. The high priest Ananus, who was responsible for this, lost his office because he had exceeded his competence (Josephus, *Antt.* 20, 200f., quoted below, p. 470).

The two non-Christian witnesses to the death of Jesus attribute responsibility to the 'procurator' Pontius Pilate (Tacitus, *Ann.* 15, 43). The (disputed) Testimonium Flavianum (Josephus, *Antt.* 18, 63f.) further emphasizes that the execution took place on the basis of a 'denunciation' by the Jewish aristocracy.[17]

2. At that time crucifixion was a Roman form of execution inflicted in particular on slaves and rebels. It was humiliating, and (officially) might not be imposed on Roman citizens.[18] There is good evidence for it as a Roman death penalty in Palestine:

---

[15]Thus the warning inscription attached to the temple, cf. Josephus, *BJ* 5, 193f.; 6, 124–6; *Antt.* 15, 417; Philo, *LegGai* 212; Acts 21.26–30. The inscription has been discovered by archaeologists, cf. Barrett §50, p.53; the Greek text is in G. Pfohl, *Griechische Inschriften als Zeugnisse des privaten und öffentlichen Lebens*, Tübingen ²1980, no.135.

[16]Müller, 'Möglichkeit', 66–9, differs: the execution of a death sentence was reserved for the Romans even in cases of crimes against the temple.

[17]For the Testimonium Flavianum see above, §3.1.2.

[18]Cf. H.-W. Kuhn, 'Die Kreuzesstrafe während der frühen Kaiserzeit. Ihre Wirklichkeit und Wertung in der Umwelt des Urchristentums', *ANRW* II 25.1, 1982, 648–793; Hengel, *Crucifixion*.

- After the 'Robber War' in 4 BCE Quintilius Varus crucified 2,000 Jews (Josephus, *Antt.* 17, 295).
- Under the procurator Felix (c.52–60 CE) the 'robbers (λῃσταί) whom he crucified, and the local inhabitants in league with them whom he caught and punished, were too many to count' (Josephus, *BJ* 2, 253).
- Jesus, too, was executed among 'robbers' (λῃσταί, Mark 15.27 par.).[19]

Of only one Jewish king, Alexander Jannaeus (103–76 CE) is the use of the penalty of crucifixion reported, around 90 BCE. This was against 800 political opponents, and was regarded as being particularly wicked (*BJ* 1, 97f.). Had a Jewish authority condemned Jesus to death, the execution would presumably have been by stoning (as in the case of his brother James, *Antt.* 20, 200) or by beheading (as in the case of his predecessor John the Baptist, Mark 6.21–29).[20] In this case, too, John alone has retained the connection between the form of execution and the condemnation by the Romans: because the Jews did not have the *ius gladii*, Jesus was crucified (18.31f.).

3. The legal proceedings against Jesus before Pontius Pilate can legally be evaluated as a *coercitio* or *cognitio*.

- *coercitio* (= 'punishment', 'compulsory measure') is the authority of any Roman governor to employ all compulsions which are necessary to maintain public order. This is nothing short of legalized arbitrariness (H. Last, *coercitio*).
- *cognitio*, by contrast, is a formal procedure according to the rules of law[21] – with accusation, interrogation, confession (in which silence was regarded as a confession) and verdict (a confession made a verdict superfluous). The verdict was given on the basis of an existing law.

---

[19]These 'robbers' were probably rebels who fought against the Roman occupation forces out of political and religious conviction, cf. Hengel, *Zealots**, 24–45, 340f.

[20]Certainly the Qumran Temple Scroll (second/first century BCE) called for the penalty of crucifixion or 'hanging on a stake' in cases of betrayal of land or people – however, this was at a time before crosses in Palestine became symbols of the hated Roman rule (cf. 11Q Temple LIV, 6ff.).

[21]According to Sherwin-White, *Roman Society*, 24–7, the trial of Jesus before Pilate was a *cognitio extra ordinem*. The Roman legal procedure originally had two parts. The state judge (praetor) determined on the basis of his investigations (his *cognitio*) the legal formula according to which the case was to be fought and decided by lay people. In civil law the proceedings were then taken over by a lay judge, and in criminal law by a sworn court under the direction of the praetor, but without his taking part in the judgment. This 'ordinary' procedure (formulary procedure) was increasingly replaced after Augustus with a procedure in which state officials controlled the whole of the proceedings and themselves passed judgment. In the provinces this

Probably the proceedings were formal. The *titulus* on the cross, which will be discussed later, indicates a violation of the law which has been noted formally. Here, too, John has probably preserved an accurate memory: Pilate sits on his judgment seat (βῆμα, 19.13; cf. Matt. 27.19) to pronounce judgment.[22]

3.2 The substantive reason for the Roman proceedings against Jesus

The *titulus* on the cross describes the basis for the accusation and condemnation of Jesus: Jesus was executed as 'king of the Jews' (βασιλεὺς τῶν Ἰουδαίων), i.e. as someone who wanted to seize political power. The historicity of the *titulus* is disputed, but the following arguments support it:

- The custom of indicating the reason for a punishment on a shield is attested (e.g. Suetonius, *Caligula* 32.2; *Domitian* 10.1; Dio Cassius 54, 3, 7) – not, however, so frequently that it could have been invented by any narrator as a natural element in an execution.
- The *titulus* is formulated from a Roman perspective. The Jews who mock do not speak of the 'king of the Jews' (Mark 15.26), but of 'Christ, the king of Israel' (15.32). The post-Easter community had no interest in inventing a royal claim on the part of Jesus which would have been open to political misunderstanding and would have caused it difficulties (cf. Acts 17.7).

In this case, too, the Gospel of John retains the political character of the accusation against Jesus most clearly. Only in John do disciples and followers call Jesus a 'king' (cf. 1.49; 6.15; 12.13). Only here do the Jews who accuse him claim that 'Anyone who makes himself king opposes Caesar' (19.12). If Jesus was

---

cognitio extra ordinem was the usual procedure. In the second century CE it replaced the old formulary procedure almost completely. In the trial of Jesus, Pilate himself judged that the case was one of *cognitio extra ordinem*. Cf. J. Bleicken. *Verfassungs- und Sozialgeschichte des Römischen Kaiserreiches* I, UTB 838, Paderborn ²1981, 262ff.

[22]L. Wenger, 'Noch einmal zum Verfahren *de plano* und *pro tribunali*', *ZSRG* 62, 1942, 366–76, thinks that Pilate first of all negotiated *de plano* because he would have preferred to end the proceedings without passing sentence. Only at the end did he ascend the judgment seat and open a proceeding *pro tribunali*. The tribunal was the elevated official seat (in the open air) on which the governor and state officials performed their official actions. Only when a judge occupied his judgment seat did a procedure *pro tribunali* begin; this had to end with a judgment, which was not necessary in a procedure *de plano* (on the floor before the tribunal).

depicted for Pilate as a 'royal pretender', two closely related crimes could have been attributed to him: on the one hand *perduellio* (from *duellio* = *bellum*?), i.e. being a major public enemy, and on the other the *crimen lasae maiestatis populi romani*, i.e. detriment to the reputation of the Roman people and those holding its mandate. As trials on a charge of *lasae majestatis* were on the increase at that time (Tacitus, *Ann.* 2.50; 3.38; Suetonius, *Tiberius* 58), it is often assumed that Jesus was accused on a charge of *lasae maiestatis* on the basis of the Lex Julia – to the degree that the Roman prefect Pilate took the law seriously at all. Jesus was a provincial of lower rank and not a Roman citizen. One could make short shrift of him.

3.3 The basis in Jesus' activity

It is usually disputed that the charge of *crimen lasae maiestatis* was justified because Jesus made political claims. Three hypotheses are possible as a historical explanation of it – with a growing agreement between the accusation against Jesus and his understanding of himself.

1. Jesus' message of the 'kingly rule' of God must have aroused the expectation among the people (and his disciples) that he himself was the messianic king who would introduce this rule (cf. Mark 11.9f.: on Jesus' entry into Jerusalem the people cry 'Blessed is the βασιλεία of our father David which is now coming'). This expectation became Jesus' fate, regardless of how he understood himself.

2. Jesus understood himself as 'Messiah', but in an unpolitical sense. His religious claim to messiahship was reinterpreted politically by his opponents in terms of the *crimen lasae maiestatis*.

3. Jesus understood himself as 'Messiah' in the political sense, and along with his disciples dreamed of a revolt.[23] However, the evidence cited for this is insufficient:[24]

- The cleansing of the temple was not an attempt at revolt but a prophetic symbolic action which endorsed the prophecy about the temple.
- The fact that there was a 'Zealot' among Jesus' disciples (Simon surnamed Ζηλωτής, Luke 6.15) does not indicate that the group of disciples were

---

[23]Thus e.g. Brandon, *Trial*, esp. 140–50. Cf. the survey of the history of research by E. Bammel, 'The Revolution Theory from Reimarus to Brandon', in Bammel and Moule (eds.), *Jesus*, 11–68.

[24]Cf. Cullmann, *Jesus and the Revolutionaries*; Hengel, *Was Jesus a Revolutionist?*.

Zealots, but quite the opposite.[25]

- Luke understood the acquisition of two swords in Luke 22.38 not as a preparation for revolt but as a repeal of the rules for mission and of the renunciation of any possibility of defence on journeys which they called for.[26]
- None of Jesus' disciples was arrested with him, as would certainly have been expected were his movement a rebel one.

Because there is a tension between the activity of Jesus and his execution as a political messianic pretender, it is probable that Jesus' accusers (and judge) reinterpreted his claim. That raises the question of the involvement and motives of the Jewish authorities in the proceedings against Jesus.

4. The role of the Jerusalem local aristocracy in the proceedings against Jesus

By all accounts the Jerusalem local authority was involved in the trial of Jesus as a kind of first instance, whereas Pilate was responsible for the execution in the last instance. We find an analogy to this series of 'instances' in the proceedings against Jesus son of Ananias, the prophet of disaster, which are reported by Josephus. This Jesus merely had a hearing before the local aristocracy and was then handed over to the procurator Albinus; however, Albinus released him (*BJ* 6, 300–9, quoted below, p. 470). Pilate would also have had this possibility. The role of the Jerusalem authorities in the proceedings against Jesus of Nazareth could have been limited to a denunciation, as in the case of Jesus son of Ananias. But in that case the trial reported by Mark and Matthew would be unhistorical. Some formal legal aspects also suggest this.

4.1 Formal legal aspects: the law relating to trials in the Mishnah

The 'trial' before the Sanhedrin as depicted by Mark and Matthew runs counter at many points to the procedure known from the Mishnah (Blinzler, *Trial*, 122ff.; R.E. Brown, *Death I*, 357ff.):

---

[25]If someone in a group is nicknamed 'the Finn', one can conclude that the others are not Finns. Brandon, *Zealots*, who argues that Jesus was closely connected with the Zealots, has a different interpretation: the fact that Jesus acceped a Zealot into the inner circle of disciples shows that the basic Zealot convictions were compatible with being a disciple of Jesus (355). Hengel, *Zealots*, 337–41, differs.

[26]The Essenes also allowed weapons on journeys, cf. Josephus, *BJ* 2, 125.

The law relating to trials in the Mishnah (Sanhedrin IV, 1 etc.)	The proceedings against Jesus
Capital trials may only take place in daylight.	The proceedings against Jesus take place by night (exception: Luke 22.66ff.).
Court proceedings may not take place on the sabbath, on festivals and the corresponding days of rest.	According to the Synoptics, Jesus' trial takes place in Passover night; according to John in the night of the day of rest.
A death sentence may not be passed on the first day of the trial, but only in a new session on the following day.	Jesus is condemned in the first session of the proceedings against him (is that why Mark 15.1 is indicated as a second session?).
According to Sanh VII, 5, blasphemy (according to Mark 14.64 the reason for the condemnation of Jesus) consists in speaking the name of Yahweh.	Both the high priest and Jesus only use periphrases for the divine name. Jesus speaks of the 'Power' at whose right hand the Son of Man will sit (Mark 14.62).
The regular place of assembly is the hall of cut stone within the temple. The temple gates are closed at night.	The session of the Sanhedrin takes place in the palace of the high priest.

Four hypotheses which attempt to resolve this contradiction between the rules for trials in the Mishnah and the 'trial' of Jesus before the Sanhedrin are currently under discussion:

1. *The trial before the Sanhedrin was historical.* Either Jesus was condemned in accordance with Sadducean law, which was harsher than the Pharisaic law that was incorporated into the Mishnah.[27] Or, while Pharisaic law was valid, it did not apply because an 'extraordinary penal procedure' was attempted against Jesus.[28]

2. *The trial before the Sanhedrin was unhistorical.* It was 'invented' to

---

[27]Thus Blinzler, *Trial,* 134ff. However, in that case the offence against the commandment relating to the feast would also remain; cf. Lohse, *The Death and Suffering of Jesus,* 80fx.

[28]Thus A. Strobel, *Die Stunde der Wahrheit,* WUNT 21, Tübingen 1980, 46–61, 85, etc. Such a procedure, in which all the usual regulations are relaxed because of the 'demand of the hour', is attested often in the later Talmudic literature, cf. Blinzler, *Trial,* 149–57. However, Blinzler regards these passages as 'pure fiction' on the part of the rabbis to justify earlier trials which were not carried out in a 'regular' way.

exonerate the Romans. H. Lietzmann put forward a variant on this theory which has become a classic:[29] at the time of Jesus the Sanhedrin had the unrestricted right to pass a capital sentence and could have had Jesus executed by stoning. But as Jesus was crucified by the Romans, the involvement of the Sanhedrin is completely unhistorical.

3. *An interrogation before the Sanhedrin has been restyled as a trial at a later stage.* The interrogation of Jesus by the high priest and some members of the Sanhedrin which prepared for a charge presented to Pilate could be historical.[30] This interrogation was reshaped under the impact of the period between 41 and 44 CE when Jewish authorities had the *ius gladii* and also executed Christians (like James the son of Zebedee, Acts 12.1f.). In the light of these experiences the interrogation of Jesus was reinterpreted as a regular trial.

4. *Several processes have been fused into a trial.* R.E. Brown (*Death* I, 362f.; 553ff.) argues that a formal session of the Sanhedrin which resolved on Jesus' death took place (long) before his arrest (cf. John 11.47ff., but also Mark 11.18; 14.2f.). After the arrest there was then an interrogation (as described in John 18.19ff. and Luke 22.66ff.). Mark's account has fused several processes into a kerygmatically impressive narrative.

4.2   The substantive basis for the Sanhedrin proceedings

Regardless of whether the Sanhedrin proceedings were an interrogation or a trial, the substantive and legal reasons for it need to be assessed. Mark 14.55ff. sees Jesus' prophecy about the temple and his claim to be Messiah as the motive for the proceedings against him. Since neither charge was necessarily a crime punishable by death (and 'blasphemy', cf. Mark 14.64), some scholars assume that Jesus was condemned as a false prophet and one who misled the people, or because he claimed divine status.

1. *Jesus' prophecy about the temple.* From Jer. 26.1–19 on there is evidence that criticism of the temple was a crime punishable by death. According to Josephus (*Antt.* 13, 79), Samaritans who defended the legitimacy of their temple against the Jerusalem temple were executed. The 'Teacher of Righteousness' was persecuted, among other things, because of his criticism of the temple (1QpHab IX, 9f.; 4QPs 37 4, 8f.); the 'Wicked Priest' even attempted to kill him on the Day of Atonement (1QpHab XI, 4–8). Jesus the son of Ananias was accused because of his prophecy against the temple and the city, but was released by the Roman

---

[29]H. Lietzmann, 'Der Prozess Jesu' (1931), 'Bemerkungen zum Prozess Jesu I + II' (1931/32), in *Kleine Schriften* II, TU 68, Berlin 1958, 251–63, 264–8, 269–76. This thesis, which is probably untenable historically, was again put forward by Winter, *Trial*.
[30]Thus e.g. J. Gnilka, *Das Evangelium nach Markus*, EKK II/2, 1979, 284–8.

procurator (Josephus, *BJ* 6, 300ff.). However, these examples also show that most critics of the temple survived – from Jeremiah through the 'Teacher of Righteousness' to Jesus the son of Ananias. Criticism of the temple was grounds for hostility, but not for a death sentence. A decisive factor in the hostility against Jesus was that with the temple the interests of the Sanhedrin were directly affected. By contrast, for Pilate, for understandable reasons, the temple played no role: he could have regarded a prophecy against the temple as an internal Jewish matter – and Pilate was certainly no 'zealot' for the sanctity of the temple.[31]

2. *False prophecy and leading the people astray* according to Deut. 13 and 17. But could not the prophecy about the temple explain a death penalty if it is assessed as false prophecy and leading people astray? Here the Mishnaic law differentiates between a *mesith* (Greek πλάνος), who leads a private individual astray into idolatry, and a *maddiach* (Greek ἀποστάς), who leads the whole people astray. The charge of false prophecy and witchcraft can be combined with the charge of leading the people astray into idolatry. The notion that Jesus was accused as a *mesith* or *maddiach* is so attractive because in such a case the usual rules for a trial might be set aside (tSanh X, 11). One might proceed with guile (Sanh VII, 10) and kill the person concerned at the time of a festival (tSanh XI, 7). According to a Jewish source (bSanh 43, quoted above, p. 75) Jesus was in fact executed as a *mesith,* and according to Christian sources, too, he was accused of leading the people astray (Matt. 27.63f.; John 7.11f., 47; Justin, *Dial.* 69.7; 108.2). But this charge does not appear in the earliest sources (Mark 14.55ff.). In Mark it does not appear in the account of the trial itself. In Luke it refers to political agitation, not to leading people astray on religious matters (Luke 23.2). Above all, the central charge laid against a *mesith* – that of leading an individual astray into idolatry – would be absurd in the case of the historical Jesus. The evidence cited belongs in a time in which Jews and Christians had separated and Jews could have seen Jesus as someone who had led people astray and who had made his followers apostates from the Jewish law.[32]

3. *Jesus' messianic claim* (cf. Blinzler, *Trial*, 125–34; Betz, 'Probleme', 633ff.). The second point in the accusation given in Mark 14.61f. is Jesus' claim to be Messiah. However, apart from this passage there is no indication that a claim to be Messiah was a crime according to Jewish law or even amounted to blasphemy. The messianic pretender Simon Bar Kochba, who led the resistance in the Jewish

---

[31]Müller, 'Moglichkeit', 71f., differs. He postulates two technical exceptions to Roman criminal law in the province of Judaea: entering the inner temple precinct and prophesying against the temple required the involvement of the Jewish Sanhedrin in the proceedings, but the Romans passed the decisive verdict. In that case Pilate could also have intervened because of Jesus' prophecy about the temple.

[32]Cf. J. Maier, *Jesus von Nazareth in der talmudischen Überlieferung*, EdF 82, Darmstadt 1978, 210–35.

war of 132–13 CE, was recognized by Rabbi Akiba as Messiah. His claim was not blasphemy, but it was politically explosive. Therefore a messianic claim on the part of Jesus would have been likely to lead to Jesus being charged before Pilate and would have contributed to his execution. For an 'unpolitical' Messiah would have been difficult to imagine at that time. To this degree Jesus' messiahship could have played a role before the Sanhedrin. But it remains open whether this messianic claim was attributed to Jesus, whether he asserted it, or whether a post-Easter projection of the messianic faith of the community back on to Jesus has not coloured memories. Since Jesus was executed as 'king of the Jews', at all events before Pilate he did not distance himself from the messianic expectations which were focussed on him (cf. §16.3).

4. *Jesus' claim to divine status.* According to Mark 14.63 Jesus is condemned for 'blasphemy'. Even if Mishnaic law defines blasphemy as pronunciation of the name of Yahweh, in New Testament times the concept had a wider significance: it means cursing, mocking or despising God – and claiming a status which only God has (Brown, *Death* I, 520–6, 531ff.). While a claim to be Messiah was not intrinsically blasphemous, a claim to divine dignity was. According to John 19.7, Jesus is to die because he claimed to be 'son of God'. In Mark 14.62 one could see a comparable claim in Jesus' announcement that he is sitting at the right hand of God (Catchpole, *Trial*, 271). However, there is much to suggest that this statement presupposes the post-Easter confession of Jesus: Jesus was 'divinized' only on the basis of the Easter experience. Such a 'divinization' would especially be blasphemy if it implied the exaltation of a *crucified* man to God. Moreover the combination of the three most important christological titles, Messiah, Son of God and Son of Man, in Mark 14.62f. suggests a post-Easter perspective and can be hardly historical (cf. already Lietzmann, 'Prozess', 255f.).

4.3   The basis in the activity of Jesus

Either the motive for the hostility of the Sanhedrin is sought in Jesus' religious message (whether in his criticism of the Law or of the temple), or political and pragmatic grounds are assumed: in that case Jesus would have been executed as a political risk-factor. Both could also have been the case.

1. Traditionally, Protestant exegetes above all see *Jesus' criticism of the Law* as the real cause of his death. According to Mark 3.6 the first resolve to kill Jesus comes after a conflict over the sabbath: 'Jesus died because of the convictions of his Jewish opponents, because in all his behaviour he had rebelled against the will of God in the law which they had advocated . . .'[33] Against this widespread theory it has to be argued that:

---

[33] J. Roloff, *Neues Testament*, Neukirchen ⁴1985, 184f.

- The conspiracy of the Herodians and Pharisees in Mark 3.6 to kill Jesus could be a redactional link created by Mark to relate Jesus' conflicts (over the sabbath) with the passion. In Mark 12.13 Mark makes the same groups look for a political reason for proceeding against Jesus (the question of tax!) – and thus perhaps comes closer to the historical truth. However, it is striking that neither the Herodians nor the Pharisees play a role in the passion narrative.
- In the case of the Pharisees, with whom Jesus is in conflict over questions of the Law, this is all the more striking, since they were represented in the Sanhedrin. According to later accounts, those in the Sanhedrin who 'sympathize' with the Christians are Pharisees (Nicodemus, John 3.1ff.; 7.30f., and Gamaliel, Acts 5.33ff.). Joseph of Arimathea with his eschatological expectation is certainly also closer to the Pharisees than to the Sadducees (cf. Mark 15.43).

2. The immediate occasion for the intervention of the local aristocracy was *Jesus' criticism of the temple.* The lofty status and a large part of the income of the local aristocracy depended on the temple. The analogy of Jesus son of Ananias who prophesied against the temple and Jerusalem (*BJ* 6, 300–9) shows that the aristocracy proceeded against such 'prophets' – if only to avoid disturbances which often broke out, particularly at the time of the great temple festivals (Theissen, 'Tempelweissagung').

3. In any case, Jesus therefore drew upon himself the hostility of the local aristocracy as a *possible factor of political unrest*: 'Jesus was executed because Jerusalem's city council or some of its members feared that he would cause unrest, prompting the Romans to act. He did not die because his attitude to the Torah and to Israel was such that Torah-believing Jews saw no other choice.'[34]

5. The role of the people in the proceedings against Jesus

On the one hand the 'people' has the function of protecting Jesus. Because the Jerusalem authorities feared the people, he was to be executed before the feast (Mark 14.1f.). On the other hand, in the Barabbas scene the people tips the scales in favour of a verdict against Jesus. However, there is a dispute as to whether this decision between Jesus and Barabbas is historical.

5.1 A formal legal aspect: the Passover amnesty

So far no evidence has been found for the custom of releasing a prisoner at Passover, not even in Josephus, who is well disposed towards the Romans. However, an occasional amnesty is imaginable:

---

[34]Burchard, 'Jesus'*, 67.

- Such a release of a prisoner at the request for the people is attested for Egypt in 85 CE: the governor releases a certain Phibion with the words, 'You deserved to be flogged . . . but I will give you to the crowd.'[35]
- Instances of prisoners being released by the procurator Albinus are attested for Palestine (*Antt.* 20, 215).

Should such a release have coincided with the condemnation of Jesus, a story like that about Barabbas could easily have arisen without there being the custom of a regular Passover amnesty.[36]

5.2 Substantive reasons for the attitude of the people

The composition of the Barabbas pericope is hardly imaginable without a hostile attitude on the part of the people to Jesus (which was historical). Probably we should distinguish between the 'people' who were sympathetic to Jesus (because of whom he was to be killed before the Passover, Mark 14.1f.), which can only mean the people who did not live in Jerusalem but streamed into the city for festivals, and the Jerusalem population. The latter may have been the 'people' hostile to Jesus in the Barabbas scene, since the high priests had influence over them. The prophecy about the temple also affected the inhabitants of Jerusalem, since it was a threat to the pilgrimage sanctuary and their material existence often depended on the temple.

5.3 The basis in the historical Jesus

The historical Jesus probably aroused messianic expectations among the people. The fact that he was executed as 'king of the Jews' presupposes that he did not clearly distinguish himself from such expectations (cf. §16.3 on the title Messiah). At any rate, by executing him the Romans and the aristocracy wanted to 'crucify' not only his person but also these expectations.

6. Summary and hermeneutical reflections

The death of Jesus is the consequence of tensions between a charismatic coming from the country and an urban elite, between a Jewish renewal movement and

---

[35]Papyrus Florentinus no.61, quoted in A. Deissmann, *Light from the East*, London 1910, 267.
[36]Cf. J. Gnilka, 'Der Prozess Jesu nach den Berichten des Markus und Matthäus', in Kertelge(ed.), *Prozess*, esp. 34–6.

alien Roman rule, between someone who proclaimed cosmic change which was also to transform the temple and the representatives of the *status quo*. Religious and political grounds cannot be separated. Certainly Jesus did not want to seize rule for himself with the help of his disciples. But he proclaimed a 'rule of God' which would break in soon, in which the first would be last and the last first. God would bring it in in a miraculous way. He and his disciples would rule Israel (Luke 22.28–30). There was no place for the rule of the temple aristocracy and the Romans.

Both groups were his opponents, but they pursued different interests. The Sanhedrin took offence at his prophecy against the temple; his criticism of the temple shattered the legitimacy of their privileges. The Roman prefect must have been mistrustful of the 'kingdom' of which Jesus spoke. He must have seen it as a danger to his power. Therefore Jesus was mocked before the Sanhedrin as a 'prophet' (Mark 14.65) and before the Romans as a 'king' (Mark 15.16–18). However, both groups had the same interest in avoiding unrest. Both worked together in proceeding against Jesus.

Here small élites of Jews and Romans took action. However, ordinary people were also involved: a crowd of Jews called for Jesus' death, and pagan soldiers maltreated and crucified Jesus as 'king of the Jews'.[37] The disciples played a dishonourable role: Judas betrayed the place where Jesus was staying and made an inconspicuous arrest possible. All the disciples fled. Peter denied Jesus in order not to endanger himself.

The question who was 'guilty' of the 'death' of Jesus is not the right one. We can only answer the question who was responsible for his execution. The responsibility lies with the Romans, who acted on the initiative of the Jewish local aristocracy. Many additional causes and factors might be mentioned: Jesus himself risked his end when he went to Jerusalem. His whole activity had a self-stigmatizing character. He laid himself open and deliberately drew aggression upon himself. It is also true that he became a victim of structural conflicts between city and country, Jews and Romans, people and aristocracy. Many suffered as a result of these conflicts.

It is also legitimate to ask why Jesus attracted such aggression. Three aspects of his activity may have been the cause of this: 1. his critical attitude to the Torah; 2. his criticism of the temple; and 3. politically explosive aspects of his preaching

---

[37]The Roman cohorts whose soldiers executed Jesus were auxiliary troops in which pagan inhabitants of Palestine (e.g. from Sebaste) served. They shared the anti-Jewish attitudes of many immediate neighbours of the Jews. Their attitude to Jewish 'kings' emerges from their behaviour in Caesarea after the death of Agrippa I in 44 CE: they held celebrations and carried off pictures of his daughters to put them on the roofs of brothels (Josephus, *Antt.* 19, 356–66). Jesus was maltreated, tortured and killed by soldiers who belonged to a troop with an antisemitic attitude.

– whether the expectation of a kingly rule of God or the claim to be the Messiah. His criticism of the temple and prophecy about it may have been the decisive factor among these three. As a rule, Jesus' 'criticism of the Torah' is merely a liberal exposition of the Torah. He might have attracted attention and caused offence by this criticism, but it was no reason for executing him. The same is true of his eschatological expectations, which were also shared by other Jews. However, the way in which they were intensified by the appearance of a charismatic was a problem for the upper classes. They denied the present form of the world and society its legitimacy. But with his criticism of the temple Jesus came directly into conflict with the religious centre of the Judaism of his day. Judaism at that time was very much more temple religion than Torah religion. It was only with the loss of the temple that the Torah exclusively came into the centre of the faith. Still, the conflict with the temple could not be isolated from other aspects of Jesus' activity: his liberal interpretation of the Torah must now have become even more suspicious. For the Torah was the basis of the legitimation of the temple, the Pentateuch the ideology of the temple cult. The same is true of the political aspects of Jesus' activity: the temple was the basis for the political autonomy of the Jewish community and thus the basis for the privileges of the upper class. Anyone who criticized it was a political troublemaker. But it is important to note that with his criticism of the temple Jesus did not go beyond Judaism. Other Jews similarly dissociated themselves from the temple: John the Baptist and the Essenes, not to mention the Samaritans. It was the great 'achievement' of the Judaism of the first two centuries CE that it turned into a religion which could also live without the temple – despite the great internal bond to it. Jesus and his preaching belongs to this process of transformation. With all his conflicts he is utterly part of Jewish religious history.

His death confirmed an age-old insight of Israel: only naive faith can believe in a connection between good behaviour and happiness. Israel had recognized that the righteous, too, can suffer and sufferers can also be righteous. The conquered can be more in the right than their conquerors. God can be on the side of the outcast and the despised. Therefore the primitive Christian community soon told the story of Jesus' death with the motifs of the suffering of the righteous. In that way the disciples could cope with a death which they had not expected.

This death became influential above all in a bold new interpretation: as a sacrificial death which created the foundation for a new community among men and women and between them and God. This significance can only be sketched out briefly here.

Jesus had given his last meal with his disciples the form of the symbolic founding of a 'new covenant'. After his death his disciples interpreted this death as a 'sacrifice' which sealed this covenant. They had not offered this 'sacrifice'. Rather, the Easter appearances had made them certain that God had acted in the death of Jesus. God alone had offered a sacrifice, on their behalf, although they had all failed.

This introduced a revolutionary change into the notion of sacrifice. Usually these 'atoning sacrifices' served to assuage an angry deity or to restore a violated order. The one who sacrifices asks for God's reconciliation through the sacrifice. That applies even if the sacrificial cult is regarded as a divine institution which God has given to human beings in order to forgive sins. The new view comprises two notions:

In this new sacrifice human beings do not seek to influence God so that he desists from his wrath; rather, God acts so that human beings shall cease from their hostility towards God and their neighbours. It is not God but human beings who are to be changed through the sacrifice; it is not God who is to overcome his wrath, his anti-social and aggressive impulses, but human beings.

This sacrifice has its effect not through death but through overcoming death. In traditional animal sacrifice the individual animal is killed, but the life is symbolic-ally preserved – by returning the blood of the animal as the seat of life to God. The individual animal dies to preserve life as a whole. However, Jesus' new sacrifice became effective, not through death but through overcoming death. God gave life in order to create it anew from death.

Paul was the first one to conceptualize this new notion of sacrifice. Salvation is created, not through 'assuaging' an angry God, but through overcoming human hostility (cf. Rom. 5.6–11). Salvation is achieved, not through killing but through resurrection (Rom. 4.25). Salvation does not begin with human requests for reconciliation but with God's request, 'Be reconciled with God' (II Cor. 5.20).

For Paul, too, this salvation was realized in the face of the 'rulers of this world' (I Cor. 2.6ff.). In the struggle over the distribution of rule and power it is important to be able to sacrifice other life for one's own. But in Jesus' sacrificial death the important thing is how life that does not live at the expense of other life becomes possible through the sacrifice of the one life.

7. Tasks

7.1 Important sources outside Christianity on the legal situation

Below, three important sources – which have already been discussed under 3–5 – are given in English translation. What important information can be gathered from these texts for assessing the legality of the death of Jesus?

(a) Josephus, *Antt.* 20, 199–203:

> The younger Ananus . . . was rash in his temper and unusually daring: he followed the school of the Sadducees, who are indeed more heartless than any other Jews. He thought he had a favourable opportunity because Festus was dead and Albinus was still on the way.[38] And so he convened the judges of the Sanhedrin and brought before them a man named James, the brother of Jesus who was called the Christ, and certain others. He accused them of having transgressed the law and delivered them up to be stoned. Those of the inhabitants of the city who were considered fair-minded and were strict in observance of the law were offended at this. They therefore secretly sent to King Agrippa, urging him, for Ananus had not even been correct in his first step, to order him to desist from any further such actions.[39] Certain of them even went to meet Albinus, who was on his way from Alexandria, and informed him that Ananus had no authority to convene the Sanhedrin without his consent. Convinced by these words, Albinus angrily wrote to Ananus, threatening that he would bring vengeance upon him for what he had done. King Agrippa, because of Ananus' action, deposed him from the high priesthood which he had held for three months, and made replaced him with Jesus the son of Damnaeus.

(b) Josephus, *BJ* 6, 300–6:

> Four years before the war when the city was enjoying profound peace and prosperity, there came to the feast at which it is the custom of all Jews to erect tabernacles to God, one Jesus, son of Ananias, a rude peasant, who, standing in the temple, suddenly began to shout: 'A voice from the east, a voice from the west, a voice from the four winds, a voice against Jerusalem and the sanctuary, a voice against bridegrooms and brides, a voice against the whole people.' Day and night he uttered this cry as he went through all the streets. Some of the more prominent citizens, very annoyed at these ominous words, laid hold of the fellow and beat him savagely. Without saying a word in his own defence or for the private information of his persecutors, he persisted in shouting the same warning as before. The Jewish authorities, rightly concluding that some supernatural force was responsible for the man's behaviour, took him before the Roman procurator. There, though scourged till his flesh hung in ribbons, he neither begged for mercy nor shed a tear, but lowering his voice to the most mournful of tones answered every blow with 'Woe to Jerusalem!' When Albinus – for that was the procurator's name – demanded to know who he was, where he came from and why he uttered such cries, he made no reply whatever to the questions but endlessly repeated his lament over the city, till Albinus decided that he was a madman and released him.

---

[38]Porcius Festus (60–62) and Lucceius Albinus (62–64) were Roman procurators in Palestine. As Festus died unexpectedly, there was a power vacuum after his death until the arrival of his successor.

[39]The reference is to the Jewish king Agrippa II, who ruled Transjordan on behalf of the Romans and supervised the temple until 66.

(c) Tacitus, *Annals* 15, 44:[40]

> To suppress this rumour (that he had himself set fire to Rome) Nero fabricated scapegoats . . . and punished with every refinement the notoriously depraved Christians (as they were popularly called). Their originator, Christ, had been executed in Tiberius' reign by the governor of Judea, Pontius Pilate . . .

7.2 The question of 'guilt for the death of Jesus'

In exegetical literature, the accusation that the Jews had murdered God, which for centuries the church made indiscriminately against all Jews with reference to Matt. 27.25, is now usually said to be inappropriate in exegetical literature. Nevertheless anti-Jewish thought patterns and stereotypes are often to be found both in the historical evaluation of the circumstances of the death of Jesus and in the theological evaluation of the passion.

Criticize the following sections, which come from the closing chapters of two books on the trial of Jesus:

> To attribute the passion to God's and Jesus' will or to the action of Satan and his demonic powers is not in any way to seek to ignore, to dispute or even to diminish the guilt of those who were historically responsible.. The New Testament texts discussed give a clear answer to the question who was *historically* responsible for Jesus' death. It was the Jews, or more precisely the members of the Sanhedrin at the time and the inhabitants of Jerusalem who made common cause with them; in addition the complicity of the Roman procurator Pilate was also emphasized. Alongside the Jews . . . Pontius Pilate was responsible for the execution of Jesus. One mitigating factor is that he did both [the scourging and the condemnation to be crucified] under the pressure of the fanatical Jews . . . Although he proclaimed the death sentence which directly led to Jesus' execution, his overall guilt is less than that of the Jews . . .[41]

> In that hour of the trial of Jesus . . . it also had to be made clear that Caiaphas and his people were fatefully involved in this decision. In so far as one may speak of a guilt of the Jew, this should unconditionally prompt the notion of tragic guilt . . . [That] 'hour of truth' . . . also in no way has anything to do with defects in a few who were involved, but with a defect in human beings and their order generally . . . The role and attitude of Caiaphas stem from his unconditional attachment and loyalty to the Law.

---

[40]Translation by M. Grant in Tacitus, *Annals of Imperial Rome*, Harmondsworth 1956, 354.
[41]Cf. Blinzler, *Trial*, 289–95; however, this particular passage is not in the English translation.

He therefore also had to impose the Law on Jesus in a tragic way . . . Caiaphas stands . . . for human beings under the fatal compulsions of the law, which in truth expresses all our guilt and failure. That Caiaphas . . . tragically had to condemn the Messiah of the people to death on the basis of the law is one of the darkest and most incomprehensible elements of Jewish history. In such an event the whole hidden-ness of the history of Israel comes upon us and we recognize how much the death of Jesus may be welcomed as the key to a last mystery . . . If it is true that the experience of the tragic is dark and unfathomable and aims at the catharsis of the soul, then this Jesus offers it to us. As far as the Jews are concerned, from then on they must doubt the truth of the law as an ultimate truth.[42]

7.3 The Letter of Pilate: a second-century source on the passion

The passion of Jesus was often treated in apologetic and popular literature after the New Testament. The person of Pilate in particular stirred the imagination, as is shown by the Pilate literature which grew steadily in the course of the centuries. Justin (c.150) already refers to the 'acts composed under Pontius Pilate' (*Apol.* I, 35) in order to confirm details of the passion narrative. Whether he really knew of such acts or merely postulated their existence is doubtful, but it is striking that in chapter 48 he refers to the same acts as proof of the miracles of Jesus, which one would not expect on the basis of the New Testament, where miracles play no role for Pilate.

The following letter from Pilate to Claudius (!), which has been handed down in the Acts of Peter and Paul (chs.40–42), belongs to the earliest literature about Pilate (probably second century). Presumably it only became a letter to Claud-ius by being inserted into the present context (the controversy with Simon Magus), and was probably originally addressed to Tiberius:[43]

Pontius Pilate to his Emperor Claudius, greeting. There happened recently some-thing which I myself brought to light. The Jews through envy have punished themselves and their posterity with a fearful judgment. For their fathers had received the promise that God would send them from heaven his holy one, who would rightly be called their king and whom God had promised to send to earth by a virgin. But when he came to Judaea when I was governor, and they saw that he restored sight to the blind, cleansed lepers, healed paralytics, expelled evil spirits from men; and even raised the dead, and commanded the winds, and walked dryshod upon the

---

[42]Strobel, *Stunde* [n.28], 138f., 142.

[43]Translation in *NTApoc* 1, 1963, 575; 1991, 527. By contrast, W. Michaelis (*Die apocryphen Schriften zum Neuen Testament*, Bremen 1956, 448f.) thinks that there is an error in the textual tradition which derives either from the chronological ignorance of the copyist or from a tradition handed down in Irenaeus, *Haer.* 2, 22, 3–6, according to which Jesus was fifty and thus died under Claudius.

waves of the sea, and did many other miracles, and all the people of the Jews acknowledged him to be the Son of God, the chief priests were moved by envy against him, and they seized him and delivered him to me, and bringing forward lie after lie they accused him of being a sorcerer and transgressing their law. And I believed this was so, and ordered him to be scourged, and handed him over to their will. And they crucified him, and set guards at his tomb. But he rose again on the third day, while my soldiers kept watch. But the Jews were so carried away by their wickedness that they gave money to my soldiers, saying: 'Say that his disciples stole his body.' But although they took the money, they were unable to keep silent about what had happened. For they testified that he had arisen, and that they had seen it, and that they had received money from tile Jews. I have reported this lest anyone should lie about the matter and you should think that the lies of the Jews should be believed (*NT Apoc I*, 1991, 527).

Dating: that despite its false addressee this letter is very old is attested by the striking agreements with remarks of Tertullian (c.200) in the *Apologeticum,* 21, 15ff.: he mentions the Jewish expectation of Christ on the basis of the prophetic writings; also that the Jews regarded him as 'only a man' but because of his power saw him as a magician because of his activity of 'expelling demons from men by a word, restoring vision to the blind, cleansing the leprous, reinvigorating the paralytic, summoning the dead to life again, making the very elements of nature obey him, stilling the storms and walking on the sea'. The description of Jesus' following among the people; the hatred of the Jewish leaders; their denunciation to Pilate who hands Jesus over to them for crucifixion; the description of the circumstances of the guard over the tomb; the resurrection and the attempt at bribery largely correspond (however, Tertullian does not state that the Roman soldiers saw the resurrection). His summary is: 'Pilate, now in fact a Christian in his convictions, sent word of him to the reigning Caesar, who was at that time Tiberius.'[44]

1. What tendencies which already appear in the New Testament description of the Romans, the Jewish local authorities, the Jewish people and Jesus do the Letter of Pilate and Tertullian show?

2. What emphases in the account of the passion are new? What is their historical value?

---

[44]Quoted from Tertullian, *Apologeticum*, The Ante-Nicene Fathers, Edinburgh and Buffalo, NY 1985, 35.

The Risen Jesus: Easter and its Interpretations

J. Alsup, *The Post-Resurrection Appearance Stories of the Gospel Tradition*, CThMA 5, Stuttgart 1975;. von Campenhausen, 'Der Ablauf der Osterereignisse und das leere Grab' (1952), in id., *Tradition und Leben*, Tübingen 1960, 4–113; R. Bultmann, 'New Testament and Mythology', in id., *New Testament and Mythology and Other Essays*, ed. S.M. Ogden, Philadelphia and London 1985, 1–44; id., 'On the Problem of Demythologizing', in ibid., 95–131; H. Conzelmann, 'The Analysis of the Confessional Formula I Cor. 15.3–5', *Interpretation* 20, 1966, 15–25; C.H. Dodd, *The Apostolic Preaching and Its Developments*, London 1936, ³1963; id., 'The Appearances of the Risen Christ', in D.E. Nineham (ed.), *Studies in the Gospels (FS R.H. Lightfoot)*, Oxford 1957, 9–35; C.F. Evans, *Resurrection and the New Testament*, London 1970; W. Kramer, *Christ, Lord, Son of God*, London 1966; G. Lüdemann, *The Resurrection of Jesus*, London and Philadelphia 1994; S. Maclean Gilmour, 'The Christophany to More than Five Hundred Brethren', *JBL* 80, 1961, 248–52; H.K. McArthur, ' "On the Third Day" (1 Cor 15.4b and Rabbinic Interpretation of Hosea 6.2)', *NTS* 1, 1971/72, 81–86; W. Marxsen, 'The Resurrection of Jesus as a Historical and Theological Problem', in C.F.D. Moule (ed.), *The Significance of the Message of the Resurrection for Faith in Jesus Christ*, London 1968, 15–50; id., *The Resurrection of Jesus of Nazareth*, London and Philadelphia 1970; W. Pannenberg, *Systematic Theology*, Vol. 2, Grand Rapids and Edinburgh 1994, 343–63; C.E. Sleeper, 'Pentecost and Resurrection', *JBL* 84, 1965, 389–99.

Introduction

The Easter faith is of central importance for the understanding of Jesus and the self-understanding of human beings. Paul combines the two when he objects to those who deny the resurrection, 'If Christ has not been raised, your faith is futile and you are still in your sins . . . we are of all men most to be pitied' (I Cor. 15.17, 19). In Paul's view one's attitude to Jesus' resurrection is decisive for the meaning or meaninglessness of faith in Jesus, for imprisonment in sin or forgiveness of sins, for human misery or the overcoming of it. In fact Easter faith involves the decision whether one can see the ground of one's own existence in the story of Jesus. Easter is God's yes to Jesus, like the yes of the disciples, both men and women, to him – and that would be the case even if one did not understand the Easter faith as the basis for these 'yes'es but as the expression of them: as human affirmation of the cause of Jesus despite the cross and failure. Easter faith involves a decision about one's human 'self-understanding'. If here something ultimate is disclosed (even through 'subjective visions'), then death and anxiety about death do not have the last word. For however one thinks about Easter, it is a protest against death, and especially against violent death.

Task

To prepare for this section read the following decisive source texts: I Cor. 15.3–11; Mark 15.42–16.8 (9–20); Matt. 27.57–28.20; Luke 23.50–24.53; Acts 1.1–11; John 19.38–21.25.

Note indications which could help to answer the following questions: which appearances are mentioned both in the formula tradition in Paul (I Cor. 15.3ff.) and in the narrative traditions of the Gospels? Where are the Easter events located? What motifs in the Easter tradition can be recognized which help to dispel doubt about the reality of the Easter appearances?

1. Six phases in discussion of the Easter faith

Six phases can be recognized in historical-critical discussion of the Easter event. First of all, after H.S. Reimarus the empty tomb, interpreted in rationalistic terms, was the focus of interest (1.1). Then D.F. Strauss stimulated scholars to recognize the Easter appearances as the historical basis of the Easter faith and to interpret them in the sense of a 'subjective vision theory' (1.2).[1]

A new theological interpretation of Easter faith was given with the shift to form criticism (say from 1920 on). There is no historical explanation of it, but it is meant to explain the traditions about Jesus (1.3).

In reaction to this, in the 1950s attempts were made at a historical reconstruction (1.4). Since the 1960s scholars have concentrated primarily on the interpretative framework of the Easter appearances, since decisions about the real content of the appearances are always made within a particular construction of reality, which applies equally both to those who receive the Easter visions and to modern consciousness (1.5). But alongside this (and especially in most recent times), questions have also been asked about the Easter event itself, whether to explain it plausibly as an 'objective' event or to interpret it psychologically as a 'subjective 'event (1.6).

---

[1]P. Hoffmann, 'Die historisch-kritische Osterdiskussion von H.S. Reimarus bis zu Beginn des 20.Jahrhunderts', in id. (ed), *Zur neutestamentlichen Überlieferung von der Auferstehung Jesu*, WdF 522, Darmstadt 1988, 15–67, provides an instructive survey of the discussion in the eighteenth and nineteenth centuries. Cf. ibid., 453ff., the 'Chronological Select Bibliography on the Resurrection of Jesus' from 1770 on; citations of the older titles which follow are based on this.

1.1 Rationalistic interpretations of the 'empty tomb' from H.S. Reimarus to H.E.G. Paulus

1. *The deception hypothesis* put forward by H.S. Reimarus (1694–1768) ushered in the historical-critical debate about the Easter faith; it was set out in the fragment 'On the Purpose of Jesus and his Disciples' published by G.E. Lessing in 1778. Reimarus thinks that the charge rejected in Matt. 28.11–15 that the disciples stole the body of Jesus as an apt one. Originally the disciples had hoped for a messianic kingdom in the worldly political sense. Jesus' execution robbed them of this hope. Nevertheless, in order to be able to maintain the prospect of worldly dignity and advantage, they now interpreted Jesus as the redeemer who suffered for human sins and by stealing the body created the presupposition for preaching his resurrection.

2. *The pseudo-death hypothesis* put forward by H.E.G. Paulus (1761–1851) is similarly based on the historicity of the empty tomb, but gives this an interpretation which is 'friendly' to the church: Jesus only seemed to have died and for the moment returned to life.[2] This interpretation was widespread among theologians: K.A. Hase and F.D.E. Schleiermacher[3] considered it seriously.[4] Possibly the Markan report of Pilate's careful enquiry as to whether Jesus had really died so quickly (Mark 15.43–45) already served to dispel the conjecture that Jesus had not really died.

3. *The reburial hypothesis* offers a third rationalistic explanation for the empty tomb: Joseph of Arimathea only provisionally buried Jesus in the nearby tomb, and after the sabbath rest was over buried Jesus elsewhere without the knowledge of the disciples. This thesis was put forward for the first time in an article entitled 'An Essay on the Resurrection of Jesus'[5] which was published anonymously and later found advocates in H.J. Holtzmann (1832–1910) and J. Klausner.[6] It is perhaps already implicitly repudiated in the Gospel of John: in John 20.2, 14f. Mary Magdalene infers from the empty tomb that someone must have removed Jesus' body – until she recognizes Jesus in the person she supposes to be the gardener.

---

[2]H.E.G. Paulus, *Kommentar über die drey ersten Evangelien* III ([1]1802), 797–806, 839–931; id., *Das Leben Jesu als Grundlage einer Geschichte des Urchristentums*, Heidelberg 1828, 277–305.

[3]K.A. Hase, *Das Leben Jesu*, Leipzig 1829, 260–84, and F.D.E. Schleiermacher, *The Life of Jesus*, Philadelphia 1975, 415–65.

[4]This thesis can still be found in popular books on Jesus, cf. e.g. F. Alt, *Jesus – der erste neue Mann*, Munich [2]1989, 56.

[5]Anon., *Versuch über die Auferstehung Jesu*, Bibliothek für Kritik und Exegese des Neuen Testaments und älteste Kirchengeschichte 2, 1799, 537–51.

[6]In most detail in H.J. Holtzmann, 'Das leere Grab und die gegenwärtigen Verhandlungen über die Auferstehung Jesu', *ThR* 9, 1906, 79–86, 119–32; J. Klausner, *Jesus of Nazareth*, London 1925, 357.

All the interpretations mentioned so far presuppose the historical fact of the empty tomb, but give it an interpretation which does without the miracle of the resurrection. All explain the Easter faith with the help of the empty tomb. Things only change with D.F. Strauss.

1.2 The 'subjective vision theory' in D.F. Strauss and in liberal theology.

1. In D.F. Strauss (1808–1874) we find three important insights which continually recur thereafter in various forms (1835/36):[7]

- The appearance tradition is played off against the 'legendary' tradition of the empty tomb. The *historical origin of the Easter faith* lies in visions of the disciples in Galilee – thus far away from the tomb of Jesus, which only becomes the empty tomb in a secondary legend. The rationalistic interpretations of the empty tomb thus simply collapse.
- The reports of experiences indicate historical visions of the disciples, but are governed by mythical notions, for example when in them a divine being goes through closed doors and suddenly disappears. They are given a secondary apologetic form in order to remove doubt about the reality of the appearances, e.g. by the risen Christ speaking, eating and allowing himself to be touched.
- The visions which underlie the Easter faith can be explained psychologically by the conflict between messianic faith and crucifixion: the offence of the cross is overcome on the one hand by the interpretation of Jesus' death as being a necessary (saving) event in accordance with scripture (according to Isa. 53; Ps. 22), and on the other by visions, which can produce 'pious enthusiasm' in situations of oppression. Here D.F. Strauss puts forward a *'subjective vision theory'* as distinct from the so-called 'objective vision theory', according to which the Easter appearances would be appearances brought about by God within the disciples.

2. D.F. Strauss combines this 'subjective vision theory' with an *objective interpretation of the Easter faith*: the myth of the God-man contains at its centre the idea of the unity of God and man: this idea is not realized in a human individual but in the human genre. 'It is Humanity that dies, rises, and ascends to heaven, for from the suppression of its mortality . . . arises its union with the infinite spirit of the heavens.'[8]

3. C. Holsten (1925–1897), who like Strauss was a disciple of F.C. Baur,

---

[7]D.F. Strauss, *The Life of Jesus Critically Examined*, ed. P.C. Hodgson, Philadelphia 1972 and London 1973, esp. 709–44.
[8]Ibid., 780.

produced the version of the subjective vision theory which dominated discussion in the heyday of liberal theology.[9] The starting point for the psychological explanation was the enigmatic 'contradiction of the Messiah who was once living and was now dead', which tormented the disciples, as the 'decisive occasion for Peter's vision'.[10]

4. This presupposition of a pre-Easter messianic faith was shattered by W. Wrede.[11] According to Wrede, Jesus' life was unmessianic. Only on the basis of the Easter appearances was he worshipped as Messiah or Son of God (cf. Rom. 1.3f.). A new epoch began with Wrede: since then the Easter faith has no longer been explained as a consequence of the (pre-Easter) Messianic faith; rather, messianic faith (after Easter) is explained as a consequence of Easter.[12]

1.3 The inexplicable eschatological Easter faith as an explanation of the formation of the Synoptic tradition

In the heyday of dialectic theology (c. 1920–1960), its adherents deliberately dispensed with an' explanation' of the Easter faith. Bultmann programmatically stated: 'The church had to surmount the scandal of the cross and did it in the Easter faith. How this act of decision took place in detail, how the Easter faith arose in individual disciples, has been obscured in the tradition by legend and is not of basic importance' (*Theology* 1*, 45). But this unexplained event now became the central explanation for the formation of the tradition and the theological self-understanding of primitive Christianity. Form criticism and kerygma entered into a firm alliance here.

1. The *form-critical scepticism* about the historicity of the traditions about Jesus paradoxically led to a historical revaluation of the Easter event: the less sayings about his own lofty status could be attributed to the historical Jesus, the more plausible it was to explain them by the Easter faith. The Synoptic tradition about Jesus seemed to be completely permeated by the Easter faith. Belief in the 'Risen One' had recast all pre-Easter memories, but had also given the decisive impulse to the formation of the tradition.

---

[9]C. Holsten, 'Die Christus-Vision des Paulus und die Genesis des paulinischen Evangeliums' (1861), and 'Die Messiasvision des Petrus und die Genesis des petrinischen Evangelium' (1868), in id., *Zum Evangelium des Paulus und Petrus*, Rostock 1868.

[10]Id., *Zum Evangelium des Paulus und Petrus*, 231. This discussion in liberal theology was concluded by two summary works: P.W. Schmiedel, 'Resurrection and Ascension Narratives', *Encyclopedia Biblica* IV, 1901, 4039–86, and A. Meyer, *Die Berichte über Auferstehung, Himmelfahrt und Pfingsten, ihre Enstehung, ihr geschichtliche Hintergrund und ihre religiöse Bedeutung*, Tübingen 1905.

[11]W. Wrede, *The Messianic Secret in the Gospels* (1901), Cambridge 1971.

[12]This is stated most clearly by R. Bultmann, 'Die Frage nach dem messianischen Bewusstsein Jesu und das Petrusbekennnis', *ZNW* 19, 1919/20, 165–74.

So the Easter faith implicitly stands behind all the traditions; it is explicitly handed down in various 'forms' and 'formulae', and in them scholars hoped to get back to the original in the 'simplest' form (completely along the lines of form-critical methodology).

- In connection with the *'forms'*, in 'The Appearances of the Risen Christ', in analogy to the 'paradigms' and 'novellas' described by Dibelius, C.H.Dodd distinguished among the accounts of appearances between earlier *'concise narratives'* (like Matt. 28.8–10; 28.16–20; John 20.19–21) and *'circumstantial narratives'* with a developed story (like Luke 24.13–35; John 21.1–14), which belong to a later stage.
- The investigation of *'formulae'* by W. Kramer (*Christ, Lord, Son of God*) and others led to simple statements like 'God has raised Jesus from the dead', which were already a general pre-Pauline conviction of primitive Christianity (see below, pp. 482ff.).

2. The *interpretation of the Easter faith in kerygma theology* begins from the historical recognition that Jesus and his disciples expected a new world which would very soon replace the old one. Therefore the disciples had to see the Easter appearances as an 'eschatological event', i.e. as an event in which God is bringing in a new world (or, in existentialist terms, a new human existence). Easter is misunderstood as an eschatological event if it is 'explained' within the framework of this world. One has access to an eschatological event only if one enters a new world oneself, i.e. oneself becomes the eschatological existence which is newly created by God. Easter faith is faith that one 'stands in the eschatological event' (Bultmann, 'Auferstehungsgeschichten', 246). This eschatological event continues to take place 'in the word' and in believers, in so far as 'in Christ' they experience the power of the resurrection and communion with his suffering (Phil. 3.10). Therefore Jesus is 'risen in the kerygma' (Bultmann, 'Kerygma'*, 42, in so far as the word is the continuation of the eschatological action of God in Christians (see below, pp. 505f.).

1.4 The new quest for the events which led to the Easter faith

The programmatic dismissal of any rational discussion of the foundations of Easter faith could not be sustained. Since the exegetes had 'refused', the discussion was started again by a church historian and a systematic theologian.

1. The church historian Hans von Campenhausen argued for *the priority of the empty tomb*. He began from the discovery of the empty tomb as the decisive stimulus to the 'course of the Easter events', the title of his 1952 article:

- After Jesus' arrest the disciples went into hiding in Jerusalem, and there they learned from the women that these had found the tomb open and empty 'on the third day'.
- Thereupon Peter believed in the resurrection of Jesus, gathered the disciples and led them to Galilee, where he hoped to meet Jesus again (von Campenhausen finds an account of this role of Peter in Luke 22.31ff.).
- In Galilee the appearance took place, first of all to Peter and then to the Twelve. The later tradition has put this sequence of events in the mouth of the angel at the empty tomb in the form of a command (Mark 16.7).

2. By contrast, the systematic theologian H. Grass emphasized *the priority of the appearances*. He rejected the tradition of the empty tomb as unhistorical (in *Ostergeschehen und Osterberichte*, Göttingen 1962, esp. 173–86, 233–49); probably Jesus had been buried with the two others as a criminal in an unknown place. Instead of this Grass argues for an 'objective vision theory' as the most plausible interpretation of the evidence as a whole.

The old opposition between the objective or the chronological priority of the tomb or the appearance tradition thus arose again; here in general the appearances were regarded as the starting point of the Easter faith.

1.5   The new quest for the interpretations which are at work in the Easter faith

In parallel to the discussion which was being carried out by a church historian and a systematic theologian, a discussion developed among New Testament scholars, who were not content with the view that Easter faith was inexplicable; however, they did not want to 'explain' the events behind it but the interpretations which are contained in it.

1. *Resurrection as interpretation*: W. Marxsen gave the real keyword for this new phase of the discussion about Easter in his 1968 article 'The Resurrection of Jesus of Nazareth as a Historical and Theological Problem'. He distinguished between the 'seeing of the crucified' which the disciples experienced and belief in his resurrection by God as an 'interpretation' of this experience. The interpretation is historically conditioned, and therefore not necessary. In contrast to the time of liberal theology, the visions (neutrally, 'seeing Jesus') remain unexplained. Only the interpretation which was immediately given to the 'seeing' is explained.[13]

2. *The horizon of expectation of the Easter faith*: other scholars, going beyond Marxsen, were concerned to demonstrate the intrinsic necessity of this interpretation:

---

[13]For the hermeneutical consequences see below, pp. 503ff.

appearances only become the Easter faith when they are experienced within the framework of particular expectations. Two variations of such expectations have been discussed:

- *The resurrection of individuals as the horizon of expectation of the Easter faith*; K. Berger (*Auferstehung*, see n.17) wanted to demonstrate that the resurrection of individuals was independent of the general resurrection of the dead in the horizon of expectation of the Jews of the time. He refers to Mark 6.14 (Jesus is regarded as John the Baptist *redivivus*) and Rev. 11.11f. (the resurrection and ascension of the two witnesses).[14]
- *The resurrection of all the dead as the horizon of expectation for the Easter faith*: as a member of the Pannenberg circle, U. Wilckens (*Auferstehung*, Stuttgart 1970) accepts the apocalyptic expectation of the general resurrection of the dead as the interpretative framework of the Easter appearances which was given by the tradition. What is new by comparison with the tradition is the anticipation (prolepsis) of the general resurrection of the dead in an individual figure.

1.6 Attempts at a comprehensive interpretation of the Easter event as objective or subjective reality

Kerygma theology bracketed off the Easter event from historical consideration. The Easter faith was accepted as the basic fact. But once the sequence of events which prompted the Easter faith had been reconstructed, along with the interpretations which were at work in it, it was natural to attempt a synthesis of event and interpretation – with statements about the Easter event itself. At present, two opposed schemes have been offered here.

1. The systematic theologian W. Pannenberg[15] emphatically argues for the *objectivity of the Easter event*. According to him the tradition about the tomb is historically as original as that about the appearances, but is dependent on it in content. For only in the light of the appearances does the empty tomb become the witness to the resurrection; without them it remains ambiguous. But this second (= confirmatory) testimony is so important because it guarantees the objectivity

---

[14]This thesis was published earlier, on the basis of Berger's material, by R. Pesch, 'Zur Entstehung des Glaubens an die Auferstehung Jesu', *ThQ* 153, 1973, 201–8, and provoked an intense discussion. For many scholars, one stumbling block seemed to be that in this interpretation the Easter appearances were no longer given the all-important role of providing the basis for faith. As in the time of liberal theology, this again brought down upon them the suspicion of being products of the disciples' expectation.

[15]*Systematic Theology* 2, 343–63 (and many earlier publications).

of the Easter event. What is confirmed by two different circumstances cannot be the product of subjective fantasy. Pannenberg is also concerned to increase the plausibility of Easter faith by recourse to analogous experiences in encounters with death, e.g. the appearances in the form of light of those who have just died, and so on. He seeks signs in the world of experience which point beyond an immanent view of reality.

2. The New Testament scholar G. Lüdemann (*Resurrection*, 1995) argues just as emphatically for a *subjective vision theory*. For him the tradition of the empty tomb is an unhistorical apologetic legend. The two appearances to Peter and Paul as individuals, which he attempts to interpret psychologically, are the foundation for Easter faith: he explains Peter's vision in terms of a mourning process blocked by Jesus' sudden death, a process in which Peter is overcoming his guilt feelings towards the Lord whom he has betrayed. In the persecutor Paul an unconscious fascination with Jesus which has previously been repressed breaks through. All the other visions are dependent on these primary visions and – as in the case of the vision of the 500 – can be explained only by mass suggestion. Lüdemann combines this subjective vision theory with an attractive theological interpretation which sees a theological 'truth' in these visions: 1. forgiveness of sins, 2. experience of life in the present, and 3. 'belief in the end', i.e. encounter with eternity.

2. The sources of the Easter faith and their evaluation

2.1 The genres and forms of the Easter texts

In the history of the tradition, among the New Testament Easter texts a distinction needs to be made between the earlier *formula tradition* (letters, speeches in Acts, summaries of the passion, see below, §2.1.1 + 2.3) and the later narrative tradition (Gospels, accounts of the appearances of Jesus in Acts, see below, §2.1.2 + 2.4). There are decisive differences between the two strands of tradition over the identity of those to whom the Easter appearances were given.

2.1.1 The formula tradition

Within the formula tradition, statements about the *Easter event* as an act of God in Jesus are independent of statements about the *Easter experience/knowledge* of the first witnesses. These are combined only at a secondary stage in more developed formulae (cf. I Cor. 15.4f., where 'risen' and 'appeared' stand side by side).

1. Statements about the *Easter event* refer either only to the resurrection of Jesus from the dead or also to his death:

- The formula 'God has raised Jesus from the dead' is regarded as the earliest nucleus of the resurrection tradition. It occurs as a statement (ὁ θεὸς αὐτὸν / Ἰησοῦν ἤγειρεν ἐκ νεκρῶν, Rom. 10.9; I Cor. 6.14; 15.15) and as a participial divine predicate ([θεὸς] ὁ ἐγείρας αὐτόν/Ἰησοῦν ἐκ νεκρῶν, Rom. 4.24; 8.11a, b; II Cor. 4.14; Gal. 1.1; Col. 2.12). The strictly theological structure is a characteristic. God is the subject who acts in Jesus.
- The rising/raising of Jesus is also mentioned in numerous two-member and multiple-member formulae, the subject of which is usually Christ/Jesus:[16]
  – As a combination of formulas about dying and rising: Ἰησοῦς ἀπέθανεν καὶ ἀνέστη (Jesus has died and risen, I Thess. 4.14; cf. I Cor. 15.3f.; II Cor. 5.15).
  – As a combination of formulas about being given up and being raised: Rom.4.26.
  – As a combination of a raising formula and a statement about Jesus' present exalted position: Eph. 1.20 and I Peter 1.21.
- The *passion summaries* in Mark 8.31; 9.31; 10.33f., the subject of which is the Son of Man, are based on an independent tradition. It is said of the Son of Man that he will be killed (ἀποκτείνω in the passive) and after three days (μετὰ τρεῖς ἡμέρας) will rise again (intransitive ἀνίσταμαι).[17]

Alongside these three typical statements about the Easter event there are formula statements about the *Easter experience* and *Easter knowledge* of the first Christians. Paul is the only eye-witness to mention his own Easter experience in writing. At the same time he reports further appearances of Jesus by repeating already formed traditions. We can distinguish three forms of statement about knowledge of the risen Christ in Paul:

- *The revelation statement* (Gal. 1.12, 15f.): Paul was called to be the apostle to the Gentiles in a revelation (ἀποκάλυψις Ἰησοῦ Χριστοῦ). The content of this revelation is the disclosure of the lofty position of Jesus as son of God (ἀποκαλύψαι τὸν υἱὸν αὐτοῦ ἐν ἐμοί), and this includes his resurrection (cf. Gal. 1.1).
- *The appearance statement* (I Cor. 15.5–8): this form (ὤφθη + dative of the person) is given to Paul by the traditional formula in I Cor. 15.3ff., but he

---

[16]At present there is no consensus among scholars over the demarcation, traditio-historical derivation and nomenclature of these formulae.

[17]The historical background for this notion is possibly a Jewish prophetic tradition about the killing, raising and ascension of the eschatological prophet, which also underlies Rev. 11.3–12, and has been transferred to Jesus; cf. K. Berger, *Die Auferstehung der Propheten und die Erhöhung des Menschensohnes*, Göttingen 1976, 133–6, and Pesch, 'Enstehung' (n.14), 222–6.

applies it to the vision that he received at his own call: ἔσχατον ... ὤφθη κἀμοί (last of all he also appeared to me). For the significance see pp. 489f. below.

- *The knowledge statement* (Phil. 3.8ff.): in Phil. 3 Paul describes the fruit of his encounter with the risen Christ as the knowledge of Christ Jesus (γνῶσις Χριστοῦ Ἰησοῦ) on the basis of which he came to a complete reassessment of his life. Instead of relying on the righteousness which was to be gained through his own power, he now seeks 'to gain Christ' in order by participating in his suffering also to participate in the power of his resurrection.

2.1.2 *The narrative tradition*

Within the narrative tradition the *narratives about appearances* and the *reports of the empty tomb* are regarded as mutually independent strands of tradition, which have been combined only at a late stage of the formation of the tradition by narratives of appearances at the empty tomb.

  1. Although the narratives of appearances in the Gospels take a great many forms, two formal types can be recognized:[18]

- *Appearances which contain a command*, in which Jesus appears in a recogniz-able form and in which the words of the command form the focal point (Matt. 28.16–20; Luke 24.36–49; John 20.19–23).
- *Recognition/ἀναγνώρισις appearances*, in which Jesus appears in an unknown form and the recognition of him is the point of the narrative (Luke 24.13–31; John 20.11–18; John 21.1–14).

  2. Scholars judge the genre and purpose of the (pre-Markan) narrative about the empty tomb (Mark 16.1–8) in very different ways. In addition to the position of von Campenhausen reported above (p. 480), the following assessments are given:

- It is a *tendentious secondary legend* without historical value, the point of which is the empty tomb as the proof of the resurrection (Bultmann, *HST**, 287).
- It is regarded as an *aetiological cult legend*, probably (not necessarily) with a historical nucleus which in the primitive community in Jerusalem served for the cultic celebration of the resurrection of Jesus. The point is the message of the angel in 16.6: 'He is risen . . .'. Here the 'Behold the place where they laid him' has a concrete cultic reference (Schenke, *Auferstehungsverkündigung und Leeres Grab*, Stuttgart 1968).
- It is a *transportation legend* to proclaim the resurrection (with no basis in

---

[18]According to Hoffmann, *Auferstehung* (n. 1), 501; cf. also the earlier distinction made by C.H. Dodd, above, p. 479.

history). The open tomb, the women's quest and the disappearance of the body are elements of an ancient transportation legend which was put at the service of the message of the resurrection of Jesus from the dead (E. Bickermann, 'Das leere Grab', *ZNW* 23, 1924, 281–92; P. Hoffmann, 'Auferstehung Jesu Christi', *TRE* 4, 1979, 449).

- For the question whether the empty tomb can be demonstrated to be a historical fact, see §2.5.3 below (pp. 496ff.).

2.1.3 *Summary survey of the genres and forms of the Easter texts*

Summary statements (usually formulae)		Narrative traditions	
Statements about the event	Statements about 'knowing'	Appearance accounts	The tomb tradition
Resurrection formula ὁ θεὸς αὐτὸν ἤγειρεν ἐκ νεκρῶν/God has raised him from the dead (Rom. 10.9 etc.) God is subject	*Revelation statement* ἀποκαλύψαι τὸν υἱὸν ἐν ἐμοί/It pleased God to reveal his son in/to me (Gal. 1.16) A commission follows	*Narrative of Paul's conversion*, Acts 9; 22; 26	
Dying and rising formula Ἰησοῦς ἀπέθανεν καὶ ἀνέστη/Jesus has died and is risen (I Thess. 4.14) Christ is subject	*Appearance statement* ὤφθη + dative of the person/he appeared/was seen (1 Cor. 15.5–8) Preaching follows	*Appearances conveying a command* Matt. 28.16–20 Luke 24.36–49 John 20.19–23	
Passion summaries Mark 8.31 etc. The son of man is subject	*Knowledge statement* γνῶσις Ἰησοῦ Χριστοῦ/knowledge of Jesus Christ (Phil. 3.8) A transformation of all values follows	ἀναγνώρισις/ *recognition appearances* Luke 24.13ff. John 20.11–18 (John 21.1–14)	*Empty tomb tradition* Mark 16.1ff. par. Transportation narrative with typical motif of the body which cannot be found

2.2 Formula and narrative tradition – parallels and differences in content

Now that we have made a first survey of the textual basis for all the statements about the Easter faith, we shall demonstrate by a table which compares the formula and the narrative traditions that the two agree sufficiently for us to be able to draw conclusions about experiences of appearances – but that at the same time they are hardly dependent on each other.

I Corinthians 15.3–8	Narrative tradition
15.4f.: ὅτι Χριστὸς . . . ἐγήγερται . . . καὶ ὅτι ὤφθη Κηφᾷ (that Christ was raised and appeared to Cephas)	Luke 24.34: λέγοντας ὅτι ὄντως ἠγέρθη ὁ κύριος καὶ ὤφθη Σίμωνι (they said that the Lord had truly risen and appeared to Simon). Cf. reflections of this appearance in Mark 8.26 (messianic confession); Luke 5.1–11/John 21.1ff. (appearance on the fishing trip?); Luke 22.31f. Rival tradition: *first appearance to Mary Magdalene*: John 20.11–18; Matt. 28.1, 9f.; Mark 16.9–11 (see below, §2.5.2, pp. 496ff.).
15.5: εἶτα τοῖς δώδεκα (then to the Twelve)	Appearances containing a command: Matt. 28.16–20 (Galilee): mission; Luke 24.36–49 (Jerusalem): mission John 20.19–23 (Jerusalem): foundation of the church
15.6: ἔπειτα ὤφθη ἐπάνω πεντακοσίοις ἀδελφοῖς ἐφάπαξ . . . (after that he appeared to more than 500 brothers at once)	No parallel? Some conjecture that the Pentecost story (Acts 2) is a reworking of this tradition[19]
15.7: ἔπειτα ὤφθη Ἰακώβῳ (then he appeared to James)	Only attested very late in Gospel of the Hebrews 7 (see n.35 below, dependent on I Cor. 15.7).
15.7: εἶτα τοῖς ἀποστόλοις πᾶσιν (then to all the apostles) – without ἐφάπαξ and therefore in succession?	No parallel, unless 'all the apostles' is identical with 'the Twelve' and we have a doublet to 15.5 (which is improbable. See below, p. 488). Or is there a parallel in Luke 24.13ff.; John 20.11ff. (see below)?
15.8: ἔσχατον δὲ πάντων ὡσπερεὶ τῷ ἐκτρώματι ὤφθη κἀμοί (last of all he also appeared to me [= Paul] as one born out of due time)	Acts 9.1ff.; 22.3ff; 26.9ff.
No parallel	The empty tomb (Mark 16.1–8 par.; John 20.1–15)
No parallel, unless there is one in 15.7	ἀναγνώρισις – appearances (Luke 24.13ff.; John 20.11–18)

2.3 The formula tradition of the appearances: I Cor. 15.3–8

Since the narrative tradition about the resurrection of Jesus only appears in the Gospels, which are later than the letters of Paul, the earliest testimony to the resurrection in I Cor. 15.3–8 occupies a key position in the historical question of what happened at Easter. Therefore we shall discuss it in detail.

> 1. *The character of I Cor. 15.3ff. as tradition* is undisputed. Arguments for this and indications of it are: the formula indicating a tradition, the language of the tradition and the stereotyped form.

- The *formula indicating a tradition* in the introduction (15.3): παρέδωκα . . . ὃ καὶ παρέλαβον (I have handed on what I have also received). Here Paul is saying explicitly that he is handing on tradition that he has received. That is confirmed by the assurance at the end that he is in agreement with the other apostles: 'Whether then it was I or they, so we preach and so you believed' (15.11).
- *Un-Pauline phraseology*: 'sins' in the plural is un-Pauline, as elsewhere Paul speaks of 'sin' in the singular; κατὰ τὰς γραφάς (according to the scriptures) is unique, since Paul usually writes γέγραπται (it is written); ὤφθη (he was seen/ appeared) does not occur elsewhere in Paul; 'he was raised' (ἐγήγερται) is in the perfect, while elsewhere Paul prefers the aorist. 'The Twelve' (οἱ δώδεκα) appear only here.
- The stereotyped form (using brief formulae attested elsewhere in Paul), which has a meaningful parallel structure, shows: 1. Death + interpretation + κατὰ τὰς γραφάς and confirmation of the death of Jesus by ἐτάφη (he was buried); 2. resurrection∙ indication of time + κατὰ τὰς γραφάς and confirmation by ὤφθη (he appeared).

> 2. *The extent of the tradition* cannot be defined with certainty; however, vv.3b–5 are certainly tradition.

- There is no dispute over I Cor. 15.3b–5 (apart from the occasional deletion of Cephas and the Twelve). Only this part of the formula is directly dependent on παρέλαβον.
- The appearance to James and 'all the apostles' (v.7) is similarly usually regarded as tradition: here Paul seems to exclude himself from the group of 'all the apostles'.
- Verse 6b is certainly Pauline: Paul is meeting possible objections; 500 eye-witnesses to appearances are no longer present. The report about the revelation given to Paul which is attached in v.8 is clearly a Pauline expansion.

---

[19]E. von Dobschütz, *Ostern und Pfingsten. Eine Studie zu 1 Kor 15*, Leipzig 1903; Sleeper, 'Pentecost'; MacLean Gilmour, 'Christophany'.

> 3. The derivation and age of the formula point to the earliest period, close to the events themselves.

- Its *pre-Pauline origin* is certain (see 1 above); it is older than the Corinthian community, which was presumably founded around 49/50.
- Since Paul is certain that the other apostles preach in the same way, the whole tradition in 15.3–7 will go back in substance to the time *before the Apostolic Council*. There Paul spoke to Peter and James and probably also to many of the other witnesses (46/48). It follows from this that there was already a stereotyped tradition about the death and resurrection of Jesus fifteen years after his death.
- J. Jeremias attempted to attribute the formula to the *Aramaic-speaking primitive community* on the basis of linguistic indications:[20] ὤφθη in the double meaning of 'appear' and 'be seen' corresponds to the double meaning of נִרְאָה in Hebrew.
- As a counter-argument, among other things it is said that Χριστός without the article would be unusual in Aramaic. The formula could also have arisen in the Greek-speaking Jewish–Christian community (H. Conzelmann).[21]

> 4. The search for indications of the setting in the life or the history of primitive Christianity is prompted above all by the juxtaposition of 'Peter and the Twelve' (v.5) and 'James and all the apostles' (v.7), of which different interpretations are possible.

- Rivalry between Peter and James is recorded in the way in which they are juxtaposed. Both claim the first appearance for themselves. By contrast the 'Twelve' and the 'apostles' denote the same group (A. von Harnack).[22]
- The juxtaposition of appearances in Galilee and Jerusalem is expressed in the formula.
- The formula reflects the shift in leadership in Jerusalem from Peter to James. The statements containing ὤφθη are consistently regarded as formulae of legitimation: i.e. they are not the basis for belief in the resurrection but – with their help – the basis for authority.

---

[20]J. Jeremias, *The Eucharistic Words of Jesus*, London and New York 1967, 102–4. Cf. also B. Klappert, 'Zur Frage des semitischen oder griechischen Urtextes von I. Kor. 15, 3b–5', *NTS* 13, 1966/67, 168–73.

[21]H. Conzelmann, 'Zur Analyse der Bekenntnisformel I. Kor.15,3–5', *EvTh* 25, 1965, 1–11; against his view cf. J. Jeremias 'Artikellos Χριστός. Zur Ursprache von I. Kor. 15.3b–5', *ZNW* 57, 1966, 211–15.

[22]A. von Harnack, 'Die Verklärungsgeschichte Jesu, der Bericht des Paulus (1 Kor. 15.3ff.) und die beiden Christusvisionen des Petrus', *SPAW PH*, Heidelberg 1922, 62–80 (P. Hoffmann [ed.], *Überlieferung*, 89–117).

> 5. *The significance of the tradition*: the use of the formula from the tradition is meant to indicate both the meaning of the events and the fact that they happened. For the interpretation of Jesus' death and resurrection it refers to the 'scriptures'.

The interpretation of the events by scripture leaves open what specific passages of scripture were meant:

- The 'dying for our sins' naturally suggests Isa. 53.5f. (however, this passage is first applied explicitly to Jesus' vicarious death in I Peter 2.24).
- The 'third day' is probably to be explained by Hos. 6.2: ἐν τῇ ἡμέρᾳ τῇ τρίτῃ ἀναστησόμεθα (on the third day we shall rise). However, this passage is not applied explicitly to Jesus' resurrection before Tertullian, *Jud.* 13.[23]

That the events actually happened is confirmed by ἐτάφη and ὤφθη ('buried' and 'appeared'): Jesus really died, for he was buried. Jesus was actually raised, for he appeared. There is argument:

- Over ἐτάφη: must Paul presuppose an empty tomb on the basis of an inner logic (J. Kremer, 36–8)? Or is his Easter faith independent of this?
- Over ὤφθη: does this mean revelation – without the element of visual seeing (thus Michaelis, 'Erscheinungen', 108f.) – in which case I Cor. 9.1 tells against it; legitimation – which does not apply to the 500 brethren who have no special position of authority; or appearance – thus in the LXX ὤφθη etc. stands for a theophany, which would probably be the most probable interpretation (cf. Hoffmann, 'Auferstehung', 493)?

> 6. The use of the tradition in Paul. There is a dispute as to whether in using the formula Paul wants to attest that the resurrection actually happened (thus most scholars, with Bultmann)[24] or whether he merely wanted to emphasize the consensus of the apostles (thus K. Barth).[25]

- The references to appearances in chronological order and the accessibility in the present of many witnesses, only some of whom have died, supports the understanding of I Cor.15.3–11 as an attempt to *prove* the resurrection of Christ.

---

[23]Cf. McArthur, ' "On the Third Day." ' Hoffmann, *Auferstehung* (n.1), 482f., gives a survey of the various interpretations.

[24]R. Bultmann, 'Karl Barth, *The Resurrection of the Dead*' (1926), in *Faith and Understanding,* London and New York 1969, 66–94: 82f.

[25]Karl Barth, *The Resurrection of the Dead* (1924), London 1933, 132–56.

- The fact that the resurrection of Jesus was not at all disputed among the Corinthians, but only the 'resurrection of the dead' – possibly because people believed in the immortality of the soul and/or a spiritual resurrection already in the present life – supports the understanding of I Cor. 15.3–11 as an appeal to a *consensus*. There is of course no contradiction between an intended proof and an appeal to a consensus.

The analysis of the formula tradition about the resurrection of Jesus allows the following conclusion: a tradition in I Cor. 15.3b–5, which goes back very close to the events themselves, attests appearances to both individuals and groups. The credibility of this tradition is enhanced, because it is in part confirmed by the narrative tradition, which is independent, and because in the case of Paul we have the personal testimony of an eye-witness who knew many of the other witnesses. There is no doubt about the subjective authenticity of these testimonies; i.e. they come from people who attest an overwhelming experience in good faith. The appearances to individuals are particularly illuminating. Peter had denied Jesus. Paul had persecuted his followers. James (possibly) shared the scepticism of other members of his family towards Jesus (cf. Mark 3.20f.). Possibly a fourth appearance to an individual, to Mary Magdalene, has been suppressed in the sources. It could have been that the first appearance was to her. But here we are anticipating the analysis of the narrative tradition. We shall now go on to demonstrate the differences between the various Easter narratives and what they have in common in the form of a synopsis (2.4.1); after that we shall describe their theological characteristics (2.4.2) before taking the further step of a historical evaluation of them (2.5.1–2.5.3).

2.4 The narrative tradition

The following synopsis offers a survey of the structure of the Easter narratives in the four Gospels.

The Easter appearances in the Gospels: redactional tendencies

1. In *Matthew*, through the description of the attempt at deception on the part of the high priests the Easter event becomes:

- *an accusation against Judaism* (and also a defence against the 'body-snatching theory' current among the Jews): Easter is regarded as a 'sign of

Jonah' which is given to this 'wicked and faithless generation' (27.63 refers back to 12.40);

- *the beginning of the move to the Gentiles*: the mission command previously limited to Israel (10.1ff.) is extended universally and now applies to all peoples (πάντα τὰ ἔθνη, 28.19f.).

Because this interpretation sees a strongly anti-Jewish attitude in Matthew and the historical relationship between church and synagogue is disputed, here is an alternative interpretation:

- The Risen Christ appears as *universal ruler*, to whom all authority is given in heaven and on earth. His superior power is shown in the fact that the conspiracy of *Jewish and Gentile powers* (the high priest and Roman soldiers) cannot do anything to him.
- The reference back to the teaching of the historical Jesus (as it is contained in the Gospel of Matthew) could be directed against 'enthusiasm' and a strongly pneumatic understanding of Christianity.[26] Matthew seeks to make the commandments of the Jewish Torah as interpreted by Jesus binding on all nations, *Jews and Gentiles*.

2. In *Mark*, the 'epiphany of the angel' is the last of the three Markan epiphany stories (the voice of God at the baptism, the transfiguration and the angel's appearance at the tomb) and stands at the centre of the narrative about the tomb.

- In all the epiphany scenes a divine voice confirms a preceding confession; the prophecy of John the Baptist, the messianic confession of Peter and the confession of the centurion by the cross that Jesus is the son of God.
- All the epiphanies remain veiled in secrecy and misunderstanding (in any case the first is addressed only to Jesus); the women take over the role of the disciples who do not understand.

---

[26]G. Bornkamm, 'The Risen Lord and the Earthly Jesus: Matthew 28.16–20', in J.M. Robinson (ed.), *The Future of Our Religious Past*, London and New York 1971, and reprinted in Bornkamm, Barth and Held (ed.), *Tradition and Interpretation in Matthew*, London ²1983, 301–27.

Synopsis of the Easter appearances: a comparison of the texts of the four Gospels

Matthew	Mark

27.62–66 Guard on the tomb

28.1–8 The empty tomb • The stone is rolled away by an angel before the women's eyes • The women do not keep silent about the message, but are afraid and joyful.	16.1–8 The empty tomb • The tomb is open, and in it is an angel with the Easter message • The women flee and say nothing to anyone because they are afraid.

Appearance to three women (including Mary Magdalene): • Command to tell the disciples	16.9–20 Secondary conclusion to Mark 16.9–13 Appearances to individuals: • Appearance to Mary Magdalene, unbelief of the others. • Appearance to two disciples, unbelief of the others.

28.11–15 Deception by the high priest

28.16–20 Appearance to the eleven as a group: • Command to engage in world-wide mission, baptism and teaching	16.14–16 Appearance to the eleven as a group: • Rebuke for unbelief; • Command to engage in world-wide mission, baptism and teaching.

+ 16.17f. Confirmation of faith by signs:
• driving out demons,
• speaking in new tongues,
• treading on snakes and
• drinking poison without harm,
• healing the sick
16.19 Jesus is received into heaven and sits at the right hand of God.

Luke	John

Luke	John
24.1–12 The empty tomb • The tomb is open: two angels proclaim the Easter message, referring back to Jesus' words. • The women hand on the message, but meet with unbelief from the 'apostles'. • v.12: Peter runs to the tomb (lacking in D it).	**20.1–10 The empty tomb** • Only Mary Magdalene goes to the tomb. • Race between the two disciples: Peter gets to the tomb after the Beloved disciple.
24.13–15 Appearance to two disciples (on the road to Emmaus): ἀναγνώρισις motif: instruction from the scriptures.	**20.11–18 Appearance to Mary Magdalene:** ἀναγνώρισις motif: instruction of the disciples about Jesus' ascension.
24.36–49 Appearance to the apostles as a group: • Reality of the one who appears shown by touching, seeing hands and feet, and eating; • Instruction from the scriptures; • Mission charge.	**20.19–23 Appearance to the disciples as a group:** • Reality of the one who appears (closed door); seeing hands and side (πλευρά, 19.34); • Command to found the church, mission, giving of the spirit, authority to forgive sins.
+ 24.50–51 Ascension from Bethany	+ 20.24–29 appearance to Thomas: overcoming of doubt. + 21.1–14 appearance by the Sea of Galilee. + 21.15–23 command to Peter to govern the church, martyrdom and his relationship to the Beloved Disciple.

The Gospel of Mark ends, after the discovery of the empty tomb and the delivery of the angel's message, with the flight and silence of the women. Despite the clear reference to the knowledge of a Galilean appearance of Jesus in Mark 16.7, no Galilean appearance is reported. The existence of the Gospel of Mark makes the closing sentence, 'And they said nothing to anyone, for they were afraid', an irresolvable paradox – for how could the evangelist have known about the events at the tomb except from the women, who allegedly said nothing to anyone? Numerous interpretations have been given to the abrupt and enigmatic conclusion to Mark. The most important are:

- Scholars postulate an originally more extensive conclusion which has now been lost or worked over, e.g. with Mark 9.2ff. as an Easter testimony (thus W.Schmithals in his basic document).[27]
- The possibility is considered of a 'deliberate break' in 16.8. Was this to invite readers to make a new reading of the Gospel?[28] Or does 16.7 not announce an appearance of Jesus at his parousia, so that the open conclusion indicates that the evangelist is indicating an immediate parousia?[29] Or does it emphasize the secret character of the revelation?[30]

3. *Luke* locates all the Easter appearances in Jerusalem (at the centre of salvation history) and concentrates them in the forty days before the ascension.

- During this time *the risen Christ himself* interprets the event: the angels at the tomb refer back to his prophecy (24.5–8). He teaches the disciples on the Emmaus road and the apostles from the scriptures the need for him to suffer. The Risen Christ himself changes their notion of the 'Messiah'.
- *Anti-docetic motifs* shape the accounts of the appearances: Luke emphasizes that the Risen Christ can be touched (24.39b) and refers to his wounds (24.39a) and the fact that he eats (24.41–43). Does he imagine the resurrection as a new combination of spirit ($\pi\nu\epsilon\tilde{\upsilon}\mu\alpha$) and flesh ($\sigma\acute{\alpha}\rho\xi$, Acts 2.25–31; 13.34–41)?[31]

---

[27]W. Schmithals, 'Der Markusschluss, die Verklärungsgeschichte und die Aussendung der Zwölf', *ZThK* 69, 1972, 379–411.

[28]M. Horstmann, *Studien zur markinischen Christologie*, NTA 6, Münster [2]1973, 132.

[29]E. Lohmeyer, *Das Evangelium des Markus*, KEK 1/2, Göttingen, 1959, 356.

[30]W. Nauck, 'Die Bedeutung des leeren Grabes', *ZNW* 47, 1956, 243–67: 251f., 257f.

[31]Cf. P. Hoffmann, 'Auferstehung Jesu Christi II/1', *TRE* 4, 1979, 478–513.

4. The *Gospel of John* locates the appearances in Jerusalem and in Galilee. They are distributed between two conclusions to the Gospel which probably arose in succession (John 20 and 21).

- The Easter tradition is shot through *with the rivalry between Peter and the Beloved Disciple*. The latter is first to believe (20.8) and recognizes the Lord (21.7). His death is presupposed (21.22f.). The Beloved Disciple voluntarily lets Peter go into the tomb first (20.5). He is appointed the 'good shepherd' and rehabilitated by his martyrdom; he 'follows' Jesus without betraying him (21.15–19).
- The story of 'doubting Thomas' deals with *problems of the second Christian generation*, which has the Easter testimony only in the form of the Gospel of John (as the testimony of the Beloved Disciple, 20.24–29). The Johannine mission command is focussed on the foundation of the church: Easter and Pentecost appear as a unity (20.19–23).

2.5   The Easter narratives of the Gospels: historical evaluation

The survey of the redactional tendencies in the Easter stories shows that each Gospel has reshaped the Easter stories with motifs from its own theology. These stories comprise not just an account of the Easter experience but also further experiences of Easter down to the time of the evangelists. At first sight the contradictions seem to predominate and a historical evaluation seems to be impossible. One feels reminded of Reimarus, who exploited the contradictions between the Easter accounts to deny their historicity and explained them by saying that after the disciples had stolen the body they did not reach a very clear agreement as to the version of events that they were all to disseminate. Today we have a different view of the agreements and differences between the various Easter stories. The comparison shows that all the Gospels depict the Easter event in three comparable 'units'. First there is a story about the tomb with a relatively large agreement over the course of events; secondly there is a first appearance story which varies considerably: the appearance takes place before Mary Magdalene (John) or before three women (including Mary Magdalene, Matthew), before the two disciples on the Emmaus road (Luke), or Peter, Andrew and Levi (Gospel of Peter).[32] In third place stands an appearance to the disciples as a group with a command which is given to them. The historicity of each of these 'units' is to be judged differently.

---

[32]The appearance to the group is not preserved in the Gospel of Peter, and the Akhmim fragment breaks off after the introduction to an appearance by the lake (in analogy to John 21.1ff.). However, the immediately preceding verse reads: 'But we, the twelve (!) disciples of the Lord, wept and mourned, and each one, very grieved for what had come to pass, went to his own home [i.e. to Galilee, as the sequel shows]' (Gospel of Peter 14.59). It is probable that this verse creates the narrative presuppositions for an appearance to the Twelve. In that case the Gospel of Peter would have offered the following sequence: guard on the tomb with an account of the resurrection (see below, pp. 509f.) – the empty tomb – appearance to Peter, Andrew and Levi (+ further disciples?) by the lake – a group appearance to the Twelve . . .?

2.5.1 The appearance to the disciples as a group

We can explain the fact that the story about the tomb corresponds relatively well in all five accounts from the literary dependence of Matthew and Luke on Mark, and in the case of John from a dependence on a pre-Synoptic passion narrative (or on the Synoptics themselves); the Gospel of Peter is familiar with Synoptic and Johannine traditions (or with the Gospels themselves). But after that the narratives differ, since after the narrative about the tomb there is no common basis. But precisely for that reason the accounts of appearances have great historical importance. Especially in the case of the appearance to the group of eleven disciples, the differences between the various versions are too great for it to be possible for them to be dependent on one another in literary terms. However, the agreements are clear enough for it possible for us to infer a real event behind the accounts. Since a similar appearance to the Twelve (or to all the apostles?) is attested in the formula tradition independently of these narratives,[33] in our view there is no doubt that it really happened.

2.5.2 The disputed first appearance: Mary Magdalene or Peter?

Between the narrative connected with the tomb and the appearance to the disciples as a group there are stories of appearances to individuals, to Mary Magdalene (John, secondary ending to Mark), three women (Matthew), the disciples on the Emmaus road (Luke), and Peter, Andrew and Levi (Gospel of Peter). The element of truth here is that alongside the appearances to the disciples as a group there were further appearances – above all to individuals. However, not all of these entered the general narrative store of primitive Christianity. In the Gospels we hear of the appearance to Peter only in Luke 24.34. The appearance to James is first related in the Gospel of the Hebrews (frag.7).[34] The Gospels pass

---

[33]The following considerations suggest the independence of the formula contained in I Cor. 15.3ff. from the narrative tradition in the Gospels: no narratives in the Easter accounts in the Gospels correspond to the appearances to Peter, to the 500 brethren, to James and to Paul which are mentioned in I Corinthians. Only the appearance to the Twelve is handed down in both spheres of tradition, albeit with slight differences: in the narrative tradition the 'Twelve' sometimes become eleven disciples (Matt. 28.16; Luke 24.9, 33). The appearance to them is always associated with a command. There is nothing of that in I Cor. 15.5 – unless the 'Twelve' are identified with the 'apostles' and a mission charge is inferred from the title 'apostle'. But even then it is striking that 'apostles' are mentioned only by Luke in the narrative tradition (24.10); elsewhere the term is 'disciples' (Matt. 28.16; Mark 16.7; John 20.19f.; 21.1, etc.) – a term which is absent from the formula tradition. At any rate Luke could have known I Cor. 15.3ff., because we cannot exclude the possibility that he knew the letters of Paul. However, in Luke 24.34 he mentions the appearance to Peter as an appearance to 'Simon' and not to 'Cephas' as in I Cor. 15.5. Even if there possibly were (subsequent) contacts between the different traditions, we unmistakably have autonomous traditions, each with its own linguistic tradition.

[34]In Jerome, *Vir inl* 2: the Lord went 'to James and appeared to him. For James had sworn that he would not eat bread from the hour in which he had drunk the cup of the Lord until he should see him rising from among them who sleep.' Jesus gives James bread and says: 'My brothers, eat your bread, for the Son of Man has risen from the dead' (quoted from *NTApoc* I, 1991, 178).

over the appearance to Paul, although it is the best-documented appearance in the New Testament: we have authentic testimony to it from the witness himself! Evidently such appearances to individuals were always retold and handed down only in particular strands of tradition. So we cannot rule out the possibility that the appearance to Mary Magdalene also represents such a special tradition, which appears in the Gospel of John but could also underlie the appearance to the three women. Perhaps it was even the first appearance of all. Granted, usually the protophany to Peter attested in I Cor. 15.5a is regarded as the first historically tangible appearance. But equally good arguments can be advanced for the rival tradition of the first appearance to Mary Magdalene, as the following arguments for and against the consensus show.[35]

1. *Pro*: The historicity of the protophany to Peter is supported by the fact that there is no mention of Mary Magdalene in the earliest list of witnesses to the resurrection (I Cor. 15.3ff.).

Con: In I Cor. 15.3ff. no women are mentioned at all, because according to Jewish law women were not fully qualified as witnesses and because a legitimation of the recipient of the appearance was bound up with the appearance. As the recipient of the first appearance Mary Magdalene would have been had the same authority as Peter.

2. *Pro*: Mark does not report an appearance of the risen Christ, but the angel announces that Jesus will show himself in Galilee. The women are to tell 'his disciples and Peter this' (Mark 16.7). The emphatic mention of Peter reflects his role as the one who received the first appearance.

Con: The explicit announcement of an appearance of Jesus in Galilee by the angel is addressed to the women and the disciples[36] (Matthew has already changed this in

---

[35]M. Hengel, 'Maria Magdalena und die Frauen als Zeugen', in O. Betz et al., *Abraham unser Vater (FS O. Michel)*, Leiden 1963, 243–56, and P. Benoit, 'Marie Madeleine et les disciples au Tombeau selon Jean 20,1–18', in M. Eltester (ed), *Judentum, Urchristentum, Kirche (FS J. Jeremias)*, Berlin 1960, 143–52, argue for the historicity of the protophany to Mary Magdalene, which has been eliminated from the tradition.

[36]It cannot be inferred from the text with complete certainty that the women are to be included among those persons who are told 'There (in Galilee) you will see him' (Mark 16.7c), but it is very probable. Grammatically the ὅτι in Mark 16.7 can introduce information about the content of the preceding verb: '*Tell* his disciples and Peter *that* he is going before you (all) to Galilee.' The last part of the verse, 'There you will see him, as he told you', is then again what the angel says to the women, who represent the absent disciples (to whom the prediction in 14.28 had been given). This solution best fits the compositional structure of Mark 16.1–8. For the 'there' (ἐκεῖ) in it stands in direct semantic opposition to the 'not here' (οὐκ . . . ὧδε) of v.6, and the verbs of seeing also have a key function in the pericope. The women, who had come to the tomb in order to anoint the dead Jesus, *look up* and *see* that the heavy stone had been rolled away in a miraculous way (v.4); they then *see* the young man (v.5), who tells them that they were looking in the wrong place: Jesus has risen and is '*not here*' (v.6). He sends them (with the disciples) to Galilee with the promise '*there* you shall *see* him'. The reference 'as he told you' is not meant to identify a particular group to which the saying is addressed, but has the function of

favour of the women, cf. Matt. 28.10!). By contrast, it cannot be inferred from the text that a special appearance to Peter was intended (cf. also Mark 14.28).

3. *Pro*: Luke also attests that the tradition of the first appearance to Peter was known; Luke 24.34 is inserted against the real flow of the Emmaus story.[37]

Con: It can be doubted whether Luke 24.34 is an independent tradition; presumably the evangelist knew the formula in I Cor 15.3ff. Luke is the only one of the four evangelists to report (or announce) an appearance to women – that could be an indication of the suppression of this tradition (for apologetic reasons).

4. *Pro*: The first appearance to Mary Magdalene is first mentioned in very late, i.e. historically worthless, strata of the tradition: Mark 16.9–11 comes from the second century; in text-critical terms the ending of Mark (16.9–20) can clearly be shown to be secondary. However, since Irenaeus (died c.202) explicitly cites Mark 16.19 as the conclusion of the Gospel of Mark (*Haer* 3, 10, 6), the section must have been composed in the second century. John 20.11–18 is a special tradition of the Johannine community with no historical nucleus. Matthew 28.1, 9f. derives from a concern, late in the history of the tradition, to combine the tomb tradition (in which the women have their fixed place) with the appearance tradition.

Con: Despite its offensive character (see below), the appearance to Mary Magdalene has been handed down in three independent sources, which probably go back to earlier traditions: the secondary Markan conclusion is an independent kerygmatic summary of the Easter events (in form comparable only with I Cor. 15.3ff.), which is not completely dependent on the Gospels and therefore could have preserved much earlier traditions.[38] John 20.11–18 also goes back to earlier traditions. That is shown by Matt. 28.9f., where the same tradition is evidently taken up. The recollection of an appearance to Mary Magdalene is older than the Matthaean redactional combination of the tomb story (several women) with the christophany (originally to one woman, Mary Magdalene).

Conclusion: it is more probable that an original tradition of a protophany to Mary Magdalene has been suppressed than that it first came into being at a later date. Mary Magdalene appears in first place in all the lists of women in the Gospels (Mark 15.40f., 47; 16.1 par.; Luke 8.2f.; 24.10).[39] That too is an indication of her

---

recalling Jesus' own prediction of his resurrection (14.28 says 'but *after I am risen* I shall go before you to Galilee').

It would be possible as an alternative to this reconstruction to define the ὅτι in Mark 16.7 also as a recitative ὅτι and translate: 'Go and tell his disciples and Peter, "He is going before you to Galilee. There you will see him as he has told you."' But in this case, too, the women might be included, since the report in fact presupposes the preceding message, 'You seek Jesus . . . he is not here', continues it and give the women's quest a new goal.

[37]The reason why Luke does not report an appearance to Peter alone could be that he limits the appearances wholly to Jerusalem, and the appearance to Peter presumably took place in Galilee (possibly Luke 5.1–11 is a version of this appearance tradition).

[38]Cf. J. Gnilka, *Das Evangelium nach Markus* II, EKK II/2, 1979, 353.

[39]John 19.25 is only an apparent exception: this list puts the women under the cross in order of their kinship with Jesus (beginning with his mother). Mary Magdalene is the only woman to be mentioned who is not a relation – thus this passage also confirms her prominent place among the male and female disciples of Jesus.

towering significance in the primitive Christian movement. This can be explained most easily by the appearance of the Risen Christ which she was granted.

2.5.3 The dispute over the empty tomb

The tradition about the empty tomb is certainly contained in a comparable way in all four canonical Gospels and in the Gospel of Peter. Some secondary elements can easily be recognized, like Peter's race with the Beloved Disciple in John. The problem is that there is no parallel tradition in the formula tradition, although this mentions the burial of Jesus in I Cor. 15.4. Time and again attempts have been made to give the empty tomb a key role in the reconstruction of the course of the Easter events (H. von Campenhausen) or of their theological significance (W. Pannenberg). In these cases the historicity of the empty tomb is of decisive importance. The following seven arguments pro and con are meant to demonstrate what possibility there is of *proving the historicity* of the empty tomb.

1. *Pro*: The resurrection message could not have been proclaimed in Jerusalem, had the body of Jesus been in an unopened tomb. The success of the Easter message in Jerusalem is inconceivable without an empty tomb.

Con: Resurrection faith is compatible with the knowledge of an unopened tomb. According to Mark 6.14, Herod Antipas believed that Jesus was John the Baptist *redivivus*, who had been 'raised from the dead', although John had been buried by his disciples (6.29). As this was a 'return' to earthly life (not a resurrection to eternal life), in this case it would have been very natural to ask whether the tomb was empty. We hear of no such question. Furthermore Jesus himself expressed the belief that the patriarchs of Israel – Abraham, Isaac and Jacob – are risen and are with God (Mark 12.18ff.). Already in the time of Jesus, however, the tombs of the patriarchs were being venerated without people assuming that they were empty (cf. the tomb of Abraham in Herod, which was enclosed within a wall by Herod the Great).

2. *Pro*: In I Cor. 15.4 Paul reliably bears witness to a burial of Jesus. According to the logic of his resurrection faith, which is orientated on a transfigured and transformed body, he must have presupposed an empty tomb, even if he does not explicitly mention one. Generally speaking, Jewish belief in a bodily resurrection – in contrast to Greek-Hellenistic belief in an immortality of the soul – leads with intrinsic necessity to the assumption of an empty tomb.

Con: If the Jewish (and especially the Pauline) resurrection faith intrinsically needs to postulate an empty tomb, the tradition of the empty tomb could have arisen on the basis of such a postulate and have been clothed with a narrative – without any basis in the discovery of an empty tomb. Quite apart from that, however, Paul's resurrection hope and that of Judaism is far too variable for us to have to postulate belief in an empty tomb as necessary for Paul (and other Jewish Christians). According to Phil. 1.21ff. Paul hopes to be with Christ immediately after his death – regardless of the fate of his body (cf. Luke 23.43). Judaism knew the idea that the bodies of the dead rest in their tombs until the last day, whereas their spirits are already preserved in heavenly chambers (Ethiopian Enoch 22). According to Jub. 23.31 the dead lie in the earth, while their spirits already experience joy in God. However, in both cases there is a future resurrection – not one that has already taken place.

3. *Pro*: The charge that the disciples had stolen Jesus' body presupposes the existence of an empty tomb. It is not the fact but the interpretation of this empty tomb that was disputed by adherents to and opponents of the message of the resurrection.

Con: What is presupposed is not the fact of an empty tomb but the claim that there was such a fact. But even if the fact of some empty tomb were presupposed in Matthew – and it is only here that the charge of stealing the body is made – it need not have been the tomb of Jesus. There were many tombs in the area of Golgotha (as archaeology can demonstrate). Possibly they were no longer used because the place was used for executions. The story of the empty tomb could have been associated with one of the empty and unused tombs – that is, if an already-existing empty tomb there had not given rise to the story in the first place.

4. *Pro*: The well-attested Jewish custom of venerating the tombs of martyrs and saints[40] must have led to the rise of a 'cult of the saints' around the tomb of Jesus – if his people knew where that was. The fact that such a custom did not develop can be explained by the fact that the tomb was empty and there was no saint to be venerated.

Con: The place where the miracle of the resurrection took place could even more have become the place of cultic veneration – a hypothesis which has in fact been put forward. L. Schenke (see above, p. 484) has argued that the story of the empty tomb is a cult aetiology of an annual celebration at the tomb of Jesus. Quite apart from that, the custom of a secondary burial of the bones after the decay of the flesh, which was only practised around Jerusalem and only in New Testament times, was a bad presupposition for the rise of a cult associated with tombs: it was not the tomb but the ossuary in which the bones were kept which would have had to be the focal point of such a 'cult of relics'.

5. *Pro*: The burial by Joseph of Arimathea is well attested in Mark. As the discovery of the body of a crucified man in Givʻat ha-Mivtar (in the north-east of present-day Jerusalem) shows, it is conceivable that the body of an executed man could have been given to his relatives (or other close friends) and have been buried by them.[41] But if the tomb of Jesus was known, the Easter message could have been refuted in Jerusalem had this tomb not been empty.

---

[40]Cf. J. Jeremias, *Heiligengräber in Jesu Umwelt*, Göttingen 1958.

[41]Cf. H.W. Kuhn, 'Der Gekreuzigte von Givʻat ha-Mivtar. Bilanz einer Entdeckung', in *Theologia crucis – signum crucis (FS E. Dinkler)*, Tübingen 1979, 303–34.

Con: In fact those who dispute the tradition of the empty tomb as a rule also tend to put in question the burial by Joseph of Arimathea. There is a rival tradition in Acts 13.29 according to which 'the people in Jerusalem' (in the plural) took Jesus down from the cross and buried him. According to John 19.31, these were primarily 'the Jews', who asked Pilate to take those who had been crucified down from the cross in good time in view of the sabbath that was dawning. Possibly Jesus was buried anonymously along with the two criminals who were crucified with him. No one knew his precise grave. In that case the story of the burial would have come into being because the first Christians could not bear the thought that Jesus had not had an honourable burial. Here they could have associated this burial with an unused tomb of a Joseph of Arimathea which was in the neighbourhood of the place of execution.

6. *Pro*: The tradition of the empty tomb is handed down in such a contradictory form in the various Gospels that here we must have independent traditions which confirm one another: in Mark 16.1ff. the young man proclaims that Jesus' body is not in the tomb, and only after that do the women see that the tomb is empty. In contrast to the account in Matthew and Luke, they keep quiet about the angelic message. But according to Luke 24.1ff. the women first vainly seek Jesus' body in the tomb, and only then are they given an explanation for the empty tomb by two men: the message of the resurrection. As in Matthew, they pass on this message.

Con: The differences between Mark and Luke are not great enough for us to be able to presuppose independent traditions. In the case of Mark, the motif of silence in particular can be explained as an apologetic one: the women say nothing about the discovery of the empty tomb out of fear, thus giving a plausible explanation why people knew nothing of the empty tomb for such a long time. Accordingly, the story of the empty tomb would only have been introduced at a secondary stage. Matthew and Luke delete the silence of the women, because the tradition is already familiar to them. The counter-question runs: if the story of the empty tomb were a secondary 'invention', would it not have been possible to refer to men who were capable of attesting the fact of the empty tomb? Was not Joseph of Arimathea available from the tradition?

7. *Pro*: The archaeological evidence[42] of the 'tomb' in the Church of the Sepulchre in Jerusalem corresponds in a more than fortuitous way with the literary evidence:

• The tomb 'discovered' in the time of Constantine cannot be an 'invention'. It

---

[42]Cf. A. Parrot, *The Temple of Jerusalem*, London 1957; id., *Golgotha and the Holy Sepulchre*, London 1957; O. Nicholson, 'Holy Sepulchre, Church of', *ABD* 3, 1992, 258–60 (with bibliography).

was discovered in the midst of the Byzantine city – under a temple of Venus connected with the foundation of Aelia Capitolina in 136 CE. In antiquity tombs lay outside the city. No one would have looked for Jesus' tomb within the city without an old local tradition. It is highly probable that in the time of Jesus the tomb of Jesus lay outside the city walls. It was not until the period between 41 and 44 CE that Herod Agrippa I had a 'third wall' built, as a result of which Golgotha and the tomb came to lie within the walls. So it is probable that already in the first century there was a local tradition which located Jesus' tomb there, where it is now venerated in the Church of the Sepulchre.

• The tomb in the church of the sepulchre is a 'new tomb'. There are none of the many additional *loculi* which usually extend from the main chamber. Moreover it is situated near Golgotha in an abandoned quarry which could have served as a garden. All this fits John 19.41. The Johannine tradition presupposes the kind of tomb that we can see today.

Con: In principle the agreement between the literary and the archaeological evidence can also be explained in another way: the story of the discovery of the empty tomb became attached at a secondary stage to the existence of an unused tomb in the neighbourhood of Golgotha. Of course this story then corresponded to local conditions in a 'more than fortuitous' way.

Conclusion: the empty tomb cannot be either demonstrated or refuted with historical-critical methods. We must reckon with two possibilities.

The resurrection faith called forth by Easter appearances led to a search for the tomb of Jesus. An unused tomb near Golgotha was interpreted at a secondary stage as the tomb of Jesus – no one knew where Jesus had really been buried. The New Testament tradition about the empty tomb then attached itself to this tomb.

However, possibly people did know about Jesus' tomb. Joseph of Arimathea had buried him in an unused tomb (perhaps his own). The women found this tomb empty on Easter morning. They kept quiet, because they did not want to be accused of grave robbery. The account of Easter appearances first gave the enigmatic 'empty tomb' an interpretation. This interpretation was then put on the lips of the 'angel' by the tomb.

Despite this open result, it must be stated that both the possibilities which we think probable presuppose an 'empty tomb', whether in that its existence explains the origin of a corresponding story or that conversely the narrative was an apt explanation of its existence. By contrast, most historical reconstructions which regard the story of the empty tomb as an unhistorical legend feel compelled to attack both the existence of an empty tomb and the burial of Jesus. For had it been known where Jesus was buried, it is hard to imagine how the Easter message could have been preached in Jerusalem without reference to this tomb. So if one wanted to arrange the considerations developed here into a spectrum of different views, the balance would tilt towards the possibility that the tradition of the empty tomb has a historical nucleus. But only a little way. For at the same time we are attempting to show that even if Christians in Jerusalem in the forties or fifties could have pointed to an empty tomb, this is no proof for the resurrection. At all events this state of affairs shows that the story of the empty tomb can only be illuminated by the Easter faith (which is based on appearances); the Easter faith cannot be illuminated by the empty tomb.

3. Summary and hermeneutical reflections

The historical data which can still be ascertained can be quickly summarized. The disciples had fled at the arrest of Jesus. Only a few women disciples ventured to look on the crucifixion from afar. Probably the fugitives had removed themselves to Galilee. There they had the first appearances (thus still Mark 16.7; Matt. 28.16ff.; Gospel of Peter 14.59f.), which were relocated in Jerusalem at a secondary stage (in Luke and John). Mary Magdalene could have had the first appearance independently of this; it did not enter the general memory of primitive Christianity, but was suppressed by the appearance to Peter, who was regarded as the first witness to the resurrection at a very early stage (I Cor. 15.5). Probably he brought together the other members of the Twelve. Together they experienced a well-attested appearance to them as a group, in which the primitive Christian narrators saw the beginning of the earliest Christian community, since they always relate this appearance along with a command to found communities. Further appearances to individuals followed, those to James and Paul. Possibly ecstatic experiences of large groups (the 500 'brethren') were also experienced as resurrection appearances. Very soon the conviction that Jesus was alive must have become associated with an empty tomb in the neighbourhood of the place where he was executed. Such a tomb could really have been discovered there by the women who remained in Jerusalem. In the light of the Easter appearances it became testimony to the resurrection. But we cannot exclude the possibility that an empty tomb near to Golgatha attracted such traditions to itself at a secondary stage.

The resurrection of Jesus who had been executed on the cross, which is unanimously asserted by the New Testament, runs counter to the modern picture of the world. Measured by Troeltsch's axioms of historical method,[43] the resur-

---

[43]E. Troeltsch, 'Historical and Dogmatic Method in Theology' (1898), in id., *Religion in History*, Edinburgh 1991, 11–32. The three axioms of criticism, analogy and correlation mean: 1. any tradition is subject to methodological doubt and must be subjected to criticism of its historical probability, since there are no absolute judgments in historiography, but only probable ones; 2. the fact that all events are in principle of the same kind conditions them and makes it possible to compare them; 3. all phenomena in culture and history are correlated with one another.

rection of Jesus cannot be a historical event: it is by definition without analogy in history; it has no cause within history (and therefore contradicts the principle of correlation), and, as believers understand it, it may not be measured by the criteria of probability, because this would include the recognition that it is possibly not historical. So in translating Easter faith for our time, in principle there are two possibilities: either the Easter event is interpreted in such a way that it can be integrated into the world of modern convictions, or modern premises are modified in the light of the Easter faith. The rationalistic explanations of the empty tomb at the time of the Enlightenment (theft of the body by the disciples, only an apparent death, reburial) and their modern variants (see above, p. 476); the subjective vision theory in liberal theology and the present (see above, pp. 477f., 481f.); and the thoroughgoing view of the resurrection as an interpretation with which we can dispense today (W. Marxsen, H. Braun, D. Sölle, et al.), belong to the interpretations of the Easter event within modern premises. The objective vision theory, which assumes that the Easter appearances were brought about by God and reveal an objective state of affairs, and the objective appearance theory, which reckons with real appearances from another world, belong to the interpretations of the Easter event which modify modern premises until they correspond with the Easter faith. We can also put here the approaches by R. Bultmann, K. Barth and W. Pannenberg, which will be discussed as important contributions to the hermeneutics of Easter in the twentieth century (see 2–4 below). First of all, however, we shall sketch out W. Marxsen's interpretation of Easter.

1. Marxsen's formula that Easter is the 'ongoing appropriation of the kerygma of Jesus' contains not only a historical interpretation but also a hermeneutical programme:

- For Marxsen, the 'resurrection of Jesus' is *not a historical event* but a time-conditioned *interpretation* which may not be historicized. 'In historical terms it can only be established . . . that witnesses, after the death of Jesus, claimed that something had happened to them which they described as seeing Jesus, and reflection on this experience led them to the interpretation that Jesus had been raised from the dead.'[44]
- The *ongoing appropriation of the Jesus kerygma* in the primitive community was the consequence of this experience (in principle independently of its interpretation as resurrection). The witnesses to Easter experienced that the nearness of God which they had experienced in the encounter with Jesus had been given to them anew. 'The cause of Jesus goes on', in that the witnesses carry it on in place of Jesus: 'As the Father has sent me, so I send you' (John

---

[44]Marxsen, 'Resurrection of Jesus', 31.

20.21). The material of the Synoptic tradition is the literary deposit of this ongoing proclamation of the message of Jesus.

- Easter faith is therefore at all times *orientation on the earthly Jesus*, his earthly claim and his proclamation, which are appropriated by the present and orientated on it. The personal Christ kerygma (i.e. the preaching of the birth, cross and resurrection of Jesus Christ as saving events) must similarly be interpreted in the service of the cause of the earthly Jesus and for Marxsen does not have any objective weight of its own.
- Proclaiming Easter in the community means *continuing to proclaim the message of the earthly Jesus*. Through this the eschaton is anticipated and Jesus still proves himself to be the living one even today.

With the interpretation of Easter as an expression of the continuation of 'Jesus' cause', Marxsen remains within the framework of modern premises, but with the statement that the 'eschaton' takes place in this cause he leaves them and comes close to Bultmann's eschatological interpretation, albeit with the decisive difference that he connects the breaking in of the eschaton not with Easter but with the earthly Jesus. By contrast, the approaches by R. Bultmann, K. Barth and W. Pannenberg which we shall go on to discuss are agreed that it is only the Easter faith which discloses to the believer a new self-understanding or understanding of the world and that this partially modifies modern premises. Easter makes manifest:

- the nature of human beings in their situation before God (existentialist interpretation);
- the nature of revelation, which in principle is a miracle removed from human insight (interpretation in terms of the theology of revelation);
- the nature of history, which discloses itself in the light of its end, and which anticipates the resurrection of Jesus (interpretation in terms of universal history).

2. Existentialist interpretation (R. Bultmann): according to Bultmann's famous article 'New Testament and Mythology', talk of the resurrection of Jesus does not relate to a historical event but rather makes use of a mythical idea which along with the picture of the world to which it belongs is 'finished' for modern men and women. Today the resurrection must be preached in such a way 'that this does not appear to be an allegedly historical or mythical event but a reality which affects our own existence' ('Auferstehungsgeschichten', 245). This abiding truth of the Easter message can only be brought out through existentialist interpretation. Confronted with it, modern men and women too are offered a new self-understanding which remains closed to the natural person.

- Easter faith is *'an expression of the significance of the cross'*, faith in the cross as the saving event in which the world is judged and the possibility of authentic life has been created.
- Easter faith is *belief in the world of preaching*: the crucified and risen Christ is encountered only in the word of proclamation, in the kerygma. In God's address the event of Jesus Christ is present as the event which always affects me in my existence ('Problem', 120f.).
- Easter faith is the *decision of faith in the face of the cross*: knowledge and affirmation of the failure of attempts to live one's own life, seizing the new self-understanding, yes to life as gift.

For Bultmann, in accord with the New Testament, the Easter faith has a central position: it is an answer to an address by God and has no immanent explanation. It contains a truth about individuals: the offer of true life – already in this life. Easter faith reveals the human condition before God: true life is radical gift – a creation from nothing.

3. The interpretation in terms of a theology of revelation (K. Barth): Barth denies that historical criticism is competent to deal with the event of the resurrection which, while not being 'historical', did 'really happen'.

- Revelation as the *sole act of God*: whereas all other events relating to Jesus have a 'historical' character because they stand in the context of human decisions and actions and can be misunderstood in the framework of this context (in so far as people fail to recognize that God is at work in them), the resurrection is exclusively God's action without any element of human action. Its only 'analogy' is creation as a sovereign act of God. Therefore in principle the resurrection is not a 'historical fact', the probability of which would be accessible to historical analysis.
- *Resurrection as the real and new act of God*: nevertheless the resurrection 'has happened . . . in the human sphere and human time, as an actual event within the world with an objective content', as a 'new act of God' over against the event of the cross' (*CD* IV, 1, 334, 304). That means (against Bultmann) that it may not be understood as the 'noetic reverse side' of the event of the cross (as a disclosure of the 'significance of the cross') but must be maintained as a real event that underlies the coming to faith of the disciples, which can be ascertained historically.
- *Resurrection faith as revelation*: as an exclusively divine action the resurrection cannot be understood and communicated by human beings. It becomes accessible to them only through divine revelation, which is accepted in faith.
- *Resurrection as a paradigm for revelation* generally: the resurrection of Jesus is the 'true and original and typical act of revelation' (*CD* IV/1, 304), which

discloses itself only through God's initiative. Therefore it may not be historically verifiable at all, so that faith remains the sovereign act of God. Easter faith shows the nature of revelation – an event exclusively brought about by God, which can be comprehended only by God himself.

4. Interpretation in terms of universal history (W. Pannenberg): Pannenberg's concern is to show the probability of the New Testament message of the resurrection of Jesus as a historical event.[45] To achieve this he formulates three postulates which modify the modern picture of the world in such a way that it becomes compatible with belief in the resurrection:

- *The postulate of universal history*: history as a purposive process can be understood only as a totality. But the whole can only be surveyed in the light of the end. The key to universal history would therefore be an event in which the end is anticipated (prolepsis). If the modern understanding of history becomes aware of its implicit presuppositions, it is open to proleptic end-events – though their ultimate verification is still to come.
- *The anthropological postulate*: 'appearances' of a dead person become the prolepsis of the general resurrection only against an apocalyptic horizon of expectation. This horizon of expectation can be verified anthropologically: personal life does not fulfil itself in this life but seeks an unlimited continuation. Therefore 'resurrection', too, is an anthropological postulate of meaning.
- *The scientific postulate*: parapsychological phenomena show that our picture of the world is incomplete. According to Pannenberg, the sciences cannot give a definitive verdict that the resurrection of a dead person to eternal life is impossible.

These three postulates are combined with a historical analysis of the sources in which the Easter event is attested historically by 'visions', which Pannenberg attempts to demonstrate as probably having a trans-subjective content, and by the 'empty tomb', which provides confirmation independently of that. Easter faith verifies a general apocalyptic horizon of expectation (relating to universal history). In it what universal history is about becomes clear.

The distinction between interpretations of Easter which keep within modern premises and those which break through them that has so far been dominant cannot be sustained consistently. If according to Marxsen the 'cause of Jesus goes

---

[45]W. Pannenberg, *Systematic Theology*, Vol.2, Grand Rapids and Edinburgh 1994, esp. 343–63; id., *Jesus God and Man*, Philadelphia and London 1968, esp. 53–114; *Basic Questions in Theology* I, London 1970, 15–80; *Grundfragen sysytematischer Theologie* II, Gettingen 1980, 66–79, 160–73, 174–87; id., *Revelation in History*, London 1969, 123–58.

on', there are many analogies to this in the case of significant individuals. But when he identifies this cause with the eschaton, there are no analogies. For Pannenberg the Easter event transcends a scientific view of the world, but he wants to explain the universal-historical and anthropological premises which are decisive for his understanding within the framework of our world of experience. The basic question is: should the Easter event be interpreted with analogies from our world of experience – or as an unparalleled breakthrough of something 'wholly other' should it widen that world? This alternative would be less sharp if there were a reason for leaving the world of our analogies from experience in particular when confronted with the Easter faith. There is one such reason: Easter is a grappling with death. In the resurrection of Jesus an enigmatic power manifests itself which overcomes death. Now we have no experience of death, but only of life to the point of death. Our understanding of analogies from the world of experience is *a priori* limited to phenomena from this world of experience. Where, as in death, we leave it and enter realms beyond the world of our experience, we are inevitably left stranded by analogies to our experience. Just as we cannot penetrate death with analogies from experiences of our world, so we cannot understand the power of the Easter event to overcome death by means of them. This power either breaks into our life without analogy – or it is not what it seems to be. In so far as it towers *into* life, it is meaningful to seek analogous visions and extranormal information beyond death. But in so far as it towers into our world *from beyond* the frontier of death, our analogies must necessarily fail.

4. Tasks

4.1 Location in the history of research

1. Attach to the texts below the headings 'subjective vision theory', 'objective vision theory' and 'resurrection as an interpretation which is no longer binding today', and identify their authors (from H. Grass, J. Weiss and H. Braun).

Text 1:

'Belief in the resurrection is an early Christian form of expression, a form of expression governed by the world of its time, for the authority which Jesus gained over those men [the disciples]. We today cannot feel that this form of expression is binding on us. However, the authority of Jesus indicated by this form of expression can certainly be binding on us . . . Jesus' resurrection is the *expression* that what Jesus willed is alive and can support people . . . *That* his cause is supportive – in primitive Christian language, *that* he is risen . . . we cannot take from anyone else, not even an apostle. Only those who allow the testimony of Jesus to run through their hearts and consciences gain this conviction.'

Text 2:

> The Easter appearances are 'not the basis of their [the disciples'] faith, though so it seemed to them, as much as its product and result . . . Under the lasting impact of the religious personality of Jesus the disciples formed the bold belief that their Master was risen. The visions arose out of this faith.'

Text 3:

> 'At any rate a theological consideration must maintain that in the experiences of the disciples, however they may be thought to have been communicated, we have an action of God in them and not merely products of their own fantasy or reflection . . . this revealing action has . . . a quite definite content . . . that Christ appears as the Risen and Living One . . . these visions and this faith determine that God also and indeed primarily acted in Christ . . . It is impossible to affirm the Easter faith of the disciples and the Easter preaching that arose out of them as an act of God and at the same time to leave open the question whether what this faith believed and proclaimed corresponds to a reality.'

4.2 The earliest account of the resurrection of Jesus (Gospel of Peter 8.28–11.49)

> But the scribes and Pharisees and elders, being assembled together and hearing that all the people were murmuring and beating their breasts, saying, 'If at his death these exceeding great signs have come to pass, behold how righteous he was!', were afraid and came to Pilate, entreating him and saying, 'Give us soldiers that we may watch his sepulchre for three days, lest his disciples come and steal him away and the people suppose that he is risen from the dead, and do us harm.' And Pilate gave them Petronius the centurion wiith soldiers to watch the sepulchre. And with them there came elders and scribes to the sepulchre. And all who were there, together with the centurion and the soldiers, rolled thither a great stone and laid it against the entrance to the sepulchre and put on it seven seals, pitched a tent and kept watch. Early in the morning, when the sabbath dawned, there came a crowd from Jerusalem and the country round about to see the sepulchre that had been sealed. Now in the night in which the Lord's day dawned, when the soldiers, two by two in every watch, were keeping guard, there rang out a loud voice in heaven, and they saw the heavens opened and two men come down from there in great brightness and draw nigh to the sepulchre. That stone which had been laid against the entrance to the sepulchre started of itself to roll and gave way to the side, and the

sepulchre was opened, and both the young men entered in. When now those soldiers saw this, they awakened the centurion and the elders – for they also were there to assist at the watch. And whilst they were relating what they had seen, they saw again three men come out from the sepulchre, and two of them sustaining the other, and a cross following them, and the heads of the two reaching to heaven, but that of him who was led of them by the hand overpassing the heavens. And they heard a voice out of the heavens crying, 'Have you preached to those who sleep?' and from the cross there was heard the answer, 'Yes'. Those men therefore took counsel with one another to go and report this to Pilate. And whilst they were still deliberating, the hevens were again seen to open, and a man descended and entered into the sepulchre. When those who were of the centurion's company saw this, they hastened by night to Pilate, abandoning the sepulchre which they were guarding, and reported everything that they had seen, being full of disquietude and saying, 'In truth he was the Son of God.' Pilate answered and said, 'I am clean from the blood of the Son of God, upon such a thing have you decided.' Then all came to him, beseeching him and urgently calling upon him to command the centurion and the soldiers to tell no one what they had seen. 'For it is better for us,' they said, 'to make ourselves guilty of the greatest sin before God than to fall into the hands of the people of the Jews and be stoned.' Pilate therefore commanded the centurion and the soldiers to say nothing (quoted from *NTApoc* 1, 1991, 224f.).

1. What special features does the narrative of the Gospel of Peter display as compared with the canonical Gospels, in respect of form, the event reported and the persons involved?

2. What narrative and theological tendencies are expressed in these peculiarities?

3. According to H. Koester,[46] the account is based on an old Easter epiphany narrative. After detaching secondary and redaction passages he reconstructs it as follows:

The elders came to Pilate and said. 'Give us soldiers so that we can guard his tomb for three days, lest his disciples come and steal him and the people think that he rose from the dead, and do evil to us.' And Pilate gave them the centurion Petronius with soldiers to guard the tomb. And with the centurion and the soldiers [all who were] there rolled a big stone and placed it before the door of the tomb. And after they had affixed seven seals and pitched a tent they kept guard. Now in the

---

[46]H. Koester, *Ancient Christian Gospels*, London and Philadelphia 1990, 232–8.

night in which the Lord's day dawned, when the soldiers, two by two in every watch, were keeping guard, there rang a loud voice in heaven and they saw the heavens opened and two men came down from there in great brightness and drew near the tomb. That stone which had been laid against the entrance to the tomb started of itself to roll and gave way to the side, and the tomb was opened, and both the young men entered in. When now the soldiers saw this, they awakened the centurion (and the elders, for they also were there to assist at the watch). They saw again three men coming out from the tomb, and two of them sustaining the other, and a cross following them, and the heads of the two reaching to heaven, but that of him who was led by them by the hand overpassing the heavens. When the centurion and his company saw this, . . . they said, 'In truth, he was the Son of God.'

Fragments of this epiphany story are said to have been worked over at a secondary stage in the Gospels of both Mark and Matthew. Compare Mark 15.39; 9.2–8 and Matt. 27.62–66; 28.2–4; 28.11–15.

(a) According to Koester there is little motivation for the confession of the centurion in Mark 15.39, whereas the Gospel of Peter contains its original content. What do you think?

(b) Koester conjectures that the epiphany part of the appearance of the tomb has been used in Mark 9.2–8. Does this interpretation seem plausible to you?

(c) Compare Matt. 27.62–66; 28.1–4. According to Koester, the request for a guard on the tomb (to prevent the theft of the body and rumours of resurrection) as a narrative continuation requires this guard to become a witness to the resurrection – as in the Gospel of Peter. Are there observations on the text which suggest the opposite conclusion, namely that the narrative in the Gospel of Peter is a further development of the narrative motifs from Matthew?

(d) Sum up your view on the theory that the epiphany at the tomb in the Gospel of Peter in the form reconstructed by Koester is earlier than Mark and Matthew.

16

The Historical Jesus and
the Beginnings of Christology

W. Bousset, *Kyrios Christos* ([2]1921), Nashville 1970; C. Colpe, *Die religionsgeschichtliche Schule. Darstellung und Kritik ihres Bildes vom gnostischen Erlösermythos*, FRLANT 60, Göttingen 1961; id., ὁ υἱὸς τοῦ ἀνθρώπου, *TDNT* 8, 1972, 400–77; E. Dinkler, 'Peter's Confession and the "Satan" Saying: The Problem of Jesus' Messiahship', in J.M. Robinson (ed.), *The Future of Our Religious Past*, London and New York 1971, 179–202; M. Hengel, *The Son of God*, London and Philadelphia 1975; B. Lindars, *Jesus Son of Man. A Fresh Examination of the Son of Man Sayings in the Gospels in the Light of Recent Research*, London 1983; J. Neusner, W. S. Green and E. Freerich, *Judaisms and Their Messiahs at the Turn of the Christian Era*, Cambridge 1987; N. Perrin, *A Modern Pilgrimage in New Testament Christology*, Philadelphia 1974; G. Theissen, 'Gruppenmessianismus'*; P. Vielhauer, 'Gottesreich und Menschensohn in der Verkündigung Jesu', in *FS G. Dehn*, Neukirchen 1957, 51–79 (= id., *Aufsätze zum Neuen Testament*, Munich 1965, 55–91).

Introduction

This chapter will describe the development from the way in which the historical Jesus understood himself to the worship of him in primitive Christianity. Of course a section on the way in which the historical Jesus understood himself belongs in an account of the period before Easter, by virtue of its content. However, it is not fortuitous that here it follows a discussion of the Easter faith. Nowhere is what Jesus himself said and what his followers said after Easter so indissolubly fused together as in sayings about Jesus' status. For his person was seen retrospectively in a completely new light on the basis of the Easter faith. Here three sets of problems may be mentioned in advance.

1. *The Easter gulf.* The consensus is that Christians said more (i.e. greater and more significant things) about Jesus after Easter than the historical Jesus had said about himself. This 'surplus value' of post-Easter christology by comparison with the pre-Easter self-understanding of Jesus is grounded both historically and in terms of content in the Easter event. Through this event the historical Jesus became the 'kerygmatic Christ', i.e. a saviour and redeemer who was proclaimed. There is a dispute as to how strong the continuity between the historical Jesus and the kerygmatic Christ is despite this 'Easter gulf'.

2. *The break in the tradition.* There is also a consensus that the 'honorific titles'

which the historical Jesus possibly used to express his status must have come from Jewish tradition (or have been mediated through Jewish tradition). The titles 'Son of Man' and 'Messiah' (= Christ) in particular arise in connection with the historical Jesus, since the former would have been misunderstood outside Palestine and the latter was soon used as a proper name. There is a dispute as to how far the sense of the titles changed when they were adopted by Jesus or his disciples and whether this marks a break with Jewish tradition.

3. *Jesus' consciousness of his authority*. Finally, there is a consensus that Jesus had a sense of eschatological authority. He saw the dawn of a new world in his actions. Here he goes beyond the Jewish charismatics and prophets known to us before him. There is a dispute over whether Jesus expressed his consciousness of authority implicitly without using christological titles, whether his consciousness of authority aroused ('evoked') expectations which were attached to him by contemporaries and his disciples in the form of traditional honorific titles, or whether he explicitly applied one or more honorific titles to himself. So in what follows we shall distinguish between implicit, evoked and explicit christology.

The question of the christological titles and their basis in the historical Jesus probably does not have the theological importance that is sometimes attached to it. The whole story of Jesus (the historical Jesus and the Christ believed to have risen) is the foundation of Christian faith; the titles are summary abbreviations of the claim contained in this story. The claim is decisive. It sets all the individual stories in a new light. What a different significance Jesus' execution on the cross has, depending on whether the one who is suffering here is an 'ordinary' person or a figure with a claim to eschatological authority, or even the 'Son of God'! The titles are abbreviations for the claim to authority which indicates the pre-understanding in which the individual parts of the story of Jesus are perceived.

Tasks: 1. The 'Easter gulf' between the historical Jesus and the kerygmatic Christ

Read the Emmaus story (Luke 24.13–27). What titles do the disciples give Jesus before their encounter with the risen Christ? What notion of a redeemer is implicit in v.21? What transformation does this expectation of a redeemer undergo?

2. The break in tradition: Ethiopic Enoch 46.1ff. and the sayings about the Son of Man

According to Dan. 7.13f. and the Similitudes of Ethiopic Enoch which take it up (46.1–8 etc.), the Son of Man is a heavenly judge who appears only with the dawn of the new time.

Enoch reports on his heavenly journey: 'At that place, I saw the One to whom belongs the time before time. And his head was white like wool, and there was with him another individual, whose face was like that of a human being. His countenance was full of grace like that of one among the holy angels. And I asked the one from among the angels who was going with me, and who had revealed to me all the secrets regarding the One who was born of human beings, "Who is this, and from whence is he who is going as the prototype of the Before-Time?" And he answered me and said to me, "This is the Son of Man, to whom belongs right-eousness and with whom righteousness dwells. And he will open all the hidden storerooms; for the Lord of the Spirits has chosen him, and he is destined to be victorious before the Lord of the Spirits in eternal uprightness. This Son of Man whom you have seen is the One who would remove the kings and the mighty ones from their comfortable seats and the strong ones from their thrones. He shall loosen the reins of the strong and crush the teeth of the sinners. He shall depose the kings from their thrones and kingdoms"', Ethiopian Enoch 46.1–5). Of the end-time it is said: 'At that hour, that Son of Man was given a name, in the presence of the Lord of the Spirits, the Before-Time; even before the creation of the sun and the moon, before the creation of the stars, he was given a name in the presence of the Lord of the Spirits. He will become a staff for the righteous ones in order that they may lean on him and not fall. He is the light of the Gentiles and he will become the hope of those who are sick in their hearts. In those days, the kings of the earth and the mighty landowners shall be humiliated on account of the deeds of their hands. Therefore, on the day of their misery and weariness, they will not be able to save themselves . . . On the day of their weariness, there shall be an obstacle on the earth and they shall fall on their faces; and they shall not rise up (again), nor anyone (be found) who will take them with his hands and raise them up. For they have denied the Lord of the Spirits and his anointed. Blessed be the name of the Lord of the Spirits' (Ethiopian Enoch 48.2–3, 8, 10).

Which of the Synoptic Son of Man sayings correspond to this traditional picture? Which contradict it? Read Mark 2.10, 27f.; 8.31f.; 13.26ff.; 14.62.

3. Jesus' sense of authority

Read Mark 6.14–16; 11.9–10; Matt. 11.2–6; 12.28. Where do we have explicit, where implicit and where evoked christology?

1. Three phases of research into New Testament christology

1.1 The discussion of Jesus' messiahship from Reimarus to c.1900

We can say that the beginning of historical-critical research into Jesus was not marked by disputing the messiahship of Jesus but rather by rediscovering it. H.S.

Reimarus (1694–1768) made it the centre of his interpretation of Jesus: Jesus was thought to have understood himself to be the Jewish Messiah – namely, the national king who would free Israel; the disciples overcame the collapse of these hopes by replacing belief in a political Messiah with belief in a 'spiritual' Messiah (the Messiah as the one who saves from sin).

The conviction of the messianic consciousness of Jesus continued to remain unshaken in the further course of historical research in the nineteenth century. D.F. Strauss was firmly convinced of it. However, the liberal quest of the historical Jesus modified the discovery of a reshaping of the traditional Jewish messianic expectation which ultimately goes back to Reimarus.

- It was not the disciples but Jesus himself who developed a more sublime concept of the Messiah with which he corrected the Jewish nationalist expectation.
- This 'correction' did not happen all at once; a development can be noted in Jesus: only at a late stage did he openly confess his messiahship and combine it with an awareness that he had to suffer.

1.2   The synthesis of form-critical scepticism and history-of-religions transference theories after c.1900

1.2.1   The rise of form-critical scepticism

In 1901 W. Wrede was the first to challenge the hitherto unassailed premise of historical criticism, that Jesus had understood himself to be Messiah. Wrede argued that the life of Jesus had been un-messianic. Messianic faith was rooted in Easter faith (cf. Rom. 1.3f.; Acts 2.36) and the projection of it back into the life of Jesus was 'community dogmatics' (see above, p. 6). When form criticism went on to demonstrate that all the Synoptic traditions were shaped by their 'use in the communities' (and therefore by the faith and needs of those communities), to begin with all the expressions of worship of Jesus (and thus above all the christological titles) were suspected of being projections backwards of the faith of the community.

1.2.2   History-of-religions transference theories

At the same time, history-of-religions research showed that the titles have a pre-Christian history. Some could have been transferred to Jesus at a secondary stage. The classic work for such transference theories is W. Bousset's *Kyrios Christos* (1913). He by no mean shared a radical scepticism, but assumed that Jesus understood himself as Messiah and spoke of himself as Son of Man (in some sense). But it was decisive for Bousset that after Easter, belief in Christ was shaped by two (successive) transferences of pre-formed conceptions of a redeemer. Belief in particular redeemer figures already existed in the environment: Jesus had only to enter these expectations of a redeemer.

1. The apocalyptic expectation of a Son of Man – i.e. the expectation of a future universal judge – was transferred to Jesus in *Palestinian primitive Christianity*. Only this variant of the messianic hope of Judaism was still possible after the crucifixion: 'The messianic faith of the primitive community *could* be formed after the death of Jesus in no other form than that of the ideal of a transcendent Messiah. The hope that Jesus as an earthly man would take over the role on earth of the king from David's tribe had been been once and for all shattered. That heavenly figure which in the Jewish tradition was indissolubly joined with the picture from the prophet Daniel was the name of the Son of Man' (ibid., 17).

2. By contrast, in *Hellenistic primitive Christianity* (thus in Antioch, Damascus and Tarsus), Jesus was worshipped by analogy with pagan deities. Bousset mentions three types of divine figures who became important for christology:

- *Kyrios deities* like Osiris, Isis, Sarapis, Atargatis who were worshipped in the mysteries (mystery cults). Whereas the expectation of the Son of Man assumed a future exaltation of Jesus, now the weight was shifted to the present: 'But the *Kyrios* of the Hellenistic primitive community . . . is a being who is *present* in the cult and in the worship. He permeates and surrounds his community in worship with his presence, and fills them from heaven with his miraculous powers' (ibid., 151). The Kyrios cult, worship and the sacrament belong together. There are then two further 'transferences' or reshapings (along the lines of analogies from the history of religion) in Paul:
- The *Gnostic myth of the primal man* who has fallen and has to be redeemed underlies the Adam–Christ typology (ibid., 195f.).
- *Pagan son of god deities* (within a divine triad of father, mother and son) shape the possibly originally messianic title 'Son of God' in Paul (ibid., 207).

1.2.3 *The combination of form-critical scepticism and history-of-religions transference theories in R. Bultmann*

Bultmann basically summed up already existing theories in a synthesis (*Theology* I*, 26–32, 42–53, 121–33; id., 'Frage'):

1. He continues to display historical scepticism. In his view the historical Jesus did not claim any honorific titles for himself (here Bultmann differs from Bousset). If Jesus spoke of the 'Son of Man' he meant a future judge who was different from himself. He did not understand himself as Messiah, but he was accused as 'Messiah' and perished because of a political misunderstanding. So Jesus only 'implicitly' put forward any claims to a lofty status.

2. What is decisive for Bultmann is not how Jesus understood himself but how God acted in him in the cross and resurrection. The decision of faith is made over this action of God. The 'kerygma' of the action of God made use of notions available in the contemporary world but radically transformed them. Thus for example the Gnostic redeemer myth was historicized, i.e.

- linked with a historically unique person who was crucified (historicity in the sense of a historical event).
- and thus the relationship of Jesus and believers was understood not as a 'physical' affinity but as 'faith' which is a decision (something 'historical' in the sense of an expression of human action).

1.2.4   *The transformation of this synthesis in the phase of the new quest of the historical Jesus (after 1953)*

The 'new' turn towards the historical Jesus after Käsemann's 1953 lecture 'The Problem of the Historical Jesus' led on the one hand to even greater scepticism about the roots of the titles in the life of Jesus and on the other to an intensive search for an 'implicit christology' which was not tied to titles.

- In 1964, in his article 'Peter's Confession and the "Satan" Saying', E. Dinkler came to the conclusion that Jesus directly rejected Peter's messianic confession (Mark 8.29), which he regarded as historical. The Satan saying ('Get behind me, Satan,' Mark 8.33), which in the present context refers to Peter's protest against Jesus' announcement of his suffering, was originally a reaction to Peter's confession.
- In his 1957 book on 'The Kingdom of God and the Son of Man in the Preaching of Jesus', P. Vielhauer denied that Jesus spoke any of the Son of Man sayings, including the logia about the future Son of Man. The expectation of the kingdom of God (which was already beginning) did not allow any eschatological intermediary who would come beforehand. Moreover the two expectations (Son of Man and kingdom of God) were separate both historically and in the tradition (i.e. the Synoptic tradition).

Whereas Bultmann had still thought that Jesus uttered the sayings about the future Son of Man, now these, too, were dropped as authentic sayings of Jesus. Jesus' deliberate distancing of himself from the title Messiah removed him from all preconceived Jewish role-expectations. This intensified the quest by the Bultmann pupils for an 'implicit christology', i.e. a claim to authority which was not bound up with a specific title. As long as this was sought in the framework of Jewish expectations (and titles), Jesus could be located in Judaism as the one who fulfilled these expectations. But such an 'implicit christology' almost necessarily led to people seeing a break with Judaism in as many of Jesus' ethical and eschatological sayings as possible. His 'authority' was understandable historically only as a 'breaking apart' of the frontiers of Judaism. The 'new quest' of the historical Jesus therefore led to a problematical (and historically vulnerable) contrast of Jesus with Judaism and against Judaism.

> As an illustration here are just a few sentences from Käsemann's fundamental article. He comments on the antitheses: 'To this there are no Jewish parallels, nor indeed can there be, for the Jew who does what is done here has cut himself off from the community of Judaism . . . certainly he was a Jew and made the assumptions of Jewish piety, but at the same time he shatters this framework with his claim' (37f.). This contrast is only slightly toned down by bringing in all antiquity (in view of Mark 7.15): 'This sovereign freedom not merely shakes the very foundations of Judaism and causes his death (*sic!*), but cuts the ground from under the feet of the ancient world view . . .' (40).

1.3   The revision of christological research (from c.1961)

Whereas a large part of (German-speaking) New Testament scholarship only slightly modified the picture worked out by the Bultmann school, it was fundamentally put in question by C. Colpe and M. Hengel.

1.3.1   *The revision of the history-of-religions derivations*

The classical transference theories related above all to the primal man-redeemer myth, and the assimilation of Jesus to (dying and rising) son deities and the Kyrios cults in the pagan environment. All three derivations were put in question:

- *The Gnostic redeemer*: in his 1961 book on 'The History of Religions School' (*Die religionsgeschichtliche Schule. Darstellung und Kritik ihres Bildes vom gnostischen Erlösermythos*, FRLANT 60, Göttingen 1961), C. Colpe demonstrated that the pre-Christian redeemer myth presupposed by the Bultmann school is a scholarly construct. It appears for the first time in the post-Christian period among the Manichees.

- *The Son of God*: in *The Son of God* (1975), M. Hengel showed that it is much more natural to derive the title Son of God from the messianic expectation of Judaism (Ps. 2.7 etc.) than from Hellenistic son-deities.

- *Kyrios*: in the same book Hengel stated that the title Kyrios was a transference of the Old Testament divine predicate ΚΥΡΙΟΣ to Jesus. Kyrios is only rarely attested in the mystery religions (outside the cult of Isis). Where the title is common (as in the case of the 'Baalim' of Syria), we do not have the mystery deities.

On the basis of these revisions in the history of religion, nowadays most exegetes assume that primitive Christianity expressed the status of Jesus after Easter with Jewish linguistic patterns. But there were also revisions within the sphere of Jewish religious history (among other things on the basis of the Qumran discoveries).

- The *Son of Man*: it became questionable whether there was an apocalyptic mediator figure with the title 'Son of Man'. In Dan. 7.13 'son of man' is not a title but a comparison referring either to a collective or an angel with an appearance 'like a man'. So did the Christians first create the apocalyptic Son of Man from Dan. 7 by scriptural exegesis (thus N. Perrin in 1974 in *A Modern Pilgrimage in New Testament Christology*)?[1]

- *The Messiah*: Jewish and Christian scholars corrected the notion that there was a messianic expectation in Jerusalem which was central for all. There are eschatological hopes with and without a Messiah, messianic figures with or without the title Messiah and – as the Qumran discoveries show – a great degree of variety in 'messianic notions' (thus J. Neusner et al., *Judaisms and Their Messiahs*, 1987).

1.3.2 *The revision of historical scepticism*

Whereas the corrections made to the history-of-religions approach met with wide consent, many hesitated also to revise the widespread scepticism towards the Jesus tradition.

- *The Son of Man*: in 1969 in his *TDNT* article on the Son of Man (υἱὸς τοῦ ἀνθρώπου), C. Colpe argued for the authenticity of Son of Man sayings from all three groups (the Son of Man at work in the present, the suffering Son of Man and the future Son of Man [see below, pp. 545ff.] and argued that the sayings about the future Son of Man were a 'symbol of Jesus' certainty of fulfilment' (*TDNT* 8, 441).
- *The Messiah*: Hengel even once again attributed a messianic consciousness to

---

[1]As the Similitudes of the Ethiopian book of Enoch which speak of the 'Son of Man' have not yet been found in the Qumran Enoch literature, they could even date from after the New Testament.

Jesus ('Jesus, der Messias Israel', 1992), not least on the basis of the history-of-religions insight that the title of 'Anointed' in Judaism had a much more varied meaning than had been assumed earlier. In addition to the royal Messiah, in Qumran for example we also find the prophets as 'those who have been anointed by the spirit'. So we need not assume any radical reshaping of a political Messiah concept if we are to regard it as possible that Jesus had a messianic self-understanding.

1.3.3 The revision of the exclusivist understanding of titles

The revisions of the history-of-religions transference theory and historical scepticism were (also) governed by the motive of safeguarding the status of Jesus as seen in traditional church christology by demonstrating authentic titles. At the same time doubt arose as to whether a claim to the disputed titles (which was historically quite possible) needed to be understood as an exclusive status or whether the distinctive character of Jesus' claim did not lie in an open use of the expression 'Son of Man' and traditional messianic expectations.

- *The Son of Man*: H. Lietzmann, *Der Menschensohn* (1896), had argued that 'Son of Man' [Aramaic *bar-nāsh(ā')*] was a general term for 'man' or 'a man'. Only at a secondary stage did it become a messianic title through the translation and influence of Dan. 7. G. Vermes took up this argument again in 1965 (summarized in *Jesus** 177–91) and attempted above all to demonstrate that the Aramaic *bar-nāsh(ā')* can also be a periphrasis for 'I'. B. Lindars interprets this periphrasis for 'I' as 'a man like me' or 'a man in my position' (*Jesus Son of Man*, 1983). The title would then lose its exclusivist sense
- *The Messiah*: in 1992 G. Theissen argued that while Jesus took up messianic notions, he modified them in the sense of a 'group messianism': Jesus transfers the royal Messiah's function of judging the tribes of Israel (Ps. Sol. 17.26) to the collective of disciples (Matt. 19.28/Luke 22.28–30).

1.4 A systematic survey of the main problems: the historical Jesus and christological titles

The central problem is still: do the christological titles have a basis in the life and self-understanding of Jesus or are they post-Easter interpretations? The discussion has shown that one can understand a variety of things by 'having a basis in Jesus'. Here are five possibilities and an example of each:

1. *Explicit christology*: possibly Jesus himself expressed his authority with a christological title. This is discussed in connection with the title 'Son of Man' and also the title Messiah. The following questions then remain open:

- By 'Son of Man' does Jesus mean himself or another, future figure as a representative of whom he has his authority?
- Is 'Son of Man' a title for a lofty apocalyptic figure or a periphrasis for 'I' or 'human beings' generally?
- Are the sayings about the Son of Man at work in the present, the future Son of Man, or both, authentic? At all events most of the sayings about the suffering Son of Man are usually taken as prophecies after the event.

2. *Evoked christology*: possibly Jesus already aroused christological expectations among others during his lifetime. This is discussed in connection with the messianic expectation, and also 'Son of David' and 'Prophet'. Then these questions remain open:

- Did Jesus accept positively, reject or correct the messianic expectations of his followers (the disciples or the people)?
- Was Jesus executed as a royal pretender because of a political misunderstanding of his messiahship, or did his opponents understand his claim rightly?

3. *Implicit christology*: possibly Jesus expressed his status without a title, but in fact fulfilled the conditions of a 'Messiah'. Then these questions remain open:

- Does the authority of Jesus show itself in contradiction to Jewish messianic expectations or as their fulfilment?
- Can Jesus' authority be understood as 'immediacy', 'criticism of the law', 'preaching of grace', 'certainty of faith' or as a paradoxical combination of 'intensification and relaxation of the Torah'?

4. *A heightened use of titles*: possibly the post-Easter community took up a title used by the earthly Jesus but gave it a transcendent claim which it did not have before. This is discussed in connection with the title Kyrios (Aramaic *mare'* = Lord) and 'Son of Man'. In that case it is necessary to explain:

- Was the respectful address 'Sir' heightened after Easter so that it denoted a Mare-Kyrios expected in the future (cf. the cry Maranatha, 'Lord, come'), or is the title Kyrios (say in the form of the so-called Kyrios acclamation, cf. Phil. 2.6–11) independent of the address 'Sir'?
- Is the heightening of the title Kyrios, which verges on the transcendent, derived from the Old Testament name of God, or is it based on the title used in pagan Kyrios cults?

5. *An exclusivist use of titles*: possibly the post-Easter community referred titles exclusively to Jesus which he understood inclusively, i.e. under which he also included others. This is discussed in connection with the title Son of God, which is used in Matt. 5.9, 45 in an inclusive way. In that case it is necessary to explain:

- Was the title Son of God first associated with the resurrection after Easter (Rom. 1.3f.) and then successively dated to Jesus' baptism, birth and pre-existence? Or did various views of the Son of God develop simultaneously and side by side after Easter?
- Does the concentration of the term 'Son of God' on Jesus derive from Jewish messianic expectations (Ps. 2.7; II Sam. 7.14f.) or (also) from a transference of pagan notions of son deities?

In an explicit, evoked or implicit christology, the claim associated with a title is in fact attributed to the historical Jesus. Only in these three cases can one speak of a real 'basis' of post-Easter christology in the historical Jesus. By contrast, the intensified and exclusivist use of a pre-Easter title after Easter dates the real claim to status to a lofty status to Easter: only the term used in the titles would have a pre-Easter forerunner, not the claim itself. Therefore within a book on the historical Jesus we shall deal only briefly with the titles Kyrios and Son of God.

The following diagram illustrates the most important alternatives in a clarification of the relationship between the historical Jesus and christology:

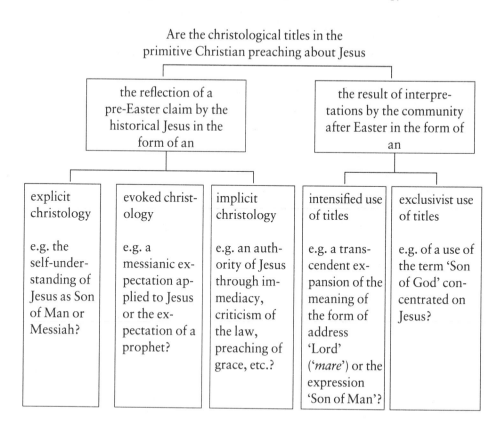

Are the christological titles in the primitive Christian preaching about Jesus

the reflection of a pre-Easter claim by the historical Jesus in the form of an			the result of interpretations by the community after Easter in the form of an	
explicit christology	evoked christology	implicit christology	intensified use of titles	exclusivist use of titles
e.g. the self-understanding of Jesus as Son of Man or Messiah?	e.g. a messianic expectation applied to Jesus or the expectation of a prophet?	e.g. an authority of Jesus through immediacy, criticism of the law, preaching of grace, etc.?	e.g. a transcendent expansion of the meaning of the form of address 'Lord' ('*mare*') or the expression 'Son of Man'?	e.g. of a use of the term 'Son of God' concentrated on Jesus?

A moderate historical criticism assumes an explicit, evoked and implicit christology for Jesus himself (especially for the titles Messiah and Son of Man) but sees the titles 'Lord' (Kyrios) and 'Son of God' as post-Easter transferences of Old Testament/Jewish traditions to Jesus (and secondarily with an elaboration by pagan analogies).

A more radical historical criticism denies Jesus all titles, and sees only an implicit christology as the substantive basis for late christology. In that case the titles were transferred to Jesus in two stages:

(a) The transference of the titles 'Messiah' and 'Son of Man' in Palestinian Jewish primitive Christianity.

(b) The transference of the titles 'Kyrios' and 'Son of God' in Hellenistic-pagan primitive Christianity; here the influence of pagan analogies is taken more seriously than it is by 'moderate' criticism.

2. Jesus the charismatic: implicit christology in the historical Jesus

There is a dispute as to whether Jesus wanted to fulfil contemporary expectations of redemption bound up with particular titles. There is no dispute about his sense of authority, but it is an open question whether all the indications of this really go back to Jesus and whether they are always so unusual that they attest a singular claim. Here, too, such indications cannot be completely unique, if one wants to give them a historical explanation and attach them to Jesus. Do the analogies point to comparable Jewish charismatics?[2]

2.1 The 'amen' formula

K. Berger, *Die Amen-Worte Jesu*, BZNW 39, Berlin 1970; B. Chilton, 'Amen', *ABD* 1, 1992, 184–6; J. Jeremias, 'Amen', *TRE* 2, 1978, 386–91.

There is frequent evidence of 'amen' as a response in Judaism. 'Amen' indicates assent to someone else's statement – whether this is a curse, a command or a prayer (cf. Deut. 27.15; Neh. 8.6; I Kings 1.36; Sotah II, 5). Primitive Christianity also knows this response (I Cor. 14.16; II Cor. 1.20; Rev. 5.14 etc.). There is always an unusual emphasis on it. An 'amen' which is not a response is characteristic of the Jesus tradition – always at the beginning of statements,

---

[2]We already discussed the charisma of Jesus in §8, as an irrational aura which influenced others. Religious charisma is always based on a special closeness of the charismatic to God, on the presence of a power in his activity which goes beyond the everyday. Charisma has both a horizontal and a vertical dimension. Indications of the vertical dimension of Jesus' charism will be collected in his section.

always combined with 'I say to you (singular or plural)', and always on the lips of Jesus. The instances appear in various complexes of tradition (Mark; Matt.[s]; Luke[s]; Q), but these do not include the Gospel of Thomas. So far attempts to find evidence for 'amen' outside the Jesus tradition at the beginning of a statement, endorsing it or giving it authority, have proved fruitless:

- An ostracon from the period before 600 BCE contains the assertion of a harvester who knows that he has been wrongly accused. He claims: 'My brothers (i.e. those working with him) will bear witness for me (and say): Amen (it is true), I am free of guilt.' Here too the 'amen' is a response.[3]
- In the Testament of Abraham there is an instance in a form of address to God (ch.8) and a speech by a personification of death (ch.20), but only in a revision of the text by a Christian scribe (recension A) first attested in the thirteenth century. Contrary to K.Berger ('Amen-Worte', 4ff.), one cannot argue from this to a pre-Christian origin of an 'amen' which does not take the form of a response.

An 'amen' which does not take the form of a response could in fact be a linguistic creation on the part of Jesus (Jeremias). It was prepared for by individual features in Judaism: in Tobit 8.8 a couple endorse their own prayer by adding an 'amen'; in Jer. 28.6 and Rev. 7.12 we find a prefaced 'amen' as a response to a statement by someone else. Other assertive formulas used at the beginning of a statement served as a pattern. There is much to say for the assumption that for Jesus the prefixing of an 'amen' which did not take the form of a response replaced the prophetic messenger formula 'Thus says Yahweh' (thus T.W. Manson, *The Teaching of Jesus*, Cambridge 1931 = 1948, 207). So it would contain the claim: here speaks a prophet – indeed perhaps more than a prophet!

2.2 Jesus' emphatic 'I' in the antitheses and the sayings about his having come

We can find a special consciousness of authority on the part of Jesus both in the antitheses which set Jesus' 'I' against the Law of Moses and also in his statements about why he has come, which express the aim of his mission (in ἦλθον sayings). The antitheses have already been discussed in §12 (3.3.1, pp. 363f.), so we can be brief here.

1. The *antitheses* (Matt. 5.21f., 27f., 33f.) do not seek either to criticize or to abolish the Torah but to supplement it by commandments which take it further. Their special feature is not their content, but the natural way in which Jesus sets his 'But I say to you' against the Torah. He speaks neither in its name nor in the name of God, but emphatically in his own name. In so doing he appears as an independent 'lawgiver'. That recalls the Hellenistic ideal of a king, according to

---

[3]Cf. J. Naveh, 'A Hebrew Letter from the Seventh Century BC', *IEJ* 10, 1960, 129–39.

which the king is 'living law' (νόμος ἔμψυχος), D. Zeller). An authentic antithesis has even been handed down about the Spartan king Ariston, in which he dissociates himself from a traditional ideal of kingship: 'When someone commended the maxim of Cleomenes, who on being asked what a good king ought to do, said, "To do good to his friends and evil to his enemies," Ariston said, "How much better, my good sir, to do good to our friends and to make friends of our enemies?"' (Plutarch, *Moralia* 218A).[4] Jesus also formulated similar self-confident antitheses.[5] Since his 'But I say to you' is without a real analogy among the rabbis, who always only differ from other interpretations of the Torah with this formula and never from the Torah itself (E. Lohse), it expresses a marked consciousness of authority.

2. *The ἦλθον sayings about the coming of Jesus*. These sayings are often regarded as retrospective summaries of the mission of Jesus which presuppose a post-Easter standpoint. However, 'I have come' is not an expression from post-Easter christology.[6] It does not appear once in the prophets. Rather, it is attested as a messenger formula for human messengers in Job 1.15ff. and for superhuman messengers in Dan. 9.23; 10.14 etc. Other figures could speak of themselves to similar effect in contemporary Judaism. Josephus reports on his prophetic forecast to Vespasian, which promised that Vespasian would be emperor: 'You suppose, sir, that in capturing me you have merely secured a prisoner, but I come as a messenger of the greatness that awaits you (ἐγὼ δὲ ἄγγελος ἥκω σοι μειζόνων). Had I not been sent by God himself, I knew the Jewish law and how a general ought to die' (*BJ* 3, 400).[7] At another point he makes John of Gischala, one of the charismatic leaders in the Jewish war, make a similar remark: 'He added that it was by divine providence that he was the one commissioned to arrange a truce (αὐτὸς εἰσπεμφθείη κατὰ θεοῦ πρόνοιαν ὡς πρεσβευτής)' (*BJ* 4, 219). As the 'I am come' cannot be derived from post-Easter christology, but can easily be imagined in Judaism, Jesus will have spoken of himself in this way. The sayings in Luke 12.49f., 51; 7.34 and Mark 2.17b could be authentic. Matthew 5.17; Mark 10.45 and Luke 19.10 could have been formed in analogy to them

---

[4]Quoted from M.E. Boring, K. Berger and C. Colpe, *Hellenistic Commentary to the NT*, Nashville 1995, 274, p.196.

[5]To avoid misunderstanding it should be emphasized that the antitheses spoken by Jesus are not to be derived from such analogies; parallels in content are merely meant to illuminate the claim of these antitheses.

[6]The phrase 'I am come . . .' appears in John 5.43; 10.10; 12.47; 16.28; 18.37 – but without any christological emphasis on the formula itself. John the Baptist speaks of himself in the same way in John 1.31: διὰ τοῦτο ἦλθον ἐγὼ ἐν ὕδατι βαπτίζων (therefore I am come to baptize with water).

[7]The last apologetic clause (which probably convinced only Josephus himself) refers to the fact that Josephus – unlike all his soldiers, who had fallen in battle or had killed themselves rather than be taken prisoner – had handed himself over to the Romans alive.

after Easter (M. Sato). At all events we can infer from them that Jesus had a sense of his mission.

2.3 The use of the metaphor of father

J. Ashton, 'Abba', *ABD* 1, 1992, 7–8; R. Hamerton-Kelly, *God the Father*, Philadelphia 1979; J. Jeremias, 'Abba', in *The Prayers of Jesus*, London 1967, 11–65; J. Schlosser, *Le Dieu de Jésus*, LD 129, Paris 1987, 179–209.

That God is 'father' (and acts like a mother) is part of the collective imagery of Judaism. The image stamps some of the most intense statements of the Old Testament about the mercy of God: 'Yet it was I who taught Ephraim to walk, I took them up in my arms . . . How can I give you up, O Ephraim! How can I hand you over, O Israel' (Hos. 11.1; cf. Jer. 31.20). In New Testament times God is addressed in the prayers of the community as 'Our Father, our King . . .' and in individual prayers as 'Father'. The latter happens not only in the Diaspora (cf. Joseph and Asenath 12.14f.) but also in Palestine (Sir. 51.10). Contrary to Jeremias,[8] one can make Jesus' address to God as 'Father' a singular and unparalleled expression of trust only by reinterpreting the evidence. But two points need to be made.

1. The Jesus tradition differentiates in a striking way between 'my Father' and 'your Father', not only in Matthew, where this terminology is immediately striking, but also in Luke, where 'my Father' (Luke 10.22; 22.29; 24.49) stands alongside 'your Father' (6.36; 12.30, 32). Even John makes the Risen Christ say: 'I go to my Father and your Father' (John 20.17). Nowhere does Jesus associate himself with his disciples in order to address God as 'our Father' – except in the Our Father, which has been formulated for the disciples and from their perspective. In any case the Lukan version has only 'Father' (Luke 11.2). As this stylization of Jesus' discourse about God is in tension with the 'family of God' metaphor and is too incidental to be the result of a deliberate post-Easter christology, the distinction between 'my Father' and 'your Father' could indicate a special relationship of Jesus to God.[9]

2. The designation of God as 'Abba' (Aramaic 'father') is attested for a Jewish charismatic, Hanan ha-Nehba, a grandson of Honi the Circle-Drawer, who lived at the turn of the eras and was regarded as a charismatic man of prayer endowed with supernatural powers:

---

[8]Schlosser, *Dieu*, 179ff., defends Jeremias, but emphasizes that if 'Abba' is the original form of address in the Our Father, the nearness to God which is expressed in it cannot be interpreted in christological terms. It also applies to the disciples.

[9]According to Schlosser, *Dieu*, 123ff., however, the sayings which contain 'my Father' are usually post-Easter.

When the world was in need of rain the rabbis would send to him schoolchildren and they would take hold of the hem of his garment and say to him, 'Abba, Abba, give us rain.' But he said before Him, 'Ruler of the world, do it for the sake of these who are unable to distinguish between the Abba who can give rain and the Abba who cannot give rain' (bTaan 23b).[10]

We may leave open the question whether this story is historical or very old. For us it is important that in primitive Christianity, too, the addressing of God as Abba is attributed to a supernatural power of the spirit (Gal. 4.6; Rom. 8.15). The term can imply charismatic intimacy. Since it is related of Jesus that he himself addressed God in prayer as 'Abba' (Mark 14.36), we may not exclude the possibility that this form of address goes back to him: it is conceivable in Judaism and among charismatics – and in primitive Christianity is noted as an extraordinary phenomenon. By contrast, comments that here the language of early childhood (like 'Daddy') is deliberately taken up or that this is an absolutely singular phenomenon, are wrong.

2.4 The forgiveness of sins

The promise of the forgiveness of sins is attested only twice in the case of Jesus – in the healing of the paralysed man (Mark 2.1–12) and in the encounter with the 'woman who was a sinner' (Luke 7.36–50). As the latter story could have been developed from Mark 14.3ff., it can be left out of account (except for 7.41–43). Despite the sparse attestation, a recollection of the historical Jesus could have been preserved here. The theme of the forgiveness of sins had been given to Jesus by John the Baptist; it occurs in Jesus' parables (Matt. 18.23–35; Luke 7.41–43; 15.11–32; 18.9–14), in the Our Father, and in admonitions (cf Matt. 6.14f.; Mark 11.25) The way in which Jesus ate with toll collectors and sinners shows that here his words and his behaviour corresponded. If the personal promise to the paralysed man, 'Your sins are forgiven', seems to stand in isolation in the Jesus tradition, we must remember that so far there is only one instance of the pronouncement of the forgiveness of sins spoken by a human being in Judaism outside the Jesus tradition – in the prayer of Nabonidus, an anonymous Jew (perhaps Daniel) heals the Babylonian king by forgiving his sins (4QprNab). To this degree it would be understandable why such a promise is also unique in the Jesus tradition and is criticized as 'blasphemy', even if the forgiveness of sins in Mark 2.5 is clearly attributed to God by a divine passive and not to the Son of Man – as in the secondary insertion 2.6–10.

---

[10]It is striking that Hanan ha-Nehba does not address God as 'Abba' but as 'Ruler of the world'. Abba does not appear as a form of address to God but as a designation of God. But cannot any personal designation of God very soon become a form of address?

The Old Testament and Judaism know both a cultic and a non-cultic forgiveness of sins. There is a dispute as to whether after atonement sacrifices the priest promised the forgiveness of sins in declamatory formulae. There is no direct evidence. But there is no disputing the fact that there was confidence in God's forgiveness on the basis of confession and repentance: 'He will cleanse from sins the soul in confessing, in restoring . . . and your goodness is upon those that sin, when they repent' (PsSol. 9.6). Here there is no trace of a cultic mediation of the forgiveness of sins. So Jesus does not do anything unprecedented in Judaism when he speaks of the forgiveness of sins independently of the temple. Nevertheless, his promise of the forgiveness of sins causes offence. That is understandable. If (perhaps) the priest did not even communicate the forgiveness of sins in the cult through his word, and if it was attributed to God independently of the cult, but not personally promised (in place of God), then the criticism 'Who can forgive sins save God alone?' (Mark 2.7) would have been an apt one. Jesus could have called on people to trust in God's forgiveness of sins without causing offence; he could have expressed his own personal confidence in God's mercy. But he does more: he says that God has in fact forgiven. In so doing, though, he attributes to himself no greater authority than that anonymous Jew who forgives sins in 4 QprNab. John the Baptist basically claims an even greater authority when he associates the forgiveness of sins with a rite which rivals the temple cult. Here, too, the authority of Jesus has analogies in other Jewish charismatics.

2.5 The causal attribution of the miracles

In the Jesus tradition, in the miracle stories we find the statement that healings stem from the faith of those who seek help (Mark 5.34; 10.52; Luke 17.19; Matt. 9.29; 15.28). In addition there is the saying about the faith which works miracles (Mark 11.22ff.). In two sayings traditions this causal attribution of the miracles to faith is rivalled by an implicit and explicit attribution of causes to God.[11]

It is contained implicitly in John the Baptist's question (Matt. 11.2ff.): Jesus replies to the question whether he is the one who is to come by pointing to the miracles which are taking place in the present, but without emphasizing that they are done by him. Miracles by his disciples could also be meant. There is a parallel to this in a Qumran fragment which speaks at the same time of the Messiah and the miracles that God performs.

> '. . . and the Lord will accomplish glorious things which have never been as [the . . .]. For he will heal the wounded, and revive the dead and bring good news to

---

[11]Especially Stegemann, *Essener**, 323ff,. has put the indications of a direct causal attribution of miracles to God at the centre of his interpretation of Jesus.

the poor/(the humble) . . . He will lead the uprooted . . .(?)]' (4Q 521 frag 2. ii 11–13).

The combination of healings, raisings of the dead and the good news recalls Matt. 11.2ff. – but above all the attribution of these miracles not to the Messiah but to God's action in the messianic era. Since in Matt. 11.2ff. the christology is ultimately brought under a lowest common denominator, 'Blessed is he who does not take offence at me', here we may not have a post-Easter construction: Jesus himself took up expectations of the messianic age without calling himself 'Messiah' in the process.

There is an explicit causal attribution to God in the saying about exorcisms. The driving out of demons is regarded as the work of the 'finger" (Luke 11.20) or the 'spirit of God' (Matt. 12.28). However, it is carried out by Jesus. God is directly at work in him (Stegemann, *Essener**). But Jesus perhaps also attributes thesa me power to other exorcists when he asks, 'But if drive out demons by Beelzebul (as is wrongly supposed of me), by whom do your sons drive them out?' (Luke 11.19). The charism of exorcism is probably not exclusively attached to Jesus (cf. above, p. 258).

We may ask whether there are links between these two causal attributions of miraculous power to God and to human beings: once it is said 'Everything is possible to him who believes' (Mark 9.23); even a share in divine omnipotence is attributed to (human) faith. The faith which works miracles is itself a charisma – a sign of the effective presence of God in the concrete individual. But Jesus sees even more in this: the dawn of the ultimate intervention of God in history. This awareness that with him the end-time is dawning might underline all the phenomena of charismatic authority. There is at least one indication of this: Jesus' attitude to John the Baptist.

2.6 The assessment of John the Baptist

Remarkably, the implicit christology in Jesus' sayings about John the Baptist is rarely investigated. Everyday experience tells us that any praise says a good deal about the one who is formulating it. That is also true here: the greater the light that Jesus casts on John the Baptist, the more reflects indirectly back on him. For the Jesus tradition leaves no doubt that Jesus lived in the awareness of surpassing John. And this was the case although for him John was already a figure who could hardly be surpassed: a prophet, but more than a prophet (Matt. 11.9), the greatest of those so far born of human beings (Matt. 11.11), with whom a new age had dawned. For since the days of the Baptist the kingdom of God had been stormed by men of violence (Matt. 11.12). However one understands this saying, it asserts that now the kingdom of God is here, and only because of that can one storm it. Furthermore, in a dispute Jesus associated his authority closely with the authority of John the Baptist (cf. Mark 11.27f.), and certainly not just for tactical advantage.

All these sayings about John indirectly contain a tremendous claim to a high status: if John stood on the threshold of the kingdom of God, surpassing all the prophets, how much more must Jesus be, who had already crossed this threshold! The thesis of an implicit claim to high status implied in the relationship between John the Baptist and Jesus can be substantiated by analogies from the history of religion. Elsewhere, too, messianic figures appear in pairs, in succession. K. Koch has collected the evidence for such a two-stage messialogy:[12]

- The animal apocalypse (EthEn. 85–90) first of all describes a sheep which grows a great horn and saves the threatened sheep from the ravens (the Seleucid oppressors, 90.9–12). After it the time of salvation begins. During this time a white bull with large horns is born. All the animals again become bulls – i.e. they assume the form which Adam and his descendants up to Isaac had (89.11). With him the primal time returns.
- IV Ezra knows the activity of the Messiah and the Son of Man one after another – distributed between two epochs. The Messiah comes at the end of the world age, rules 400 (?) years and dies. The world returns to silence (7.28f., 39). However, at the beginning of the new world age the 'man' appears and conquers the Gentile peoples (13.1ff.). There is a dispute as to whether he is identical with the Messiah mentioned previously or represents a second figure.
- In the last world age the Apocalypse of Abraham knows a man from the seed of Abraham. He gathers together the righteous, brings judgment for part of the Gentiles and hope for the others (Apocalypse of Abraham 29). He is followed by terrible plagues. Only after that does God send his 'elect' (Apocalypse of Abraham 31). Again we find two figures, one at the end of the world age and the other at the beginning of the new time.
- The Syrian Apocalypse of Baruch expects a two-stage activity of the same Messiah: according to 29.3 the Messiah reveals himself at the end of time; according to 30.1ff. he will appear anew – after a cosmic turning-point!
- According to the majority opinion among exegetes, the Similitudes of Ethiopian Enoch (37–71) identify Messiah and Son of Man. However, these could also be two separate figures. If the kings and mighty men are judged by the Son of Man because they 'had denied the names of the Lord of the Spirits and his anointed' (48.10, cf. above, p. 514), the question arises: how could they have denied the Son of Man, since he was revealed only at the judgment?
- 11 QMelch knows a messianic messenger of joy who announces the rule of

---

[12]Half the instances (IV Ezra; Apocalypse of Abraham; Syrian Apocalypse of Baruch) are later than the Jesus tradition, but the other half may be earlier than it.

Melchizedek. The messenger of joy carries on his activity on earth. By contrast, the rule of his prince Melchizedek (also) embraces the heavenly sphere.

It is in keeping with the patterns of expectation of the time that two messianic figures (who need not be called 'Messiah') follow each other.[13] If John the Baptist already grew up into such a decisive prophetic role, how much more must his 'successor' have been a messianic figure! At least one can understand how he evoked messianic expectations. The next section is concerned with them.

3. Jesus as Messiah: evoked christology in the historical Jesus

J.H. Charlesworth (ed.), *The Messiah. Developments in Earliest Judaism and Christianity*, Minneapolis 1992; J.H. Charlesworth, 'From Jewish Messianology to Christian Christ-ology. Some Caveats and Perspectives', in J. Neusner et al. (ed.), *Judaisms and Their Messiahs* (see above), 225–64; C.A. Evans, *Jesus**, 53–212, 437–56; M. Hengel, 'Jesus, der Messias Israels. Zum Streit über das "messianische Sendungsbewusstsein" Jesu', in I. Gruenwald et al. (eds.), *Messiah and Christus (FS D. Flusser)*, Tübingen 1992, 155–76; M. Karrer, *Der Gesalbte. Die Grundlagen des Christustitels*, FRLANT 151, Göttingen 1991; G. Theissen, 'Gruppenmessianismus'*.

If Jesus was a charismatic who claimed to be bringing in the eschatological turning-point, would he not then necessarily have been seen as the fulfilment of messianic expectations? Would he not have had to understand himself as 'Messiah'? We could answer such questions better if we knew what messianic expectations existed at that time, how widespread they were and in what variations they could appear. The sources give a confusing impression. Here we shall discuss some fundamental differentiations.

3.1 The two Old Testament roots of messianic expectation

The messianic expectation of the New Testament period derives the term 'Messiah' from the anointed kings, priests and prophets of the Old Testament, but its content from the expectation of future redeemer figures in the Old Testament, who are not given the name 'Messiah'.

3.1.1 *The anointed of the OT*

The name 'anointed' (from the Hebrew מָשִׁיחַ, *māshiaḥ*), points to a ritual of anointing which is attested for kings, high priests and prophets. It makes the

---

[13]Half the examples (IV Ezra; Apocalypse of Abraham: Syrian Apocalypse of Baruch) are later than the Jesus tradition; but the other half may be older than it.

anointed persons taboo (I Sam. 24.11). All the evidence for anointed figures relates not to future redeemer figures but to historical figures.

- The books of Samuel and the Psalter mention *kings* as 'Yahweh's anointed' (cf. I Sam. 12.3, 5; Ps. 2.2; 18.51, etc.). The transference of the term 'anointed' to Cyrus king of Persia is unique (Isa. 45.1). Otherwise the term 'Messiah' does not appear in the prophets, as though they were afraid of associating the expected king of salvation conceptually with an act of consecration which had been performed by the earthly kings whom they had criticized.
- In or after the exilic period the title of 'Messiah', which had been orphaned by the collapse of the monarchy, was applied to the *high priest* (Lev. 4.3, 5, 16), who was consecrated by anointing (Ex. 29). This concept of a priestly Messiah occurs only in late texts (I Chron. 29.22; Sir. 45.15; Dan. 9.25f.; II Macc. 1.10).
- We rarely hear of the *anointing of a prophet* (I Kings 19.16). According to Ps. 105.15 the patriarchs are prophets and anointed by God. According to Isa. 61.1 it is said in a transferred sense that God has anointed the prophets with spirit.

We may begin from the assumption that the ritual of anointing ceased with the Hasmonean monarchy, which was formed on Hellenistic models: Hellenistic kings were not anointed, but crowned with a diadem.

3.1.2 *Messianic figures of the OT*

Three criteria must be fulfilled for it to be possible to speak of messianic figures:

- They usher in an eschatological turning point, i.e. a definitive new state in the world which goes beyond anything previous.
- They have a soteriological function: they bring salvation to Israel (and often to all humankind through Israel).
- They have a charismatic status and tower above other human beings by virtue of their nearness to God.

The classic messianic texts of the OT are texts without the term 'Messiah'. In them, what the royal ideology of the ancient Near East attributed to present kings as a superhuman aura and a saving power was reformulated as the expectation of a saving king who will defend Israel against his enemies and bring peace (Isa. 8.23–9.6; 11.1ff.; Micah 5.1ff.; Zech. 9.9f.). Other texts were interpreted secondarily in a messianic sense: the blessing of Jacob in Gen. 49.10; the saying of Balaam in Num. 24.17; Nathan's prophecy in II Sam. 7.12ff.; and Ps. 2; along with Amos's saying about the tabernacle of David in Amos 9.11f.:

OT	Messianic interpretation in subsequent history
II Sam. 7.12ff.	4Q174 III, 10ff.[14]
Ps. 2.1ff.	4Q174 III, 18f. (probably); PsSol 17.23f., 30
Amos 9.11f.	4Q174 III, 11–13
Gen. 49.10	LXX Gen. 49.10; 4Q 252 frag.1, v.1ff.
Num. 24.17	CD VII, 19–21

In the period after the New Testament, the messianic interpretation of these Old Testament texts (now with the term 'Messiah') is attested above all by the Targumim, i.e. the Aramaic translations of the Hebrew Old Testament.[15] The conclusion to be drawn for the Old Testament period is that we know either messianic expectations without a messianic concept or historical figures called 'Messiah' to whom no messianic expectations are attached.

3.2 The plurality of messianic expectations in New Testament times

Messianic figures who bear the name 'Messiah' appear first around the turn of the ages. Here for the first time there is evidence of the absolute usage of the name 'the Messiah' (perhaps in 1QSa II, 12; also in the NT). Psalms of Solomon 17/18 can be clearly dated (middle of the first century CE). Under the impact of the Roman occupation of Palestine and the failure of the Hasmonean kings a future king of salvation is expected as 'the Lord's anointed' (or 'his anointed', 17.32; 18.1, 5, 7), at a time when the ritual of anointing had long ceased to be practised. In deliberate opposition to the earthly king, the term 'Messiah', which had newly been revived, emphasizes the divine legitimation of the hoped-for king of salvation. It fits well with this that in Greek, too, Christos (anointed) was also full of associations of a consecrated nearness to God (M. Karrer). However, this renaissance of the concept of Messiah in a far-reaching political crisis did not lead to a unitary messianic expectation. Typically, four forms of eschatological and messianic expectations can be distinguished; we shall go on to discuss them.

3.2.1 Eschatological expectation of messianic figures with the term 'Messiah'

Even if the expectation of a royal Messiah is attested most frequently, we find all three types of 'anointed', as in the Old Testament – but now as messianic figures in the eschatological sense defined above. The table below gives a survey of the pre-

---

[14]Numbering as in Vermes*.
[15]Cf. the texts and the interpretation of them in Evans, *Jesus**, 155–81.

Christian evidence for 'Messiah'; it is limited to passages in which 'Messiah' or 'Christos' in fact occurs.

It is clear that outside Qumran the expectation is predominantly only of a royal Messiah. The messianic dyarchy of a priestly and royal Messiah is opposition to the Hasmonean rule which combined the two offices. Elsewhere we find a comparable juxtaposition of a priestly and a royal messianic figure only in the Testaments of the Twelve Patriarchs, on the one hand in TestLevi 18, where the eschatological high priest reopens paradise, and on the other in TestJudah 24, where a royal Messiah without military features and with an ethical orientation appears. The term 'Messiah' is not used at either point.

	High priest	King	Prophet
Qumran[16]	1QS IX, 9–11: 'Messiahs of Aaron and Israel' (in the plural!). CD XII, 22; XIV, 18f.; XIX, 10f.; XX, 1: 'Messiah of Aaron and Israel' (in the singular). Where both figures appear, the priest has the pre-eminence (cf. also 1QSa II, 11ff.)	4QPatr (4Q 252): interpretation of the blessing of Jacob in terms of the 'Messiah of Righteousness', the shoot of David. 1QSa II, 11ff.: God has the Messiah of Israel born in the community: he appears alongside the eschatological priest. 4Q521 frag.2 ii 1: '[Hea]ven and earth will hearken to his anointed.'[17]	CD II, 12: prophets are 'anointed'. 11QMelch: the messenger of joy from Isa. 52.7 is identified with the anointed of Isa. 61.1f. He announces the rule of Melchizedek, a heavenly figure.

[16]Further messianic texts in the Qumran writings are 4Q 161 (a *pesher* on Isaiah) III, 12–25 (Branch of David); 1QSb V, 20–29 (the Prince of the Congregation); 4Q 285 frag.5 (the Prince of the Congregation); 4Q 541 frag 9; 4Q 246 I/II (son of God II, 1); CD VII, 18–21 (Interpreter of the Law and Prince of the Congregation); 4Q 174 III, 10–13 (Branch of David); 4QTest (a royal, priestly and prophetic form side by side). F.G. Martinez, *Messianische Erwartungen in den Qumranschriften* and Evans, *Jesus**, 83–154, give a survey of these Qumran texts.

[17]Another possible translation is '. . . to his anointed', but in that case the reference would be to the prophets (cf. Stegemann, *Essener**, 50).

LXX		I Kingdoms 2.10: Hannah prays: 'He will exalt the horn of his anointed.'	
PSSol. 17/18		The Messiah is the son of David, who drives the sinful Gentiles from the land, and on the other hand sets off the pilgrimage of the peoples to Zion.	
Similitudes of Ethiopic Enoch		In 48.10 and 52.4 the Son of Man is (perhaps?) identified with the Messiah (see above, pp. 513f. and 530).	

3.2.2 *Eschatological expectation of messianic figures without the term 'Messiah'*

In the New Testament period messianic figures did not necessarily bear the title 'Messiah' – regardless of whether we encounter them in utopian literary schemes or as historical figures who claim or suggest the fulfilment of messianic expectations. The following table brings together the most important instances – and at the same time also takes post-New Testament sources into account:

Messianic figures	with the title of Messiah	without the title of Messiah
as expectation	Qumran writings (see above) Ps Sol. 17/18 (see above) EthEnoch 48.10; 52.4 (see above) IV Ezra 7.28 SyrApocBar 29.3; 30.1, etc.	Dan. 7.14: Son of Man; Ethiopic Enoch 90.9ff., 37f. Sib. 3.49f., 286f., 652f. Philo, *Praem.* 95 Test Lev 18; Test Jud 24
as historical figures	Jesus the so-called Christ (Josephus, *Antt.* 20, 200) Bar Kochba, the Messiah in the Third Jewish War (132–135 CE)	Simon and Athronges in the 'Robber War' (4/3 BCE) Menahem and Simon ben Giora in the First Jewish War (66–70 CE)

3.2.3   *The usurping of messianic expectations by political rulers*

Not only rebels and charismatics from the people but also the political rulers of Palestine claimed that they were the fulfilment of messianic hopes. Only at first sight may it be surprising that here a pagan ruler also appears in the role of the 'messianic ruler'. But Deutero-Isaiah already saw Cyrus as 'Yahweh's anointed' (Isa. 45.1): Sib. 3, 652ff. similarly thinks of a pagan king 'from the East'! In transferring messianic expectations to Vespasian (*BJ* 3, 400ff.), Josephus by no means breaks with the traditions of his people:

- The Maccabean ruler Simon (143/2–135/4) is depicted with messianic colours in I Macc. 14.4–15: 'He restored peace to the land, and there were great rejoicings throughout Israel. Each man sat under his own vine and fig-tree, and they had no one to fear. Those were days when every enemy vanished from the land and every hostile power was crushed. Simon gave his protection to the poor among the people; he paid close attention to the law and rid the country of lawless and wicked men. He gave new splendour to the temple and furnished it with a wealth of sacred vessels' (14.11–14).
- His son John Hyrcanus (134–104) wanted to be not only prince and high priest but also prophet, although the rule of the Hasmonaeans was limited 'until a prophet should appear' (I Macc. 14.41). He wanted to do away with the eschatological 'proviso' and thus claimed to be fulfilling an eschatological hope.

- Herod I (36–4 CE) probably began the renewal of the temple in order to legitimate himself as a 'new Solomon' – as a legitimate successor to David. The reason he gave for restoring the temple to the extent it had under Solomon was that only alien rule had prevented the Jews under Zerubbabel from restoring it fully. Thus he was suggesting that under his rule the old freedom was restored (cf. *Antt.* 15, 380ff.). He had the reputation of 'being the darling of heaven' (*BJ* I, 331).

When the first Christians claimed that Jesus was the Messiah, that he alone was the messianic figure who was bringing redemption and deliverance, they rivalled political ideologies with their claim. They reclaimed for a victim of the rulers a fulfilment which the rulers claimed for themselves.

3.2.4 *Eschatological expectations without a messianic figure*

We saw that the messianic expectations of the time were very different. Alongside a messianic dyarchy we find the expectation of only one Messiah; alongside redeemer figures with the title 'Messiah' we find figures without such a title; alongside future expectations we find the emphatic claim that these expectations were being fulfilled in the present. Moreover many circles in Judaism shared an eschatological expectation. But they were focussed wholly on God. Such theocratic expectations without a messianic figure are attested for the book of Jubilees (cf. 23), for the book of Baruch (cf. 2.34f.; 4.36f.; 5.5ff.), the book of Tobit (13.11ff.; 14.4ff.) and above all for the Assumption of Moses. Here a sharp criticism of the Herodian princes is combined with the hope that the kingdom of God will soon break through (AssMos 10.1ff.).

Our conclusion must be that there was no such thing as Judaism and its messianic expectation in the singular; there were many Judaisms with different eschatological and messianic expectations.[18] Therefore if primitive Christianity deviated from some Jewish messianic traditions, it did not forsake 'Judaism'. It moved within the spectrum of messianic notions. If there is no typical Jewish messianic expectation, there cannot be any correction of Jewish messianism either.

3.3 Jesus and the messianic expectations of his time

The inner variety within Judaism shows that not all its hopes pointed in the direction of the Messiah. However, messianic hopes were alive among the people – probably more alive than appears from the sources. The Greek word *Messias* (cf. John 1.41) is a transcription of the Aramaic *meshīḥā* (מְשִׁיחָא), not the Hebrew word *māshīaḥ* (מָשִׁיחַ); i.e. it comes from the popular vernacular and not from the

---

[18]Cf. the title of the book edited by J. Neusner, *Judaisms and Their Messiahs*, 1987, where both terms appear in the plural.

sacral language of scholars and the educated. The people always had fewer opportunities to express their expectations in texts than did the upper class, in whose interest it was to give to keep messianic unrest under control. When two royal pretenders popular with the people appear with a messianic aura in the Robber War (4/3 BCE) and throw the whole country into uproar, these events show better than many literary texts that messianic expectations were alive among the people.[19] It is historically probable that Jesus was confronted with them.

3.3.1 Texts on the attitude of the historical Jesus to the title Messiah

The primitive Christian tradition in its various forms offers a very variegated picture:

- The title Messiah is sparse in the *sayings tradition*. In all probability it is absent from Q, and it certainly is from the Gospel of Thomas, although it occurs often in Gnostic writings and writings close to Gnosticism. It almost never occurs on the lips of Jesus. Mark 9.41; Matt. 16.20; Luke 4.41; Matt. 23.10; Luke 24.26 are exceptions here.
- The *narrative tradition* knows that the title 'Christ' or the expectations associated with it were attached to Jesus, indeed by his followers (Mark 8.29, Christ; Mark 10.46ff., son of David; Mark 11.10, the rule of our father David), his opponents (Mark 14.51, the Christ, the Son of the Most High), and finally by the Romans: he is executed as 'king of the Jews' (Mark 15.26), which in content is identical to 'Christ, king of Israel' (cf. Mark 15.32).
- The *formula tradition* in the letters of Paul clearly associates the title Christ with Jesus' death – but now with a soteriological interpretation: Christ has died for us or for our sins (cf. Rom. 5.6, 8; I Cor. 15.3ff., etc.).

On the basis of this evidence, in our view the following hypothesis can be advanced: Jesus had a messianic consciousness, but did not use the title Messiah. He aroused messianic expectations among the people and among his followers, and because of that was executed as a royal pretender. After Easter his disciples attributed a new messianic dignity to him as the suffering Messiah whose death had saving significance.

3.3.2 Jesus' confrontation with messianic expectations during his lifetime

That historically Jesus confronted messianic expectations is suggested by the fact

---

[19]Cf. *Jesus**, 53–81, with a good survey of all 'messianic claimants'. Cf. also above, §5.3.1, p. 122.

that very different circles express similar expectations or fears: on the one hand followers (Mark 8.29; 10.46f.; 11.10) and on the other opponents (Mark 14.61; 15.26). A certain distinction can be made between a confrontation with messianic expectations in Galilee and one in Judaea.

Peter's confession (Mark 8.27–30), which does not take place in public, is located in *Galilee*. The saying about Satan (8.33) could originally have followed this confession. The Johannine parallel also combines Peter's confession with a saying about Satan (which has now been reminted and applied to Jesus, cf. John 6.67–71). What stands in Mark between Peter's confession and the saying about Satan can be understood as a secondary expansion: the command to keep silent which is usually understood as Markan redaction (8.30) and the first prophecy of the passion (8.31f.). Jesus could originally have replied to the confession that he was Messiah, 'Get behind me Satan! For your thoughts are not divine but human.' The saying about Satan is not a rejection of the title Messiah, but criticism of the disposition which is connected with it. The tradition can be understood to mean that if a disposition in keeping with God is associated with the title Messiah the title is acceptable, otherwise not. Mark has made it clear what kind of understanding of the title Messiah is in keeping with God: the affirmation of suffering for the Messiah.

In *Judaea* the messianic theme is discussed publicly: Bartimaeus greets Jesus as 'son of David' in Jericho, and the festival pilgrims in Jerusalem expect the 'rule of David'. Jesus was accused and executed on charges relating to his kingship. Was the (Davidic) messianic expectation more lively in the south of Palestine? Already in the Robber War, royal pretenders with a messianic aura appear only here (Simon: Josephus, *Antt.* 17, 224; Tacitus, *Hist.* 5, 9; and Athronges: Josephus, *Antt.* 17, 279f.). Judas son of Hezekiah did not express any comparable pretensions in Galilee at that time (*BJ* 2, 56). Most evidence about the Messiah for the pre-Christian period comes from Qumran – i.e. more from the south. But the decisive thing is that the royal Messiah was expected to take up rule in his city of Jerusalem. That explains why this expectation is clearly intensified with Jesus' arrival in Jerusalem.

In our view, the saying about the Twelve who will rule over Israel shows that Jesus took up messianic expectations but did not endorse them by using a messianic title. According to PsSol. 17.26 it is the task of the Messiah to gather the people (from the dispersion) and to judge his (twelve) tribes. In the logion about the Twelve this particular task is transferred to the disciples. The material common to Matt. 19.28 and Luke 22.28–30 says that one day they will sit on thrones and judge the twelve tribes of Israel. They form a messianic collective. Jesus is so terse about the 'messianic' title, not because he rejected it but because he was more than a Messiah: he gave the status and dignity of a Messiah to others. He reshaped the messianic expectation which was focussed on an individual into a 'group messianism', to use Theissen's term.[20] Ordinary people, fishermen and farmers, were to rule as representatives of the twelve tribes – exercising a representative popular rule.

This transformation of the notion of Messiah points to an inner conflict within Jesus over the messianic expectation which had revived in Palestine only after it had become part of the Roman empire – even if it aroused only parts of the population. Jesus must have been confronted with a messianic expectation above all in the trial before Pilate. For the *titulus* on the cross shows that he died as a Jewish royal pretender. Probably this messianic expectation also played a part in the deliberations of the Sanhedrin in which the charge against Jesus was prepared. If Jesus was executed as a royal pretender, one thing is certain: he did not distance himself from the messianic expectations of his followers (and the corresponding fears of his opponents) before his accusers and judges. However, he need not have identified with them. According to Mark 15.2–5 Jesus was silent on this point. That is possibly in keeping with the historical situation. Jesus probably kept silent not only before Pilate but also at other times, and this was then 'condensed' in the scene before Pilate. According to John 10.24, too, he kept those around him in the dark as to whether he was the Messiah. Today we know how open the concept of Messiah was at that time. Would not any position on it inevitably have provoked misunderstanding?

3.3.3 *The new interpretation of Jesus' messiahship after the cross and Easter*

It is historically improbable that the title Messiah was transferred to Jesus only after Easter: the cross and resurrection had now become the most important events, which put everything else in a new light. The title Messiah would have been unsuitable for interpreting a life which focussed on the cross and resurrection. There is no evidence prior to the New Testament for the notion of a suffering Messiah; moreover, there is no evidence of anyone becoming the Messiah through resurrection. Therefore the title Messiah must already have been associated with Jesus if it was to live on after Easter: it could not have interpreted the cross and resurrection, but the cross and resurrection could have given it a deeper meaning.

Sometimes it is nevertheless conjectured that there is a pre-Christian notion of the suffering Messiah. The evidence known so far is not sufficient to substantiate this.

- Isaiah 53 is indeed interpreted in terms of the Messiah in the Targum of the

---

[20]There is a plea for accepting that Jesus understood himself as Messiah in *Jesus**, 437–56; Jesus is regarded as a prophet in Galilee (e.g. Mark 6.4), and is executed in Jerusalem as 'king of the Jews' (Mark 15.26). Only the combination of the Davidic king and prophet as it is attested in Josephus, *Antt.* 6, 156f.; 11QPs^a 27, 11 (= 11Q05 XXVII, 11) and the targumim on II Sam. 23.1–4,8; I Kings 5.13; 6.11 etc., would explain both aspects of Jesus' activtity.

Prophets, but the statements about suffering which it contains are reinterpreted as statements about exaltation; the sayings about suffering are interpreted in terms of the peoples; and the vicarious suffering is interpreted away (cf. *BJ* I, 281f.).

- Test Benj 3.8 is a general statement about the soteriological significance of dying for others. Thus in view of Joseph's fate Jacob is made to say: 'The innocent will be stained for the lawless, and the sinless will die for the godless.'
- 4Q 541 frag.9, I, 2 speaks of cultic atonement, not of atonement by a death, in the context of burnt offerings. It is then said: 'and he does atonement for all the sons of his generation'.
- 4Q 285 frag.5.4 – according to R. Eisenman the central evidence for the idea of a crucified Messiah – probably does not speak of the death of the Messiah but says that the Messiah, the Prince of the Congregation and the 'Branch of David', has the Wicked Priest killed: 'and the Prince of the congregation', the Br[anch of David], has him killed.'[21]

Of course one day evidence for a pre-Christian conception of the suffering Messiah could emerge. But even then it remains improbable whether the disciples lived in the expectation of such a suffering Messiah: the disciples on the Emmaus road had not been prepared for the death of Jesus. The risen Christ had to show them by means of the scriptures that the Messiah had to suffer in order to enter his glory (Luke 24.25ff.). The reference to scripture is illuminating: the new conception of the Messiah, deepened by suffering, is grounded in Jewish traditions – not against them. It re-actualizes a possibility which was latently present in Jewish convictions.

4. Jesus as Son of Man: an explicit christology in the historical Jesus?

J.J. Collins, 'The Son of Man in First-Century Judaism', *NTS* 38, 1992, 448–66; C. Colpe, ὁ υἱὸς τοῦ ἀνθρώπου, *TDNT* (see above); J.R. Donahue, 'Recent Studies on the Origin of "Son of Man" in the Gospels', *CBQ* 48, 1986, 48–98; A.J.B. Higgins, *The Son of Man in the Teaching of Jesus*, SNTS MS 39, Cambridge 1980; R. Leivestad, 'Exit the Apocalyptic Son of Man', *NTS* 18, 1971/2, 243–63; B. Lindars, *Jesus Son of Man* (see above); H. Merklein, *Jesu Botschaft von der Gottesherrschaft*, SBS 111, Stuttgart 1983, 152–64; G.W.E. Nickelsburg, 'Son of Man', *ABD* 6, 1992, 137–50; R. Otto, *The Kingdom of God and the Son of Man*, London 1943; N. Perrin, *A Modern Pilgrimage* (see above); id., *Rediscovering the Teaching of Jesus*, London 1967; T.B. Slater, 'One Like A Son of Man in First-Century CE Judaism', *NTS* 41, 1995, 183–98; P. Stuhlmacher, *Biblische Theologie des Neuen Testaments* I, Göttingen 1992, 107–25; H.E. Tödt, *The Son of Man in the Synoptic Tradition*, London 1965; G. Vermes, 'The Use of בר נש/נשא in Jewish Aramaic', in M.

---

[21]Cf. R. Eisenman and M. Wise, *The Dead Sea Scrolls Uncovered*, Harmondsworth 1992, 24–9.

Black, *An Aramaic Approach to the Gospels and Acts*, Oxford 1967, Appendix E, 310–28; id., *Jesus the Jew*, 161–91.

The term which Jesus is most likely to have used of himself is at the same time the most enigmatic:[22] on the one hand 'son of man' is an everyday expression which means 'the or a man'; on the other hand 'son of man' is a figure entrusted by God with judging the world, who appears in visions 'like a son of man'. The first possibility seems to have too little theological significance to do justice to Jesus' sense of authority; the second to claim far too much to be historically realistic. Did Jesus really believe that he was the future judge of the world, where he did not in any way appear in this role? Unfortunately the two linguistic and literary traditions which could give us a clear understanding provide no clear information about how the term is to be understood.

4.1 The two linguistic traditions behind the Son of Man sayings: everyday language or visionary language

4.1.1 *The everyday expression 'son of man'*

'Son of man' (ὁ υἱὸς τοῦ ἀνθρώπου) is a translation of the Aramaic בַּר־נָשָׁא *[bar-nāshā]*,[23] the Hebrew equivalent of which is בֶּן־אָדָם (*ben-'ādām*), and means 1. human beings generally (in the 'generic' sense); 2. some human being (in the indefinite sense); 3. (rarely) 'I' as a periphrasis. This third usage is disputed for two reasons.

- There is a dispute as to whether it is really a periphrasis for 'I' or a generic and indefinite usage which is deliberately left ambiguous in order also to include the speaker. Here is one of the examples discussed:

  'Rabbi Simeon ben Yohai said: "If I had stood on Mount Sinai when the Torah was given to Israel, I would have asked the Merciful One to create two mouths for *bar nasha*, one for the study of the Torah and one for the provision of all his needs"' (jBer 3b).[24]

---

[22]G. Haufe, 'Das Menschensohnproblem in der gegenwärtigen wissenschaftlichen Diskussion, *EvTh* 26, 1966, 130–41; Donahue, 'Studies', and M. Müller, *Der Ausdruck 'Menschensohn' in den Evangelien*, AThD 17, Leiden 1984, give surveys of the discussion on the title Son of Man.

[23]The undetermined form בַּר־נָשׁ(*bar-nāsh*) was used with the same meaning in place of the determined form בַּר־נָשָׁא (*bar-nāshā*). Moreover the linguistically more original forms with the initial *aleph* were in use: בַּר־אֱנָשָׁא (*bar-'enāshā*) and בַּר־אֱנָשׁ (*bar-'enōsh*); presumably not, however, in Galilee, as the dropping of initial gutturals was a characteristic of the Galilean-Aramaic dialect (cf. C. Colpe, ὁ υἱὸς τοῦ ἀνθρώπου, 400–77; Vermes, *Jesus* *, 188ff).

[24]Quoted from Vermes, *Jesus* *, 166; cf. Colpe, υἱὸς, 403 n.20.

Here the speaker is making a general statement about human beings, but includes himself in it: it is his personal wish to be able to devote himself wholly to the Torah. It is therefore usually assumed that there is no purely periphrastic use of *bar nasha*, but that it is always associated with a generic sense.

- There is also a dispute over the age of the evidence. The Targums come from the period after the New Testament. In one version of them, for example, Cain's words in Gen. 4.14 are rendered 'I cannot hide myself' (Targ Neofiti on Gen. 4.14), and in another '*Bar nash* cannot hide himself from you, O Lord' (Cairo Targum fragment on Gen. 4.14). That recalls the terminology in the Synoptics: there many Son of Man sayings have parallels in which an 'I' takes the place of 'Son of Man' (J. Jeremias).

4.1.2 *The term 'like a son of man' in visionary language*

In Jewish apocalypses a heavenly figure appears who is compared with a 'son of man'. 'Son of man' here is not a title which is already honorific in itself, but a comparison, which indicates the exalted figure of a judge. The basic text is Dan. 7; the two other texts relate to it.

1. *The basic text for the expression in visionary language* (Dan. 7). Daniel 7 (which was written between 167 and 164 BCE) deals in a vision with the overcoming of the world powers by God: a lion, a bear, a panther and a monster which surpasses all of them symbolize the ungodly world powers of the Medes, Persian, Babylonians and Syrians. They are annihilated by God. After that rule is transferred to a being who looks 'like a son of man':

> 'and behold, with the clouds of heaven there came one like a son of man ['someone in human form'], and he came to the Ancient of Days and was presented before him. And to him was given dominion and glory and kingdom, that all peoples, nations and languages should serve him; his dominion is an everlasting dominion, which shall not pass away, and his kingdom one that shall not be destroyed' (Dan. 7.13f.)

An interpretation following the vision interprets the event first as the transference of power to the 'Holy of Holies', which probably means angels (7.18), and secondly to the people of Israel (7.27). In our view the figure like a human being is more than a symbolic cipher for the people of Israel.

- Because the beasts in Dan. 7 are symbols for world powers, their counterpart, the 'one like a man', has also been seen as a symbol for a collective, the people of Israel. But just as the beasts appear only 'like' a lion, bear and panther, because behind them are not lions, bears and panthers but real human beings, so at all events behind the one who appears 'as' a human being stands a figure who is not a human being – probably an angel (cf. Dan. 8.15; 10.16, 18; ApocAbr 10.5).[25]

---

[25]Cf. Slater, 'One Like a Son of Man'.

- This angel represents (in a way comparable to the notion of angels of the peoples) the people of Israel in heaven. There is a social mythical parallelism between heaven and earth. Soon a take-over of power will come about on earth parallel to the transfer of power in heaven: Israel will come to rule over the world. The 'one like a man' in heaven is the representative of a group persecuted on earth which is helped to gain its rights.

There is no dispute that the 'one like a man' in Dan.7 also expresses a symbolic sense: the kingdoms of the world so far have had a bestial character; the new world rule will be humane.

2. *Two developments based on Dan. 7* (EthEnoch 37–71 and IV Ezra 13): referring back to Dan. 7, two further apocalyptic texts speak of the figure of a judge as 'man' or 'son of man'. IV Ezra can be dated to the end of the first century CE, but the dating of the Similitudes of Ethiopic Enoch (37–71) is disputed. Since all the parts of Ethiopic Enoch apart from the Similitudes are attested in Qumran, we could even suppose that they were composed after the New Testament. They are certainly a Jewish work; there are no specifically Christian features. The destruction of the temple is not mentioned. Therefore many scholars think that they were composed before 70 CE. Moreover Ethiopic Enoch 37ff. and IV Ezra 13 correspond in many features – usually against Dan. 7, which indicates a common tradition. It follows from this that at least this tradition goes back to New Testament times.

	Similitudes of Ethiopic Enoch 37–71 (see above, p. 514)	IV Ezra 13 (see below, p. 565)
The reference to Dan. 7.13: introduction by comparison	The Son of Man is introduced on the basis of Dan. 7.13 as one 'whose figure had the appearance of a man' (46.1). Further passages refer back to this, e.g. 'this Son of Man whom you have seen' (46.4; cf. 62.5, 7 etc.). This is an individual figure.	The 'Man' is introduced on the basis of Dan. 7.13 as 'as it were in the form of a man' (13.3). The further instances of 'this Man' (13.3) and 'that Man' (13.12) refer back to this. This is an individual figure.
The identification with the Messiah	Twice the Son of Man is identified with the 'Messiah' (48.10; 52.4), but this is not certain (see above, p. 530).	God twice calls the 'Man' 'my son;' (13.37, 52) and thus identifies him (probably) with 'my son, the Messiah' (7.28).

The pre-existence of the Son of Man	The Son of Man already exists in primal times: Enoch can see him in heaven. His name was named before God prior to the creation (48.3).	The 'Man' was 'kept a long time' by God (13.26): he exists long before his eschatological appearance.
His active role in the judgment	Whereas in Dan. 7 the Son of Man accedes to rule only after the annihilation of the world powers, in 46.4ff. the Son of Man is involved in the judgment of kings and sinners. Here he appears as judge (cf. 62.1ff.)	The 'Man' appears as a warrior of the end-time who annihilates the Gentiles. His militant features are accentuated by comparison with EthEnoch 37ff. The eschatological judgment has become an eschatological war, but this is not an irreconcilable opposition.

We can also conclude from the fact that the last three features common to EthEnoch 37–71 and IV Ezra 13 agree against Dan. 7 that the notion of an apocalyptic judge was less read out of Dan. 7 than read into it and elucidated with the help of this basic text (Collins, *Son of Man*).[26] There are no reasons for disputing the existence of such an apocalyptic mediator figure (*pace* N. Perrin). But it is right to say that this mediator figure is compared with a 'son of man' and not given the firm title 'Son of Man'? The question now is: are Jesus' sayings about the Son of Man to be understood more in terms of the everyday language tradition or the visionary language tradition?

4.2 The Son of Man sayings in the Jesus tradition: the evidence[27]

All Jesus' sayings about the Son of Man are characterized by three striking characteristics:

1. They appear only on the lips of Jesus – with few exceptions: on the one hand

---

[26] 4Q246 is another possible text for the continuation of Dan. 7 in messianic hopes (see below, p. 566).

[27] In Dan 7.13 (LXX), υἱὸς ἀνθρώπου stands without an article. In the Gospels this form appears only in John 5.27 (because of the reference to Dan. 7.13?). Elsewhere there is the doubly determined 'the son of the man' (ὁ υἱὸς τοῦ ἀνθρώπου).

in two visions of the Son of Man in heaven (Acts 7.56; Rev. 1.13; 14.14; Eusebius, *HE* 2, 23, 13) and on the other in John 12.34, before which a saying of Jesus is cited. Jesus always speaks of the Son of Man as if he were another figure. Yet thirty-seven of the fifty-one Son of Man sayings in the Gospels have competing parallels with 'I' (Jeremias).

2. They are limited to the Gospels, where they appear in all strata, in the Synoptics and in John, and once even in the Gospel of Thomas (86 = Matt. 8.20), where the term can be understood generically: the saying is about human beings as distinct from beasts. The term is absent from the epistolary literature with the exception of Barn. 12.10, where it is the counterpart to 'Son of God'.

3. The term 'Son of Man' is not explained and does not provoke any dispute. Only in John 12.34 do Jesus' audience ask, 'Who is this Son of Man?' No primitive Christian confession uses the term Son of Man; yet it has a *Sitz im Leben* in the *status confessionis*, cf. Mark 8.38; Acts 7.56; John 9.35ff.; Eusebius, *HE* 2, 23, 13: the confession of the Son of Man means conflict with the outside world.

In addition, three groups of Son of Man sayings can be distinguished, each of which displays specific features in addition to these general characteristics: these are sayings about the Son of Man active in the present, about the future Son of Man, and about the suffering Son of Man.

4.2.1 *The sayings about the Son of Man active in the present*

These have rather different tendencies in the two earliest sources (Mark and Q):

- *Sayings about the authority of the Son of Man appear in Mark.* This emphasizes his authority to forgive sins and to break the sabbath (2.28). The Son of Man who is at work on earth is subject to the universal norms and restrictions.
- *The Logia source contains sayings about the outsider role of the Son of Man.* Unlike the animals, the Son of Man has no home (Matt. 8.20 par.), is criticized as a glutton and a winebibber (Matt. 11.18), and is reviled (Matt. 12.32).

It is natural to understand the sayings about the Son of Man active in the present in terms of the everyday-language tradition: in Mark 2.27f., 'man' and 'son of man' are in parallel. Both have authority over the sabbath. Matthew 8.21 emphasizes the difference between human beings and animals; here too the sense is generic. The fate of the homeless man is evident in Jesus' fate. Matthew 11.18 could have an indefinite meaning: John the Baptist came and was rejected as an ascetic; then came (some) man (like Jesus) and was criticized as a glutton and a winebibber. The thought in the background is that the stronger one announced by the Baptist did not come, but a man like Jesus. The saying about the authority of the Son of Man (Mark 2.10) is understood in a generic sense in Matthew: the crowd praises God for giving such authority to 'man' (Matt. 9.8).

4.2.2   *The sayings about the future Son of Man*

Whereas the everyday-language tradition explains some sayings about the Son of Man active in the present, some sayings about the future Son of Man can be understood only against the background of the visionary-language tradition. The most important statements are:

- *Eschatological correlatives*: they put the Son of Man in a typological relation-ship to figures of the past. The Son of Man is compared directly with Jonah (Luke 11.30). His 'days' are correlated with the days of past catastrophes in the time of Noah (Luke 17.26) and Lot (17.28). A visionary element is retained in the comparison of the Son of Man with a flash of lightning which illuminates the whole heaven (Luke 17.24).
- *An eschatological legal maxim*: Mark 8.28 emphatically contrasts Jesus in the first person with the future Son of Man: 'Whoever is ashamed of me and my words . . . of him will the Son of Man be ashamed . . .' There are allusions to Dan. 7.13: the Son of Man comes in the glory of his Father with his holy angels! Luke 12.8 similarly attests the striking differentiation of 'I' and Son of Man: by contrast, Matt. 10.32 has an 'I' in both halves of the logion, probably a secondary assimilation.
- *Sayings about the future 'seeing' of the Son of Man*: Jesus announces to his judges that they will see the Son of Man seated at the right hand of God and coming with the clouds of heaven (Mark 14.62). Here there is a direct reference to Dan. 7.13, except that a figure who is compared with a 'son of man' has become 'the Son of Man'. The future 'seeing' of the Son of Man is depicted with more strongly apocalyptic colours in the Synoptic apocalypse (Mark 13.26) – here too as an actualization of Dan. 7.13f. A comparison with the Jewish apocalyptic visionary texts shows important differences:

Apocalyptic texts	Sayings of Jesus
The Son of Man is *always* spoken of in a comparison: 'one like a son of man', etc. The reference is always to an angelic figure who is not a human being but can only be compared with one.	The NT always speaks of '*the* Son of Man'. There is a comparison only in Rev. 1.13 ('one who is like a son of man'/ὅμοιον υἱὸν ἀνθρώπου). The articles which otherwise always occur are absent here.

The one in human form is always seen in visions. All Son of Man sayings are combined with the form of the account of a vision.	In primitive Christianity there are only isolated visions of the Son of Man, in the cases of Stephen (Acts 7.56), James (Eusebius, *HE* 2, 23, 13) and the seer John (Rev. 1.13; 14.14). The bulk of the sayings occur in 'everyday' sayings. However, there are visionary elements: references to a future (real) seeing (Mark 14.62; 13.26).
The Son of Man accedes to his rule *after the annihilation of the enemies of God* (Dan. 7) or is actively involved in their destruction (EthEnoch 37ff.; IV Ezra 13).	The Son of Man has more a task of saving than of destroying: he appears in Mark 13 only to bring together the elect.

Common to the apocalyptic and primitive Christian texts is their socio-mythical parallelism: the fate of the Son of Man stands in parallel to the fate of his followers: the authority and outsider role of the Son of Man, his suffering and his exaltation, correspond to the experiences and hopes of the followers of Jesus.

4.2.3 *The sayings about the suffering Son of Man*

The sayings about the suffering Son of Man appear in different variants. On the one hand they speak of the Son of Man being 'delivered up' (παραδιδόναι, cf. Mark 9.31; 14.41; Luke 24.7) and on the other of his 'suffering' (παθεῖν, Mark 8.31; 9.21; Luke 17.25). John offers a remarkable variant on these sayings about the suffering Son of Man when Jesus speaks there of the 'exaltation' and 'glorification' of the Son of Man and means by it his crucifixion (as the way to the Father, John 3.14; 12.23, etc.). The term 'Son of Man' is appropriate for the prophecies of suffering in so far as the term 'Son of Man' in any case suggests mortality (cf. Isa. 51.12; Ps. 146.3f.; Job 25.6; 1QS XI, 20; 1QH IV, 30). However, the use of it in prophecies of the quite particular fate of Jesus is unmistakably a further development.

4.3 The historical Jesus and the term Son of Man

It is certain that Jesus used the expression 'son of man'. It derives from Aramaic and is attested in all the complexes of the Jesus tradition (Mark; Q; Matt.[s] cf. 10.23; 25.31ff.; Luke[s] cf. e.g. 18.8; John; Gospel of Thomas 86). Already in primitive Christianity it was regarded as a characteristic feature of Jesus' language and appears only in sayings of Jesus. However, for that reason it has also been introduced into sayings which were not originally Son of Man sayings (cf. e.g. Luke 6.22 with Matt. 5.11; Luke 22.28ff. with Matt. 19.28). The criterion of plausibility on the basis of multiple attestation clearly supports the authenticity of the term 'Son of Man'. There is a dispute as to which group of Son of Man sayings is to be attributed to Jesus and also what and whom Jesus meant by the expression. To begin with, here are two solutions which either assert or dispute the authenticity of Son of Man sayings from all three groups.

1. *The authenticity of sayings from all three groups* – the present, suffering and future Son of Man – has been argued for by e.g. C. Colpe[28] – albeit with the qualification that the title Son of Man has found its way into authentic prophecies of suffering only at a secondary stage. Colpe cites the history-of-religions criterion of 'underivability' for his thesis: the Synoptic notion of the Son of Man cannot be derived from Dan. 7.13; references to Dan. 7 have rather all been introduced by the primitive community; the notion of the Son of Man in the Similitudes remained limited to an esoteric circle; that of IV Ezra belongs to a political idea of the Messiah. It follows 'that we find here a fourth tradition, which is independent of Daniel, IV Ezra and Enoch, becomes visible, and which thus indicates the variability of Son of Man expectation in Judaism' (υἱός, 438). In terms of content it has striking features: Jesus speaks of himself as the present Son of Man, thus contrasting himself with God (Mark 2.20), with another man (Matt. 11.18f.), or animals (Matt. 8.20). At the same time he speaks of a future apocalyptic Son of Man as a 'symbol' of his 'certainty of fulfilment' (ibid., 443). He emphasizes the suddenness and public nature of the appearance of the Son of Man (Matt. 24.27, 30, 37; Luke 17.30), who secures justice for the oppressed (Luke 18.8), will judge his judges (Luke 22.69), and will come before the disciples have reached all Israel with their message (Matt. 10.23). Therefore constant watchfulness is called for (Luke 21.36). Colpe regards only the eleven Son of Man sayings just mentioned as authentic.

2. By contrast, P. Vielhauer argues *that none of the sayings about the Son of Man is authentic.*[29] Jesus put forward a purely theocentric eschatology. He thought that the kingdom of God was so near that there was no room for an intermediary figure between himself and God's coming. Nowhere are sayings about the kingdom of God and the Son of Man organically related to one another

---

[28]Colpe, υἱός. Further schemes which reckon that all three groups of Son of Man sayings are authentic are P. Stuhlmacher, *Biblische Theologie* 1, 1992, 107–25; V. Hampel, *Menschensohn und historischer Jesus* (1990).

[29]P. Vielhauer, 'Gottesreich und Menschensohn in der Verkündigung Jesu' (1957) and 'Jesus und der Menschensohn', in *Aufsätze zum Neuen Testament*, Munich 1965, 55–91 and 92–140.

in a logion. To this it has been objected that 'Son of Man' and 'kingdom of God' are already associated in Dan. 7.13f. There is no incompatibility in principle.

3. *Differentiations between different groups of Son of Man sayings.* Usually the three groups of Son of Man sayings are differentiated. Here there are three possibilities, if one leaves aside the sayings about the suffering Son of Man as prophecies after the event. Either sayings about the present Son of Man are authentic, or those about the future Son of Man, or both (see the table on the facing page).

Despite a vast amount of work, scholars are not yet in a position to make a well-founded decision between the possibilities sketched out above. So we have to content ourselves with a few comments which do not give a solution but could point the way towards a solution.

1. The Easter experience is hard to understand as the origin of the Son of Man christology if we accept that 'Son of Man' was not a fixed title for a lofty heavenly figure but meant 'human being' – and the comparison in Dan. 7 (like a son of man'), as distinct from this, is specifically meant to bring out the supernatural character of the heavenly figure. Now Dan. 7.13 is never echoed in the sayings of Jesus in a form which speaks of a figure who is 'like a son of man', i.e. merely has a human likeness. Rather Jesus speaks of 'the Son of Man', i.e. of a man. But such a term was far from indicating exaltation, since it emphatically stresses the 'human'. Titles like 'Son of God' and Lord were more appropriate (cf. Rom. 1.3f.; Phil. 2.12) because they expressed better the nearness of the exalted one to God. So the term Son of Man must have been previously associated with Jesus if it was to describe the Easter experience as the appearance of the 'man' and reinterpret the 'one like a son of man' in Dan. 7.13 as a 'man'.

2. The association of the term 'son of man' with Jesus cannot be derived from everyday language alone. Why should an expression which in principle anyone could use and which could mean anyone be so clearly associated with Jesus that it was retained even after Easter, when for Christians Jesus had already long since been more than a man? Jesus must have used the everyday expression emphatically so that it could become his 'title' – say by using it to correct excessive expectations: other people might expect miracles of him, other people might hope that he was the stronger one expected since John the Baptist, others might throng after him – but as a correction of such expectations he emphasized his human status as 'son of man' (Mark 2.10; Matt. 11.18f.; Matt. 8.20). So among other things the expression became a christological title because Jesus opposed it to christological expectations and thus made it a mysterious honorific title first for his followers. In the Gospel texts after they have been subjected to redaction, this corrective function of the term 'Son of Man' can still be detected: Peter confesses Jesus as the Messiah, but Jesus answers by prophesying the suffering of the Son of Man (Mark 8.29ff.). Jesus is asked about his messiahship before the Sanhedrin, but replies with a saying about the Son of Man (14.61f.).

	A. Sayings about the present Son of Man	B. Sayings about the future Son of Man
The expression 'son of man' in everyday language is authentic; the sayings about the future son of man are secondary: A → B	Sayings about the earthly Son of Man are original: (a) as a periphrasis for 'I' (G. Vermes); (b) in the general sense as a statement about human beings; (c) as a combination of a periphrasis for 'I' and emphasis on the universal role, 'I as a human being' (B.Lindars).	The sayings about the future Son of Man are post-Easter interpretations on the basis of the Easter faith: (a) as scriptural exegesis of Dan. 7.13f. (in combination with Ps. 110.1, etc., N. Perrin) (b) as the transference of a general idea of the apocalyptic Son of Man to Jesus.
The sayings about the apocalyptic Son of Man are authentic; the sayings about the present Son of Man are secondary A ← B	Only after Easter were saying about the present Son of Man were created: (a) By misunderstanding and reinterpreting universal statements about being human; only now were they understood 'messianically'; (b) by the transference of the future title 'Son of Man' into sayings about the present Son of Man which sometimes were new creations.	Jesus expected an apocalyptic judge different from himself (Mark 8.38) – taking up the Baptist's expectation of a 'stronger one'. This future, heavenly Son of Man can be imagined: (a) as an exclusive exalted figure who is contrasted with human beings or (b) as an 'inclusive' heavenly figure who represents and symbolizes the new people of God. Only after Easter was Jesus identified with this figure – demonstrably first in Q (H.E. Tödt).
Jesus combines the everyday- and the visionary-language tradition in his sayings about the Son of Man: both groups contain authentic sayings: A + B	Jesus spoke of both the present and the future Son of Man. The relationship between the two sets of sayings can be defined as follows: (a) as the relationship between two stages in the activity of one and the same figure). Just as Enoch himself is appointed to the role of Son of Man in EthEnoch 70/71, so Jesus expected that he would be appointed to be Son of Man in the kingdom which would soon dawn. He had a futuristic self-awareness (R. Otto). (b) as a representative relationship (in the sense of a socio-mythical parallelism). Just as the one like a human being in Dan. 7 represents the people of God in heaven and in the Similitudes the 'community of the just', so Jesus knows that he is (now the only) representative of the heavenly Son of Man on earth (Mark 8.38f.) (H. Merklein).	

3. This christological revaluation of the everyday expression 'son of man' was encouraged above all by the fact that Jesus spoke of a future Son of Man who would suddenly be made manifest with the eschatological turning-point. He did not mean anyone else by this. Rather, like Paul in II Cor. 12.1ff. he meant himself. In that passage Paul speaks of himself as another 'man' (in the third person) who for a moment belonged to the heavenly world as a result of a rapture. What Paul writes about a past ecstatic experience, Jesus says about a future ecstatic experience: with the dawn of the kingdom of God he expected to assume the role that he attributed to the Son of Man. The turning-point will come unexpectedly and suddenly. With it he too will be changed, like the whole world. Therefore he speaks of this changed man as of a third person, but in so doing is thinking of himself as a changed person. The suddenness and miraculous character of this change is so great that the Son of Man sayings leave a gap here. They say nothing about how the present Son of Man will become the future Son of Man. Only prophecies after the event say that the transformation takes place through cross and resurrection. But that is a retrospective interpretation by the community. When Jesus proclaimed the present beginning of the kingdom of God he expected it to come during his lifetime.

4. In our view the interpretation mentioned last is therefore the most probable one: Jesus spoke of both the present and the future Son of Man. He combined the expression 'son of man' from everyday language with the visionary-language tradition of a heavenly being 'like a son of man'. This combination revalued the everyday expression, and the visionary-language comparison with a son of man was replaced by the direct designation 'Son of Man'. No angel, no heavenly being, no one who was only *like* a man, but a concrete man will take over his role in the kingdom of God which is breaking in: Jesus himself. He is at the same time the present and the future 'man'. This 'double' concept of Son of Man is analogous to the 'double' kingdom of God eschatology. However, the combination of present and future eschatology in the kingdom of God is more easily understandable than in the case of a person who is speaking about his own future as though about another person. The two proposed solutions discussed by scholars – the assumption of a two-stage activity of the same person and that of a representative relationship between heavenly and earthly person – do not *a priori* contradict each other: mythical thought understands the future as the present which already exists in heaven. To say that Jesus represents in the present the future Son of man amounts to the same thing. Except that in relating himself to an already existing heavenly figure Jesus could not be referring to himself, whereas in relating himself to a future figure he could. At all events, it is certain that Jesus thought in terms of a symbolic representative relationship. When he chose the 'Twelve', they represented the twelve tribes of Israel. This presupposes that Jesus himself represents Israel as a whole. He, a human being, was destined to lead Israel into the kingdom of God.

Jesus was reticent about all titles. Even the term 'Son of Man' was not a firm title for him, but came to have the connotations of dignity as a result of Jesus' preaching. For Jesus, the Son of Man could occupy that place which in some apocalyptic visions was reserved for a heavenly being who was not a human being, but one like a human being. An everyday expression which simply meant the human being or a human being was evaluated in 'messianic' terms by Jesus. Only because of that could it become the characteristic way in which he described himself.

5. The transformation of the picture of Jesus by the cross and Easter

F. Hahn, *The Titles of Jesus in Christology*, London 1969; M. Hengel, *The Son of God*, London and Philadelphia 1975; W. Kramer, *Christ, Lord, Son of God*, London 1966; I.H. Marshall, *The Origins of New Testament Theology*, Leicester 1976; R.P. Martin, *Carmen Christi: Philippians 2.5–11*, Cambridge 1967; G.E.W. Nickelsburg, 'Son of Man', *ABD* 6, 1992, 137–50.

Already before the cross and Easter Jesus was seen in the light of 'messianic' expectations. The cross and Easter were experienced both as a contradiction to these expectations and as a fulfilment of them. The expectation that the kingly rule of God would break in as a miraculous transformation of the world and that Jesus and the messianic collective of his disciples would rule Israel was thwarted. The resignation of the disciples on the Emmaus road shows the failure of such expectations. They were fulfilled in quite a different way. The Easter appearances made the disciples certain that Jesus was alive. However, this certainty alone would not have led to the origin of post-Easter christology: no one becomes Messiah, Son of God or Kyrios because he rises from the dead. The origin of christology can be understood only if already before Easter there was a debate over a claim to an exalted position (implicit, evoked or explicit) which was confirmed in the resurrection by God. This confirmation comprised the renewal of the original expectations and a transcending of them. They were renewed to the degree that the hope was intensified that Jesus would soon bring about his kingdom. People expected his 'parousia' not as his return but as his (first) advent as eschatological ruler. However, the expectations were surpassed in that with the Easter event the bounds of death were transcended: according to the ideas of the time (and not only them) that is possible only through God's action. The present aspect of Jesus' eschatology – the destruction of the evil one which had already begun – could be revived in a new way. The whole world of angels and demons was subject to the Risen Christ. The one who was stronger than death was stronger than all other powers. It is understandable that post-Easter christology went beyond all the claims to authority made by the earthly Jesus. Within the framework of this book on the historical Jesus, however, the development can be sketched out only briefly.

5.1 From the Messiah to the Son of God

The title Son of God was given to Jesus only on the basis of the Easter experience. The most important evidence of this is:

- *The pre-Pauline formula in Rom. 1.3f.:* here Paul sums up his gospel as the preaching of the son of God 'who was descended from David according to the flesh and designated Son of God in power according to the Spirit of holiness by his resurrection'. The messianic son of David becomes 'Son of God' through (or with) the resurrection. Previously he was expecting his lofty position; now he enters it in 'power'. The designation of the Davidic Messiah as 'Son of God' is Jewish tradition (cf. Ps. 2.7; II Sam. 7.13–14, quoted in 4Q174 III, 11–13; probably the son of God in 4Q 246 [see pp. 566f. below] is also the Messiah – and not an ungodly king who divinizes himself).
- The use of Ps. 2.7 in Acts 13.33: Acts sometimes displays remnants of an archaic christology. This includes the interpretation of Ps. 2.7, 'You are my son, today I have begotten you' in terms of the resurrection in 13.33. Elsewhere in the Gospels a divine voice (comparable to Ps. 2.7) is moved to the period before Easter: it rings out at the baptism (Mark 1.11) and the transfiguration (Mark 9.7). As the motifs of an Easter epiphany have been worked into the story of the transfiguration, it is natural to follow Acts 13.33 in seeing the original point of reference of Ps. 2.7 in the resurrection of Jesus.
- *The combination of omnipotence and the title of son in Matt. 11.27:* finally, the (absolute) title 'son' already appears in the Logia source: 'All things have been delivered to me by my Father; and no one knows the son except the Father, and no one knows the Father except the son and any one to whom the son chooses to reveal him' (Matt. 11.27). In this logion the transference of divine omnipotence to Jesus is presupposed, as it is first attributed to the risen Christ in Matt. 28.18 when he says, 'All power is given to me . . .' Therefore we may also understand Matt. 11.27 as a saying of the risen Christ (spoken by inspired Christians). The transference of the title Son of God to Jesus could certainly take up pre-Easter aspects of Jesus' preaching, but it transcends all points of contact.

Jesus spoke of God as 'Father', but not exclusively of 'my' Father'; he also spoke of the Father of the disciples. Though his use of the metaphor of father may be more intensive and direct than elsewhere in Judaism, there is an immediacy here which he wants to make possible for all others. It is not limited to him. It is also in keeping with this that Jesus could speak of 'sons of God' in the plural: as a promise for the men and women who make peace (Matt. 5.9) and love their enemies (5.45; cf. also Matt. 17.25f.). This collective use of the title Son of God lived on after Easter. All those driven by the spirit are υἱοὶ θεοῦ, sons and daughters of God (Rom. 8.14; cf. Gal. 4.6f.). This corresponds to Jewish tradition: in the end-time all Israelites will be 'sons of God' (Jub. 1.24f.; PsSol. 17.27, 30; EthEnoch 62.11; AssMos 10.3; Test Jud 24.3); in the present they can become sons through ethical behaviour and wisdom (cf. Sir. 4.10; Wisdom 2.18; JosAs 7.2–6; 13.20; 21.3; cf. Philo, *Conf.* 143–8; *SpecLeg* I, 317f.).

When Jesus became *the* 'son of God' in primitive Christianity, a traditional title (which was not necessarily meant exclusively) was being used exclusively. The transition from the inclusive to the exclusive use of the title is a consequence of the Easter insight that Jesus is the messianic 'Son of God'. This messianic and exclusive use of the title goes back to early Jewish Christianity. But as the pagan world was familiar with the idea of sons of God, it also found wide dissemination in Gentile Christianity, whereas the title Messiah paled into becoming a proper name in the form of 'Christ'. The growing significance of the title 'son of God' in a pagan milieu clearly emerges from the Gospel of Mark: in that Gospel a demon in pagan territory is the first to address Jesus as 'son of the Most High' without a subsequent command to silence (Mark 5.7). The first human being to confess Jesus as son of God is the pagan centurion under the cross (Mark 15.39). The continuity with Jewish messianic expectations is still also visible here: the crucified Jesus is the 'king of the Jews' (15.26). In the Gospel of John this continuity is expressed by the model Jewish Christian Nathanael: for him Jesus is 'the Son of God, the king of Israel' (1.49). But increasingly the title Son of God detached itself from this Jewish-messianic tradition. The notion of the virgin birth and a divine sonship through procreation can themselves no longer be explained on the basis of Jewish presuppositions.

In fact at a very early stage there was already a special motif which on each occasion was associated with the titles of Messiah and Son of God: the title Messiah usually appears as an expectation which is attached to Jesus by others: as Messiah Jesus is the fulfilment of the expectations of Israel. By contrast, the title Son of God often appears on the lips of superhuman subjects: demons and the voice of God attribute to Jesus the dignity of a son of God. As Son of God Jesus is the one who has access to the supernatural world and can communicate a divine revelation (cf. Matt. 11.27).

After Easter both titles were necessarily deepened by the integration of the cross and passion into them. That the Messiah has to suffer is the insight that the disciples on the Emmaus road are taught by the risen Christ (Luke 24.26f.). Pre-Pauline formulae emphasize that he had to die 'for our sins' (Rom. 5.8; 14.15; I Cor. 8.11; I Thess. 5.10). He was delivered up for us (Rom. 8.32; cf. Gal. 1.4; 2.20) (Vielhauer, *Geschichte**, 126ff.).

Thus the cross and Easter transformed the messianic expectations attached to Jesus in three ways: the title attached to Jesus in the sense of an evoked christology was firmly associated with him in the sense of an explicit christology. The inclusive terminology of 'sons (which also includes daughters) of God' was concentrated in messianic terms on the one Son of God. 3. The one who was exalted to be the messianic 'Son of God' was identified with the one who suffered and was crucified.

5.2 From the Son of Man to the new man

Whereas after Easter the title of Messiah which was attributed to Jesus from outside was taken up as 'Son of God' and developed further to great effect, the title 'Son of Man', which was first given messianic connotations by Jesus himself, faded into the background and finds only a broken echo. After Easter Jesus was more than a 'man' or 'son of man'. But the conception that in him there is a new human being who is typologically contrasted to the first human being is in continuity with Jesus' own designation of himself. In the Easter appearances Jesus had appeared as heavenly man – as the perfect image of God, who radiated God's glory (cf. II Cor. 4.4f.; 3.18). This experience could be articulated with the help of speculations about a heavenly man who had already been the model for the earthly Adam at creation (Philo, *All.* I.31f.; *Op* 134). Except that the sequence had to be reversed: it was not the heavenly primal man who was the first man but his earthly copy, Adam. However, the Risen Christ was the second man who had appeared at the end of time. Paul interprets the Easter experience in these terms in I Cor. 15.20–56. His remarks contain echoes of the Son of Man tradition (G.E.W. Nickelsburg). He speaks of the 'human being' (I Cor. 15.47) as the counterpart of Adam. This 'human being', who is identified with the Messiah, subjugates all the powers opposed to God: all rules, powers and authorities – and lastly death. This recalls the victory over kings and powers by the 'Son of Man' in the Similitudes of Ethiopian Enoch. After his victory Jesus hands over the rule to God, whereas the 'Son of Man' in Dan. 7 receives an eternal kingdom. It is important for us that this is a new man transformed by resurrection (15.44–49). All other believers hope to be transformed into his spiritual being (15.49, 50–52). The hope that with the dawning kingdom of God as 'man' he will suddenly be transformed into the 'Son of Man' appointed eschatological judge by God appears here as a universal Christian hope which has now been reinforced by the Easter experiences: as the firstfruits of the dead (15.23), Jesus has already been transformed into his heavenly nature: all others will follow him. All others will participate in his lofty position. They will even judge the angels (I Cor. 6.2).

This dream of the new man, reinforced and given wings by Easter, was soon associated with the earthly Jesus (and at the same time became the model for the earthly existence of Christians). In Rom. 5.12ff. the Adam–Christ typology is no longer related to Adam as mortal man and to the Risen Christ as his counterpart who overcomes death. Rather, the disobedience of Adam on the one hand is contrasted with the obedience of Christ on the other. So the mortality of the first man is no longer (as in I Cor. 15) the consequence of his earthly being but the consequence of his sin. The opening up of the way to the overcoming of death is not (just) grounded in the resurrection but in the obedience of Christ, whether here the thought is of the obedient acceptance of earthly life by the pre-existent Christ or of the way of the earthly Jesus to the cross (cf. Phil. 2.6–11).

The belief that with Christ a new man and a 'new creation' has appeared has consequences in Paul for the way in which Christians understand themselves: by 'putting on Christ' or becoming members of his body they overcome the traditional social differences between Jews and Greeks, slaves and free, men and women (Gal. 3.28; cf. I Cor. 12.13; Col. 3.11). As a 'new creation' they stand on the other side of the differences between circumcised and uncircumcised (Gal. 6.15). All this presupposes the conviction that Jesus is not just an exclusive being distinct from all other human beings, but '*the* human being', with whom a new humankind begins. This view would not have come into being without the messianic revaluation of the concept of 'man' by Jesus himself.

At the same time, after Easter the suffering of Jesus had to be integrated into the concept of the 'Son of Man'. Only now did the prophecies of the passion come into being which speak of the necessary suffering of the Son of Man (Mark 8.31; 9.31; 10.32ff. etc.). In the Pauline sphere this is matched by the transference of the Adam–Christ typology to the sin and obedience of the first and second man; for the obedience of Christ consisted in the acceptance of suffering. We then find a synthesis between the humiliated and the exalted Son of Man in John: here the Son of Man is on the one hand a pre-existent heavenly being who has descended from heaven (cf. John 3.13); at the same time, as a sufferer he is the 'exalted' (John 3.14; 12.34) and glorified one (12.23 etc.).

Thus after Easter the Son of Man christology was transformed in three ways: 1. Jesus is depicted as the prototype of a new humanity. 2. This new humanity is determined by a spiritual 'new man' who has transcended the frontiers of death. 3. Suffering becomes a firm part of the Son of Man conception.

5.3 From discipleship of Jesus to worship of the Kyrios

The earthly Jesus called a narrower group of disciples, men and women, to follow him and regarded a wider group of followers as his 'family of God'. He did not expect to be venerated. On the contrary, while he was addressed respectfully – as rabbi (Mark 10.51; 11.21), teacher (Matt. 8.19; Mark 4.38; 10.17; 12.14, etc.) or as 'Lord' (Matt. 8.2; Mark 7.28 etc.) – he rejected even being addressed as 'good teacher', since in his view only God is good (Mark 10.17). This rejection of an overestimation of him is certainly historical. The use of the term 'Man' as a messianic title by the historical Jesus is also in keeping with this. It arises out of the conviction that God will carry out his will in salvation and judgment, not through a supernatural figure but through a human being (specifically through Jesus).

After Easter this restraint on the part of Jesus was given up by his followers. That is shown most clearly by the christological title 'Kyrios' (Lord). It signalizes a qualitatively new relationship of the followers of Jesus to their exalted Lord, since it serves as the form of address to a divine being who is worshipped in a cult. None of the other titles are basically a problem in Judaism, in which even speculations about a second divine being alongside God were conceivable. Philo comes to see a 'second God' in the Logos (*QuaestGen* 2.62). The Jewish tragedian Ezekiel could depict Moses occupying the place of God in a dream (frag.28ff.). The decisive step with which the later separation of Jews and Gentiles begins is not theoretical speculation about a second being alongside God, but the worship of this being in the cult. Worship and veneration of him are offensive and have to be criticized as apostasy from strict monotheism, a criticism which is first attested in the Gospel of John (cf. John 10.30ff.).

This step towards the worship of Jesus is closely bound up with the title Kyrios. It has its roots in the Easter faith. It emerges from a pre-Pauline formula that the resurrection of Jesus from the dead was the basis for his worship as 'Kyrios': 'Because if you confess with your lips that Jesus is Lord and believe in your heart that God raised him from the dead, you will be saved' (Rom. 10.9). The confession of the Kyrios can be heard outwardly; belief in the resurrection is its inner basis. Generally speaking the title Kyrios is attested in three (pre-Pauline) forms and formulae:

- The *cry maranatha*: the cry for the coming of the 'Lord' (Aramaic *māre'*) which has been translated into Greek in Rev. 22.20 as 'Come, Lord' occurs independently in I Cor. 16.22 and Did. 10.6 (in a eucharistic framework). The preservation of an Aramaic formula in Greek texts indicates the great age of this cry. It goes back to early Palestinian primitive Christianity and expresses the expectation of an imminent end there: it longs for and calls in the accession of the Lord to rule.
- The *acclamations of the Kyrios* are cited often in Paul: in Rom. 10.9 (see below); I Cor. 12.3; and within the Philippians hymn 2.11. The veneration of the Kyrios in the cult associated with this title emerges especially from Phil. 2.11: the knees of all those who are in heaven, on earth and under the earth are to bow before this Kyrios and they are to confess his exalted status. There is a dispute as to whether there is also a thought here of demonic powers in the underworld which already subject themselves to the Kyrios in the present, or

only of the dead human beings in the underworld who in the near future will acknowledge Jesus as Lord along with the angels (thus O. Hofius).

- The Εἷς acclamation: the acclamation 'there is one God' (εἷς θεός) originally applied exclusively to God himself. It is also transferred to Jesus in I Cor. 8.6. There Paul asserts: 'For although there may be so-called gods in heaven or on earth – as indeed there are many gods and many lords –

> yet for us there is *one God* (εἷς θεός), the Father,
> from whom are all things and for whom we exist,
> and *one Lord* (εἷς κύριος) Jesus Christ,
> through whom are all things and through whom we exist (I Cor. 8.5–6).

Whereas the historical Jesus still explicitly applied the formula 'there is one God' (εἷς θεός) strictly to God and firmly put himself on the human side (Mark 10.17f.), this formula was now transferred to Jesus himself.

With this transfer of the title Kyrios Jesus is in fact brought near to God: that is shown not only by the parallel formulation in I Cor. 8.6 but also by the assurance in the Philippians hymn that God has given the exalted Christ a name which is above all other names (Phil. 2.9). This is a reference to the name of God, especially since the Old Testament passage used immediately beforehand clearly refers to God (Isa. 45.23) but here is referred to the exalted Jesus: '. . . that at the name of Jesus every knee should bow, in heaven and on earth and under the earth' (Phil. 2.10). The name bestowed on Jesus is the title 'Kyrios'. Since Paul also quotes Isa. 45.23 LXX in Rom. 14.11 as a statement of God, he will have been aware that in the Philippians hymn Jesus was praised with statements which really apply to God. Furthermore, the second part of the Philippians hymn shows that the first Christians were aware that Jesus attained his divine status definitively only with his exaltation.

Nevertheless, the assumption that the title Kyrios represents the transfer of an Old Testament divine predicate is not undisputed. The history-of-religions school derived it from the mystery deities (thus the classical thesis of W. Bousset). Against this it can be objected (Hengel, *Son of God*, 77ff. n.135).

- Kyrios is not a characteristic name for Hellenistic mystery deities – with the exception of the Isis cult in Egypt. Here Isis is often addressed as Kyria.
- Kyrios corresponds to 'Baal', a title which has its place above all in the popular religions of Syria and Mesopotamia.
- In addition Kyrios was a respectful form of address to distinguished persons, e.g. the emperor. When Agrippa was mocked as a Jewish king in Alexandria, the man who represented him was addressed as '*Marin*' ('Lord', Philo, *Flacc.* 39)! Paul too speaks of 'Kyrioi' in heaven and on earth, and is thus also thinking of authoritative figures on earth – in which case he could only have the emperor cult in mind. Only here were earthly 'Kyrioi' divinized.

In the light of the New Testament texts an alternative to the history-of-religions derivation from mystery cults would be the more natural derivation from Jewish worship of God. But there are also difficulties in this theory of a transference of the Old Testament divine predicate to Jesus.

- Jesus was demonstrably called on as '*mare*' (cf. Maranatha). The question is: was YHWH also called *mare*? The name Yahweh itself was never pronounced. When reading scripture, people replaced the tetragrammaton יהוה with an equivalent term, in Hebrew with '*ādōnāy* (as *qere*, i.e. the spoken version of the written word for the *kethīb yhwh*). Was there an analogous Aramaic *qere*, namely *mare*'? At any rate *mārēh/māryā*' is now attested as a divine name in the Qumran writings (11QTgJob XXIV, 6f.; 1QGenAp XX, 12f.).
- The same question arises for the LXX. In the old LXX manuscripts the tetragrammaton is not rendered by Kyrios but by a Greek rendering of the tetragrammaton. It is possible that 'Kyrios' was read in Greek, but there is no certain evidence of this. It can only be demonstrated, quite generally, that among Greek-speaking Jews 'Lord' was a divine predicate (cf. Josephus, *Antt.* 10, 90): here God is the 'Lord of all', τῶν πάντων κύριος).

Our conclusion must be that the acclamation of Jesus as 'Kyrios' was the most far-reaching innovation after Easter. The Risen Christ was worshipped alongside God. He sat at God's right hand (Ps. 110.1; cf. Mark 12.36; Acts 2.34; I Cor. 15.25 etc.). He participated in divine power. But above all, from now on he was called on and worshipped as a divine being, albeit as a divine being who, as the Philippians hymn shows, had experienced human life in extreme lowliness – to the point of suffering a shameful death on the cross – before his exaltation.

6. Summary and hermeneutical reflections

Who was Jesus? The first answer is that he was a Jewish charismatic who independently of any messianic expectations had a power to attract and provoke far beyond the normal. His *charisma* showed itself in the way in which he implicitly attributed to himself a special nearness to God. He endorsed his words by putting an 'amen' in front of them as though he had received them from God. His antitheses deliberately transcended the Torah without contradicting it. He reactivated the traditional metaphor of father in a way which indicated a special relationship to God. He promised that forgiveness of sins which as a rule was hoped for from God himself. And he was active in the awareness that God was doing miracles through him. Though he did not develop a doctrine about himself, he spoke clearly about John the Baptist, whom he set above all other human beings. But he knew himself to be the 'coming one' who was announced by John the Baptist, except that he was quite different from the one whom John had announced. He transcended the prophet who in his eyes was more than all other prophets. His sense of himself can hardly be underestimated.

This awareness of authority transcended the role-expectations with which he was confronted – above all the *messianic expectation* which was alive in many variants among the people, alongside other eschatological expectations. It was by no means clear in what sense anyone understood Jesus' messiahship if they saw him as the 'Messiah'. Therefore Jesus could reject a confession of himself as Messiah without generally repudiating the title Messiah: what he repudiated was the conviction expressed in a specific messianic expectation (cf. Mark 8.29 along with 8.33). Probably Jesus had a messianic self-understanding in the broadest sense. But he wanted to exercise the role of Messiah not exclusively, but along with his disciples, whom he saw as a messianic collective to rule Israel. He activated their messianic hopes, but this very activation of messianic expectations was fateful for him: he was crucified by the Romans because of the messiahship attributed to him by the people. They were not so concerned to strike at him and his teaching: they wanted to 'crucify' the messianic expectations of the people in him.

As John the Baptist had not associated his messianic expectation with a title, Jesus could dispense with any existing honorific title. The only term which he explicitly applied to himself was the expression '*son of man*' – and this was not a title but an everyday expression which was first given messianic connotations by him – however, Jesus linked it with visions of a heavenly being who was like a son of man. It is not a modern anachronism to note that Jesus made the term 'man' the decisive honorific title. He gave human beings themselves a dignity which transcended all other honorific titles: Messiah, Son of God and Kyrios. He put forward a human christology. The vision contained in Dan. 7 said that it was Israel's destiny to replace the bestial kingdoms of the world by a humane kingdom. Jesus did not expect this from someone who was only 'like a human being', but from a real human being. He was convinced that he himself was this human being and would become so in the near future. In a world of mythological symbols a kind of 'humanism' is expressed with such images. In the fate of Jesus this human christology was fulfilled in a way different from what had been expected. When Jesus preached the kingdom of God in Galilee and went up to Jerusalem, he hoped that the kingdom of God would soon break in. But he was executed. The kingdom of God did not come. God's final intervention to lead Israel and the world to salvation did not take place. God intervened in another way: according to the faith of the disciples he raised the crucified Jesus from death. The 'Son of Man' had attained his lofty position only through suffering and death. All that Jesus had said previously about himself implicitly and explicitly, all that others had hoped or feared from him, had to be reformulated in the light of the cross and Easter.

That part of the picture of Jesus which survived this 'Easter break' became decisive for a deeper understanding of him. For with Jesus all implicit, evoked or explicit expectations had been crucified, to be raised to new life at Easter in the faith of the first Christians. The three titles which acquired new meaning after Easter were 'Messiah', 'Son of God' and 'Son of Man' – supplemented by the worship of Jesus as Kyrios, something which did not have a forerunner before Easter. No way leads from the everyday form of address 'Lord' to the worship of the exalted Jesus as the 'Lord' who sits at God's right hand.

From a post-Easter perspective the *title Messiah* was associated with Jesus even more closely than before. Now Jesus was not just confronted with messianic expectations; he became the Messiah. The messianic expectations had been fulfilled in him, albeit in a paradoxical way, through suffering and death. The suffering of the Messiah was interpreted as the acceptance of sin and guilt. That opened up the way to the Gentiles. For in the eyes of the Jews these lived with the terrible guilt of having turned away from the one and only God. In this way, as Messiah of Israel Jesus confirmed the old promises – he confirmed that they apply in the midst of a world governed by suffering and are addressed to all peoples. In this way, too, he created the presupposition for a Christianity which today is again discovering Judaism as its mother religion and no longer sets itself above Judaism, but along with Judaism looks for the fulfilment of the promises they share in the midst of the unredeemed world.

The *title Son of God* took up messianic expectations, but emphasized Jesus' bond with God in a unique way. No human expectations were fulfilled here. Jesus was Son of God because a divine voice made him so. Already in the New Testament the title 'son' designates Jesus as the revealer who represents the voice of God in the world. It is not by chance that the Gospel of John, which understand Jesus entirely as God's emissary whose coming and presence in the world contains the decisive message, is governed by a 'Son' christology. As 'Son', Jesus is the representative of God in this world – an opportunity to enter into dialogue with the hidden God through him.

But the *title Son of Man* should stand at the centre of christological reflection. Jesus himself shaped it and was the first to make it a messianic title. Through his human christology he bestowed messianic dignity on human beings themselves. The Easter faith led to belief in a transformed 'human being' who does not cease to be God's creature even beyond the frontier of death. These new perspectives released a utopian power, so that by the assimilation of all men and women to this 'new human being' traditional differences between peoples, classes and sexes could be overcome: differences between Jews and Greeks, slaves and free, men and women (Gal. 3.28). Reflection on Jesus today may see him as a kind of metamorphosis of the human. Daniel's vision was already applied to Jesus in primitive Christianity: the kingdom of God brought in by the 'one like a man' is to replace the bestial kingdoms. In a great vision human history is interpreted as a transition from beasts to 'one in human form' who has not yet appeared. Jesus was cast in the role of the 'one in human form'. And time and again the question is whether there are people who allow themselves to be grasped by the transformation embodied by Jesus, and despite the failure of all hopes through death and violence, trust in the midst of an unredeemed world that a humane life is possible in covenant with God.

All the titles discussed so far are surpassed by the worship of Jesus as *Kyrios*. Through it, for the people who worship him, Jesus is brought near to God. It is all the more decisive that this worship never loses a connection with the earthly Jesus – and the substance of what is expressed by the other christological titles. As Messiah Jesus is a son of Israel, and any relationship to him is a relationship to Israel. As Son of God Jesus is representative of the voice of God in this world, and any relationship to him is a relationship to God. As Son of Man Jesus is a new form of the human, and belief in him is participation in the incomplete project of God in this world: the human being whose history and development is not yet finished. What is problematical about the title Kyrios is that through it Jesus can be exalted to become a formal authority. Human beings have an unquenchable need to give themselves absolute authorities. The history of religion and of Christianity shows that dedication to absolutized 'Lords' can activate dangerous energy. The Lordship of Jesus – in other words his authority – must therefore always remain bound to the Galilean and Judaean Jesus, to the friend of toll collectors and sinners, the critic of the self-righteous, the one who proclaimed the grace of God, the victim of priestly hostility and state power. In the first half of this century Christian theology was in danger – not least because of its contact with a widespread authoritarian mentality – of developing a Kyrios christology with minimal reference to the earthly Jesus. The kerygmatic Christ, i.e. the one who after Easter was worshipped as Kyrios, was preached as an absolute power who makes demands and bestows grace. The human face of the earthly Jesus was lost. His Jewish features faded. The God revealed by him threatened to become an authoritarian God. The quest for the historical Jesus was regarded as a failed undertaking by liberal theology. This book makes an interim stocktaking in a new orientation of theology which has come about in the second half of the twentieth century. It seeks to provide information about who Jesus was. And it also wants to make possible to him an access which is not distorted by authoritarian demands.

7. Tasks

7.1 The title Messiah: PsSol 17

First of all PsSol 17.4 recalls Nathan's prophecy in II Sam. 7: 'Lord, you chose David to be king over Israel, and swore to him about his descendants forever, that his kingdom should not fail before you.' Then mention is made of the sins of the people and the establishment of a kingdom (probably the Hasmonaean kingdom) which despoiled the throne of David, of a man from an alien race (Pompey?), who swept away this kingdom, and of an alien rule which subjugates the land and desecrates Jerusalem. The state of the people of God is said to be lamentable: sin, disobedience and lawlessness prevail. Then follows the prayer for a king of salvation, which turns into a description: 'See, Lord, and raise up for them their king, the son of David, to rule over your servant Israel in the time known to you, O God. Undergird him with the strength to destroy the unrighteous rulers, to purge Jerusalem from Gentiles who trample her to destruction; in wisdom and in righteousness to drive out the sinners from the inheritance; to smash the arrogance of sinners like a potter's jar; to shatter all their substance with an iron rod; to destroy the unlawful nations with the word of his mouth. At his warning the nations will flee from his presence; and he will condemn sinners by the thoughts of their hearts. He will gather a holy people whom he will lead in righteousness and he will judge the tribes of the people that have been made holy by the Lord their God. He will not tolerate unrighteousness (ever) to pause among them, and any person who knows wickedness shall not live with them. For he shall know them that they are all children of their God . . . And he will have Gentile nations serving him under his yoke, and he will glorify the Lord in (a place) prominent (above) the whole earth. And he will purge Jerusalem (and make it) holy as it was even from the beginning, (for) nations to come from the ends of the earth to see his glory, to bring as gifts her children who had been driven out and to see the glory of the Lord with which God has glorified her. And he will be a righteous king over them, taught by God. There will be no unrighteousness among them in his days, for all shall be holy, and their king shall be the Lord Messiah . . . Blessed are those born in those days to see the good fortune of Israel which God will bring to pass in the assembly of the tribes. May God dispatch his mercy to Israel; may he deliver us from the pollution of profane enemies. The Lord himself is our king for evermore' (17.21–27, 30–32, 44–46).

1. What are the characteristic properties and tasks of the Messiah according to this text?

2. Numerous Old Testament motifs have found their way into PsSol 17. The links with Ps. 2 are particularly striking. Describe the relationship of the two texts. Are there common traditions? What elements are taken up from Ps. 2? Are there striking gaps?

7.2 The title Son of Man: IV Ezra 13

Ezra has a dream: 'And lo, there arose a violent wind from the sea, and stirred all its waves. And I beheld, and lo the wind caused to come up out of the heart of the seas as it were the form of a man. And I beheld, and lo this Man flew with the clouds of heaven. And wherever he turned his countenance to look, everything seen by him trembled . . . And after this I beheld and lo there was gathered together from the four winds an innumerable multitude of men to wage war against the Man who had come up out of the sea. And I beheld, and lo he cut for himself a great mountain and flew upon it . . . And lo, when he saw the assault of the multitude as they came he neither lifted his hand, nor held spear nor any warlike weapon; but I saw only how he sent out of his mouth as it were a fiery stream, and out of his lips a flaming breath . . . and it fell upon the assault of the multitude which was prepared to fight and burned them all up, so that suddenly nothing more was to be seen of this innumerable multitude save only the dust of ashes and smell of smoke. When I saw this I was amazed. Afterwards I beheld the same Man come down from the mountain and call unto him another multitude which was peacable. Then drew nigh to him the faces of many men, some of whom were glad, some sorrowful; while some were in bonds, some brought others who should be offered' (IV Ezra 13.2–3, 5–6, 9–10a, 11–13). The vision is interpreted by God: 'Whereas you saw a Man coming up from the heart of the Sea: this is he whom the Most High is keeping many ages, and through whom he will deliver his creation, and the same shall order the survivors . . . Behold, the days come when the Most High is about to deliver them that are upon earth. And there shall come astonishment of mind upon the dwellers on earth; and they shall plan to war one against another, city against city, place against place, people against people, and kingdom against people. And it shall be that when these things come to pass, and the signs shall happen that I showed you before, then shall my son be revealed whom you saw as a Man ascending' (13.25–32). The mountain which was cut out is interpreted as Zion, from where the son will annihilate the nations (13.33–39). The peaceful crowd consists of the ten tribes who had been carried off by the Assyrians (721 BCE), and those left behind in the land of Israel; the son will protect all these (13.39–50).

Using this text, remind yourself of the most important characteristics of the apocalyptic Son of Man, taking up and developing Dan. 7; collect the decisive differences from the Jesus tradition and the features which are shared with it (no solution, see 4.1.2 and 4.2.2).

7.3 The title Son of God: 4Q 246

J.J. Collins, 'The Son of God Text from Qumran', in M.C. de Boer (ed.), *From John to Jesus: Essays on Jesus and New Testament Christology in Honour of Marinus de*

Jonge, JSNT Supp 84, Sheffield 1993, 65–82; C.A. Evans, *Jesus**, 107–10; J.A. Fitzmyer, 'The Contribution of Qumran Aramaic to the Study of the New Testament', *NTS* 20, 1973/74, 382–407; id., '4Q246: The "Son of God" Document from Qumran', *Bib* 74, 1993, 153–74; G. Vermes, *The Complete Dead Sea Scrolls in English*, London 1997, 576–7.

There is a vigorous argument about the significance of the Aramaic fragment from the first century BCE or early first century CE which we shall go on to discuss. Unfortunately the first column is badly damaged, and thus completely opposite supplements to the text, and differences about its content, are possible. Column II has been preserved complete, but because the preceding context is uncertain, it is not clear at many points to what the statements relate and how their content is to be understood (and translated).

Evidently a seer prophesies the future to a king (on the basis of a vision in a dream, I, 1–3). Oppression on earth and riots in the provinces are announced (I, 4–5). It is impossible to reconstruct with certainty the context in which the 'king of Assyria and Egypt' is mentioned (I, 6). The the text goes on, after a large gap: '. . . he will be [gr]eat on the earth' (I, 7). In the following lines there is (again?) mention of a powerful figure; here it is unclear whether it is identical with the Seleucid ruler (the 'king of Assyria and Egypt') or whether another (Israelite) king is meant, whose appearance is reported in one of the gaps in the text.

8 [all] . . .will serve [him] 9 . . . he will be called great and by his [God's] name he will be designated. Column II: 1 'The son of God he will be proclaimed and the son of the Most High they will call him. Like the sparks of the vision, so will be their kingdom. They will reign for years on 3 the earth and they will trample all. People will trample people and one province another province . . . 4 until the people of God will arise [God/the son of God raises up the people of God] and all will rest from the sword. 5 Their (the people of God's) kingdom will be an eternal kingdom (Dan. 7.27) and all their paths will be in truth. They [He] will judge 6 the earth in truth and all will make peace. The sword will cease from the earth, 7 and all the provinces will pay homage to them [him]. The Great God is their helper. 8 He will wage war for them. He will give peoples into their hands and 9 all of them (the peoples) he will cast before them (the people of God). Their [His] dominion will be an eternal dominion (Dan. 7.14) and all the boundaries of . . .'[30]

---

1. A widespread interpretation sees the figure described in I, 7–II, 1 as a pagan king (e.g. Alexander Balas or Antiochus IV Epiphanes), whose attributes are 'son of God' and 'son of the Most High'. What understanding of 4Q 246 as a whole follows from this presupposition?

---

[30]The translation is based on Vermes, 576–7 (with alternative renderings).

(a) What course for the final events is presupposed?

(b) What interpretation of the Daniel fragment follows?

(c) Compare Luke 1.32–35 and draw parallels with 4Q 246.

How are they to be interpreted in this case?

2. An alternative interpretation of 4Q246 is a messianic one. This understands 'son of God' and 'son of the Most High' as titles of the Messiah, whose rule is described in II, 4–9. What overall understanding of 4 Q 246 follows on this presupposition?

(a) What course of the end events is presupposed? What parallels can you recognize for the individual activities of the Messiah (cf. e.g. PsSol 17; IV Ezra 13; and Isa. 10.20–11.16)?

(b) What understanding of the Daniel quotations follows from this? Are there analogies to this understanding in contemporary texts?

(c) 4Q 246 would be the earliest evidence for the designation of the Messiah as 'son of God'? Some scholars dispute that this title fits within the framework of Jewish messianic notions. What traditions and messianic texts can be cited to the contrary?

(d) In this case the parallels to Luke 1.23–35 can be further increased. How is the relationship between the texts to be interpreted?

3. Weigh up the two possibilities of understanding 4Q 246 sketched out above against each other.[31] Is the 'son of God' the Messiah or a pagan king?

---

[31]These two interpretations – an earthly king hostile to God or a divinized Messiah – are the most common. But there are further possibilities of understanding the text. For example, D. Flusser regards the 'son of God' as the 'Antichrist', i.e. not an earthly but a supernatural (satanic) power hostile to God ('The Hybris of the Antichrist in a Fragment from Qumran', *Immanuel* 10, 1980, 31–7). J.A. Fitzmyer interprets the 'son of God' in terms of a successor to David, without wanting to understand the text messianically. The two alternatives, 'son of God' as an usurped or legitimate title on the one hand and 'son of God' as an earthly or heavenly form on the other (here the boundaries are fluid), structure the field of possible interpretations.

Retrospect: A Short Life of Jesus

Historical scholarship does not relate what happened, but reflects on sources, levels of research, methods and problems. And yet history ultimately deals with events that can be narrated – even if any narration of them curtails them. So in conclusion we shall attempt a brief narrative: a short life of Jesus. The whole of the book which has gone before can be regarded as an introduction to this life with question marks, qualifications and alternatives. We give this summary with great hesitation. The results indicated here are less important to us than the problems which underlie them; the answers given by those who research into Jesus are less important than the questions which lead to them. At present our answer to the question 'Who was Jesus?' would take the form of the following short narrative.

Jesus was born in Nazareth shortly before the end of the reign of Herod I (37–4 BCE), the son of Joseph, a craftsman in wood and stone, and his wife Mary. He had several brothers and sisters. We know the names of some of his brothers. He must have had an elementary Jewish education, was familiar with the great religious traditions of his people, taught in synagogues and was called 'rabbi' during his public activity.

In the 20s of the first century CE he joined the movement of John the Baptist, who was calling on all Israelites to repent and promising them deliverance in the imminent judgment of God by a baptism in the Jordan. Here John offered the forgiveness of sins in ritual form – independently of the possibilities of the temple in providing atonement. This was a vote of no confidence in the central religious institution of Judaism, which had become ineffective. Jesus, too, had himself baptized by John. Like everyone else he confessed his sins. Like everyone else he, too, expected the imminent judgment of God.

Soon Jesus made an appearance independently of John the Baptist – with a related message, but one which put more emphasis on the grace of God that still gives everyone a chance and allows more time. Perhaps this was the way in which Jesus used his experience that the judgment announced by John did not break in immediately. The world went on, and that in itself was a sign of the grace of God. Jesus' basic certainty was in fact that a final shift in the direction of the good had taken place. Satan had been conquered, and in essentials evil had been overcome. One could experience this in exorcisms, in which the demons had to flee.

With this message Jesus travelled through Palestine as a homeless itinerant preacher, focussing his attention on small places north-west of the Sea of Galilee. He chose twelve disciples from among ordinary people, fishermen and farmers, with Peter at their head. They were representatives of the twelve tribes of Israel with whom he wanted to 'rule' the Israel that would soon be restored. His idea was a kind of 'representative popular rule'. Moreover others from among the people followed him, including women, which was unusual for a Jewish teacher. Mary Magdalene had a special position among them. For a while Jesus' family thought that he was mad, though later, after his death, they joined his followers.

At the centre of Jesus' message stood Jewish belief in God: for Jesus, God was a tremendous ethical energy which would soon change the world to bring deliverance to the poor, the weak and the sick. However, it could become the 'hell-fire' of judgment for all those who did not allow themselves to be grasped by it. Everyone had a choice. Everyone had a chance, particularly those who by religious standards were failures and losers. Jesus sought fellowship with them, the 'toll collectors and sinners'. He found prostitutes more open to his message than the pious. He was confident of his power to move people to repentance. He did not call for any demonstration of repentance, nor any baptism. For him God's grace was certain without such rites.

In his picture of God Jesus combined two traditional images in a new way. For him, God was father and king. However, he never spoke of God as king but always only of God's 'kingdom'. He was confident that the goodness of the Father would establish itself in his kingly rule and that this process began in the present. He proclaimed that in words and deeds.

The most impressive of his words were the parables, little poetic narratives which ordinary people could also understand. However, in them he inculcated an 'aristocratic' self-confidence: everyone had infinite responsibility before God, and in view of that all could risk their whole lives. Salvation and damnation were now near.

At the same time Jesus was active as a charismatic healer. People flocked to him in order to profit from his gift of healing. He saw these healings as signs of the kingdom of God which was already beginning, and at the same time as an expression of the power of human faith. At a very early stage people attributed incredible things to him: his fame as a miracle-worker made him independent of reality even during his lifetime, as when for example people told of his miraculous multiplication of loaves of bread.

The great transformation of the world by God was also to change human wills: Jesus' ethical teaching was the pattern for a human being who was governed entirely by the divine will. He intensified the universalist aspects of the Jewish

Torah and dealt in a 'liberal' way with those ritual aspects which distinguished Jews from Gentiles. But all his teaching remained grounded in the Torah. He put the commandment to love God and neighbour at the centre of his ethic, but he radicalized it so that it became an obligation even to love enemies, strangers and the religious outcasts. In ritual questions he was demonstrably non-fundamentalist. He extended the recognized exceptions to sabbath regulations when it was a matter of saving a life to cases where life was enhanced. He showed his scepticism towards the distinction between clean and unclean things, which could separate people from God, without drawing specific consequences for behaviour in the present. In any case, his vision of the future rule of God was that of a great shared meal in which Jews and Gentiles were no longer divided by commandments about food and cleanness.

What he taught to all has to be distinguished from the demands he placed on his followers, men and women: here in individual instances he could require trans-gressions against the Torah, including contempt for the commandment to honour one's parents and (probably) for the commandments about cleanness. Here he called for a radical ethic of freedom from family, possessions, home and security. As an itinerant preacher, along with his followers he could avoid the domesticat-ing power of everyday duties.

Jesus attracted attention and provoked opposition by his teaching and life. He discussed his behaviour with the Pharisees, precisely because in many things he was close to them. They both wanted the whole of life to be penetrated by the will of God, but argued over the way in which this should be done. Such a dispute did not create any deadly hostility. It was Jesus' criticism of the temple which was fateful for him when he went up to Jerusalem for the Passover. John the Baptist had already denied the legitimacy of the temple, but Jesus attacked it directly: he prophesied that God would replace the old temple with a new one. By a symbolic action, the so-called cleansing of the temple, he disrupted the temple cult and deliberately provoked the aristocracy associated with the temple. For his disciples (as a substitute for the sacrificial rites in the temple?) at the last meal that they shared he instituted a new rite: a simple meal which he shared with them one day before the beginning of the Passover in expectation of a dramatic escalation of the conflict with the Jerusalem aristocracy. Probably (as is expressed in his prayer in Gethsemane, in a scene composed in poetic fashion) he hovered between expect-ing death and the hope that God would intervene before his own death and usher in his rule. Judas, a member of the most intimate circle of disciples, betrayed the place where Jesus was staying so that he could be arrested inconspicuously by night. The aristocracy which arrested him took steps against him because of his criticism of the temple, but accused him before Pilate of a political crime, of having sought power as a royal pretender. In fact many among the people and his followers expected that he would become the royal Messiah who would lead

Israel to new power. Jesus did not dissociate himself from this expectation before Pilate. He could not. For he was convinced that this God would bring about the great turning-point in favour of Israel and the world. He was condemned as a political troublemaker and crucified with two bandits (very probably in April 30 CE). His disciples had fled. However, some women disciples were braver, and witnessed the crucifixion from afar.

After his death Jesus appeared first either to Peter or to Mary Magdalene, then to several disciples together. They became convinced that he was alive. Their expectation that God would finally intervene to bring about salvation had been fulfilled differently from the way for which they had hoped. They had to reinterpret Jesus' whole fate and his person. They recognized that he was the Messiah, but he was a suffering Messiah, and that they had not reckoned with. They remembered that Jesus had spoken of himself as 'the man' – specifically when he was confronted with excessively high hopes in himself. He had given the general term 'man' a messianic dignity and hoped that he would grow into the role of this 'man' and would fulfil it in the near future. Now they saw that he was 'the man' to whom according to a prophecy in Dan. 7 God would give all power in heaven and on earth. For them Jesus took a place alongside God. Christian faith had been born as a variant of Judaism: a messianic Judaism which only gradually separated from its mother religion in the course of the first century.

Thus far our attempt at a short narrative about Jesus. Narratives form the basis of identity. The narrative about Jesus is the basis for Christian identity. If our narrative is correct, then the self-understanding of Christianity must change on one point. Historically and theologically, Jesus belongs in Judaism. Through Jews who believed in him, at the same time he became the foundation of Christianity. Thus today he belongs to two religions, which developed out of each other only after his death. Their common theme is life in dialogue with the one and only God and ethical responsibility for the world and society. A Christianity which in the footsteps of Jesus is concerned with both these things can remain true to itself only if it remains true to its Jewish roots, if it perceives its social responsibility, and if it understands the Jesus tradition as a chance to keep beginning the dialogue with God all over again.

Solutions

1. The Quest of the Historical Jesus

Five phases of the quest of the historical Jesus

Text 1: E. Käsemann, 'The Problem of the Historical Jesus', in *Essays in New Testament Themes*, London 1964, 15–47: 37f. ('New quest')

Text 2: D.F. Strauss, *The Life of Jesus Critically Examined*, ed. P.C. Hodgson, Philadelphia 1972 and London 1973, 85f. (mythical approach to the sources about the life of Jesus)

Text 3: R. Bultmann, *Jesus and the Word*, London 1934 reissued 1958, 14f. (collapse of the quest of the historical Jesus)

Text 4: C. Burchard, 'Jesus of Nazareth', in J. Becker et al., *Christian Beginnings*, Louisville 1987, 15–72: 15f. ('third quest')

Text 5: H.J. Holtzmann, *Die synoptischen Evangelien. Ihr Ursprung und geschichtliche Charakter*, Leipzig 1863, 458f. (liberal quest of the historical Jesus)

2. Christian Sources on Jesus

Extracanonical sources and research into Jesus

Text 1: J. Jeremias, *Unknown Sayings of Jesus*, London 1957, 33.

Text 2: J. Gnilka, *Jesus von Nazareth*, HThK Suppl. III, Freiburg, Basel and Vienna 1990, 25.

Text 3: H. Koester, *Introduction to the New Testament*, Vol.2, 1ff.

The following objections might be made:
to Text 1 (J. Jeremias): First of all the circular argument is a methodological weakness: as the extra-canonical texts are thought only to be worth investigating

if they 'fit the framework of the tradition offered by the Synoptic Gospels', the result, namely that decisive material about Jesus is to be found only in the canonical Gospels, is hardly more than a confirmation of the presupposition. At best it proves that virtually all the Jesus traditions of a Synoptic kind are contained in the Synoptic Gospels. A second point of criticism is that the circular conclusion is based on the unexamined priority which is accorded to the canonical or Synoptic Gospels: this stands above criticism. That leads to extra-canonical Gospels always being seen as supplements to the picture of Jesus that can be gained on the basis of the New Testament sources and never as corrections to it.

to Text 2 (J. Gnilka): See the three objections made under 1.1 (above, p. 21). It is hardly true that the Gospel of Thomas belongs to a later stage in the tradition than the late representatives of the Apostolic Fathers. A verdict on the orthodoxy of a work should not be seen as a verdict on the traditions which it incorporates.

to Text 3 (H. Koester): Individual instances have to be examined to see whether the relatively early dates to which Koester inclines can be sustained. Purely quantitatively, at any rate, the presumably old sources among the extracanonical sources are clearly inferior to the canonical texts and therefore can hardly be quantitatively 'equivalent' sources, though they can be qualitatively. If applied to research into Jesus, Koester's approach in some instances runs the risk of reconstructing an 'anti-canonical picture of Jesus' as opposed to the previous 'canonical' one.

3. The Non-Christian Sources on Jesus

1. Josephus' testimony about Jesus according to the Religious Dialogue at the Sasanid court

1. The *language* of Josephus' testimony according to the religious dialogue shows virtually no agreements with the Testimonium Flavianum and the testimony of Agapius; a direct literary dependence is to be excluded.

In terms of *content* there are agreements and differences as compared with the Testimonium Flavianum and the testimony of Agapius, both in the statements which are there and those which are not:

(a) The emphasis on virtue has parallels in Agapius, John Malalas,[1] and Josephus' testimony about John the Baptist (*Antt.* 18, 116–19). In Luke 23.47 the

---

[1]The relationship between John Malalas (491–577) and the religious dialogue, which dates from about the same time, is unclear. It is uncertain whether he is presenting a mixture of the variants of Eusebius and the religious dialogue when he writes of Jesus (*Chronographia* X; P G 97, 377): ὃς ἦν ἄνθρωπος ἀγαθὸς καὶ δίκαιος, εἴπερ ἄρα τὸν τοιοῦτον ἄνθρωπον δεῖ λέγειν καὶ μὴ θεόν (who was a good and righteous man, if one may call him a man and not God).

evangelist attributes to the pagan centurion under the cross the judgment that Jesus was a 'just man'.

(b) The Testimonium Flavianum also mentions signs and wonders, but in different terminology; there are no miracles in Agapius.

(c) The attestation from divine grace by signs and wonders and the characterization of the miraculous healings as benevolence in part agree word for word with texts from Acts (2.22; 10.38).

(d) There is no questioning the humanity of Christ in Agapius either.

(e) The absence of the title Christ (for περὶ Χριστοῦ is not part of the quotation) has no parallels; nor have the designation 'wise man' and the report about the disciples, the death of Christ and the testimony of the prophets.

The tendency of the text, like that of the Testimonium Flavianum and Agapius, is markedly friendly; like Agapius the lines contain nothing that a Jew could not have written (this is not the case with the Testimonium Flavianum). The tendency to depict Jesus as a model of virtue and a philanthropic benefactor, which has its closest parallel in the description of John the Baptist by Josephus, is striking, but is formulated in a way which suggests closeness to the Acts of the Apostles.

2. In favour of the authenticity/inauthenticity of the text:

The language and tendency fit Josephus and correspond to his description of John the Baptist (see below).	The echoes of Acts are difficult to explain: the text does not fit the context of *Antt.* 18, 62, 65 and is thus at least quoted incompletely.
The context of the religious dialogue makes it clear that the author is quoting all the positive Jewish testimonies that he can find. The Eusebian Testamentum Flavianum would have fulfilled this aim far better than the 'innocuous' text of the religious dialogue. That suggests its authenticity.	This can also be an earlier Christian interpolation or revision, i.e. a parallel version to the Testimonium Flavianum which had not yet established itself everywhere in the fifth/sixth century.

Its content can be defined in the following ways:

• The text of the religious dialogue corresponds to Josephus' original (thus the 'early' E. Bratke)[2] – this solution calls for an explanation of the parallels to Acts by a dependence of some kind (literary?).
• The text is a free and abbreviated rendering of the original testimony of Josephus (thus J. Klausner);[3] here we must suppose that the author involuntarily allowed common phrases from Acts to influence him.

---

[2] E. Bratke, *Zeugnis*, from the year 1894.
[3] J. Klausner, *Jesus of Nazareth*, 61f.

- The text is a moderate Christian revision or interpolation independent of the Testimonium Flavianum, inspired by Luke–Acts and Josephus' testimony about John the Baptist, which could not establish itself because of the popularity of the version handed down in Eusebius (thus E. Schürer and the 'late' E. Bratke).[4]

2. The Old Slavonic version of the Jewish War as a source for the teaching and death of Jesus and the original form of the Testimonium Flavianum

1 (a) Jesus' nature is developed in the terminology of christological reflection with reference to a developed doctrine of two natures: he participates in the nature common to all human beings and his form is human, therefore he cannot have been an angel (repudiation of a Jewish–Christian angel christology?); his works are divine, so his whole appearance is to be called 'more than human'. This could be said of Jesus Christ *at the earliest* after Nicaea (325 CE), and by Christians, since a Jew for whom it is 'not possible to call' Jesus 'a man' would be a Jewish Christian.

That the Jews bribed Pilate and then themselves inflicted the Roman penalty of crucifixion on Jesus is a historical impossibility which Josephus, who had been confronted with the terrible reality of mass crucifixions as a Roman deterrent, often under his very eyes, would never have handed on.

1 (b) Throughout, the text shows the Christian interest in the glorification of Jesus, often combined with a negative description of the Jews and an implicit argument with charges which are known to have been made against Christians in Jewish polemics:

- There is a marked emphasis on the miracles, but it is manifestly stressed against the charge of magic and witchcraft that Jesus performed them all through the word and an invisible power, and despite his transgression of the law did nothing shameful in healing on the sabbath.
- No ambitions of rebellion are imputed to Jesus and his followers but to the Jewish mob; the innocence of Jesus is asserted by Pilate himself against the Jewish authorities who are blinded by hatred and envy, and Jesus himself is even at first released again.
- Jesus' followers, too, are portrayed in a positive way: they do not act out of ambition and perform miraculous signs.

2 (a)–(b) The most important points of contact with the NT and the further development of tendencies and motifs which occur there:

---

[4]E. Bratke, *Religionsgespräch* (1899), and Schürer, *Geschichte* I*, 549.

- For Jesus as the risen 'first lawgiver' cf. Mark 6.14–16, where he is John the Baptist *redivivus* or Elijah or a prophet; for Jesus as the second Moses cf. John 1.17; 6.32.
- The many healings and arts recall summary reports of healings, e.g. Mark 3.10; Matt. 9.35; 12.15; John 3.2; 11.47; 20.30.
- Healings through the word are mentioned in Matt. 8.16; Mark 4.39; 9.25, etc. In the New Testament there is also occasional mention of manipulations and touchings (e.g. Mark 7.33; John 9.6), which are disputed in the Testimonium Slavianum (evidently because of the likelihood of a charge of witchcraft).
- Healings on the sabbath are regarded as a breach of the law: Mark 3.1–6; Luke 13.10–17; 14.1–6; John 5.1ff.; 9.1ff.
- Many from the people follow him: Mark 3.7; 5.24 etc.
- For the custom of staying on the Mount of Olives cf. Luke 22.39; 21.37.
- The crowd wants Jesus to rule over it as king because of the demonstrations of power that have taken place in the miracles: John 6.15; that this means war against the Romans is at most hinted at in the Gospel of John (11.48; 18.36), but is vividly elaborated in the Testimonium Slavianum.
- The assembly and deliberation of the Jewish leaders and high priests about the political danger posed by Jesus; miracles and the enthusiasm of the crowd as the basis for their denunciations to Pilate: the passage is clearly based on John 11.47–53, but with an accentuated anti-Jewish tendency. Whereas John makes only the high priest speak out of sheer concern for the people and the land and interprets his words as a high-priestly prophecy – albeit an unconscious one –, in the Testimonium Slavianum all speak and express less noble motives (the loss of possessions).
- The hearing before Pilate in which Pilate asserts Jesus' innocence is based on John 18.33ff., in particular the fact that Jesus is not striving for political rule. The attempt of Pilate to release Jesus (19.12), which is vain there, becomes an actual release. The apologetic against the political charge is depicted much more broadly (no transgressor, rebel, striving for power).
- Pilate's wife is mentioned in Matt. 27.19.
- That Jesus glorified himself through his miracles sounds Johannine, as δοξάζειν (glorify) occurs often in John with reference to Jesus. But significantly there Jesus refuses to glorify himself; rather, he is glorified by God and to the glory of God (cf. John 8.54). This happens above all through his crucifixion and resurrection (e.g. John 7.39; 12.16; 13.31f); in connection with a miracle (of resurrection!) only in John 11.4; 13.31f. The Testimonium Slavianum thus offers a crude reminiscence of the Johannine motif.

- Envy as the motive of the Jewish leaders: already Mark 15.10.
- The thirty talents to bribe Pilate could have been constructed on the basis of Judas' reward of thirty pieces of silver (Matt. 26.15).
- That Pilate lets the Jews do what they want and that they thereupon crucify Jesus is a transposition of John 19.6 into narrative form (Pilate says there: 'Take him and crucify him'). Here the ambiguity of John 19.16 may have played a part where it says: 'Then he delivered Jesus up to them to be crucified.' The sentence immediately preceding had spoken of the high priests, so they could have been envisaged; of course this was historically impossible and is excluded by 19.23, where the soldiers are mentioned as the ones who carry out the execution.
- In essentials, the section about Jesus' disciples runs parallel to Acts 5.12–42: preaching of Jesus' resurrection, numerous miracles performed by the 'servants'; a great following among the people, followed by the wish of the scribes to kill Jesus; the general feeling of all that a decision should be postponed so that it can be shown whether the miracles are from God; release, and then later persecution. For the disciples' hope of political liberation by the one who is to return cf. Acts 1.6; for the 'expulsion' to Antioch and distant lands cf. Acts 11.19ff.; for the emperor see Acts 25.9–12.

The observations assembled here are reinforced by the fact that many special features of the Testimonium Slavianum have parallel motifs in the apocryphal Pilate literature. Various writings are brought together under this collective title; the date of their composition ranges from the second century CE to the Middle Ages. The Testimonium Slavianum clearly shows parallels with the presumably much earlier part of the collection, Pilate's letter to the emperor Claudius (quoted above, pp. 472f.), which is closely related to or identical with (apart from the name of the recipient) the letter of Pilate to the emperor Tiberius which is mentioned by Tertullian (c. 200, *Apol.* 21.24, cf. p. 473 above). Acts of Pilate are already mentioned by Justin (c. 150 CE), but it is uncertain whether and in what form he knew them. The *Acta Pilati* usually handed down under the title Gospel of Nicodemus claim in the prologue (which is certainly fictitious) to be a translation from the Hebrew which was made in 425; this gives the *terminus ad quem*. In particular chapters 1–8 have points of contact with the Testimonium Slavianum (they can be read in *NTApoc* 1, 505ff.). There are also links with the latest parts of the Pilate literature, above all the so-called *Anaphora Pilati*:

- Miracles play a central role in the Letter of Pilate and even more in the Acts of Pilate (chs.1–6, 8, etc.), in the proof, brought against Jewish objections, that Jesus' claim is justified.
- The triad of Jewish polemic presupposed in the Testimonium Slavianum against Jesus' miracles, transgression of the law (= healings on the sabbath) and the charge of doing shameful things (= making use of magical practices) appears at

length in the first chapter of the Acts of Pilate[5] and is summed up briefly in the Letter of Pilate.

- In later legends Pilate's wife comes more markedly to the fore (Gospel of Nicodemus/Acts of Pilate 2); the fact that she has been healed is reported first by the late *Anaphora Pilati*.
- The letter of Pilate and Tertullian also mention the hostility of the Jewish leaders as an envious reaction to the miracles of Jesus and his following among the people.
- Tiberius accuses Pilate of venality in the *Anaphora*.
- There are parallels to the crucifixion of Jesus by the Jews in Gospel of Peter 2.5, 3.6; in the Letter of Pilate and in Tertullian, *Apol.* 21, 18.

3 Points of contact with other Josephus texts:

There is a word-for-word parallel to the Testimonium Flavianum only in the first sentence; the greatest similarity is to be found in the second part, which might already be a Christian insertion ('if it is fitting to call him a man'). Elsewhere the Testimonium Slavianum runs largely parallel in content to the Testimonium Flavianum (with some transpositions), but is longer: cf. the mention of miracles, teaching and the many followers, reflection on Jesus' status in salvation history (Christ, Moses *redivivus* or an emissary of God), denunciations by the Jewish leaders, death on the cross, loyalty of followers, the claim that he is alive.

Striking contradictions: in the Testimonium Slavianum there is no mention of pagan followers; Jesus is first released by Pilate and then crucified by the Jews.

Parallels to the report on the Egyptian: he himself plans what according to the Testimonium Slavianum the people requires of the miracle-worker, namely to defeat the Romans from the Mount of Olives and rule as king. In both cases the attack is put down in a bloody way by the governor (Pilate/Felix), though the messianic pretender himself and his closest followers escape unscathed. The parallels are very close, so that it seems improbable that two different historical events form the basis. Rather, the account in the Testimonium Slavianum will have been formed on the model of the Mount of Olives episode.

4. In our view, the simplest explanation of the observations collected under 1–3 above is that the Testimonium Flavianum from *Antt.* 18.63f., already with Christian interpolations, has been expanded by the inclusion of canonical and

---

[5]The Jews accuse Jesus before Pilate: '"Moreover he pollutes the sabbath and wishes to destroy the law of our fathers." Pilate said: "And what things does he do that he wishes to destroy it?" The Jews say: "We have a law that we should not heal anyone on the sabbath. But this man with his evil deeds has healed on the sabbath the lame, the bent, the withered, the blind, the paralytic and the possessed." Pilate asked them: "With what evil deeds?" They answered him: "He is a sorcerer, and by Beelzebub the prince of the devils he casts out evil spirits, and all are subject to him"' (*NTApoc* 1, 506). The point of dispute is mentioned on several other occasions.

extracanonical traditions about Jesus (especially relating to the passion) and the Mount of Olives episode from *BJ* 2, 261–263. The insertion can be explained above all by the interest in glorifying Jesus as God-man, miracle-worker and benefactor, guarding him against Jewish attacks (that he was a magician and political rebel), putting the blame for his death on the Jews and exonerating the Romans.

Two arguments above all tell against the alternative theory that this is an account of Jesus with a negative tone which comes from Josephus or an unknown Jewish author and has been subjected to Christian revision:

- The same defence, anticipating Jewish charges of witchcraft and instigation to riot, that occurs in the Testimonium Slavianum can also be found in the Letter of Pilate and in Tertullian. This proves that there is no need of any negative Jesus basic account (but only of a corresponding climate of Jewish-Christian polemic) to produce an account of Jesus which is so steeped in apologetic tendencies.
- Chronological considerations: the Testimonium Flavianum was presumably composed between 230 (Origen does not know it) and 300 (Eusebius quotes it) as the revision of an authentic text of Josephus. On the basis of its christological remarks the Testimonium Slavianum is to be put at the beginning of a later stage in the history of dogma (and is only attested much later).

Conclusion: the Christian revisions of the Testimonium Slavianum show an advanced stage of legendary, christological, anti-Jewish and unhistorical tendencies as compared with the Testimonium Flavianum. Formulations of a version of the Testimonium Flavianum which has already been subjected to a Christian revision glimmer through. Therefore this and not an unknown authentic Josephus text will have been the literary basis of the Testimonium Slavianum.

4. The Evaluation of the Sources: Historical Scepticism and Research into Jesus

1. 'Taking the kingdom by storm' – an authentic logion of Jesus?

1. The attestation of the logion is simple: apparently Matthew, Luke and Justin have taken it over from Q.

It belongs to the broad Jesus tradition about the kingdom of God which is represented in all the early strands of tradition (Mark, Q, Paul, Matt[s], Luke[s], Gospel of Thomas, John, Epistle of James) and occurs in a large number of genres (see above, p. 117).

Kingdom of God traditions which use metaphors (of violence) with a similarly negative connotation are particularly close to this saying: for example the parable which compares the kingdom of God with an intruder (Gospel of Thomas 98), the sayings about those who have made themselves eunuchs for the sake of the kingdom of heaven (Matt^s 19.12), about binding the strong man and plundering his house (Mark 2.27), about the fishers of men who call others to repentance in the face of the kingdom of God (Mark 1.17).

Tendencies which go against the tradition are the dating of the kingdom of God by John the Baptist (from a post-Easter perspective Jesus himself would surely have been chosen) and the metaphor of violence. The latter fits Jesus well and would certainly not have been chosen later because of possible political associations (the Christians as resistance fighters who fight for the kingdom of God against Roman rule).

2. Sayings about the kingdom of God appear in a contemporary Jewish context either as an apocalyptic future expectation that God will establish his kingdom against all the enemies of Israel or doxologically as a confession of God's eternal kingship (see above, §9.2–9.3). By contrast, the logion is only one of a few sayings which understands the kingdom of God as present: the kingdom is already there and can be 'stormed'. Thus Jesus shows an individual profile within widespread Jewish notions.

The saying about taking the kingdom of God by storm may therefore go back to an authentic saying of Jesus.

2. Is Jesus an invention of the third Christian generation?

(a) The argument that 'brothers of the Lord' in the passages mentioned means brothers who are especially zealous in the service of the Lord is intrinsically contradictory: in the Gospels, as is clear from the context, the brothers are the eleven apostles or the disciples, and Peter is always included with them. In I Cor. 9.5, however, the 'brothers of the Lord' are distinguished from the 'other apostles and Peter'; in Gal. 1.19 James, and not Peter, is called 'brother of the Lord'.

(b) The breadth of the tradition is impressive: physical brothers of Jesus occur in different strands of tradition and literary contexts within Christianity and once even outside it.

- A Jewish contemporary, *Josephus*, hands down the date (62 CE) and the circumstances of the stoning of James, whom he identifies as the brother of Jesus, the so-called Christ (*Antt.* 20, 200). There are no solid grounds for assuming that this passage is an interpolation. Here alone Wells's thesis proves to be ungrounded speculation [literary context: historical note].
- *Paul*: James appears as brother of Jesus in I Cor. 9.5; Gal. 1.19 (also without

the designation 'brother' in Gal. 2.9, 12; I Cor. 15.7). Where he appears as a brother, the context, in which other apostles are mentioned by name and/or as a group, does not allow the term to be used as a general designation for Christians or apostles (a group of apostles) with a special emphasis (see above) [literary context: letters].

- *Markan tradition*: brothers of Jesus appear in Mark 3.31ff. par. (cf. Mark's 3.21, where the same persons are meant); also Mark 6.3 par.; Matt. 13.55, where four brothers are mentioned by name: James, Joses [Joseph], Simon and Jude [literary context: narrative tradition].
- *Johannine tradition*: brothers of Jesus are mentioned without being named in John 2.12; 7.3, 5, 10, but are clearly physical brothers of Jesus [literary context: narrative tradition].
- *Acts*: Mary and the brothers of Jesus appear in 1.14 [literary context: summary note about members of the community]; James appears in 12.17; 15.13; 21.18, but is not called a brother of Jesus.
- *Gospel of Thomas*: James is mentioned in logion 12, but is not called a brother.

Evaluation: the instances are historically credible. This impression arises from a mixture of aspects which are coherent and go against the tendency: thus on the one hand it is quite understandable that after the resurrection of Jesus his brothers should have been members of the Jesus movement (Acts 1.14; Gal. 1.19; I Cor. 9.5) and that on the basis of a vision of Christ (I Cor. 15.7) James quickly gained high esteem (Gal. 2.6–9; Acts 12.17; 15.13; 21.18; Thomas 12); later, he and Jude later were even chosen as fictitious authors of early Christian letters (James and Jude). The fact that James became the object of Jewish persecution and ultimately a victim of lynch law because of his exposed position, also accords with this (Josephus *Antt.* 20, 200). By contrast, the reports that the brothers of Jesus had tried to take him away because they thought him mad (Mark 3.23, 31ff.), that they had not believed in him (John 7.3–5), and that Jesus himself had publicly distanced himself from them (Mark 3.31ff.) go so much against the grain that they certainly would not have been invented. They were known facts which were handed down despite some pain, at least for a while (Mark 3.21 is already omitted by the other Synoptic evangelists). The numerous sayings of Jesus which are critical of the family further confirm the substance of this attitude of Jesus to his family or his brothers, which was later felt to be a problem.

If we had only the letters of Paul, which even G.A. Wells accepts as early sources, we would still know the following about Jesus. He was a Jew from a Davidic family (Rom. 1.3f.) and had several brothers (I Cor. 9.5), one of them called James, who long survived him (Gal. 1.19). He taught a prohibition against remarrying or the requirement for those who were separated to be reconciled (I Cor. 7.10); he required missionary preachers to earn their living from their message (I Cor. 9.14). He was betrayed one night, but celebrated a meal with his followers at which he interpreted his impending death (I Cor. 11.23–25). He was executed, indeed crucified. Some Jews (I Thess. 2.15) and some 'rulers of the world' (I Cor. 2.8) were involved in his death. After his death his followers, especially Peter and a group of 'Twelve', received appearances which convinced them that he was alive (I Cor. 15.3ff.).

5. The Historical and Religious Framework of the Life of Jesus

2. The 'Teacher of Righteousness' and the 'Wicked Priest'

1. The 'Teacher of Righteousness' is a priest (1QpHab II, 8). He has a close connection to the new covenant which is not described in more detail here (II, 3, 4, 6) and his followers regard his sayings as 'sayings from the mouth of God' (II, 2–3), i.e. prophetic sayings (e.g. II Chron. 35.22; 36.12, etc.); by contrast they are not to believe the 'Liar' and all the 'apostates'. In substance this is an interpretation of the mysterious sayings of the prophets, which contain all that will come upon the land and its people in the near future (II, 9–10; VII, 4f.). It can be inferred with some certainty from numerous other passages and his further titles that he was high priest and after his illegitimate deposition founded the Essene new covenant.

2. *(a)* The 'Wicked Priest' is a priest who has a ministry at the Jerusalem sanctuary, and because of his exalted status (and because he is twice called *the* priest: 1 QpHab VIII, 16; XI, 12) is probably the high priest in office there. From the perspective of the Qumran community his exercise of office is an abomination and defiles the temple (XII, 7–9). He has offended against the 'poor' (the term the Qumran community uses to designate itself) or the 'Teacher of Righteousness and the men of his council', and has apparently appropriated their possessions (XII, 9–10; IX, 9–10). He has fallen into the hands of his enemies, and has been humiliated and destroyed, i.e. probably killed (IX, 10–11). In VIII, 9–10 (not printed) it is said that 'he was named after the name of truth when he entered into his office' and that God only abandoned him when he 'had attained to rule'.

The sum of these features best fits Jonathan, the first of the Maccabees, who had himself appointed high priest in 152 BCE, after asserting himself for some years as a successful general. He was lured into a trap in 143 by Trypho, the general and spokesman of Antiochus VI, and executed (I Macc. 11.39–52; Josephus, *Antt.* 13, 209–212). However, other identifications have been put forward.

2 *(b)* The purpose of the meeting between the 'Wicked Priest' and the 'Teacher of Righteousness' (1QpHab XI, 5–7) cannot be determined clearly, since it is not certain in what sense the verbs 'persecute', 'swallow up' and 'ensnare' are used.

Either the Wicked Priest attempted to dissuade the Teacher from his deviant view and thus 'destroy' his community, or – more probably – there was a murder attempt on him, which is mentioned elsewhere in the Qumran writings (4Q 171, iv, 8–9). Probably it failed, but that is not completely certain. It happened 'in the place of his banishment'; thus the 'Teacher of Righteousness' was not living in Jerusalem, where the 'Wicked Priest' was exercising his ministry, but had fled (after his deposition as high priest?) or had officially been banished. The Day of Atonement is given as the date of the event (XI, 7). Now it would be quite inconceivable for a high priest in office to have been outside Jerusalem on the Day of Atonement. However, there were many disputed questions between the Essenes and the Jerusalem priest relating to the calendar and the dating of individual feasts. So the passage is usually interpreted to mean that the Jerusalem high priest exploited the difference in the calendar and took the Teacher of Righteousness by surprise when he was celebrating the most important Jewish feast day with his community on a day which differed from the official calendar.

3. Against the various ways of identifying figures from primitive Christianity with the 'Teacher of Righteousness' or his opponents can be adduced:

Archaeology. The archaeological evidence itself clearly tells against any theory of this kind: Qumran was founded around 125 CE and the 'Teacher of Righteousness' or the 'Wicked Priest' belong to the period in which the Essene movement came into being (possibly clearly before the settlement in Qumran).

Palaeography. On the basis of palaeographical evidence which has meanwhile been confirmed all along the line by radio-carbon investigations, most Qumran manuscripts are to be dated to the second/first century BCE, and only a very few to the first century CE. For example, the Habakkuk commentary is to be dated to around 50 CE, and already makes a distinction between the past time of the 'Teacher of Righteousness' and the most recent political developments; it attempts to explain the 'delay' in the end-events announced by the teacher.

The sources. Josephus mentions the Essenes for the first time in connection with political events from the time of the Maccabee Jonathan (*Antt.* 13, 171–173). The dating of the foundation of the community by the 'Teacher of Righteousness' in the Damascus Document points to around the same time: 390 = 20 years after the fall of Jerusalem, i.e. the first half of the second century BCE (CD I, 5–7, 9–11).

The intrinsic improbability, given the content of the Qumran writings. This cannot be developed at length here (see the literature mentioned on p. 148). The information given in the passages from 1QpHab only has to be checked. Even from these few examples it is clear that the disputes must have been between rival groups of priests. That *a priori* excludes Jesus and James (on either side), since there is never any mention of their priestly descent in the reliable early sources. James perished in Jerusalem (Josephus, *Antt.* 20, 200), so the murder attempt 'at the place of his punishment' cannot in any case have referred to him. John the

Baptist possibly came from priestly circles and perhaps could have had contacts with the Qumran community. However, on chronological grounds alone he was certainly not the 'Teacher of Righteousness'. The Jewish and Christian sources about him (see §8.4.1) depict him as a prophetic individual, an eschatological preacher of repentance, who publicly addresses the Jewish people who flock to him, not as the founder of an elitist community.

6. The Chronological Framework of the Life of Jesus

The day of Jesus' death

Arguments for the correctness of one of the two New Testament chronologies for the day of Jesus' death (cf. Meier, *Marginal Jew* 1*, 429f.).

Methodologically, the assumption of just any day of death is based on a 'conjecture' which goes against the statements of two independent sources which in agree in some respects – namely over the days of the week of the last supper and death and the imminence of the Passover, but in others do not – namely as to whether the death took place before the feast or on the first day of the feast, and whether or not the last supper was a Passover meal. The dates confirmed by the two sources would also fall victim to such a conjecture with no basis in the sources.

In terms of content, I Cor. 5.7 confirms that already in the 50s the death of Jesus on the cross was interpreted as the sacrificing of the true Passover lamb. Both the Johannine and the Synoptic chronology agree in different ways with this early dating, which came into being when numerous eye-witnesses were still alive. Therefore it will presumably take account of the historical facts. The Barabbas pericope also shows (regardless of its historicity) that the pre-Markan and pre-Johannine tradition saw the condemnation of Jesus as being immediately before the evening in which the Passover lamb was eaten.

Thus in principle we cannot rule out the possibility that the chronology of both the Synoptic Gospels and John is wrong. But it is far more probable that one of the two is right than that the day of Jesus' death would have remained completely unknown.

7. The Geographical and Social Framework of the Life of Jesus

1. Petronius and the rebellion against the emperor's statue

Josephus' account of the Jewish protests against Caligula's attempt to have his statue set up in the Jerusalem temple indicates the following structural tensions within Palestinian (and Galilean) society:

- *Ethnic and cultural tensions between Jews and Gentiles.* The conflict over the erection of the statue of the emperor concerns the centre of Jewish faith and Jewish identity, the uniqueness of YHWH, who tolerates no other gods (or divinized human beings) alongside him and does not allow any images of human beings or animals which could be understood as idols. The emperor or the representatives of his power in Palestine saw themselves confronted with the theocratic conviction of the broad Jewish population that absolute obedience was to be given to God and his Law – even at the cost of extreme sanctions.
- *Socio-political tensions.* The mediating position of King Agrippa I, represented by his brother Aristobulus, the rest of the Herodians and the aristocracy allied with them, between the Romans who held power and the Jewish population, can clearly be recognized. The population first of all offered resistance; thereupon the aristocracy took over the role of negotiators. Since Jewish identity had been fundamentally put in question and broad masses of the people had adopted an uncompromising attitude, they attempted to convince the representatives of the Roman military of the fatal consequences that their action would have and thus at any rate secured a postponement. Josephus, who himself was a member of the priestly aristocracy, presumably gives an accurate account of the distanced tone of their intervention – see the talk of the 'stubbornness of the people'.
- *Socio-economic tensions.* The main concern of the aristocracy was a complete end to the agricultural strike. The refusal to sow seed by some thousands of Jewish and Galilean smallholders (and tenants) threatened to bring about an economic catastrophe, since we must presume that they had no stores: the taxes would not be paid, people would starve, and plunder on a large scale would be the inevitable consequence. Evidently the aristocrats also saw their own privileged status endangered by this, and even Petronius seems to have taken the matter very seriously. An extremely shaky social and economic equilibrium threatened to collapse through some minority measures by the poor masses.

2. Jesus and Sepphoris

On Bösen's argument it should be noted that a methodological approach which isolates Sepphoris without treating the analogous case of Tiberias does not go far enough and must be criticized.

Particularly in view of the fact that the failures of Jesus in such insignificant places as Nazareth, Capernaum, Chorazim and Bethsaida have left a mark on the tradition, the last two even being contrasted with the world cities of Tyre and Sidon, the silence about the two greatest and most significant cities of Galilee is all the more evocative.

As for the charge of passing by those in need, from which Bösen wants to protect Jesus, one should remember scenes like those presupposed by the stories of feedings and the summaries of healings (cf. e.g. Mark 6.32–37, 53–56; 8.1–3). Although these are redactional in form and exaggerated, they will give an essentially accurate picture of Jesus' activity: news of his presence in an area spread rapidly, and interested people made long journeys to see him. John the Baptist, who preached an imminent judgment from which nothing but the baptism of repentance that he performed could bring deliverance, naturally expected 'all the land of Judaea and all of Jerusalem' (Mark 1.5) to come to him in the wilderness. By that standard, Jesus hardly expected the inhabitants of Sepphoris and Tiberias to go very far.

In view of the silence of the sources and the towering significance of Sepphoris and Tiberias, S. Freyne is probably right in assuming that Jesus decided against any public activity in them. His comparison between the Hellenized Jewish cities and the Gentile cities which surrounded Galilee is also appropriate. However, Freyne does not note that Jesus also always stops at the outskirts of cites and never enters them. Finally, the explanation that he wanted to avoid a confrontation with the Herodians is insufficient – at least as a sole reason. Antipas had had John the Baptist arrested in southern Peraea; he could also have seized Jesus anywhere. That Jesus himself expected a confrontation with government circles if he thought it necessary for the sake of his message is shown by his appearance in Jerusalem during Passover week – the authorities were never more nervous than at the great pilgrim festivals.

Meanwhile S. Freyne has clearly changed his position. In 1994 he regarded the two cities built by Antipas as 'signs of social change' (*Geography*, 104), since they functioned as mercantile, financial and administrative centres and were the seat of the elites, who were interested in increasing their own prosperity, necessarily at the expense of the rural population. The Jesus movement grew up as Galilee was becoming more intensively orientated on a market economy; this can also be observed in the growth of particular 'industrial centres' like the fishing and pottery industry. The movement shared the antipathy of the rural population to the symbols of this new market economy. But whereas in the face of the theocratic ideal the rural population attempted to maintain a life which concentrated on the possession of land acquired in the extended family, loyalty to the temple and obedience to the Torah, Jesus proclaimed the vision of a new family in the restored Israel of the dawning kingdom of God.

5–7. Chronological survey

Roman emperors: 1. Octavianus Augustus; 2. Tiberius; 3. Gaius Caligula;
4. Claudius.

Rulers in Palestine: 5. Herod I (the Great); 6. Archelaus; 7. Pontius Pilate;
8. Agrippa 1; 9. Herod Antipas; 10. Philip.

Legates of Syria: 11. Quintilius Varus; 12. Quirinius.

8. Jesus as a charismatic

1. John the Baptist and Jesus: abiding agreements

1. John the Baptist and Jesus have the following features in common: 1. in their
appearance and their teaching; 2. in the way in which they were perceived by
outsiders; and 3. in their fate:

1.1 As prophets, both led a reform movement concentrated on Israel which
called for repentance in the face of God's judgment and the restoration of Israel.
Both (in different ways) regarded themselves as God's last human messengers.

1.2. Although both addressed the whole people and attracted great masses,
they gathered a small group of disciples around themselves with whom they
shared their life-style (which differed in details) and by whom they were called
'rabbi' – in a way without analogy in contemporary sources.

1.3. Both show detachment from the religious and political establishment:

- They are in opposition to the temple: if the baptism of John mediates
  purification from sins, the temple cult is not enough. Jesus' saying about the
  temple and the symbolic action of the cleansing of the temple similarly imply
  the inadequacy of the existing temple.
- They are in opposition to the rich Hellenized upper class: John's criticism of
  Herod Antipas (Mark 6.17f.) is carried on by Jesus in a veiled form (Matt.
  11.7–9). Criticism of riches is attributed to both. Probably there was a
  continuity in their ethics which can no longer be recognized because the
  sources (for John the Baptist) are so bad.

2. To outsiders, John the Baptist and Jesus seemed so alike that they could be
confused: thus Jesus was taken to be John the Baptist *redivivus* (Mark 6.15,16;
8.28); Jesus and John were thought to be Elijah (John: Mark 9.11–13; Luke 1.17;
Matt. 11.4; John 1.21; Jesus: Mark 6.15; 8.28). Opponents accused them both of
being possessed by demons (John: Matt. 19.18; Jesus: Mark 3.22; John 8.48.52;
10.20). Striking differences between John (and his disciples) and Jesus (and his

disciples) were registered by the public and needed to be justified (Mark 2.18 par.; Matt. 11.16–19/Luke 7.31–35) – evidently because the two were otherwise close.

3. Both suffered a similar fate: although they were prophetic leaders of a reform movement with a religious motivation, they were thought to be politically destabilizing and were executed by political authorities (Herod Antipas; the Sanhedrin/Pilate) in order to avoid the danger of a revolt.

2. John the Baptist and Jesus: incompatible?

Haenchen's account is stamped by one anti-Jewish and two anti-Catholic stereotypes:

1. The God of 'pious Jews' is 'the zealous God, the God of retribution' (58), whereas the God of Jesus (and of Christians) is the demanding but merciful God. This loses the sight of the fact that Jesus, too, was a pious Jew who had come to know the merciful God whom he experienced and preached not least in the scriptures of Israel, and the fact that in principle Jesus maintained John the Baptist's expectation of judgment.

2. Even more marked are the two anti-Catholic stereotypes of righteousness by works and sacramentalism in the light of which John the Baptist is perceived. Thus John is said to be trapped in the error 'that human beings can decide for themselves' (59) and thus have a free will – to fulfil God's demand through asceticism, repentance and obedience, in order then to be able to 'put merits in the scales against him' (59). Moreover John is in danger of perverting baptism 'into a means which works by magic' (59), i.e. a saving means which works *ex opere operato* – through which claims can be made against God (which is what Catholics – in the hostile perception of Protestant theologians, and not just in the sixteenth century – allegedly do with the sacraments). By contrast, Jesus preaches 'law and gospel', in the proper order: like a Lutheran penitential preacher he confronts people with God's total demand 'which no human good will can meet' (59), and then proclaims God's salvation and mercy to those who are 'no longer trapped in the delusion' of all righteousness by works, namely that they can earn the forgiveness of God through an exemplary life 'within the framework of human possibility' (59).

Here confrontations, even down to the very wording, are projected back on to the time of Jesus which presuppose the complicated history of the rise of the scholastic doctrine of sacramental grace and the way in which it was put in question by the Reformers. The presuppositions for the thought of John the Baptist and Jesus are different. In view of the demand for true penitence and the forgiveness of sins followed by good works, there can certainly be no question of the danger of a magical understanding of baptism. Moreover, after John the Baptist's harsh preaching of judgment ('You brood of serpents' . . . is the way in which he addresses those to be baptized), none of his hearers would have dared to advance any 'claims' on God or appeal to 'merits'. Indeed, one of John's concerns was to shake the way in which people counted on privileges from salvation history and supposed righteousness. Baptism as a gracious act of God was necessary because there was no longer any time to do any good worth measuring. Jesus evidently put more emphasis on proving one's conversion by doing God's will because he saw himself confronted with a delay in the judgment announced by John. For John and Jesus are utterly and completely Jews in that in fact they require people to do good works 'within the framework of human possibilities' and to trust in the mercy of God, knowing how limited such works are'.

For the baptism of Jesus as a fact which is historically well attested cf. under §4.2. In particular Jesus' ongoing high esteem for John, which is reflected in countless of his sayings, is incompatible with Haenchen's two suggestions (Jesus turned away radically from John's picture of God; John did not baptize).

But the main objection to be made to Haenchen's alternative reconstruction is that it cannot explain plausibly how the primitive community, 'contrary to the action of Jesus, could have made baptism the condition for entry into the Christian community' (62) had Jesus had distinguished himself so plainly from John in his teaching and had he never been baptized.

3. Jesus and his opponents: Pharisees

Texts which do not put in question the righteousness of the Pharisees before God but which emphasize Jesus' special mission to those who cannot live up to the Pharisaic criteria of righteousness are: Mark 2.16f./Luke 5.30–32; Luke 15.(2,)7; Luke 15.(2,)29–32; Luke 7.36, 41–43.

Texts which dispute that the Pharisees could succeed in achieving their goal along the way that they took – obedience to the Torah, righteousness and holiness – are: Matt. 5.20; Mark 7.1–15; Luke 11.37–44; Luke 18.10–14.[6]

---

[6]K. Berger, 'Jesus als Pharisäer und frühe Christen als Pharisäer', *NT* 30, 1988, 249, also thinks that in this text the righteousness of the Pharisee 'in so far as it is expressed in 18.12' is not disputed; 'there is also the question whether according to v.14 it is totally denied him'. However, there is no argument in confirmation of this which can be checked.

9. Jesus as Prophet: The Eschatology of Jesus

1. The history of research

	Present statements	Future statements
1. Ethical eschatology (A. Ritschl)	The kingdom of God is inwardly present as the loving community which begins in human beings and which will establish itself in history.	The future statements are an unemphasized adoption of apocalyptic notions which were not particularly important to Jesus.
2. Thoroughgoing eschatology (J. Weiss/ A. Schweitzer)	The present sayings are an expression of an anticipation of the future in a prophetic enthusiasm which is certain of victory.	In accordance with apocalyptic thought the kingdom of God is envisaged by Jesus as being in the future and transcending the world, albeit immediately imminent. It comes in cosmic catastrophes.
3. 'Realized eschatology' (C.H. Dodd)	The present sayings are authentic: in Jesus' person all eschatological statements are fulfilled.	Future statements derive from misunderstandings on the part of the community.
4. Double eschatology (W.G. Kümmel)	The present statements are an expression of the certainty that Jesus is already in the present what the kingdom of God will bring in the future.	Future statements derive from Jesus' assumption of a short time between his death and the coming of the kingdom.
5. Existentialist eschatology (R. Bultmann and pupils)	The present statements express the immediacy of the presence of God, as the future which already transforms the present.	Future statements are an expression of the prophetic-apocalyptic tradition in which Jesus stands.

2. Does Jesus' notion of judgment 'leave behind the process of judging'?

1. According to the present text, Jesus merely made use of the mythological notion of the last judgment in order to express his 'real theme': the present nearness of God. So this interpretation is a variant of existentialist eschatology, which attributes to Jesus himself the demythologizing of the apocalyptic notions of his environment. The future eschatological sayings merely have the function of changing attitudes and conduct in the present. Another example is the use of spatial metaphors to interpret Jesus' understanding of time: 'His real theme is the journey of life as the place where one can adopt an attitude to the rule of God.' Extracts are taken from H. Weder, *Die 'Rede der Reden', Eine Auslegung der Bergpredigt heute*, Zurich 1985. Quotations come from 222 (heading), 109, 217–19 (extracts) and 243–5 (extracts).

2. In our view, the theory that Jesus did not expect an eschatological judgment by God and did not imagine God as judge is untenable.

- Matthew 7.1f. alone rules out this interpretation. Here, rather, the coming judgment is taken for granted as the horizon of expectation, and the debate is only about the criterion. Furthermore, Jesus' message of God's unexpected readiness to forgive in the present is presupposed. However, this requires human beings to act accordingly (cf. Matt. 6.12; 18.23–25, etc.).
- In particular the broad attestation to Jesus' preaching of judgment, which is discussed under §5.1–5.4 above, tells against Weder's interpretation. The examples show that Jesus was in fact 'imprisoned' in an apocalyptic notion of judgment of a kind that was natural for a Jew of his time. Here it is characteristic of Jesus that in God's saving action in the present his kingly rule is already dawning and that the main emphasis is on that – and not on the judgment.
- As for the question of 'righteousness by works', the generalization that 'in contemporary Judaism . . . the person is created by his or her works' is untrue, nor can Jesus be denied the view that doing the will of God will be a criterion in the last judgment. Like every Jew, he knows that human beings nevertheless remain dependent on a gracious verdict.[7] Certainly one can ask whether it does not follow from Jesus' message of salvation that – mythologically speaking – in the end hell remains empty. That would be the greatest possible intensification of the grace with which God declares the unrighteous righteous and accepts them into his rule. But Jesus did not say that. He called on sinners to repent and

---

[7]For a criticism of Weder's false alternative 'between the just and the loving God' (H. Weder, *Gegenwart und Gottesherrschaft*, BThSt 20, Neukirchen 1993, 245), i.e. between the Jewish God of judgment and the God of Jesus, see also M. Hengel, 'Zur matthäischen Bergpredigt und ihrem jüdischen Hintergrund', *ThR* 52, 1987, 398–400.

subject themselves now and in the future to the rule of God, and threatened those who refused with final exclusion. At the same time he forbade people to pass any judgment on who would be included or who would be excluded (cf. Matt. 7.1).

10. Jesus as Healer: The Miracles of Jesus

Introduction: 2. The motifs of the New Testament miracle stories

On 1.: The structure of motifs in Mark 1.39–45:

1.39:   1. The coming of the miracle-worker
1.40:   3. The appearance of the distressed person; 8. description of the distress; 10. falling to the knees; the plea and expression of trust
1.41:   15. Pneumatic excitement of the miracle-worker; 22. touch; 24. miracle-working word
1.42:   26. Recognition of the miracle
1.43:   28. Dismissal
1.44:   29. Command to secrecy; 27. demonstration
1.45:   33. The spread of the news

The structure of motifs in Mark 2.1–12:

2.1:   1. The coming of the miracle-worker
2.2:   2. The appearance of the crowd
2.3:   4. The appearance of representatives and 3. the distressed person; 8. description of the distress
2.4:   9. Difficulties in the approach
2.5:   18. Assurance
2.6.   6. The appearance of opponents
2.7:   15. Criticism
2.8–10:   19. Argument
2.11:   24. Miracle-working word
2.12:   27. Demonstration; 30. Wonder; 31. Acclamation

On 2: Some examples of motifs (motifs which occur very frequently are not included):[8]

4. The appearance of representatives: e.g. Mark 2.3 (bearing the sick person);

---

[8]All the examples come from Theissen, *Miracle Stories* *, 49–72, which also contains further references.

Mark 7.25f. (the Syro-Phoenician woman, the mother of the sick child); Matt. 8.5f. (centurion of Capernaum).

5. The appearance of emissaries: Luke 7.1–5, 6 (embassy of the centurion of Capernaum); Mark 5.35 (those who bring the news of the death of the girl to Jairus).

7. Motivation of the appearance of opponents: Mark 5.27; 7.25 (the woman with an issue of blood and the Syro-Phoenician woman have heard of Jesus).

8. Description of the distress: in especial detail e.g. Mark 5.25f. (the woman with an issue of blood); Mark 9.20–22 (the epileptic boy).

9. Difficulties in the approach: Mark 2.4 (the paralysed man is let down through the roof); Mark 10.48 (Bartimaeus is first of all rejected by the disciples); Mark 7.27 (Jesus at first rejects the request for healing).

13. Misunderstanding: Mark 6.37 (the disciples believe that they should buy bread); Mark 5.39 (Jesus' remark 'the girl is not dead but sleeping' is misunderstood); John 5.7 (the sick man of Bethesda is waiting for someone to put him in the water at the right time); cf. *VitAp* IV, 45 (the crowd thinks that Apollonius wants to make a speech).

14. Scepticism and mockery: Mark 5.35, 40 (those who bring the news of the death ask, 'Why trouble the master further?' – the bystanders mock Jesus, who says that 'the girl is only sleeping'); Mark 9.22 (scepticism: '*If* you can, help us').

15. Criticism (by opponents): Mark 2.5ff. (forgiveness of sins); Mark 3.1ff. (breach of the sabbath)

16. The resistance and submission of the demon: at great length, Mark 5.6–13.

17. Pneumatic excitement: Mark 1.41; 3.5; 6.34.

18. Assurance: Mark 2.5; 5.36; 6.50.

19. Argument: Mark 2.9; 3.4; Matt. 17.25.

20. Withdrawal: Mark 4.38 (Jesus is sleeping while the boat is in distress); John 4.48 (Jesus rebukes those who ask).

21. Setting the scene: Mark 5.40; 7.33; 8.23 (exclusion of the public); Mark 3.3 (the sick person comes into the centre); Mark 10.49 (the blind man is brought).

22. Touch: Mark 1.21, 41; 5.27; 7.33.

23. Healing substances: Mark 8.23; John 9.6 (spittle).

24. Miracle-working word: Matt.8.16; Luke 4.38f. (threats and words of power); Mark 5.41; 7.34 (foreign language).

25. Prayer: John 11.41.

27. Demonstration: Mark 1.31 (minister); 2.12 (carry the bed); 5.43 (eat).

29. Command to secrecy: Mark 1.44; 5.42; 7.36.

32. Rejection: Mark 3.6; 5.17; Matt. 9.33f. (divided reaction).

33. The spread of the news: Mark 1.28, 45; 5.14, 20; Luke 7.17.

Task 1. Belief and unbelief

In both stories the connection between miracle and the trial of belief or unbelief is the topic. In both the healing takes place despite the ἀπιστία (the unbelief) of the person concerned. But behind this feature which both superficially have in common there are clear differences. The sick man of Epidaurus is healed although he does not believe; the miracle takes place independently of belief or unbelief, and leads to the removal of his unbelief. Mark 9.14ff. is more complicated, since as in numerous New Testament miracle stories faith is regarded as the presupposition of the miracle. That is shown by the saying 'Your faith has saved you', which occurs often; it is confirmed in the logion about faith moving mountains (Mark 11.22–24 par.) and is also presupposed in Mark 9.23, which says that anything is possible to those who believe. Jesus even attributes to the sick people or their representatives the capacity to transcend their human limitations by faith and to gain a share of the power of the creator God to whom everything is possible (πάντα δυνατά is a divine predicate). Here Jesus is to some degree the catalyst of this incredible event which is made possible by faith. This also emerges clearly in Mark 9.22f., where first of all the father had asked Jesus to help, *if he could*; thereupon he is asked by Jesus about his own faith, which can do anything. The father reacts to this belief which transcends all that is humanly possible with his desperate, 'I believe, help my unbelief', and the miracle takes place. The point of this miracle story is not the removal of unbelief but the recognition and perfection of the faith which is tried by a need that cannot be overcome.

2. Miracle-worker and favourite of God

1. With obvious irony, Tacitus describes the creation of a miracle-worker by the expectations of the sick person and the credulous crowd: Vespasian initially rejects the crowd's suggestion and only allows himself to be persuaded to make an attempt by the urgings of many who are persuaded that the miracle will take place and by the positive consequences it will have.

2. In the perception of the sick person and the people, whom Tacitus depicts as superstitious, the deity commands the emperor as its instrument to perform a healing which is humanly impossible. From the perspective of the 'enlightened' and more sceptical upper class the miracle can be described in a different way. The request for a medical opinion is particularly illuminating for its assessment of the miracle: Vespasian wants to venture only something that in principle is humanly possible. But then – according to Tacitus' interpretation – he exploits the crowd's belief in miracles and deities: he hopes that once the healings have proved successful people will think that nothing is impossible for him, and thus attribute divine omnipotence to him (see the previous task). The mediating role of the

doctors is particularly interesting – they vacillate between a rational argument forced on them by the emperor (the diseases can be cured) and an interpretation stamped by religious ideas (the emperor as the instrument of the gods). Finally, they give cynical and opportunist advice: if the healings do not succeed, they will lead to mockery of the superstition of the crowd; otherwise a divine aura would surround the emperor.

3. This divine aura is meant to reinforce the political power of the emperor, who had no dynastic legitimation. Moreover, even the sceptical Tacitus is not entirely free of this attitude, as is shown by his remark at the beginning of the text about the favour of heaven and the proclivity of the gods towards Vespasian. The intensity and vividness of the belief in miracles differs, depending on the class; it is introduced 'from above' and 'from below' in ways which are ideologically different, but it is a constitutive part of the perception of reality in antiquity.

4. The historicity of the miracles. Tacitus clearly indicates that he is basing himself on the oral reports of eye-witnesses who are still alive and is himself clearly detached from what is reported. But he regards it as an indication of the reliability of what is related that after the replacement of the Flavian dynasty there seems little reason why an invented story which serves as propaganda should continue to be handed down. Given what is reported, it is to be presumed that there were many eye-witnesses. Since Suetonius knows both miracles with slight divergences (a lame leg instead of a damaged hand), in this aspect he is independent of Tacitus and is reproducing a variant of the same (probably oral) tradition which, while differing in details, preserves the same basic facts. Neither the critical Tacitus nor Suetonius seems to have heard accounts to the contrary, which cast doubt on the historicity of the miracles. So we think it highly probable than in Alexandria the trust of helpless people in the successful general Vespasian, who seemed to them to be the darling of the gods and therefore an appropriate instrument, made possible healings which further confirmed his reputation.

11. Jesus as Poet: The Parables of Jesus

1. Forms of figurative speech

1. The sower could be a fixed metaphor as an image for God; an unusual detail is the appearance of the enemy who sows tares. There is perhaps an overlapping in the servants' question whether they are to let the tares ripen, since it incorporates the probable reaction of a community to 'sinners' in its own ranks into the parable and goes on to reject it.

2. Similitudes (in the strict sense): Luke 6.43–45; 11.11–13; 11.34–36; 17.7–10.

Example stories: Luke 10.30–37; 12.16–21; 16.19–31; 18.9–14.
Parables: Luke 7.41–43; 15.8–10;[9] 15.11–32; 18.1–8.
3. Allegories: Ezek. 17.3–10; Rev. 17.1–6.
Allegorizing: Matt. 22.1–10; Mark 12.1–11.[10]
Allegorizations: Matt. 13.36–43; Gal. 4.21–31.
4. On the basis of the definitions given here, the 'Parable of the Ring' is to be defined as allegory, since one needs a key to decipher the metaphors (sons = peoples; ring = world religion) and interpret the picture correctly.

2. The generous employer (Matt. 20.1–16): merit there, grace here?

The text is taken from J. Jeremias, *The Parables of Jesus*, 136–9. Without doubt Jeremias made an inestimable contribution to research into rabbinic Judaism. To that extent he belongs among those scholars who first laid the scholarly foundation for a new concern with Judaism, free of Christian claims to superiority. But for the same reason his life-work obliges us to make a critical assessment of the anti-Jewish stereotypes which are contained in it. So the aim of the following critical objections is not to measure Jeremias by today's insights but to engage in a critical reading of exegetical standard literature in order to break through the widespread and disastrous way in which theological anti-Judaism is automatically handed on without reflection.

Methodological perspectives. An examination of the rabbinic parable to see whether it is a reworking of Jesus' parable is inappropriate, given the large number of rabbinic parables about recompense. Rather, these are independent creations from a rich field of imagery in the tradition: its leading metaphor is 'recompense', around which other metaphors are grouped. Parables of quite different kinds, saying quite different things, could be created from this reservoir (employer, lazy or diligent worker, the nature and duration of the work, the payment of equal/unequal wages, reactions to the payment, etc.).

Views of content. Jeremias's aesthetic verdicts are extremely arbitrary. Why should the king's long walk with the diligent worker be 'more artificial' than the five times (!) at which workers are recruited in Matt. 20? Both features serve to build up the narrative tension and are equally 'improbable'. Nor can one see why the 'murmuring' of the workers who are underpaid (in the comparison) is better motivated in one case than in the other.

The theological interpretation ('merit there, grace here') is based on an anti-

---

[9]Here Bultmann vacillates between classifying it as a similitude or as a parable.
[10]Some exegetes regard Mark 12.1–11 as an early Christian allegory, which may either go back to Jesus himself or have been formed as a real allegory. However, usually the pericope is regarded as an allegorized parable of Jesus.

Jewish prejudice and is untenable, If we look at Jesus' parable in the context of all the rabbinic parables about recompense, it is clear that it occupies a middle position, under the aspect of the goodness of God. The rabbis could depict God both as a 'just' employer who rewards people for their services and as one who graciously gives full wages even to lazy workers who have not deserved them. Therefore the goodness and righteousness of God are no more mutually exclusive among the rabbis than they are with Jesus, who does not dispute that those who have worked for a long time have deserved their reward. The only remarkable thing is that Jesus expresses both aspects in one parable and that they are to be referred to different groups within Israel.

12. Jesus as Teacher: The Ethics of Jesus

1. Jesus' education

In our view the self-glorification of Josephus, who is known to tend towards exaggerations, cannot be used as an argument to defend the historicity of the story of the twelve-year-old Jesus in the temple. At the beginning of his autobiography, Josephus takes pains to apply the theme of the unusually gifted youth to himself and in so doing arouses the expectation among his readers that they will be reading the history of someone who is equal to the other great figures of whom similar stories were told. So Josephus' (often questionable) diplomatic and military activities in Galilee before the beginning of the Jewish War and in its early days, which stand at the centre of the *Life*, are to be seen in the light of the actions of a Cyrus, a Cambyses or an Alexander! Josephus confirms the literary convention of attributing to a significant figure exceptional knowledge in his early youth as a foretaste of his later greatness. In the case of Jesus, too, this will have led to a corresponding legend.

2. Jesus' ethic as a protest against Jewish legalism?

Bultmann's text is a variation of the first of the four stereotyped prejudices listed in the introduction and refuted under §3.1 (and indeed throughout the chapter): the absolutizing of the Law, casuistry, a morality of recompense, and formalism. Although in religious terms Bultmann puts Jesus in Judaism, he makes Jesus' ethic stand out against 'the' Jewish ethic, the image of which represents a tradition of decadence invented out of prejudices and false judgments with a long form-critical tradition. The problems and consequences of this approach are discussed at length by W. Stegemann, 'Das Verhältnis Rudolf Bultmanns zum Judentum. Ein Beitrag zur Pathologie des strukturellen theologischen Antijudaismus', *Kirche und Israel* 5, 1990, 26–44.

3. Religion and concern for daily bread

Common to Kidd. IV. 14 and Matt. 6.24ff. is recourse to an argument from wisdom about the goodness of creation and the possibility of drawing analogies from it. The metaphors agree in details, and the form of argument (from the lesser to the greater) is the same. There is also agreement over the basic assumption that human beings are created to serve God (cf. Matt. 6.24b, 32f.). The only explanation of this is that here Jesus is participating in a widespread Jewish tradition of imagery and argument.

The evaluation of the argument differs. R. Eleazar is justifying the fact that he must nevertheless work for his living: because of the fall humankind has lost the original privilege of eating its daily bread without toil (cf. Gen. 3.17–19). By contrast, Jesus calls for a life without working for one's daily bread in the service of the kingdom of God which is dawning, the kind of life that he and his followers are leading. This expresses the conviction that they are already living in the end-time in which God is restoring the state of the beginning, which was damaged by sin. His eschatological consciousness alone thus distiguishes Jesus from Rabbi Eleazar.

4. Jesus' ethics and the Essenes

On divorce. The rejection of a second marriage (described as fornication or adultery) is common to CD IV, 20–V, 2 and Mark 10.2–12; reference is made to the beginning or the creation ordinance in scripture, 'male and female he created them' (Gen. 1.27 quoted in CD IV, 21; Mark 10.6). However, the context is different: Jesus prohibits divorce and subsequent remarriage; the Damascus Document prohibits any second marriage.[11] Accordingly, Jesus and the Essenes share an understanding of Gen. 1.27 or the creation ordinance generally (cf. the reference to the flood story in CD V, 1) as the divine institution of monogamy, though this could be used as an argument in various ways. There is a divergence in the reference to other biblical passages: Jesus disputes the validity of Moses' regulation about a letter of divorce (Deut. 24.1) with a reference to the creation ordinance. In Qumran, the various scriptural proofs are evidently presented to confirm one another in accordance with the rule of three witnesses (Deut. 19.15).

The hallowing of the sabbath. CD X–XII illuminates the framework of the discussion in which Jesus' argument stands. Here Jesus presupposes for his conversation-partners (Pharisees and scribes in Luke 14.1f.; the synagogue president and those attending the synagogue in Luke 13.10f.) in part a more

---

[11] An alternative interpretation sees CD as a polemic against polygamy, i.e. it refers to the wife 'during her lifetime'. Jesus evidently presupposes monogamy as the rule.

liberal understanding than the Damascus Document attests for the Essenes: of course on the sabbath one may get a child or an ox out of the well from which cattle drink. However, there was evidently a widespread view (cf. Luke 13.14 and the prohibition in CD XI, 9f. against carrying medicine around) that healing was a work forbidden on the sabbath. Jesus' argument focusses on a further relaxation of the sabbath commandments in the service of human beings; here – making common cause with his audience against the strictest interpretation of the sabbath commandments in his time – he takes up existing exceptions, and by so doing indicates that he does not in any way want to abolish them in principle.

Since the violation of the rigorous sabbath regulations in Qumran is explicitly not punishable by death, we may regard the historicity of Mark 3.2, 6 – the decision of the Pharisees and Herodians to kill Jesus because of a healing on the sabbath which was performed without the use of medicine and physical manipulation – as extremely questionable, even if Pharisees and Herodians possibly featured in the original pericope. As the Herodians play no role in Jesus' passion in Mark, they were probably not first inserted here by him.

Loving one's enemies. Regardless of the question whether the heightening of love of neighbour and hatred of enemy in an antithesis in Matt. 5.43, which possibly indicates a direct reference to Essene obligations, goes back to Jesus (which is improbable), the extension of the commandment to love one's neighbour by Jesus to loving one's enemies must be set in the context of discussions which seek to define the scope of Lev. 19.18. Here the Essenes are that group within the spectrum of Judaism which is clearly attested in the sources as having combined an intensification of the love of fellow members of the community with a call to hate others. The obligation to hate enemies (because they are God's enemies) is clear in the Old Testament tradition.

13. Jesus as Critic of the Cult and Founder of a Cult: The Lord's Supper

Introduction: 1. Forms of the presence of Christ

The following forms of the presence of Christ are dominant:
  I Cor. 10.3f.: causal presence;
  I Cor. 10.16f.: social presence;
  I Cor. 11.25: remembered presence;
  John 6.51–58: real presence.

2. The eucharist in the Didache

The eucharistic liturgy in the Didache does not have a reference either 1. to the death of Jesus or 2. to a last meal held by him, so there are no words of institution, etc. 3. The sequence of bread and wine has been reversed. 4. No real presence of Jesus in the elements can be recognized, but a causal presence of Jesus is presupposed.

Tasks: 1. Forms of meals in primitive Christianity: conditions for taking part in the eucharist

1. *Paul*: 1. No participation in meals in the 'temples of idols'; 2. All are to examine themselves to see whether they are 'worthy'; the only concrete point mentioned here is concern for poor members of the community. In both cases the reason for this is the idea of the body of Christ, i.e. the social presence of Christ in the community which is celebrating the eucharist. This excludes fellowship with idols and contempt for one's neighbour. There is no mention of baptism, and the understanding of the elements plays no role!

2. *Didache*: 1. Baptism; 2. Holiness (if not, confession of sins, repentance, reconciliation with one's neighbour); reason: the holiness of the individual guarantees the purity of the community's sacrifice.

3. *Ignatius*: 1. Belief in the real presence of Christ in the elements; 2. Works of love (presumably the thought is of the collection which is made before the eucharist; anyone who did not come had no opportunity to give); 3. Subordination to the bishop: the basis of the social presence of Christ in the real presence is that the unity of the community gained through union with the flesh and blood of Christ is conceivable for Ignatius only as a hierarchical gradation.

4. *Justin*: 1. Baptism; 2. Belief in the doctrines of the church and life in accordance with Christ's instructions; 3. Belief in the real presence[; at another point mention is made of the collection, but only as everyone can afford, not as a condition (*Apol.* I, 67)].

2. Jesus as a critic of the cult?

1. *Well disposed to the temple/cult*: Mark 1.44f.par; Matt.ˢ 17.24–27; 23.16–22; Lukeˢ 2.21–52; 21.1–4; Acts 2.46–3.1ff.; 5.12–42 etc.; Matt. 23.35f./Luke 11.50f. Q.

2. *Hostile to the temple/cult*: Gospel of the Ebionites, frag 6; Matt. 9.13 (but cf. 12.7 in context).

3. *Despite a fundametal recognition of the institution*, critical and qualifying its importance: Mark 7.6–13 par.; Matt. 23.23f./Luke 11.42; Markˢ 12.32–34; Mattˢ 5.23f.; 12.3–7.

1. It is evident that there is a markedly positive tendency towards the temple in Luke–Acts. But there are also examples in Mark, Matthew and Q of a basic recognition of the holiness of the temple and priestly control in the case of the

healing of lepers by Jesus, and of the payment of the temple tax by his followers. The nucleus of these traditions will be historical, for unless Jesus had such an attitude it would be impossible to understand why the first Christian community had an important centre in Jerusalem and continued to take part in the temple cult.

2. By contrast, the only instance of Jesus being hostile to the cult in principle, which is in the Gospel of the Ebionites, is late, and is to be assessed as a prophecy after the event, following the destruction of the temple. The quotation from Hosea (I want mercy, not sacrifice, Hos. 6.6), which is redactional, appears in isolation in Matt. 9.13, but in Matt. 12.7 in connection with a statement about something more than the temple that logically presupposes the goodness of the temple which has been surpassed.

3. Finally, several passages (like Matt. 12.5–7) indicate a critical attitude to the cultic institutions on the part of Jesus. Here the tendency is always to set the moral above the cultic: care of parents has priority over assigning goods to the temple (Mark 7.6ff.); tithing cooking herbs is not on the same level as a concern for law, mercy and faith (Matt. 23.23f.); love of God and neighbour are more important than sacrifice (Mark 12.32–34 – this conclusion is drawn by a scribe and Jesus acknowledges it in 12.35); and a sacrifice is worthless unless it has been preceded by reconciliation between the parties in a dispute (Matt. 5.23f.). This attitude of Jesus and his followers has its models in the prophetic tradition of Israel (cf. I Sam. 15.22; Isa. 1.11ff.; Hos. 6.6; Ps. 40.7; 51.18ff.; Prov. 21.3, etc.); it is no coincidence that quotations from Hos. 6.6; Isa. 29.13 appear in Matthew. Such an ambivalent attitude to the cult could fit both with a recognition of cultic institutions in principle and also with the idea that God will destroy the temple which human beings have alienated from its purpose and put a new one in its place. It also explains how different attitudes to the temple and cult could have been taken by followers of Jesus after Easter.

14. Jesus as Martyr: The Passion of Jesus

1. Important extra-Christian sources on the legal situation

(a) Josephus, *Antt.* 20, 199–203:

First of all, the text contains an account of the strict Sadducean legal norms which some scholars believe would have played a part in the trial of Jesus. Secondly, it clearly shows how the high priest exploited a vacancy in the procuratorship which evidently meant that no capital sentences were passed in the land, in order to hold capital trials of 'transgressors of the law'. After the objections of some Jews who were loyal to the law (Pharisees?), he then lost his office. The text shows that the supreme council did not have the *ius gladii* in 62 (and there is no reason to suppose that this was not the case for the whole period from 6 CE to 70 – apart from the reign of Agrippa I, 41–44 CE).

(b) Josephus, *BJ* 6, 300–306:

Here we see an 'established chain of authorities'[12] in the collaboration between Jewish and Roman authorities. Members of the Sanhedrin interrogate the prophet of doom. When his behaviour does not change even after the punishment (a beating) which the Sanhedrin was allowed to inflict, they hand him over to the procurator. There apparently capital proceedings are held against him, recognizable by the flogging which always preceded crucifixion (though it could be imposed as an independent punishment). However, Albinus is not convinced of the guilt of Jesus the son of Ananias and releases him. This again shows that the Sanhedrin had no competence to impose the death penalty or to carry it out; and that the procurator could have decided on acquittal even after denunciations from the supreme Jewish authorities.

(c) Tacitus, *Ann.* 15, 44:

The text shows that Tacitus makes the holder of the Roman mandate in the province of Judaea (who is wrongly called a procurator instead of a prefect) responsible for the execution of Jesus. This verdict corresponds completely to the legal proceedings that we know from elsewhere in the Roman empire.

2. Who is to blame for Jesus' death?

The historical and theological questions connected with the death of Jesus are highly explosive for most Christians. Therefore they are particularly controversial and clarify the individual profile of anyone giving an answer to them. The church and theology always have to cope with the legacy of theological anti-Judaism when the question arises as to who is to blame for the death of Jesus, and they must always keep it in mind. This anti-Judaism has firmly established itself in our tradition, beginning with the New Testament texts; it is often only belatedly recognized, and takes much effort to remove. The following remarks on the texts by J. Blinzler and A. Strobel are meant to help towards the sensitizing which is needed here.

Blinzler: positively, it has to be said that Blinzler is concerned to distinguish theological statements about the salvation-historical necessity of the death of Jesus from historical verdicts on those who were responsible for his death. A

---

[12]Müller, 'Möglichkeit', 70.

differentiation of the groups involved is part of the assessment of the historical question: 'the Jews' are defined precisely as 'the members of the Sanhedrin of the time and the inhabitants of Jerusalem who made common cause with them'. Blinzler also remembers that it was Pilate who had the competence to pass the death sentence. That makes all the more astonishing his overall verdict that Pilate was only an 'accomplice' who is less to blame than 'the Jews' (as they are sweepingly called in the end). Blinzler leaves no doubt as to how he arrives at this verdict. 'The New Testament texts give a clear answer to the question who was historically responsible for Jesus' death. It was the Jews.' Even worse, these were 'the fanatical Jews', to whose pressure Pilate had to bow. However, it has to be doubted whether this pro-Roman and anti-Jewish verdict does justice to the historical events. For example, it is striking that the two non-Christian historians who make statements on this question, who come from the ruling classes and were familiar with legal conditions, clearly make Pilate responsible for Jesus' execution. Tacitus (see the previous task, under [c]), mentions only him; Josephus limits the involvement of the Jerusalem aristocracy to a denunciation to Pilate (*Antt.* 18, 63f.; see above, §3.2.1). The analogous case of Jesus, son of Ananias, who was released by Albinus because he thought him harmless (see the previous task under [b]), clearly shows that the governor was free to decide and that a denunciation from the local aristocracy did not necessarily have to lead to a death sentence. It is historically highly improbable that Pilate in particular, of whom Josephus reports many instances of behaviour which takes no account of Jewish interests, bowed to Jewish 'pressure' against his better judgment.

Accordingly, the members of the local aristocracy who denounced Jesus bear the blame for the death of Jesus in the first instance and Pilate in the last instance. On both the Roman and the Jewish sides, individuals acted out of particular group interests and motives of a religious, political and economic kind. We should attempt to describe these as precisely as possible, instead of resorting to anti-Jewish stereotypes like 'the fanatical Jews', which are not least the legacy of a pernicious Christian exegesis of scripture.

Strobel: Here inaccurate statements about historical events and anti-Jewish theological interpretative categories produce a highly questionable picture of the trial of Jesus as the 'hour of truth' for Judaism:

It is historically unjustifiable for Caiaphas to be depicted as the sole judge who believed that he had to 'condemn the Messiah of the people to death on the basis of the Law'. Pilate, who in fact pronounced the death sentence and had it carried out by his soldiers, is not even mentioned! Furthermore, it is improbable that an obligation to the Jewish Law provoked the deadly hostility of the local aristocracy to Jesus (see in the section under §4.2–3, 6). Even less can there be any question that there was no other choice to a high priest loyal to the Torah than to condemn Jesus, as Strobel suggests, and that in so doing he was obeying 'the fatal compulsions of the Jewish law'. Even if we assumed what in our view is the improbable case that it was Jesus' attitude to the Torah which motivated the supreme council to denounce him to Pilate, we would have a clash between two of the numerous contemporary interpretations of the Jewish law, namely that of the temple aristocracy and that of the Galilean rabbi Jesus, but not *the* (fatal) Jewish law and the one who overcame it. Here we have a projection backwards of dogmatic abstractions from later times which will not stand up to a historical examination, the anti-Jewish substance of which has long been recognized (see §12). But does not Strobel counter the charge of anti-Judaism when he emphasizes that 'the guilt and failure of us all', 'a defect in human beings and their order generally' is expressed in the person of Caiaphas and his people? Hardly. Here Strobel is using a pattern of theological argument which unfortunately is still common, when he depicts Jews as examples of unredeemed humanity that becomes tragically guilty under the compulsions of the Law and can only be redeemed by the catharsis which Jesus offers. This makes Jewish existence *the* embodiment of the form of life which is to be rejected and overcome. In this view Judaism no longer has a theological right to exist. According to it, there are only two possibilities for Jews: the Jew must either 'doubt the truth of the Law as an ultimate truth', and that means become a Christian – or the Jew largely stands 'under the fatal compulsions of the Law', and that means being involved with the powers which allegedly put Jesus to death. To this degree, Strobel's view that it is still necessary to speak of 'a guilt of the Jew' in connection with the death of Jesus, even though this may also be defined as tragic, is not a linguistic aberration but a logical consequence of this structurally anti-Jewish theological argument. This is none other than the old charge of being God's murderers, in a rather more respectable garb: in our view, even in this form it is ruled out of theological discussion and, as has been shown, its historical foundation is untenable.[13]

3. The Letter of Pilate: a source on the passion from the second century

1. Tendencies which also occur in the New Testament but which are massively reinforced:

(a) The *Romans* are acquitted of any guilt in the death of Jesus: the *Jewish leaders* are depicted as the sole culprits:

- The Jewish leaders manage to hand over Jesus by deceiving Pilate; thus Pilate does not give way against his better judgment – as in the canonical Gospels – but because he has been deceived.

---

[13]For further detail see D. Catchpole, *The Trial of Jesus*, Leiden 1971; S. Légasse, *The Trial of Jesus*, London 1997.

- The Jewish leaders crucify Jesus – contrary to any historical probability. Hatred and wickedness are mentioned as the only motives; the 'lies of the Jews' are mentioned three times in the Letter of Pilate (before Pilate, to the guard and to Claudius, i.e. the Roman authorities generally).
- The guard on the tomb and the Jewish attempt at bribery (cf. Matt. 27.62–66; 28.11–15) are now documented by the Roman governor as facts: contrary to Matt. 28.15, the Roman soldiers do not incriminate themselves by silence but record the lies of the Jews.
- The fact that the title 'king' does not play any role at all accords with the tendency to dispute the Roman involvement in the execution of Jesus.

(b) The *Jewish leaders* and the *Jewish people* are on the one hand distinguished in retrospect: the whole people is said to have recognized Jesus as Son of God because of his miracles, but the Jewish priests dismissed this with hatred. As in the Gospel of John, however, the Jewish leaders are then identified with 'the Jews' (already in the bribery), clearly with an eye to current Jewish–Christian hostility, as the last clause indicates.

2. New and certainly secondary tendencies as compared with the New Testament:

(a) The accusation is of *'magic and transgressing the Law'*. As the detailed documentation of the miracles of Jesus (with a clear emphasis on the nature miracles, which are particularly powerful) shows, the underlying question is whether these prove that Jesus is Son of God or brand him a magician. In the context of the miracles, we should see transgressions of the sabbath above all as the healings on the sabbath, but, bearing in mind the author's day, also as the Christian abolition of the Law with an appeal to Jesus Christ.

(b) *Roman soldiers as witnesses to the resurrection of Jesus.* Whereas according to the canonical Gospels there were no witnesses at all to the resurrection, and according to Tertullian even the guards fled at it, in the Letter of Pilate (and at even greater length in the Gospel of Peter 9–11), the guards attest the resurrection of Jesus and Pilate himself sees to it that the emperor is informed. Thus Pilate is transformed from being a witness to Jesus' innocence (the tendency of the Synoptic Gospels) to being a witness to the resurrection.

(c) Of course these sources have no historical value for the reconstruction of the passion of Jesus, as they are extremely tendentious (anti-Judaism, the attempt to claim the Roman authorities positively for the Christian concern, the desire for documented eye-witness evidence to the resurrection from outside Christianity). Accordingly, the Letter of Pilate is an important source which gives us information:

- about the controversy between Christians and Jews over the worship of Jesus as the risen Son of God (and the status of miracles in this debate) and the legitimacy of Christian freedom from the Jewish law based on this;

- about the Christian apologetic towards the Roman state in the second century which was not afraid to make *the* Roman official who ordered Jesus' execution a Christian in his innermost convictions.

15. Jesus as the Risen One: Easter and its Interpretation

1. Form-critical classification

Text 1. Cf. H. Braun, *Jesus of Nazareth. The Man and His Time*, Philadelphia 1979 (however, this English translation is of an earlier edition which does not contain the chapter on the resurrection).

Text 2: J. Weiss, *Earliest Christianity* 1, London 1937 reissued New York 1959, 30f.

Text 3: H. Grass, *Ostergeschehen und Osterberichte*, Göttingen ²1962, 243–5: objective vision hypothesis.

2. The earliest account of the resurrection of Jesus (Gospel of Peter 8.28–11.49)

1. *The form*. The independence of the narrative of the empty tomb from the traditions about the appearances, which can be observed in the canonical Gospels, has been done away with. Jesus appears from the tomb.

The event. First of all the process of the resurrection itself is described, and even Jesus' preaching in Hades which precedes it (cf. I Peter 3.19) is mentioned. However, this preaching is not depicted but is the content of the dialogue between the risen Christ and the heavenly voice.[14]

The persons present. Romans and hostile Jews are witnesses to the resurrection, whereas in the canonical Gospels Jesus always appears only to disciples, male and female.

2. *Narrative tendencies*. By comparison with the other sources, the wealth of detail reported and the vivid and dramatic depiction of the mysterious events are striking. Elements of faith which are difficult to grasp are thus illustrated. But in fact the historical distance has visibly increased, and therefore the deliberately

---

[14]Later apocrypha continue this tendency to describe all the phases of the revelation. Thus for example the Gospel of Nicodemus after 425 CE is expanded by a lengthy description of Christ's descent into Hell, of which various versions are extant (cf. *NTApoc* 1, 1991, 521ff.).

detailed description presents anachronisms and historical impossibilities. For example, the resurrection takes place in the night in which 'the Lord's day dawned'; i.e., a later liturgical development is used in an unthinking way to date the event which first produced it. A crowd of Jews is said to have come out from Jerusalem to the tomb on the previous day – such a mass violation of the sabbath regulations is hardly imaginable.

Theological tendencies. As elsewhere in the Gospel of Peter, the tendency to blame the Jews and exonerate the Romans is marked. In addition, a central position is occupied by a solid demonstration that the resurrection of Jesus in fact happened, as is shown by the numerous Jewish and Roman witnesses who are mentioned as being present at every stage from the sealing of the tomb to the resurrection.

3. (a) Against Koester it can be objected that the formulation in the imperfect 'this man was a son of God' (Mark 15.39) is far more likely as a reaction to the death of Jesus accompanied by a heavenly voice and the rending of the curtain of the temple than as a fitting commentary on his resurrection, which would rather call for a confession formulated in the present tense.

(b) The common features shared by the Easter epiphany in the Gospel of Peter and the transfiguration narrative in Mark 9.2–8 are not very specific: shining white garments or a shining light are characteristic of epiphanies generally; the fact that in both cases two heavenly figures stand by Jesus can hardly be seen as sufficient proof of a connection between the two narratives. A decisive difference weighs much more heavily: in Mark 9.2–8 *disciples* are witnesses to the appearance, whereas in the Gospel of Peter the witnesses are a Roman guard on the tomb!

(c) Two motifs in the Gospel of Peter are novellistic developments of Matthaean elements: whereas according Matt. 27.65 Pilate sets a guard, in the Gospel of Peter this is led by a centurion (cf. Mark 15.30) named Petronius. The tomb is not simply sealed (Matt. 27.66), but given *seven seals*. This precision at a linguistic level which takes the detail further may have run parallel to the elaboration of the content of the narrative: whereas according to Matthew the guard on the tomb merely makes sure that the tomb was closed until the epiphany of the angel and its discovery by the women, the guards in the Gospel of Peter become witnesses to the event of the resurrection.

In our view it is quite improbable that the epiphany at the tomb in the Gospel of Peter (even in the pre-redactional form, free of expansions, which has been reconstructed by Koester) is a tradition which is earlier than Mark and Matthew. In addition to the individual observations made in (a) to (c) above in favour of the priority of the Markan and Matthaean version, in sum it must be maintained that in all the canonical Gospels we can recognize that the tomb narrative and the appearance tradition initially had independent histories in the tradition. According to the earliest tradition, only followers of Jesus (and a converted persecutor) experienced visions. Appearances to women disciples at the tomb (Matt. 28.9f.; John 20.11ff.) form the beginning of a link between the two traditions. The appearance of Jesus from the tomb to uninvolved or hostile witnesses stands at the end of this development.

By contrast, the development postulated by Koester is hardly imaginable: the real climax of the old Easter epiphany, namely the appearance of the crucified Jesus from the tomb, is said to have been passed over by Mark and Matthew. Both would have also kept silent about the fact that there were credible witnesses to the resurrection among the Roman soldiers responsible for the execution of Jesus. And yet they would have integrated far less central elements into their account. That hardly seems plausible.

16. The Historical Jesus and the Beginnings of Christology

Introduction: 1. The 'Easter gulf' between the historical Jesus and the kerygmatic Christ

The disciples on the Emmaus road give Jesus the title 'prophet', which is explained as 'mighty in deed and word before God and the whole people' (Luke 24.19). When in 24.21 the disciples say, 'But we had hoped that he would be the one who would redeem Israel', the fundamental expectation is one of the royal Messiah who will restore the greatness of Israel with military force. It is therefore logical that the risen Christ should make the title Messiah/Christ the object of his interpretation of scripture and show from Moses and the prophets 'that the Christ had to suffer this and enter into his glory' (24.26). Thus it is not a prophet capable of acts of military redemption but the Christ who has undergone suffering and risen who is the Lord (24.34).

2. The break in the tradition: Ethiopic Enoch 46.1ff. and the Son of Man sayings

Of the passages mentioned, the sayings about the present (Mark 2.10, 27f.) and the suffering Son of Man (Mark 8.31) contradict the notion which is shaped by apocalyptic. Mark 13.26f. and 14.62 are comparable to the apocalyptic tradition in that the Son of Man is a figure standing in the immediate presence of God (Mark 14.62), who comes from heaven at the end of days (Mark 13.26f.). There are striking differences: according to Mark 13.26f. the primary function of the Son of Man is redemption, whereas in Dan. 7.14 and Ethiopic Enoch his prime task is to judge and rule on the one hand and to punish the powerful on the other.

Moreover only in the NT do we have a clear use of the term as a title, whereas in apocalyptic all the statements about 'that son of man' (etc.) go back to the initial comparison (one whose form was like the appearance of a man, EthEnoch 46.1).

3. Jesus' sense of authority

There is *explicit christology* only in Mark 14.62, where Jesus confesses that he is 'Messiah' and 'Son of the Most High' and says that in the future he will sit at God's right hand (as Son of Man) and appear from there. In Matt. 11.2–6; 12.28 there is *implicit christology*: Jesus expresses awareness of having a high status without using traditional tittles. *Evoked christology* appears in Mark 6.14–16; 11.9–10; traditional titles are applied to Jesus.

Tasks: 1. On the title Messiah: PsSol. 17

1. The Messiah is a son of David and is distinguished by his immediacy to God. He owes all other properties like military strength, wisdom and justice to this close relationship to God. He has military and administrative tasks, both of which have a strongly religious dimension. As the general appointed by God he drives away the enemy, frees Jerusalem from the alien rule which profanes it and subjugates Gentile nations. The purified Jerusalem becomes the religious centre of the world, to which the nations stream.

2. The relationship between Ps. 2 and PsSol. 17. Both texts are rooted in the traditional royal ideology of Israel, which is set down in most concentrated form in Nathan's prophecy in II Sam. 7. PsSol. 17.4 conjures up the promise of an eternal kingdom (II Sam. 7.12f.) in the face of the loss of political autonomy; Ps. 2.7 actualizes the promise that the king is God's son (II Sam. 7.14) and derives his military supremacy and the right to have the nations as his possession from this.

Psalms of Solomon 17 takes up elements of Ps. 2.2, 6, 8–9 and interprets them messianically – like II Sam. 7.12f. What Ps. 2 promises the anointed (cf. v.2) in the present (2.6, 8–9) in PsSol. 17 becomes the hallmark of salvation in those days in which the good fortune of Israel before God is recreated in the assembling of the tribes. The king reigns on the holy mount of Zion, rules over the nations, shatters them with an iron bar, and breaks them like potters' vessels. Granted, the promise to the son in Ps. 2.7 is not transferred to the Messiah. However, it appears in 'democratized' form: the people hallowed by God consists of pure 'sons of God'.

3. On the title Son of God: 4Q 246

1 (a) If one thinks that the 'son of God' is a pagan ruler, then the course of the end-events corresponds to the usual apocalyptic scheme: the ruler who is

venerated as God's son belongs to the era of kingdoms, wars and tribulations which is passing away (I, 4–II, 3); after that the people of God arises, and once it has subjected its enemies with the help of God, the time of eschatological peace dawns (II, 4–9). According to this interpretation, the disputed third-person pronominal suffixes from II, 5 on all refer to the people of God. This is a collective subject and thus also takes over tasks which elsewhere were assigned only to the promised king of salvation (like judging in righteousness, II, 5–6; cf. Isa. 11.4; PsSol. 17.26–29).

(b) According to Dan. 7.14 the eternal rule will pass to the one who is 'like a Son of Man'. In Dan. 7.27 the eternal kingdom is given to 'the people of the saints of the Most High', i.e. Israel. According to 4Q 246 (as understood here) both promises are applied to the people as a whole. Thus 4Q 246 is the first known extra-biblical piece of evidence for a collective understanding of the one like a son of man in Dan. 7.13.

(c) The parallels to Luke 1.32–35 are impressive: 'He will be great' (Luke 1.32/4Q 246 I, 7); 'He will be called son of the Most High' (Luke 1.32/4Q 246 II, 1); 'He will be called the son of God' (Luke 1.35/4Q 246 II, 1). If 4Q 246 has attributes of Hellenistic rulers, then Luke, by transferring them to the promised son of David, is making the political statement that Jesus Christ in fact fulfils the claim which political propaganda wrongly attributed to the great king.

2. (a) If the 'Son of God' is the eschatological bringer of salvation to Israel, which is also the subject of the action in II, 4 (5)ff., then II.1 (end) –3 causes certain difficulties, because here after the appearance of the son of God, whom all serve (I, 8), there is still talk of war and the confusion of the nations for several years. However, given the fragmentary state of the preceding lines this cannot be a decisive argument against the messianic interpretation, especially as a strict chronological sequence is not always observed in other apocalyptic texts, and there are repetitions of or variations on what has already been reported (J.J. Collins, *Son*, 70f.). The close parallels to other messianic texts, e.g. to PsSol. 17, and in part also to IV Ezra 13, also support the messianic interpretation: the Messiah (or in IV Ezra the Son of Man, who is nevertheless identified with him), appears as the warrior who with God's support wages the eschatological wars, subjects the peoples, brings eternal peace and judges the people in righteousness (see above, Tasks 1–2).

There are particularly close parallels with Isa. 10.20–11.16, above all with the Aramaic Isaiah Targum, which interprets the passage eschatologically (C.A. Evans, *Jesus**, 108): Assyria and Egypt are regarded as Israel's main enemies (Isa. 10.24; 11.15f.; 4Q 246 I, 6); the royal heir 'judges in righteousness' (TargIsa 11.4; 4Q 246 II, 5); he brings peace to the land (TargIsa. 11.6; 4Q 246 II, 7).

(b) If the 'son of God' is the subject of the action in II, (4,) 5ff., then both quotations from Dan. 7 refer to him as an individual figure. Here (again EthEnoch

37ff. and IV Ezra 13) we would have an interpretation of the Son of Man from Dan. 7 in terms of an individual superhuman figure who wages war and has the function of a judge. Granted he is not called Messiah (as in Ethiopian Enoch and IV Ezra), but he assumes the Messiah's role. In that case the text would be the first clearly pre-Christian piece of evidence for the individual ('messianic') interpretation of Dan. 7. Here we cannot exclude the possibility that the ambivalence of the point of reference for the pronominal suffixes from II, 5 on has a deeper significance. They could be a linguistic expression of a representative relationship. The Messiah represents the people of God and his rule is a rule of the people, etc.

(c) The notion of the Messiah as son of God is prepared for in the Old Testament tradition of the king (who is also called' anointed'); cf. Ps. 2.2, 7; 89.26f.; I Sam. 7.12–14). However, the title 'son of God' does not occur in any of these passages; we always read only of 'my son' (or, on the side of the king, of 'my father'). Reference should also be made to 4Q 174 I(III), 10f., 18 for the messianic interpretation of these passages; there I Sam. 7.11–14 and Ps. 2.1 are quoted and the 'son' is interpreted in terms of I Sam. 7.14 and the 'Branch of David' (the exegesis of Ps. 2 has not been preserved). Psalm 2 also has a messianic interpretation in PsSol. 17.23f., 30, but the promise to the son is not related to the Messiah (see Task 1 above). However, in IV Ezra 13 the Messiah-Son of Man is called 'my son' by God. Certainly IV Ezra is not pre-Christian, but the book does represent a Jewish messianology roughly contemporaneous to the NT. The messianic interpretation of the Old Testament traditions about the king in Qumran and beyond shows that 'son of God' could easily be imagined as a messianic title in the framework of Jewish ideas of the Messiah.

(d) Two further parallels (one implicit and one explicit) can be added to those mentioned under 1 (c) ('be great', 'son of God' , 'son of the Most High'). 'God will give him the throne of his father David' (Luke 1.32) corresponds to the depiction of the 'son' as royal Messiah in 4Q 246, even if neither Davidic sonship nor the title Messiah are explicitly mentioned. 'He will reign as king over the house of Jacob for ever and his reign will have no end' (Luke 1.33; cf. 4Q 246 II, 5, 9). If 4Q 246 is to be understood in a messianic sense, then Luke has transferred current Jewish messianic titles and expectations to Jesus.

3. The conclusion must be that while good arguments can be put forward for both interpretations, certainty will probably not be achieved until new texts are found. However, because of the close parallels to various messianic texts in Judaism and early Christianity, the messianic interpretation seems to us to be the more probable.

Index of References

Extra-biblical sources quoted in the text are printed in bold with an asterisk.

Select Index of Names and Subjects

In the case of long entries, the most important pages are printed in italics